Europe, the State and Globalisation

Europe, the State and Globalisation

Simon Sweeney

York St John College,
a college of the University of Leeds

PEARSON
Longman

Harlow, England • London • New York • Boston • San Francisco • Toronto • Sydney • Singapore • Hong Kong
Tokyo • Seoul • Taipei • New Delhi • Cape Town • Madrid • Mexico City • Amsterdam • Munich • Paris • Milan

Pearson Education Limited
Edinburgh Gate
Harlow
Essex CM20 2JE
England

and Associated Companies throughout the world

Visit us on the World Wide Web at:
www.pearsoned.co.uk

ISBN 0 582 47291 1

British Library Cataloguing-in-Publication Data
A catalogue record for this book is available from the British Library

Library of Congress Cataloging-in-Publication Data
Sweeney, Simon.
  Europe, the state, and globalisation / Simon Sweeney.
    p. cm.
  Includes bibliographical references and index.
  ISBN 0-582-47291-1 (alk. paper)
  1. European Union. 2. State, The. 3. Regionalism—European Union countries. 4.
Nationalism—European Union countries. 5. Globalization—Economic aspects—European
Union countries. I. Title.

JN30.S92 2005
341.242′2—dc22   2004063356

10 9 8 7 6 5 4 3 2 1
08 07 06 05

Typeset in 9.5/12.5pt Stone Serif by 35
Printed and bound by Bell & Bain Ltd, Glasgow

The publisher's policy is to use paper manufactured from sustainable forests.

A proportion of royalties from sales of this book goes to the Medical Foundation for
the Care of Victims of Torture, Registered Charity No. 1000340, 111 Isledon Road,
London, N7 7JW.

I dedicate the book to my family, to Lyn – who ensured that I remember the other things closer to home that really matter – and our children Jude, Ruth and Neil, all of whom have tolerated my absences and my distraction. Lyn also provided a valuable sounding board for ideas that found their way into the book, or were – fortunately – discarded. If I may also dedicate this book to a place, it is to the Ryoan-ji Zen garden in Kyoto.

Brief contents

Contents

Acknowledgements

I would like to thank Dr Ian Greener, Department of Management Studies, University of York for suggestions leading to many improvements to the manuscript. Ian has been a valuable colleague, provocateur and critic over several years. Thanks also to Nicola Smith and Thomas Diez at the Department of Political Science and International Studies, the University of Birmingham and Professor W.L. Miller, Edward Caird Professor of Politics at Glasgow University. They commented on earlier versions of the manuscript and made many useful suggestions. I make the usual plea that none of them should be held in any way responsible for any errors or weaknesses that remain in the text. Thanks also are due to Lyn Wait, Dr Judy Giles, Dr Phil Ross, Richard Thurley, Wayne Johnson, and Jon Neale, all of whom provided valuable help with source material.

Thanks too to colleagues at Pearson Education, especially Morten Fuglevand and Emma Travis for their commitment in seeing the project to completion, and Aylene Rogers, Helen Hodge and Barbara Massam for their magnificent editorial help. I am indebted to colleagues in the School of Management, Community and Communication at York St John College, including Dr Stuart Billingham, Jackie Mathers and Tish Hamill. I also thank Toshimi Kawashima and Chizuru Horado for their generous welcome on my numerous visits to Japan; Dr Patrick Griffiths, formerly of the University of York and now of Beppu University in Japan, and the best teacher I ever had; friends in Spain, Italy and Poland including Mark Wilson, Araceli Sanz, Marta Berraondo, Ramón Cabestany, Juan Carlos Aguinaga, Guido Fornaro, Cesary Wosinski and Janusz Szpala. I also thank colleagues and friends at Meiji University in Tokyo, and at Wyższa Szkoła Lingwistyczna in Częstochowa.

Above all I am grateful to my students. I thank my postgraduate students in Japan, based in Osaka and Tokyo, and in Poland, in Częstochowa, as well as undergraduates at York St John who have braved my international and European-related modules, and postgraduate students at the University of York. All of them have demonstrated their wish to learn about things that matter, and in so doing encouraged me to write this book. One of the greatest pleasures that I gain from teaching is participating in the learning process with my students. It is through them that I learn, and their warmth, hospitality and enthusiasm enriches my work. I shall refer to just one by name, in recognition of his contribution to Unicef in Tokyo and worldwide. He is Yoshihisa Togo, President of the Japan section of Unicef and a graduate of our MA in International Studies in 2003.

Abbreviations and acronyms

A-10	Accession Ten, the states joining the Union in 2004
ACP	African, Caribbean and Pacific (region)
APEC	Asia Pacific Economic Cooperation
ASEAN	Association of South East Asian Nations
BMD	Ballistic Missile Defence
CAP	Common Agricultural Policy
CEE	Central and Eastern Europe
CEECs	Central and Eastern European Countries
CFI	Court of First Instance
CFSP	Common Foreign and Security Policy
CIA	Criminal Intelligence Agency
CIS	Commonwealth of Independent States
CMEA	Council for Mutual Economic Assistance (also known as COMECON)
CoR	Committee of the Regions
COREPER	Committee of Permanent Representatives
CPSU	Communist Party of the Soviet Union
CSCE	Conference on Security and Cooperation in Europe
DDR	German Democratic Republic (East Germany)
DG	Directorate General
EA	Eusko Alcartasuna (Basque Solidarity)
EBRD	European Bank for Reconstruction and Development
EC	European Community, European Communities
EC-6, EC-9, EC-10, EC-12	European Community, European Communities and number of member states
ECB	European Central Bank
ECHR	European Convention on Human Rights
ECJ	European Court of Justice
Ecofin	Council of Economics and Finance Ministers
ECOSOC	Economic and Social Committee
ECSC	European Coal and Steel Community
EEA	European Economic Area
EEC	European Economic Community
EFTA	European Free Trade Association
EMU	Economic and Monetary Union
EPC	European Political Cooperation
ERDF	European Regional Development Fund
ERM	Exchange Rate Mechanism

ESF	European Social Fund
ETA	Euzkadi ta Askatsuna (Basque Homeland and Liberty)
EU	European Union
EU-15	European Union of 15 members (pre-2004 enlargement)
EU-25	European Union of 25 members (post-2004 enlargement)
FBI	Federal Bureau of Investigation
FDI	Foreign Direct Investment
FRG	Federal Republic of Germany (West Germany)
FTAA	Free Trade Area of the Americas
FYROM	Former Yugoslav Republic of Macedonia
G-7	The group of the world's leading industrialised nations (US, Jap, Ger, UK, Fr, It, Can)
G-8	The G-7 plus Russia
GATT	General Agreement on Tariffs and Trade
GDP	Gross Domestic Product
GDR	German Democratic Republic (see also DDR)
GNP	Gross National Product
HIPC	Heavily Indebted Poor Country
HST	Hegemonic Stability Theory
IBRD	International Bank for Reconstruction and Development (the World Bank)
ICC	International Criminal Court
ICJ	International Court of Justice
IGC	Intergovernmental Conference
ILO	International Labour Organisation
IMF	International Monetary Fund
IPE	International Political Economy
IR	International Relations
JHA	Justice and Home Affairs
LDC	Less developed country
LI	Liberal Intergovermentalism
Mercosur	Mercado Común del Sur (Southern (American) Common Market)
MLG	Multilevel governance
MNC	Multinational corporation (see also TNC)
NAFTA	North American Free Trade Agreement
NATO	North Atlantic Treaty Organisation
NGO	Non-governmental Organisation
NIC/NIE	Newly Industrialising Country/Economy
OAU	Organisation of African Unity
OCA	Optimal Currency Area
OEEC	Organisation for European Economic Cooperation
OECD	Organisation for Economic Cooperation and Development
OPEC	Organisation of Petroleum Exporting Countries
OSCE	Organisation for Security and Cooperation in Europe

PHARE	Poland and Hungary Aid for Economic Restructuring
PJCCM	Police and Judicial Cooperation in Criminal Matters
PNV	Partido Nacional Vasco (Spain, Basque Nationalist Party)
PP	Partido Popular (Spain, Popular Party)
PRI	Partido Revolucionario Institucional (Mexico, Institutional Revolutionary Party)
PSOE	Partido Socialista Obrero Español (Spanish Workers Socialist Party)
QMV	Qualified Majority Voting
RRF	Rapid Reaction Force
SAPs	Structural Adjustment Programmes
SEA	Single European Act
SEM	Single European Market
SMP	Single Market Programme
TACIS	Technical Assistance for the Commonwealth of Independent States
TEU	Treaty on European Union (Maastricht Treaty)
TNC	Transnational Corporation
ToA	Treaty of Amsterdam
ToN	Treaty of Nice
Triad	NAFTA + EU (EEA) + Japan/Asia Pacific region
UKIP	United Kingdom Independence Party
UNCTAD	United Nations Conference on Trade and Development
UNDP	United Nations Development Programme
UNEP	United Nations Environment Programme
UNESCO	United Nations Educational, Scientific and Cultural Organisation
WEU	Western European Union
WMDs	Weapons of Mass Destruction
WSF	World Social Forum
WTO	World Trade Organisation

Publisher's acknowledgements

We are grateful to the following for permission to reproduce copyright material:

Independent Newspapers for a series of responses to eurosceptics published in *The Independent* 21st June 2004; Oxford University Press for extracts from *Introduction to International Relations: Theories and Approaches* 2nd edition, edited by R. Jackson and G. Sørenson, 1999; Time Warner Books and Curtis Brown Group for extracts from *Open World: The Truth about Globalisation* by P. Legrain, 2002; Granta Books and The New Press for extracts from *False Dawn: the Delusions of Global Capitalism* by J. Gray, 1998; and Polity Press Ltd for extracts from *Globalization and Anti-Globalization* by D. Held and A. McGrew, 2002.

Figures 1.5 and 7.1 from *A Political History of Western Europe*, Addison Wesley Longman, (Urwin, D.W. 1997), with permission of Pearson Education; Figures 4.1 from chapter by H. Wallace and 4.4 from chapter by Stephen Woolcock in *Policy Making in the European Union*, (Wallace, H. and Wallace, W. (eds) 2000), by permission of Oxford University Press; Figure 4.3 from *Introduction in European Politics*, (Cini, M. 2003), by permission of Oxford University Press; Figure 8.1 from *Introduction to International Relations: Theories and Approaches*, 2nd edition, (Jackson, R. and Sørenson, G. 2003), Box 4.8 (p. 118), by permission of Oxford University Press, original source: *Verden 2000: Teorier og tendenser i international politik*, Gyldendal, Copenhagen (Heurlin, B. 1996), © Gyldendalske Boghandel, Nordisk forlag A/S, Copenhagen; Figures 8.2 and UF 8.1 (Discussion 8.5) from *Introduction to International Relations: Theories and Approaches* 2nd edition, (Jackson, R. and Sørenson, G. 2003), Boxes 5.6 (p. 146) and 7.1 (p. 199), by permission of Oxford University Press; Figure 10.1 from Ballard Street Comics, 08 July 2004, Copyright © 2004 Creators Syndicate, Inc., by permission of Jerry Van Amerongen and Creators Syndicate, Inc.; Figure 10.2 from Inequality of world incomes: what should be done? from www.openDemocracy.net, (Wade, R. 2001), with permission of openDemocracy.net; Figure 10.3 'Illustration, p. 94', from *The Return Of Depression Economics* by Paul Krugman. Copyright © 1999 by Paul Krugman. Used by permission of W.W. Norton & Company, Inc.; Figure 10.4 'Feature 1.1, p. 11', from HUMAN DEVELOPMENT REPORT 2001 by United Nations Development Programme, copyright © 2001 by the United Nations Development Programme. Used by permission of Oxford University Press, Inc.; Figure 11.2 'Figure 1.1, p. 26', from HUMAN DEVELOPMENT REPORT 1999 by United Nations Development Programme, copyright © 1999 by the United Nations Development Programme. Used by permission of Oxford University Press, Inc.; Figure 11.3 reprinted by permission of Sage Publications Ltd, from Dicken, P., *Global Shift*, Copyright (© Peter Dicken, 2003); Figure 12.2 from

Globalization/Anti-Globalization, Polity Press, (Held, D. and McGrew, A. 2002), p. 99.

Photograph 1.1 reprinted by permission of Archivo Iconografico, S.A./Corbis; Photograph 1.2 reprinted by permission of Michael St. Maur Sheil/Corbis; Photograph 1.3 reprinted by permission of Bettmann/Corbis; Photograph 3.1 reprinted by permission of Ed Kashi/Corbis; Photograph 3.2 reprinted by permission of Jonathan Blair/Corbis; Photograph 3.3 reprinted by permission of Hulton-Deutsch Collection/Corbis; Photograph 4.1 reprinted by permission of Corbis Sygma; Photograph 5.1 reprinted by permission of Bettmann/Corbis; Photograph 6.1 reprinted by permission of Warwick Sweeney, www.warwick-sweeney.com; Photograph 7.1 reprinted by permission of Philippe Wojazer/Reuters/Corbis; Photograph 8.1 reprinted by permission of Bettmann/Corbis; Photograph 9.1 reprinted by permission of Jacques Langevin/Corbis Sygma; Photograph 10.1 reprinted by permission of Lyn Wait; Photograph 10.2 reprinted by permission of Mark Renders/Getty Images; Photograph 11.1 reprinted by permission of Touhig Sion/Corbis Sygma.

Table 1.1 extract from *Europe: A History* by Norman Davies published by Pimlico. Used by permission of The Random House Group Limited; Table 4.1 from European and regional integration (Christiansen, T.) from *The Globalization of World Politics*, 2nd edition, (Baylis, J. and Smith, S. (eds) 2001), by permission of Oxford University Press; Table 6.1 from *Finance in the European Union*, October 1998, Annexe 8, Table 5. Reprinted by permission of the European Community, Office of the Official Publications of the European Communities; Tables 8.1 and 8.3 from *Introduction to International Relations: Theories and Approaches* 2nd edition, (Jackson, R. and Sorenson, G. 2003), Boxes 1.2 (p. 6) and 6.11 (p. 192) by permission of Oxford University Press; Table 8.2 from *International Relations Theory: A Critical Introduction*, p. 16, Routledge, (Weber, C. 2001), by permission of Thomson Publishing Services; Table 12.1 based on The World in 2004 from The Economist, © The Economist Newspaper Limited, London, 2003; Table 12.2 from *Globalization/Anti-Globalization*, Polity Press, (Held, D. and McGrew, A. 2002), p. 99.

In some instances we have been unable to trace the owners of copyright material, and we would appreciate any information that would enable us to do so.

Map of the book

	Chapter 1 EUROPE: THE ORIGINS OF NATIONALISM AND THE STATE EXPERIENCE	Chapter 2 THE STATE, SOVEREIGNTY, AND NATIONALISM	Chapter 3 NATIONALISM IN CONTEMPORARY EUROPE	Chapter 4 THE EUROEPAN UNION AND THE STATE	Chapter 5 INTEGRATION THEORY AND THE STATE	Chapter 6 THE EU AND THE REGIONS: MULTILEVEL GOVERNANCE IN AN ERA OF GLOBALISATION
CHAPTER CONTENTS	The Enlightenment	The concept of state	Identity	Pooling sovereignty	Federalism	Regionalism
	French Revolution	Sovereignty	Former Yugoslavia	Single European Market (SEM) and Economic and Monetary Union (EMU)	Confederalism	Regional development
	Nationalism	International institutions and the state	Nationalism – 8 contexts		Functionalism	
	War and dicatorship	Defining nationalism				
	History of European integration	Types of nationalism	Integrating Europe	Institutions of the EU	Neo functionalism and spillover	Multilevel governance (MLG)
	Cold War	Culture	Sovereignty	Policy making	Intergovernmentalism	Regionalism in Spain and Germany
		Nation building			The EU – a federal state?	
	Multinational institutions	Culture and ethnic nationalism	Euroscepticism			
		EU and citizenship				
	Euroscepticism					
KEY CONCEPTS	THE STATE	SOVEREIGNTY	EUROPEAN INTEGRATION PROCESS	INTERGOVERN-MENTALISM	FEDERALISM	SUBSIDIARITY
	DICTATORSHIP	NATIONALISM	EUROSCEPTICISM	SUPRA-NATIONALISM	NEOFUNC-TIONALISM	EUROPEANISATION

Chapter 7 EU ENLARGEMENT AND THE CHALLENGE TO THE STATE	Chapter 8 INTERNATIONAL RELATIONS THEORY AND THE STATE	Chapter 9 GLOBALISATION AND THE EU IN TRANSITION	Chapter 10 GLOBALISATION AND ITS CONSEQUENCES	Chapter 11 GLOBALISATION, THE STATE AND MULTINATIONAL CORPORATIONS	Chapter 12 MULTILATERALISM AND THE EUROPEAN UNION AS A GLOBAL ACTOR	CHAPTER
History and process of EU enlargement	IR theory	Defining globalisation	Postmodernism	The state – in relation to globalisation	Multilateralism	
Copenhagen criteria	Realism/neorealism	Americanisation	Challenge to the Enlightenment	Washington consensus	Institutions	
Rationale for enlargement	Cold War	History and process of globalisation			September 11, 2001	
	Liberalism	EU and globalisation	Consequences of globalisation	Multinational corporations (MNCs)	Human rights post-9/11	
Democracy and human rights	Multinational institutions	Single European Market (SEM) and Economic and Monetary Union (EMU)	Asian Crisis 1997–8	Global economy	EU as global actor	CHAPTER CONTENTS
	International society		Defending globalisation	Business and governance	Weaknesses of the EU	
Costs and benefits of enlargement	International Political Economy (IPE)			Trade	The new security context	
					Regionalism	
Single European Market	Mercantilism			The Triad	Responding to globalisation	
	Economic liberalism				Public goods	
Common Agricultural Policy (CAP)	Marxism			Foreign Direct Investment (FDI)	Institutions	
	Hegemonic Stability Theory (HST)				Cosmopolitan social democracy	
Future enlargements	US hegemony				Feminism/gender issues	
The global context						
HUMAN RIGHTS WIDENING AND DEEPENING	CAPITALISM LIBERALISM MARXISM HEGEMONY	GLOBALISATION POWER	POSTMODERNISM CULTURE	TRANSNATIONAL MULTINATIONAL CORPORATIONS WASHINGTON CONSENSUS	MULTILATERALISM TRANSATLANTIC PARTNERSHIP HARD/SOFT POWER	KEY CONCEPTS

Introduction

'Europe is the best example in the history of the world of conflict resolution.'

John Hume (b. 1937), winner of the Nobel Peace Prize, 1998
(from David McKittrick, 'Tributes to giant of peace process as Hume bows out', *The Independent*, 5 February 2004)

There are many books which examine the state and state sovereignty, and many devoted to the theme of nationalism. Books on European integration are even more numerous, while new books on globalisation seem to appear every week. *Europe, the State and Globalisation* attempts the perhaps foolhardy task of combining all of these issues in a single text. The rationale for this is that it is surely vital to have an overview of how these processes interrelate. It is hoped that this book provokes readers to further study. Indeed the book asks many questions and by no means provides full or complete answers. It aims instead to provide essential foundations as well as stimulating and useful arguments about the relationship between the state, European integration and globalisation.

Outline

- A summary of the main argument of the book
- A brief discussion on defining Europe
- An overview of the book's structure
- Suggestions for readers

● ● ● ● The argument presented in *Europe, the State and Globalisation*

The modern state emerged in the seventeenth century following the Treaty of Westphalia of 1648 which settled the shape of Europe for the following century and beyond. This book provides an analytical description of the role of the state in contemporary Europe, a subject of increasing relevance not only in Europe itself but also beyond, as experiments in **regionalism** appear elsewhere. There may be lessons to be learned from the European experience, now spanning seven decades. The state is undergoing considerable change. The book argues that two related processes, European integration and globalisation, are important to this change. European integration centres on the European Union and its various institutions, but other international governmental organisations besides the EU also affect the role of the state. These include NATO, the UN and the WTO. Globalisation is a multifaceted process that embraces not only social and technological change, but also institutional change. International organisations like the ones just referred to may be seen as responses to, as well as products of, the globalisation process. Indeed, this book argues that the continued progress of European integration may be interpreted as a response to factors involved in globalisation, notably the internationalisation of markets, privatisation and liberalisation, increased competition, **regionalisation** and the ITC revolution.

Globalisation is a highly contested phenomenon. Some writers emphasise the positive outcomes of the globalisation process (Micklethwait and Wooldridge, 2000; McRae, 2004), while others are more critical (Monbiot, 2000; Klein, 2001; Callinicos, 2003). Still others indicate various ways in which globalisation should be made to work better (Soros, 2002; Legrain, 2002; Held & McGrew, 2002). Meanwhile on the streets protest has built up with major anti-capitalist demonstrations at Seattle and Genoa, and on the Internet, campaigns for a global civil society have attracted massive support. Even the notion of globalisation is contested: some writers have argued that the term is inappropriate, because the process it describes is international, and far from global (Hirst & Thompson, 1999; Goldmann, 2001). The issue of defining globalisation is examined in detail in Chapter 9, but for now we present a single definition from a prominent exponent of globalisation theory, Anthony Giddens. He defines globalisation as the:

> intensification of worldwide social relations which link distant localities in such a way that local happenings are shaped by events occurring many miles away and vice versa (Giddens, 1990:64).

This book, however, adopts an interpretation of globalisation which treats it as a primarily economic phenomenon, identified with the neo-liberal project of promoting *laissez-faire* (free market) economics around the world. This approach is the same as that of John Gray in his book *False Dawn* (1998). Gray considers globalisation to be a political project driven by the **Washington consensus** that favours the uninterrupted flow of private capital, free markets, a reduced role for the state, and an absence of regulatory control on private markets. The political project of globalisation is to extend this market system to as many countries as possible.

It is often suggested that the two processes that are the focus of attention in this book, European integration and globalisation, indicate that the **state** is in decline. However, a central claim in the book is that the state should not be seen as a passive victim in this decline. On the contrary, governments have been willing participants in these processes which have to a considerable degree changed the nature of the state. In other words, it is national governments which have been the agents of the 'altered state', and some would argue diminished authority of the state. One may also ask to what extent has this been a 'good thing', and while this is certainly touched upon, it is outside the scope of this text to examine this in detail. Instead, the question is asked – and hopefully answered in the final chapter – what can the state do now; what are its responsibilities in the context of the onward march of globalisation?

While the main theme of the book – the relationship between European integration, the state and globalisation, is reflected in the title, a fourth theme, **nationalism**, is examined in the early part of the book. The approach taken is one of examining a series of concepts and experiences that interrelate like tectonic plates (see Figure 0.1). Indeed, as in geology, where tectonic plates clash, earthquakes occur. Thus it is argued that where state powers and nationalist sentiment clash, violence is invariably the result. The book begins by looking at the origins of the state and at the related notion of **sovereignty**. Next we examine the foundations of nationalism established after the French Revolution of 1789. Nationalism, 'a doctrine invented in Europe' (Kedourie, 1966:9), tends to be accompanied by extreme violence.

In order to understand European integration, we must first examine the notions of state, sovereignty and nationalism, and recognise how these have on occasions combined to devastating effect. Chapter 1 argues that the process of European integration is a 'response to conflict'. Chapters 2 and 3 provide an

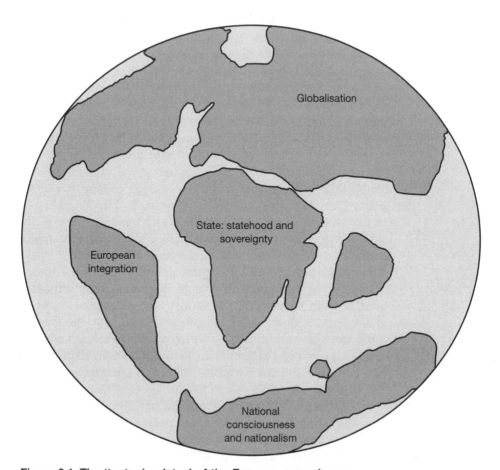

Figure 0.1 The 'tectonic plates' of the European experience

overview of the contemporary relevance of nationalism in Europe. The subject of Chapters 4 to 7 is the core characteristics and consequences of European integration. Then the book moves to the wider global context, and especially those factors attributed to globalisation, the phenomenon now shaping the direction, not only of Europe, but of the world. The last chapter is concerned with the implications of globalisation post- 11 September 2001, and examines possible responses from the EU and its member states. The book ends with a summary of how national governments and the leaders of the European Union, as well as other IGOs, might respond to the challenges presented by globalisation.

To return to the analogy of tectonic plates shown in Figure 0.1, the concepts and processes studied in this book are the state and its attendant notions of statehood and sovereignty; national consciousness and nationalism; European integration and the European Union; and globalisation. There is of course a substantial risk of instability in all these relationships. One particular clash, disastrously familiar in Europe, is the risk of conflict between state and nation. The clash occurs where there is a mismatch between the two phenomena, where one does not mirror the other. In fact state and nation are rarely ideally matched and there is often at least potential conflict within states for this reason.

One of the core arguments of *Europe, the State and Globalisation* is that since the Second World War, European political elites, with support from the USA, have sought to resolve the historical conflict between state interests on the one hand, and national consciousness on the other. The product of this elite-driven endeavour has been the **European integration process**, the third of our 'tectonic plates'. While European integration has achieved much in terms of bringing peace and reconciliation between former enemies, it continues to harbour many risks. It too can become vulnerable to the stirrings of those restless beasts, the state and nationalism. If the European Union fails to reconcile its constituent parts to the whole, it will disintegrate. Some commentators, such as Hutton (2003), have warned that it is by no means certain that Europe's comparative peace since 1945 will continue indefinitely. The Union has major problems, identified in Chapter 12, that it shows little creative energy in resolving, but if it does prove able to overcome these and avoids succumbing to reactionary atavistic tendencies that seek a regression along national lines, then the Union offers significant grounds for optimism about the future track of globalisation.

The end of the Cold War brought new nationalist threats as well as opportunities. Wars occurred in the former Yugoslavia and in the former USSR, and in the Persian Gulf region to Europe's south. But the greatest challenge may come from the multifaceted process of globalisation, with its attendant economic and political pressures, including increased economic disparities, migration and international terrorism, as well as climate change and environmental degradation.

Why does the EU offer grounds for optimism? The answer lies partly in its economic strength – the Single European Market is the world's largest trading block with some 40 per cent of world trade – and it is a vital partner to the US. If consumer strength is a possible source for change, the EU has significant potential. It comprises over 450 million people. The Union is a unique experiment in governance, being a combination of state interests expressed through

intergovernmentalism in the Council of the European Union (the former Council of Ministers) and the European Council, and supranational authority based on legislative agreements among its member states, and sustained by the European Commission and European Court of Justice.

> The European Union is [. . .] a stateless market which is not controlled at its own level but by the various states, united in permanent negotiation (Kapteyn, 1996:131).

It is the combination of both national and supranational pressures that can be a force for enlightened and innovative thinking, most likely in response to lobbying from non-governmental organisations (NGOs) at the European and at the state level. In one area the EU holds a certain trump card in its relations with the US. The latter is the one surviving superpower, but it is unlikely to continue with this role indefinitely. The costs, material as well as in terms of criticism at home and abroad, will chip away at the US's will to continue as world policeman. The US has long required the Europeans to take greater responsibility for their own security. This of course has major tax implications and political repercussions for the European states, and for the European integration process. However, the usual pattern will assert itself: where integration serves state interests, integration will happen. There will eventually be acceptance by member state governments that greater integration in the area of defence and security makes economic as well as military sense, and such integration will be a prerequisite to building credibility as a counterbalance to American hegemony. The choice that the UK makes is a moot point, for on this issue above all else, the UK traditionally aligns with the US, as in the recent Iraq conflict. The EU may also finally achieve the kind of institutional reform and constitutional framework that a body of its scope and impact must surely require. If these changes come about, then the EU can begin to share in the global responsibilities that should be its destiny.

The response to globalisation must be both reformist and highly innovative in the institutional sense. A major difficulty is that there is no enthusiasm for creative solutions, either among governing elites in developed states, or among their electorates. Indeed, institutions worldwide are under attack, and are very much seen as part of the problem, part of the 'democratic deficit'. Thus the EU and the World Trade Organisation (WTO) are two of the most high-profile and most contested of the international organisations, as protests in Seattle, Genoa, Gothenburg and elsewhere demonstrate. Clearly, there is good reason for this, given their deficiencies. However, the protests may be misdirected. It is state governments that hold the key to planning and enforcing reform and yet they have thus far proved incapable of doing much more than acquiescing in the status quo.

A major claim in the book is that the role of the state has greatly altered over the past 300 years and in particular through the most recent stage in the process of globalisation. It is argued that two phases of globalisation have occurred since the Second World War. The first was immediately after the war, when statesmen set about reconstructing a world order based on multilateral institutions that would provide greater stability than the environment that emerged from the ashes of the First World War. Despite the Cold War divisions, this proved broadly successful. The second phase of globalisation, which we may describe as post-Cold War, has had a more profound impact on the lives of ordinary people. It is the burgeoning technological change following the launch of the World Wide Web in 1990, and the huge increase in capital movement that has been such a striking feature of the past decade and a half. Through all this the state has survived, but its influence, its call on citizens' loyalty, its direct impact on people's lives, and above all its power to control or influence matters that it formerly controlled or influenced, has declined.

This book examines questions of both responsibility for this decline, and its consequences. It also looks at the altered role of the state in the context of the current phase of globalisation. Some fundamental arguments surrounding European integration are examined, in particular the prospects for an effective settlement of the ongoing conflict between integrationist tendencies and preferences for some repatriation of authority to the member states. Specific EU policy areas such as Economic and Monetary Union, EU enlargement and regional policy, are referred to in the light of this dispute between federalists and intergovernmentalists. Figure 0.2 illustrates the main subjects covered by the book and demonstrates the relationship between them.

It is perhaps opportune to comment on the term 'European integration process' which is commonly used in the literature. Cini (2003:95) reports that intergovernmentalists – by which we may mean those preferring a more nationalist perspective on European politics – tend to prefer the term 'cooperation' to 'integration' since the latter may be interpreted as implying a reduction in state authority, whereas 'cooperation' would affirm the centrality of governments in the Union. Nevertheless, throughout this book the term integration process is used. However, one should not infer from this term that the process has been unopposed, or uniform. The arguments over a federal or an intergovernmental model for European integration have ensured that the process has often been heavily contested.

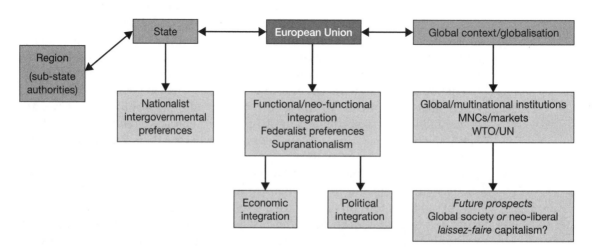

Figure 0.2 Europe in the global context: participants, processes and preferences

Globalisation is just as contentious. The term is normally understood in a fairly restrictive fashion, referring to economic globalisation, a process driven by neo-liberal preferences emanating from the United States supported by its closest allies in rich countries, as well as elites elsewhere. According to Gray (1998) globalisation is a political project designed to impose a neo-liberal free market economy throughout the world. Opponents of globalisation argue that the southern hemisphere is mostly left behind by the process, and that even in rich countries, society is left fractured and damaged by increased social inequalities. It is argued in the final chapter that September 11 forces a wider conception that takes account of other phenomena including the 'internationalisation of illegitimate violence' (Keohane, 2002).

The book does adopt a critical stance towards globalisation but uses prescriptions from various writers to argue for a constructive approach towards making globalisation work for the common interests of all humanity. Soros, for example, claims that the WTO effectively serves the interests of private goods, but he laments the lack of an equivalent body representing 'public goods' (Soros, 2002). He advocates that states accept responsibility for establishing and sustaining an institution, or group of institutions, tasked with defending 'public goods', such as environmental protection, food safety, human rights and labour rights. Such an institution, or group of institutions, can only emerge if states have the will to pursue such innovations and accept eventual jurisdiction of supranational authorities. The position of the United States is crucial to such a reformist agenda, because its leadership is an established fact of present-day international relations. But if the US is not prepared to accept the need for such change, then the EU must lead and find alliances elsewhere, including among liberal opinion in the United States, and from business interests which support efforts to maintain a more stable commercial and trading environment. Institutional reform in defence of public goods will require financial support as well as unflinching political commitment. The financing of such innovation may come from a so-called Tobin Tax on currency exchanges or a levy on corporate mergers, or from direct taxation. Gray says that such a reform might lead to a more managed global economy but 'so long as the United States remains committed to a global free market it will veto any such reform' (Gray, 1998:200). The commitment of a sufficiently large coalition of states, together with leading NGOs, is critical to any such reformist agenda, not least because it will require substantial resources.

The WTO, stung by widespread revolt and criticism, has attempted to increase its transparency and accountability. However, improvements to its website, publication of procedures and decisions, and greater access to meetings for NGOs, are superficial steps that fail to fully address the concerns of civil society organisations and the public. Wilkinson (2002) reports that member state governments tend to deny the WTO a greater role in precisely those areas that civil society, NGOs and the wider public would wish it to take more responsibility, namely international labour regulation, the environment and human rights. In these areas the progress of the EU has been good, through the social chapter of the Treaty on European Union (TEU), employment measures, the incorporation of the European Convention on Human Rights and through minimum standards relating to health, safety and the environment. In the WTO, linkage between trade and these issues is more limited, though, according to Wilkinson, likely to increase. He reports that since the Seattle debacle in 1999, the WTO has been more proactive in matters of public health, the manufacture and distribution of generic drugs, genetic engineering, and the fight against HIV/AIDS. These 'issues confronting the world trade system' are likely to gain prominence within the WTO, extending both its role and its effectiveness.

There may be scope for NGOs to enhance their influence in the WTO, although it is inevitably the northern-based larger and better equipped ones that have the most access to and influence on the Organisation, and the EU for that matter. In terms of public opinion, web campaigning and information dissemination are potentially powerful tools in developed countries where web access is high. While the low density of computers in less developed countries is a major concern, it is in OECD countries where governments must be persuaded to respond proactively to assist less developed countries (LDCs) and ensure progress in respect of public goods.

Clearly NGOs will encounter the usual problems of resources, both financial and logistical, as well as the difficult task of alerting sufficient people to identify with direct material advantage from campaigning for and setting up structures that can defend public goods. There is a major problem of message: how to get sufficient numbers of people, with sufficient resources, to commit to the idea of reform through existing institutions like the EU and the WTO, if not through new ones. The alternative is to continue with current policy and the current direction of globalisation, a path with all too obvious consequences: large numbers of relatively rootless migrants, increased poverty and marginalisation, rising crime, increased prison populations, widely divergent wealth differentials, environmental despoliation and international terrorism. Even a cataclysmic event like the 9/11 attacks on New York and Washington does not seem to alert a wider public in the richer developed countries to ask what could possibly be questionable about the current direction of globalisation. Instead there appears to be a retrenchment behind old convictions that are made increasingly redundant by the unpredictable, volatile and uncharted directions of the globalisation process.

The final chapter of the book argues that the European Union has a critical responsibility in shaping any reforms to global governance. The Union is the most significant example of multilateral institution building and has experience of marrying the conflicting needs of state governments and their populations with supranational authorities. It also has a powerful strategic position with ties to the west, east, north and south. The downside is that the Union itself is vulnerable to the twin spectres of nostalgia and racism. Its own unity is threatened by recidivist tendencies. It has other major weaknesses too, including its failure to deal adequately with concerns over political legitimacy and its subsidy regime in the field of agriculture, which is damaging to the reputation of the Union internationally, as well as internally. It is essential that the Union resolve these contradictions and others before it can effectively contribute to the much bigger challenge of contributing to a wide coalition of interests that can fashion a more equitable and sustainable global governance.

● ● ● ● Defining Europe

Europe's boundaries are well defined on its western edge facing the Atlantic, but while the Americas and most of Africa are entirely surrounded by sea, Europe is part of the Eurasian landmass and its Eastern limits are less obvious. Russia and Turkey are normally considered part of the European family, although both extend deep into Asia (see Discussion 0.1 and Figure 0.3). Europe's eastern edge is normally considered to run from the Bosporus, across the Black Sea and north to the Volga River and onward in a north-easterly direction to the Ural Mountains, and then north to the Arctic Ocean.

Chapter 2 refers to Europe's cultural heritage, essentially built on a Greco-Roman-Christian tripod. Such commonality serves to justify a claim for a specifically European culture, though it has been successfully exported via colonisation to North America and to Australasia. With each geographical extension a culture undergoes further change, assuming new layers as new identities are forged. Thus the culture of the United States, while having a European heritage, is markedly different. This discussion has gained fresh impetus under globalisation, with the question emerging of the extent to which globalisation is actually no more than Americanisation. Europe, meanwhile, has established its own socio-political characteristics, which make it distinctive, with different preferences from the US for example (Hutton, 2003; Micklethwait & Wooldridge, 2004). Contemporary European states, as well as the European Union, are largely built on the basis of a social contract between the state and the citizens that involves substantial state responsibility for welfare, education and health provision, as well as the more fundamentalist, or realist concerns such as security and protection from crime. Nevertheless, as McLean and McMillan suggest in Discussion 0.1, any sense of civic responsibility and community in Europe is tempered by the twin threats of nostalgia and racism. Nostalgia is a significant component in nationalist sentiment and remains under the surface of Europe's perhaps fragile unity.

Discussion 0.1

What is Europe?

Europe remains powerful though ill-defined. Some of its members, Russia and Turkey, extend beyond its accepted geographical limits. Such unity as it possessed by the early twentieth century rested equivocally upon a shared though divisive Christianity and a rationalist philosophical and scientific tradition (both owing much to the Arab world), a common history of sustained internecine warfare, a fiction of racial homogeneity, and an original responsibility for industrialisation and modernity. This tense unity was first effectively projected beyond its own boundaries in the sixteenth century, reaching its greatest extent in the early twentieth century, before dissolving in the great European civil wars of 1914–45. Its greatest continuing vulnerabilities are to nostalgia and racism (from McLean & McMillan, 2003:178).

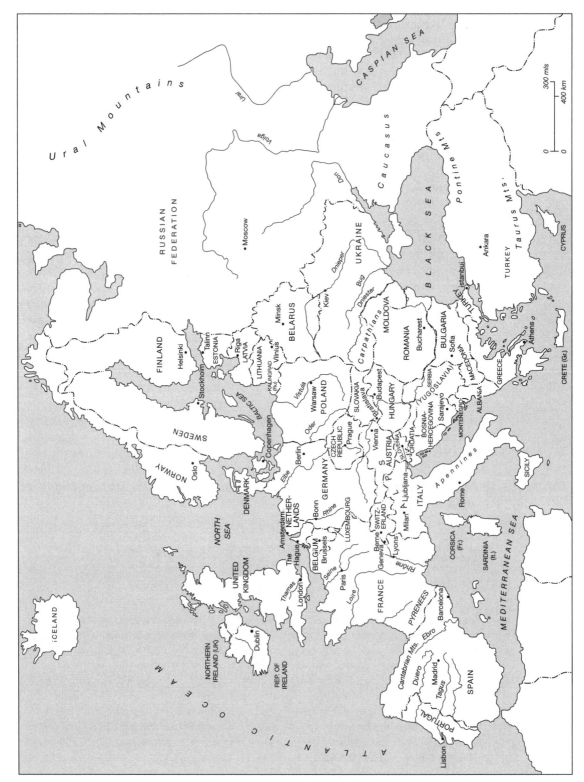

Figure 0.3 Geographical Europe – from the Atlantic to the Urals

●●●● The structure of the book

Overview

The book passes from history, the role of the state and nationalism to the European context before addressing the wider global context in the final third.

Chapters 1–3 are concerned with laying down a foundation to better understanding of the complex relationships between state, sovereignty, nationalism, European integration and globalisation.

Chapters 4–7 examine the European Union in detail, focusing first on its institutions, then on integration theory, then regional policy and multilevel governance, and finally EU enlargement.

Chapter 8 is about International Relations (IR) theory.

Chapters 9–11 are about different aspects of globalisation, from defining the term and the EU response, arguments for and against globalisation, and the role of the state, and of transnational corporations (TNCs).

Chapter 12 is about how to meet the challenge of transnational governance in the context of globalisation.

●●●● Summary

Chapter 1 focuses on the history, and establishes the foundation for the development of nationalism in Europe. It is argued that the French Revolution stirred national consciousness and precipitated a period of war and then competition to establish powerful empires, sustained by increasing military capability. As the Ottoman Empire disintegrated and the Austro-Hungarian Empire collapsed under the weight of its internal pressures, Europe erupted in its long civil war of 1914–45. The second part of the chapter describes the transition after 1945 towards a more integrated Europe, albeit initially in the context of Cold War division. The end of the Cold War and the emergence of a new phase in the development of globalisation provide the two contexts within which the integration process has continued.

Chapter 2 lays further foundations for the rest of the book with an examination of the relationship between the state and sovereignty, and it explores the idea of nationalism in detail.

Chapter 3 examines the notion of identity before exploring the relevance of nationalism in contemporary Europe. Eight contexts are considered with the conclusion that nationalism remains a powerful force across the continent.

Chapter 4 is a detailed study of the processes and institutions involved in European integration. Described throughout as a process, European integration is presented as an intergovernmental attempt to resolve the tensions which have torn Europe apart over centuries. The chapter explores the nature of European integration and examines the institutions which comprise the European Union. These are described in relation to the member states, thus retaining the key focus on how the state relates to the EU and vice versa.

Chapter 5 examines the theoretical background to European integration, again focusing on the relationship between the state and the integration process.

Chapter 6 looks at the regional dimension to European integration and places the state in a continuum between sub-national authorities, or regions, and the European level, or EU institutions. This relationship, and its role in decision-making, is referred to as 'multilevel governance' (MLG).

Chapter 7 examines the 2004 Eastern Enlargement of the Union, taking in ten new states including eight former members of the communist bloc. The chapter details the role of the state in the enlargement process and the likely consequences of this historic step.

Chapter 8 again has a theoretical focus, summarising key theories of International Relations (IR). The chapter has a state-level focus but it examines how different IR theories regard the role of the state in international affairs. A key dispute in IR concerns the extent to which the state is the primary actor in international politics, or whether international institutions, such as the EU, have become more powerful at the expense of the state. While by no means comprehensive, the chapter picks out core approaches from the IR tradition and relates them to the role of the state.

Chapter 9 is concerned with defining and understanding globalisation and an examination of the response of the European Union to globalising tendencies. It is argued that Europe's broadly federating progress since Maastricht, consisting of the consolidation of the Single European Market, Economic and Monetary Union, and the 1995 enlargement as well as the Eastern Enlargement in 2004, are all closely related to, or responses to, globalisation.

Chapter 10 examines consequences of economic globalisation and contains critical perspectives from a number of writers as well as a passionate defence of globalisation from two writers for *The Economist*, John Micklethwait and Adrian Wooldridge.

Chapter 11 looks at the role of the state in the process of economic globalisation and also the contribution from multinational corporations, once seen as emblematic of the power and wealth of industrialisation, and now universally recognised as badges of globalisation itself.

Chapter 12 analyses the direction of globalisation post-September 11. It begins with an exploration of the nature of multilateralism and the role of international governmental organisations. The chapter examines responses to 9/11 and then returns to a focus on the European Union. It examines the major weaknesses of the Union that may not only undermine its possible contribution to shaping global governance, but also risk provoking the abandonment of the Union's achievements of the past six decades. The chapter also examines the prospects for a continuation of the EU/US strategic, political and economic partnership.

The conclusion of the chapter, and of the book, is in two parts. First a survey of how the reform of existing institutions can assist in maximising the benefits from globalisation while minimising the risks. The idea of a partner organisation to the WTO charged with defending public goods is explored. Finally, the concept of a cosmopolitan social democracy (Held & McGrew, 2002) is described. This proposal calls for an international coalition of liberal states and international governmental organisations, embracing support from NGOs and private businesses, that can reach a just settlement suitable for the effective conduct of transnational governance in a globalising world.

How to use the book

Most readers may wish to read the book in strict chapter order. This is of course a perfectly logical and unsurprising approach. It is also possible, however, to choose to read selected chapters to match your specific interests, for example one might seek an overview of integration theories (Chapter 5) or International Relations theory (Chapter 8), or want a perspective on EU institutions (Chapter 4) or regions (Chapter 6) or enlargement (Chapter 7). However, some readers might prefer a more thematic approach, selecting to read the first three chapters on the state and nationalism, or Chapters 4–7 on the European Union, or Chapter 8 on IR theory, or the final four chapters on globalisation.

Still another approach is to dip into various chapters following thematic links across several of them, which is also possible, given that there is naturally some cross-over between chapters in relation to certain themes. For example, the question of the possible decline in the role of the state is looked at in Chapters 2, 3, 5, 6 and 9. A thematic map of the book is provided on page xviii to facilitate cross-referencing.

Each chapter includes highlighted words which signal an important topic. This is useful for speedy location of information you need. There are several key terms that recur throughout the book and when these are introduced they appear as *Key concepts* presented at the end of each chapter. While the meaning of some key concepts may be disputed, it is helpful to at least establish a framework within which discussion of these concepts can take place. The further discussion at the end of each chapter also helps to consolidate your understanding. Examples of these key concepts include the state, nationalism, sovereignty, European integration, hegemony and globalisation itself, as well as a raft of terms relating to integration theory and international relations. An A–Z glossary of these key terms, as well as other important concepts, is provided at the back of the book. Words included in the glossary are printed in bold, usually the first time they appear in the book.

The main theoretical context for the discussion comes from two sub-disciplines of political science, integration theory and International Relations theory. Both areas require an understanding of a number of key terms that enable us to talk more coherently about the phenomena that impact upon the state and are responsible for its changing role. Again, this is not a book to provide a detailed explanation of IR theory, and nor is it a book about integration theory. Far more suitable texts are available to give you a more full understanding of these complex and fascinating areas of enquiry. Nevertheless, it occurs to this author that any discussion about the role of the state in an international context has to touch upon these areas, and it is hoped to provide a useful introduction. For further learning about these and other issues raised here, key texts are recommended at the end of each chapter.

Each chapter is divided into sections and at the end of each section there is a *Review* task designed to check your understanding of some of the main points established in the preceding pages. These review questions are intended for either class discussion or personal reflection.

At the end of each chapter there are several important features of the book:

- a summary, listing main points presented in the chapter;
- key concepts – with definitions and further discussion;
- recommended further reading – often referring to texts already mentioned and quoted in the chapter concerned;
- film suggestions – most chapters include films for suggested viewing. These have been selected on account of their relevance to issues discussed in the chapter and present an alternative way of thinking about questions discussed in the book.

At the end of the book is a complete list of source references and a full index by subject.

I hope you enjoy using the book.

Simon Sweeney
York, December 2004

Chapter 1

Europe: the origins of nationalism and the state experience

Outline

- The impact of the French Revolution
- The European state: towards the abyss
- Recreating Europe: the emergence of European integration

Key concepts

1.1   State

1.2   Dictatorship

● ● ● ● Introduction

It is important to trace the major events in the recent history of Europe in order to understand the development of the modern state and the changes that affect the state in the context of both European integration and contemporary trends in globalisation. The concept of **state** relates to questions of national identity and consciousness, and it is surely not a matter of dispute that somewhere in an analysis of the meaning of state one needs to consider these issues. Looking at the history of Europe can help us to understand the development of national consciousness, the advent of states and the notion of statehood. Later in the book we shall refer to how in some respects European integration has impacted upon these older notions, and at how globalisation in some way erodes the very consciousness and identity that has developed in European states over the past 300 years.

The Treaty of Westphalia of 1648 marked the end of the German phase of the Thirty Years War and settled a pattern of separate states that valued **sovereignty** and independence, as well as mutual recognition. The stability that followed the Treaty was eventually disrupted by the social and then political turmoil of the late eighteenth century, and the emergence of early forms of class consciousness. This class consciousness, combined with the intellectual force for change stemming from the **Enlightenment**, created the revolutionary environment that drove the *ancien régime* from power in the French Revolution of 1789–94.

The French Revolution was a revolt against the privileges of the ruling elite comprising the monarchy, the aristocracy and the church. It was spurred by the ideals of the eighteenth-century Enlightenment, especially those that questioned established beliefs, hierarchies and privileges, all of which appeared to be for the benefit of the monarchy and organised religion. The Enlightenment promoted the power of reason, affirming faith in man's ability to resolve problems, whether technological or political. Gray (2003) describes this as a new humanism, placing humanity at the centre of all life on earth, superior to all other life forms and uniquely in control of events, a proposition he roundly dismisses as futile and at odds with the facts. Gray's views are discussed at length in Chapters 9 and 10. Nevertheless, the Enlightenment provided a powerful and ultimately irresistible challenge to the 'old order'. Although the middle classes had benefited from improved education and the onset of technological change in pre-revolutionary France, social conditions were deteriorating for the population as a whole, including the new urban working class. Even more significantly, the growing bourgeoisie and intellectual elite found itself isolated from the privileges of power, still zealously protected by the establishment (see Figure 1.1).

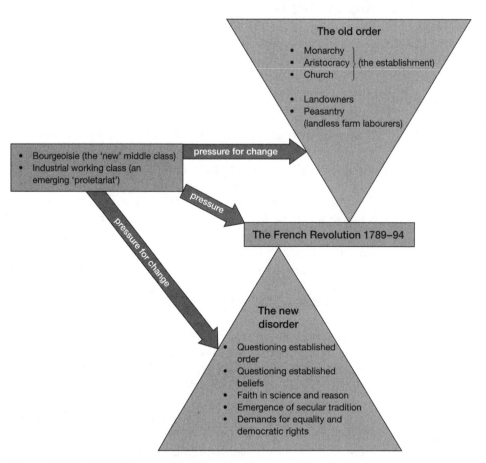

Figure 1.1 The Enlightenment challenge: the pressure for change

This chapter provides the historical background to the more theoretical discussions that follow in later chapters. It begins with a discussion of the impact of the French Revolution and its contribution to the development of the state and nationalism in Europe, as well as other legacies including republicanism and secularism. The second section develops the historical background to European integration, referring mainly to the years of war and **dictatorship** between 1914 and 1945. The third part begins with the claim that European integration is a response to conflict. A core dimension to this conflict is not simply war, but also the experience of dictatorship, hence the inclusion of dictatorship as a key concept (1.2). If you are in any doubt as to what this term means, look at this before reading the chapter.

The rest of the final section explains the changing context within which European integration has occurred, beginning with the post-war years when the role of the United States was decisive in providing the environment in which European states could cooperate. The **Cold War** provided an ominous backdrop and the first fundamental change to the context of integration occurred with the ending of the Cold War in 1989–91. This coincided with the emergence of the most recent phase in globalisation, a phenomenon which has had enormous consequences for the European integration project.

The chapter presents the first two key concepts, 1.1 State and 1.2 Dictatorship.

● ● ● ● The impact of the French Revolution

Louis XVI had begun modest social reforms, but many writers on revolutionary theory describe how attempts at reform are frequently the precursor to upheaval. Alexis de Tocqueville in his *L'Ancien Régime et la Révolution Francaise* (1856) claimed that many aspects of governance were improving under Louis XVI and that the king was genuinely committed to reform:

> 'The social order which is destroyed by a revolution is almost always better than that which preceded it; and experience shows that the most dangerous moment for a bad government is generally that in which it sets about reform' (the slightest acts of arbitrary power under Louis XVI seemed harder to endure) 'than all the despotism of Louis XIV' (de Tocqueville, cited in Davies, 1996:689).

A combination of social forces engulfed France at the end of the eighteenth century. While the rural peasantry was suffering acute food shortages and continued injustices at the hands of detached and arrogant landowners, the urban poor were increasingly hungry and jobless. The bourgeoisie were angered by their exclusion from power and by the excesses and privileges of the nobility.

The French Revolution swept the *ancien régime* from power and went on to have a profound impact on the development of the state in Europe. Far from ushering in a democratic system of government dedicated to *liberté, fraternité et égalité*, the events of 1789–94 gave rise to Napoleonic despotism and the widespread use of military force as a political weapon, and as an instrument of state policy, on a scale hitherto unknown. The response was a virtual call to arms across the continent. War fed the emergence of national consciousness and generated particularly virulent forms of nationalism. A vicious circle of nationalism, militarism and imperialism engulfed the continent.

The Revolution had already employed conscript armies and the numbers killed were testimony to the prevailing belief that armies could be used to crush political opposition. Napoleon's conviction that he could achieve what he required through the use of huge conscripted armies pitched Europe into a protracted period of war, involving all the major continental powers as well as Britain. Conscript armies were created, although Britain had less immediate need since its naval superiority and ability to inflict defeat on Napoleon at sea meant that Britain had much less risk of suffering a land invasion. Britain did not introduce conscription until shortly before the outbreak of the First World War.

Between 1804 and 1815 the Napoleonic Wars raged, and while the Holy Roman Empire collapsed, the continuing crisis prepared the ground for Germany's unified national identity under one flag, embracing the German-speaking peoples of Germany and Austria. Napoleon also spurred a sense of national solidarity in Britain. Free from invasion, Britain managed to enhance and develop its overseas territories, aided by a powerful navy. The British economy improved and Britain prospered, even winning control over certain French, Spanish and Dutch colonial territories. It is pertinent to point out that Britain's perspectives in the nineteenth century always had a global orientation, a position echoed by Churchill and other British politicians in the years following the Second World War, when the emphasis once again was on Britain's global role as head of the Commonwealth and an interlocutor between Europe and the USA. Even a casual observer of Britain's relationship with the experiment in European integration since 1945 would conclude that old habits die hard. Britain has often seemed a 'reluctant European' (Gowland & Turner, 1999) or an 'awkward partner' (George, 1998), and some explanation for this can be found in history as far back as the French Revolution and its aftermath.

The final years of Napoleon's leadership brought disaster to France, as between 1812 and 1814 the Russian campaign led to the conquest of Moscow, but ultimately 600,000 French troops faced starvation and were forced to retreat. Barely 1 in 20 made it back to Paris. In those two years Napoleon lost over a million men and the British, the Russians and the Prussians managed to occupy Paris. Napoleon was finally defeated by Britain, with decisive support from the Prussians, at Waterloo in 1815.

Even after 1815, a ferocious level of competition between rival powers intent on empire building continued throughout the next 100 years. The French Revolution had contributed to a sense of national identity in European countries, as well as nationalist ambition among political elites. This combination had a particularly malign effect on an unstable continent, already experiencing huge social upheavals as a consequence of industrialisation. Industrialisation had a twin impact: firstly, the wealth generated by economic progress under industrial capitalism sustained increased militarism and the imperialist adventures of the Great Powers, which in turn fostered national consciousness. Secondly, industrialisation contributed to the rapid development of political consciousness related

© Archivo Iconografico, S.A./Corbis

Photograph 1.1 Francisco Jose de Goya y Lucientes: The Executions on Pio Hill (3rd of May). Napoleon's soldiers execute rebels in Madrid in 1808 . . . and spur nationalist sentiment in the process. Goya's dramatic painting reflects the horrors of the French occupation of Spain, and the painter's disillusionment with the French Revolution.

to the emerging class system. This came to underpin the great ideological conflict of the twentieth century, **capitalism** versus communism. Meanwhile, drawing on the ideals of the Enlightenment and nurtured by industrialisation, liberalism became a powerful intellectual tradition. The complex and often contradictory legacies of the French Revolution are summarised in Figure 1.2.

As well as a growth in national consciousness and **liberalism**, other important legacies such as **republicanism**, human rights, democratic participation and **secularism** would become entrenched over the following two centuries. While some of these might be considered relatively benign, others were more obviously controversial. Republicanism developed throughout nineteenth-century France for example, but never gained momentum in Britain. **Nationalism**, on the other hand, became arguably the most powerful influence of all, and its emergence signalled a decisive turning point in the development of modern Europe. It bolstered a sense of statehood, reinforcing the development of modern

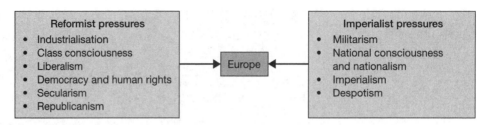

Figure 1.2 The aftermath of the French Revolution: pressures and divisions

states. Italy, for example, only achieved unification in 1861 following the successful nationalist campaigns led by Garibaldi and Cavour in the south of the peninsula. Nationalism underpinned much of the conflict that scarred European history between 1789 and the end of the Second World War. Given that the growth in nationalism can be traced to these revolutionary origins, it seems reasonable to pay a brief visit to this part of European history in seeking to understand both the significance of nationalism and the role of the state in contemporary Europe.

It should be apparent from this introduction that many of the legacies of the French Revolution are deeply intertwined. Militarism, a hallmark of the Napoleonic Wars, certainly contributed to competition and suspicion between states across Europe that was to have lasting impact. It also sustained and supported its common bedfellows, nationalism and imperialism, which flourished during the nineteenth century. The revolution greatly increased a sense of nationality and nationhood. As rumours swept Paris of a Prussian invasion in 1792, Robespierre asserted that the 'fatherland is in danger'. The remark shows how the French Revolution required and achieved identification with nationhood, something which was relatively undeveloped in pre-Revolution Europe. This was by no means peculiar to France. The emergence of such identification would strengthen the *idea* of independent sovereign states across the continent. See Figure 1.3 below.

Thus while the French Revolution boosted the concept of the state, the Revolutionary Wars of 1805–15 laid the foundations for the internecine conflicts of the twentieth century. A growing identification with nationhood emerged from national consciousness not only among rulers, but just as importantly, among the ruled. Competition between nations continued even during a century of relative peace. Militarism and imperialism boosted national consciousness

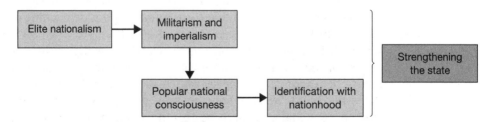

Figure 1.3 Developing state power in post-1789 Europe

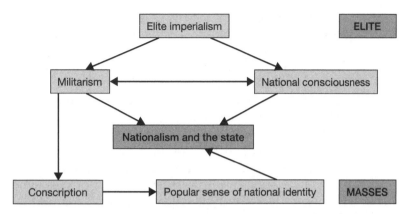

Figure 1.4 Emerging concepts of nationalism and the state in post-1789 Europe

among elites, and the use of conscription helped to do the same among the general populations of Europe (see Figure 1.4).

Apart from the nationalist and imperialist legacies already referred to, the French Revolution awakened a widespread sense of political awareness more than any previous event in Europe. Arguably the most important change in this respect was the emergence of republicanism. For many the enduring image of the French Revolution is the widespread use of the guillotine, used to execute Louis XVI and Marie Antoinette. But despite their gruesome end, the monarchy was not finished. This is less significant than the fact that the revolution marked the beginning of the end for the French monarchy (see Discussion 1.1).

As populations became more politicised this had an effect on individual and collective rights. Rousseau had written about the 'general will' in the *Social Contract* in 1762 but after 1789 it became much more of a conscious expression. It combined with a sense of individual rights as citizens had much higher expectations, beginning with the educated middle classes but eventually filtering

Discussion 1.1

Republicanism in France

After 1815 most European monarchies were still in place, even in France. Although the French Republic was declared on 20 September 1792, the monarchy returned in 1814 under Louis XVIII. Republicanism briefly reasserted itself 1848–51 but did not finally take permanent hold until after the Franco-Prussian War in 1871. Nevertheless, the *idea* of republicanism had taken root following the events of summer 1789, most obviously in France but also elsewhere. This did not immediately give rise to a universal demand for constitutional republics, or even for constitutional monarchies, but the idea was now discussed (see Davies, 1996:713). Change was perceived as possible: after 1789, the world *could* be turned upside down. This spurred both hope in those seeking change and panic in those who preferred the status quo.

through all levels of society. Despotism was far more likely to be opposed, constitutions demanded and rights articulated and defended. Furthermore, awareness and expectations relating to human rights were more widespread, though the American War of Independence and Thomas Jefferson's Declaration, which included reference to human rights, had already had an impact, even on the French Revolution itself. Thomas Paine produced his famous tract, *Rights of Man*, in 1791 as a response to the French Revolution, with an impact that spread throughout Europe.

In Germany there was considerable political and social progress even under the authoritarian Prussian leadership. Universal suffrage and social insurance appeared, together with a federal system of government, an interesting precursor to the German Basic Law that is the foundation of the modern Federal Republic. In Britain on the other hand political and social reforms emerged much more slowly. Queen Victoria's huge family retained massive privileges and there was no concerted effort towards republicanism, or even any form of federalism. Indeed, it was as if the French Revolution had never happened. Religious toleration never quite progressed and divorce was not allowed until 1857. The church was never disestablished in England and the two-party system prevailed. Whigs and Tories became Liberals and Conservatives and, most significantly, social legislation was minimal and the labour movement barely developed, despite Britain's earlier industrialisation than on the continent. Unlike in Germany and France, universal suffrage was nowhere to be seen, not emerging until 1928. This conservatism coincided, however, with a stronger degree of politicisation among

---

Discussion 1.2

Secularism and the French state

The French Revolution also marked the beginning of the end of church influence in the affairs of the French state. It contributed to a process that by the late nineteenth century had established secularism as a core principle of the French Republic. While widely accepted by the majority of the population, secularism also brings controversy. In February 2004 the French National Assembly passed a law banning the wearing of the traditional hijab, or veil, by Moslem school girls in state schools. The government sees the ban on overt religious symbols as important in upholding the secular traditions of the French Republic. Religion has no part in French schooling, and this now extends to a ban on the 'ostentatious' wearing of faith symbols, such as the hijab, the Jewish skullcap or 'large' crucifixes. The French government has argued that it must uphold a fundamental tenet of the French system: religion has no place in state affairs, including schools and education. This shows that secularism is deeply entrenched in the concept of state in France.

The policy is seen as draconian and illiberal by many commentators in Britain for example, which has tended to promote the ideal of a multi-faith, multi-ethnic society, while at the same time retaining the Church of England as the established church of the realm, with many attendant privileges. This is one reason why a policy such as that adopted in France would be much more difficult to introduce in English schools.

the middle class in Britain than in Germany. In Britain the middle class enjoyed privileges and improving living standards which created an acceptance of the status quo. Davies (1996) argues that this undoubtedly benefited a certain maturation of democracy, and aided greater middle-class participation in politics and the development of liberal traditions. The industrial working class on the other hand, without political representation, endured conditions of abject poverty and exploitation.

Russia was especially resistant to liberal ideas. The Tsar remained authoritarian and surrounded by a privileged aristocratic elite. Access to politics was denied to the mass of the peasant population, and even in the cities, a Russian middle class barely emerged, with the result that there was very little pressure towards reform.

In summary, the French Revolution is a defining moment in modern European history. It shaped developing rivalries across the continent and fuelled the use of militarism as a political tool. Militarism was emboldened by ever more strident nationalism. Nationalism won ever wider acceptance; emergent national identities helped to consolidate the institution of the modern state. Finally, the Revolution spurred political and social consciousness, as well as secularism (see Discussion 1.2), that would have enduring impact to the present day.

Review   *What were some significant legacies of the French Revolution? How did it impact upon the development of the state in Europe?*

● ● ● ● The European state: towards the abyss

This section briefly explores the historical experience of the state in Europe. There is no need to provide more than a brief survey of the state experience prior to 1945, but it is important to recognise the context of what has happened since the Second World War. The core claim is that the process of institution building that occurred after the war, and which had such enormous consequences for Europe, was a response to the conflict which had gone before. This section outlines the main characteristics of that conflict.

The state gained full expression in the period following the French Revolution, as during the nineteenth century the idea of nationalism became established throughout Europe. The role of the state was central to political affairs in a period of colonialist expansion, increased trade and growing military capability, driven as always by changes in technology. The nineteenth century saw relative stability in trade as economies expanded, benefiting from the framework of the international Gold Standard. Currency stability helped to maintain both growth and low inflation. During the twentieth century, however, competitive nationalism increased and was accompanied by a growing arms race. A volatile situation was made worse by an increase in territorial ambitions among the Great Powers, Austria-Hungary, France, Germany, Russia and Britain. The break-up of the Ottoman Empire and the weakness of Austria-Hungary led directly to the First World War. Furthermore, the Treaty of Versailles of 1919 failed to resolve the tensions unleashed by nationalism.

[The Treaty] created states which were too small for successful defence or economic management, regimes which were oppressive or illiberal, and ethnic grievances which have proved persistent (McLean & McMillan, 2003:362).

Gray (2003:94) is critical of the United States' policy of promoting nationalism in the Balkans and Eastern Europe after the First World War (see Chapter 3). Indeed, further turmoil followed as Europe lurched into a period of economic instability then collapse. Amid widespread social upheaval, weak democratic governments were swept from power across the continent. Versailles had put together a patchwork of nominally sovereign and mostly democratic states but the result was a contagion of dictatorship, beginning with the Bolshevik Russian Revolution in 1917, but followed by many others, including fascist regimes in Italy and Germany. The extent of the democratic meltdown is extraordinary. Table 1.1 summarises the collapse of European democracies in the period 1917–39.

The roll-call of disaster continued once war broke out with the Nazi invasion of Poland on 1 September 1939. By 1942 Nazi Germany had achieved its high point of conquest and occupation:

The extent of the [German advance] undertaken during the Third Reich is astounding. The Saar was re-incorporated as the result of a plebiscite in 1935, the Rhineland remilitarized in 1936, Austria annexed [. . .] in 1938, the Sudetenland annexed in 1938, the area around Memel on the Baltic coast annexed in 1939, and a protectorate established in the rest of what is now the Czech Republic in 1939. The subsequent war saw German troops occupying the Netherlands, Belgium, Luxembourg, much of France, Denmark, Norway, Estonia, Latvia, Lithuania, Poland, the USSR to a line running roughly from Leningrad to Rostov, Yugoslavia and Greece, all by the end of 1942 (Blacksell, 1997:2–3).

In 1945 Europe lay shattered by the twin horrors of fascism and war. Not only had the Third Reich wrought death and destruction to most of the continent, it had spawned the uniquely grotesque machine killing of human beings on a scale hitherto unknown. The Holocaust destroyed 6 million European Jews as well as at least 1 million others – Roma, political detainees, homosexuals, handicapped people and others who merely got in the way. The trauma of the Holocaust is a stain on European consciousness that can never be erased.

Among many shocking aspects of the European experience in the 1930s and 40s, one of the most striking is that while Hitler set about establishing a German Reich throughout continental Europe, a few score miles to the east Stalin was engaging in his own murderous project. The forced collectivisation of agriculture generated famine in Russia and the Ukraine on an appalling scale. Opponents of the Communist dictatorship, or mere critics of Stalin or his policies, were routinely killed or sent to labour camps where they died from starvation and maltreatment. Stalin's rule resulted in the deaths of approximately 30 million civilians (Davies, 1996:1329).

Table 1.1 Dictatorships of inter-war Europe 1917–39

	Duration	Dictator(s)	Description
Soviet Russia (USSR)	25 Oct 1917–1991	Lenin (to 1924) Stalin (to 1953)	Bolshevik *coup d'état*, totalitarian, Communist Party state. Terror.
Hungary	21 Mar–Sept 1919 1919–1944	Bela Kun Admiral Horthy	Soviet Communist Republic. Terror. Proto-fascist dictatorship. Terror.
Italy	28 Oct 1922–1943	Mussolini	Fascist takeover. Constitutional monarchy replaced by 'corporate state'. All opposition parties disbanded in 1926.
Bulgaria	9 Jun 1923–1944	Tsankov	Military *coup d'état*. Authoritarian regime, dissolution of opposition: from 1934, royal dictatorship of Boris III.
Spain	23 Sept 1923–1920 Jan 1930	Primo de Rivera	Authoritarian regime allied to King Alfonso III. Military directorship. Constitution suspended.
Turkey	29 Oct 1923–1938	Kemal Pasha	Personal dictatorship, one-party national state.
Albania	Jan 1925–1940	Ahmed Zogu (king post-1928)	Authoritarian regime, presidential then royal.
Poland	15 May 1926–1939	Marshall Pilsudski	Military *coup d'état*: left-wing military regime: dictatorship behind a parliamentary façade.
Portugal	28 May 1926–1975 from 1932	De Oliveira, A. Salazar, Caetano	Authoritarian regime, dissolution of parliament, constitution suspended.
Yugoslavia	Jan 1929–1941	King Alexander	*Coup d'état*, royal dictatorship.
Lithuania	19 Sept 1929–1940	Smetona	Nationalist one-party state.
Romania	9 Jun 1930–1941	King Carol II	*Coup d'état*, royal dictatorship.
Germany	30 Jan 1933–1945	Hitler	Nazi electoral success; one-party state through 'emergency powers'. Terror.
Austria	Mar 1933–1937	Dollfuss	Dictatorship by the semi-fascist 'Fatherland Front', rule by emergency decree.
Estonia	12 Mar 1934–1940	Pats	Authoritarian regime, state of emergency, rule by decree, parliament dissolved.
Latvia	15 May 1934–1940	Ulmanis	Authoritarian regime, government of national unity, parliament dissolved.
Greece	Oct 1935–1941	Metaxas	Authoritarian military-royal regime, dissolution of parliament.
Spain	Sept 1936–1975	Franco	Military fascism: totalitarian regime. Terror.

Source: from *Europe: A History*, 1996, Norman Davies, published by Pimlico. Used by permission of The Random House Group Limited.

McLean and McMillan (2003:362) suggest that the years following the Treaty of Versailles indicate that multinational entities such as the Austro-Hungarian Empire or the Soviet Union, and by implication the European Union, have significant advantages over independent states. Certainly multinational entities have proved more stable in the west European context, and arguably in the

© Michael St. Maur Sheil/Corbis

Photograph 1.2 Europe's history: the killing fields. In Tyne Cot British military cemetery tombstones mark the graves of British soldiers killed in the 3rd battle of Ypres, at Passchendaele, in the First World War.

volatile Balkan region as well. However, as Chapter 4 makes clear, the European Union is a unique polity and comparisons with Tito's Yugoslavia or the former Soviet Union are not revealing. It is the democratic structures, imperfect though they may be, the respect for human rights, toleration of diversity, and devolution of authority that makes the EU attractive to Central and East European Countries (CEECs) emerging from the yoke of Soviet-style communism.

Indeed, for the populations of the CEECs which were freed from Nazi occupation, but found themselves under Soviet-style rule after 1945, there remained a mismatch between the 'national plate' and the 'state plate' (see Introduction and Figure 0.1). The Soviets installed puppet governments. The fault line of the Cold War was confirmed as the opposition between communism and capitalism dominated Europe. This ideological split appears to have submerged the earlier fragmentation of competing forms of nationalism. However, the Soviet system merely suppressed nationalism, as the experience of Yugoslavia and parts of the former USSR post-1991 vividly demonstrate. The original mosaic of national cultures across the continent remained in place. Only in Czechoslovakia was a mutual divorce achieved without bloodshed, as the Czech Republic and Slovakia divided in 1993.

Meanwhile, in Western Europe, a significant experiment spanning seven decades has taken place. This is the process of accommodating difference within the European integration process, what federalists call 'unity in diversity' (Burgess, 2003:67). The future prospects of this experiment are of vital concern and are explored in later chapters.

Review	*US Secretary of State John Foster Dulles famously referred to Europe as 'the world's worst fire hazard'. Is/was this reasonable?*

● ● ● ● Recreating Europe: the emergence of European integration

This section explains the context within which European integration has occurred, beginning with the immediate post-war situation and the devastation of the continent, and then examining the impact of American engagement in Europe. The argument presented is that the US enabled integration to happen. States responded in different ways, notably Britain by pursuing a traditional approach, defending and asserting its sovereign independence. Others in contrast sought to cooperate more closely. The context of integration remained broadly similar until the end of the Cold War, which is referred to at the end of the chapter, and the acceleration in global capitalism, widely described as globalisation.

Given the history described above, the claim that the process of European integration post-1945 is first and foremost a response to conflict is hardly contentious. This conflict should be seen as encompassing not only wars between states, but also conflicts within states, especially those marked by dictatorship. The serial disasters of 1914–45 meant that a mere handful of European states did not experience dictatorship, military defeat or occupation. Only the United Kingdom, Switzerland, Sweden and Iceland avoided this trinity of horrors. Ireland endured occupation by the British until partition in 1921 and even then part of Ireland remained under British rule, giving rise to a protracted republican campaign against continued British authority in part of the island of Ireland. Finland was successively occupied by both the Nazis and the Russians during the war, although it achieved relative independence post-1945. The hallmark of the European state experience has been conflict, entwined with dictatorship, military defeat and occupation. This is crucial to the history of the modern state. It has also been a critical factor underlying the post-1945 **European integration process**, because on the one hand it demonstrates the volatility and danger inherent in the state experience in Europe, and on the other it provided the motivation for a complete break with the past after the Second World War.

In March 1946 Churchill spoke in Fulton, Missouri, of an 'Iron Curtain that had descended across [Europe]'. His striking metaphor for the post-war division of Europe between East and West, between communist and capitalist economic systems, between so-called Peoples' Democracies and liberal democratic systems, between those who were under the **hegemony** of the Soviet Union and those who were economically and militarily dependent on the United States, was a new nightmare for Europe to live with. This scenario gave rise to the grim and ever-threatening term, the **Cold War**.

A group of European leaders coalesced around the idea, first articulated by Winston Churchill, to create 'a kind of United States of Europe', at the heart of which would be France and Germany. In September 1946, Churchill made a speech in Zurich in which he stated that Europe had to move forward to a new future of cooperation:

> The first step in the re-creation of the European family must be a partnership between France and Germany. [. . .] There can be no revival of Europe without a spiritually great France and a spiritually great Germany. The structure of a United States of Europe, if well and truly built, will be such as to make the material strength of a single state less important. Small nations will count as much as large ones and gain their honour by their contribution to the common cause (quoted in Bainbridge, 2002:545).

Incidentally, Churchill did not imagine that the United Kingdom would be part of such a formation. He envisaged Britain's role as primarily centred around global responsibilities stemming from the Empire, the new Commonwealth, and the partnership with the United States (Jones, 2001:7). Perhaps Churchill, like so many other Britons, saw the continent as 'somewhere else', a continent that Britain, an island nation, would keep at arm's length. Indeed the history of Britain's relations with its neighbours, and the integration process in particular, suggests that this has been an enduring habit. Britain's long history of relatively stable parliamentary democracy surely contributes to a sense of separateness. It might be argued that British euroscepticism owes much to psychological differences between the UK and the continent, given the very different UK experience, especially during the twentieth century (see Discussion 1.3). The lack of dictatorship, military defeat or occupation means that Britons have little understanding of the concept of 'fearing the knock at the door' – unless they happen to be members of Amnesty International, or the Medical Foundation, a London-based organisation that provides care and rehabilitation to victims of torture. Instead, for continental Europeans, and especially those living in the former East Germany and in other ex-communist states, and others for whom the transition from dictatorship is relatively recent, such as Spain, Portugal and Greece, this is not only part of the national psyche, it is part of living memory. Learning about the Third Reich and the Holocaust is central to the curriculum for all students in Germany, where, at least since the mid-1960s, the exploration of the Holocaust and the Third Reich has been a massive industry spanning the arts, publishing and visual as well as print media, leaving no aspect of German society untouched by reflection on the catastrophe of Nazism (Ardagh, 1995). Thus Europe's various traumas have been significant vectors in the push towards integration. States have survived as important political entities, but they are deeply entwined in a complex web of institutions, mutual obligations and related responsibilities.

Discussion 1.3

British euroscepticism: why is Britain reluctant to fully engage with Europe?

Geography: Britain is an island and 22 miles of water separate England from France – some have suggested it can seem wider than the Atlantic Ocean.

History: Long tradition of parliamentary democracy, political stability and constitutional monarchy.

War and dictatorship: British perception of the continent as a zone of conflict and war; Britain 'won' both world wars, so did not experience occupation or military defeat; Britain has no relevant experience of living under a dictatorship.

Traditional global perspective: Britain looks beyond Europe, and historically views the European continent as 'competition'; former imperial power with colonies in Asia, Africa, America and Australasia; highly 'globalised' economy, with high capital inflow (FDI) and outflow.

Culture and language: Shares much in common with the USA and is naturally 'transatlanticist'; overwhelmingly monolingual population, low level of expertise in other European languages; English is a global language.

Historical sense of importance: Global 'power', Head of Commonwealth, nuclear power, 'special relationship' with the USA; permanent member of UN Security Council; cannot be 'top dog' in the EU.

Question of sovereignty: Britain clings to a traditional notion of 'sovereign independence', aligned to its self-image as a 'global power'.

Late entrant to the EEC: did not benefit from the 'growth years' in the European continental economy; not involved in setting up the founding institutions of the EEC, nor even in establishing EMU and the ECB; critics point to the entire integration venture as 'a Franco-German project'.

Social and ideological separation: More individualist society; weaker family networks; less committed to social welfare model; tradition of centralised authority; antipathy to federalism; little sense of 'European' identity; traditionally anti-Catholic, dating back to 1535; more protective of traditional interpretations of sovereignty.

Media: Overwhelmingly anti-European press, much of it foreign-owned; significant corrosive impact on public opinion over thirty years; persistence of negative stereotypes.

Post-1945 integration

The integration process that ensued post–1945 contrasts markedly with the experience of the 1920s and 1930s, as it has involved significant institution building, and not only through the construction of the EEC and the EU. Other institutional initiatives stemmed primarily from the USA, the one country which emerged from the Second World War stronger than it had been at the beginning. The USA abandoned its preference for unilateralism that had precipitated the economic collapse of 1929, and its indifference towards world events that characterised the 1930s. A decade and 60 million deaths later, the US provided the vital lead in constructing a political economy that was based more on international partnership and mutual dependency.

The institutional innovations involving the US coincided with an understandably much changed mood in Europe. The preference for a more multilateralist approach to international relations facilitated innovations that would lay the foundations for post-war economic recovery. The Bretton Woods Accords of 1944 created a framework for an international monetary and payments system. European currencies were locked to the dollar at a fixed exchange rate, without which heavy capital flows into Europe would have risked severe inflation and collapsing currency values. Bretton Woods also established the International Monetary Fund, the International Bank for Reconstruction and Development, which became known as the World Bank, and the General Agreement on Tariffs and Trade (GATT). GATT was a multilateral agreement to liberalise trade within a rule-based system. It came into force in 1947.

This institutional framework would enable the development of international trade and facilitate European recovery. Meanwhile the US proceeded with further initiatives on two fronts, in the fields of defence and economy. First, European security was guaranteed by the Truman Plan in 1947 which pledged US support for 'free peoples who are resisting subjugation' – a direct reference to insurgency in Greece that was attracting the attention of the Soviets. The Western Allies had already determined that Stalin had got as much as he was going to get from the post-war settlement. The Truman Plan was consolidated by the creation of North Atlantic Treaty Organisation (NATO) in 1949, the central instrument in the US determination to resist the threat of Soviet expansionism.

Sandwiched between the Truman Plan and the creation of NATO was the 1948 Soviet blockade of West Berlin. This was an early example of Cold War tension. The US, supported by Britain, carried out the Berlin airlift which supplied materials, resources and food to beleaguered West Berliners in the heart of Soviet-occupied East Germany for ten months. It was a remarkable illustration of the West's logistical competence and political will (Walker, 1994).

In the economic domain, the US gave substantial aid towards the reconstruction of Europe. Having seen that the resources available to the IMF and the World Bank were inadequate to stimulate economic recovery, the US invoked the Marshall Plan (McLean & McMillan, 2003:52). The distribution and spending of Marshall Aid would be coordinated by the Organisation for European Economic Co-operation (OEEC), an early example of an intergovernmental body involving various European states.

The American post-war occupation of both Germany and Japan, and later financial support, secured long-term influence for the US over the emergence of liberal democratic and capitalist systems in both countries. US aid helped to develop a pro-American business environment in which US multinational corporations could, and did, play a major part. It is clear that US aid was not purely altruistic. Many writers (Peterson, 1996; Piening, 1997) have argued that the US required the reconstruction of Europe as part of a Cold War order that would ensure reliable European allies for the US in the development of the capitalist liberal democratic order. It would also provide a large market for US exports. A strong European economy would also bring rising living standards that would undermine the appeal of counter-capitalist propaganda in Western Europe. The US was always nervous about the electoral appeal of Europe's socialist and communist parties, especially in France and Italy. There were also strategic imperatives, especially the need to ensure that the Soviet system extended no further than what was agreed at Yalta. Central to the post-war settlement in Europe was the position of the Federal Republic of Germany (FRG), which attained full sovereignty only in 1955 when it joined NATO and began rearmament. It was critical for the US that West Germany remained within its sphere of influence and that it was not incorporated into communist East Germany (GDR).

British reluctance towards integration

Urwin comments that in the early years after the war, the US role was decisive in providing an environment conducive to European integration, all the more so because the continental states had tended to rely on Britain to advance integrating initiatives.

> It was widely assumed across Western Europe that the lead in any moves towards closer collaboration, because of its wartime role, would be taken by the UK, and that, with Germany prostrate and militarily occupied, a British-French alliance would lie at the core of European integration [. . .] while other countries and federalists alike looked to Britain to take a lead, the British attitude towards anything more than cooperation between independent states was consistently negative, at best deeply sceptical, and at worst totally hostile (Urwin, 2003:13–14).

British lack of interest in the integrating initiatives undertaken by France, Germany, Italy and the **Benelux** states had everything to do with British reluctance to engage in any institution building that might affect traditional notions of sovereignty. Defence of the national interest was Britain's overwhelming priority and the early post-war governments in the UK were convinced that their interests did not lie with continental Europe. On the contrary, Britain looked to its disintegrating Empire and the emerging Commonwealth. The Attlee government (1945–51) prioritised domestic concerns and Britain's ambition to become a nuclear power. The latter was a further indication of Britain's undiminished global pretensions, despite its much reduced economic circumstances. The British political establishment tended to equate sovereignty with military power (see discussion of realism in Chapter 8). From the outset, Britain's only interest in European multinational institutions after the Second World War was limited to strictly intergovernmental organisations. A somewhat conventionally strategic and backward-looking alliance, the Treaty of Brussels in 1947, signed with France and the Benelux states was acceptable to Britain, as was the OEEC. So too was the Council of Europe, created on the initiative of Winston Churchill, who became its first chairman. It was, and remains, purely intergovernmental.

This was the context in which six Western European states could begin to follow a very different path to that taken after the First World War. With economic support and an emerging security guarantee provided by the US, France and Germany, together with Italy, Belgium, the Netherlands and Luxembourg, began to look for ways to cooperate. Britain, spurning invitations to contribute or take part, remained on the margins of the continent both geographically and metaphorically. With US military protection through NATO, and economic support through GATT and Marshall Aid, West European leaders could focus on achieving some degree of integration between their states. Thus the French diplomat Jean Monnet created the Schuman Plan, a blueprint for the Treaty of Paris in 1951 which set up the European Coal and Steel Community (ECSC). Britain was invited to take part but chose not to. Five years later, with the ECSC already operative, the UK position remained unchanged when Anthony Eden succeeded Churchill as Prime Minister. Ministers of the ECSC planned a meeting at Messina to discuss closer and wider cooperation, leading to a customs union, or common market, between the signatory states. According to Young, 'Most [British] government officials thought nothing at all would happen' (Young, 1999:82).

The Messina Conference in 1955 set up a committee to plan for a wider, more ambitious project involving a European economic community. This led to the eventual Treaty of Rome and the launch of the European Economic Community (EEC) in 1958. Young is immensely critical of the prevarications on the part of Britain in the 1950s, referring to 'sharpening vanity', 'fear-filled diminishment'. What is also striking is the failure of judgement in underestimating the consequences of the Messina meeting, a pattern which would be repeated many times over subsequent decades. However, it should be admitted that the different paths taken by Britain and its continental neighbours in the 1950s are not surprising. Britain was reluctant to engage in organisations that might cause it to lose its 'sovereign independence'. Discussion 1.3 suggests some explanations for this but one in particular can be contrasted with the experience of France and Germany. Britain had maintained its sovereignty during the war years and emerged victorious. Germany on the other hand had not only endured dictatorship and defeat, but had been deprived of its sovereignty for the immediate post-war years. It was also divided, so in many respects sovereignty for Germany appeared a much tarnished commodity. France, too, had suffered defeat and loss of sovereignty during the war years. Later though, the French position on sovereignty began to resemble that of Britain (see Chapter 3, pp. 94–5).

Both the ECSC and the EEC presented a challenge to traditional approaches to sovereignty from the outset, as they contained a supranational (above the level of state) dimension. The ECSC included a High Authority to manage the production and supply of coal and steel throughout the signatory states. Likewise the EEC established a supranational Commission to coordinate integrationary initiatives of the Community. However, although the signatories of the Rome Treaty aspired to create a customs union, the notion of a Single Market was only in embryonic form at this time. Furthermore, the EEC was a long way from establishing a political community. An attempt to create one in 1953, known as the European Political Community, together with an integrated defence policy, the European Defence Community, collapsed when the latter was vetoed in 1954 by the French National Assembly. These failures were interesting in the context of sovereignty, because they foundered on the rocks of declared 'national interests' taking precedence over community aspirations. Table 1.2 summarises the institutional developments described above.

A few years after shunning the ECSC and the EEC, Britain set up the European Free Trade Association (EFTA) with Austria, Denmark, Norway, Portugal, Sweden and Switzerland. EFTA also involved no loss of sovereignty. EFTA

Photograph 1.3 The past is history. The EEC is created by the signing of the Treaty of Rome on 25 March 1957.

helped cut some tariffs, but achieved relatively little in the long term, mainly because several of its members did more trade with the EEC than with their EFTA partners (McCormick, 2002:69).

Once the British government saw that the EEC was actually working, and its economic performance was far outstripping that of Britain, it applied to join the EEC in 1961. Pressure to do so came from British industry, which was losing export opportunities from being outside the EEC (McCormick, ibid.). Eventually, five of the original seven members of EFTA did join the EC/EU.

The end of the Cold War

Within 40 years the EEC had become the European Union with a membership of 15 states, and it was preparing to launch a single currency among 12 of them. Now the EU has 25 member states and over 450 million inhabitants. It has a

Table 1.2 Post-war context: institutional initiatives 1944–57

Military/strategic	Global/involving the US	European integration process
	1944 Bretton Woods Accords 1945–52 US occupation of Japan	
1947 Treaty of Brussels 1947 Truman Plan	1947 Marshall Plan – Marshall Aid to Europe 1947 General Agreement on Tariffs & Trade International Bank for Reconstruction and Development (World Bank) International Monetary Fund (IMF)	1947 Organisation for European Economic Cooperation (OEEC)
1949 North Atlantic Treaty Organisation (NATO) 1955 Germany joins NATO		1949 Federal Republic of Germany created with new Constitution 1949 The Council of Europe 1951 Treaty of Paris (ECSC) 1955 Messina Conference 1957 Treaty of Rome (EEC)
Remarks Security umbrella provided by US involvement in Europe. Germany's incorporation into NATO in 1955, and the beginning of its rearmament, prompted the formation of the Warsaw Pact by the Soviet Union.	**Remarks** US central to establishing a stable international trading environment with a view to building up US trading partners in Europe and Japan.	**Remarks** OEEC is intergovernmental; later expands to include US, Japan, Canada and is renamed OECD. The Council of Europe is also intergovernmental.
Military protection against Soviet threat and economic aid to reconstruct war- torn European economies enables European states to focus on cooperation.		Britain remained resolutely outside all cooperation and integration initiatives between 'the Six'.

share of world trade that is greater than that of the US, and a GDP that is almost as large. Just a generation after the Second World War, European integration represents a formidable achievement without parallel in history.

The most recent developments in European integration have occurred against a rapidly changing political and economic environment. As we have seen, the support from the US for increased European cooperation coincided with specific strategic aims of the US during the early years of the Cold War. Fundamentally, this context remained unaltered, despite some policy reversals such as President Nixon ending the Bretton Woods commitment to fixed exchange controls in 1971. The major geopolitical earthquake to change the whole basis of European integration, and the relationship with the US, came with the revolutionary upheaval in Central and Eastern Europe between 1989 and 1991. The Cold War ended. The implications of this are looked at in more detail in later chapters.

For four decades Europe and the world had lived through the ideological schism of the Cold War (see Table 1.3). It was a considerable paradox that while Western Europe achieved greater integration over 40 years, the wider

Table 1.3 Cold War division of Europe 1945–91

WEST		EAST
United States of America (USA)	Leading protagonist/ military power	Union of Soviet Socialist Republics (USSR)
NATO (from 1949) USA/Canada/UK/France/Netherlands/ Denmark/Norway/Belgium/Luxembourg/ Italy/Portugal/Iceland/Greece (from 1952)/ Turkey (from 1952)/Federal Republic of Germany (from 1955)/Spain (from 1982)	Defence alliance	Warsaw Pact (from 1955) USSR/Albania (until 1968)/ Bulgaria/Czechoslovakia/ German Democratic Republic/Hungary/Poland/Romania
Liberal democracy	Dominant ideology	Marxist-Leninism
Capitalism	Economic system	Communism/command economy
GATT, EEC	Major institutions	COMECON

continent had remained more marked by division than unity (see Figure 1.5). The Berlin Wall was the most striking symbol of this division. The end of the Soviet Union has, understandably, had enormous consequences. One of these is that there is arguably more uncertainty now, in an age of global terrorism, and threatened ecological disaster, than was the case during the years of *détente*. But there *was* uncertainty during the Cold War, the great stand-off between two superpowers and ideological rivals. Both were capable of destroying the planet several times over.

So if the Cold War provided some sense of security, one has to use the term with a degree of irony given the risks attendant on nuclear arsenals capable of destroying all life on earth. In reality the Cold War was a constant threat, a slumbering giant. There was widespread fear of nuclear war. It was a recurrent theme in films, books, comics, popular music and popular protest. Dylan's 1963 song *A Hard Rain's A-Gonna Fall* spoke for a generation living under the shadow of nuclear catastrophe. As the cities of Hiroshima and Nagasaki discovered in 1945, nuclear weapons could bring instant annihilation to many thousands. Terrorism generates mass fear but relatively few actual deaths, and global warming brings a gradual threat that is too easy to ignore.

The second context within which European integration has continued concerns the third major theme of this book, globalisation. In the late 1980s a new wave of computer technology emerged, at least comparable with other great technological shifts in previous epochs. The launch of the World Wide Web in 1990 coincided with innovative economic and socio-cultural processes, some driven by policy changes from the UK and US governments. Notably, the liberalisation of financial markets and the telecommunications sector enabled huge expansion by multinational businesses. These developments are hallmarks of the modern era of globalisation. The profound social consequences of globalisation continue to generate considerable debate (see later chapters).

It is against this background of fundamental shifts in the wider political and social contexts, embracing all aspects of human society, that modern state

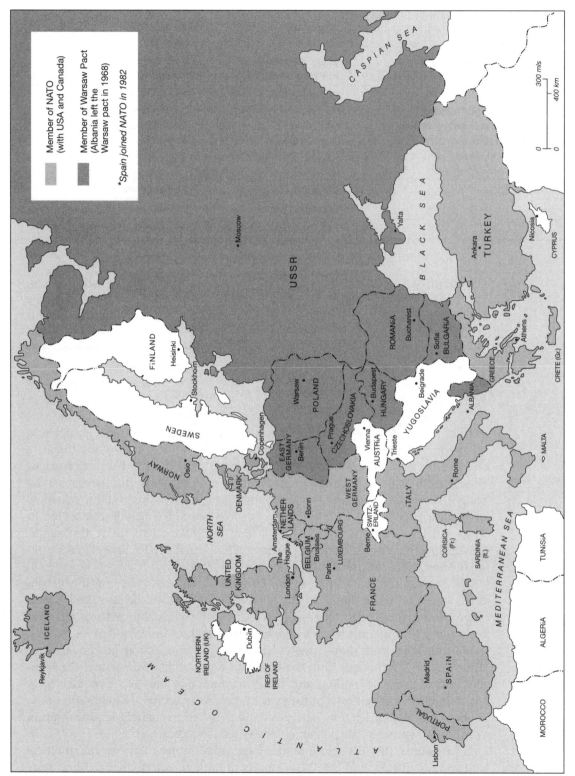

Figure 1.5 Cold War Europe 1945–91

Source: based on Urwin, 1997

governance has undergone, and is still undergoing, dramatic changes. The central concern is to address what these changes mean and how they affect the responsibilities of governments and international institutions.

Review *What were the motives for US engagement with Europe after the Second World War?*
Why would it be wrong to think of the period 1945–89 in Europe as being solely about the integration of Europe?
Suggest explanations for British euroscepticism.
What major changes occurred in the late twentieth century that have had such an impact on the European integration process?

Summary

This chapter has made the following key points.

The impact of the French Revolution

- The French Revolution advanced the cause of nationalism in Europe as states established conscript armies, encouraged a sense of identity with nationhood, and struggled to establish supremacy in a changed international environment as well as a rapidly industrialising one in the nineteenth century.

The European state: towards the abyss

- Great Power rivalry, militarism and unconfined nationalism provoked the First World War.
- Weak states fell prey to dictatorship in the inter-war years.
- Dictatorship is a significant part of the European twentieth-century experience and a factor in the drive towards integration among European states.

Recreating Europe: the changing context of European integration

- The different historical experience of the UK to continental Europe may explain the lukewarm British approach to European integration.
- Following the Second World War, Britain had a more traditional view of sovereignty than did France, Germany and others in continental Europe.
- European integration owes much to the US policy of providing a security umbrella for Western Europe during the Cold War.
- The US sponsored Western European economic recovery, a further prerequisite to integration.

- The US had strategic and economic motives for supporting the recovery of Western Europe.
- The end of the Cold War and the latest phase of globalisation have coincided with the transition from EEC to European Union, and the enlargement of the EU to 25 member states.

Key concepts: discussion and other definitions

Key concept 1.1   State

A political entity that is coterminous with a territory and represented by a government that is recognised as having legitimate authority, or sovereignty, over that territory and the people who live in it.

In most instances, this book uses the word *state* based on the above definition. However, as Held points out (Held, 1995:49), definitions in political analysis are controversial. One problem with this definition, and most other attempts to define the term, is that obviously different entities are routinely described as states. When one asks 'Is California a state?', the answer is clearly yes, it is one of the states of the United States of America. To claim that California is not a state would be absurd. 'Is the USA a state?' Yes, since it matches the definition above. Clearly we are using the same word to signify two very different entities, California and the USA.

Perhaps we should not be too upset by this, since we know that the English language accepts two meanings for words like *bank* or *mug*. The fact that two signified items such as California and the USA are not completely unrelated merely indicates that the word *state* is less like the words *bank* or *mug* than it is like the word *branch*, which also has different applications, but with a cognitive relationship (branch of a tree, branch of a company).

The commonly used term *nation state* is unhelpful, and it may make matters worse. The reason is that many states, such as the UK, contain different nations. This is obvious in the case of the UK, or the former Federal Republic of Yugoslavia, but many who describe themselves as 'Americans' (citizens of the USA) would object to the notion that the US contains many 'nations', though surely no one would deny that it contains many 'ethnic groups'. The US Constitution clearly presents the USA as a single nation, and in fact fuses territory with people in that single word, nation, as did, for example, the League of Nations, or the United Nations does now.

Held appears to accept a close relationship, even synonymy, between the two terms. He writes:

> Modern states developed as nation states – political apparatuses, distinct from both ruler and ruled, with supreme jurisdiction over a demarcated territorial area, backed by a claim to a monopoly of coercive power, and enjoying legitimacy as a result of a minimum level of support or loyalty from their citizens (Held, 1995:48).

This definition includes the useful reference to the source of legitimacy coming from inside the state itself, albeit perhaps from a 'minimum level of support'. This perhaps equates to the recognition referred to in the first definition above, though that also implies that the recognition is external, in other words coming from international institutions and from other states.

Here is another definition of the (modern) state:

> A centralised administration applying common laws uniformly to all citizens over the whole territory (Davies, 1996:715).

This description might be applied to a local authority or a region in a federal system of government. It does not explicitly refer to the international aspect of the state, its bordering other territories, or its requirement to have some form of legitimate authority.

Another brief definition is 'a sovereign body dominated by a single nation' (McLean & McMillan, 2003:364). This fits with the description of the United Kingdom of Great Britain and Northern Ireland, which is a state, dominated by the (majority) nation, the English.

The *Shorter Oxford English Dictionary* defines the 'state' as 'a body of people occupying a defined territory and organised under a sovereign government' (*Shorter Oxford English Dictionary*, 1973, reprint 1992, Vol. II, p. 2112).

Perhaps it is best to interpret the phrase *nation state* through its constituent parts. A **nation** is:

> a named human population which shares myths and memories, a mass public culture, a designated homeland, economic unity and equal rights and duties for all members (Smith, 1995:56–7).

while a state is 'a defined territory under the governance of a recognised authority or authorities' (Smith, ibid.). The term *nation state* conflates both ideas, thus it comprises a territory with internationally recognised borders, with a government that exercises authority over that territory and its people. Confusion arises when we attempt to reconcile this use of the term *nation state* with the apparent reality that many so-called nation states contain different nations reflecting different identities.

Equally, a country may be a nation but not a state. Scotland, part of the UK since the Act of Union in 1707, is an example. Tito achieved the political unity of the multinational state the Socialist Federal Republic of Yugoslavia, but after his death in 1982 the country disintegrated along ethnic lines in the 1990s. Clearly the state is often a contested entity, as history has shown in Spain, the UK/Ireland, Yugoslavia, and elsewhere (see Chapter 3).

Identity is a complex component within the state, since within one state there may be different identities, nationalities, beliefs, and also different languages.

Thus a state may comprise different nations, as does the United Kingdom, within which the English, the Scots and the Welsh are nations, while Northern Ireland contains a variety of identities including Irish and Northern Irish. The Republic of Ireland offers a clear example of a state, but not all the people living in the island of Ireland who proclaim themselves to be 'Irish' live in the state known as the Republic of Ireland. The former Federal Republic of Yugoslavia under Tito was a state, but it comprised different nations or, perhaps better, one can say different ethnicities, where ethnicity is rooted primarily in matters of identity pertaining to race, religion and language. Switzerland is a federal state composed of at least three national groups, while Belgium is a federal state containing six constituent units, broadly delineated along ethno-linguistic lines. Many UK citizens have no problem in describing themselves as British, including some Scots. However, many Scots certainly prefer to call themselves Scottish, and would recoil from the term British, while they might accept that they are also Europeans. We can see therefore the potential for accepting multiple identities. Clearly we have to accept that defining terms such as nation state, nation and state is always controversial because of different people's perceptions and different identities.

Smith (1995) calls ethnic communities *ethnies*, and defines these as

> named units of population with common ancestry myths and historical memories, elements of shared culture, some link with a historic territory and some measure of solidarity, at least among elites (Smith, 1995:57).

The question of identity is explored further in Chapter 3.

Key concept 1.2 Dictatorship

An authoritarian form of government that does not have democratic legitimacy and is not subject to the law.

The above definition begs the question: what is democratic legitimacy? In Western terms, a democracy is rule for the people, by the people. This is achieved by having free and fair elections where the electorate, composed of all members of the community who have reached the age of majority (i.e. they are considered adults) have a vote. The electorate is offered a free choice from a variety of candidates, typically presenting alternative programmes offered by different political parties. Likewise, in a democracy, the formation of political parties and the right to campaign are regarded as fundamental rights. In a democracy, this process is protected by the rule of law and any resulting government or ruler is subject to the rule of law. The judiciary is therefore independent of the government. Laws are made by the freely elected parliament and upheld by independent courts. In a democracy there is usually an absolute separation of authority between the government, the courts, the military and the police. All are subject to the law.

On this basis we can define a dictatorship by what it is not. A dictatorship is none of the above and a deficient democracy may be weak in one or more of the criteria above. Thus, the arch liberal critic of the current US government, Michael Moore, among others, criticised the administration of George W. Bush for having 'stolen' the 2000 presidential elections, because in Tallahassee, Florida at least, the elections were not conducted according to democratic principles – namely hundreds of black voters were denied the right to vote; extraordinary lengths were undertaken to include the votes of military service personnel overseas even if they failed to register their votes by the due date, and even if they had long since ceased to live in Florida; counting procedures were mired in irregularities; and above all a recount was suspended by the Supreme Court in which there was a Republican majority when it was clear that the count was going to produce the 'wrong' result. Moore actually questions whether the US is any longer a democracy, given the extent to which political advancement is dependent on the patronage of big business (Moore, 2002).

Here is another definition of dictatorship:

> Absolute rule, unrestricted by law, constitutions or other political or social factors within the state (McLean & McMillan, 2003:150).

A dictatorship normally presents a number of characteristics:

- The ruling elite is self-selecting and relatively permanent.
- There is no distinction between the government and the organs of state security, i.e. the police and the military.
- A dictatorship secures and retains power by force or coercion.
- It controls the media and other means of communication.
- Freedom of speech, association, and thought are severely restricted.

Examples of European dictatorships are given in Table 1.1. A particularly pure form of dictatorship is one that is **totalitarian**. A totalitarian dictatorship has all the above characteristics and is able to control virtually all aspects of the state and society. This is possible on account of its complete control over three core areas of society:

1. Politics and power (governance, political parties, local and central administration, military and police).
2. Capital and ownership (property, industry, agriculture).
3. Thought and culture (education, publishing, association, language, religion – the latter is often suppressed).

A totalitarian dictatorship is often accompanied by a 'cult of the personality', whereby the leader is deemed to be endowed with special, almost superhuman qualities that mark him out as an outstanding servant of his people, to be revered and respected, if not worshipped as a quasi-religious figure. Mass orchestrated demonstrations of public and military support are common hallmarks of totalitarian dictatorships. The major totalitarian dictatorships in history are those of Stalin, Hitler and Mao, all of whom employed mass demonstrations of support to sustain the myths of their leadership. These regimes, together with the Khmer Rouge in Cambodia or Saddam Hussein's Iraq under the rule of the Ba'ath Party, were also marked by terror, the sustained and widespread use of violence, including the elimination of opponents or those suspected of plotting against the state. Dictatorships do not stop at simply limiting freedom of expression by controlling the media. Persecution and intimidation, as well as arbitrary imprisonment without trial, show trials, torture and disappearance of opponents or anyone suspected of crimes against the state is routine. Other totalitarian regimes include those of Ceauşescu in Romania, Honecker in the GDR and Zhivkov in Bulgaria. North Korea under Kim Il Sung and now Kim Jong Il is a contemporary example of totalitarian governance, while China retains many features of totalitarian government despite its dramatic embracing of capitalism and private enterprise. The ruling Communist Party still dominates the political landscape, freedom of speech is sharply limited and there is widespread intimidation and abuse of human rights.

It is sometimes a mystery to people who have never had to endure dictatorships why people do not rise up and throw out their appalling governments. Such a question is naïve and betrays a failure to understand the extent to which fear and intimidation are used by dictatorships – or to put this more bluntly, they fail to appreciate what life (and death) might be like in a country where torture and extrajudicial killing by the state are endemic. It is estimated that half the adult population of the former German Democratic Republic was in the service of the secret police, the *Stasi*, the eyes and ears of the ruling Communist Party. All employment, housing, education and health care is distributed according to party patronage. In a society where even your own children can be indoctrinated into informing if you criticise the regime, dissent is more than an act of courage. It may be a foolhardy move that leads to your own demise, or worse, that of your loved ones. Having said this, it is extraordinary that most dictatorships are faced by movements of political resistance, or at the very least courageous individuals who become dissidents, often at extreme personal risk. There was a considerable resistance movement to Nazi occupation in France and also in Norway, and even in Germany itself there were attempts to aid the escape of Jews to safe havens and occasional plots to assassinate Hitler.

It is worth devoting a couple of pages of a book on European politics to the meaning of dictatorship for two reasons. Firstly, as this chapter has made clear, dictatorship was a major European experience of the twentieth century, and those of us who forget our history, to coin a phrase, are condemned to repeat it. Secondly, in the context of European integration and in particular the most recent enlargement of the European Union, the recent experience of dictatorship is a powerful motivating factor for joining an EU, which, despite its evident weaknesses, is still widely perceived to be an organisation which upholds democratic and broadly inclusive values.

Further reading

Davies, N. (1996) *Europe: A history*, Oxford: Oxford University Press. The book provides a short account of the key events in the French Revolution, an overview of its nineteenth century aftermath and useful survey of the lead up to war in 1914. This book is a superb historical account of European history, especially during the period post-1789 to 1945.

George, S. (1998) *An Awkward Partner. Britain in the European Community*, Oxford: Oxford University Press. George provides a comprehensive survey of successive British governments' policies towards European integration, from initial indifference to eventual reluctant engagement. The book is considered a classic text on UK relations with the EEC/EU.

Held, D. (1995) *Democracy and the Global Order: From the Modern State to Cosmopolitan Governance*, Cambridge: Polity. See in particular Chapter 3 'The development of the nation state', pp. 48–72; Chapter 4 'The interstate system', pp. 73–98 describes the changes affecting the international environment, especially in the context of globalisation.

Hibbert, C. (1982) *The French Revolution*, Penguin. This is an excellent introduction to the shifting tides of the French revolutionary period from 1789 to the coup d'état by Napoleon Bonaparte in 1895.

Young, H. (1998) *This Blessed Plot: Britain and Europe from Churchill to Blair*. London: Macmillan. This outstanding book adopts a quasi-biographical approach to explaining British policy towards Europe. It is a fascinating and highly readable account that traces the history of British policy through successive prime ministers.

Film suggestions

The two films described below provide powerful portrayals of different aspects of European history. The rationale for choosing them is to identify films which demonstrate aspects of that history in a less than conventional or purely historical fashion. Spielberg's masterful *Schindler's List* might have been selected if one was looking for a vivid and harrowing portrayal of the meaning and consequences of the Holocaust, but I have chosen to recommend films with a non-conventional and not especially historical approach, but that nevertheless present an atmosphere and a message that is deeply revealing about Europe's past.

Roberto Rossellini, *Germania Anno Zero* (Germany Year Zero), 1946, Italy

Have you ever wondered about the progress that Europe has made since the devastation created by the Second World War? A good reminder of how things were can be obtained by watching a classic of Italian neo-realism. Try to find a copy of *Germania Anno Zero* (Germany Year Zero, 1946) by Roberto Rossellini. Rossellini, who married the actress Ingrid Bergman after she wrote to him asking to be in one of his films, shot *Germania Anno Zero* amid the ruins of bombed-out Berlin just as the war ended. It tells the story of a young boy and his family scratching a living amid the chaos of rubble and broken relationships as Germany begins its emergence from Nazism. Bear in mind that the rubble-strewn streets of Berlin were typical of the devastation wrought on several German cities, not just its burnt-out capital. More importantly, the film highlights the psychological and material degradation that Nazism brought to the German population. It is a wonderful, though intensely harrowing, film. (Ingrid Bergman isn't in this film, by the way. If you appreciate *Germania Anno Zero*, see *Stromboli* – her first Rossellini film.)

For more on this film, see http://www.bbc.co.uk/bbcfour/cinema/features/germany-year-zero.shtml

Andrej Wajda, *Danton*, 1982, France

This film is a vivid portrayal of the turmoil in Paris following Robespierre's seizure of power during the French Revolution and the beginning of the Reign of Terror. Wajda, who was Polish, was always preoccupied with the terror of dictatorship, and many of his films, including this one, echoed events in his homeland as martial law was imposed under General Jaruzelski in 1981. Wajda denied explicitly modelling the character of Danton on the shipyard electrician Lech Walesa, who later became Polish president, and who led the emerging *Solidarnosc* trades union against the communist authorities, but it is hard to resist the parallel. Again the film is a powerful illustration of the history that Europe has spent 50 years getting away from, or only 15 in the case of the Central and Eastern European countries.

As you watch the film's eponymous hero, memorably played by Gérard Dépardieu, having his head removed, reflect on the startling fact that the guillotine was used in France as recently as 1977 and capital punishment was only abolished, by President Mitterrand, in 1981.

For a more detailed synopsis and comment on *Danton*, see Issue 212 of *Socialist Review*, October 1997, or visit http://pubs.socialistreviewindex.org.uk/sr212/picture.htm

Chapter 2

The state, sovereignty and nationalism

Outline

- The state and sovereignty
- State sovereignty and international institutions
- The meaning of nationalism
- Three types of nationalism: state nationalism; civic nationalism; ethnic nationalism
- Promoting cultural identity and the problem of ethnic nationalism
- The EU, nation building and citizenship

Key concepts

2.1   Sovereignty

2.2   Nationalism

Introduction

The first chapter presented the historical context for understanding the European integration process. This chapter contains more detailed discussion of two contentious issues that are central to that process, namely (1) the role of the state and its relationship to sovereignty, and (2) the meaning of nationalism. Both themes run throughout the book but they are especially pertinent to the early chapters on Europe and the European Union.

This chapter begins with a discussion of the relationship between the **state** and **sovereignty** and then examines how sovereignty is affected by involvement with international institutions. This demonstrates that the notion of sovereignty has changed since the Second World War, and how this has important implications for the state itself.

The second part of the chapter focuses on the meaning of **nationalism** and explores three different forms of nationalism, namely civic nationalism, state nationalism, and ethnic nationalism. The promotion of local cultural identity is also looked at in relation to ethnic nationalism.

The chapter concludes with a brief examination of the notion of European citizenship. The apparent interest of the EU in nation building is strongly criticised. An alternative approach is recommended that is more constructive and complimentary with the traditional role of the state.

● ● ● ● The state and sovereignty

European integration has provoked a lot of argument over what kind of model should be developed, how this integration should be achieved, or even, from nationalists, whether it is desirable at all. At the core of this debate in recent times is the relationship between the state and the European Union. To understand this, let us first establish what the state is and what the related concept of sovereignty is about.

In Chapter 1 the state was defined as 'a political entity that is coterminous with a territory and represented by a government that is recognised as having legitimate authority, or sovereignty, over that territory and the people who live in it' (see discussion in key concept 1.1, pp. 38–9). Recognition is a key aspect of this definition, since it means that states and their governments have legitimacy in the eyes of other governments.

> **Definition   The modern state**
>
> A centralised administration applying common laws uniformly to all citizens over the whole territory (Davies, 1996:715).

States are recognised in international law, as upheld in international courts such as the International Criminal Court established in 2003, and supported or recognised by international institutions such as the United Nations, the World Trade Organisation, or by treaties, conventions and institutions such as the Geneva Convention, the North Atlantic Treaty Organisation or the European Union. States typically have other defining characteristics, such as formal legal identity associated with the constituted government, a **legislature** and a judiciary, an army, a police force and tax-raising powers. Government is exercised through a **constitution** that defines how the territory is governed, and government representatives usually have relations with other governments' representatives. States are also frequently identified with an official language, or a number of languages, in common use by its citizens, and certain symbols that are uniquely associated with the territory and people, such as flags, anthems and government buildings. Many of these criteria are referred to in Discussions 2.3 and 2.4.

The state possesses an attendant linkage to the question of sovereignty. Sovereignty means the ability of a state, or a constitutionally recognised body acting on behalf of the state, to exercise authority over its territory and its people without being subject to any higher authority. A further implication behind the concept of state is that it is in some way connected to the identity or identities of the people living within it.

The concept of state therefore often assumes an integrated and closely matching relationship with nationhood, or national consciousness. This provides the state with a form of legitimacy, in that it is tolerated, or supported, by its people. It follows therefore that there should be a close fit between the entity described as a state and the people within it, meaning that together they should constitute a **nation**. In reality, however, people's chosen identities, even within a state, are many and various, or contingent upon circumstances. Nevertheless, the term nation implies a people with a shared national identity. From such an assumption stems the commonly used term nation state. This phrase is problematic, since in practice many states contain many national identities. Nevertheless, a certain form of nationalism, state nationalism, eschews this uncomfortable fact and promotes the notion of the state as comprising a single nation, something which is rarely the case, as 'contemporary states only rarely have a population made up of a single ethnic group' (Goldmann et al., 2000:7). This is discussed in more detail later in this chapter.

The next chapter considers different examples in Europe where the relationship between state and nation as described above has been or remains highly conflictive, leading all too frequently to appalling violence. This has especially been the case where state powers have sought to expand or consolidate their authority at the expense of national groups. This has been Europe's spectacular tragedy in modern times.

The traditional, or classical interpretation of the state can be traced to the Peace of Westphalia of 1648 which clarified the nature of the inter-state system and established an understanding of international order. This is frequently referred to as the 'Westphalian model' and is based on the entrenchment, through the treaty, of the principle of territorial sovereignty in inter-state affairs.

> The [Westphalian] model covers a period from 1648 to 1945, although many of the assumptions underpinning it are still operative in international relations today. It depicts the development of a world community consisting of sovereign states which settle their differences privately and often by force (or the threat of force); which engage in diplomatic relations but otherwise pursue minimal cooperation; which seek to place their own national interest above all others; and which accept the logic of the principle of effectiveness, that is, the principle that might eventually makes right in the international world – that appropriation becomes legitimation (Held, 1995:77–8).

The Westphalian model informs the realist perspective within the discipline of **International Relations** (see Chapter 8). **Realism** assumes the primacy of the state in the conduct of international affairs. It is based on the assumption that

> international politics is composed of sovereign nation-states and that these sovereign nation-states are beholden to no higher power. That is what it means to be sovereign – for a state to have absolute authority over its territory and people and to have independence internationally (Weber, 2001:14).

A further crucial example of how sovereignty rests with the state is its having a 'monopoly on the legitimate use of violence' (see Discussion 2.1). This

---

Discussion 2.1

The state and the legitimate use of violence

Gellner reports Max Weber's terse definition of the state as the 'agency within society which possesses the monopoly of legitimate violence' (Gellner, 1983:3). Some states may exercise violence against their citizens, or ethnic minorities, that other states or international authorities might consider illegitimate. In recent years, this has been used as the precept for condemnation by the United Nations, and even for armed intervention by outside authorities, as in the case of UN and NATO involvement with Serbia in the 1990s. Gray (2003:72) has pointed out that this 'monopoly of violence' has broken down, commenting on how weapons of mass destruction may have leaked away to terrorist groups, and similarly the diffusion of science and technology has undermined traditional state authority. These trends have altered the nature of war. He is right, but the point does not undermine Weber's definition, which includes the vital qualification 'legitimate'.

---

typically applies to independent sovereign states, but not to entities at a sub-state level such as the *Länder* in Germany, the four nations that make up the UK, or the (non-sovereign) states of the USA. Another way to express this idea is to affirm that only sovereign states can deploy armed forces against an enemy, or declare war.

Review   *What is a state? What is meant by the 'Westphalian model'? What is sovereignty?*

● ● ● ● State sovereignty and international institutions

How is sovereignty affected by states' involvement with international organisations? This is crucial in assessing the dynamics of the member state–European Union relationship, as well as the impact of globalisation. This section examines three examples: the North Atlantic Treaty Organisation (NATO), the European Union (EU) and the World Trade Organisation (WTO).

Bainbridge (2002:479) argues that 'most treaties curtail the freedom of action of the signatory states in certain specific areas'. The impact on sovereignty has been a contested issue during the development of European integration since 1945. In significant respects member states are indeed 'beholden to a higher power', given that European Community law has been created at the European level and is backed by the authority of the European Commission and the European Court of Justice (ECJ). The signatories to the Washington Treaty that established NATO in 1949 are bound to meet their obligations under the treaty. Similarly, parties involved in WTO negotiations contract to abide by agreed trade rules. In all cases, the nature of sovereignty has moved on from Westphalian principles, or classical realist interpretation. On the other hand, Bainbridge points out that states are in fact free to leave the European Union if they so desire – a stipulation potentially enhanced by the proposed Constitutional Treaty signed by the EU heads of government in Rome in October 2004 (though pending ratification by the member states). Within NATO states have a veto on policy decisions in the North Atlantic Council, its supreme governing body. Since the NATO treaty obliges the signatories to come to the aid of any member threatened by aggression, and if necessary to go to war, this may indeed entail a loss of sovereignty. However, since in international law part of any understanding of state sovereignty is the freedom to enter into treaty obligations, then clearly joining NATO is the sovereign right of any state invited to do so. It can hardly be used as an argument for the irrelevance of sovereignty.

What makes the EU qualitatively different for Bainbridge is that once states accept the EU treaties and accede to membership, the Union does have judicial authority in the form of dedicated institutions that can draw up legislation binding on member states. The EU has assumed powers over its members that go beyond the actual treaties in force at the time of accession. However, the EU is not the European Commission alone: the Commission cannot make substantive laws without state agreement and the legislative process requires state participation. Laws are made in the European Council, or in the Council of the European Union (formerly the Council of Ministers), and it is in this forum that member states have the opportunity to either veto proposals, or, in areas of policy where Qualified Majority Voting has been approved by previous Treaty accords, to muster a sufficient minority opposed to the policy initiative to prevent it becoming law. Even where this endeavour is unsuccessful, and a member state is outvoted, it is still up to the state to introduce the law in its own territory. The legislation has to be passed by the national parliament, admittedly within a timeframe laid down by the European Commission. Frequently legislation is incorporated into member state law with exceptions and allowances to accommodate local preferences (see Chapter 4). See Discussion 2.2 for a further discussion relating to the sovereignty of national parliaments.

The WTO offers another example of how sovereignty is dealt with. Membership of the WTO is voluntary and the rules it seeks to uphold are, in theory, freely negotiated. Individual states or groups of states acting in cohort, perhaps through the auspices of international organisations such as the EU or NAFTA, negotiate trade agreements. Such agreements usually impose some restrictions on members' freedom of action, for example on the right to unilaterally impose trade barriers or additional non-negotiated tariffs.

However, in practice, it is questionable to what extent WTO negotiations are freely conducted. Individual states and their representatives are often bound by limitations to do with specific circumstances or the preferences of third parties. Powerful members of the WTO may exert pressures on the less powerful, persuading them to accept certain conditions. For example the US can persuade representatives of South American states, worried about US disinvestment if they do not accede to Washington's expectations, to accept certain conditions. This acquiescence to US preferences where the WTO is concerned is even more marked in negotiations with the International Monetary Fund, where the US has voting rights that effectively provide the US with a veto on IMF policy. The WTO

Discussion 2.2

How much sovereignty should reside with national parliaments in approving EU Directives?

Would it be reasonable for national parliaments to have a vote on whether to incorporate EU directives into national law? Such a change in the member state–EU relationship would indeed amount to the 'repatriation' of sovereignty that many critics crave. In April 2004 the UK government proposed such a measure for the draft European Constitution. There are two problems with this idea:

1. The measure would create unevenness in the application of European Community law within the Single European Market. On the other hand, if rejection by a single member state parliament could trigger the fall of the directive right across the Union, then the proposal would mean giving national parliaments a veto on directives applying to the entire Single European Market. Such a veto would go beyond what is currently permitted within the Council (see Chapter 4), and it would effectively paralyse the decision-making process of a 25 member state Union.

2. The second observation is that there is no certainty that such a power would actually deliver real authority to national legislatures. It is more likely that it would simply lead to more 'rebellions' and more discontent at the national level. In the case of the UK, which put forward this suggestion, the national legislature is to a large extent a rubber-stamping device for the executive. The UK party system ensures voting discipline among Members of Parliament, so individual MPs vote according to the wishes of their party leaders. This undermines the co-called sovereignty of Parliament.

Critics of the UK political system argue that the extraordinary power of the prime minister's office means that the national parliament is hardly the sovereign authority it is supposed to be according to the UK's (unwritten) constitution. Therefore the request for national parliaments to be given this decisive vote on EU directives may be a red herring. National parliaments would rarely be able to use it, or if they did, they could conceivably be on a collision course with their own executives if the ministers responsible, or the heads of government, had already voted in favour of the European directive becoming law. If they hadn't, then the first – more substantial – objection applies.

The proposal is, however, interesting in that it harks back to Westphalian notions of state sovereignty. One is tempted to suggest that such a measure would so paralyse the EU that any state that seriously seeks such an innovation should instead consider whether its future lies inside or outside the European Union. The most enthusiastic eurosceptics in Britain would endorse such a conclusion.

See Chapter 4 for more on the decision-making processes within the European Union.

is sometimes open to a similar criticism given the practical if not theoretical power of its largest and most influential members. Despite this criticism, the WTO is a form of treaty negotiation that sovereign states may, in theory, reject. Arguably, as with NATO, acceptance of an agreement may compromise sovereignty, but a different way of looking at this is to consider that multilateral negotiations that reach common agreements do not simply involve the giving up of sovereignty. Instead, they may indicate that sovereignty is 'pooled' or 'shared', a notion developed in Chapter 4. In the WTO, once agreement is reached in the form of a trade round, states that renege on agreements may expect sanctions from other states, which the WTO may endorse. In summary, the WTO is a rule-based system constructed by sovereign states or their representatives, but participation in the WTO inevitably restricts freedom of action to some degree.

The central claim from this discussion is that state sovereignty is at least to some extent compromised by participation in international organisations. This means that the notion of sovereignty has undergone significant changes, and it therefore implies that the state itself has changed. Some organisations compromise state sovereignty more than others, and in different areas. In the conduct of international relations circumstances and conditions vary and require different responses. Nevertheless, at least where democracies are concerned, reaching compromises with the representatives of other states ought to present few insurmountable problems. It is clear, however, that for those of a strongly nationalist or realist disposition, compromise might be judged as a sign of weakness. There have been several watershed moments in the history of European integration where the defence of state sovereignty provoked serious problems (see Discussion 2.3).

The classical realist perspective asserts a preference for unilateralist decision-making and a defence of the Westphalian principle that state sovereignty is inviolable. Even involvement with traditional defence-related treaties might be

---

Discussion 2.3

Defending the state against EEC/EU encroachment: four examples

1 The Empty Chair crisis in 1966

The so-called Empty Chair crisis in 1966 occurred when De Gaulle objected to limitations on the use of veto by member states in the Council of Ministers. France sent no representatives for five months and held out for the Luxembourg Compromise which confirmed the right of veto where 'national interests' prevailed.

2 Thatcher's Bruges Speech

In 1988 the Franco-German axis in the Community was seeking to extend political and economic integration. It was supported by an assertive Commission under the dynamic leadership of Jacques Delors. The British premier Margaret Thatcher delivered a blistering attack on the 'Community method' in her famous Bruges Speech. She affirmed the primacy of states in shaping policy direction.

3 The Treaty on European Union and the innovation of the 'opt out'

Agreeing the terms of the TEU at Maastricht was difficult and ratification was tortuous. The Treaty survived only because of the inclusion of the 'opt-out' device which allowed Britain and Denmark to stand outside some of the provisions of the Treaty. The chapter on EMU was presented as a separate protocol and the UK and Denmark were given opt-outs on the final stage of EMU which involved adopting the Single Currency. The UK also opted out of the Social Chapter, which contained provisions relating to employment and workers' rights.

4 The Schengen Agreement

The Schengen Agreement was intended to enshrine the free movement of people into Community law. Initially created in 1985 as an intergovernmental accord between France, Germany and the Benelux states, it was designed to remove border controls between them. It later incorporated other member states of the EU, and when Denmark, Finland and Sweden joined, so too did the non-EU states Norway and Iceland, as these five already constituted a passport union. The Schengen Agreement was incorporated into the structures of the EU by the Treaty of Amsterdam in 1997. However, the UK and Ireland remain outside the agreement, thus benefiting from a further opt-out. The UK, in particular, has argued that its right to control its ports of entry is a fundamental necessity and a mark of its sovereignty against encroachment by 'Brussels'.

viewed as a threat to sovereignty. Indeed members of the non-aligned movement during the Cold War showed a preference for remaining outside any such alliances. This was, however, not simply to protect their sovereign independence; there were other political and strategic factors involved. We shall see in Chapters 4 and 8 that the *neo*-realist position does accept that states may voluntarily accept a reduction in sovereignty *where it is in the state's interest to do so.*

One of the main contentions of this book is that the concept of state sovereignty has altered since the Peace of Westphalia. In a more interconnected international environment, with around 200 states and a similar number of international institutions to which states delegate representatives, the classical principles of sovereignty require revision. Naturally in the post-Westphalian world, nothing is especially straightforward in defining states, or in settling on the meaning of sovereignty. This argument is further developed in Chapter 4, which describes how European integration has led to a reassessment of traditional interpretations of sovereignty. The notion of 'pooled' or 'shared' sovereignty has emerged as a characteristic feature of involvement with multinational institutions. For various reasons this has proved attractive to many states' political leaders in Europe since 1945.

Discussion 2.4 examines the extent to which the European Union has assumed the characteristics of a state. It highlights some of the features of a prototypical state and signals issues analysed in more detail in Chapter 4. Discussion 2.4 concludes that the EU has assumed 'state-like characteristics'. It is opportune, however, to emphasise that these should not be underestimated. In three respects the Union has gathered considerable powers, all of which hugely compromise state sovereignty. By focusing on specifics, rather than on the generalities of state relationships to international institutions, it becomes evident that EU member state sovereignty has diminished. Weiler reports that the EU has the capacity, among other things, to do the following:

- To enact norms which create rights and obligations both for its member states and their nationals, norms which are often directly effective and which are constitutionally supreme;

Discussion 2.4

The state test: 1. Is the EU a state?

The EU compromises the traditional notion of sovereignty whereby states are 'not subject to any higher authority'. This is because European Community law, which applies to the Single European Market, has primacy over member state law.

But does the EU constitute a state? Its critics often imply that it is becoming something similar to a state, and in fact something much more terrifying, a 'super-state'. This term was used by Margaret Thatcher in her 1988 Bruges speech (Thatcher,

1988:4). Kapteyn (1996) describes the EU as a 'stateless market' which seems more accurate (see Chapter 11).

The table below lists criteria for assessing statelike characteristics and highlights some discussion points before giving an assessment of whether the EU meets each particular test.

From the table, we may conclude that in several important respects the European Union has 'statelike' characteristics but it is more accurate to

Discussion 2.4 (*continued*)

Criteria/state characteristic	Comments	Assessment
A political entity coterminous with a territory	Unlike most states the EU can extend its borders through enlargement – and has done so several times.	Yes – but unusual in the respect indicated
Has a government/ institutions of governance	Clearly so, including courts.	Yes
Internationally recognised as 'sovereign'	The EU has full membership of the WTO and is a fully recognised international institution. However, it is not recognised as 'sovereign' in the sense that the US or the UK are. It cannot be member of the UN.	No
Legislative functions	It does, but these are in proscribed areas (SEM) and shared with member state authorities.	Partial
Army, monopoly of legitimate use of violence, right to declare war	The EU does not possess its own army in the way that a sovereign state does. The RRF can be deployed on behalf of the EU, but states may opt out of its missions. The Union has neither of the other two features.	No
Constitution	The Council confirmed the text for a Constitutional Treaty in 2004, although it requires ratification by all 25 member states.	Yes (provisionally)
Police force	The EU has Europol, an organ concerned with police and criminal matters, but it is not a police force analogous to national forces.	No
Foreign policy	The EU has a limited role in foreign policy and the TEU signalled this through the CFSP in Pillar II.	Partial
Identity with a national group	The national group of 'Europeans' is poorly defined and does not have a strong pull on people's identities.	Partial
Common language	The EU describes the main languages of all its member states as 'official languages' and accords primary status to three: English, French and German.	No
Common economic policy and currency union	Full EMU applies across 12 member states, the discipline of economic union – the stability and growth pact – in theory extends to all EU members.	Partial
Political union	Relatively underdeveloped. States have powerful political roles.	No
Symbols of unity: flag, anthem, coins, physical evidence	The EU has created various such symbols, e.g. its flag and Schiller's 'Ode to Joy' from Beethoven's Choral Symphony, and the ECB is responsible for the circulation of euro notes and coins in 12 member states.	Yes

describe the EU as an organisation comprising several member states and having a significant institutional framework that makes it a prominent actor in international politics. It is an organisation composed of several institutions and by its member states that contribute to the wider whole. The EU cannot create substantive legislation except in partnership with its member states' governments and legislatures. The member states share sovereignty in many significant areas and, significantly, they have chosen to do so. They may also, in theory, leave the Union, if they so desire.

- To take decisions with major impact on the social and economic orientation of public life within the member states and within Europe as a whole, considerably enhanced with Economic and Monetary Union;
- To engage the Community and consequently the member states by international agreements with third countries and international organisations (Weiler, 2000:181).

A second application of this form of 'test of statehood', Discussion 2.5, looks at a sub-state region, the Basque Country, in Spain. Spain illustrates a frequently disputed aspect of the state conundrum, namely the mismatch between state authority and national identity within the constituted polity known as the state. Spain seeks to resolve the tensions flowing from its many identities by recognising various regions in a quasi-federal system. The view that there are in fact 'many Spains' (Ellingham & Fisher, 2002:v) reflects not only Spain's 17 autonomous regions, but also the different identities carried by individuals. It is not difficult for the people of Andalucia to be both Andaluz and Spanish. It is more problematic for some Basques to accept this kind of shared identity. The question of national identity is further explored in the next chapter.

Discussion 2.5

The state test: 2. Is the Basque Country a state?

A second test looks at a sub-state entity, the Basque Country (*Euskadi*), situated in Northern Spain and South West France. For the purposes of this analysis it is simpler to apply the test only to the larger (and more contested) 'Spanish' Basque Country.

The conclusion is that the Basque Country is also not a sovereign state, but for different reasons. It is an autonomous community within the Kingdom of Spain. It lacks international recognition as a sovereign state.

As is well known, the Basque Country is a highly disputed territory. It is clear that a section of the community feels that the only reason the Basque Country is not a sovereign state is that it is not *allowed to be one* by the Spanish state, despite Basques constituting a nation. However, it should be pointed out that there is no clear consensus on whether the majority of Basques, let alone other nationalities living in the region, actually want full separation from Spain. In the March 2004 election, 54 per cent voted for non-nationalist parties, comprising PSOE (33.71 per cent), PP (18.8 per cent), and EB-IU (8.0 per cent) – a non-nationalist left-wing Basque party. Meanwhile, 34 per cent voted for the moderate nationalist PNV, but it is not clear how many of its

supporters actually want full independence. The election indicated a maximum of around 10 per cent support for more extreme nationalist parties seeking outright separation (6.5 per cent support for EA and some 3 per cent of spoiled papers, deemed to be expressions of support for the banned pro-ETA party, Batasuna).

Some Basque nationalists demand a referendum on the future status of the disputed territory and in 2003, the President of the Basque Parliament, Jose Ibarretxe, presented a plan for 'free association' between the Basque autonomous region and the Spanish state. Fernando Savater, the founder of a citizens' opposition to ETA called *Basta ya* (Enough is enough) declared that the plan threatened the integrity of the Spanish state: 'The idea that we are citizens of a country and not merely a part of that country is in peril [. . .] the proposal amounts to saying "If you accept this idea, we'll try to persuade ETA to stop killing people".' Savater also expressed concern about an alliance between local socialists and members of the Republican Left in Catalonia – a combination that would, according to Savater, cause problems for Spain's new Socialist government (Savater, 2004).

Discussion 2.5 (*continued*)

Criteria/state characteristic	Comments	Assessment
A political entity coterminous with a territory	Yes, although it extends into South West France as well. Under the Spanish Constitution, the Autonomous Region of the Basque Communities has an established regional government.	Yes – with the proviso noted
Has a government/ institutions of governance	It has a Parliament and a government with specific delegated authority. Clearly governance is shared with the Spanish state.	Partial/ shared
Internationally recognised as 'sovereign'	The Basque Country does not have international recognition in the way that Spain, for example, does. It is not a member of the UN and nor can it be invited to join while it is part of Spain. The Basque Country is not recognised as a member state of the EU and is therefore excluded from voting in the European Council/Council of the European Union.	No
Legislative functions	These are strictly limited according to the statutes of autonomy within the Spanish constitution.	Partial
Army, monopoly of legitimate use of violence, right to declare war	The Basque Country has no authority in this area.	No
Constitution	There is no autonomous and independent Basque constitution. The region is incorporated into the Spanish state.	No
Police force	The Basque Country has its own police force but again policing is shared with the Spanish state.	Partial
Foreign policy	The Basque Country has only very limited scope for independent representation, for example in the EU's Committee of the Regions (CoR).	No
Identity with a national group	Basques represent a significant majority of the Basque Country's population. Like Catalans and Galicians, the Spanish Constitution recognises Basques as a 'nationality'.	Yes
Common language	*Euskera* is widely spoken and is commonly used in public affairs, government offices and schools. However, Spanish is more widely used among the general population.	Partial
Common economic policy and currency union	The Basque economy is fully incorporated into that of Spain and the EU. The regional government has limited tax-raising powers.	No
Political union	As an Autonomous Community within the Spanish state, the political independence of the Basque Country is heavily proscribed by a 'higher authority'.	No
Symbols of unity: flag, anthem, coins, physical evidence	The Basque Country has all these symbols except coins, and has a highly developed sense of its own distinctive culture, including language.	Yes

It is unlikely that a referendum campaign would resolve the problem of the Basque Country no matter what the result. A campaign would merely expose the deep divisions in Basque society. Doubtless the issue would be more conflictive than the in some ways – at least in the eyes of Basque nationalists – analogous situation of Greenland, where its voters were given a choice through a referendum on their country's continued membership of the European Union (see Discussion 2.6).

> ### Discussion 2.6
>
> ### Leaving the EU: the case of Greenland
>
> No member state has as yet left the EU. However, Greenland provides an interesting caveat to this statement. An island larger than France, Germany, Italy, Spain and the UK combined, and with a population of only 50,000, Greenland was formerly an integrated part of the Kingdom of Denmark and as such joined the EU, or the EEC as it then was, in 1973 with Denmark. In 1979 Greenland was granted a substantial measure of home rule including the right to hold a referendum on EEC membership. The result was a vote to leave the EEC and Greenland finally seceded from the Community in 1986 (Bainbridge, 2002:313).
>
> The proposed EU Constitutional Treaty contains a provision asserting the right of a member state to secede from the Union if it so desires. Naturally, state constitutions afford no such right to disputed territories.

> **Review**   *Can you identify some of the key characteristics that help to define the meaning of the word state?*
>
>   *How does membership of international institutions compromise sovereignty?*

● ● ● ● The meaning of nationalism

Chapter 1 argued that the French Revolution spurred a significant territorial consciousness and associated reaction against foreign occupation. Conscription appeared in Europe for the first time, and militarism contributed to the rise in national sentiment. Droz (1967:143–4) argues that this coincidence of national and liberal aspiration had an important impact on the nineteenth and twentieth centuries. He describes two nationalist models: first, the French concept of nationality was based on the consent of the various elements within the population determined to live under the same laws. Another was the Herder concept, adopted by German Romantic writers, which compared nationality to a living organism and held that it was based on an unconscious community of race, language or customs.

Napoleon appears to have been a prophet of nationalism. Droz quotes his saying after defeat at Waterloo, 'I would have liked to make a single national body out of each of these peoples', meaning the unification of Germany and Italy. The legend of Napoleon contributed to the idea of him as a teacher leading Europe towards unity. In Britain, such a message would seem to confirm the worst nightmares of any eurosceptic opponent of European integration in recent times.

What is nationalism? Here are two definitions:

> [Nationalism is] an ideological movement for the attainment and maintenance of autonomy, unity and identity on behalf of a population deemed by some of its members to constitute a 'nation' (Smith, 1995:149–50).

Kedourie, in a seminal work on the subject, defines nationalism as:

> a doctrine invented in Europe at the beginning of the nineteenth century . . .
> [which] holds that humanity is divided into nations, that nations are known by
> certain characteristics which can be ascertained, and that the only legitimate type
> of government is national self-government (Kedourie, 1966:9).

In general terms, and one is obliged at times to use such imprecision where
no broadly accepted consensus is readily available, in most states the majority
of citizens are conscious of a degree of shared identity and share the same culture. This does not preclude the possibility of different minority cultures co-
existing with the dominant one, and in fact contributing to its evolution, as
can be observed in the UK, for example.

> The nation is a soul, a spiritual principle. [It] consists of two things. One is the com-
> mon legacy of rich memories from the past. The other is the present consensus, the
> will to live together [. . .] in order to create that consensus, the members of a com-
> munity will have to forget the injustices and oppressions that once divided them.
> *L'oublié*, the act of forgetting, and one might even say historical falsehood, are neces-
> sary factors in the creation of nations (Renan, quoted in Davies, 1996:813).

This reference to the aspect of delusion which attaches to the nation implies a
certain subjectivity, even artificiality, about the whole notion of nationalism.
Nationalism depends on shared myths, and this concept of myth should be
interpreted as beliefs or sentiments that may or may not be true: indeed, their
truth is less important than their existence in shared culture (this idea of myth
returns in the discussion of International Relations theories in Chapter 8).

It is worth remembering that the concept of the sovereign state is relatively
modern, as Chapter 1 suggested. It has become an accepted feature of contemporary society and political discourse, and is obviously central to the discipline
of International Relations. Nationalism then, is an ideology strongly associated
with the concept of state. It assumes, not unreasonably, that nationhood and
statehood are attributable to the same geographical area and that the idea of the
state has historical and sociological legitimacy. Furthermore, the concept is
sustained by modern geopolitical organisation, whereby states are identifiable
in relation to other states, or to any perceived external threat. This implies a
certain characteristic defensiveness among nationalists and proponents of the
state. In recent years there has indeed been evidence of this, especially among
those who assert the value of classical notions of sovereignty, and 'national interests' in respect of the process of European integration. Before addressing the
specific context of European integration, let us look further at the historical
evolution of nationalism by examining various different types.

Review   *Using your own words, explain what nationalism is. How does nationalism relate to
the concept of the state?*

● ● ● ● Three types of nationalism: state, civic and ethnic

Davies (1996:812) writes that nationalism was boosted by the French Revolution and from there exported around the globe. 'The idea', he says, 'is that the nation has a collective of interests which are the supreme good.' During the nineteenth century nationalism developed in various forms: state nationalism and civic nationalism, which are different manifestations of nationalism both sponsored by ruling elites; a third kind is ethnic nationalism, which is sponsored by the mass of the population that shares a particular national identity, or by a community within the state. In the latter case, the community may confront the dominant state authorities which do not reflect the same aspirations in terms of nationhood. Indeed, they may represent another opposing set of nationalist aspirations. This section seeks to explain in some detail how these forms of nationalism are distinguished.

Doubtless, the nineteenth-century combination of modernisation and political oppression spurred national sentiment – of different kinds. Davies (1996:821) describes nationalism as underlining the essential differences between civilisation and **culture**. European civilisation is the result of the sum total of influence over centuries from previous ideas and traditions, inherited from the ancient world – from Ancient Greece and the Roman Empire – and from Christianity. These historical epochs have shaped local cultures throughout Europe and created a broadly common and dominant heritage, albeit one that includes other traditions as well.

> So at the roots of the culture of Europe are the curiosity, open-mindedness and rationality of the Greeks, the civic responsibility and political individualism of the Greeks and Romans and the sense of the significance of the free individual spirit to be found in the main tradition of Christianity (Gowland et al., 2000:280).

This Greco-Roman-Christian tradition might be described as a chassis on which various distinctive but related models have developed, together constituting the broad mass of a European, as opposed to local, culture. However, like identity – which is discussed in the next chapter – this European culture is often best described contrastively, in opposition to that which it is not. Therefore Japanese culture and European culture are distinct because one is built on an Eastern Buddhist tradition, on Samurai traditions of hierarchy and military discipline, and was shaped by several centuries under a relatively closed body politic, controlling a markedly local and inward-looking culture, until the Meiji Restoration in 1852 opened Japan to a wave of foreign influences and rapid industrialisation. In contrast, European culture is founded on the religious traditions of Judaeo-Christianity, and on the broadly open and trade-orientated, or mercantilist, legacies of Ancient Greece and Roman society, a heritage which assisted a relatively early industrialisation. European culture evolved as a complex web of local habits, speech, folklore, religious deviations, and other idiosyncrasies. Europe achieved a pan-European civilisation over several centuries, which nationalism, according to Davies, broadly opposed, because nationalism promoted local culture rather than a pan-European civilisation.

Civilisation, represented in the European context by the arts and sciences, by learning and language – even multilingualism – was extolled as local culture was despised during the Renaissance, and even more so during the seventeenth-century Enlightenment. Subsequently nationalism did the opposite. National cultures were extolled and what was common between them was relatively neglected. The educated, multilingual, cosmopolitan elite in Europe was fragmented, while half-educated national masses who thought of themselves as British, French, Russia, German or Italian, grew stronger.

State nationalism and civic nationalism

State nationalism is initiated 'at the top' by elites anxious to build the nation according to a specific national image. It asserts the dominance of a particular ethnicity. **Civic nationalism**, on the other hand, is more tolerant of diversity and is marked by a recognition of different ethnicities, even multi-culturalism. States may exhibit one or other of these types of nationalism. Spain under Franco aggressively prosecuted a form of state nationalism, suppressing regional identities and linguistic diversity, and promoting a form of Spanish nationalism. Even the dominant language was consistently referred to by the regime as *Español*, as opposed to the more usual *Castellano*. In contrast, one of the hallmarks of Spain's transition to democracy after the dictator's death in 1975 was its accommodation with diversity. The new Spanish constitution (1978) recognised the existence within Spain not only of different languages but also different nationalities. It affirmed the creation of 17 Autonomous Communities within Spain, and is thus more consistent with the civic nationalism.

A second example is the UK, where British state nationalism, dominant during the eighteenth and nineteenth centuries, has given way to a more tolerant civic nationalism. This trend has accelerated in recent years. There is now a greater acceptance of different national entities within the UK, leading to significant changes in the political institutions of Scotland and Wales in particular. Another trend is also significant: Britain seeks to develop its self-image, as well as its image abroad, as a multicultural society, with London as a world city. Over 60 languages are used in London's primary schools, and it is striking that the government has enabled different religious groups to receive state funding to set up maintained faith-specific schools, whether Moslem, Hindi or Christian of any particular denomination. The policy is controversial, and it is in marked contrast to that of France reported in the previous chapter. It is nevertheless evidence of an elite commitment to the notion of multi-culturalism. A further example within the UK of how civic nationalism is in the ascendancy is the gradual transition towards power-sharing in a devolved assembly between the two opposing communities in Northern Ireland. The 'peace process' has been attempting the difficult task of building an accommodation between Protestants and Catholics since 1994, handicapped, it might be argued, by the strict segregation of both housing and education in most areas of the province.

Table 2.1 State building: four examples of state nationalism

State	Dates	Characteristics
Great Britain	Post-1707	Promotion of national symbols, anthem, flag, empire, notion of 'Britishness', identification with monarchy and Parliament.
The United States of America (USA)	Post-1787	War of Independence, identification with America, anthem, flag, founding of Washington as capital city, George Madison and the creation of a constitution, individualism.
Turkey	1923–38	Banning the traditional fez, secularism, modernisation, Westernisation, cult of the personality of Kemal Pasha known as 'Ataturk'.
Israel	Post-1948	War of Independence against the British colonial power, immigration policy, rebirth of Hebrew, promotion of Judaism, national service, Zionism.

There are certain features that are fundamental to national identity. Smith (1991:14) specifies five characteristics spanning both state and civic nationalism: an historic territory or homeland; common myths and historical memories; common mass public culture; common legal rights and duties for all members; a common economy with territorial mobility for members.

One may contrast state building with nation building, the former initiated 'at the top', the latter at grass roots level among the masses. Examples of the former are shown in Table 2.1.

As Table 2.1 shows, state nationalism is illustrated by eighteenth- and nineteenth-century Great Britain. Until 1707 there was no British nation, but the elite created it. During the nineteenth century symbols of British identity were heavily promoted and regional identity suppressed. The anthem and the flag would be cemented in the minds of all the monarch's subjects along with a sense of 'Britishness'. In the United States the government and state agencies acted similarly to suppress the various ethnic identities among a diverse immigrant population and to promote a sense of 'American-ness'. Thus the state may seek to create identity and to promote loyalty. Still nowadays American schoolchildren and college students are expected to swear allegiance to the Constitution, salute the flag and stand to attention during the national anthem, which is regularly played at public events. Immigrants to the United States also have to speak English and swear allegiance to the constitution in just the same way as the schoolchildren. Manifestations of national sentiment, found on a regular basis in the US, are anathema to most Europeans and European governments. The idea of swearing allegiance to the state or singing the national anthem in school assemblies is absolutely unheard of in most European countries, although not entirely, since such expressions of commitment to national territory and the constitution are discussed in respect of immigrants and asylum seekers wishing to take up residence. Bizarrely, the singing of the national anthem and the swearing of allegiance to the Queen is touted as a test of an immigrant's credentials for admission to Britain. This worrying proposal, were it to be made mandatory, would appear to contravene the cherished, though at times strained ideal of free speech in the UK. It seems odd to demand of an immigrant something which would be mightily difficult for a committed republican.

It may be illustrative of different interpretations of modern democracy to observe that for a German resident in Britain to be granted British citizenship requires swearing an oath of allegiance to the British Crown. For a Briton living in Germany, acquiring German citizenship merely requires a commitment to the principles of democracy.

Ethnic nationalism

Various European states in the nineteenth century promoted nationalism and national cohesion. The Ottoman Empire, in contrast, always granted rights to minorities and the Austro-Hungarian Empire gave up trying to forge a single identity between its diverse elements as popular nationalism increased. Popular nationalism was grounded in Rousseau's doctrine of popular sovereignty. It assumed that the proper forum for the expression of the 'general will' was provided by a national or ethnic community, not by artificial frontiers of the state. Popular nationalism, therefore, is synonymous with **ethnic nationalism**. This generated a linkage between blood of nation and soil of territory. Massimo d'Azeglio, at the opening of the Italian state parliament in 1861, commented 'Now that we have created Italy we must start creating Italians' (Davies, 1996:814). The remark is a clear example of state nationalist thinking, although Italy in fact achieved national unity through a more inclusive civic nationalism, tolerant of the regional diversity throughout the peninsula, at least until the advent of Fascism after 1922.

The concept of ethnic nationalism requires some clarification of the meaning of ethnicity.

> The term ethnicity [is reserved] for groups and group identities that are in fact recognised in social life on the basis of a mixture of perceived cultural and social inheritance [...] an ethnic identity is 'passed down': you have the identity of your parents and ancestors, and this tends to make ethnicity a matter of lay under-standings of kinship and biology. On the other hand, one tends to recognise ethnic membership in terms of particular behavioural markers, which are interpreted to signify a shared and more or less enduring group culture (including, at different times and in different places, religion, language, customs and so forth) (Goldmann et al., 2000:7–8).

Goldmann admits that there is potential for ambiguity and arbitrariness in this understanding of ethnicity, but the term is never going to be satisfactorily defined in ways which meet every circumstance and usage. Another description of ethnicity is:

> The physical and cultural differences covered by the term ethnicity – language, customs, religion, territorial affiliation, and physical type – represent various ascriptive characteristics often perceived as [...] inherited (Greenfield, 2000:25).

Understanding ethnicity provides a basis for understanding the notion of ethnic nationalism. The substantive point is that ethnic nationalism is rooted in the common characteristics of an ethnic group and in mass identification with a political programme that underlies nationalist sentiment. The definition of nationalism presented at the beginning of this chapter refers to nationalism as an ideological movement that seeks to attain and maintain autonomy, unity and identity. Nationalism therefore clearly carries a political mission for independence.

Ethnic nationalism, rooted in popular consciousness, indicates an aspiration held by the masses, and is therefore especially potent. Ethnic nationalism and state nationalism may therefore be diametrically opposed. State nationalism promotes the idea that governments forge nationality while it normally abhors the idea that nations, or ethnic groups, can forge states. Significantly, ethnic nationalism may also present a direct threat to the civic values found in liberal understanding of democracy. Greenfield writes that, in Western discourse, democracy is based on 'the primacy of the individual over the group and affirms individual liberty as an inalienable right' (Greenfield, 2000:27). This view uncovers a powerful dilemma in the debate over different nationalisms and how Western democracies might respond to nationalism. Greenfield claims that the

> rights of communities and rights of individuals cannot be ensured in equal measure; either the former or the latter must become subordinate. [. . .] Plainly put, cultural validation and empowerment of ethnic identity and ethnic diversity endanger liberal democracy. [. . .] [T]he best way to ensure that such democracy will thrive within *ethnically diverse populations* may be by rejecting the principles of ethnicity and ethnic diversity and, instead, encouraging civic identities and commitment to pluralism, or diversity, of a civic nature (Greenfield, 2000:28–9).

This view is supported by Gray, who uses historical evidence to make a similar claim. He writes that the US policy after the First World War of promoting nationalism in Eastern Europe and the Balkans could only have disastrous consequences, because the nationalism there was not of the civic kind that had unified countries like France and Italy. It had a strong ethnic component, 'a dangerous divisive factor in regions where populations are mixed and borders disputed' (Gray, 2003:94). Not only in the Balkans but throughout Eastern Europe the Treaty of Versailles made a volatile situation worse, disturbing ethnic consciousness like a stick in a hornets' nest.

The popular revolutions that overthrew despotic communist governments across Central and Eastern Europe in 1989 were energised by a popular national consciousness. In the former German Democratic Republic, Hungary, Poland, Czechoslovakia, Bulgaria, as well as in the Baltic States of Estonia, Latvia and Lithuania, there was a strong element of ethnic nationalism against the communist authorities. These were regarded almost as quisling governments, having ruled since 1945 thanks largely to Soviet patronage, and on occasions sustained in power by armed Soviet intervention against popular uprisings – in the GDR in 1953, in Hungary in 1956 and in Czechoslovakia in 1968. Romania is a slightly different case because the Ceauşescu regime had already distanced itself from the USSR. There, the revolution was not marked by a sense of liberation from Soviet-backed oppression, but it was celebrated as an escape from tyranny. These popular revolutions across Central and Eastern Europe were all inspired in part by nationalist uprisings, and all were naturally applauded in the West.

While Marx estimated that nationalism was a class-related phenomenon and would disappear under socialism, the reality is that it survived, and to a considerable extent, contrary to common assumption, it was not even especially suppressed in the Soviet satellite states.

> The opinion that xenophobia, previously suppressed by Communism, was released by the shift towards democracy in [. . .] eastern and central European countries cannot be maintained. In reality, the Communist system – contrary to Communist ideology – encouraged chauvinism in selected areas of political life and exploited it as a convenient political weapon (Tomaszewski, 2000:84).

Nevertheless, the former Federal Socialist Republic of Yugoslavia from 1945 until the death of Tito in 1982 provides an example of state nationalism. Events after 1989 showed that conflicting radical ethnic nationalism in Yugoslavia could be stirred up, despite Tito's attempt at nation building. Chapter 3 (pp. 79–81, 86–9) refers to the disastrous break-up of Yugoslavia during 1991–95.

Kedourie (1966) admits that nationalism derives from the need to belong to a stable, coherent community. Various levels of communality and allegiance, to family, village, region, religion or language or other cultural and historical factors may satisfy this need. It does not have to find expression in a state. Nevertheless, in times where identities and communities such as those listed are threatened, or suppressed, especially by force, or where economic conditions create insecurity and instability, then reaction happens. This reaction may be reflected in the creation of external scapegoats or the framing of internal conspiracies. Nationalism can thus be used as a convenient nostrum for establishing a new sense of purpose. Hitler's Germany is the most spectacular example of this in Europe, but there are plenty of others, including various dictatorships that emerged in the inter-war period, such as those of Mussolini in Italy and Salazar in Portugal (see Table 1.1 on p. 25). In Spain, Franco blamed international Jewry for Spain's economic woes, and attacked any possible internal dissent, targeting former republicans. Franco's security forces crushed any intimations of socialism or regional identity, while at the same time the regime assiduously promoted, through nationalist rhetoric, the ideal of the Spanish nation (see Preston, 1996). This was happening in a country which for centuries had comprised a variety of regional identities. In the early years of the Franco dictatorship, after the successful overthrow of the short-lived Republican government and victory in the Civil War 1936–39, repression continued in those regions where resistance to Franco's forces had been strongest, with ruthless reprisals against former opponents. Salazar dealt with opposition to his fascist regime in Portugal in a similar manner. More recently, Milosevic in Serbia, Tudjman in Croatia, Gamsakhurdia in Georgia all asserted nationalist claims against perceived threats from would-be insurgents, minorities or separatists. Meanwhile, and in contrast to the aforementioned state nationalisms, other regionalist and separatist movements employed the trappings of nationalism to pursue separatist agendas, for example in the Russian Federation, in Northern Ireland and in the Basque Country. All rely on a nationalist backlash against state entities, and all present the state as an occupier and as an oppressor.

Nationalism leads to problems within and between national groups; there may be conflicts between state nationalism and more local varieties aspiring to statehood. The United Kingdom has for years been troubled by the aspirations of Northern Irish Catholics to secure a united Ireland. Scottish and Welsh nationalists have tended to be considerably less violent, but while the UK has these three potential sources of conflict, and even a fourth if one is to take seriously the claims of Cornish nationalists occasionally expressed in the letters columns of London-based newspapers (Holmes, 2003), the Russian Federation has no less than 89. The most notorious instability in Russia involves the Chechen campaign against the Russian state, ongoing since former President Boris Yeltsin sent in Russian troops to quell an uprising in 1994. There is a sense that should Russia accede to the separatist demands from Chechnya then the entire Russian Federation would face disintegration. Nationalism may also conflict with other beliefs and ideologies in a state. Socialists or liberals may disagree with nationalism *per se*, or argue that it has the wrong priorities. Modern democratic systems should be able to accommodate such diversity of opinion, but nationalism presents disagreements that may cross ideological boundaries. The dominant party in the Spanish Basque Country for example, the Partido Nacional Vasco (PNV), is both conservative – in an economic and ideological sense – and nationalist. A point of embarrassment to some Basque Nationalists might be the reluctance on the part of the PNV to defend republicanism against the Franco-led uprising that disposed of the democratic Republican government during the Spanish Civil War (Fusi, 1990).

Discussion 2.7 summarises the three main types of nationalism described in this chapter. Note that the summary of civic nationalism includes toleration of diversity – although, as we have seen, some writers indicate that this carries substantial risks for liberal democratic government.

Review	*How is state nationalism different from ethnic nationalism? Give examples of where governing elites have used nationalism to promote a sense of national belonging.*

Discussion 2.7

Three nationalisms summarised

State nationalism

- Elite-driven 'from above'
- Associated with nation building
- Promotes sense of common nationality
- Promotes linkage between the state and symbols of state nationalism (flag, army, head of state, coins, anthem, etc.)
- Identifies with the state and state institutions
- Typically centralised and bureaucratic

Civic nationalism

- Elite-driven 'from above'
- Tolerant of diversity
- Encourages multiculturalism
- Promotes linkage between the state and symbols of state nationalism (flag, army, head of state, coins, anthem, etc.)
- Identifies with the state and state institutions
- Approves sub-state representation, as for example in federations

Ethnic nationalism

- Rooted in popular consciousness
- Based on ascriptive characteristics such as language, customs, religion, territorial affiliation and physical type
- Emerges from the masses
- Privileges symbols of local culture
- Opposes state authority and contests its incorporation into the wider political entity

---

Promoting cultural identity and the problem of ethnic nationalism

A related concern to this examination of nationalism is the extent to which localised promotion of culture extends into nationalist ambitions. We have seen that ethnic nationalism requires common reference to specific symbols of local identity. Many of these symbolic references are typical of what is promoted as heritage and the trappings of identity for national groups, or what Smith (1995) refers to as *ethnie*, using the French word. In English there is no word for the collectivity of people to whom the adjective ethnic is applied.

The promotion and celebration of cultural identity is rightly viewed as a legitimate activity, and is part of socialisation and the development of a sense of community. In many cases it can also have economic benefits relating to tourism. Such endeavours may include the promotion of folk symbols, history

(1)

(2)

(3)

(4)

(5)

(6)

and tradition, as well as the teaching and learning of minority languages, local sports, fairs, the arts – including music, poetry and song, and other customs which uphold traditions, even including gastronomy for example. All this may be accompanied by toleration of others and peaceful coexistence. It may celebrate heritage and nourish a sense of belonging. This is evident in many contexts across Europe, including Cornwall and Wales in the UK, Brittany in France, Andalusia in Spain and Bavaria in Germany. The *cornomuse*, a form of bagpipe, is as much a symbol of Brittany as the *cesta*, a woven basket used in the spectacular sport of *remonte*, is a symbol of Basque culture.

Such peaceable promotion of the characteristic markers of local communities can be contrasted with the more politically assertive ethnic nationalism which demands separation from a dominant state power. The critical difference between promoting local cultural identity and ethnic nationalism is that the former has no pretension to impose the culture and the identity on anyone else. In fact, it is accompanied by a genuine respect for other cultures.

Ethnic nationalism may of course use all the same kinds of cultural symbols and cultural markers to promote identity. But it is accompanied by a nationalist, separatist agenda. If the promotion of cultural identity becomes fused with the political ambitions of separatism then the result is potentially violent. Ethnic nationalism does not respect diversity and instead seeks to impose identity on others. In different contexts the balance between the promotion of cultural identity and the overtly political challenge of nationalism may be very different. In the French Basque Country for example, Basque identity is celebrated in all the ways indicated above, but ethnic nationalism is relatively absent. Just across the border in Spain, Basque nationalism has a more assertive and politically charged character. It is a vocal expression of opposition to the Spanish state. This creates a dilemma for those Basques who are proud of their heritage but are not inclined to seek separation from Spain. The result is that the Spanish Basque region remains divided and questions of Basque identity and nationalism are hard to reconcile.

Promoting cultural identity may indeed have little to do with political assertiveness, or the 'armed struggle' of more militant nationalists. However, the distinction between the celebration of local culture on the one hand and separatist nationalism on the other is critical. The former risks being subverted and can lead to intolerance. For example, the insistence that members of different communities must speak the local language in order to gain employment or civil rights might seem a relatively benign measure, but it is controversial in Catalonia as well as in the Basque Country. A commitment to local identity becomes extremely dangerous when it is accompanied by a chauvinism that asserts

Photograph 2.1 (*opposite*) (1) Carving *kaiku*, milk jugs from birch wood; (2) *Harrijasoketa*, stonelifting; (3) *Remonte*, a spectacular version of handball; players use long curved woven baskets strapped to the wrist to hit the ball; (4) Traditional folk music; (5) *Aitzkolaris*, wood chopping; (6) *Txalaparta*, a form of drumming with sticks of wood, used over centuries to communicate across the valleys of *Euskalherria*.

The word *aitzkolaris* is sometimes mentioned as evidence of the great antiquity of the Basque language as etimologically it refers to the axe as made of stone.

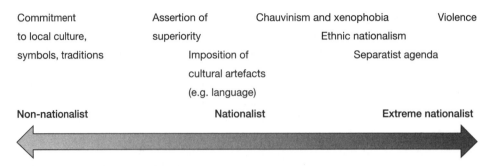

Figure 2.1 A nationalist continuum

superiority or exclusivity. Perhaps nationalism exists in a continuum from affection for local symbols and culture, through to chauvinism and **xenophobia**. This has been part of Europe's enduring tragedy (see Figure 2.1).

Where racist champions of nationalism are able to build on people's sense of grievance, and can create scapegoats for their problems, then the slide into anarchy and conflict is all too easy. When these elements combine with charismatic leadership, it is clear from history that a potent mix emerges. The former Yugoslavia shows how such chemistry can be exploited by the ruthless and the ambitious. Individuals such as Milosevic in Serbia, Tudjman in Croatia, or Karadic, the leader of the Bosnian Serbs, in Bosnia Herzegovina, sought a great deal more than the promotion of a few historical and cultural symbols.

Nationalism appears less likely to lead to conflict where the consensus among the group concerned is that they are free to express their cultural identity and where they are optimistic about their material prospects. This suggests that the civic nationalist model, with its toleration of diversity, ought to be most successful in curbing the excesses of ethnic nationalism. This is especially the case if there is some acceptance that co-existence with the larger state is materially advantageous and that separation might threaten prosperity. This would appear to fit the situation of Scotland for most of its history since the Act of Union in 1707, and especially for the greater part of the past 200 years. Scotland and especially the densely populated Glasgow/Strathclyde area prospered from the early industrialisation of the United Kingdom. Benefits also accrued from Britain's empire building in the nineteenth century. The discovery of North Sea oil off the coast of Scotland provided a fillip to the cause of Scottish nationalism during the 1980s, although supporters of the status quo, and those in government in London, have argued that Scotland benefits from a net transfer of resources to north of the border. More recently, since the election of a Labour government in 1997, Scotland has achieved its own Parliament, and thus increased autonomy within the UK. A further example of a relatively peaceful nationalism is provided by Catalonia. This is discussed in the next chapter.

Review	*What are the risks associated with promoting local cultural identity? When do these risks seem least problematic?*

● ● ● ● The EU, nation building and citizenship

The European Union has, as Discussion 2.4 points out, created for itself some classic symbols of state building enterprises throughout history, a flag, an anthem, a currency, even a capital city in Brussels, albeit not officially described as such. It has attempted to promote a sense of belonging among its member states and its *demos* – its public. The term *demos* is central to the concept of **democracy** and this leads us to a major criticism of the Union: it suffers from a democratic deficit. The Union has extended its reach and increasingly impinged upon the role of the state and the lives of the European peoples. Criticism of the lack of democratic accountability has grown, even in states formerly most sympathetic to the integration ideal. The EU has, in Brussels-speak, extended its '**competence**'. Meanwhile it has become more remote from the citizens whose lives it increasingly affects. Many, and in some countries perhaps most, feel disenfranchised, disillusioned and disinterested. A growing minority feels angry. Furthermore, the Union appears to make increasing demands on its member states, for example in respect of the austerity measures required by the convergence criteria stipulated for Economic and Monetary Union. Unemployment has risen and living standards have ceased to rise. The Union seems to offer less than it did in its early years, when the overwhelming payback was peace and security, benefits which by the late 1990s were simply taken for granted.

The EU appeared to suffer a crisis of nerve during the drafting of the Treaty on European Union (TEU) at Maastricht. In what appeared to be a highly visual assault on state sovereignty, the Union planned to take away national currencies and replace them with the euro (although the impact on sovereignty is disputed – see Chapter 4). Weiler reports that, perhaps as an afterthought, the Maastricht IGC rushed to insert a chapter on citizenship which contains the phrase 'Citizenship of the Union is hereby established. Every person holding the nationality of a member state shall be a citizen of the Union.' The 1997 Treaty of Amsterdam modified this phrase by adding the phrase '[c]itizenship of the Union shall complement and not replace national citizenship'.

Weiler writes that

> This is a trite, banal phrase. [. . .] For many the concept [of citizenship] is considered one of the least successful aspects of Maastricht, trivial and empty and hence irrelevant. From this perspective, those who believe in it are engaged in wishful thinking, and those who fear it suffer from paranoid delusion. On this view [the Amsterdam revision] was another unnecessary and empty gesture placating dreamers and loonies (Weiler, 2000:171).

Weiler is scathing about the Union's flirtation with citizenship. He points out that citizenship is a concept which has to be understood in relation to nationality, and yet the EU from its foundation has been presented as the antithesis of nationhood. Indeed it has been created, as this book consistently points out, as a counter movement against the entire concept of nationality. And yet Maastricht sees the Union playing with a fundamental cornerstone of the concept of nationhood, which Weiler equates with 'belonging' (ibid., 183). The Union has from its inception been about 'building an ever closer union among the European peoples'. It has not, asserts Weiler, been about creating a single European people, as a notion of citizenship implies.

> If citizenship classically postulates a sovereign state, is it not anachronistic to introduce it in an age in which [. . .] sovereignty itself has become fragmented, and states constitutionally cannot even pretend to have control over their most classical functions: Provision of material welfare and personal and collective security? (Weiler, ibid., 174)

In a postmodern globalised world, in which the 'market place' renders everyone a consumer, in which citizenship is deprived of any real meaning, in which individuals' sense of helplessness is increased by job insecurity, and in which people feel increasingly alienated from their ever weaker national polities, as well as entirely remote from the juggernaut of multinational institutions like the European Union (and other far-off international bodies), the Maastricht sop looks like a cheap gimmick. Weiler calls it an empty gesture that is 'closer to a market culture and the ethos of consumerism' (ibid., 179). He asks whether it is

> an unacceptable caricature [to suggest] that the Union has become a product for which the managers, alarmed by customer dissatisfaction, are engaged in brand development (ibid.).

Weiler asserts that in the turbulence and uncertainty of market-driven globalisation, citizens will naturally return to their local allegiances in search of some constancy and security. The state is not about to disappear. In fact, globalisation offers the state salvation. In an echo of Milward (2000), the state finds a second unlikely saviour.

> Once [nationality] sheds its ethnic and culturally repressive baggage, [it] has an altogether more poignant meaning in the age of multiculturalism. Precisely in an epoch in which individuals and groups develop myriad identity referents and in which a culture of rights and entitlements invites social dislocation, its artificiality gives it bridging potential (Weiler, ibid., 184).

Weiler continues that we have also to recognise the appeal of place, land and local community as an 'antidote to the fragmentation of the post-modern condition' (ibid.). He proposes an interesting solution to the nationality and citizenship issue in respect of the EU. He suggests a decoupling of citizenship from nationality that allows a notion of citizens of the Union who do not share the same nationality. Citizenship can imply not nationality – as its usual meaning does – but a shared set of values, common duties and rights within a civic society, a commitment or membership of a polity which privileges exactly the opposites of nationalism.

> European citizenship should explicitly not be thought of either as intended to create the type of emotional attachments associated with nationality based citizenship (ibid., 190).

The result of such a conceptualisation is that one may be 'a European citizen in terms of European transnational affinities to shared values which transcend the ethno-national variety' (ibid.). At the same time, the European citizen retains other identities of a more traditional kind and expressed by allegiance to region, to state and perhaps to any number of other callings including religion, or ethnic group.

Weiler concludes that the notion of European citizenship can only become effective, and achieve its potential as a civilisatory constraint on the demonic aspects of classical nationalism, if it is accompanied by a genuine solution to the chronic problem of democratic deficit. That remains a major challenge to the Union (see Discussion 12.7, p. 397).

Review *What does Weiler propose as a new concept in citizenship? Why is this so different from the traditional understanding of the term, as used (so ineptly, according to Weiler) in the Treaty on European Union?*

Summary

This chapter has made the following key points.

The state and sovereignty

- The traditional notion of the state has altered since the Treaty of Westphalia laid down the basis for the inter-state system.

State sovereignty and international institutions

- Sovereignty can be shared with other states in international institutions.

The meaning of nationalism

- Nationalism is in part composed of a common legacy of memories, myths and beliefs, shared experience, and the will to live together.
- Nationalists claim to promote the interests of their identified group or community and its identification with a territory.

Three types of nationalism

- Nationalism is always in opposition to perceived external threats.
- There are at least three different kinds of nationalism: state nationalism; civic nationalism; ethnic nationalism.

Promoting cultural identity and ethnic nationalism

- The promotion of cultural identity focuses on symbols shared in the perceptions of ethnic nationalists.
- Ethnic nationalism may be associated with politically assertive and separatist agendas.

The EU, nation building and citizenship

- The European Union employs some of the tools of nationalism to assert a notion of European citizenship, but it privileges a different set of values to traditional nationalism.
- The EU has somewhat maladroitly engaged in classic nation-building gimmicks, most notably in the TEU.
- An improved strategy might consist of resolving first and foremost the problems of democratic deficit in the Union, and then constructing a notion of citizenship that is entirely separate from any notion of nationality.
- A concept of European citizenship can co-exist with national citizenship and be complementary, modern, rational and civilisatory.

Key concepts: discussion and other definitions

Key concept 2.1 Sovereignty

The ability of a state, or a constitutionally recognised body acting on behalf of the state, to exercise authority over its territory and its people without it being subject to any higher authority.

For a (nation) state to be sovereign means having 'absolute authority over its territory and people and to have independence internationally' (Weber, 2001:14). As has been argued, the nature of sovereignty has altered from its Westphalian origins. However, sovereignty is a core dimension of the 'state system' defined by Jackson and Sørensen as

> relations between politically organised human groupings which occupy distinctive territories, are not under any higher authority or power, and enjoy and exercise a measure of independence from each other. International relations are relations between such independent groups (2003:11).

The point is reinforced by McLean and McMillan:

> Sovereignty is the claim to be the ultimate political authority, subject to no higher power as regards the making and enforcing of political decisions. In the international system, sovereignty is the claim by the state to full self-government, and the mutual

recognition of claims to sovereignty is the basis of international society (McLean & McMillan, 2003:502).

Nevertheless, any understanding of sovereignty has to take into account its logical contradiction.

> While internal sovereignty refers to a supreme decision making and enforcement authority with regard to a particular territory and population [. . .] [e]xternal sovereignty on the other hand refers to its antithesis: the absence of a supreme international authority and hence the independence of sovereign states. Paradoxically therefore the doctrine of state sovereignty necessarily leads to the concept of international anarchy (Evans, 1998:504).

The concept of international anarchy was articulated by Waltz in his seminal work *Man, the State and War*, first published in 1954. In essence, Waltz argued that states existed in a context of perpetual anarchy given the absence of any higher authority. Later Waltz developed the view that it was the international system itself rather than any intrinsic characteristics of people or states that ensured the inevitability of war (Waltz, 1979). Waltz is credited as the central figure in the neo-realist tradition that emerged after the onset of the second Cold War post-1979 (see pp. 242–3).

Walker highlights two important respects in which the nature of sovereignty has altered:

> The cardinal principle of sovereignty in international affairs, the right to declare war, [has] been constrained by nuclear caution and alliance responsibilities. The cardinal principle of sovereignty in domestic matters, the right to regulate the currency, to decree national taxation and to manage the economy in order to establish social priorities, is now constrained by the enforcement mechanism of the new global economy, the markets (Walker, 1994:355).

A traditional understanding of sovereignty, then, certainly indicates a decline in the role of the state. However, such a view ignores other processes whereby globalisation/internationalisation has produced a net gain in influence for the state. This is especially the case for small and medium-sized states that have forged alliances in order to achieve more impact collectively than they otherwise would, as is the case in the European Union. Giddens has argued that globalisation actually enhances the role of the state, and refers to the increase in sovereignty experienced by former Warsaw Pact members following the end of the Cold War (Giddens, 1998:32). Several writers on the European Union refer to 'shared' sovereignty – sometimes described as 'pooling' sovereignty – involving simultaneous loss and gain (see Jones, 2001:36–8).

Baun describes the

> logic of interdependence and economic necessity [where the] sacrifice of some authority and policy independence to European institutions has enabled national governments to better perform the economic and social tasks required of democratic welfare states and has thereby actually bolstered, rather than undermined, the sovereignty and legitimacy of European nation states (Baun, 1996:159–61).

Others refer to the extent to which European integration has contributed to the survival of European nation states, in particular Milward (2000:18–19) who refers to 'the European rescue of the nation state'. Sovereignty remains a highly contentious concept, especially in the context of European integration and globalisation. In later chapters we shall examine how different interpretations of sovereignty affect both these processes.

Finally, here's another definition:

> Sovereignty is power (Anon.)

If a state appears to have sole authority over its monetary policy, one would assume this is an illustration of its having sovereignty. If global events, or any other events exert stronger impact than government policy, presumably this illustrates the diminished value of sovereignty. If there is no power, sovereignty is compromised, perhaps damaged irrevocably. Chapter 9 looks at the impact of globalisation on state power, while power itself is defined in Key concept 9.2.

Key concept 2.2 Nationalism

An ideological movement for the attainment and maintenance of autonomy, unity and identity on behalf of a population deemed by some of its members to constitute a 'nation' (Smith, 1995:149–50).

Nationalism evokes widely different reactions. Not unreasonably, the phenomenon has been regarded somewhat warily in the European sphere. The association between nationalism and war is indelibly marked on the history of the continent. But nationalism was widely applauded in the West when it contributed to the overthrow of despotic regimes on the other side of the East–West divide of Cold War. Unfortunately, as we have seen in this chapter, following the end of the Cold War there was an outbreak of regional tensions across the former Yugoslavia that had appalling consequences. Nationalist fervour erupted in parts of the former Soviet Union, particularly in Russia itself, and in Georgia. In Chechnya, nationalist rebellion continues, bringing havoc to Moscow and other parts of the Russian Federation. Chechen separatists have been conveniently linked by President Putin, for example, to the global problem of 'terror' that has been a watchword of the US and its allies since the attacks on the World Trade Center and the Pentagon on 11 September 2001.

Gellner provides some explanation for the passions aroused by nationalism:

> Nationalism holds that [nations and states] were destined for each other; that either without the other is incomplete, and constitutes a tragedy (Gellner, 1983:6).

It follows from this that the denial of sovereignty to nations may indeed provoke conflict, but Gellner (ibid., 45) also points out that the number of communities who might in theory claim identity as separate nations, and thus seek statehood as well, is virtually limitless. That they do not is perhaps fortunate.

Echoing the distinction made in this chapter between state and ethnic nationalism is an interesting claim about the inverse relationship between the two in Gellner's work, cited above. It is worth quoting an extract from Gellner at length:

> The basic deception and self deception practised by nationalism is this: nationalism is, essentially, the general imposition of a high culture on society, where previously low cultures had taken up the lives of the majority, and in some cases of the totality, of the population. It means that generalised diffusion of a school-mediated, academy-supervised idiom, codified for the requirements of reasonably precise bureaucratic and technological communication. It is the establishment of an anonymous, impersonal society, with mutually substitutable atomised individuals, held together above all by a shared culture of this kind, in place of a previous complex structure of local groups, sustained by folk cultures reproduced locally and idiosyncratically by the micro-groups themselves. That is what really happens (Gellner, ibid., 57).

Such a description appears to fit with practically any example of nation building from above. Gellner goes on:

> But this is the very opposite of what nationalism affirms and what nationalists firmly believe. Nationalism usually conquers in the name of a putative folk culture. Its symbolism is drawn from the healthy, pristine, vigorous life of the peasants, of the *Volk*, the *narod*. There is a certain element of truth in the nationalist self presentation when the *narod* or *Volk* is ruled by officials of another, an alien high culture, but it does not then replace it by the old local low culture; it revives, or invents, a local high (literate, specialist transmitted) culture of its own, though admittedly one which will have some links with the earlier local folk styles and dialects (Gellner, ibid.).

Gellner says that the nationalist conducts a

> self deception, a vision of reality through a prism of illusion [. . .] society no longer worships itself through religious symbols; a modern, streamlined, on-wheels high culture celebrates itself in song and dance, which it borrows (stylizing it in the process) from a folk culture which it fondly believes itself to be perpetuating, defending and reaffirming (Gellner, ibid., 58).

This analysis, while inappropriate to contemporary manifestations of Islamic or Hindu nationalism, in Chechnya or Kashmir for example, surely also fits any European context referred to in this chapter.

Finally, nationalism may also be interpreted within the context of integration theory, as a preferred approach in seeking cooperation between states. The nationalist approach to European unity extols the interests of the member state above those of the community as a whole. It supports integration only where it is demonstrably the case that cooperation is in the national interest. A nationalist approach to integration pursues intergovernmentalism and eschews federalism.

Nationalism is sometimes considered in relation to patriotism:

Nationalism turns devotion to the nation into principles or programmes. It thus contains a different dimension from mere patriotism, which can be a devotion to one's country or nation devoid of any project for political action (McLean & McMillan, 2003:361).

Patriotism . . . the last refuge of the scoundrel (Samuel Johnson).

Further reading

Bainbridge, T. (2002) *The Penguin Companion to the European Union*, 3rd edition, London: Penguin. Pages 478–80 contain a good short discussion on sovereignty. The book is an excellent reference guide to the European Union, being especially informative on the institutions and treaties of the EU.

Gellner, E. (1983) *Nations and Nationalism*, Oxford: Blackwell. A classic text on nationalism, one to which just about all works on the subject appear to make frequent reference.

Goldmann, K., Hannerz, U. & Westin, C. (eds) (2000) *Nationalism and Internationalism in the Post-Cold War Era*, London and New York: Routledge. This book is a fascinating edited collection of quite challenging essays on nationalism, including the one by Weiler which is reported extensively in the last section of this chapter.

Gowland, D., O'Neill, B. & Dunphy, R. (2000) *The European Mosaic. Contemporary Politics, Economics & Culture*, Harlow: Addison Wesley Longman. See Chapter 13, 'How Europeans see themselves: culture, belief and writing'. This is an excellent account of key aspects of European culture.

Smith, A.D. (1995) *Nations and Nationalism in a Global Era*, Cambridge: Polity. Smith examines the relationship between nationalism and the state and argues that globalisation has reawakened ethnic conflict and nationalism. See in particular pp. 97–102 for a description of the problems of civic and ethnic nationalism.

Film suggestion

Wolfgang Becker, *Goodbye Lenin*, Germany, 2003

Goodbye Lenin is both funny and extremely moving. Brilliantly acted by a relatively unknown cast, the story revolves around a mother who suffers a heart attack just before the Berlin Wall falls in 1989. A devout Communist living in the German Democratic Republic (GDR), she remains in a coma for eight months and so entirely misses the epic transformation of her country in the months prior to German reunification in November 1990. When she finally emerges from her coma the doctors reluctantly accede to her son's request that she be allowed to return home, on condition that she suffers no shocks, as these could be life-threatening. Her children embark on a massively elaborate hoax, to recreate the former GDR around their mother, pretending that the Wall had never fallen. The film shows the acute ideological divide between East and West, and highlights the enormity of the transformation that the collapse of communism in Eastern Europe brought about. Above all though, it shows the lengths that people will go to construct a fantasy to protect those that they love. It is a triumph.

The political content of the film takes a back seat to the human drama. However, it is a good illustration of the artificiality of the concept of state, as the German Democratic Republic, an unloved political artefact born of the Cold War, disintegrates in a massive outpouring of emotion under a sky lit up by celebratory fireworks. Germans reunited Germany – though the task of integrating the two halves economically and psychologically has proved more difficult, as Marsh (1995) predicted it would.

For a detailed review of *Goodbye Lenin* see http://www.iofilm.co.uk/fm/g/goodbye_lenin_2003.shtml

Chapter 3

Nationalism in contemporary Europe

Outline

- Identity and difference, real and imaginary
- Nationalism in contemporary Europe: eight contexts
- Integrating Europe and issues of state sovereignty
- Defending sovereignty – nationalism and euroscepticism

Key concepts

3.1   The European integration process

3.2   Euroscepticism

Introduction

The preceding chapters have already referred to the need to understand state-hood in relation to identity, as well as the vexed question of the match between the state and nation, meaning the ethnic group or *ethnie* that comprises the population of the state. There is rarely a close match between the state and a single national group within its borders, a state of affairs which might indicate inherent instability in all states. However, whether there is in fact instability probably depends on the extent to which distinct communities coalesce to create distinctive ethnic identities that then assume nationalist ideology. If instead communities, or the *demos* within a particular polity, choose to coalesce around common civic values such as democracy and tolerance of diversity, then the risk of instability is so much less.

This chapter presents further discussion of nationalism, looking first at a particular dimension to the issue of identity. Identity is usually considered to be objectively ascribed to individuals and communities. However, this chapter uses the examples from Bosnia Herzegovina and Croatia to show how ascribing identity to communities can be disastrous. Identity can be less real than is often assumed.

The second, longer part of this chapter looks at the continuing relevance of nationalism, based on eight contexts in different regions of the continent. It should be remembered that these are just some manifestations of nationalism in Europe and there are plenty of others which are not mentioned, notably in Scandinavia involving Laps, in the Russian Federation, where the example of Chechnya is best known, and in Eastern Turkey where Kurds have long sought separate statehood. This section demonstrates that nationalism remains a potent force.

The final section suggests that the European integration process has attempted to constrain nationalism, while it has itself been subject to a counter movement that is resistant to further integration. This trend has been variously labelled 'eurosceptic', 'nationalist', and even 'anti-European'. The latter may be unfair. Many would argue they are not 'anti-European', but simply anti the drift towards a more federal European Union, which is not the same thing. Nevertheless, the tensions are real, and some writers estimate that how the EU responds to its critics may have a decisive role in determining the future of the Union. Hutton (2003) for example has warned that one should not take the survival of the EU for granted, nor underestimate the consequences of any major redesign of its role or of its architecture (see Discussion 12.7, p. 397). Enlargement, the subject of Chapter 7, may be especially significant in this respect.

● ● ● ● Identity and difference, real and imaginary

Identity is often subjective, and individuals carry multiple identities (see Discussion 3.1). One might describe oneself as Scottish, European, a Glasgow Rangers supporter and a fan of *The Simpsons*. Someone else might consider themselves German, Roman Catholic and a BMW driver (the last is mentioned only half in jest – the wide-ranging but increasingly sophisticated field of marketing emphasises branding, brand image and brand identity – the latter closely associated with the self-identity of the consumer). Only the ethnic dimension in these descriptions might be guessed at or assumed by another person on first acquaintance. Ethnic identity is often understood *ascriptively*. This means that a specific ethnic identity is ascribed to individuals and communities by others, using objective criteria that are often visible and beyond dispute, such as eye or skin colour, territorial association, language or religion. However, ascribing identity in this way may also be subjective and fraught with danger, as the post-1991 conflict in the former Yugoslavia demonstrated. Greenfield writes that

> Cultural significance attached to ethnic differences is rarely proportionate to their 'objective' magnitude. Very often these differences are minimal or virtually non-existent, but when perceived as culturally significant, they are magnified (2000:26).

The result may make peace untenable, differences unbridgeable and violence a possibility at any given moment. Bosnia provides an example of such minimal differences being magnified and turned murderous by the cultural significance attached to them.

The differences between Serbs, Croats and Bosnian Muslims are mostly in the imagination. These three groups of Southern Slavs belong to the same race and

Discussion 3.1

Multiple identities

Most people would accept that they possess different identities. Some identities are 'ascriptive' – meaning they are ascribed to an individual by others. For example, society at large may describe someone as an Arab, a Moslem, an immigrant, a citizen of Birmingham, and a member of a particular mosque. That individual may claim or accept all those descriptions, or dispute them, for example if he happens to have been born in Solihull, a prosperous suburb of Birmingham, he might easily contest the notion that he is an immigrant. He may also add others, for example that he is Qatari, or British-Qatari, or simply British, or English, or Qatari-English. These identities are subjective and may be subject to others' disagreement, even quite unreasonably so, and on spurious or racist grounds, such as the claim that this individual 'cannot be British' or is 'not properly British', but is simply and straightforwardly 'an Arab'. In fact, nothing is simple and straightforward where identity is concerned.

Someone from Northern Ireland, a place redolent with the sulphurous odour of disputed, or passionately defended, identity, might claim to be Irish and not Northern Irish, and certainly not British, and Catholic and not Protestant. This chapter argues that identity is often constructed in this way, on the basis of opposites, or exclusion. Identity marks not only what one is, but what one is not. Someone from Northern Ireland cannot be both Protestant and Catholic, though he/she might be neither. It is certainly conceivable to be both Irish and Northern Irish, though such a configuration is less likely to be acceptable to an Ulster Unionist than a nationalist.

Multiple identities are common. Consider for example an individual who presents a set of identities comprising European, Spanish, Catalan and member of the Catholic Church, of a particular gastronomic society and as a supporter of *Barça*. Certain of these identities may become more manifest at certain times such as on St George's Day, a national holiday for the patron saint of Catalonia, or when the individual attends a football match at *Nou Camp*.

The point of these musings is to highlight several key observations:

- identity is subjective as well as ascriptive;
- individuals carry several different identities;
- identity may shift according to context;
- identity is frequently composed of characteristics that are shadowed by opposites.

Given the last of these points, it is hardly surprising that identity has so often been at the root of conflict. One might argue that the more inclusive identities are less likely to lead to conflict. It is on these grounds that an idealist might prefer to proclaim one's identity as a human being, and leave it at that.

look the same; they speak Serbo-Croatian – the same language; their religion, which has been made so much of recently, cannot, in practice, be used to distinguish between them, because overwhelming majorities in each of them are (or were until the eruption of the recent conflict) non-believers. These facts are overlooked because the identities of Serbs and Croats have traditionally been defined as ethnic identities (Greenfield, ibid.).

The point is that these identities are bestowed on these communities ascriptively, and as such are not easily denied or avoided. The tendency to impose identity on others on the basis of more or less significant characteristics might be seen as unfortunate. Indeed, Greenfield implies that what happened in Bosnia demonstrates that these communities could become divided by the virtual *manufacturing* of difference by opportunist and ambitious, not to say ruthless politicians, and by naïve outside observers. The Bosnian experience, far from highlighting the fundamentally absolutist nature of nationalism, as is often

Discussion 3.2

Balkan identities, Balkan rubbish

It's four in the morning. I'm in the command post of the local Serbian militia, in an abandoned farm house, 250 metres from the Croatian front . . . not Bosnia but the war zones of central Croatia. The world is no longer watching, but every night Serb and Croat militias exchange small arms fire and the occasional bazooka round.

This is a village war. Everyone knows everyone else: they all went to school together; before the war, some of them worked in the same garage; they dated the same girls. Every night they call each other up on the CB radio and exchange insults – by name. They go back to trying to kill each other.

I'm talking to the Serbian soldiers – tired, middle aged reservists, who'd much rather be at home in bed. I'm trying to figure out why neighbours should start killing each other. So I say I can't tell Serbs and Croats apart. 'What makes you think you're so different?'

The man I'm talking to takes a cigarette packet out of his khaki jacket. 'See this? These are Serbian cigarettes. Over there they smoke Croatian cigarettes.'

'But they're both cigarettes, right?'

'You foreigners don't understand anything', he shrugs and begins cleaning his Zastovo machine pistol.

But the question I've asked bothers him, so a couple of minutes later, he tosses the weapon on the bunk between us and says, 'Look, here's how it is. Those Croats, they think they're better than us. They think they're fancy Europeans and everything. I'll tell you something. We're all just Balkan rubbish' (M. Ignatieff, cited in Woodward, 1997).

claimed, may instead illustrate how the inherent *fantasy* of nationhood can erupt into something as tangible as a civil war.

The tragedy of Bosnia, which is referred to repeatedly in this chapter, is all the more shocking once the full meaning of Greenfield's claim is understood. It is substantiated further, perhaps, by the extract in Discussion 3.2, in which Michael Ignatieff reports on a meeting with Serb militiamen during the Bosnian War 1991–94.

The extract in Discussion 3.2 presents identity as a set of opposites. The Serbian soldier is seeking to explain difference. He feels he is a Serb because he is not a Croat. The brand of cigarette serves as a useful symbol of this difference, no matter that it is entirely trivial. However, clearly he is challenged by Ignatieff's question and the implication that in fact there is not much difference between Serbs and Croats. He ends up admitting as much, but again through reference to difference, though this time the difference is not between Serbs and Croats, but between all Serbs and Croats together, and other – presumably northern, Europeans. In comparison, Serbs and Croats are just 'Balkan rubbish'.

'They smoke (different) cigarettes.' The phrase reduces nationalist division to the level of absurdity, but absurdity is a phenomenon often found in great tragedies, as in Shakespeare's *Othello*.

Identity, then, is constructed on the basis of difference. One is (usually) male, or female, and being one proscribes the other. One might be Chilean, which means – among other things – not Argentine, or an individual may be a native Flemish speaker in Belgium and therefore not a native French speaker. A Canadian may pointedly assert his or her Canadian identity should you make the mistake of assuming (s)he is from the United States, while to ask a Scot if he is English in an Edinburgh pub might be considered tactless.

Review *How do you ascribe identity to the people in the place where you last spent a holiday? How do you define your own identity? What are the risks attached to ascribing ethnic identity to communities?*

Nationalism in contemporary Europe: eight contexts

Since the Second World War perhaps the two salient features of the European political scene have been the division of the continent through the Cold War and the creation of an institutionalised cooperative framework in Western Europe, namely the European Union, now incorporating eight former communist states, once part of the Soviet bloc. However, despite this remarkable exercise in regional consolidation – the EU now contains 25 states – nationalism remains a potent force in many areas across the continent, inside and outside the EU. By no means all nationalist campaigns are underscored by violence, but in Spain, the UK and Yugoslavia in particular conflict has been ongoing, and in the latter case, catastrophic, erupting in a full-scale civil war in 1991. This section contains a brief summary of some manifestations of nationalism in Europe, referring not only to Spain, the UK/Ireland and Yugoslavia, but also several other countries with less violent recent histories.

Spain

The Spanish Constitution, created in 1978 less than three years after the death of Franco and the end of dictatorship, decrees that Spain consists of 17 Autonomous Regions. Three of these, the Basque Country, Catalonia and Galicia, benefit from a high degree of devolved powers. Nevertheless, Basque nationalism has been underscored with violence throughout the democratic era. The separatist campaign has resulted in over 800 killings since 1969. Injustice, violence, and denial of human rights have been hallmarks of the Spanish state response to the Basque problem. This reached its nadir in the early 1980s through the activities of GAL, a shadowy counter-terrorist group with direct links to the Ministry of the Interior in the Socialist government of Felipe Gonzalez. GAL was implicated in extrajudicial executions (murders) of ETA suspects. The difficulty in the Basque Country is that even where the Madrid government has been more thoughtful, for example in granting further autonomy and in setting up specifically Basque security services, this has not always met with the support of Basque Nationalists. Those who seek independence from Spain are certainly not satisfied and demand further autonomy if not outright separation. The Spanish government, mindful of undermining the Constitution, is unlikely to accede. Nor is it keen to offer a referendum on independence, not because they fear it would be lost to the separatists, but because it would expose the fault lines in the Basque Country itself. There would surely be grave risks in such a campaign, splitting families as well as communities, exacerbating tensions and ultimately, whatever the result, not resolving the issue. When issues of sovereignty are at stake, referenda rarely seem to be decisive in ending disagreement – British member- ship of the EEC/EU, on which there was a referendum in 1975, is a case in point. Other possible concessions on the part of the Spanish state, such as the trans- fer of convicted Basque separatists to prisons nearer home, instead of up to 2,000 miles away from their families, would be constructive steps as well as consistent with a respect for the rights of prisoners and their families. This issue remains a key demand for nationalists, as well as human rights campaigners.

In recent years, those seeking a complete separation from Spain have experi- mented with an extended cease-fire as part of a different strategy in attempting to wring further concessions from Madrid. The Spanish government under Jose María Aznar and the Popular Party, which lost office in March 2004, was accused of intransigence when it insisted on the inviolability of the Spanish state. ETA therefore ended its two-year cease-fire early in 2000 and the killing resumed. Since the return to 'armed struggle', victims have included a PP councillor, a left-wing journalist and critic of ETA, as well as members of the judiciary and the academic community. Nevertheless, the previous suspension of direct hostilities would seem to indicate a dialogue within the ETA organisation, with at least some activists being prepared to pursue a different strategy – one of negotiation – to achieve the same objective. Similar discussions within ETA seem to be on-going following the election of a new government in the 2004 elec- tions. A cease-fire would be interpreted as following the lead of the IRA in Northern Ireland, with whom ETA has often been compared. In addition, the more moderate and largest of the nationalist parties, PNV, published in 2003 a manifesto demanding a renegotiation of the region's relationship to Spain, including the right to self-determination. The response from Madrid has been predictable: the document is a threat to the integrity of the Spanish Constitution. Critics of the nationalists argue that whatever concessions are granted, they will always come back for more (see introduction to Discussion 2.5, p. 54). It might be time to call the nationalists' bluff and ask them exactly how much inde- pendence they want. PNV supporters may learn that separation from Spain is like pregnancy: there are no half measures.

Compared with its Basque counterpart, Catalan nationalism appears relatively benign. In Catalonia, a distinctive Catalan identity has strengthened under Spanish democracy post-1975, but has not been scarred by the violence of the military campaigns waged by ETA in the Basque Country. Catalan identity and autonomy within Spain is highly developed. Autonomy seems to suit the majority of the population that would stop short of seeking secession from Spain. The confidence in their identity, or indeed identities, and the prosperity of the region seem to inhibit the extent to which the population seek full independ- ence. The Catalan language benefits from widespread use in schools and in the public sector, while Spanish remains dominant in the media and co-exists with

Catalan on the street. This alarms some Catalans who fear for the future of their language, although Catalan is spoken by some two thirds of the population of 6 million. It is also spoken in the Balearic Islands and in parts of the neighbouring region of Valencia. However, problems emerge in the treatment and rights of non-Catalans who do not speak Catalan, especially in relation to employment. The requirement to use Catalan in public offices, schools and universities has in particular been controversial. Thus, even in the least contentious contexts, nationalist sentiment carries certain *social* risks.

Ireland

Nationalism has a long and violent history in Ireland. Following British colonisation in the seventeenth century and the brutal repression of religious and property rights, Irish identity and language remained under sustained attack. The British presence in Ireland reached its most shameful apotheosis during the potato famine of 1845–49 when the British failed to offer relief. The British military even provided armed guard for grain exports to the British mainland. Up to a million people died during the famine and many emigrated, cutting the population by a quarter. The status quo held, even through the Easter Rising in 1917 against British rule when Ireland descended into virtual civil war. Following Balfour's Home Rule Bill, the Irish Free State was declared in 1921. Unfortunately this has never quite resolved the problem, as the Catholic Fenians never accepted partition and have under various guises, notably that of the IRA, demanded British withdrawal from the six of Ulster's nine counties that the British government kept for the Crown. Naturally, the majority Protestant population in the six counties does not want to be ruled by Dublin in a united Ireland. The result has been a long-running campaign of guerrilla warfare, especially since 1969, against the British state and its security forces by the IRA. The British government gifted the IRA a propaganda coup in 1972 with the so-called Bloody Sunday massacre, in which 13 unarmed civilians were allegedly murdered by the British army. The subsequent inquiry produced a whitewash, the Widgery Report, which may at last be laid to rest with a further judicial inquiry now in process some 30 years after the event. The IRA campaign involved numerous appalling atrocities, both in Northern Ireland and on the British mainland, but it has co-existed alongside a vicious sectarian conflict between republican nationalists and unionists, the latter no less marked by nationalism. During the period 1970–2000 there were over 2,000 deaths related to the Northern Ireland problem, and the numbers of Catholics murdered by unionist extremists has actually exceeded the combined numbers of British security forces and unionists/ Protestants killed at the hands of nationalists seeking a united Ireland. The conflict reflects the continuing religious divide in the troubled province. Nationalism has been just one factor – albeit a critical one – in a deadly cocktail of local hatreds and historical injustice in Northern Ireland. In recent years the republican approach has altered, towards one of a cease-fire and political dialogue, but like ETA in the Basque Country, their objectives remain the same.

© Ed Kashi/Corbis

Photograph 3.1 Catholic children play along the 'Peaceline' in Western Belfast, which separates the Catholic Falls Road and the Protestant Shankill Road communities.

Both sides, Irish republicans and Northern Irish unionists, have employed many trappings of nationalist campaigning. This has undoubtedly made any accommodation between them more difficult and an uneasy suspicion would appear to mark the positions of both sides in ongoing negotiations involving both the British and Irish governments. Establishing constructive dialogue between the major protagonists is difficult. The UK government re-established the Northern Ireland Assembly as an element of self-government in the Province, with full local representation. It has been suspended three times, sand-banked if not shipwrecked on the issue of arms decommissioning, or on accusations of spying within the offices of the regional Parliament building, Stormont, by Sinn Fein nationalists. Then in autumn 2003 elections produced the inconvenient result of increased support for the political extremes, the ultra-nationalist Sinn Fein and the ultra-conservative Democratic Unionists. Normal democratic political processes are to say the least difficult, especially in a region where cautious returns to devolved government have tended to be marked by disputes over what flags fly from certain government buildings. The symbolism matters: flags, badges, uniforms or the name of the local police force have tremendous significance in the cauldron of animosities that is Northern Irish politics. What seems clear is that the British government position has changed and that withdrawal is now a real option, if not now, at some time in the future. The issue may ultimately revolve around the simple issue of demography: when nationalists outnumber unionists, the British government will leave Northern Ireland. Unfortunately, withdrawal without the consent of the unionists is not likely to resolve the issue.

It should not be concluded from the above that nationalism lies at the root of the Irish Question. It is instead a symbol and a consequence of the historical and cultural imperialism that has dogged Anglo-Irish relations for four hundred years. Even religion, often blamed for the conflict, is simply a byproduct of the same colonialist history. Nor should one make the further assumption that the UK now maintains a presence in Ireland for colonialist or imperialist motives: history has moved beyond this facile interpretation. Rather, the UK remains inextricably linked to Ireland because of history, culture, demography and simple democracy: a substantial part – still just about the majority – of the population of Northern Ireland wish the UK to remain engaged with the province, and the Republic of Ireland has dropped the clause in its constitution that used to refer to the aspiration of a united Ireland. This change recognises that resolution to the conflict can only be achieved with the consent of all parties.

As in Spain, elsewhere in the UK nationalist sentiment has not precipitated the same violence. Wales and Scotland achieved a regional Assembly and a Parliament respectively in major constitutional changes in the UK following the election of a Labour government in 1997 but their powers are limited, especially those of the Welsh Assembly.

Yugoslavia

It is in the former Yugoslavia where nationalism has made its most serious mark in recent years. Following the end of the Cold War in 1991, the break-up of the Yugoslav Federal Republic began in earnest. Slobodan Milosevic became President of Yugoslavia in 1987 and quickly set about fanning the flames of Serb nationalism. Alarmed by the prospect of increased Serb domination, Slovenia and Croatia declared their independence in 1991, the former after a short war. Invoking their own claims to separate nationhood, one can sympathise with the actions of the Slovenes and the Croatians in wanting to promote their own sense of identity in the face of a threat from an increasingly hostile and illiberal regime in Belgrade. Unfortunately, Yugoslavia descended into chaos. Serbs living in Croatia refused to accept the split from Belgrade and war broke out, initially with significant Serb successes. But in summer 1995 'the biggest single exodus of refugees since World War Two' (Silber & Little, 1996:27) occurred, as the Croatian army drove the Krajina Serbs from what had been their homeland for centuries. Silber and Little (1996:353–60) accuse the West of complicity in this particular example of 'ethnic cleansing', but Franjo Tudjman, the President of Croatia, was quite happy for his military forces to carry out the expulsion of the Serb minority from Croatia. Tudjman of course had collaborated with Milosevic in the carving up of Bosnia Herzegovina, at the expense of the majority Moslem population. Bosnia suffered the same inter-ethnic brutality, where Bosnian Serbs under the military command of General Mladic engaged in widespread ethnic cleansing, driving Moslems out of Eastern Bosnia. The intention throughout, tacitly or openly encouraged by Milosevic and Belgrade, was to promote a Greater Serbia. After four years of chaos, Milosevic was able to claim some success as Serbia won control over swathes of Eastern Bosnia. Tudjman achieved his desire for an independent Croatia, recovering territory lost at the beginning of the war. Furthermore, Croatia was virtually free of Serbs, since they had been 'ethnically cleansed'. This grotesque phrase has become etched on the former Yugoslavia as clearly as the Adriatic coastline. It stands for burning, looting, rape, the destruction of entire villages, the indiscriminate killing of civilians, and the torture and murder of prisoners of war. This carnage occurred in a country that for over 40 years had lived relatively peacefully, had experienced considerable modernisation and had achieved a high degree of inter-communal existence, especially in Sarajevo, a modern, cultured, multi-ethnic and artistically rich city where the communities had co-existed for centuries. At the end of the Bosnian war, Sarajevo was partitioned and placed under the protection of the United Nations.

Milosevic was not finished. Unrest continued in the south of the country and reports of attacks on ethnic Albanians in Kosovo became regular news fodder for the TV channels. Eventually popular opinion accepted the need for humanitarian intervention. What happened instead was a seven-week aerial bombardment by NATO forces in 1999, led by the United States, of Serbia and Kosovo itself. The objective was to force Serbian security forces out of Kosovo. Being an integral part of the Serbian state, this was, to say the least, a controversial deployment, and unprecedented in NATO's 50-year history. The withdrawal eventually occurred, but at a desperately heavy cost in terms of the damage done to Serbian infrastructure, loss of civilian life and a strong like-lihood of severe environmental contamination in much of Kosovo. The NATO attacks were of dubious legitimacy, not being approved by the UN Security Council, where Russia would have been able to use its veto. Nevertheless, NATO's actions were tolerated, if not directly supported, by the international com-munity. Others, such as Ignatieff (2000), have criticised the campaign on moral grounds. He claims that since there was no risk to NATO personnel, the conflict was not subject to the normal democratic constraint that characterised previous wars, where there was a real risk of casualties. The operation to enable refugees to return to Kosovo was a bombing campaign against Serbia and Serbian forces. While there were scores of civilian casualties on the ground, not one NATO combatant was killed in a seven-week campaign. Arguing that this changes the normal conditions of war, Ignatieff calls this a 'virtual war'. His argument is not only interesting in its own right, but it also calls into question the role of the state in such actions, as the nature of the conflict dilutes the potential for dis-sent among the electorates of the participating countries. It is perhaps a further example of the change in the nature of state sovereignty, since it means that states can wage war with less constraint. Furthermore, the United States is the

Discussion 3.3

US and its post-Cold War and post-Bosnia assertiveness

One of the apparent consequences for the United States post-Cold War is that there is less restraint on its military adventurism. Indeed, after the attacks on New York and the Pentagon on 11 September 2001 the White House created a Plan for an All American Century which asserted the right of the US to intervene 'pre-emptively' against potential aggressors. This is a significant change in the conduct of international affairs.

The US response to 9/11 demonstrated the profound nature of this change. In 2002 the US carried out attacks on Afghanistan that were classed as 'retaliatory' against Al Qaeda. In March 2003 the US and a phalanx of allies, including the UK, attacked Iraq in a pre-emptive strike on the grounds that Iraq possessed weapons of mass destruction (WMDs). As is well known, the attack on Iraq lacked a clear UN mandate and split the European Union into two camps. Almost two years after the invasion, the former Iraqi dictator Saddam Hussein is under arrest, but no WMDs have materialised and Iraq is in chaos. US and coalition forces, as well as those of the interim Iraqi government, are under daily attack from insurgents (see Chapter 12).

sole remaining superpower. These changed circumstances may affect how the US and its allies police the world or act against so-called 'rogue states'. The implications are potentially alarming and highlight the lasting international impact of a local tribal conflict in a corner of Europe (see Discussion 3.3).

Kosovo, like Sarajevo, remains under UN protection. The positive spin on this tragedy is that Serb aggression was punished. The world did not stand by and allow the entire population of ethnic Albanians to be removed from their homes. Furthermore, Milosovic, indicted for war crimes, was arrested by the new Serb government of Vladimir Kostunica, and handed over to the International Court at The Hague to face charges relating to war crimes and genocide. There is, however, continuing instability in the region. Fresh inter-communal fighting broke out in Kosovo in early 2004, with minority Serbs attacked, their homes and Orthodox churches torched. Shepherded away from their villages under protective escort from the UN peacekeeping forces, media reports described the incidents as a fresh bout of 'ethnic cleansing'. In neighbouring Macedonia tensions remain, revolving around the treatment of the Albanian ethnic minority.

In another respect, the entire credibility of the Western Alliance has been damaged by events in ex-Yugoslavia. The West, and the European Union in particular, remained powerless to prevent atrocities on its doorstep. Germany was heavily criticised for its early recognition of the breakaway states of Slovenia and Croatia. Eventually the West was able to unleash the latest military technology on a small country without appreciable air defences able to deal with attacking planes almost three miles up. Serbia did have and still has a large land army. While arms specialists could marvel at the skill of NATO pilots and the sophistication of the latest weaponry, we are still, ten years later, unable to apprehend two of the individuals who bear the heaviest responsibility for the ethnic slaughter in the former Yugoslavia: Karadic and Mladic remain at large, presumably in Bosnia. NATO officials commented in March 2002 that their arrest was only a matter of time, but there have been no arrests.

Czechoslovakia

A more positive outcome was achieved in Czechoslovakia. After the 1989 Velvet Revolution, the Czech Republic and Slovakia achieved a mutually agreed divorce in 1993 without recourse to violence. Slovakia appeared to drift towards authoritarian government under Vladimir Meciar in 1994. As his government showed a questionable commitment to democracy and the rule of law, the European Commission signalled that prospects for Slovak accession to the Union were receding, despite the country's administrative and economic progress. The Slovak Democratic Coalition benefited from this and won the 1998 elections, being returned again in 2002 (Glenn, 2003:219).

Belgium

Elsewhere in Europe there are many areas where local national sentiments have sparked difficulties, if not outright violence. The federal state of Belgium has for a long time struggled to reconcile its two major linguistic communities of Flemish speakers in the north and French-speaking Walloons in the south. The two regions are remarkably different culturally and appear to look in opposite directions. The southern region is based around the capital Brussels, which even in a small country seems remote and detached from its Flemish community. The Flemish – who speak Dutch – despise what they perceive to be the bureaucratic arrogance of their French-speaking counterparts. The state has six federal components: the Flemish, Francophone and German communities, the Flemish region, the Walloon region, and the Brussels Capital region. Thus Belgium is a state comprising several distinct ethnic communities. However, the tensions in Belgium have remained relatively submerged and while there have been separatist movements in the north, the general prosperity and status at the heart of the European Union appear to dissipate any truly concerted efforts to break up the country.

Switzerland

Switzerland is a quintessentially democratic state retaining independence from the European Union, remaining outside NATO – Switzerland was a key member of the non-aligned movement – and the European Economic Area (EEA, comprising the EU plus Iceland, Norway and Lichtenstein). It only agreed to join the UN after a referendum in 2002. It has a unique constitution that allows for a high degree of participative democracy. The country has a population of 7.3 million and is divided into 22 cantons, or regions, that make up the national parliament.

Switzerland is a confederation, with four official languages, in which a very strong sense of local identity co-exists with an equally strong sense of national identity (Bainbridge, 2002:497).

The principal ethnic divisions are represented by three major language groups, French, German and Italian. Nevertheless, despite its varied ethnicity, Switzerland is a tight-knit homogeneous political entity enjoying stability and prosperity, as well as international prestige for its highly productive banking, pharmaceutical and tourism industries. The generally high living standards, traditional neutrality and unique democratic heritage appear to be the glue that keeps this multilingual and multi-ethnic community from disintegrating along nationalist lines. But Bainbridge emphasises the historical unity as well:

> The Swiss nation was built up gradually over some 700 years on the basis of a very particular combination of geographic, political, religious and historical circumstances. The country is governed at a federal, cantonal and communal level (with frequent referendums) under constitutional provisions introduced in 1874 as a means of limiting the power of central government (Bainbridge, ibid.).

What is most significant about Switzerland is that it is a multinational state that demonstrates civic nationalism, not state nationalism. It is tolerant of its ethnic diversity and does not seek to impose any single identity.

Italy

Potentially more serious issues arise in Italy, which was unified only in 1861, adding the Veneto region in 1871 and Trieste from the disintegrating Austro-Hungarian Empire in 1918. In Italy the historic divisions between regions have consolidated into essentially two camps, the prosperous north and the relatively dependent south. The reasons for this divide are deeply rooted in pre-Risorgimento (unification) history. Ruling elites clustered around the great cities and their respective hinterlands. Genoa, Turin, Milan and Venice were dominant in the north. Florence, Siena, Bologna and Rome, together with the Vatican City State, dominated the centre. Naples ruled much of the south, including Sicily. The other large island, Sardinia, was linked to Turin in the north. Unfortunately for the south, in modern times the entire region has remained relatively underdeveloped, not benefiting from the industrialisation that occurred in Liguria, Piedmont and Lombardy in the late nineteenth century. This was the common experience of more remote regions in Europe (Gowland et al., 2000). Brittany in north-west France, much of the Iberian Peninsula away from the Mediterranean ports of Barcelona and Valencia, and Ireland in Europe's western fringe, hardly benefited from the rapid modernisation that spread across Europe in the early 1900s. In contrast, industrialisation took firm root in the north. Modernisation brought with it a developing civic culture and a sense of participation (Putnam, 1993). By contrast, in the south the population was typically exploited by unscrupulous land owners and the region fell easy prey to protectionist clans, themselves often competing with each other for influence and authority. The consolidation of the Mafia in

Sicily and of the *Camorra* in and around Naples was easily achieved during the nineteenth century, in a climate of hardship and exploitation. Both organisations have contributed to a culture of nepotism and clientelism, which remains endemic throughout Italy, but should be understood within this historical context. The relative underdevelopment of the Italian *mezzogiorno* is ironic given its extraordinary importance in European cultural history. Any visitor commencing a tour of Italy in Florence and taking in Rome, Naples, Pompeii and the island of Sicily for example, cannot fail to be struck by the sense that the Greco-Roman-Christian traditions are overwhelmingly evident. The linguistic diversity, maritime and mercantile history, to say nothing of gastronomic excellence, is underpinned by the phenomenally rich heritage that includes the renaissance splendour of medieval Christian churches, the sumptuous art and architecture of Giotto, Botticelli, Brunelleschi, Michelangelo, Leonardo da Vinci, Bernini and their contemporaries. This is the heart of Europe's Christian heritage, but the tour will also reveal the immense contribution of the Roman Empire, still literally and monumentally evident in Rome itself and at Pompeii in particular. Continuing south, Sicily contains a staggering richness in Ancient Greek temples, unrivalled anywhere except of course in Greece itself. The

© Jonathan Blair/Corbis

Photograph 3.2 Segesta Temple is one of the best-preserved Greek monuments in Sicily. It was abandoned, unfinished, by the Elyminas 2,400 years ago, yet stands as one of the finest examples of Hellenic architecture.

overwhelming impression is that the south of Italy is Europe's cultural heart, not a remote and uncivilised hinterland, as the northern stereotypical assumptions often imply.

The problems of the Italian south were exacerbated by widespread emigration, perhaps of the fittest and most able, and certainly the most entrepreneurial. This phenomenon also affected Ireland and Spain, contributing to the enormous diaspora of all three ethnic groups, Italians, Irish and Spanish, especially throughout the USA (all three), South America and northern Europe (Spanish and Italians). Many other southern Italians headed for the factories in the northern cities of Turin and Milan, to work for the great industrial conglomerates FIAT and Olivetti, both of which were founded at the beginning of the century. This background is important, because it helps explain the reasons for the persistent underperformance of the southern Italian economy and the poorly developed sense of civic engagement. The south remains chronically underdeveloped, although still in receipt of capital shifts from the wealthy north. In spite of years of investment assisted by government schemes and development projects sponsored by EU structural funds, the wealth and productivity gap between north and south remains considerable. Worse still, the psychological gap is a veritable chasm. This has contributed to demands by sections of the northern population to break away altogether, creating a new state, which will no longer have to 'subsidise' the south. Putatively named *Padania*, this movement, under the umbrella of the so-called Northern Leagues, employs racist language and ideas borrowed from nationalist campaigns to further its cause. *Leghisti*, incidentally, have determined that the divide is south of Florence, placing Rome – regarded as the black hole of their taxes – very firmly in the unloved south. Football would appear to be the one unifying phenomenon in present-day Italy, still a country of strongly differentiated regional identities.

France

Finally, France presents interesting contrasts between Corsica and the Basque Country which of course straddles part of both Spain and France. On the one hand Corsican nationalists have kept up a low intensity campaign to secede from the French state, and there have been isolated violent incidents. In contrast, the French Basque Country, *Le Pays Basque*, claimed by 'Spanish' Basques as part of *Euskadi* (the Basque name) has remained virtually unscathed by separatist violence. There is, though, much evidence of Basque identity in south-western France where the local culture is extremely strong.

Review	*What have been the hallmarks of nationalist campaigns in Catalonia, the Basque Country, Ireland and the former Yugoslavia?*
	On what grounds might we include Italy in this list?
	What might be considered unusual about the recent history of Czechoslovakia?
	Why do Belgium and Switzerland appear to manage diverse ethnic groups so peacefully?

● ● ● ● Integrating Europe and issues of state sovereignty

As was argued in Chapter 1, given the historical context provided by the Napoleonic Wars of 1805–14, the Franco-Prussian War of 1870–71, and two world wars, plus the Holocaust and numerous dictatorships, it is surely beyond dispute that the vision presented by Churchill for a 'kind of United States of Europe', and by Monnet, Adenauer, Spaak and others for an 'ever closer union' was a response to conflict. The previous section of this chapter illustrates how nationalism is far from a spent force in Europe. One can perhaps present the integration of Europe as an attempt to settle the atavistic tendencies in Europe to resort to **racism** and **nostalgia**, components found in the most virulent forms of ethnic nationalism (McLean & McMillan, 2003:178, see also p. 8 in the Introduction).

Chapter 1 included an overview of the early history of the integration process by looking at the context of the Cold War and the support provided by the USA that enabled integration to proceed. This section examines some of the issues emerging later which have a particular bearing on sovereignty and the relationship between the state and the integration process. It is not within the scope of this book to present a comprehensive and analytical portrait of the history, but it is useful to have some historical context for Chapters 4 and 5 which examine the European Union and theories of integration in some detail.

Whatever form integration would take, the decisive need was to lock France and Germany into a position of mutual interdependency in political, economic and social spheres, in such a way that armed conflict between them would become unthinkable. In this respect, and in others, the achievements of the past 60-plus years have been remarkable. As the 'European project' continues, the motivation for further integration has undoubtedly changed. In the early years the peace-making aspect was uppermost. Lord Ismay, NATO's first Secretary General, said the purpose of NATO was to 'keep the Russians out, the Americans in and the Germans down'. During the 1970s and détente, and more obviously after the end of the Cold War, the security aspect was less significant in popular consciousness as peace was and remains more or less taken for granted. Instead the principal concerns have become economic, and are rooted in the need for securing improved living standards, high employment, and the capacity to compete in the global environment.

Integration in Europe has not proceeded in a uniform or consistent manner. The early years were punctuated by significant disagreements and disappointments, notably the failure to achieve the planned Political and Defence Communities. The UK's lack of interest was also a disappointment to some continental states, and may well have contributed to the non-participation of Denmark in particular. The 1960s were, however, if anything, even less successful and the momentum towards deeper cooperation that was created by the launch of the EEC was dissipated within a few years. First of all, when Britain did apply to join the Community in 1961, the French were cool on the prospect. Eventually de Gaulle vetoed the application, which also included Denmark and Ireland. Better news was the signing of the Franco-German Treaty of Friendship (the Elysée Treaty) which led to increased political, economic and cultural ties between the two neighbours. But within ten days of signing the Elysée Treaty, de Gaulle unilaterally announced his veto on British accession, which not only upset Britain but some of his EEC partners as well (McCormick, 2002:70).

The reasons for the French veto of the UK's accession are probably threefold. First, de Gaulle feared a lessening of French control. The early years of the European integration project were fundamentally dominated by France and a French design (Siedentop, 2000:115–16). De Gaulle feared that Britain would be a rival and dilute French authority over the future direction of the enterprise. Secondly, de Gaulle feared that Britain would be a 'Trojan Horse' for US interests in Europe, since the UK had already consolidated its **'special relationship'** with the US, mainly through the sharing of nuclear weapons technology. Thirdly, de Gaulle felt that Britain lacked commitment to the European cause. In all these respects de Gaulle was probably right, but the final reason is deeply ironic given de Gaulle's own penchant for unilateralism and the pursuit of 'French' interests.

Indeed, two years after de Gaulle first vetoed the British attempt to join the Community, he was vehemently asserting France's sovereign interests. The Community, as a consequence, faced its first major crisis. France proved more determined than the other EEC members to protect what it deemed to be its national concerns against the federating tendencies of the EEC. From the

© Hulton-Deutsch Collection/Corbis

Photograph 3.3 De Gaulle says 'Non'. French President Charles de Gaulle twice vetoed British applications to join the EEC in the 1960s.

Discussion 3.4

Two steps forward, two steps back: the stalling of integration in the 1960s

1961	Britain, Denmark and Ireland apply to join the EEC
1963	Elysée Treaty (Treaty of Friendship) between France and Germany
1963	De Gaulle vetoes UK accession
1965	France abandons the Council of Ministers initiating the 'empty chair' crisis
1966	Luxembourg Compromise affirms veto in cases of 'national interest'
1966	France withdraws from military command structure of NATO
1967	Second French veto of UK accession to the EEC
1969	De Gaulle resigns
1970	Georges Pompidou becomes French President
1972	UK, Denmark and Ireland accession to the EEC agreed
1973	UK, Denmark and Ireland join EEC

---

mid-1960s France began to fear a tendency to determine policy by greater use of majority voting, the effect of which was to increase supranationalism in the Community. France actually withdrew from the Council in 1965 in an episode that became known as the 'empty chair' crisis. The subsequent Luxembourg Compromise affirmed the right of veto. At the same time, de Gaulle removed France from the Military Command Structure of NATO, and in 1967 he vetoed the UK's second attempt to join the EEC. French interests appeared to stymie further integration. The core dispute centred on French concerns about sovereignty, not only in Community-related matters but also in defence and foreign affairs (see Discussion 3.4). In summary, the 1960s were marked by a significant slowing down in the integration process.

In 1971 the US President Richard Nixon unilaterally abandoned the Bretton Woods framework which had secured European currency stability since it came into force after the war. The decision, which was in response to America's growing trade deficit with Europe's rapidly expanding economy, brought tumbling currency values and wage and price inflation. The 1973 Arab-Israeli Yom Kippur War followed, and so did the resultant oil crisis. The 1970s proved an extraordinarily difficult decade for heavily oil-dependent European economies. Jackson and Sørensen (2003:178) describe the oil crisis as contributing to 'a sense of lost invulnerability'. Oil prices quadrupled and inflation let rip in several European countries, while unemployment soared. This meant that Britain's entry to the EEC occurred at an extremely inauspicious time. It also appeared to demonstrate how governments only have so much control over matters that profoundly affect national economies, thus raising questions about the relationship between power and sovereignty, discussed in the previous chapter (see Discussion 3.5).

In order to enforce some exchange rate discipline, the EEC created the European Monetary System in 1979 which included the Exchange Rate Mechanism (ERM), a device that locked member state currencies to limited bands of

---

Discussion 3.5

A miners' strike, soaring petrol prices, and the three-day week

1971   End of Bretton Woods system
1973   Arab-Israeli War provokes quadrupling of oil prices
        National strike by National Union of Mineworkers
        UK government introduces a three-day working week to cut fuel demand
        Inflation rampant, declining pound, rising unemployment

The miserable condition of the economy could be blamed on any of the following, depending on your politics (tick preference):

Decimalisation □; EEC □; Government □; Unions (especially miners) □; Bosses □

The ending of Bretton Woods and the soaring oil price was an early indication, if one were needed, of how events far beyond the control of mere governments can disrupt the best-laid plans. In fact, the 1970s showed how global events (globalisation?) could affect the price of going to a football match – or at least the kick-off time: matches were played at lunchtime to avoid having to use floodlights, as electricity use was heavily restricted.

---

fluctuation against the dominant Deutschmark. The ERM clearly had profound implications for any traditional interpretation of a government having sole control over its currency management. Consistent with past form, the UK chose to remain outside the ERM. Again, the reason given was that Britain required control over its money.

It was not until the mid-1980s and the push towards the Single European Market that the drive towards closer union made much progress. The British contribution at this time was considerable, as the UK Commissioner Lord Cockfield created the Single Market Plan. The document led directly to the Single European Act (SEA) of 1986. This was the first major treaty revision since Rome. The SEM would have major implications for sovereignty because it would enhance supranational governance in matters relating to the economy and trade. The SEA provided for the precedence of EEC law over national law in matters concerning the Single Market. In addition, the SEA introduced political changes, including increased use of qualified majority voting (QMV) in the Council. As QMV was enhanced, so the use of the veto would become more restricted, meaning states could find their preferences overruled by the majority. Once again, a significant policy change had important implications for traditional notions of sovereignty. The implications of the SEA and the SEM are examined in more detail in the next chapter, together with the subsequent treaty, the 1992 Treaty on European Union (TEU), agreed at Maastricht.

After the collapse of the communist bloc between 1989 and 1991, global capitalism was entering a new and more competitive phase. The launch of the World Wide Web and other technological advances had major implications for world markets. These changes coincided with important policy directions in the late 1980s, including the liberalisation of global financial markets and the telecommunications sector. These events were signal elements in a new phase in the history of globalisation. In response, the European Community undertook further steps towards closer union. The Treaty on European Union (TEU), agreed at Maastricht in 1992 and containing the three-pillar structure of EC/Single Market (Pillar I), Common Foreign and Security Policy (CFSP, Pillar II) and Justice and Home Affairs (JHA, Pillar III), included the Economic and Monetary Union (EMU) protocol to launch a single currency. EMU was seen as a logical step in completing the Single Market. Again, the TEU, and EMU in particular, was especially contested on the grounds that it further compromised state sovereignty.

In 1997 the European Commission published *Agenda 2000*, affirming its intention to proceed to the most ambitious EU enlargement so far, whereby up to twelve more states, mainly from the former Eastern Bloc, would join the Union once they had successfully incorporated the *acquis communautaire*, the entire body of EU treaties, legislation, norms and conventions. Further treaties followed, with both Amsterdam (1997) and Nice (2000), the first a tidying-up exercise supposed to deal with weaknesses in the TEU and the latter preparing for a future enlargement. Both enhanced cooperation between EU institutions in policy making and increased the use of Qualified Majority Voting.

The Nice Treaty proved more problematic than was initially expected. First of all Ireland, to the great surprise of most continental Europeans, voted against the Treaty of Nice in June 2001. This threatened the ratification process and hence the entire enlargement. Ireland duly held a second referendum in September 2002 for which the Yes campaign argued that it would be a huge embarrassment to Ireland, a country which had benefited so much from EU membership and generous provision of Structural and Cohesion Funds in particular, if the voters now sabotaged an enlargement that would extend the Union to much poorer regions of the continent. Not only that, it would be detrimental to Ireland's economic prospects, especially the continued flow of FDI from the continent. This time the voters obliged and Nice was ratified.

But the real trouble lay ahead. Nice created new distribution of votes for the Qualified Majority Voting (QMV) system used in the Council for the post-enlargement Union. This would reduce the enormity of pre-Nice anomalies such as a weighting that meant a vote for Luxembourg equated to just 200,000 citizens, but a vote for Germany equated to 8.21 million. The post-Nice arrangement would mean a Luxembourg vote representing 100,000 citizens, and a German vote 2.83 million, which is still an enormous pro-small state advantage but is at least more reasonable. In addition, the system would introduce an innovative double majority rule, whereby the larger states would benefit. A qualified majority vote would have to represent at least 62 per cent of the total population, which naturally gives Germany new power in Council deliberations. However, the issue came to a head in discussions over the proposed Constitutional Treaty at the Brussels Council in December 2003. The summit was meant to endorse the Draft Constitution created by the Constitutional Convention under former French President Giscard d'Estaing. But it failed to do so, and it reopened the voting issue. Germany was unhappy that it would have only 29 votes in the Council, while Spain and Poland, each with half the population of Germany, would each have 27 votes.

This dispute wrecked the summit and left Poland in particular feeling much aggrieved. The package on which Polish voters had been sold EU membership in a referendum now risked being reopened, just a few months after the voters had given their approval to Poland's accession. This was bad politics. The Spanish conservative government agreed with Poland, but it lost office in March 2004. Poland, therefore, was left isolated and much weakened in the subsequent negotiations to resolve the issue. In June 2004 under the skilful presidency of Bertie Ahern, the Irish Prime Minister, the Council finally agreed the Constitution. The settlement involved a new agreement on QMV, by which most decisions in the Council will require the agreement of 55 per cent of member states, comprising at least 15 countries and representing 65 per cent of the EU population. Other contentious issues were also resolved, including the absence of any reference in the Constitution to the Union's Christian heritage – another defeat for Poland, but a significant protection of the secular nature of the Union's institutions. Despite the success of the agreement, the Constitution may yet be stillborn. It requires ratification in all member states, which might prove difficult, especially in the UK where voters tend to be either apathetic or eurosceptic.

In retrospect, it looks as if the late night arguments in Nice produced a solution that in the cold light of day proved unacceptable. Arm-twisting is common at EU summits, but perhaps at Nice it just went too far. The Eastern enlargement was achieved, but at least three serious issues remain unresolved: the Constitutional Treaty must be ratified by all 25 member states; further Common Agricultural Policy (CAP) reform must accommodate the needs of European consumers, world markets, the environment and natural justice; and there will have to be adequate provisions to enable the poorer regions of an enlarged EU to achieve economic convergence with their wealthier counterparts to the west. These are major challenges, perhaps indicating that the enlarged Union will face problems for which it is ill-prepared. The inter-state bargaining (see next chapter), so characteristic of the Union over several decades, becomes more tortuous and complex with every EU enlargement.

The pace of change has been unrelenting. While the Brussels Summit in December 2003 broke up in acrimonious failure over the proposed new Constitution and the issue of voting rights, it did confirm the intention to enhance the EU's security identity through the European Rapid Reaction Force, and to boost defence cooperation between member states. In May 2004 the EU admitted ten new members, bringing the total to 25 and the population to 453 million. One month later the Council agreed the text of a new Constitutional Treaty. All of these landmarks in the integration process can be seen as responses to the changing international environment, notably competition in global markets, the end of the Cold War, a tendency towards greater regionalisation worldwide,

Discussion 3.6

Progress towards 'Ever Closer Union' 1973–2004

1979	European Monetary System and Exchange Rate Mechanism created
	First direct elections to European Parliament
1981	Greece joins Community bringing membership to ten
1985	Schengen Agreement signed by France, Germany and the Benelux states
1986	Spain and Portugal join the Community
	Single European Act signed
1990	German reunification brings former East Germany into the Community
1992	Treaty on European Union (Maastricht Treaty) signed
	Single European Market created
1995	Austria, Sweden and Finland join the EU (bringing membership to 15)
1997	Treaty of Amsterdam signed
	Agenda 2000 sets out plan for enlargement
1999	Eleven states agree switch to euro which is launched as a currency of accounts
2000	Treaty of Nice signed
2002	Euro notes and coins introduced in 12 member states (UK, Denmark and Sweden remain outside the eurozone)
2004	Cyprus, Czech Republic, Estonia, Hungary, Latvia, Lithuania, Malta, Poland, Slovakia and Slovenia join EU
	Council agrees a proposed Constitutional Treaty, ratification of which is required by the 25 member states

and the 'internationalisation of problems' (Goldmann, 2001:26) such as environmental threat and international terrorism.

Advocates of European integration have always claimed that history demonstrates that the mosaic of separate nation states confirmed by the Treaty of Versailles of 1919 was disastrous for Europe, and would have been equally so after the Second World War. The view still holds that Europe is better off when its states are embedded in multinational organisations. The civil wars in the former Yugoslavia in the 1990s appear to confirm this. However, for most citizens of the European Union, and especially younger ones, peace is nowadays taken for granted, while extreme nationalism, despite the cautionary evidence in the previous section, is less of an issue than it once was.

Review	*What are the key landmarks in the process of European integration?*
	Has the process been linear and regular?
	What difficulties affected the European project in the 1960s and 1970s?
	How did Europe respond to the turmoil of the 1970s?
	What are the main landmarks in the development of European Union since then?
	Why did the Treaty of Nice become so controversial?

● ● ● ● Defending sovereignty – nationalism and euroscepticism

In the EU the state appears challenged both from above and below. Pressure from above is exerted by the development of supranational instruments and institutions. Pressure from below emanates from sub-state groupings such as regions. The latter might interpret the existence of a higher authority than the state as an opportunity to enhance their status. In other words, various peoples, from the Corsicans in France to Galicians in north-west Spain, may feel tempted to assert a local nationalist identity against Paris or Madrid, or whatever their unloved capital may be. This theme of sub-state representation is examined in Chapter 6. For many Europeans the issue of most concern is the relationship between their state and the European Union. Traditionally it has always been the British and the Scandinavians that are most identified with this **euroscepticism**, but in recent years the sceptics have been heard in places where they have hardly existed before, such as Italy and the Netherlands. Already there are signs of growing euroscepticism among the new member states, especially in Poland, where anti-European candidates did well in elections to the European Parliament in June 2004.

This suggests that the state-EU relationship must be resolved, or at least brought more centre-stage. Writers such as Siedentop (2000) and Habermas (2001) called for a European Union Constitution to address the issue, and as mentioned in the previous section, agreement on this has been reached, subject to ratification by national parliaments. The Constitutional Treaty is intended to clarify the relationship between the member states and EU institutions, but its ratification is by no means certain.

A traditional view of sovereignty holds that the sovereign state is not subject to any higher authority, and inevitably therefore this indicates a clash with the institutions of the European Union. Clearly while some broad areas of policy remain with the state, such as taxation, policing and education, and the state retains a monopoly on the legitimate use of force, even these areas are to some extent impinged upon by the EU. There are also other broad areas of policy where sovereignty has in fact already passed to the European level, such as in matters relating to the Single European Market, or to other bodies, such as NATO in respect of defence, or the World Trade Organisation in respect of trade agreements. For some this is simply a natural consequence of choosing voluntary participation in international institutions and is in recognition of the realities of the global economy.

However, critics of European integration style themselves as defenders of 'nation state' interests (see Discussion 3.7). Their primary concern is that too much sovereignty has been transferred to European Union institutions and this has undermined the state. They argue that too much 'daily life is controlled from Brussels' and that 'unelected bureaucrats' determine policies. Politicians such as the former Labour Energy Minister Tony Benn or the former Conservative Trade and Industry Secretary Norman Tebbit have called for the

Discussion 3.7

Defending the nation state

In the UK, the notion of defending the 'nation state' means sustaining the hegemony (power or influence of a dominant polity) of 'England' over other ethnic groups that make up the UK. A former government minister, Norman Tebbit, famously proposed a 'cricket test' for members of ethnic minorities living in the UK. Would ethnic Indians living in Britain support England or India in a test match? Unless the answer was 'England', Tebbit appeared to suggest that these 'immigrants', no matter whether they were born in the UK or not, would somehow be forfeiting their rights to full citizenship. The example is a good illustration of state nationalist assumptions.

The author's father, and the author for that matter, hopelessly fail Tebbit's test whenever Ireland play England at football.

re-negotiation of Britain's relationship to Brussels, in order to regain and defend sovereignty. The more supranational institutions – the European Commission, the European Parliament and the European Court of Justice – are regularly criticised by a passionately anti-European press in Britain, much of it owned and controlled by extra-European media magnates.

Defenders of state sovereignty clearly distinguish between their allegiance to the state and the worst excesses of nationalism described previously in this chapter. They stress the benefits in terms of democratic accountability, proximity of rulers to the ruled, and the surety of a change of regime if the electorate so desire in a general election. They also point to the historical famil- iarity with established systems of governance. The European Union on the other hand, is a much more remote, complex and exotic beast. It is the product of a process, and it remains in constant flux. Since the early 1980s the European Union has been preparing, negotiating or ratifying a new treaty, or an enlargement. The process of integration has become institutionalised, a factor which has spurred the concomitant growth in euroscepticism. Commonly cited complaints from eurosceptics about the European Union are summarised in Discussion 3.8.

As various writers have suggested (Walker, 1994; Strange, 1996), there may be other factors beyond the European level that are gnawing away at the authority – or sovereignty – of the state. The most significant of these probably relate to the various processes that contribute to globalisation. While the next chapter develops the discussion of how the European integration process affects the state, specifically examining the institutions and the decision-making process, later chapters assess the impact of globalisation to try to understand the changing role of the state in an increasingly complex world.

McDonald and Dearden (1999) describe the intergovernmental position of critics of the European integration process as a 'nationalist' position. In this respect, the label is applied to mainstream political behaviour, not to a form of ethnic protest as presented elsewhere in this chapter. Chapter 5 looks at theories of integration, so there is no need to go into detail here. Briefly,

> ### Discussion 3.8
>
> ## Eurosceptic case against the EU and further integration
>
> *The European Union . . .*
>
> - undermines state sovereignty;
> - is overly bureaucratic, unaccountable and undemocratic;
> - is a form of government but unlike national governments cannot be voted out of office;
> - creates legislation that hampers business and damages economic growth;
> - wastes taxpayers' money in the CAP, structural funding, and fraud;
> - wastes money on MEPs' expenses, unnecessary buildings, translation and interpretation;
> - plans to raise taxes and extend its authority in other ways, notably over pensions, VAT, and foreign and security policy;
> - threatens national character, local and national traditions and established 'way of life';
> - is a massive bureaucracy.
>
> *Furthermore . . .*
>
> - citizens are loyal to their states, not to the European Union;
> - there should be a referendum on any proposed EU Constitution;
> - national parliaments should have a vote on whether to accept EU directives.

intergovernmentalism is centred on the promotion of state interests, while any suggestion of a 'community' interest is usually seen as closer to a federalist position, quite the opposite of nationalist preferences. Charles de Gaulle was a particularly powerful advocate of the (French) state position and is sometimes referred to as a nationalist, as is Margaret Thatcher, formerly UK prime minister. In recent years the term eurosceptic has been applied, especially in Britain. While centred on relations between the state and the European Union, and opposed to any process towards a federal Europe, the politics of euroscepticism echoes across other policy areas too, in particular immigration and asylum, defence and foreign affairs.

A recent nationalist movement to emerge in Britain is the United Kingdom Independence Party which won 12 per cent of the vote in the 2004 European Parliament elections. The party calls for Britain to leave the European Union.

At the outer limits of peaceable politics is a set of right-wing political parties that express a more virulent form of nationalism that also includes opposition to the European Union. These include the British National Party, the National Front in France and the Freedom Party in Austria. Such parties are broadly opposed to immigration from developing countries and tend also to reject European integration outright.

Review   *What are the principal objections of eurosceptics over the European integration process? Suggest two other terms that might be used to refer to eurosceptics.*

Summary

This chapter has made the following key points.

Identity and difference, real and imaginary

- Ethnic identity is ascriptive and often considered beyond dispute.
- Ethnic identity may lie dormant and hidden for years, but it remains a dangerous phenomenon.
- Identity is constructed on the basis of difference.

Nationalism in contemporary Europe

- Violence has accompanied nationalist campaigns in recent decades, especially in Northern Ireland, the Basque Country and in the former Yugoslavia.
- Not all multi-ethnic communities or nationalist campaigns are marked by violence.

Integrating Europe and issues of state sovereignty

- The European integration process seeks to contain nationalist potential for violence.
- European integration has not been a regular, linear process; it has been marked by periods of inertia as well as several strongly federating initiatives.
- De Gaulle may be considered a French nationalist within the context of European integration.
- Britain has tended to defend state interests against incursion by supranational or federating policy initiatives.
- Volatility and weakness in European economies in the 1970s were related to global events – especially the ending of the Bretton Woods system and rising oil prices.
- The EEC responded with a series of federating or integrationary initiatives: the EMS/ERM, the SEA/SEM, the TEU/EMU and subsequent treaties.
- The end of the Cold War and the liberalisation of key sectors of the economy, together with the launch of the World Wide Web, signal a new phase in global capitalism.
- The EU has expanded to 25 member states, but not resolved underlying tensions concerning its system of governance.

Defending sovereignty – nationalism and Euroscepticism

- The defence of state sovereignty in the EU is associated with intergovernmentalism, nationalism and euroscepticism.
- Eurosceptics are critical of the EU for many reasons; foremost among these is that it is seen as an assault on state sovereignty.

Key concepts: discussion and other definitions

Key concept 3.1   European integration process

The dynamic of political change that has led national governments in Europe to cooperate in creating institutional innovations in order to achieve desired outcomes that would be less easily realised without such cooperation.

Integration [. . .] implies the act of combining parts to make a unified whole – a dynamic process of change. European integration is usually associated with the intensely institutionalised form of cooperation found in Western Europe after 1951 (Cini, 2003:419).

European history since the end of the Second World War has been marked by two contrasting phenomena: division – the overwhelming hallmark of the Cold War, and integration, the institutional partnership established between initially just six West European states, eventually extending to 15, and then moving to embrace at least ten others, mostly from the former communist eastern bloc in the most ambitious of the five enlargements that the European Union, or its predecessors, has undertaken. The Cold War had split the continent in two. Only after the fall of communism and the collapse of the USSR in 1991 could the integration process begin to involve central Europe and many of the CEECs previously tied to the Soviet Union.

The major outcome from the European integration process is the European Union. The 25-member state EU has evolved from the ECSC, EEC and EC, all of which have been landmarks in the European integration process (see Table 1.2). A feature of the process has been that it has expanded to include more participants over more than half a century and, in theory, no European state that meets the criteria for membership is barred from applying to join. European integration has in general been welcomed and encouraged by the United States, which initially sponsored European post-war recovery through the Marshall Plan and has broadly been an ideological soulmate and major trading partner of the EEC/EU.

The process has been instrumental in securing better living standards and improved international standing for many of its participants. However, between the years 1951 and 1989 the integration process was extremely one-sided in that it occurred only in Western Europe among liberal democratic countries that were (mostly) allied to the US throughout the Cold War. Nor has the process been one of simple linear progression towards greater harmony and prosperity. As we have seen, the history has been marked by disagreements, different expectations, different preferences and at times outright disagreements between the participants. These are further discussed in Chapter 5 on integration theory, and in Chapter 7 on enlargement.

Hutton (2003) describes the European integration process as 'always a fragile enterprise'. He says that since the Cold War it has experienced many new tensions. He writes that as the EU adjusts to the new Single Currency and contemplates its largest ever enlargement bringing in ten new member states, it faces crises on various fronts. It is by no means pre-ordained that the European integration process is one-way traffic towards greater harmony or greater prosperity for all its members.

As has been stated above, the term European integration may be objected to on account of its implication that integration is pre-ordained and leads to 'ever closer union'. Indeed, given that the phrase 'ever closer union' features in the preamble to the Treaty of Rome, and is repeated again in the Treaty on European Union, this is hardly surprising. Nevertheless, some prefer the word cooperation to integration, because it implies the continuing sovereign independence of nation states (Cini, 2003:95).

Key concept 3.2 Euroscepticism

Strongly critical view of the European Union and the integration process in general, tending towards hostility towards the Union, or even opposition to EU membership.

Euroscepticism is a particular brand of nationalism directed against the European Union and the European integration process. It is characterised by a highly efficient and well-funded media campaign against the EU. In the UK it has received prominent backing and financial support from entrepreneurs like the late Sir James Goldsmith and the Yorkshire-based businessman Paul Sykes. More recently it has secured a high profile through the successful campaign waged by the United Kingdom Independence Party, winning 12 seats in the European Parliament elections in June 2004.

Euroscepticism emerged in the UK in the late 1980s, especially around the time of Prime Minister Thatcher's Bruges speech in which she was sharply critical of the Delors/Kohl vision of a more politically integrated Community, with a much stronger social dimension. Thatcher, who had signed the Single European Act, tended to see economic integration and the liberalisation of the Single Market as the natural limit of integration. As the Community began to pursue the goal of a Single Currency and a greater role in employment rights, Thatcher became more openly critical, distancing herself from any such ambitions.

Thatcher's critical perspectives of the Community were already apparent from the Fontainebleau summit in 1984 when she demanded 'Britain's money back'. She did achieve a rebate on UK payments to the Community budget, which remains in place until 2006.

After the Bruges speech several Conservative politicians styled themselves 'eurosceptic', preferring to distinguish between what they claimed was a constructive though critical engagement, and the more openly hostile anti-Europeans who had always opposed EEC membership. Several of the latter were on the Labour benches in the House of Commons. Thatcherite Conservatives held back from demanding that Britain should leave the Community, but several argued that integration had gone far enough. This meant that after Thatcher had been deposed as Tory leader in 1990, the eurosceptic wing remained loyal to her and caused problems for her successor, John Major, throughout the difficult ratification of the TEU during 1993.

The term eurosceptic became common currency in the media and eventually was applied to several newspapers which were most openly hostile to the European Union. As the TEU was drawn up and eventually ratified, eurosceptics became increasingly hostile and turned their attentions to the prospects of eventual UK membership of the euro. Not satisfied with the opt-out agreed at Maastricht, eurosceptic MPs and the anti-European media campaigned to keep Britain out of the euro, either for the foreseeable future, or permanently. One newspaper in particular harangued the emerging euro as 'toilet paper' money.

By the time the Conservatives lost office and Labour entered government in 1997, eurosceptics seemed to be more anti-European than ever. Now, several years later, the euro has been replaced as the prime target of their campaign by the proposed Constitutional Treaty, which eurosceptics reject. Having demanded a referendum on the Constitution, they got what they asked for in 2003 when the Labour Prime Minister Blair unexpectedly announced a U-turn, agreeing to hold a referendum at an unspecified date (probably late in 2006). This gives Conservative eurosceptics another bone to chew on. Meanwhile, they have been trumped by the emergence of the much more overtly hostile United Kingdom Independence Party (UKIP), which campaigns on the single issue of getting Britain out of the EU altogether. However, there is evidence that some Tory MPs are increasingly inclined to this position.

Euroscepticism, meanwhile, has ceased to be a purely British affair. Various other countries have seen the emergence of eurosceptic voices, many campaigning vociferously in European parliamentary elections. Even countries with a long history of apparently total commitment to the European project have sounded more critical in recent years, notably the Netherlands, Austria and Ireland. Denmark has always had a eurosceptic fringe and has frequently followed the UK in supporting a strongly intergovernmentalist perspective on EU matters. The same is also true, if to a less marked extent, in Sweden. Euroscepticism has also been evident in Italy, and in parts of Germany, particularly Bavaria, which has a strong farming community. Perhaps the most striking development in the eurosceptic pantheon is the considerable eurosceptic wing in many of the new member states in Central and Eastern Europe. Following referenda on membership, those who campaigned against joining the EU have simply carried on where they left off, as fully fledged eurosceptics. They have also gained more support since entry and tended to do well in the June 2004 elections to the European Parliament.

In conclusion, euroscepticism, from being a minority view associated with the traditionally awkward British, has become a much stronger force in European politics. It is not, however, a united and coherent lobby. As well as extending

Answering the eurosceptics

The Independent (21 June 2004) provided a selection of quotations from prominent eurosceptic sources about the proposed EU Constitutional Treaty, and presented counter-arguments. The selection below is based on this.

"If Mr Blair signs the Constitution regardless of public opinion we will have to surrender our place at the international top table – in NATO, in the UN and at the G8 summits to name but a few."

Nick Farage, UKIP MEP, 4 June 2002

Independent response:
The UK will continue to enjoy exactly the same status in all the organisations referred to. Fantasy.

"The constitution is a gateway to a country called Europe . . . It's going to be a constitution which has supremacy over our constitution, over our laws, and this is something which we believe is highly damaging to our interests of this country."

Michael Ancram, shadow Foreign Secretary, 20 June 2004.

Independent response:
The EU is not a country. It is a collection of 25 nations which pool some of their sovereignty. The Constitution says that countries confer competences upon the EU, not the other way round. It spells out the supremacy of EU law but this restates the current position: every lawyer knows that the European Court of Justice in Luxembourg is the highest court.

"If Tony Blair puts his pen to paper today he'll be signing away a thousand years of British sovereignty. Our independence to run our own lives, make our own laws, be masters of our own destinies, will all be lost."

The Sun, editorial, 18 June 2004

Independent response:
The Constitution defines and clarifies who does what. Most EU powers already exist. There is an extension of majority voting that is small by comparison with earlier treaties negotiated by previous governments. In all sensitive new areas such as justice and home affairs or social security, Britain cannot be outvoted [. . .] To describe this as the loss of 1,000 years of British sovereignty is absurd.

"The British have done dogged and effective work to pare back the more federalist aspects of the constitution. But it still has a number of legal and institutional innovations, including the charter (of fundamental rights), the creation of a single legal personality for the EU, more majority voting, the establishment of a foreign minister and a full-time president of the European Council. Combine them, and assume that the ECJ puts a federalist spin on them, and the potential for a big EU increase in power is clear."

The Economist, 19 June 2004

Independent response:
This mixes up a host of different measures most of which are designed to increase efficiency rather than increase power. For example, the European Community already has legal personality (the ability to sign treaties) but the EU does not. This is a change, but a technical one. There is already an EU representative for foreign affairs; what the constitution does is to stop duplication with the work of the European Commissioner for external relations. There is already a President of the Council; the idea is that this job would not rotate every six months but would be in place for at least two-and-a-half years. Moreover, strengthening the Council – the place where member states take decisions – would beef up the intergovernmental part of the EU at the expense of the European Commission, something the sceptics always say they want.

"A secret clause in the constitution would give Brussels control over our oil."

The Sun, 12 November 2003

Independent response:
The Treaty contains no reference to EU control over North Sea oil. It says that natural resources are for member states to exploit.

"The constitution creates an EU foreign minister, despite British opposition, and a new EU foreign ministry and diplomatic service to support him. [It] limits our global influence by forcing Britain to surrender its seat on the UN Security Council whenever the EU foreign minister needs it. [It] creates a mutual European defence pact and army to go with it, thereby undermining NATO."

Irwin Stelzer, Daily Mail, 18 June 2004

Independent response:
The UK did not oppose the creation of an EU foreign minister (though it did not like the name) or of a team of officials to assist. The EU foreign minister will not sit on the UN Security Council. Britain keeps its permanent seat there. There is no mutual defence pact – EU nations simply promise to help each other if they suffer a terrorist attack or natural disaster. NATO remains the mutual defence organisation for the Western Alliance.

Source: The Independent, 21 June 2004

across 25 nations, it comprises campaigners who simply want to improve the way the EU is run but remain committed to its fundamentals, and others who are viscerally opposed to the entire enterprise and wish to withdraw from the Union, or worse, sabotage it from within. Eurosceptics also cover the entire political spectrum from extreme left to extreme right, including Green Party members, Italian Radicals and (some) Basque Nationalists.

Discussion 3.9 summarises claims and counter-claims about the proposed Constitutional Treaty. The extract gives a flavour of the eurosceptic arguments in Britain. In fact, the proposed Constitutional Treaty actually does *nothing* unless and until it is ratified by all 25 member state parliaments. Ratification is dependent on passing the test of a referendum in several states, including Britain.

Back in 1990, a Conservative Minister, Nicholas Ridley, was obliged to resign his post as Trade and Industry Secretary when he drew comparisons between German desire for a more integrated Europe and Hitler's Third Reich. In an interview with the *Spectator* he described European integration as 'all a German racket designed to take over the whole of Europe . . . you might as well give [sovereignty] to Adolf Hitler, frankly' (cited in Young, 1991:572). Young reports that Ridley's outburst spelt the beginning of the end for Thatcher. She held similarly visceral anti-German prejudices, so much so that she was 'appalled' by German reunification and did her best to prevent it. Together with her private secretary, Charles Powell, a faithful acolyte, she engineered a day-long conference at Chequers in March 1990 involving various academics, which reached preconceived and racist conclusions about the German 'weakness of character' that would 'prove' that 'Germans could never be trusted' and therefore German reunification should be resisted (Young, 1999:357–62).

Comparisons between European integration and Nazi Germany, and the Stalinist Soviet Union, are staple fare for eurosceptics. More recently, a prominent member of UKIP, former Labour MP and TV presenter Robert Kilroy-Silk, likened Tony Blair's support for the EU Constitution to Neville Chamberlain's appeasement of Hitler in 1938. He told the BBC 'He's waving a piece of paper saying it's OK, I've only given a little bit away of our sovereignty' (*Independent*, 21 June 2004).

But it is Thatcher who remains the fount of all truths for most eurosceptics on the political right. Young writes that she

> never [. . .] modified the fury with which she defended what she chose to depict as timeless British verities that no European could possibly be permitted to violate: in particular, parliamentary sovereignty and the pound sterling (Young, 1991:618).

Further reading

Preston, P. (1996) *A Concise History of the Spanish Civil War*, London: Fontana. Preston is author of perhaps the definitive biography of Franco. The truly committed should read that, but for a speedier and shorter insight into the nationalist campaign that overthrew the Republican government and emerged victorious in Europe's curtain raiser to the Second World War, this is a great book. It also offers insight into the emerging

Franco dictatorship, and explains how both Mussolini and Hitler lent support to Franco – including the notorious *Stukker* bombing of the market place of the Basque town of Guernika on a Saturday afternoon – vividly commemorated in perhaps the twentieth century's most famous painting, by its most famous painter, Picasso. Picasso lived in exile in Paris and took the painting with him, vowing that it should never return to Spain until democracy had been restored. His wish was granted and the painting now resides in the Reina Sofia Gallery, in Madrid. It alone is worth the trip.

Silber, L. & **Little**, A. (1996) *The Death of Yugoslavia*, revised edition, London: BBC/ Penguin. This is a harrowing eyewitness account of the disintegration of the former Yugoslavia. The book was written to accompany a BBC television series that is painful but riveting viewing. The book is a masterful illustration of the extraordinary horrors that nationalism can release. It is a brilliant example of outstanding front-line reporting with numerous interviews with soldiers, civilians and leading politicians, including those outsiders who came to clear up the mess.

Smith, A.D. (1995) *Nations and Nationalism in a Global Era*, Cambridge: Polity. A clear and concise account by an acknowledged expert on the topic.

The following books all offer excellent reading on the European integration process:

Baun, M. (1996) *An Imperfect Union*, Boulder, CO: Westview. Baun analyses the importance of the Treaty on European Union and explains not only its three-part structure but various other weaknesses that contributed to its tortuous ratification procedure.

Jones, R.A. (2001) *The Politics and Economics of the European Union*, Cheltenham: Edward Elgar. This is a highly accessible account of the institutional structure of the European Union, with excellent summaries of the key events, arguments and outcomes of various treaties, as well as the process leading up to EMU and the most recent enlargement.

Siedentop, L. (2000) *Democracy in Europe*, London: Allen Lane. This is a superb critique of the European Union in which the author calls for a Constitution and a federal future – although he is careful to point out that the EU is far from ready for the latter. Siedentop is merciless in his condemning EU leadership, attacking the venal defence of vested interests, especially French ones, and the failure to create a properly democratic and accountable institutional framework. The book is a sobering read for pro-Europeans and should be obligatory reading for students of European politics and policy makers alike. Despite the dramatic changes in the Union since Siedentop wrote this book, its central arguments remain utterly relevant.

Young, H. (1998) *This Blessed Plot: Britain and Europe from Churchill to Blair*, London: Macmillan. There are many excellent accounts of the UK's problematic relationship with European integration. This is one of the most informative and most entertaining. Young uses a great journalist's skill to brilliant effect to draw detailed portraits of the ebb and flow of British policy under successive prime ministers. Ultimately, his conclusion is that the UK managed a succession of missed opportunities. Chapter 9 'Margaret Thatcher: Deutschland Über Alles' is an excellent assessment of European policy under the doyenne of euroscepticism.

Film suggestions

Three films, none of which is an easy night's entertainment, examine nationalism and its consequences in contexts referred to in this chapter. Certainly a health warning should be attached to the film about Srebrenica. As the reviewer says below, it visits a place of horror that few of us could possibly recognise.

Julio Medem, *La Pelota Vasca* (The Basque Ball: The Skin Against the Stone), 2002, Spain

This film is presented in a documentary format and presents a range of opinions from different perspectives of the Basque problem. The film was condemned by the then Conservative Spanish government of Jose María Aznar, for being a propaganda exercise for Basque nationalism. The director, who is himself Basque, rejected the criticisms with the counter-claim that he wanted to present views of ordinary people living in the contested region. It is a frightening illustration of how polarised the community is, and how the issue of self-determination can be so powerful a force even in an outwardly prosperous and democratic Spain, more than a quarter of a century after the death of the dictator, Francisco Franco. The most celebrated terrorist act perpetrated by ETA occurred before Franco even died. In 1973 a massive car bomb exploded in broad daylight in central Madrid killing Franco's last Prime Minister and anointed successor, Admiral Carrero Blanco. The event is still recalled with modest affection by liberals throughout Spain.

For non-Spanish speakers, Medem's film requires considerable dedication to reading fairly densely constructed opinions through the subtitles. This is hard going because the format of the film is almost relentless talking heads, albeit presenting a wide variety of interesting and often controversial viewpoints.

See http://www.guardian.co.uk/spain/article/0,2763,1068933,00.html for an article about the film and the controversy it aroused in Spain.

Michael Winterbottom, *Welcome to Sarajevo*, 1996, UK

This harrowing film is about a community under siege during the Bosnian War of 1991–94. While by no means a flawless film, about a journalist who takes an orphaned child from her war-torn home to Britain, the backdrop of the Bosnian War provides a deeply shocking portrayal of a recent war in the heart of Europe. Sarajevo had been a multi-ethnic, peaceful and reasonably prosperous city, until it was torn apart by nationalist feuding.

See an article about the film at http://www.londonstudent.org.uk/7issue/film/sarajevo.htm

Leslie Woodhead, *Srebrenica: A Cry From the Grave*, 1999, UK/US

'This detailed account of the massacre of an estimated 7000 Muslim men in July 1995, at the Bosnian "safe enclave" of Srebrenica, relies not only on eye-witness testimony, but on some astonishing telltale footage. Video recordings from a variety of sources, including a British reporter, the Dutch army and even Serb camera crews, are offset against each other to form a lacerating record. The testimonies of those who are dealing with survival take this film to a place of personal horror most of us will struggle to recognise' (Morrow, 2003:1138).

A devastating portrait of the Srebrenica war crimes. There is an accompanying website at: http://www.pbs.org/wnet/cryfromthegrave/about/about.html

Chapter 4

The European Union and the state

Outline

- Pooling sovereignty
- The Institutions of the European Union
  - The European Commission
  - The European Council
  - The Council of the European Union
  - The European Parliament
  - The European Courts
- Policy-making in the European Union

Key concepts

4.1 Intergovernmentalism

4.2 Supranationalism

● ● ● ● Introduction

This chapter assesses the relationship between the European Union and its constituent parts, the member states. It examines the extent to which state interests are submerged or compromised by supranational or European-level interests.

The chapter begins with a discussion of the notion of 'pooling' sovereignty, based primarily on an examination of currency management. An overview of the principal institutions of the EU follows, in which their relationship to the question of sovereignty is addressed. There are frequent references to two contrasting concepts, supranationalism and intergovernmentalism, vital ideas both for this chapter and for the next one on integration theories. The final part of the chapter explains the basic policy-making process employed within the institutions of the Union.

If you are unsure about the meanings of intergovernmentalism and supranationalism, look first at key concepts 4.1 and 4.2.

● ● ● ● Pooling sovereignty

We have already seen that a traditional view of sovereignty holds that a sovereign state has the ability or authority to legislate without being subject to any higher authority. Sovereignty rests with the national legislature, and in democracies, by extension, with the electorate since it is the electorate which chooses its representatives to form the legislature, or parliament. European integration alters this situation because in several important respects – primarily in matters relating to the Single European Market (the so-called Pillar I in EU jargon) the EU does represent a higher authority than national legislatures. Also, the legislative organs of the EU, the European Council and the Council of the European Union (formerly the Council of Ministers) are not directly elected – they are composed of representatives elected to member state parliaments.

Defenders of the integration process argue that the EU provides for the pooling or sharing of sovereignty between members and as such the member states gain as much as they give away. This view is the conclusion of Milward in his seminal work aptly titled *The European Rescue of the Nation State* (2000). Other writers have similarly argued that states have engineered a consensus towards sharing authority in key areas of governance (Moravcsik, 1999; Baun, 1996). According to this notion of shared or pooled sovereignty, governing elites in various European countries have accepted the view that they can achieve more to defend their national interests by pooling their resources and their decision-making in common institutions. The drive towards **common policy** has always focused on the economic sphere and is characterised above all by the emergence of the **Single European Market**, which is regulated by the European Community pillar of the Treaty on European Union, Pillar I. The integrationist perspective holds that sovereignty is only of any value where it results in effective ability to defend or promote state interests, and particularly in matters of economy this had ceased to be the case.

How useful is absolute sovereignty? Two examples are instructive. North Korea is a sovereign state that operates in most respects outside or at best at the very margins of the world community. Its sovereignty is of little practical use in the world. Instead, North Korea is a pariah state with chronically low living standards, widespread hunger and an appalling human rights record. It is a police state governed by the totalitarian dictatorship of Kim Jong Il. However, it is a nuclear power and a military threat to the Asia-Pacific region. The United States is also a sovereign state, and it happens to be the world's only remaining superpower, and the largest national economy in the world accounting for about a quarter of global GDP. The sovereignty exercised by the US enables it to adopt an increasingly unilateralist position in world affairs, as demonstrated by the Bush administration's reneging on the Kyoto Accords on carbon emissions, the abrogation of the anti-ballistic missile treaties agreed with the Russians in the 1970s, the failure to recognise the newly established International Court of Human Rights and the statement by President Bush, prior to the US-led invasion of Iraq in 2003, that the US would act with the UN if possible, but 'alone if necessary' (*Economist*, 12 September 2002).

The new American defence doctrine was announced formally in a paper submitted to the US Congress on 20 September 2002. Declaring that the era of deterrence and containment was over, the paper committed the US – acting alone if necessary – to a far reaching pre-emptive campaign against terrorism (Gray, 2003:90).

Gray places this in the context of what he calls 'American universalism':

> American institutions are the only possible model for the world, [the paper] declares; the twentieth century ended with 'a decisive victory for the forces of freedom – and a single sustainable model for national success: freedom, democracy and free enterprise' (Gray, ibid.).

Such unilateralism indicates much more than the US pursuing its realist, sovereign preferences. It is a statement of the hegemonic intention that has characterised US policy since the attacks of 11 September 2001. It has also undermined the international reputation of the United States. By acting outside the framework of international institutions like the UN, the US has undermined its moral legitimacy. US sovereignty may be sustained by its overwhelming military and technological superiority but in other respects, notably economic and arguably also moral (see Chapter 12), America's power is in decline (Gray, 2003:88).

While it is commonly assumed that the European Union has compromised the sovereignty of its member states through the creation of extensive supra-national (above the level of state) decision-making institutions, a significant alternative perspective is presented in the literature on European integration. Moravcsik (1999) developed a theoretical position known as liberal intergovern-mentalism (LI). He concludes that governments are the prime actors in EU policy making, although he accepts that the EU is not a purely intergovern-mental organisation; it has significant supranational institutions, notably the European Commission, which is the principal policy initiator, and the European Court of Justice, which upholds EU treaties and legislation. Nevertheless, these bodies, according to Moravcsik, exercise authority which is delegated to them by the member states through the Council of the European Union. Furthermore, Moravcsik argues that policy is created on the basis of states recognising shared mutual interests, or responding to a convergence of national interests due to external factors. He cites the Single European Market as a prime example, being a response to global competition, notably from the US and Japan. Prior to the advent of the Single European Market, the lack of cohesiveness and the attachment to internal domestic markets was hampering the competitiveness of European industries. Bainbridge reports

> the feeling among leading European industrialists that the fragmentation of the Community market was hampering the ability of European firms to compete internationally (Bainbridge, 2002:469).

Leading proponents of the Single Market, such as the UK Commissioner Lord Cockfield and Jacques Delors, who became head of the Commission in 1984, argued that a more open European market would produce increased competition and flexibility in European business, and at the same time lead to better use of synergies through cross-border cooperation, and even mergers, especially in research and development (R&D). Inevitably this would involve some rationalisation, but the economies of scale so achieved would realise improvements and productivity gains, especially if accompanied by a general liberalisation of markets – and eventually by a currency union. This argument was especially important for major global industries such as information technology, telecommunications, pharmaceuticals, automotive and aeronautical engineering, and financial services. The eventual Single Market Programme emerged from Cockfield's White Paper of 1985, in which he identified 292 specific deregulatory measures to complete the Single European Market. This initiative proceeded alongside negotiations for the Single European Act (SEA) of 1986, which would extend the scope of **qualified majority voting** (QMV), thus making it easier to get the necessary legislation through the Council of Ministers. Through QMV, measures facilitating the Single Market would no longer be vetoed by single states, as had previously been the case. Thus the Single Market Programme (SMP) and the SEA provide a clear example of powers moving away from individual states towards a 'Community interest'. A further document from the European Commission, under the chairmanship of the Italian Commissioner Paolo Cecchini, was based on a survey of over 11,000 companies. The Cecchini Report, published in 1988, identified barriers to trade including the lack of harmonisation throughout the Community, border impediments and the absence of Community-wide product standards. The report was a further step towards the launch of the Single European Market in 1992.

It is worth noting that the SMP had the full support of the British government of Margaret Thatcher, despite the widespread impression that the UK has been routinely obstructive where any shift of sovereignty towards the EU has occurred, according to Hugo Young in his biography of Thatcher (Young, 1991). The former Prime Minister, amusingly enough, has said that she would 'never have signed the SEA had she fully understood its implications for British sovereignty'. For someone renowned for intellectual acuity and attention to detail this is an extraordinarily candid admission. Another Thatcher biography reports that it is incredible that she did not read the SEA carefully before signing it: John Campbell claims that Thatcher did not appreciate others' convictions and it was entirely her own fault that she signed the Act; there was an impetus towards social, political and economic union that she entirely misjudged. Campbell reports that at the Luxembourg IGC in 1985 she accepted reassurances from the Foreign Office that the SEA reflected their own agenda, but regardless of the interpretation placed on the Act by the FO or by Thatcher, it did

> . . . very significantly extend the powers of both the Commission and the Strasbourg Parliament, and led on logically to the Treaty of Maastricht in 1992 and eventually to the Single European Currency (Campbell, 2003:311).

Campbell asserts that Thatcher, doyenne of British eurosceptics, gave away more sovereignty than either Heath in 1973 or Major in 1992. Thatcher again demonstrated her absolute failure to understand the impetus for European integration when as late as 22 July 1988 she told BBC Radio 2 that 'EMU will never happen'. Campbell summarises his subject's approach to European policy as follows:

> Europe was the greatest challenge facing Mrs Thatcher's premiership. It was also the greatest failure [. . .]. And it was a failure directly attributable to her own confrontational, xenophobic and narrow-minded personality (Campbell, 2003:622).

Moravcsik's (1999) exploration of the genesis of the Single European Market emphasises the role of the member states. He claims that the SEM resulted from intergovernmental bargaining on the basis of mutual interests, and that supranational organisations were peripheral to policy making. The process shows that the supranational institutions are weak and can only achieve their desired objectives through having powerful allies, or a confluence of interests, at the state level. He argues that domestic economic interests primarily shaped governments' policies towards the SEM.

This view is similar to that expressed by Milward in *The European Rescue of the Nation State*. Milward (2000) argues that states have always sought to defend their interests and have accepted integrating initiatives where these clearly offer benefits to the states themselves. He gives the example of the Common Agricultural Policy (CAP), citing it as an example of an integrationary measure with a significant social dimension. The CAP, introduced in 1968, would sustain incomes and living standards for a significant group in society, namely farmers, making the entire European project more politically attractive. The CAP would therefore contribute to the social contract that integration entailed. Milward also refers, like Moravcsik, to the Single Market, where changes in the global economy, and especially competition from the USA and Japan, rendered it imperative for European economies and their businesses to engage in more partnerships in order to achieve economies of scale both in research and production, as well as marketing. The SMP developed from this perception, and proved to be a major impulse towards greater integration, ultimately leading to Economic and Monetary Union (EMU) and the single currency. In pursuing these policy objectives EU governments negotiated intergovernmentally, acquiescing in the extension of supranationalism in matters relating to economy and eventually – through a process known as **spillover** – to social welfare protection. Thus, Pillar I of Maastricht increased the authority of the Commission in relation to the Single Market. This therefore is no ambush by the Commission, but a firm policy choice by European governments.

It is clear therefore that choices by governments have indeed led to a transfer of sovereignty to supranational authorities within the EU. The integration process has been especially effective in creating the Single European Market over which a (primarily) supranational body, the European Commission, backed by the European Court of Justice, has authority. Member states and European businesses are subject to European law, although the procedures by which the Commission and the ECJ pursue non-compliance is slow and laborious. The Treaty on European Union gave the EU a legal personality which institutionalised the supremacy of EC law over national law in respect of the Single Market. It also extended the use of majority voting in the Council. The advent of the

SEM led to the highly symbolic and integrationary step of a currency union through EMU, which not only creates a single economic policy for all participating members but also delivers a single currency at the expense of 12 national ones. Furthermore, the emergence of greater EU involvement in other fields such as common foreign and security policy (CFSP) and justice and home affairs (JHA), albeit apparently ring-fenced as domains where intergovernmentalism would hold sway, alarmed eurosceptics who feared the encroaching powers of the EU. Those fears, ten years on, seem eminently justified as Pillars II and III of the TEU that dealt with CFSP and JHA have virtually collapsed. There have been significant moves towards the EU developing a much higher profile in matters of defence and security, notably the creation of a European Rapid Reaction Force and a role for a military planning organisation to co-exist with NATO confirmed at the Brussels Summit in December 2003. Much of JHA has edged its way into Pillar I. In all these respects, we see sovereignty shifting away from the state, but this should be interpreted not simply as loss, but as an inevitable and logical response to changes in the international environment.

Indeed, one might argue that the question of sovereignty is a red herring. Sovereignty is increasingly a chimera, given the trend, noted by Walker (1994) and referred to in Chapter 2 (see p. 73), towards increased globalisation and the transfer of authority in both the international and domestic spheres to private, market based interests (see also Strange, 1996), or to multinational institutions. Hutton refers to a similar impact on state sovereignty from globalisation and argues that it is only through cooperation that European states can 'regain sovereignty and re-legitimise their national political processes' (Hutton, 2002:47).

Supporters of European integration claim that pooling sovereignty at most sacrifices marginal trappings of authority, and in fact enhances influence. However, Bainbridge (2002:479) rejects this as pedantry. Any basic examination of sovereignty shows that the opponents of the European ideal are correct: there has been a real and considerable transfer of sovereignty from the states to the European Union, especially to its more supranational judicial institutions, the European Commission and the European Court of Justice. This view rejects the notion of pooling sovereignty. A state is either sovereign, or it is not, and in the case of European integration there is clear evidence of sovereignty having been compromised, as power has very definitely been transferred from once sovereign states to higher, supranational (above the level of state) authorities. See Discussion 4.1.

Walker (1994:355) claims that markets and private capital undermine sovereignty, a view shared by Strange (1996). The UK currency, pound sterling, may find itself somewhat exposed between two major global currencies, the US dollar and the euro. It has not happened yet, but another market attack on sterling, such as happened in 1992 when government borrowing of £7.25bn in foreign currency was insufficient to sustain sterling's position inside the Exchange Rate Mechanism (Griffiths & Wall, 2001:749), is not an especially fantastic future scenario. As the UK government was powerless in 1992, it could be powerless again. This suggests that while joining the euro might be seen as a risk, remaining outside is also a risk.

Discussion 4.1

Economic and Monetary Union and arguments over sovereignty

The case is made that EMU incontrovertibly compromises the sovereignty of states, or, at the very least, has led to a pooling of sovereignty if one allows that concept. The European Central Bank has taken sovereignty from those states that use the euro.

However, a counter-argument may be presented. Consider the case of Denmark. The Danish government, along with the UK and Sweden, opted out of the third stage of monetary union, the actual adoption of the euro as a currency of account in 1999. During the third stage of the transition to the euro the new currency replaced the European Currency Unit (the ECU) which had been used as a common reference value based on the basket of participating currencies in the Exchange Rate Mechanism (ERM). Thus EU institutions, states and businesses in the designated euro area were given until 2002 to prepare for the final switch to the euro when notes and coins would be introduced.

Denmark opted out of this Stage III, thus signalling together with the UK and Sweden that it would not adopt the euro. However, the Danish kroner had been tied to the Deutschmark since the inception of the European Monetary System and its currency banding instrument, the ERM, in 1979. The Danish kroner remains in ERM-2 now that the euro is a fully functioning currency. The result is that when the Governing Council of the ECB discusses interest rates and the management of the euro, it takes decisions that directly affect the Danish currency, but there is no Danish representative involved. In other words, while the governors of individual euro area member states accept that 11 other countries' representatives can provide input on decisions affecting the currency used in their countries, they also know that they can contribute to decision-making affecting the currency used in 11 other states. This *quid pro quo* is clearly a pooling of expertise and opinion and an exercise in shared decision-making.

The Bundesbank did not operate like this. But the result for Denmark, inside the ERM-2, is that Danish representatives have no input: they can only wait for the collective judgements of the ECB. Following on from the Bainbridge argument referred to above, one can interpret this as Denmark retaining sovereignty over its currency but *choosing not to exercise it*. The core aspect of Denmark's retention of its sovereignty in this arrangement is that it can withdraw from the ERM, and join Sweden and the UK on the outside. In contrast, withdrawal from the Single Currency is not usually considered to be an option for any of its members.

Some commentators interpret the advent of the single currency as a sovereignty *gain* for the participating member states, *except Germany* which loses the benefits that it formerly had from seignorage (inward investment from other currencies). This is the view adopted by Dinan (1999) and Baun (1996). The argument is that participating states had hitherto been members of the **Exchange Rate Mechanism** (ERM) which pegged currencies to the DM and so decisions taken by the Bundesbank were effectively binding on other states' currencies even though no other national central bankers or government representatives could participate in the decisions made by the Bundesbank. Once the euro was launched in 1999 the European Central Bank was established, its Executive Board comprising the governors of the participating Central Banks. Therefore for the first time states had representatives able to contribute to decisions on inflation targets, interest rates and exchange rates made by the ECB. This represents, arguably, a net gain in sovereignty.

We may conclude from this discussion that the euro provides a clear example of pooling sovereignty, and one which, according to its supporters, offers better prospects for the long-term stability of the exchange rate environment in the European Union than was possible under the ERM, and certainly under a floating currency regime, such as existed before 1979. Of course, states might have chosen to break up the ERM altogether and abandon plans for EMU, thereby taking back sovereignty lost in the ERM, but that was not a choice any of them wished to make, except Britain and Sweden, while Denmark remained in the ERM.

Currencies offer a good example of how global markets have significantly altered perceptions over sovereignty. In terms of economic management, an independent central bank such as the Bank of England can pursue low interest rates and low inflation while hoping that the currency remains stable as a consequence of prudent management by the bank, and careful stewardship of those aspects of the economy that the Treasury can affect, namely monetary policy, taxation and government spending. Nevertheless, there is an impressive array of risk from several quarters: currency speculators as suggested above, private capital disinvestment, global economic downturns extending to a recession or a slump, and economic shocks. Examples of the latter include major political crises, terrorist attacks, or natural disasters. To take just a few of these examples together, one can argue that the real decisions affecting the stability of a currency are those taken by currency speculators and businesses in determining levels of inward investment, and by consumers buying – or not buying – goods and services. Economies, governments and currencies are acutely vulnerable to economic shocks, a spectacular example of which was the quadrupling of oil prices following the Yom Kippur Arab-Israeli War in 1973. Recession followed, with a massive increase in unemployment. As the 1970s proved turbulent in

---

Discussion 4.2

Economic shock – German reunification and the ERM

The speed of political change that engulfed Germany after 11 November 1989 had dramatic consequences for its economy, the effects of which are still apparent 15 years later. It also led to the dramatic implosion of the Exchange Rate Mechanism on 16 September 1992, known as Black Wednesday.

After German reunification on 6 October 1990 Germany experienced a consumer credit and spending boom which led to an upturn in inflation. The Bundesbank raised interest rates to stem the rising borrowing, and rising prices. Together with low interest rates in the US, the result was Deutschmark appreciation against sterling and the Italian lira in particular. Sterling had joined the ERM in 1989 at a rate that was too high, and the government failed to realign sterling within the ERM (Griffiths & Wall, 2001:748–9). By 'Black Wednesday' both sterling and the lira had fallen victims to currency speculation. They both crashed out of the ERM. By October 1992 sterling had lost 20 per cent against its previous central rate inside the ERM. With interest rates at 15 per cent and inflation at 11 per cent the impact on public confidence in the government was terminal for the ruling Conservative party.

Interpretations vary, but one is that Black Wednesday occurred because there had been insufficient adjustment to the relative strengths and weaknesses of European currencies since 1987. There were dramatically divergent factors impacting on the major ERM economies, as well as between the US and Germany, where interest rates were 3 per cent and 9 per cent respectively (Griffiths & Wall, 2001:750). A further destabilising factor were the political uncertainties surrounding the Maastricht Treaty. Certainly the experience of Black Wednesday has regularly been cited by opponents of Economic and Monetary Union as evidence that fixed currency regimes for divergent economies spell major risks, if not severe economic crises.

A different view is that Black Wednesday would not have occurred had there been a single currency: in other words, the system practically blew apart *because it could*. Perhaps most significant is the fact that the break-up of the ERM occurred as a consequence of an 'economic shock'. Opponents of the euro argue that it is ill-prepared for such shocks. They may be right.

Photograph 4.1 Who cares about sovereignty? Crowds form the euro sign for the launch of the euro in Frankfurt, Germany.

currency markets the EC responded by creating the European Monetary System in 1979, a feature of which was the banding of currencies inside the Exchange Rate Mechanism, where the Deutschmark was the benchmark currency. The Bundesbank had mostly maintained stable German inflation and interest rates for 40 years. The ERM managed to provide a more stable currency environment across the continent. This lasted until the arrival of a further economic shock, the extraordinary and unexpected collapse of the Eastern Bloc and the rapid reunification of Germany, achieved in October 1990, less than a year after the Berlin Wall was dismantled by a popular revolution. See Discussion 4.2.

Sovereignty may not be the inviolable principle that a traditional Westphalian interpretation appears to suggest. A central bank may raise or lower interest rates, but only within tight limits without losing all credibility. It may choose to devalue its currency against other currencies, but such a policy has certainly lost any respectability, even if it ever had any. It is remarkable how the Conservative right in the UK clamour for the retention of the freedom to engineer the exchange rate, despite decades of commitment to low inflation and a marked preference for non-intervention where devaluation is concerned, preferring other forms of fiscal management. There may be very good economic reasons for the UK rejecting EMU and retaining the pound, and even political justification for doing so. Nevertheless, sovereignty is hardly one of them. In any case, one might be forgiven for gaining the impression from sections of the UK media that the issue that really counts is having the Queen's head on Bank of England notes. Even this is curious when compared with other countries. In Spain King Juan Carlos, after the death of Franco in 1975, ushered in a new era of democracy. Seven years later he was instrumental in the failure of an attempted military coup led by armed civil guards who invaded the Parliament. In spite of this there was no great lamenting over not having his head on the bank notes after the withdrawal of the *peseta*. Instead, ever happy to party, the Spanish happily celebrated the launch of the euro on 1 January 2002. Sovereignty evidently means different things to different people.

Review   *What is meant by 'pooling' sovereignty? How and why has this occurred? How does the advent of the euro reflect the notion of pooled sovereignty?*

● ● ● ● The institutions of the EU

Perhaps the clearest way to assess the extent to which sovereignty has shifted from states towards the European Union is to examine in more detail the main institutions of the Union and how decisions are reached. This explanation will show that the EU is a hybrid organisation, in part supranational, in part inter-governmental. This characteristic of the EU is different to other multinational organisations. The Council of Europe, NAFTA, ASEAN, NATO, the UN, OPEC, the WTO and NATO are all far more unequivocally intergovernmental, even allowing for the fact that some of them, such as NATO and the WTO, may nego-tiate binding agreements. The EU is without historical precedent, being unlike any other organisation (Burgess, 2003:73). Furthermore, the balance between supranationalism and intergovernmentalism has fluctuated over the years. The TEU agreed at Maastricht in 1992, which included the Social Contract and EMU protocols, strengthened the Commission and the supranational aspects of EU governance, but later developments, and especially the Treaty of Nice (2000), have caused the pendulum to swing back towards a more intergovernmental apparatus.

The **European Commission** currently comprises 25 Commissioners, including the President of the Commission. Commissioners are nominated by member state governments, and each is responsible for a department, or Directorate General, concerned with a discreet policy area. Each Commissioner and DG is supposed to represent the 'Community interest' and not promote any state agenda. However, there is inevitably some degree of national influence, not least from the Commissioners themselves, who are invariably career politicians with long service in domestic politics. The former President of the Commission, Romano Prodi, took steps to ensure that Commissioners staffed their offices, known as *cabinets* in the French, with different nationals (Egeberg, 2003:139).

This should assist in the avoidance of Commission portfolios becoming national enclaves.

The President of the Commission is charged with representing the Union as the face of the EU, attending ECB meetings, and he (there has as yet been no female president) also has a role in planning the direction of EU initiatives. Some presidents have had especially high profiles and a considerable impact, notably Jacques Delors (1985–95), who steered the Union through the Single European Act, the Single Market Programme and German reunification as well as the controversial Treaty on European Union.

The Commission has an external representation role, particularly since the early 1990s. The Commission staffs and runs offices around the world, and it is also the EU's main negotiator in the WTO. The Commission has only a peripheral role in CFSP, where the Council is in a stronger position, delegating a leadership role to the Secretary General of the Council who is the Union's High Representative for CFSP. This strengthening of the Council's role is an example of the tension between the generally assumed supranationalism of the Commission and the intergovernmentalism of the Council (Egeberg, 2003:133).

The Commission is 'the guardian of the treaties', having a monitoring function, to ensure that the ideals and laws (the treaties) of the Union are respected. It has a role in enforcing Community law, and may call on one of the Community Courts to assist in this process. It also has a key legislative role in that it is generally regarded as the sole initiator of policy and it draws up policy documentation, albeit in consultation with other EU institutions and with the advice of interest groups, including industrial lobbyists, trades unions, employer groups, professional bodies and other agencies. In reality, proposals may come from outside the Commission, but the Commission can decide whether to take up or disregard a proposal (Egeberg, 2003:132). This demonstrates the key agenda-setting function of the Commission, a role which is especially significant in determining the direction of policy and the overall ambitions of the Union. The Commission is also responsible for setting the EU budget and overseeing expenditure, although national authorities are mainly responsible for the implementation of correct procedures. In popular discourse, and perhaps as a consequence of the relentless implication from eurosceptic press in the UK, the Commission is the EU law-maker, but this is not the case. It does, however, issue directives; the relationship of these to legislation is as follows:

> Laws made by the Council, usually together with the European Parliament, tend to take the form of broad policy guidelines or frameworks, rather than detailed steering instruments. Thus it is up to the Commission, in close cooperation with the member states, to detail and fill in EP/Council legislation by agreeing more specific rules, often in the form of Commission directives or regulations, in what is called delegated legislation (Egeberg, 2003:133).

Thus it is clear that the legislative procedure is complex and involves a number of agents, not least the member states themselves who have to pass legislation through their own parliaments, usually taking account of local circumstances but keeping to the spirit of the initial guidelines from the EU institutions.

The Commission issues directives, regulations and opinions. Directives have to be agreed by the Council and are then passed into law by national parliaments, often with some flexibility in terms of time span and detail. Regulations, on the other hand, are directly binding once issued by the Commission and do not require approval either from the Council or from member state parliaments. This means that the European Commission can effectively create legislation that is binding on member states, albeit in narrow areas closely related to the existing treaties, or existing directives. Opinions have no binding status but they may signal views, preferences or intentions in a general way.

Although regulations created by the Commission are relatively minor compared to directives agreed by the Council, the fact that the Commission can issue regulations that are binding on signatories to the treaties is, as Bainbridge points out (2002:479), qualitatively very different to what happens in NATO, for example. No higher authority in NATO can issue binding legislation in this way, since NATO is run by its Atlantic Council which cannot impose policy on any of its 26 signatory states that prefers to dissent from the proposal. Nevertheless, the deliberations of the Atlantic Council are not made public, so there may be pressures that compromise a state's representatives from acting truly independently, and NATO is an alliance based on the principle of mutual guarantee, so there is some reason to argue that sovereignty may be restricted, even in NATO. However, the case of the European Commission, and therefore of the EU, seems more clear-cut, as in the EU higher authorities clearly can impose policy on the member states.

A major restriction applies to the role of the Commission in respect of regulations: these have to be within the sphere of competence of the Commission, which means the European Community pillar (Pillar I) of the TEU. Pillar I legislation is most obviously supranational – thereby compromising state sovereignty. However, since the TEU was agreed, its pillar architecture has suffered severe decay, if not collapse. Many aspects of Pillar III, which concerns Justice and Home Affairs, have been shunted sideways into Pillar I. What is left is now labelled, post-Treaty of Amsterdam, Police and Judicial Cooperation in Criminal Matters (PJCCM). Citizenship, immigration, asylum policy and professional qualifications all, arguably, have implications for the Single Market and so have been absorbed into EC (Pillar I) law. Even Pillar II, Common Foreign and Security Policy, has tended to take on a more supranational hue, despite the initial TEU declaration that Pillars II and III were primarily intergovernmental. Any shift towards common policy in foreign and security matters begins to take on the characteristics of supranational governance, although in theory at least the existence of the veto, zealously defended by the UK and a handful of others, notably the Scandinavians and the Irish, suggests that the intergovernmental character of Pillar II has survived. However, the EU has taken steps towards developing a defence and security identity since the TEU, especially during 2003, and therefore a greater degree of common policy in this area.

The final function of the Commission is its policy management role, an essentially administrative task, which includes the management of programmes sponsored by the Commission relating to structural development, community initiatives, education, external funding and other budgetary issues. The Commission's use of funds is monitored by the European Court of Auditors, which is responsible for ensuring that the Community budget is correctly managed. The administrative role of the Commission is considerable, including a variety of service provision to the Union, such as library and archives, legal and technical support, and communication and translation and interpretation services. Translation involves the Union's 20 official languages. Administration and services account for the majority of Commission staff of about 22,000 (Egeberg, 2003:141).

Egeberg (2003:135) stresses that the Commission is involved in virtually all EU policy processes, especially anything relating to Pillar I/EC affairs. However, to what extent does it really have influence? The answer is disputed. Intergovernmentalists believe that the Commission has a relatively marginal role, since it can exercise only delegated authority. The member states effectively call the shots through the Council of the European Union and through the European Council. On the other hand, a supranationalist perspective stresses the agenda-setting role of the Commission and points to its powerful role in establishing the SEM. Egeberg concludes that both interpretations may be 'partly correct' (ibid., 136).

The Commission and the President of the Commission are at the heart of the supranational dimension of the European Union, together with the European Court of Justice. The functions and responsibilities of the Commission and of the President are shown in Discussion 4.3. In summary, despite its scope for issuing regulations that are binding on all member states, the Commission is not able to independently create substantive new legislation. New treaties or major treaty amendments are created by Intergovernmental Conferences (IGCs), in which national delegations are led by the heads of member state governments. Furthermore, the legislative role of the Commission is secondary to the more powerful law-making authorities of the Union, the **European Council** and the **Council of the European Union**, previously known as the Council of Ministers. These are composed of elected representatives from member states, but they are only indirectly elected to the European level by their national electorates. They are first elected to national legislatures and then appointed to European level office by their respective executives, or governments. They are not *directly* elected to EU office, although in the case of heads of government or senior ministers it must surely be clear to voters that a consequence of their election at home is that they will represent the state at European level. If this is not clear, then they are most likely acutely ignorant of how the EU works or barely even know of its existence – a state of affairs which is all too common.

The Council consists not merely of ministers, but of national delegations headed by ministers. These delegations may include junior ministers, civil servants and special advisors, but their exact composition is up to member states. Of course, only the ministers, as heads of their delegations, can vote. Debate and decision-making in the Council is conducted on a government to government basis: participants negotiate as representatives of the state executive, thus

---

Discussion 4.3

Functions and responsibilities of the European Commission and the President of the Commission

The President of the Commission

- Head of the Commission
- Attends meetings of the European Central Bank and of the European Council
- Public face of the European Union, significant PR role
- Plans European Union initiatives

The European Commission

- *Diplomatic and international role*
  - 'Civil service' of the European Union
  - Staffs and coordinates EU 'missions' in Europe and around the world
  - Represents the EU in international forums such as the WTO
  - Centre of lobbying by interest groups
- *Guardian of the Treaties*
  - Represents the 'Community' interest
  - Investigates contraventions of the rules of the Single European Market
- *Legislative functions*
  - Agenda-setting function
  - Initiates policy proposals
  - Draws up legislation in partnership with other EU institutions

- Issues:
  1. Directives – must be approved by the Council and put into law by member states
  2. Regulations – immediately binding – must be within the scope of existing European Community (Single Market) legislation
  3. Opinions – no legislative authority, not binding.
- *Policy management (civil service role)*
  - Sets and allocates EU budget, oversees expenditure
  - Administrative functions
  - Policy coordination
  - Institutional coordination within the EU
  - Management of programmes
    - Structural funding and development projects
    - Common Agricultural Policy
    - Education
    - External funding, including aid programmes
  - Service unit for the Union
    - archives and library services
    - legal and technical services
    - communication, translation and interpreting services

---

the term intergovernmental is used to describe the bargaining and decision-making that occurs in the various Councils.

Nevertheless, Lewis (2003:151–2) reports that the Council is 'more than the sum of its parts'. While it is evidently a 'defender of the national interest' it is also 'a collective system of decision making'. This possible paradox blurs the traditional distinction between intergovernmentalism and supranationalism. It makes the Council, like the Commission, more of a hybrid creature than is often assumed.

The European Council comprises member-state heads of government, the Heads of State in the case of France and Finland, plus the President of the Commission, two Commission Vice Presidents as well as the Foreign Ministers of the member states. The Council meets twice a year, normally accompanied by a vast media circus. Votes are rarely taken but the role of the Council meetings, known as summits, is to chart the course of future developments for the

Union and to resolve issues that have been too problematic at the Council of Ministers level for a decision to be taken there. Members of the European Council represent their home states and they return to their capital cities to report the outcome of such summits. Council meetings may involve substantive decisions on major issues, such as reaching agreement on treaty changes or enlargement. Decisions are normally arrived at by consensus but occasionally votes may be taken. The European Council is unequivocally an intergovernmental body and as such represents the views and conscience of member state governments, each of which is answerable to its own parliament and electorate. However, the profile of the Council as a powerful European Union institution has grown. Summits, often reported as EU heads of government meetings, have a tendency to produce significant outcomes in terms of the direction of EU policy.

The Council of the European Union is arguably the most powerful EU body, and the most strident champion of member states' interests, but arguably the least well known (McCormick, 2002). It is the final decision-making body and its powers make it more like a formal legislature than is the European Parliament. The Council of the European Union is in fact a series of Councils, each concerned with a different set of responsibilities or different areas of policy (see Figure 4.1). The foremost Councils are the General Affairs Council which sets the EU agenda; *Ecofin*, which is the Council of Finance Ministers and works in close association with another EU body, the **European Central Bank**, which is based in Frankfurt and manages the single currency, the euro. A third key Council is the *Council of Agriculture*, which is especially significant on account of its disproportionately large budget, amounting to some 48 per cent of total EU expenditure. These three meet monthly in Brussels. There are various other Councils for other spheres of activity, such as the environment (environment ministers), employment (employment ministers), industry (industry ministers), and so on. These meet on average two to four times a year, again in Brussels. Each Council is primarily constituted by representatives of the different ministries of member state governments. The key members are the ministers themselves, who have voting rights. Each Council is joined by the relevant European Commissioner whose task is to ensure that the European Union view is kept in focus. Decisions are normally made without a vote but by consensus. Where voting is required, a complex system of **Qualified Majority Voting** is used, with votes distributed roughly in line with population size. In the current Council there are a total of 87 votes and 62 provides a qualified majority, while 26 represents a blocking minority. This arrangement changes in 2005 to take account of the 2004 enlargement. In some areas of policy a veto applies, thus unanimity is required to pass a proposal. Laws are created as directives or regulations. Most are directives and these are passed to national parliaments to be made law within an indicated timeframe. Thus it is the national parliaments that put EU legislation onto the statute.

Between meetings of the various Councils, there are permanent representations of about 30–40 professional diplomats working as a kind of continual representation of state interests and expertise in ongoing discussions about policy formulation and implementation. The heads of each delegation are members

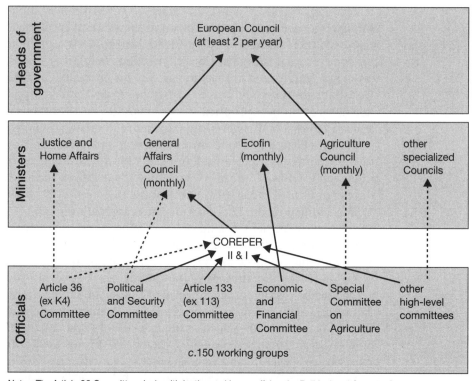

Notes: The Article 36 Committee deals with justice and home affairs; the Political and Security Committee deals with common foreign and security policy; the Economic and Financial Committee deals with EMU; Coreper ii (Ambassadors) prepares Councils and topics that are more political; Coreper i (Deputies) prepares the more technical and financial issues; the Article 133 Committee deals with trade issues.

Figure 4.1 The structure of the Council

Source: figure 1.2 (p. 16) from chapter by H. Wallace from *Policy Making in the European Union* (2000) edited by Wallace, H. & Wallace, W. Reprinted by permission of Oxford University Press.

of the powerful Committee of Permanent Representatives (COREPER) which acts as a permanent link between Brussels and the member states. COREPER also makes decisions, sets agendas and prepares ministers for Council meetings.

In summary, then, the Council of the European Union, in all its manifestations, is *primarily* an intergovernmental body. However, as Lewis points out, the Brussels-based secretariat of the Council and the surrounding culture of EU decision-making ensures that even the Council is subject to normative pressures which foster a degree of Europeanisation (Lewis, 2003:158). Lewis concludes:

> The Council is both an institution that represents national interests and a body at the supranational level that makes collective decisions. [...] [I]t blurs the traditional distinctions between the national and the European levels, between intergovernmentalism and supranationalism (Lewis, 2003:163).

The European Parliament is composed of 732 directly elected representatives from EU member states. The Parliament has no formal powers to introduce legislation but has over the years astutely increased its lobbying capability, using its moral authority as an elected body to pressure the Commission and the

Council into taking account of its opinions and proposals. Most of its work is through its various specialist committees, within which many MEPs become expert in their chosen fields. The Parliament and its committees lobby both the commission and COREPER, and scrutinise legislative proposals passed down from the Council. Significantly, the TEU created the so-called *co-decision procedure* which gave the Parliament the right to a third reading for certain laws under consideration in the Council. This role was significantly extended by the Treaty of Amsterdam (1999) giving the Parliament 'equal standing with the Council of the European Union on deciding which laws will be enacted and which will not' (McCormick, 2002:105). The Parliament also has significant powers over the budget of the Commission, and over the appointment and conduct of the College of Commissioners. In 1999 it succeeded in forcing the resignation of the Santer Commission over allegations of nepotism and mismanagement against two of its members.

In October 2004 the Parliament vetoed the new Commission proposed by its President José Manuel Barroso. This was portrayed in some quarters as evidence of the EU in chaos, but can more plausibly be interpreted as an example of the democratic will of the elected European Parliament asserting its authority over the unelected Commission. The rejection was a rebuke, not only to the Commission, but also to the member-state governments, and that of the Italian Premier Silvio Berlusconi in particular, since the Parliament's chief complaint was against his nominee, Rocco Buttiglione.

The Parliament is generally deemed to be a supranational institution, but the term is a bit of a misnomer because it is not able to impose policy on the member states: that competence is reserved to the Council, the Commission and the ECJ. Also, the Parliament has direct links to national governments and more significantly to local regions in the shape of the constituencies that the MEPs represent. Unfortunately, participation in EP elections is low at 44 per cent in 2004, which, however, is not significantly lower than for US Congressional elections. The reasons for this probably include the extent to which the work of the Parliament is little understood by electorates, its perceived lack of formal powers, and the fact that its work fails to generate much media interest – except in reporting the huge waste of money resulting from its operating from three cities: committees meet in Brussels where there are also occasional plenary sessions, the administrative headquarters are in Luxembourg, while the assembly is in Strasbourg. France has consistently blocked any attempts to relocate the assembly to Brussels, a move that would save both time and money. Scully (2003:176–7) reports that voter apathy and lack of awareness concerning the EP's role risks undermining its legitimacy, despite the fact that it has become a far more significant player, especially in terms of co-decision with the Council. Scully writes that gaining wider public acceptance, rather than more powers, would appear to be the current priority for the Parliament.

The Community Courts are the **European Court of Justice** (ECJ) and the Court of First Instance (CFI). Their task is to uphold Community law and to investigate any possible breaches of the treaties or the spirit of the Union by the EU institutions themselves. The courts have a clearly European-level brief, and are impartial where national interests are concerned, thus they are the most

Table 4.1 Institutions of the European Union: the beginnings of a political community

EU Institutions	Responsibilities	Location
European Commission	Initiating, administrating, and overseeing the implementation of EU policies and legislation	Brussels and Luxembourg
European Parliament	Directly elected representatives of EU citizens, scrutinising the operation of the other institutions and, in certain areas, sharing with the Council the power to determine EU legislation	Strasbourg (plenary sessions) Brussels (MEP offices, committee meetings and some plenary sessions) Luxembourg (administration)
Council of the European Union (formerly Council of Ministers)	Representing the views of national governments and determining, in many areas jointly with the EP, the ultimate shape of EU legislation	Brussels (some meetings in Luxembourg)
European Council	Regular summits of Heads of State and Government, setting the EU's broad agenda and a forum of last resort to find agreement on divisive issues (NB *not* the Council of Europe)	City in the member state holding the Presidency
European Court of Justice	The EU's highest court, ruling in disputes on matters of EU law between member states and EU institutions, as well as providing preliminary rulings on request from national courts in cases involving private persons (NB: *not* European Court of Human Rights)	Luxembourg
European Court of First Instance	Subsidiary court to ECJ. Sifts cases and rules on uncontroversial breaches of EU law, or rejects appeals to the court. Refers other cases to ECJ	Luxembourg
European Central Bank	Central bank responsible for setting the interest rates and controlling the money supply of the single European currency, the euro	Frankfurt/M
Committee of the Regions	Advisory committee of 317 members representing the interests of local and regional authorities in the EU	Brussels
Economic and Social Committee	Advisory committee of 317 members representing the interests of labour, employers and consumer organisations in the EU	Brussels
Court of Auditors	The EU's audit office, responsible for auditing revenues and expenditure under the EU budget	Luxembourg

Source: box 23.8 (p. 502) from 'European and regional integration' by Thomas Christiansen from *The Globalization of World Politics* 2E (2001) edited by Baylis, J. & Smith, S. Reprinted by permission of Oxford University Press.

unequivocally supranational of all EU institutions. The ECJ is the most important court. It investigates and pronounces judgment, as well as imposes penalties on those who transgress EU law or fail to enforce binding legislation. It has competence mainly within European Community law (Pillar I) and the enforcement of EU treaties. The court consists of 25 judges and eight advocates general. An advocate general is assigned to a particular case and gives an initial opinion to the ECJ on the merits or likely outcome of a case. As well as the application of Community law by states and other actors, such as companies and organisations, the ECJ is responsible for enforcing correct adherence to the treaties and the spirit of the Union by EU institutions themselves. This includes powers to enforce an action for annulment, which enables both the ECJ and the Court of First Instance to review the legality of binding Community acts (Arnull, 2003: 188). In addition, the ECJ provides advice to national courts on the application of EC law. The Court oversees the work of the CFI which gives preliminary judgments and following the Treaty of Nice is likely to have its caseload increased to relieve pressures on the ECJ. Arnull (2003:190) describes the excessive workload of the European courts and indicates that the judicial architecture of the Union is likely to undergo changes, especially following the 2004 enlargement, including the appointment of more judges and a more streamlined system for filtering appeals to the courts. While the ECJ has 25 judges, in the interests of efficiency it is able to sit as a 'Grand Chamtor' of 11, rather than in a plenary session of 25.

Table 4.1 summarises the main responsibilities of the leading EU institutions.

Review	*What are the main functions of the EU institutions? Explain the extent to which each institution can be described as intergovernmental or supranational.* *What are directives and regulations?*

Policy making in the European Union

Let us turn now to a brief overview of policy making in the EU. Policies are created through a complex process of negotiation within and between a variety of institutions and actors both inside and outside the formal structures of the Union. Perhaps the best way to gain an understanding of what happens is to first have an overview of the roles of the institutions involved and then look at the processes themselves in more detail. Figure 4.2 shows a simple overview of the core EU institutions, their functions in respect of policy making, and the relationships between them.

There are three legislative procedures in the EC pillar (Pillar I): co-decision procedure, the assent procedure and the consultation procedure (Cini, 2003:5). Co-decision is the most common, and works as follows: the Commission initiates policy and draws up proposed legislation. This is sent to the Parliament and the Council for debate. Both Parliamentary Committees and Council representation scrutinise proposals and provide detailed responses. The role of the Parliament, enhanced by the Treaty of Amsterdam, is thus one of co-legislator with the Council (Dinan, 1999:285–6; Cini, 2003:5). The Parliament and the Council may act as conduits for the views of the extensive lobbying and information services in Brussels, as well as opinion from other EU institutions such as the Economic and Social Committee and the Committee of the Regions. Parliament and the Council may point out the advantages and disadvantages of the legislation. The Commission then draws up final drafts before passing the legislation back to the Council and the Parliament for a second reading.

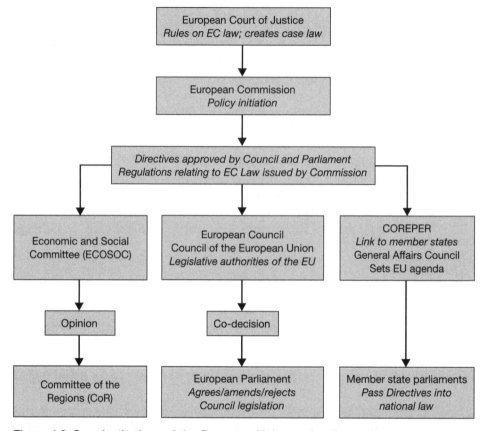

Figure 4.2 Core institutions of the European Union and policy-making functions

If the two institutions cannot agree, a 'conciliation committee' is set up. This includes representatives from both the Council and the Parliament, and also from the Commission. Once this body hammers out an agreement, the proposal is sent to the Council and Parliament for a third reading. Figure 4.3 provides a more detailed account of how co-decision works.

COREPER is also required to deliver a verdict on the political implications and practicalities of legislative proposals. Decisions taken within the Council are normally by unanimity, simple majority or by qualified majority voting (QMV). Most legislation emanating from Brussels is in the form of directives. The Commission usually sets a deadline for the implementation of the legislation by member state parliaments.

Assent procedure was introduced by the SEA in 1986 and involves the Parliament agreeing to a policy decision from the Council. The Parliament can say 'yes' or 'no' but cannot table amendments. Assent is used only in a few policy areas, such as enlargement and international agreements.

Consultation procedure is the original format outlined in the Treaty of Rome, but successive treaty amendments have increased the involvement of the Parliament and so only very few areas remain where the limited intervention of the Parliament known as 'consultation' still applies. Here the Parliament is

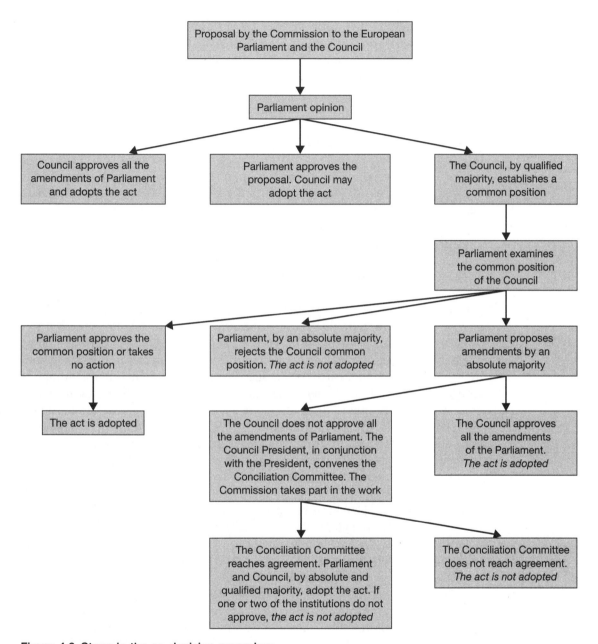

Figure 4.3 Steps in the co-decision procedure

Source: figure 1.1 (p. 6) from 'Introduction' by M. Cini from *European Politics* (2003) by Cini, M. Reprinted by permission of Oxford University Press.

consulted on Commission proposals before the Council takes a decision. The Commission may amend a proposal in the light of Parliament's opinion, before the Council amends, adopts or rejects the measure. A rejection has to be unanimous. Consultation procedure only applies 'to a small number of policy areas over which national governments are reluctant to cede control (Dinan, 1999:281).

QMV applies in votes taken by the Council, with unanimity required for particularly sensitive or constitutional matters such as treaty changes or enlargement. Unanimity also applies in Pillars II and III, with a few minor exceptions (Cini, 2003:5). Decision-making procedures in respect of Common Foreign and Security Policy (CFSP) and police and judicial cooperation in criminal matters (PJCCM) are essentially intergovernmental and subject to unanimity in the Council.

Finally, it is also important to recognise that the procedures that create EC/EU legislation are complex, and involve much detailed work by several EU institutions, including ones barely touched upon in this account. An indication of this is given by Figure 4.4, which describes the decision-making process for trade agreements. The picture demonstrates the complex flow of opinion and assessment within and between a wide variety of institutions and actors from the Commission through to member states.

Even this diagrammatic representation of the process is necessarily simplified, as there are many other actors who impact on the process. They may include a range of industry representatives, employer and employee groups, professional bodies and single issue pressure groups. Many major international non-governmental organisations (NGOs) have offices in Brussels. All of these various interests function at different levels, local, national and European, using a range of channels. They are engaged in a complex matrix of communication, and in many cases the information supplied by these external interest groups is vital to the framing of efficient and constructive legislative acts. Input of this kind is especially important at the early stages of drafting and most interest groups would seek to learn at the earliest opportunity about likely initiatives in their area(s) of interest. Informal communication channels are commonly used to signal intentions and assess opinion. (For more on lobbying and interest groups, see Greenwood, 1997; Mazey & Richardson, 1993).

From this brief description of the legislative procedure, one can see that the machinery of law making is a complex of intergovernmental and supranational involvement, but ultimately the laws are made by the Council, with in the majority of cases the Parliament having a role as co-legislator. The Council is *primarily* an intergovernmental institution representing state interests. The implementation of legislation is a member state responsibility.

It is hard to reconcile this description with the usual characterisation of 'faceless Brussels bureaucrats' forcing laws onto defenceless populations. The Commission in particular is lampooned almost daily by certain British newspapers. Unfortunately it is easier for the media to engage in defamatory propaganda than it is for them to explain complex processes to readers who are not interested. Negative and distorted reporting has a corrosive effect, but if the result is that the population becomes increasingly hostile to the EU and all things European, then the proprietors of the newspapers are satisfied (see Discussion 4.4).

This review of the decision-making procedure provides a snapshot of the relative roles of European-level institutions in policy making. However, it is also instructive to examine policy implementation to gain a perspective on the

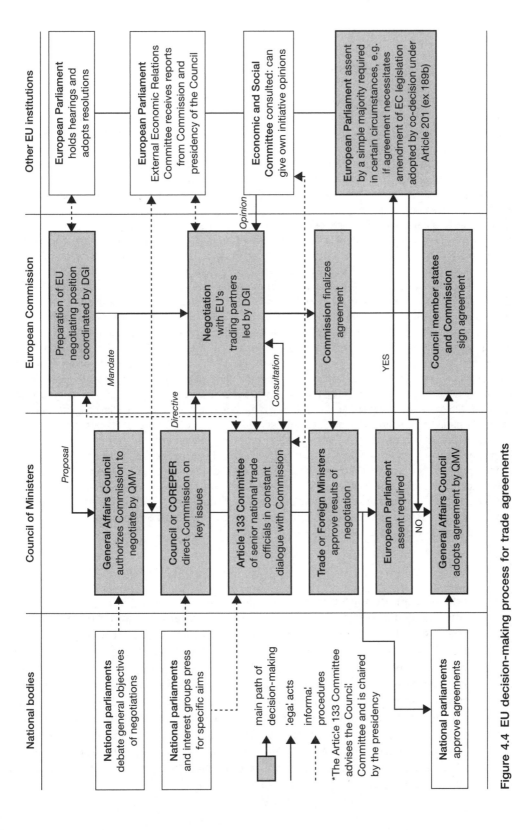

Figure 4.4 EU decision-making process for trade agreements

Source: figure 14.1 (p. 378) from chapter by Stephen Woolcock from *Policy Making in the European Union* (2000) edited by Wallace, H. & Wallace, W. Reprinted by permission of Oxford University Press.

Discussion 4.4

The Commission v. the Council – the stability and growth pact

In 2003 the European Commission ruled that France and Germany were in breach of the stability and growth pact set up as a framework for the smooth running of the euro under EMU. The pact was established as part of the TEU and its terms were agreed by the Council, specifically through Ecofin, the Council composed of EU finance ministers. The pact sets rules concerning borrowing and fiscal deficit, limiting states' annual borrowing requirement – or deficit – to no more than 3 per cent of GDP. Germany and France both exceeded this limit in 2003, which was embarrassing for them and for the Union, since it was France and Germany that had most vociferously insisted on the need for such a limit, apparently to restrain more profligate smaller economies, as well as the notoriously lax Italians, from jeopardising the stability of the entire euro area by running up big deficits.

In fact, Germany argued that its continuing difficulties in coming to terms with reunification should allow for German exceptionalism where the pact was concerned. France argued that specific cultural and structural issues demanded extra flexibility from the pact.

Under the terms of the pact, the Commission, on the advice of the Council, could fine member states that breached the limits imposed. However, the Council of Ministers opted not to impose any penalties on the offending governments. This was seen as a further example of the states asserting their authority over the Commission. However, the Commission took the case to the European Court of Justice. On 13 July 2004 the ECJ ruled that the Council was in breach of EC law in not imposing fines on France and Germany.

The judgment can be interpreted in one of two ways. Firstly, while it does not mean that France and Germany will actually be fined, it is a moral victory for the Commission and is likely to exert pressure on states to abide by the rules laid down for the operation of the euro in future. This could help to build credibility in the euro and enhance the standing of the ECB. The stability and growth pact is due for revision in early 2005, and it is widely expected that it will allow for greater flexibility in future.

A second interpretation is that the decision shows how the Union interferes in states' freedom of action and that the supranational organs of the Union (Commission, ECJ, ECB) take precedence over sovereign states' competence in running their own economies according to their individual circumstances.

Both interpretations are correct, although the ECJ is merely ruling that the states should adhere to the rules that they themselves have agreed. No one should be under any illusions that adopting the euro involves passing a very substantial measure of control over currency management and fiscal policy to the ECB.

effectiveness of European-agreed legislation. The Single European Market is often lauded as one of the Union's central achievements, and indeed, following the SEA of 1986, the Community set 1992 as the target for the 'completion' of the SEM. However, the ambitions of the SEM have not quite squared with reality. Thus the Lisbon Summit in 2000 set further targets that would enable the Union to 'become the world's most competitive and dynamic knowledge-based economy by 2010' (*Financial Times*, 22 January 2004). The *Financial Times* points out that new targets agreed in Lisbon were behind schedule four years later, and that in various respects the Single Market was still incomplete. The newspaper cited a European Commission study deploring the failure on the part of member states to implement an extraordinary 40 per cent of SEM legislation (Parker, 2004).

The implications of such an assessment are significant not only for the European economy – lack of full integration is seen as a partial explanation for poor economic growth – but also the politics of how the EU operates. This chapter has examined the institutional balance in the EU and also the balance of power between EU institutions and the member states. The SEM is one of the central features of European integration and widely understood as one of the Union's core achievements. But the states are clearly stymieing the Commission which, as we have seen, has a key role in monitoring the implementation of EU/EC directives. Indeed, the report just referred to is part of that monitoring process, but what it highlights is that the Commission, and effectively the Union, is a prisoner of the political will of the states. Implementation and enforcement is primarily a state responsibility. The *Financial Times* rates as 'good' the performance of only five states in raising competitiveness through the implementation and enforcement of EU law – the UK, the Netherlands, Denmark, Austria and Luxembourg – while four are rated as poor: Italy, Spain, Portugal and Greece (Parker, ibid.).

Review   *How is EU legislation created? Where does power appear to be primarily located? How does this relate to the implementation of policy?*

Summary

This chapter has made the following key points.

Pooling sovereignty

- States pool or share sovereignty where it is believed cooperation is more likely to achieve desired outcomes than acting alone.
- The creation of the SEM and EMU offers significant examples of pooling sovereignty; in both instances participating states judged that cooperation would best serve their interests, especially in the light of economic competition in an increasingly global trading environment.

Institutions

- Cooperation between national governments has created significant integration involving supranational institutions and policy instruments, especially in Pillar I, the European Community pillar.
- EU institutions may be described in approximate terms as supranational (Commission, Parliament, Courts) or intergovernmental (European Council, Council of the European Union) but in reality the distinction is not as clear-cut as traditional interpretations of the EU and its institutions would imply.

- The European Commission is the 'guardian of the treaties', and is responsible for the administration of the Union and has a key role in the legislative process as it initiates and draws up policy proposals.
- The European Council, composed of member-state heads of government (or heads of state for France and Finland), is the driving force of new treaties and treaty amendments, for which unanimity is required. Such major initiatives require an intergovernmental conference (IGC), a special meeting of the European Council.
- The Council is also the prime actor in EU foreign and security matters; it is a intergovernmental institution.
- The Council of the European Union consists of many councils responsible for a wide range of policy areas; it is the primary law-making institution; most legislative measures are directives which are passed into national law by national parliaments; regulations issued by the Council are immediately binding and do not need to be channelled through national parliaments.
- The European Court of Justice and the Court of First Instance are responsible for investigating possible breaches of the treaties and of European Community (Pillar I) law; they are supranational institutions and both suffer from an excessive caseload.

Policy making

- The Commission proposes and drafts legislation; the Council of the European Union and the European Parliament, who are co-legislators, amend, reject or approve legislative measures; the Council signs off legislation.
- There are in addition to the formal institutions of the EU many other public, private and NGO organisations that influence policy formulation; these work at a regional and national as well as European level.
- Policy implementation, primarily a member-state responsibility, is incomplete; even in respect of the SEM, many states do not meet the commitments they have agreed to.
- The advent of Economic and Monetary Union passes substantial control over monetary and fiscal policy to the ECB, although individual currencies outside the euro zone may also be subject to forces that are beyond the control of their governments.

Key concepts: discussion and other definitions

Key concept 4.1   Intergovernmentalism

An approach to policy making based on the principle of negotiation between one or more sovereign states pursuing their individual interests but tending towards cooperation to common advantage.

> A theory of European integration which privileges the role of states (Cini, 2003:419).

Intergovernmentalism, like its antithesis supranationalism, refers to a process by which power is exercised in decision-making processes within multinational organisations. Intergovernmentalism means *between governments* of member states, indicating a government-to-government decision-making process, although it may involve a multilateral negotiation, not just bilateral one, or a combination of several such negotiations.

Here is another definition of intergovernmentalism:

> both a theory of integration and a term used to describe institutional arrangements and decision-making procedures that allow governments to co-operate in specific fields while retaining their sovereignty (Bainbridge, 2002:329).

Intergovernmentalism by definition limits supranationalism and is therefore the opposite of **federalism**. Nevertheless, 'it may be in states' interests to share or pool sovereignty and to delegate it to European institutions' (Cini, 2003:97).

Moravcsik proposed an important variant on intergovernmentalism. He examined the intergovernmental bargaining processes that led to the establishment of the Single European Act (SEA) and formed his theory of Liberal Intergovernmentalism (LI). However, Moravcsik subsequently modified his stance and declared that his formulation was less than a theory, but was instead a description of policy process, applicable in some instances of EU policy making, albeit important ones (Moravcsik, 2001).

Intergovernmentalist preferences imply that policy processes in the EU should be overwhelmingly controlled by national governments. Historically, the Council of the European Union has represented state interests and thus consistently manifested an intergovernmental approach to deliberating and approving policy. Intergovernmentalism implies that states should be able to veto policy proposals they did not agree with, a point which the French government under de Gaulle pursued to the point of withdrawing from the Council for six months in 1965. De Gaulle stood out for the right of veto where 'national interests' were at stake, and on this basis France returned to the Council in January 1966 following the so-called Luxembourg Compromise which approved the right of veto to member states. De Gaulle spoke of *L'Europe des patries*, a phrase which has resonated well with nationalist politicians ever since, and the current French President, Chirac, has called for a 'Union of states' which implies much the same thing. Even Joscher Fischer, the German Foreign Minister and member of the Green Party, who is far more federally inclined, has spoken of a 'confederation of states'. All these nuances imply a pre-eminent role for states and a weakening of supranational tendencies. Margaret Thatcher, naturally, went further than even de Gaulle, claiming in a BBC Radio interview that there was 'no such thing as a Community interest', since society was made up of individuals, and did not contain communities. This bizarre and depressing view of human nature is often recalled, but most intergovernmental viewpoints do not go quite this far.

Indeed, eurosceptics appear happier with participation in more overtly intergovernmental organisations than the EU. One example of such is the Council of Europe, where member-state governments act independently without being subjected to any higher authority. The Council of Europe, founded in 1949, is a debating forum in which governments talk to other governments, and there is little by way of policy implementation, and no formal legislation. The Council of Europe did have an important advisory role in CEECs following the collapse of communist regimes in 1989–90. In addition the Council of Europe established the European Court of Human Rights which drew up the European Convention on Human Rights. This has been incorporated into European Union law through the Treaty of Nice in 2001.

NATO, the WTO and the UN are all intergovernmental organisations, with significantly less complex structures than the EU, which as we have seen is a hybrid organisation, partly intergovernmental and partly supranational.

Key concept 4.2   Supranationalism

An approach to policy making and enforcement through which a higher authority can enforce legislation and determine policy practice in those states which are bound by its legal framework.

Supranationalism applies to decision-making that is *above the level of the state* and it produces decisions that are binding on state governments. It implies the imposition of authority from above. Clearly supranational governance presents a major challenge to sovereignty, since definitions of sovereignty usually include reference to there being 'no higher power' (Weber, 2001:14).

> That is what it means to be sovereign – for a state to have absolute authority over its territory and people and to have independence internationally (Weber, ibid.).

Walker (see Chapter 1) argues that sovereignty is reduced by participation in international organisations and Bainbridge cites the European Union as a specific example (Bainbridge, 2002:478–9). McCormick (2002:10) argues that this is not the case, since sovereignty in a democracy rests not so much with governments but with the people who elect the legislature and that in reality sovereignty has not been lost, but 'redistributed'. This smacks of sophistry and it seems evident that while it is true that pooling or merging sovereignty redistributes it, there is also little doubt that the European Union has built up a body of power that once rested with the states but now lies very definitely with EU institutions. Walker argues that the discussion is academic: sovereignty has diminished even more than it has been redistributed. He says that governments' ability to shape domestic economic policy is restricted by global markets, a view shared by Strange (1996) and Monbiot (2000). This seems consistent with experience: as governments have lost power over economic policy, various other actors have assumed those powers, from currency speculators, to large investment houses and multinational corporations. If Nissan decides to close down a car plant in Sunderland in the UK's north-east, 2,000 employees and countless support industry workers lose their livelihoods. The entire city and region would be massively affected. There is nothing a UK government minister can do to prevent such a choice. Similarly, when George Soros decided to cut and run on his sterling investments in 1992, his actions contributed to the massive fall in the value of the pound.

The TEU produced something of a dog's breakfast in terms of clarifying the relative ascendancy of either intergovernmentalism or supranationalism, and required revision through the Treaty of Amsterdam (ToA) in 1997. In the TEU, Pillar I enhanced supranational policy making, especially by increasing the use of QMV. The EMU protocol, attached to the treaty as a device to permit the British, Danish and Swedish opt-outs, also signalled a major advance for the federalist, or supranational cause. However, the ambition to create a political community to accompany the economic one in Pillar I was shelved in favour of the Pillar II and Pillar III architecture, both of which implied a form of intergovernmental ring-fencing. The compromise, together with the innovation of opt-outs, helped to buy off nationalist governments like that of John Major's UK Conservative Party. But in fact, post-Maastricht, the fears of eurosceptic opponents of the TEU have been more or less confirmed as the intergovernmental nature of Pillar III in particular has come under sustained attack. The ToA moved various aspects of JHA into Pillar I.

Different international organisations have different impacts on sovereignty. As its detractors ceaselessly complain, the EU has had huge implications for sovereignty. They do, however, appear to ignore other respects in which sovereignty has been compromised, especially in relation to the management of the economy, but also in the domain of security.

Walker comments on the limitations placed on states by treaty obligations and nuclear caution, or the fear of retaliation (Walker, 1994). This may be so, but in the context of NATO it is reasonable to point out that a fundamental right of a sovereign state is the freedom to engage in treaties. One can hardly argue the tautology that to use this fundamental right is to give up sovereignty. NATO remains an intergovernmental organisation where states sign up voluntarily and can leave if they no longer wish to be part of the club, or reject the responsibilities associated with membership.

Further reading

Cini, M. (ed.) (2003) *European Union Politics*, Oxford: Oxford University Press. This outstanding collection provides comprehensive descriptions of key aspects of EU institutional form and policies and processes. See in particular Part III, Institutions and actors, containing five chapters on the main institutions of the EU. This book has frequently referred to these chapters.

Jones, R.A. (2001) *The Politics & Economics of the European Union*, Cheltenham: Edward Elgar. This is a particularly good and very comprehensive book on the European Union, with a particular emphasis on major policy areas. See Chapter 5, 'Institutions and Policy Processes', pp. 105–181, for an excellent description of the institutions of the Union.

McCormick, J. (2002) *Understanding the European Union*, Basingstoke: Palgrave. A short book that serves as an excellent introduction to the EU, it contains a single chapter (pp. 84–114) on 'The Institutions of the EU'.

Milward, A. (2000) *The European Rescue of the Nation State*, London: Routledge. As the title indicates, Milward's contention is that the process of integration has ensured the survival and prosperity of the states involved. He claims that the motivation for integration is the desire to ensure that Europe could maintain a good standard of welfare support for its citizens. Thus the CAP is based on the notion of supporting the way of life of farmers and rural populations. The entire integration process is geared towards sustaining the European social welfare model and is in marked contrast to the free market-oriented *laissez faire* preferences of the USA. This is a fascinating though detailed and challenging read. In many respects it is a seminal work on the European integration process.

Moravcsik, A. (1999) *The Choice for Europe*, University College London. Moravcsik contends that European nation states pooled sovereignty in a conscious attempt to realise benefits through the Single Market that they judged less achievable if they pursued them separately. Moravcsik's contention is that the Single European Act and the Single European Market emerged from a long process of intergovernmental bargaining that was understood to be in everyone's mutual interest. A significant driving force behind this process was pressure from European business. The book is the clearest presentation of Moravcsik's theory of liberal intergovernmentalism, which he presents less as a theory of European integration than as a description of policy-making procedures in key areas, specifically in respect of the SEA and the SEM.

Nicol, W. & **Salmon**, T. (2001) *Understanding the European Union*, Harlow: Addison Wesley Longman. Part 2 'The Institutions of the European Union', pp. 79–171, is another excellent survey of EU institutions.

Nugent, N. (2000) *The European Commission*, Basingstoke: Palgrave. Probably the best recent study of the Commission.

Peterson, J. & **Bomberg**, E. (1999) *Decision Making in the European Union*, Basingstoke: Macmillan. A detailed research-based study of policy-making processes in the Council.

Films

To this author's knowledge, no film yet exists on policy making, or even whistle-blowing, inside the EU.

Chapter 5

Integration theory and the state

Outline

- Destinations: federalism and confederalism
- Theories of integration: functionalism, neo-functionalism and intergovernmentalism
- Other theories of European integration
- Conclusion

Key concepts

5.1 Federalism

5.2 Neo-functionalism

● ● ● ● Introduction

This chapter is concerned with the principal theories of European integration. Understanding these theories can be helpful in considering the prospects for more integrated regional structures in other areas of the world, especially in the context of accelerating pressures from globalisation. We shall return to this later in the book. Here the emphasis is firmly on the European experience.

We have seen that the process of European integration began after the Second World War, and was set in train by the vision of a handful of eminent Europeans, among them Winston Churchill, Jean Monnet, Robert Schuman, Alcide de Gasperi, Paul-Henri Spaak and Konrad Adenauer. Monnet espoused an 'incrementalist' approach to European integration (Jones, 2001:46), but there has always been and remains support for a federal Europe. Monnet's genius was in recognising that a sudden rush towards federal institution building would probably fail, but that a more gradual approach might get there in the end anyway. Monnet is often referred to as the 'father of Europe', or more accurately, as McLean and McMillan (2003:353) point out, of the European Union.

A consistent theme throughout the chapter is the relationship of European integration to the state and the vexed issue of sovereignty. The chapter explores two possible destinations of an integration process, federalism and confederalism.

Then it examines different approaches to achieving unity, namely functionalism, neo-functionalism and intergovernmentalism. These are presented as theories of integration. Finally there is a brief survey of some more recent perspectives, among them normative and institutional, and bureaucratic policy-based approaches, and multilevel governance (MLG). In thinking about these different theoretical approaches, it is helpful to assess the extent to which they reflect intergovernmental or supranational tendencies to governance in the context of Europe.

Historically integration theory has tended to focus on 'grand theories' – an attempt to produce an overarching explanation for how European integration has occurred. This usually involved comparing and contrasting federalism with functionalism and evolved into a neo-functionalist description. Such an approach no longer seems especially fruitful. It tends to oversimplify the history, producing at times facile judgements about what was/is intergovernmental and what was/is supranational. As the previous chapter showed, while an intergovernmental approach predominates in the Council, supranationalist tendencies are important as well even in those supposedly ring-fenced areas of intergovernmental bargaining. Likewise, in the Commission there is evidence of pushing national, as opposed to European or Community preferences.

As well as these institutional complexities, there are historical changes as well. European integration has not proceeded in a regular and uniform manner (see Chapter 3). Trends have shifted depending on circumstances and personalities. Initiatives have been driven by external pressures for peace, for trade and competitiveness, for stability within the region, or in response to the geopolitical or strategic environment. A largely unforeseen event such as German reunification, for example, created a much stronger motivation, not least among German political elites, for more integration both through an extension of EU **competences** and a deepening of institutional integration. More integration or less integration has often depended on the personalities involved. The 'ever closer union' has made its most significant advances under the influence of visionary and powerful personalities, or combinations of two or three such figures being around at the same time, such as Delors, Mitterrand and Kohl in the late 1980s and early 1990s. In contrast, de Gaulle in the 1960s stalled deeper integration.

In place of grand theories, then, in recent years, as Rosamond (2000, 2003) has made clear, a more nuanced approach is more accurate.

The chapter ends with the conclusion that the integration process followed a broadly neo-functional, gradualist approach in its early years, stalled in the 1960s and 70s, before switching towards intergovernmentalism in the 1980s. Since then it has become increasingly evident that policy making is the result of a complex range of different interrelated pressures. Although over 50 years have elapsed since Jean Monnet drew up plans for the European Coal and Steel Community as the first step towards a federal Europe, the EU remains some way distant from being a fully federal system. Perhaps the sceptics should relax: it looks unlikely to become one.

© Bettmann/Corbis

Photograph 5.1 Jean Monnet (1888–1979), the architect of the Schuman Plan which formed the blueprint for the European Coal and Steel Community in 1951. Monnet is sometimes referred to as the 'father of the European Union'.

● ● ● ● Destinations: federalism and confederalism

Federalists favour the creation of a political community founded on strong constitutional and institutional frameworks. Burgess (2003:66) says that a 'federal Europe' refers to:

> a conception of the EU that is constantly changing, but which has at its core a set of basic principles or assumptions that indicate a voluntary union of states and citizens committed to the shared goals of welfare, security and prosperity, and which is structured in a manner which is specifically designed to preserve nation states' identities, cultures and interests, where these are consistent with the overall well-being of the union (Burgess, 2003:ibid.).

Burgess interprets this as 'common solutions to common problems', with the broad conception being 'unity in diversity'. Critical to the construction of the EU is that membership is voluntary and 'based on political consent and legal agreement' (Burgess, ibid.). He also refers to the moral basis in **federalism**, being rooted in a set of values and beliefs that intrinsically reflect a moral imperative, drawing on the conviction to work for the common good. There is a basic principle of reconciliation of the interests of individual parts to the totality of the union or state (Burgess, 2003:67).

However, according to McDonald and Dearden, a federal body politic requires institutional innovation:

> [a federation has] supranational powers that take precedence over the powers of member states. Therefore, achieving European unity is seen as requiring the creation of new federal structures (McDonald and Dearden, 1999:4–5).

Indeed, federalists favour major constitutional changes to bring about a supranational framework in which states are left with only very limited powers. A federal politic normally involves

> authority being dispersed into two or more levels of government . . . a division of authority between central and regional or state government (Rosamond, 2000:24).

But Rosamond highlights weaknesses in federalist governance that tend to undermine public acceptance and thus legitimacy:

> The advantage of nation states is that they have a very powerful claim on the loyalties of peoples and in many respects constitute viable political communities in ways that powerfully federated communities cannot (Rosamond, 2000:30).

Indeed for some, European integration has always been scary, and Rosamond points out a further danger that follows from a projection of federalist logic. Federalism can lead to wider **regionalisation** which may

> [lead] in some eyes, to an Orwellian nightmare of interregional rivalries as 'superstates' reproduce the flaws of a state-based international system – but on a bigger scale (Rosamond, ibid.).

Federalism espouses a fully-fledged government with its own parliament. The government of a federation has direct control over key areas of policy, but permits regional or local authorities to determine policy in other areas. The USA and the Federal Republic of Germany are federal unions with a clearly constitutionally defined separation of powers between the federal (central) government and the states/*Länder*. The logical outcome in Europe to a federalist agenda is the creation of a United States of Europe, with a central government possessing supranational authority over the territory and the citizens living within the territory. It would, however, allow member states and sub-national regions to retain competence or authority in certain designated policy areas. The inclusion in the Treaty on European Union of a commitment to the principle of **subsidiarity** is consistent with this approach. Subsidiarity aims to have decisions made at the lowest practicable level between Union, member state, regional and local government. Federalism also implies a constitutional settlement, formally described in a written constitution, and a set of institutions with designated responsibilities. The federal system of government delegates areas of governance to regional elements within the federation. In the case of a federal European Union these would be the member states and sub-national regions. Member-state governments and regional authorities would retain competence in specified areas. It is, however, likely that such a federalist agenda would extend the competence of the (central) supranational authorities far beyond the current Single European Market remit of the European Community pillar, perhaps including significant aspects of foreign and security policy, immigration, refugee and asylum policy, human rights, judicial and criminal matters, prisons and even policing, as well as taxation and social security. Such a vision has always been the worst of all horrors envisaged by the most dedicatedly anti-European Union sceptics. Napoleon could not have dreamt up anything worse.

The fears of eurosceptics are understandable. The phrase 'ever closer union' in the preamble to the Treaty of Rome is, in the eyes of opponents of the European federalist agenda, the clearest indication of federalist ambition. A curious side issue in the negotiations of the Maastricht Treaty was the evident delight of the British Prime Minister at securing the removal of the word 'federal' from an early draft of the Treaty. It was replaced by the phrase 'ever closer union' which, for some reason known only to himself, enabled Major to sleep more soundly. Many thought the phrase 'more centralist than the original formulation' (Rosamond, 2000:24). Indeed such confusion over terminology has been common. In the UK the emergent media and government interpretation of the word 'federal' has focused only on its centralising aspects (Jones, 2001:40). Burgess (2003:71) says British interpretations of the term reflect experience from the Empire, where the British applied federal ideas to the colonies, and as a consequence associate the experience with nation building, and link federalism to centralisation. In contrast, the usual understanding of the term on the continent, and especially where there is a greater federal tradition (for example, in Germany), has emphasised the division of authority and a more benign understanding of the concept. So federalism according to usual German interpretation represents:

> [a dispersal of] authority and power between the centre and the periphery, creating a political system which protects local autonomy in the absence of aristocracy (Siedentop, 2000:79).

Siedentop argues that federalism might seem

> [to be] 'the most natural form of the state' in so far as its defining characteristic is the resolve to leave to each locality and region enough authority and power to manage its own affairs, while carrying to the centre only enough authority and power to deal with matters of general interest (Siedentop, ibid., 94).

Siedentop describes federal government as a very complex and demanding form of government. It requires

> considerable moral and intellectual development . . . because [it] seeks to minimize the need for coercive power and to maximize willing obedience to laws, which are perceived to match local, regional and national interests (Siedentop, ibid.).

It is not surprising, as Burgess (2003) and others have pointed out, that given the centralised and unitary traditions of French and British democracies, a federal construction of the EU is not popular in these countries. De Gaulle used to trumpet the virtues of *L'Europe des patries* and successive British governments, especially Conservative ones – see for example Mrs Thatcher's Bruges speech attacking the federal vision of Jacques Delors (Thatcher, 1988:4; Young, 1991, 1999) – and aided by a press hostile to the EU, have for years railed against 'the

Brussels federalist agenda', often invoking the image of a 'super-state', although what this is supposed to entail, and whether it has anything in common with the EU's future direction, is never fully explained. There is, however, always an implication that somehow the EU is destroying not only the sovereignty of its member states, but also identities, as if with every directive approved in Brussels, Italians become less Italian and the French less French. In other circumstances a cynic might suggest that for newspapers not averse to voicing scarcely disguised xenophobia, such an outcome might be highly desirable.

However, despite Siedentop's soothing interpretations of the term federalism, and Major's delight at securing the change in wording in the Maastricht Treaty, many critics of further integration are concerned by the idea of federalism and the phrase 'ever closer union'. At what point, they ask, does the Union decide that integration has gone far enough? The answer is by no means clear. It is evident that since the Treaty of Paris in 1951 there has been gradual evolution towards the federal Europe described above. Sometimes described as a train, this train has hardly sped like a Japanese *Shinkansen* from Nagasaki in the south to Sapporo in the north with just a few stops to take on new passengers. This train has taken detours, stopped for repairs, sometimes gone into reverse, but mostly it has kept going and it has certainly taken on extra passengers. Table 1.2 and Discussions 3.4 and 3.6 summarise the main institutional steps of European integration.

Nevertheless, it would be wrong to characterise the EU as federal, and more wrong still a federal state. Jones (2001:39) says the EU is not a state of the Westphalian variety. It has a weak centre and does not have a central governing authority. Nevertheless, it does have some state-like features, including

a Union title, some supranational institutions, including an increasingly powerful Parliament, a Court of Justice and a seemingly ever widening range of common policies (Jones, 2001:41).

However, Jones goes on to describe many ways in which the EU is quite unlike a federation.

Firstly, the EU does not have a written constitution and is based on treaties negotiated by governments. Secondly, the power exercised by member states in EU decision-making has no parallel in any existing federation. For example, state governors in the US federal system are not key decision makers at central level. Nor, in contrast with EU governments, do they play any significant role in foreign and defence policy (Jones, 2001:41).

While the substance of Jones's position is correct, it should be noted that the EU may be close to having a written constitution, following the Brussels Council in June 2004 which agreed the text of the Constitutional Treaty, now subject to ratification by the member states. Furthermore, a mood change is apparent in recent years over the federal ambitions of the European Union. When the Single European Act was agreed in 1986, Jacques Delors was disappointed at its lack of federalist content. This is in spite of its central achievement in establishing the framework for the Single European Market comprising the four freedoms of movement for goods, services, people and capital, and the removal of physical and technical barriers to trade. The Act also extended Qualified Majority Voting

(QMV) in key areas. It is significant that even Margaret Thatcher pronounced satisfaction at the outcome although, as mentioned in the previous chapter, she later confessed to regret at signing the Act, ultimately judging it too federalist, especially in respect of QMV and the cooperation procedure which enhanced the role of the European Parliament. When the Treaty on European Union was agreed in Maastricht, the German Chancellor Helmut Kohl regretted that it lacked a stronger commitment to political union. He wanted foreign and security policy to be placed under the aegis of the Union, rather than pointedly left in the hands of member-state governments.

During negotiations, the British insistence on removing the word 'federal' from the text signalled a change in language that has endured to the present. Nowadays there is no Delors or Kohl advocating more federalism. Recent pronouncements have not only avoided any reference to the term federal, but there has been a concerted effort to highlight the role of member-state governments. The Treaties of Amsterdam and Nice are seen by Jones (2001) as reaffirming the centrality of member-state governments in decision-making, and represent a slowing down or even a reversal of the federalist ambition signalled in the Maastricht Treaty by the inclusion of a route map towards Economic and Monetary Union and the Single Currency. However, the tortuous negotiations over Maastricht are evident in the result: the three pillar architecture was a compromise. Pillar I represents the more federalist and supranational aspect of the treaty, with its additional protocols relating to EMU and social policy permitting opt-outs for those states unwilling to accept their inclusion in the main body of the treaty. In contrast, Pillars II and III signalled a reaction against the federalist ambition. These were decisively marked as domains of state or intergovernmental competence.

Nevertheless, the picture remains unclear. While Amsterdam and Nice signalled a strengthening of the intergovernmentalist position, the advent of the Single Currency and the strengthening of the social policy protocol agreed at Maastricht suggest that the federalist agenda has made progress as well. Current initiatives also send a variety of signals: enlargement indicates a widening of the Union, while a Constitutional Treaty, if ratified, would signal further, or deepening, political union. The mechanism by which the ECB operates, the Stability and Growth Pact, has been undermined by its primary architects, Germany and France. According to Hutton (2003) this sends worrying signals about the authority of the ECB and the European Commission, and the discipline required to maintain the viability of the infant currency. Further weakness of the Commission was demonstrated during 2003 in its failure to persuade France in particular – but tacitly supported by others – to accept substantial reform of the Common Agricultural Policy. As the Union enlarges, the viability of the current CAP regime is increasingly questioned, but ultimately its reform depends on the will of the member states to push for changes, if necessary by removing existing veto rights.

Finally, there is one other reason for the fading profile of federalism: it has become evident that not only have Europe's political elites lost enthusiasm for a federal outcome to the European project, it is also utterly apparent that electorates have no appetite for a more federalist European Union either. The last great shout for federalism may be Economic and Monetary Union and the euro. It is true that most Euroland populations have accepted the euro with a degree of equanimity, a Gallic shrug perhaps. Nowadays the currency is seen for what it is: a technicality, a means to buy things. But it is also a symbol of European unity. Most citizens in Euroland are happy enough with this outcome, but it does not indicate any general enthusiasm for greater federal ambitions. Discussion 5.1 shows the key features of a typical federal system.

The discussion above implies that there are forms of federalism that might be described as strong federalism, and others that are weak federalism. Indeed, federalism might be placed on such a continuum together with confederalism, which represents a more state-centric, intergovernmental alternative to federalism.

Confederalism might offer an alternative architecture for the EU. The clearest rendition of the EU as a confederation is Murray Forsyth's *Unions of States* (1981), in which the Union is portrayed as a 'voluntary association of states with a common interest in building larger markets' (Rosamond, 2000:148). Confederalism places the participating states in a flat matrix shape with the supranational and hierarchical aspect much less in evidence. The focus of decision-making and power rests with the states as sovereign members of the confederation. They may accept high levels of integration, and even some degree of supranational authority over the states, but the bulk of affairs are

---

Discussion 5.1

Key features of a federal system of government

A federal political system has a clear division of competence between the higher level federal government and the states or regions that are its constituent parts.

Federal/central government

Seat of sovereign state government

Central government institutions/National parliament or legislature

Administrative centre and higher courts

Policy areas: Sole responsibility for defence, national security, foreign policy, social welfare, policing, economic policy, currency control, legal system, national infrastructure.

Finance: Sets taxation levels, national budget and core areas of government spending.

Regional/local level (states/regions/*Länder*/*Comunidades Autonónomas*)

Local assembly/council/regional or local government offices

Responsibilities: Education, local transport, local services including leisure, street maintenance, refuse, health provision, emergency services, museums and parks.

Finance: Limited tax raising powers, responsible for local budget.

Examples of federal systems: USA, Federal Republic of Germany, Spain, Belgium, Switzerland.

managed at state level and negotiations and agreements are carried out intergovernmentally.

Thus the hallmarks of a confederal arrangement are its flat architecture and the egalitarian relationship between states that are locked in a kind of permanent negotiation. Secondly a confederal arrangement has a clearly intergovernmental character.

Confederalism involves a much looser relationship between the parts of a union. It is less binding, less regulated and has less direct impact on the citizens. Burgess says

> Confederation is [...] a form of union where the constituent units rather than the central authority remain the decisive force, and institutionalised diplomacy takes the place of federal government (Burgess, 2003:69).

Such an arrangement might at first sight appear likely to calm the fears of anti-federalists or eurosceptics. The difficulty is that in many respects the European Union, as presently constituted, is rather more federal than it is confederal. The Single Market aspects of EU governance are firmly in a federalist framework, and while the TEU placed CFSP and JHA in a confederal/intergovernmental structure, we have already seen how this is breaking down. There has been considerable encroachment by the EU into both these areas. For example, the EU has a Commissioner for External Affairs, Javier Solana, who in theory can appear as an EU spokesman on matters of CFSP. The fact that he has rarely done so has more to do with the divisions within the EU in matters of foreign policy than with any lack of ambition on the part of the Union, or even Mr Solana himself. Indeed the phrase CFSP implies an 'EU foreign policy', something that the UK in particular has always felt uneasy about.

Rosamond (2000:148–9) provides an interesting comment on confederalism based on work by Øhrgaard (1997). Øhrgaard describes the case of foreign policy coordination through the processes of European Political Cooperation (EPC). EPC originally arose outside the formal structure of the treaties and is an example of the supranational institutions of the EU playing no role whatsoever. Rosamond says that neo-functionalism cannot explain the emergence of the EPC and that Øhrgaard demonstrates that intergovernmental integration is in this context based around three processes of socialisation, cooperation and formalisation.

> Integration through socialisation becomes a precondition for the establishment of a sufficient level of trust. The level of trust allows for cooperation on the basis of upgrading common interests, which might eventually create a platform from which further formalisation – in scope or level – might be undertaken (Øhrgaard, 1997:18).

Rosamond points out that Øhrgaard's explanation places a lot of emphasis on the agency of states in setting these integrationary processes into action. It might be added that this kind of informal socialisation aspect to policy making has a long tradition in Brussels and is established practice at the biannual summit meetings of the European Council and in Council meetings, both of which are primarily intergovernmental forums. The contribution of informal socialisation and networking to all aspects of the integration process and the work of the EU should not be underestimated, and is also a significant aspect to the lobbying that goes on continually involving politicians and interest groups ranging from NGOs through to industry representatives and MNCs. Nevertheless, the confederal model is probably less likely to suit the objectives of external lobbyists and pressure groups because an advantage of a more hierarchical and clearly delineated structure is that it is easier to identify one's preferred target for lobbying. In some ways the more dispersed power and authority is, the more difficult it is to access.

While a confederal system might offer some attractions for those seeking to limit the trend towards greater supranationalism, there could be unforeseen consequences, such as less transparency rather than more, less efficient decision-making procedures, and a risk of institutional paralysis, especially in a Union of 25 member states. Certainly, these criticisms seem to fit with current concerns over 'democratic deficit', for example.

However, one might be tempted to assume that the intergovernmental dimension to the EU, especially through the Council and in Pillar II, implies a confederal union. But Burgess points out:

> the confederal dimension to the EU (the Council) is subject to a wide variety of federalist forces and influences at both the EU and member state levels, pressures that emanate from within both the Commission and the European Parliament (EP) at the EU level and from a host of interest groups, public organisations and civil associations at the member state level (Burgess, 2003:69).

Indeed, the case for arguing that the EU is more federal than confederal is summed up in the evolution from a 'Community' towards 'Union'. Burgess calls this development both a quantitative and a qualitative change. The Union has undertaken economic, social, political and legal change. There is plenty of evidence that political integration is developing strongly in the wake of decades of economic integration. The objective, says Burgess, is not just an economic one of promoting capital accumulation.

> Rather, European integration involves the construction of a viable, working political union founded upon peace, order, security and welfare. In short, the EU as a federal union is supposed to represent a new moral force for good in European and world affairs (Burgess, 2003:70).

Nevertheless, according to the description of federalism presented here, the EU is not a federation, nor necessarily a confederation. This is on account of its especially complex institutional design where there are clearly aspects that match a more federal description, while others correspond more closely to the principles of confederation. In order to unpack this more satisfactorily, it is necessary to go beyond the constraining prototypical formations of 'confederation' and 'federation' and look at the different approaches to unity that have contributed to the European project over time. That is the subject of the next section of this chapter.

In conclusion, we return to the notion that confederalism and federalism might be placed on a continuum between weak association and strong union.

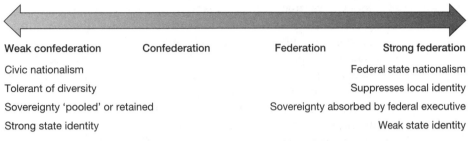

Figure 5.1 Confederation and federalism: a continuum between different integration goals

This idea is represented in Figure 5.1. The picture also attempts to link the federal/confederal relationship to the issues of sovereignty and nationalism discussed in Chapter 2. In it we see an association between extreme federalism and state nationalism, as well as a strong accumulation of sovereignty by the federal government at the expense of the constituent parts of the federation, the states. The USA offers an example of this, where throughout history there has been an attempt to create and maintain federal state identity – American-ness. On the other hand, confederalism privileges sovereignty at the state level and assumes a more tolerant civic nationalism. Sovereignty is retained on the basis of its being 'pooled', as discussed in Chapter 4 (Milward, 2000; Moravcsik, 1999).

Local or state identity is strongly preserved in a confederal polity, whereas in the federal arrangement the unifying federal identity is promoted at the expense of local identity. Such a project would seem ill-advised and utopian in the European context, where local identities are strong. It is on this basis that federalism presents such an unrealistic goal for those sympathetic to European integration and is so absolutely welcome to critics of the process. The European Union is a long way from being a strongly federal entity as represented at the polar end of Figure 5.1, or as demonstrated by the USA for example. This is not surprising: there remains a strong allegiance to the national identities of Europeans. The 'masses' undoubtedly provide a brake on the federal tendencies of elites engaged with the European project.

Review *Is the EU a federalist organisation? Give reasons for your answer.*
What are some disadvantages of a confederal arrangement in the context of the EU?

Theories of integration: functionalism, neo-functionalism and intergovernmentalism

Functionalism is based on the strategy of 'gradually undermining state sovereignty by encouraging technical co-operation in specific policy areas across state boundaries' (Jones, 2001:44). Referring to the founder of the functionalist school, David Mitrany, whose *A Working Peace System* was first published in 1943,

Jones says that functionalism opposes the creation of regional authorities, preferring a global approach, but is fundamentally flawed by its failure to take account of political realities. He cites UNESCO as an example of a body 'torn by political disputes' (Jones, ibid.). Functionalism describes 'a form of integration between states that is based upon practical cooperation in well-defined areas with a minimum of institutional apparatus' (Bainbridge, 2002:299). Functionalism, unlike federalism, does not overtly seek the creation of supranational institutions, preferring instead to aim for technical and pragmatic cooperation in defined policy areas. There is a distinction between political forces and 'economic, social and technical imperatives' (Bainbridge, ibid.). A consequence of the gradualist, incremental approach towards unity implied by functionalism is further integration.

However, in the context of European integration, it is **neo-functionalism**, an approach that evolved out of functionalism, that is much closer to offering an effective description of how European integration has evolved. As stated above, Jean Monnet reckoned that the gradualist approach implied in functionalism was more practical than an overtly federalist ambition from the start. But Monnet was not a functionalist. His interest clearly focused on Europe, and his blueprint for the ECSC did include a substantial measure of institutional innovation at a supranational level, in that the High Authority, which gestated into the European Commission by 1958, was central to the structure of the ECSC. Monnet's approach is better described as employing a gradual, incrementalist and neo-functional approach to integration.

Neo-functionalism involves states acquiring the habit of cooperation after which they are then prepared to extend that cooperation into other policy areas, a phenomenon known in the literature as **spillover** (Jones, 2001:45). This may lead to the creation of supranational institutions in order to provide some measure of control, transparency and legitimacy. Spillover may also lead to unintended consequences, as where political cooperation conducted with a specific policy goal in mind leads to the formation of new goals in order to secure the originally envisaged benefits. This also leads to cooperation being extended over time (Strøeby Jensen, 2003:84). Examples of this are the abolition of border controls through the Schengen Agreement influencing subsequent steps towards improved cooperation in cross-border policing and shared intelligence between national police forces, or the SEM eventually providing the impetus for EMU (though EMU had been signalled as early as 1970 by the Werner Report).

Neo-functionalism typically involves integration for those 'functional' activities of government such as trade rules where it is relatively easy to gain agreement. This is indeed where integration has advanced most. Such policy areas are sometimes referred to as 'low' politics, as opposed to the 'high' politics of security, defence and foreign policy, where national governments are traditionally more reluctant to surrender sovereignty. Thus:

> Neo-functionalists argue that, as functional areas of government are integrated, the political and bureaucratic elite that handles these policies will increasingly switch their loyalties, expectations and goals from the national government arena to the overall aims of the integration agencies. In this scenario a functionalist approach would

gradually move towards the goals of European political integration (McDonald & Dearden, 1999:4).

Neo-functionalists tend to adopt functional methods, including spillover, in order to achieve federalist objectives (Bainbridge, 2002:299). Neo-functionalism has been highly successful in the European context, in that it has achieved high levels of both economic and political integration. It is characterised by an incremental approach to integration, favoured by both the architects of European integration and by the majority of policy makers that have come after them.

The neo-functionalist approach is based on the work of the American scholars Haas, Nye and Lindberg. Haas (1958) is primarily concerned with the process of integration, rather than the result (Strøeby Jensen, 2003:81), and describes how integration is based on negotiation and compromise, a clear feature of how the EC/EU has operated. The approach is to reach agreement in some fields of policy, which then assists in a learning process, and so impacts on other areas. Cooperation tends to begin in areas of low politics, and later moves on to high politics. This is precisely the spillover effect of policy making that so alarms opponents of further integration. An example is the impact of JHA and CFSP being formally described as comprising 'pillars' within the TEU architecture. They may have appeared in the Maastricht Treaty as ring-fenced areas of intergovernmental policy making, but since Maastricht, Pillar III in particular has been revised by the Treaty of Amsterdam and questions of asylum, immigration and citizenship have migrated to Pillar I, so coming under EC law. Another example is the Schengen Agreement on border crossings, which was initially a separate policy initiative, but was later incorporated into the ToA and applied to more member states than the original signatories.

A further observation in the neo-functional process is that it is marked by what has been termed 'elite socialization' (Strøeby Jensen, 2003:86). This informal engagement between different nationals in the policy-making process nourishes an affinity for the culture of supranationalism and can result in a form of embedded loyalty to the integration process. This emerges in part from policy makers recognising that international relations is not a zero-sum game as a realist position would imply. Instead the culture created accepts that everybody gains from a process of economic and political integration (Strøeby Jensen, 2003:84). Neo-functionalism also makes clear the central role of governments in EU policy making. According to Jones:

> the political dimension and the role of governments in integration processes is fully accounted for. A central assumption of this approach is that functional co-operation will take place at the behest of governments (Jones, 2001:45).

However, neo-functionalism is criticised for its '[emphasis on] the importance of elites and elite bargaining rather than mass support for integration' (Jones, ibid.). It tends to be driven by technocratic or functional needs and

> [it] sees little role for democratic and accountable governance at the level of the region. Rather the 'benign elitism' of neo-functionalists tends to assume the tacit support of the European peoples – a 'permissive consensus' upon which experts and executives rely when pushing for further integration (Strøeby Jensen, 2003:82).

A more substantive criticism is that it simply fails to take account of how the EU works: while it is partly successful in explaining certain processes, much else that happens is not effectively covered by neo-functionalism. Neo-functionalism implies a regular gradualist progress of integration, but this does not match with the history. Jones comments that Haas admitted that the neo-functionalist approach would proceed unevenly, even with examples of 'spill-back' rather than spillover. The history of European integration certainly bears this out. Jones quotes Keohane and Hoffman (1991:19) denying that spillover was primarily responsible for the Single European Market, but rather a combination of factors, in particular:

> the convergence of national interest, developments in the global economy and concern about the poor competitiveness of European industry (Jones, 2001:46).

These conclusions are matched by those of other scholars mentioned previously, such as Milward (2000) and Moravcsik (1999).

Other criticisms suggested are that elite socialisation does not necessarily lead to a lessening of the member-state assertiveness in the Commission for example, and that many civil servants in the Commission are in fact on message from national governments. Secondly, Haas himself 'stepped back from the neo-functional theory he himself had been so instrumental in developing' (Strøeby Jensen, 2003:88–90) as he recognised that global factors needed to be taken into greater account and that spillover was an insufficient logic to describe what was actually happening. Finally, intergovernmentalist critics of neo-functionalism claim that it overemphasises supranationalism and undervalues the intergovernmental role in regional cooperation. This conclusion is drawn by Moravcsik (1999). **Intergovernmentalism** emphasises the extent to which 'political integration is based exclusively on the aggregate interests of the single nation state and on its determination to survive' (Strøeby Jensen, 2003:89).

Intergovernmentalism emerged as an alternative theory of European integration. It is characterised by state-centrism (Cini, 2003:94) and interprets integration as a zero-sum game, meaning the success of one party in a negotiation or deal is mirrored by someone else's loss. This interpretation is based in realist interpretations of the conduct of international relations (see Chapter 8). Intergovernmentalist perspectives on European integration are based on cost-benefit analysis and prefer to focus on the notion of European cooperation as opposed to integration – which implies greater sacrifice of sovereignty.

Intergovernmentalist theory emerged in the mid 1960s from a critique of neo-functionalism and federalism. It centred on interpretations of the French boycott of EEC institutions in 1965 – the empty chair crisis – and also on other policy choices by France relating to the UK application to join the Community, vetoed by France in 1963 and again four years later. The persistence of the veto demonstrated the centrality of member-state interests over any pooling of sovereignty or collective consensus. The European Commission adopted a more cautious role after the Luxembourg Compromise of January 1966 which affirmed the right of veto (Cini, 2003:97).

Cini reports the key role of Stanley Hoffman in articulating the intergovernmental approach. Hoffman's (1995) criticisms of neo-functionalism were that it neglected the *context* in which integration occurred, being overly focused on *process*. Nor was Hoffman persuaded by theories of spillover. He stressed instead the perpetual conflict over interests between states. Cini writes that according to Hoffman 'there was nothing inevitable about the path of European integration' as neo-functionalism implied, and there was no evidence of a generalised commitment to a federal Europe (Cini, ibid.). Hoffman emphasised the 'dialectic of fragmentation and unity', producing more diversity than integration (Cini, 2003:98). Finally, Hoffman argued the importance of the high/low politics split and said that there was no evidence that the much easier to achieve technical cooperation in economic matters would transfer to issues of citizenship, foreign policy or defence. Nevertheless, subsequent developments indicate that the integration process has indeed impacted on these areas of high politics, and others besides, including immigration, border controls and currency management in the highly symbolic area of dispensing with national currencies and adopting the euro.

This chapter has already referred to the work of Moravcsik (1999). Moravcsik bases his work on case studies in five policy areas, namely the founding Rome Treaty, the Common Agricultural Policy, the European Monetary System, the Single European Act and the Treaty on European Union. His theory of liberal intergovernmentalism (LI) presents a different perspective of intergovernmentalism, firstly by recognising that integration can have positive-sum outcomes. He identifies the EU as a successful intergovernmental regime and says that integration emphasises the importance of preferences and the power of states (Cini, 2003:103). He makes three specific claims. First, that policy choices are driven by domestic preferences, so bargaining at the EU level is influenced by domestic politics, often shaped by relatively powerful interest groups. National governments come to represent these interests in international forums. Secondly, Moravcsik stresses the inter-state relations where relative power is important and alliances are made. Supranational institutions have a peripheral role in the process. Thirdly, LI claims that states delegate authority to European-level institutions in order to enhance the efficiency of the bargaining process. Such 'pooling' improves the prospects for cooperation. This leads to substantial linkage across issues. Here Moravcsik's work draws on Keohane (1989) who views institutions as ways of facilitating positive-sum outcomes among states but not in ways that prejudice the interests of states, according to Rosamond (2000:143), as reported by Cini (2003:104).

Neo-functionalism is summarised in Discussion 5.2, intergovernmentalism in Discussion 5.3.

Review	*What is functionalism? How closely does it reflect the process of European integration?*
	Is neo-functionalism a better explanation for how European integration has developed?
	What criticisms of neo-functionalism are presented by intergovernmentalists?
	Is intergovernmentalism or liberal intergovernmentalism an adequate explanation for European integration?

Discussion 5.2

The neo-functionalist approach to unity

Main characteristics

- Gradualist/incrementalist
- Pragmatic
- Benefits from 'spillover' effect – integration in one area leads to integration in related areas
- Benefits from 'unintended consequences'
- Concentration on areas of 'low politics' (economy, trade, employment, welfare)
- Benefits from 'elite socialisation' and 'normative' policy-making processes

- Engages governments in policy making
- Focus on process

Criticisms of neo-functionalism

- Focus on elites
- Behind the scenes bargaining
- Undemocratic and unaccountable
- Technocratic and complex
- Does not engage sub-national authorities (regions)
- Disputed role of governments

Discussion 5.3

The intergovernmentalist approach to policy making

Features of intergovernmentalism

- Privileges the role of member-state governments and their representatives
- Zero-sum game (gains for integration represent loss for member states)
- Uses a cost-benefits approach to determining policy
- Focus on cooperation, not integration

- Integration is viewed as undermining sovereignty
- Protective of the veto in policy-making procedures
- Averse to emphasis on consensus-oriented politics
- Focus on content, not process
- No commitment to ideal of a federal Europe
- Privileges domestic interests
- Governments represent local interests

Other theories of European integration

Rosamond (2000, 2003) has written extensively on the limitations of the 'classical' federal/neo-functional/intergovernmental approaches to explaining European integration. To what extent do Moravcsik's conclusions confirm that intergovernmental or statist assumptions correctly match the realities of EU governance? Or, on the other hand, has the process of integration created supranational institutions and non-state actors that have superseded the role of member state governments? Rosamond says such an approach is understandable, but ultimately highlights the weakness in the 'grand theory' approach to European integration and instead stresses the complex, multifaceted nature of the process. Indeed, much recent work on the subject has examined how policy is actually made rather than attempting to characterise in simple terms the whole history of the integration process.

Neo-functionalism, according to Rosamond (2003:111), failed to capture the evident realities of state preferences that dominated in the 1960s, especially in respect of France. Similarly, the implication that progress in integration only resulted from inter-state bargaining, without any inherent involvement of supranational agencies, is at variance with reality as reported from the 'coalface' of EC/EU policy making. The genesis of the Single Market, driven according to Moravcsik by intergovernmental negotiation, is not so clear-cut an example of ascendant intergovernmentalism. Indeed, spillover and institutional involvement at the European level was also highly influential.

Rosamond refers to the claim that much of the classical debate had its origins in an International Relations (IR) approach to looking at European integration. In other words, it is rooted in the toolkit of IR, with its focus on war and peace, and relations between *states*. Either way, whether intergovernmental or neo-functional, the point of concern was the role of states and the degree to which state actors were prepared to cooperate, or integrate, in order to defend state interests. This IR context is examined in the next chapter. Rosamond cautions against focusing too much on the integration question, because to do so implies a zero-sum game between member states and a federal 'super-state'. Essentially the 'grand theory' approach has been preoccupied with the *form* of integration, when what is more useful is an examination of the *process*: how has integration come about (Rosamond, 2003:112). But he also cautions against a readiness to dump the IR approach, especially as the emergence of International Political Economy (IPE) as a sub-area of IR

> explicitly emphasises the fuzziness of the boundaries between domestic politics and international relations [. . .] [and] IR theories retain a valuable place in EU studies [because they can assist in] understanding the global environment within which the EU operates (Rosamond, 2003:113).

Rosamond introduces a range of alternative theories that shed new light on the integration process. The first of these is the institutional perspective. Evidently the EU is heavily institutionalised, possessing a number of formally constituted supranational institutions and a number of intergovernmental bodies as well. The institutional approach is in turn is divided into three quite different strands. The first is *rational choice institutionalism*, which holds that institutions are the product of 'long-run patterns of behaviour by self-seeking agents' (Rosamond, 2003:115). Rational choice theory is based on the proposition that human beings are self-seeking, and behave rationally and strategically. In this context, institutions are intervening variables, meaning that they filter and alter independent variables. The institutional context will impact on how actors pursue their goals, and any constitutional changes, such as the increased use of QMV or the emergence of the European Parliament as a co-legislator with the Council, will alter the ways in which actors pursue their objectives. Critics say that the emphasis on formal rules misses out the significance of informal socialisation and normative pressures, meaning pressures to conform to established practice. A second institutionalist strand is represented by *historical institutionalism*. This standpoint emphasises the long-term affects of institutional

Institutional approaches to policy making

Rational choice institutionalism

Characteristics: rational preferences; informal socialisation; normative pressures

Historical institutionalism

Characteristics: ongoing, permanent agendas; inherently conservative; normative culture

Sociological institutionalism

Characteristics: internal dynamics drive policy making; personal preferences count; normative culture.

choices and how agendas become relatively permanent and ongoing. Such tendencies ensure the longevity of institutions and institutional practice. Reform is rendered difficult. Rosamond refers to work by Pierson (1996) which reported that the early architects of the European Communities led them to acts of institutional design which eroded the capacities of national governments to control their economies. He inverts the thesis presented by Milward (2000) that the EC rescued the (nation) state and says instead that institution building at a European level in fact had exactly the opposite effect. Others (Armstrong and Bulmer, 1998) focus on the normative cultures that emerge in institutions over time, as ideas, norms and values become established and impact on policy-making procedures and decisions. This links to *sociological institutionalism*, an approach which focuses on the internal dynamics and deeply rooted preferences of the individuals concerned and less on the inherent rationalism implied in the other two approaches. The concern of sociological institutionalists is the normative culture that emerges, for example in different DGs within the Commission. This approach can inform understanding on the extent to which

> intergovernmental processes such as those associated with the Common Foreign and Security Policy (CFSP) conform to established patterns of interstate interaction, or whether they bring about new norms of exchange between the envoys of member states (Rosamond, 2003:117).

Rosamond points out that many studies are now being carried out on the interaction between national and European-level norms and in particular on the ways in which 'European' norms filter into the existing political cultures of the member states (Börzel, 2002).

Institutional approaches to policy making are summarised in Discussion 5.4.

Theories of policy making

So far we have looked at Rosamond's appraisal of institutional approaches to European integration studies. A second area he addresses is *theories of policy making*. Here, the EU is seen as a policy system, and therefore policy agendas, policy formulation, decision-making, and the implementation of legislation becomes the focus of interest. Rosamond suggests that this approach may also have important implications for wider studies of how governance is carried out in modern complex societies. Once again, rather than grand theorising, it may be more useful to study the EU in terms of how it addresses technical matters in relation to the Single Market, for example. What emerges is that different policy processes are found in different areas and suggests that detailed empirical studies are needed on a sector-by-sector basis to properly understand EU governance. Peterson and Bomberg (1999) suggest that different levels of policy making require different theoretical explanations. They identify three areas: super-systemic, systemic and meso (sectoral). The first looks at the wider EU environment, the second at institutional change and the third at resource dependencies (Rosamond, 2003:118). Each level requires different tools: IR works well at the super-systemic level, new institutionalist theories work at the institutional level. For sectoral analysis however, Peterson and Bomberg suggest policy network analysis. The sectoral level is marked by regulatory complexity and the varying interests of stakeholders involved in the exchange of information and resources. In this context, ideology, according to Rosamond, is less important than expertise. Politics remains important however:

> Policy network analysis deals with the politics of influence and mutual dependency in situations where power is dispersed (Rosamond, ibid.).

This area of study emerged from looking at national governance but is especially suited to European Union studies because policy making in the EU is segmented, complex and involves a wide range of stakeholders. It is especially valuable because it obliges us to focus on understanding 'the specific relations of mutual dependency that obtain in different sectors' (Rosamond, ibid.). The policy-making approach is a useful advance in EU studies because it progresses an approach to understanding how **governance** works. Rosamond defines governance as 'the range of actions and institutions that supply order' (Rosamond, 2003:119).

Government is one way in which order is delivered. What is highlighted by the policy-making approach is that

> the traditional methods of public regulation, intervention and legislation are being displaced and that authority is becoming dispersed amongst a variety of actors. The state retains a key role in governance, but its role is being reformulated, and arguably, residualized (Rosamond, ibid.).

This is a key observation and one that is especially significant in terms of wider conclusions drawn in later chapters of this book. It also points towards the next area that Rosamond addresses, that of multilevel governance, which we shall return to in more detail in the next chapter, but which is briefly introduced here.

The **multilevel governance** (MLG) approach is a position that is based on the proposition that the character of governance in Europe has changed radically over the past 50 years. Furthermore,

> The boundaries between national policy making and European policy making have been blurred to the point of insignificance. The EU policy process is not something that simply happens at the European level. It penetrates into national political and legal systems in complex ways. So while there has been an undoubted 'drift' of authority in various policy areas to the European level, we need to move away from the image of there being two distinct domains of politics in Europe – the national and the supranational/European level (Rosamond, 2003:120).

Rosamond says this MLG approach is a direct challenge to Moravcsik's liberal intergovernmentalism which is founded on the model of a two-level national and European level. For Moravcsik, national-level preferences are pursued at the European level in a process of inter-state bargaining. MLG challenges this interpretation. Hooghe and Marks (2001) write about the extent to which authority has become dispersed since the 1950s. In most European countries there has been devolution of power within the state as well as a drift of authority to the European level. The state remains important, but power is more dispersed. Therefore EU policy processes occur at European, national and sub-national levels, but it is just as important to recognise that there is fluidity across these levels, as policy actors move between them, and that the dispersal of authority is uneven in different policy areas.

Rosamond cites Marks, Hooghe and Blank in describing the MLG view of the EU as:

> A set of overarching, multi-level policy networks [where] . . . [t]he structure of policy control is variable, not constant across policy space (Marks, Hooghe and Blank, 1996:41).

He adds

> In many ways, MLG represents an attempt to capture the complexity of the EU, but it also represents a clear denial of the idea that there can be a single all-encompassing theory of the EU (Rosamond, 2003:120).

The notion of MLG is discussed further in the next chapter; see also Discussion 6.5. The main characteristics of a policy-making approach are summarised in Discussion 5.5.

The next new tool that might be used to consider European integration is *social constructivism*. It is not a theory of European integration as such, but 'a position on the nature of social reality (an ontology)' (Rosamond, 2003:122). The approach adopts a scientific method, using the neutrality of facts to highlight observable realities. Rosamond says the social constructivist approach has had an important impact on IR theory in the past decade. Constructivists examine how collective understandings emerge and how institutions constitute the interests and identities of actors. An effective constructive approach is based on research and empirical studies that demonstrate regular and therefore predictable outcomes. The constructivist approach focuses on the EU as a process, in contrast to the intergovernmentalist position of looking at inter-state bargaining. Constructivists are concerned with the transition from 'a bargaining regime to a polity' (Rosamond, 2003:122). Rosamond provides the helpful observation that

> **Discussion 5.5**
>
> ## Theories of policy making in the EU context
>
> The main characteristics of a policy-making based approach are:
>
> - The EU is seen as a policy system
> - Focus on process of policy making and policy implementation
> - Key role of influence and mutual dependency
> - Power is dispersed among actors, institutions and sectors
> - Recognition of the complexity of the policy system; many actors and agencies involved
> - Mutual dependency
> - Multilevel governance (MLG): the EU–state–region relationship demonstrates how power has become dispersed across and between levels

perhaps the simplest way to understand what this account is about is to observe that constructivism has studied questions such as how European identities emerge, through for example looking at the idea of a 'European economy', a 'European security community', or 'European citizenship'. Constructivism does not accept that such 'identities' emerge as a response to the end of the Cold War or the progress of globalisation for example, but as a consequence of how language is used, norms, and the deployment of ideas. Exactly how these norms and ideas are communicated in processes of socialisation and learning among actors is of paramount importance. Norms are central to the vocabulary of constructivists, and can be defined as 'collective explanations for the proper behaviour of actors with a given identity' (Katzenstein, 1996:5).

> It is through the internationalisation of norms that actors acquire their identities and establish what their interests are' (Rosamond, 2003:122).

Constructivism has much in common with sociological institutionalism, outlined earlier, which also focuses on norms and normative behaviour. The main characteristics of the social constructivist approach are summarised in Discussion 5.6.

> **Discussion 5.6**
>
> ## Social constructivism in the EU context
>
> The key characteristics are:
>
> - Scientific, research-based approach to understanding policy processes
> - Analysis of institutional behaviour
> - Focus on key role of individual actors
> - EU is viewed as a process
> - Focus on emergent identities and normative behaviour in various policy areas or sectors
> - Assumes collective explanations for behaviour of individuals within a sectoral identity

The final section of Rosamond's overview of new theories of European integration is concerned with International Relations and IPE in particular. Since this is the subject of the next chapter little is said about it here. Nevertheless, Rosamond points out that recent renewed interest in IR in the field of EU studies may be a result of the apparent growth in regionalism in the global political economy of which the EU itself is a prime example. Regionalism refers to 'state-led projects of institution building' (Rosamond, 2003:123). The extent to which the EU has become an international actor challenges traditionally state-centric approaches of IR, but IR does appear to demonstrate more interest in regionalisation, meaning the emergence of regional economies, and regionalism with its attendant transnational organisations, than used to be the case.

Review   *What are the main new approaches suggested by Rosamond?*
What are the main characteristics of these approaches?

● ● ● ● Conclusion

Most writers on European integration have tended to emphasise the neo-functionalist approach to unity (Jones, 2001; Baun, 1996; Dinan, 1999). Neo-functionalism highlights how agreements between states have resulted in pooling sovereignty in designated areas. Both Moravcsik (1999) and Milward (2000) have described how European integration has been primarily driven by member-state governments seeking or accepting integrating initiatives as the best means to achieve desirable outcomes, and have underlined how these outcomes match or emerge from domestic preferences, such as improved living standards, better social welfare, and increased employment. In other words, there has been less European idealism than nationally determined self-interest.

Federalism has lost its zeal. A federalist approach to unity would prefer to build a federal, supranational architecture and have states adapt to this in a kind of 'big bang' approach. However, there is not and probably never has been much appetite for this ambition. Instead, integration has been achieved in a gradualist, piecemeal manner, beginning in the economic sphere and extending into other areas through spillover. Pinder (2001) cites the example of European leaders forming first the ECSC and then later, finding considerable but insufficient benefits in the first initiative, creating the EEC. More than 30 years later the SEM lead to the final preparations and eventual launch of the single European currency. Pinder, a federalist by instinct, criticises neo-federalism for its lack of openness in setting clear objectives, and for the manner in which agreements are reached through intergovernmental bargaining and spillover, leaving citizens at the very least confused and alienated. He implies that this process is fundamentally flawed because it is neither effective nor democratic enough to satisfy the citizens' needs. Furthermore, he argues that the steady transfer of powers to the Union is less because of a conscious application of spillover theory, but more because states acting alone are unable to respond adequately to changes in the international environment.

It is, however, one thing to argue the weaknesses of neo-functionalism, and quite another to assume that a federal approach would be more successful. It is hard to accept the implied assumption that 'big bang' federalist supranationalism with broadly enhanced powers for the European Parliament would be more acceptable to European publics. The issue demonstrates the difficulties faced by the EU in resolving problems of 'democratic deficit'. These include overly complex decision-making processes, lack of transparency, poor sense of engagement with citizens, low public participation, and poor public awareness of what the EU does and why.

Any attempt to construct a single overarching explanation for European integration seems doomed to failure. Furthermore, the classical opposition between neo-functional and intergovernmentalist approaches also seems unsatisfactory. Theoretical explanations have become much more complex and this probably reflects the need for a more sophisticated interpretation of how policy processes are undertaken at a national and European level. Several newer approaches to studying how integration has occurred indicate that a policy-based examination of processes is more fruitful than traditional explanations. These approaches also look at the importance of normative behaviour, institutionalised cultures, and the significant variation that is observable between policy areas. An especially important trend is the interest in multilevel governance. An MLG perspective holds that the common assumption that the EU involves a straightforward split between the national and the supranational/European level is out of date. Not only does this traditional view fail to take account of the interests and roles of sub-national actors – regions and cities for example – it appears to deny that a process of 'Europeanisation' is occurring at the national level too. There is much fluidity in terms of personnel working across and between different levels. Policy development often involves preferences that emerge across and between different levels. Furthermore, there is considerable variation between different sectors or policy areas, so what appears to be a marked tendency in one sector may not reflect tendencies in another area.

European Union studies have tended to marginalise the discipline of International Relations, especially as the dominant schools of thought in IR have themselves struggled to take account of a regional grouping like the EU, composed of apparently sovereign states. However, in recent years there has been some movement in these respects as IR develops a greater interest in regionalisation in the context of globalisation, especially in the sub-area of International Political Economy (IPE). Chapter 8 presents a discussion of IR theories and assesses their relevance to the European context.

In summary, new approaches are especially important because they challenge commonly held assumptions, including the basic assumption of a straightforward win/lose argument between intergovernmentalist or nationalist preferences, and European integrationists. Perhaps the very longevity of the 'European project', as it is sometimes known, has created an environment that is more nuanced, more complex and more challenging than we have hitherto been asked to consider.

Rosamond, whose work has been extensively referred to in this chapter, sums up the efforts to understand integration theories in the context of the EU:

> We might continue to be confused about the complexity of the EU, but the present vibrant theoretical culture in EU studies at least gives us a chance of being confused in a relatively sophisticated way (Rosamond, 2003:126).

In terms of the foregoing discussion on integration theories, it is evident that the EU has established itself as a formidable entity, but it is not likely to become a United States of Europe and it will never become 'one country'. The high water mark of federalism has probably passed.

Review	*What is meant by the 'classical approach' to integration theory?*
	What are some of Pinder's criticisms of neo-functionalism?
	What is appealing about an MLG approach to theorising about European integration?

Summary

This chapter has made the following key points.

Destinations of integration: federalism and confederalism

- Federalism offers a moral foundation for European integration and is based on a division of authority between centre and the periphery, or between (broadly) supranational EU institutions and the member states. The core of the federalist approach is expressed in the phrase 'unity in diversity'.
- Confederalism is a more intergovernmental arrangement but in the EU context would appear to suffer from significant weaknesses, such as weakening the informal socialisation influences that surround policy making, making access more difficult, creating paralysis in an enlarged Union and lessening, rather than enhancing, transparency.
- It is possible to construct a continuum between 'weak confederalism' and 'extreme federalism'. The latter would create a model similar to the United States of America. The EU does not remotely correspond to such a description.

Functionalism, neo-functionalism and intergovernmentalism

- Neo-functionalism, of which the concept of spillover is a vital part, presents a state-driven gradual, incremental approach towards 'closer union'.
- Critics of neo-functionalism claim that it overestimates spillover and underestimates the context in which integration occurs, in other words the global environment.
- Intergovernmentalism privileges the role of the state and argues that integration occurs because states pursue self-interest. A sub-theory of

intergovernmentalism developed by Moravcsik emphasises inter-state bargaining, especially in establishing the Single European Market.

Other theories of European integration

- The 'grand theory' approach of a single overarching explanation for European integration does not match with reality.
- The 'classical' opposition between neo-functionalism and intergovernmentalism is similarly deficient.
- New approaches focus more on policy-making processes than on the form that integration has adopted.
- Institutional theories include rational choice – participants weigh up alternatives in pursuing strategic objectives; historical institutionalism – the institutions themselves evolve in ways that create an institutional culture that has its own relatively unchanging ethos; sociological institutionalism – a normative culture emerges among the individuals working within institutions.
- Policy-making theories – with an emphasis on the process from inception to implementation; the approach recognises how power is dispersed and that expertise is more important than ideology.
- Multilevel governance (MLG) is a direct challenge to intergovernmentalism. MLG claims that the traditional view of a split between state-level governance and the European-level is breaking down; power is much more dispersed; MLG highlights the fluidity and flexibility across sub-national, national and European/supranational levels; there is also variation between sectors.
- Social constructivism – a scientific research-based approach which sees the EU as a policy-making process; it focuses on the normative pressures in different sectors.
- International Relations – especially the sub-area of International Political Economy (IPE); IPE can take account of regionalising tendencies in the context of advancing globalisation.

Key concepts: discussion and other definitions

Key concept 5.1   Federalism

A system of integration which suggests that everybody can be satisfied by combining national and regional/territorial interests within a complex web of checks and balances between a national or federal government, and a multiplicity of regional governments (based on McLean & McMillan, 2003:195).

Cini suggests a very similar definition but stresses the ideology behind the concept, which seems appropriate in the European context where federalism has been such a contested phenomenon.

> An ideological position that suggests that everyone can be satisfied by combining national and regional/territorial interests in a complex web of checks and balances between a central government and a multiplicity of regional governments. In a European Union context it tends to imply an ideological approach that advocates the creation of a federal state in Europe (Cini, 2003:418).

There are of course different forms of federal state. In the USA, for example, the presidential system privileges the position of the president but gives considerable power to the Congress, which is composed of representatives delegated by the federal states. Certain powers are located very firmly at the federal government level, for example taxation and welfare, and all matters relating to foreign and security policy. In both these respects, as well as the considerable powers of the President, the European Union appears quite unlike the US conception of a federal state.

In Germany, the tradition of federal government probably contributes to the historical sympathy for a more federal arrangement at the European level than is evident in more unitary or centralised states, like Britain and France.

As the chapter has pointed out, federalism is interpreted differently by different people, and there is a generally different perception of what it means in Britain, compared with the continent. In Britain the emphasis is placed on its centralising functions, whereas quite the opposite is the case in Germany or elsewhere in Europe. In fact, federalism stresses the decentralising character of federal arrangement, where considerable powers are retained at a local and regional level. Federalism is presented as a way of ensuring close links between the people and their representatives and different levels of government.

Nevertheless, the concept is highly contested and it is now generally assumed that the EU, while showing some of the characteristics of a federation, is far from being a federal state, or even a 'super-state' as some would argue.

While not a definition of federalism as such, a noted anti-federalist in the government of Margaret Thatcher provided a concise and pithy account of Economic and Monetary Union, describing it as: 'a German racket' (Ridley, 1990 cited in Young, 1991: 572; 1998: 361). Nicholas Ridley offered this entertaining assessment in an interview with the *Spectator* political weekly. In the same article he drew parallels between the German Chancellor Helmut Kohl and Adolf Hitler. His remarks, swilling around in a gutter of xenophobic stereotypes, caused widespread embarrassment. They also cost him his job. It is, however, a common view among British eurosceptics, and for critics of the EU elsewhere, that the EU has historically been based on a French design and paid for by German economic success (Siedentop, 2000), at least up to the end of the Cold War. This grates in the UK, and is one reason for widespread anti-EU sentiment. The fact is, however, as many writers have pointed out (Denman, 1997; George, 1998; Young, 1998), Britain chose to sit on the sidelines while France and Germany constructed the European Economic Community with support and engagement in the process from Belgium, Italy, the Netherlands and Luxembourg. Britain seems to have joined the club late and complained about the rules ever since.

This is not to say that the rules should not be changed, but that Britain, as a country of comparable size to France and the pre-unification Federal Republic of Germany, might easily have had a more equal relationship with its continental neighbours had it not turned down the invitation to participate in the Coal and Steel Community and then, even more short-sightedly, rejected an invitation to attend the Messina Conference in 1955. Young (1998) reports that Britain felt Messina would not lead to anything significant, so sent a minor official as an observer. In fact Messina was a road that really did lead to Rome.

Key concept 5.2   Neo-functionalism

A theory of regional integration that maintains that 'political integration and the growth of authority at the supranational level occur as a long term consequence of modest economic integration. Integration in one sector creates pressures for integration in related sectors, and so on. This process is called functional spillover' (Rosamond, 2000:202).

Cini defines neo-functionalism as follows:

> A theory of European integration that views integration as an incremental process, involving the spillover of integration in one sector to others, ultimately leading to some kind of political community (Cini, 2003:421).

Rosamond says that

> the success of integration initiatives draws self-interested groups of actors into the game (political spillover) [and both this form and functional spillover] are promoted by purposeful supranational institutions (Rosamond, 2000:202).

Neo-functionalists therefore describe integration as occurring as a consequence of pressures both from actors within governments and from within supranational institutions. The process is often described as incremental, or gradualist.

Neo-functionalism was substantially challenged by intergovernmentalists, who stress the role of governments and tend to downplay the significance of supranational institutions. Intergovernmentalism appears to present a higher degree of self-interest on the part of governments than neo-functionalism implies. Jones (2001:47) points out that Moravcsik's theory of liberal intergovernmentalism centred on 'intergovernmental bargaining and the influence of supranational actors is generally marginal'.

Similarly, Jones writes that

> Keohane and Hoffman (1991:19) deny that spillover was primarily responsible for the SEM – rather they attribute it to a combination of factors, in particular to the convergence of national interests, to developments in the global economy and to concern about the poor competitiveness of European industry (Jones, 2001:46).

However Jones does suggest that the transition from SEA/SEM to TEU and EMU can indeed be interpreted as spillover effect. It seems reasonable to argue that neo-functionalism remains a useful and relevant instrument in seeking to explain the integration process.

Finally, it should be recalled that neo-functionalism, unlike federalism, is a theory of regional integration as opposed to a kind of blueprint for an emerging global government. Neo-functionalism is ideally applied to the early steps of the European integration process, and remains relevant to more recent developments as well. In this respect therefore the neo-functional approach can be relevant to other regions where a process of regionalism may be occurring. This is further discussed in Chapter 10.

Further reading

Cini, M. (ed.) (2003) *European Union Politics*, Oxford: Oxford University Press. This major work is a comprehensive overview of the EU. Part Two, Theories and conceptual approaches, contains four excellent chapters on Federalism, Neo-functionalism, Intergovernmentalism and a chapter by Rosamond (see below) on New theories of European Integration.

Moravcsik, A. (1999) *The Choice for Europe: Social purpose and state power from Messina to Maastricht*, University College London. The book is the seminal text on liberal intergovernmentalism and offers a decisive alternative to neo-functionalism. Moravcsik uses a case study approach to argue that states have been the driving force in major policy initiatives. 'European integration can best be explained as a series of rational choices made by national leaders' (Moravcsik, 1998:18).

Rosamond, B. (2000) *Theories of European Integration*, Basingstoke: Palgrave Macmillan. This is probably the best recent survey of integration theory.

Films

No films seem to encapsulate the finer concepts of integration theory. Hollywood awaits . . .

Chapter 6

The EU and the regions: multilevel governance in an era of globalisation

Outline

- The practical significance of regional development policy
- Funding EU regional policies
- Theoretical implications of regional development policy: multilevel governance
- Comparison of the EU–region relationship in Spain and Germany

Key concepts

6.1 Subsidiarity

6.2 Europeanisation

● ● ● ● Introduction

It is not uncommon to hear the claim that the European Union and the European integration process seeks to create a common European identity *at the expense of* national identities. The claim perhaps stems from insecurity, but it would seem to imply that the French have become less French and the Italians less Italian since their governments signed up to the Treaty of Rome in 1957, or that Latvians, having recently shaken off the yoke of Russian imperialism endured since the Red Army occupied Latvia in 1940, have committed to mass national identity oblivion by joining the European Union as one of its smaller member states. In fact, for many individuals, if not all, their experience is one of possessing multiple identities (see Discussion 3.1).

Even a superficial understanding of the European Union should make it obvious that such fears exaggerate both the powers of the Union over its citizens, and the effects of membership. Nevertheless, it is still common for the EU's most rabid critics to portray it as some kind of monster that gobbles up unwary states and obliterates centuries of culture, language, identity, history, experience and allegiance. The Union, as has been stated elsewhere, has instead tended towards the notion of unity in diversity, and has played a significant role in promoting the regions through a range of policy initiatives that have a primarily, though not exclusively, economic rationale. The most important of these is the European Regional Development Fund, which is concerned with structural funding projects. These include regeneration and support for less advantaged areas, or with managing recovery following industrial decline. A second fund is the Cohesion Fund, which promotes transport infrastructure development and measures relating to the environment in the poorer member states. Regional policy initiatives are wide-ranging. Some are large and high profile, while many others, particularly with a significant social dimension, are small and may go broadly unnoticed.

This chapter discusses the role of regions within the EU and describes attempts to reconcile the tensions that exist between the different levels of EU governance. The EU state relationship is much more widely discussed, but the impact of integration on the third level – that of sub-state regions – is often absent in popular discourse, although it attracts considerable interest among EU scholars, especially since the Treaty on European Union (Maastricht) of 1992.

An important claim in this chapter is that the European Union has attempted to incorporate a regional dimension into policy making since the late 1980s, mainly as a response to criticism that major integrating policies, such as the Single European Market and EMU, undermined member-state governments' capacity to conduct their own regional development policies (Bourne, 2003:284). The EU response to this criticism has been to try to provide a counterbalance to its centralising tendencies, specifically through measures to help the regions of the Union.

The chapter also refers to the question of how much actual authority resides at a sub-state level. Despite a developed regional policy, it does not necessarily follow that there is much actual power below the state level. This point is important and the issues it raises have had significant impact on theorising about EU governance.

The previous chapter noted that classical federalism does take account of a division of responsibilities between centre and periphery. But the EU has never been truly federal. Were it so, then there might be a stronger case for arguing that the Union was moving towards a form of 'Europe of the Regions', but this claim is largely discounted in the discussion that follows. Instead, the locus of power in the Union has tended to be in Brussels, albeit through a complex interplay between predominantly supranational institutions, led by the Commission, and the representatives of member-state governments, through the Council. It is here where authority actually resides, and where most decision-making takes place. The role of regions is more marginal. Nevertheless, there is evidence to support the view that a third level has emerged, and that this sub-state level is not insignificant. In the 1990s, interest in the role of the third level gave rise to a theory of multilevel governance (MLG). Power within the multilevel model is not clearly subdivided, nor even hierarchical; it is dispersed. The claim is made in this chapter that the emergence of a stronger profile for regional policy in general has much to do with inter-state bargaining, but perhaps not quite so much to do with policy making at a sub-state level. On the contrary, central governments appear to act as gatekeepers where sub-state interests are involved.

To summarise, the regions of Europe have played a significant and visible role in the history of European integration. Especially since the early 1990s, the main vehicles for regional policy have been structural funding mechanisms. These are explained in what follows.

The chapter provides a background to the issue of regional development policy within the European Union. It then looks at its current role, including some budgetary implications. Some theoretical considerations of regional policy are examined, including the notion of multilevel governance (MLG), which was briefly introduced in the previous chapter. The chapter concludes with a comparison of the EU–region relationship in Spain and Germany.

● ● ● ● The practical significance of regional development policy

The Treaty of Rome had little to say about the regions of the European Economic Community. It merely signalled an ambition to 'reduce the differences existing between the various regions and the backwardness of the less-favoured regions', but did not create any formal mechanism to achieve this aim. Nor were there any institutional or treaty frameworks to provide sub-national representation within the decision-making process or in EEC governance. Any regional opinion brought to bear at a European level necessarily depended on the ministers of member-state governments choosing to present arguments emanating from regional interests. The extent to which this might happen would vary and clearly some member states, notably the more federally constituted ones, such as Germany and Belgium, would be more inclined to express sub-national aspirations in this way (see Discussion 6.1).

A mechanism intended to assist in achieving the aims referred to above in the Rome Treaty finally emerged in 1975. The European Regional Development Fund was set up, mostly at the behest of Britain, as the ERDF was designed to bring assistance to poorer regions, especially ones affected by industrial decline. The UK had several such regions, and indeed these were among the poorest areas in the Community. However, the ERDF began with a mere 5 per cent of the Community budget. It was the Single European Act of 1986 that established a foundation for a genuine EU regional policy. Between 1984 and 1999 structural funding rose from 18 per cent to 33 per cent of the total EU budget (McCormick, 2002:75). A second funding initiative was established at Maastricht, known as cohesion funding. The Cohesion Fund was designed to support initiatives in the field of the environmental and transport infrastructure, and was targeted at whole states, rather than to regions. The recipients were those states with a per capita GDP of less than 90 per cent of the Community average, which in 1992 meant Greece, Portugal, Spain and Ireland, the same states that had already benefited from increased structural funding pushed through by Commission President Jacques Delors. Pinder (2001:85) emphasises Delors's prominent role in these initiatives, motivated out of a strong sense of social justice, but also

Discussion 6.1

Different national approaches to regions

France, under the 1958 constitution of the Fifth Republic, is a highly centralised state, the 'one and indivisible French Republic', despite de Gaulle's apocryphal quote that a 'country with 365 cheeses is ungovernable'. The remark, whether de Gaulle actually said it or not, tells us a lot about France: it is a highly regionalised country, with strong local identities, diverse cultures and a myriad variety in its renowned cuisine (including cheeses). However, the Constitution emphasises the singular, unitarian nature of the French body politic. In this respect, France is similar to the United Kingdom, although since 1997 the UK has taken steps towards a more devolved constitution. The Labour government established a Scottish Parliament, a Welsh Assembly and it has tried to breathe life into Stormont, the Belfast-based Northern Ireland Assembly, still suspended in late 2004 due to local disagreements. Further devolution to the English regions is under consideration in some quarters, but at the current time there are no elected regional governments in England (not to be confused with district, city or county councils). Keating and Hooghe comment that there is merely 'a system of functionally specific agencies for economic development' (Keating and Hooghe, 1996:240).

In contrast to France, Germany has a clearly federal arrangement, consisting of 16 *Länder*, or region-states, each with its own parliament, and represented in the lower house of the German federal legislature, the *Bundesrat*. Belgium is also federally constituted, with six regions. Spain is constituted by 17 Autonomous Communities, some with more autonomy than others. Italy has been historically similar to France, broadly unitary and centralised, but it has recently 'extended broad autonomy to all of its twenty regions' (Padoa-Schioppa, 2003:18). It contains 20 *regioni*, each with a range of administrative powers and responsibilities. Levy (1996) reports that the powers of Italian regions are limited to consultative meetings between the government in Rome and representatives of the regions, although regional presidents do take part in Cabinet meetings when EU legislation is discussed. Certain regions in Italy have a greater degree of devolved responsibility than others, and these have more latitude in the implementation of EU directives than do the 'ordinary regions' (Levy, 1996:17). Keating and Hooghe (1996:240) describe the 'weak, administrative regionalism' of France compared with the 'fully-fledged federalism of Germany, Belgium and Austria'. The *Länder*, *regioni* and *régions* are important in the context of EU regional policy because they often correspond to EU administrative areas.

from a conviction that the Mediterranean states in particular might obstruct progress towards the Single Market unless there were visible benefits coming their way. The expansion of regional development funding through these devices considerably raised the profile of the EU in the regions. It also made EU policies more region friendly, and 'turned regional actors into both lobbyists and stakeholders in the EU decision process' (Bourne, 2003:279).

Pinder reports on the success of structural funding:

> The four states for which the expansion of the structural funds was designed have performed for the most part well, with the Portuguese and particularly the Irish economy expanding faster than the Union's average, Spain also successful, and Greece, after faltering for a number of years, meeting the Maastricht convergence criteria in 2000. While it is not possible to say how much of this can be attributed to the structural funds, their contributions can hardly have been negligible, given that Ireland received in the mid-1990s the equivalent of some 3 per cent of its GDP from them, Greece and Portugal 4 per cent each, and Spain 2 per cent (Pinder, 2001:85–7).

It is notable that the major increase in regional development funding came with the SEA, and other initiatives benefiting the regions followed with the TEU. The SEA heralded the process leading to the Single European Market. It was also probably the most centralising piece of legislation agreed in Brussels and ratified by the 12 member states since the Treaty of Rome. Together with the Cecchini Report (1988), the Act set about facilitating a greater level of harmonisation throughout the Community, especially in terms of removal of frontier formalities and common Community-wide technical standards (Bainbridge, 2002:41). The effect of this legislation was to abolish rafts of nationally imposed impediments to trade, or restrictive practices within specific industries, and to deliver unprecedented powers to the European Commission and the European Court of Justice to enforce common policies in respect of the Single Market. The political impact was dramatic: the EC/EU would experience a massive quantitative and qualitative increase in its powers at the expense of the state. This process is sometimes described as '**Europeanisation**' (Olsen, 2003:333–48), though there are several other applications of the term (see Key concept 6.2).

This shift of gear towards strongly integrating initiatives marked a watershed in the development of the EC/EU after a couple of decades of virtual inertia, bar the enlargements of 1973, 1981 and 1985. The impression of a centralising Community was not lost on supporters of greater integration, nor on its critics. Together with the ambition to create a single currency – a vision nurtured by member states since the late 1960s – the SEA was powerfully centralist. It was therefore potentially highly detrimental to the regions. By the time negotiations for the TEU were under way at Maastricht, it was widely understood that the Union would need to supply some returns of a decentralising nature in order to achieve greater harmony in respect of the Single European Market, Economic and Monetary Union and the Single Currency. This was the conjuring trick that Maastricht aimed to carry off.

The Maastricht Treaty included the EMU protocol, part of which set out the convergence criteria required to meet the exigencies of the single currency (annual government borrowing to be below 3 per cent of GDP, total debt no more than *or falling towards* 60 per cent, plus inflation, exchange rate and interest rate targets). In order to meet these fiscal restraints governments would be required to implement tight austerity packages, significantly reducing freedom of manoeuvre in respect of their own regional policies. Hitherto, governments may have been more inclined to manipulate exchange rate policy or provide subsidies to support their regions. Now, member states would find their policy options much reduced. Keating and Hooghe (1996:241) report on the widespread consensus that 'market integration exacerbates territorial disparities'. To counter this negative impact, the TEU included measures to boost regional development. Maastricht enhanced structural funding through the European Regional Development Fund and introduced the Cohesion Fund. The logic of regional funding is simple. It is designed to assist underdeveloped or declining regions to raise their levels of productivity and employment towards the national (or in the case of the EU, European) average. If the SEA, and to an even greater extent the TEU, were going to compromise member-state governments in this respect,

---

Discussion 6.2

Structural funds objectives (from Bourne, 2003:288)

The 1988 Structural Fund reforms established six objectives under which regions might obtain funds. Three of these were limited in their geographical scope to disadvantaged regions. These were:

- Objective 1 development and structural adjustment of least-developed regions
- Objective 2 conversion of regions facing industrial decline
- Objective 5b development of rural areas

The remaining priorities were focused on the whole EU:

- Objective 3 combating long-term unemployment
- Objective 4 combating youth unemployment
- Objective 5a adjustment of agricultural structures

When Sweden and Finland joined the Union a new objective was added:

- Objective 6 help low-population density regions

The *Agenda 2000* round of structural fund reforms cut the number of objectives from seven to three:

- The new Objective 1 remained unchanged in its focus on the regions whose development is lagging behind, although it did come to incorporate the aims of the old objective 6.
- The new Objective 2 brought together the old Objectives 2 (industrial decline) and 5b (rural development) and became broader in scope, aiming 'to support the economic and social conversion of areas facing structural difficulties'.
- The new Objective 3, a horizontal objective focusing on all of the EU and not just disadvantaged regions, brought together the social aims of the old Objectives 3 and 4 to focus on 'supporting the adaptation and modernisation of policies and systems of education, training and employment'.

---

then the Union would need to compensate. Discussion 6.2 explains the objectives of structural funding in more detail.

Bourne summarises the relationship between EU regional policy and the impact of the Union's wider Single Market and EMU objectives by referring to the functional spillover effects inherent in regional policy implementation. In the previous chapter spillover was described as the phenomenon whereby integration in one area tends to lead to integration in other areas, a process which has been characteristic of the European integration process over the years.

> Part of the explanation for EU regional policy lies in functional imperatives captured by the metaphor of functional spillover. Justifications include the negative effects of market integration on peripheral regions and the fact that European integration restricts the range of policy instruments that member states can use to combat such differences (Bourne, 2003:289).

The Commission has traditionally been closely involved in the monitoring and implementation of regional development projects. It has emphasised the importance of partnerships involving multiple actors, from the Commission itself, to local agencies and businesses, and even involving transnational co-operation. Throughout the 1990s the role of partnership initiatives increased, although Allen (2000:254) reports that a streamlining of procedures in relation to regional development projects effectively reduced the role of various partners in policy planning and implementation, and instead reasserted the dominance of central governments in the process.

Discussion 6.3

The Single Market, competition policy and support for regions

There is an interesting dilemma in respect of the ideal of a Single Market and the need for political control. Free-marketeers tend to approve of trade liberalising measures but reject the political mechanisms necessary in order for the market to work. Obvious examples of political mechanisms at the European level include EU competition policy, Commission directives relating to the Single Market and rulings by the ECJ. In respect of regional policy, the Commission would argue that it has to have a role in the maintenance of a level playing field within the Single Market. The Commission holds that the efficiency and competitiveness of the Single Market is undermined by national governments subsidising their regions or specific industries. Therefore, the Union – through the Commission and its Competition Policy watchdog – is mindful of such activities. In fact, the Union takes on a partially supranational role in regional development through structural funding. It is only partially supranational, since decisions on management and actual deployment of funds are taken locally. Clearly, all this is anathema to eurosceptics and amounts to Brussels 'interference' in domestic affairs. It might be pointed out, however, that for some on the political right the whole question of structural funding or even domestic support for regions, or for struggling industries, is undesirable. It runs counter to the normal processes of supply and demand. Equally, the notion of 'free market' is a chimera. No market is actually 'free' in the way a lot of rhetoric around trade might imply, and certainly not the Single European Market.

The notion of fair competition within the SEM, monitored by the Commission, is, however, just one of the responsibilities of the Commission, albeit an important one. The Commission needs to fulfil this role while simultaneously meeting other responsibilities, among them regional funding and the desire to assist the 'less advantaged' regions of the Community. Squaring this particular circle is one of the Commissions more difficult balancing acts.

The rationale for the Single Market throws up a dilemma relating in the wider sense to political control, and specifically where regional funding is concerned – see Discussion 6.3.

A useful spin-off from the Union having a regional development policy, at least as far as the Commission is concerned, is that successful regional development and greater integration of the peripheral regions could also achieve a better level of integration for the Union's citizens, and even improved understanding of the benefits of the Union. Examples of regional development initiatives include transport infrastructure through the Cohesion Fund, such as the high speed rail link between Madrid and Seville in Andalucia, an area designated as one of the more disadvantaged regions of the Union. Environmental improvements, from protection of local habitats to major land reclamation projects, can also have a positive and regenerating impact. A spectacular example of this is the Eden Project in Cornwall, located in an area severely damaged by a now redundant industry, tin mining. The Eden Project benefited from the European Regional Development Fund. At a more mundane level, tourism, retraining the unemployed, and study opportunities in remote areas are all examples of Community involvement in local communities. Few would dispute the benefits of cleaner beaches, improved infrastructure, protected habitats and land reclamation. It is through projects like these, large and small, that the Commission aims to bring benefits to regions and to villages, and in doing so, hopes to justify the existence of the European Union for the individual citizen.

Photograph 6.1 EU structural funds assisted in land reclamation and creation of the Eden Project in Cornwall, UK, on the site of a disused tin mine.

As well as a significantly enhanced role for regional development funding, the TEU contained a number of other innovations designed to benefit regions. One of these was the formalisation of a policy known as **subsidiarity**, whereby policy decisions would be made at the lowest appropriate level between Brussels, member-state governments or regions. This concept was not new, but it attained formal status in the TEU. Subsidiarity is an important component of multilevel governance and again it would reinforce the status of regions. The TEU also provided a key institutional innovation, the Committee of the Regions (CoR), composed of 317 members, all drawn from Europe's regions and appointed by member-state governments in consultation with local regional authorities. The Committee of the Regions was intended to provide the regions with a direct voice in Brussels, as well as through the European Parliament. The CoR has a limited role, however. It has no formal powers, but it is an advisory chamber, able to influence other more powerful institutions and therefore the legislative process. Many of its members are experienced local or regional politicians, bringing significant expertise as well as a knowledge of local and regional issues. Its emergence has significance, not only because it represents the regional voice at a European level, but because it offers the opportunity for regions to exchange experience, to network, to engage in synergies that bring mutual benefits. As a result, some of the positive impact of the CoR may be difficult to quantify, but it is nevertheless an important innovation in the institutionalisation of the European project. Bourne points out that establishing the CoR represented a breakthrough:

> It recognised regional authorities as legitimate participants in EU decision making and represented a significant departure from the hitherto prevalent idea that only central governments ought to represent their state in the EU (Bourne, 2003:281).

The CoR has attempted to make subsidiarity a more meaningful benefit for the regions, as its members judged that the TEU mostly set out a principle of subsidiarity which applied to the EU–member-state relationship (Bullmann, 1997:15). However, Bullmann also points out that the CoR is not exactly united in its approach to achieving higher profile, as there have been divisions between the more assertive representatives from larger, more powerful regions and others from more peripheral or smaller regions. Keating and Hooghe (1996:246–7) report that the CoR is especially weak: it is divided between sectional and geographical interests, the latter cutting north–south. Representatives from the German *Länder*, for example, whom one might expect to have the greatest influence, often find it easier to channel their influence through different means. Another weakness is that some national governments, notably France, exert powerful control over the French delegates to the CoR, while others leave regional authorities to choose their own representatives. Another significant innovation at Maastricht was acceptance that member states might 'delegate their vote in the Council to a ministerial representative of a sub-national tier of government' (Bullmann, 1997:15–16). Germany, Austria and Belgium, as well as representatives from the Scottish Parliament and the Welsh Assembly, have made use of this, but Bourne (2003:282) reports that Spanish regional representatives have yet to do so. The issue is still a matter for negotiation with Madrid (see below). It is likely that possible regional participation in the Council is the most productive route for regions to gain greater influence in the policy-making process, but it is also likely that national governments will remain 'gatekeepers' where access to the Council is concerned. It is therefore important to recognise the limitations of the Maastricht initiatives, rather than to necessarily see matters such as subsidiarity, or the arrival of the Committee of the Regions, as a great leap forward for regional participation in the EU policy-making process.

The late 1980s and 1990s also saw the development of cultural initiatives with a regional dimension, for example in education. Education policy at the Union level is barely developed, but through the Socrates Programme the Commission has encouraged student mobility between universities in different member states, as well as teaching staff exchanges. The Lingua Programme focuses on transnational projects involving language teachers in joint professional development initiatives. In these fields, too, the value of partnerships across regions and between states, as well as from local communities to the Commission, are a vital part of the rationale for engaging in such projects. In addition, more recently the Union has taken measures to provide greater support to minority languages.

Finally, Maastricht also increased the powers and the profile of the European Parliament, the only directly elected body composed of local or regional, rather than specifically national, representatives.

Review   *What was the rationale for the European Community (as it then was) to develop a regional policy?*

What have been the main instruments of this policy?

What are the strengths and weaknesses of the Committee of the Regions?

● ● ● ● Funding EU regional policies

One of the significant areas of dispute relating to an increased structural funding budget is, of course, the question of who pays, and who gets what. The EU annual budget is €89.6bn, or 1.13 per cent of the entire GDP of the Union. It is projected to remain less than 1.2 per cent throughout 2000–2006 (figures from Pinder, 2001:88). The budget is highly contested, especially as the costs are not borne equally. There are net contributors and net recipients (see Discussion 6.4). The major contributors have been Germany and the Netherlands, and since the 1995 enlargement Austria and Sweden. The UK, thanks to the continuing 'rebate' – amounting to €3.1bn in 1999 – achieved by Margaret Thatcher at Fontainebleau in 1982 and regarded as inviolable by British governments ever since, is a small net contributor. France benefits from the enormous largesse of the CAP, a factor which underlines French obstructionism whenever meaningful reform of the CAP is broached. France emerges an even smaller contributor to the budget than Britain. At the opposite end of the scale are the Mediterranean member states, Italy, Spain, Greece and Portugal, plus Ireland, all net recipients from the EU budget, and significant beneficiaries from regional development funding. The critical question now is how will enlargement impact on budgets? *Agenda 2000*, agreed after the Treaty of Amsterdam in 1997, set out the Commission's requirements for both member states and the applicant states planning to join the Union. One of the major implications of the 2004 enlargement is the impact of ten new members, mostly from Central and Eastern Europe, on the Community budget. *Agenda 2000* determined that new member states would receive much less from the CAP than they might have wished for. Were they to get payments proportional to existing beneficiaries, the Union's finances would implode.

It appeared that enlargement would have significant implications for those member states already benefiting from structural funding, since their receipts would be significantly reduced or removed altogether once the poorer Eastern European states joined the Union. Furthermore, Bourne (2003:286) cites a Commission study that estimated that benefits accruing from the Eastern enlargement would be enjoyed mainly in Germany, France and the UK, and the Mediterranean states were significantly less likely to secure advantages from the accession of the CEECs. As *Agenda 2000* made clear, it was inconceivable that

Discussion 6.4

Funding the EU: who gets what and who pays?

The vexed question of funding the EU budget has long dogged the EU and is becoming an ever more controversial issue, much exploited by the EU's opponents. The major contributor to the Community/EU budget has always been Germany, with – as Table 6.1 shows – a contribution of over 6 per cent of its GDP throughout most of the 1990s. This burden is one that Germany is increasingly reluctant to meet, especially since it has had to meet the extra cost of German reunification. A key dispute concerns the UK – a net contributor, albeit not by very much, on account of the substantial rebate it receives from other Union members. The rebate was secured in part as a back payment on account of increased food costs that Britain endured after joining the EEC, a result of UK incorporation into the CAP instead of continuing to enjoy cheaper food imports from the Commonwealth. The UK benefits from structural funding support but gains little from the CAP because of its relatively small agricultural sector.

Given the likely cost implications of enlargement there will have to be reform of the budget, including a reassessment of the British rebate. One source of revenue that might be increased is the current 1 per cent of VAT levied across the Union which is diverted to the Union and currently raises about 36 per cent of the budget – the approximate cost of structural funding. State budgetary payments raise about half of Union funds, enough to cover the costs of the CAP. Germany tolerated its high contribution for years, but it has become customary for all net contributors to complain about the scale of their payments. Pinder (2001:92) comments that this is a dangerous development, indicating a lack of community spirit, especially as the Union enlarges to take in significantly poorer states to the east. The current perspective until 2006 of expenditure amounting to less than 1.2 per cent of GDP may not be enough, and Pinder wonders if the statutory ceiling of 1.27 per cent of Union GDP may have to be raised if the CEECs are to be helped to succeed in the Union.

Table 6.1 Member-state net budgetary payments or receipts 2000 (Percentage of GDP average 1992–99, minus sign net payment)

Belgium	−0.31
Denmark	0.20
Germany	−0.67
Greece	4.45
Spain	1.07
France	−0.12
Ireland	5.15
Italy	−0.12
Netherlands	−0.60
Austria (1995–97)	−0.34
Portugal	3.06
Finland (1995–97)	−0.03
Sweden (1995–97)	−0.49
United Kingdom	−0.30

Source: *Finance in the European Union*, October 1998, Annexe 8, Table 5. Reprinted with permission from the Official Publications of the European Communities.

existing budgetary arrangements be retained after enlargement. The costs of both the Common Agricultural Policy and of structural funding would be much too high if the new member states were to be treated in the same way that Greece, Spain and Portugal have been treated since they joined the Union – and Ireland and Italy, for that matter.

In the event, the mood among existing members, especially the Mediterranean states, hardened. In 2002 the Berlin European Council affirmed bad news for the applicants: the overwhelming proportion of structural funds (€213bn out of a total of €258bn) would be distributed among current members, and applicant states would only get €45bn. The existing 15 member states concocted a 'take it or leave it' message for the applicants. But enlargement happened anyway and the issue of budgetary reform is still outstanding. It is clear that there is no spirit of largesse towards the new members, where the average GDP is around 40 per cent of the Union average. There have been unfortunate repercussions: in the June 2004 elections to the European Parliament, anti-European and eurosceptic parties performed strongly in the new member states where voter turnout averaged a feeble 26 per cent. Across the Union the figure was only 44.2 per cent, and governing parties generally took a hammering, while eurosceptic parties did well. Clearly the Union is suffering for its failure to address long-standing problems. Institutional reform, arguments over the proposed Constitution, an effective and workable framework for the 2004 enlargement and budgetary reform are all unresolved issues. In addition, growth remains low and unemployment persistently high, especially in Germany.

Review   *What are some of the major issues concerning the funding of the European Union? Why did the new member states joining in 2004 get such a poor deal from structural funding?*

Theoretical implications of regional development policy: multilevel governance

One of the topics of interest to scholars emerging from the growth in European regional development policy has been a concept of an emerging 'Europe of the Regions'. This model suggests that European integration is projected towards a network of interrelated regional authorities engaged with supranational European-level institutions. The model is attractive both to federalists, and to regions with a highly developed sense of identity and with more developed and formal institutional apparatus – for example the *Länder* in Germany, or Spain's Autonomous Communities. For some regions, such as the Basque Country, it even presents an appealing solution to the 'state problem' represented by the Madrid government.

However, the idea of a Europe of the Regions is not well developed. As the last chapter suggested, federalism is not an ascendant force in European politics despite EMU, enlargement, and the continuing efforts to create a constitution for the Union. The idea of a Europe of the Regions is contested by theorists more inclined towards the intergovernmentalist perspective, such as Moravcsik. He reports that any influence that regions may have in the EU policy-making process are effective only if they are easily subsumed into the negotiating positions of their central government's representatives (Moravcsik, 1993:483–5). According to this view, a form of filtering occurs, and the whip hand is firmly with the states. One possible interpretation of this is that in the Committee of the Regions, for example, regional representatives may present their depositions to policy makers, but they will only listen if they want to. This may be overly cynical as there is evidence of how regional opinion can be effectively channelled. Bourne (2003:281) cites a Basque government report stating that a Basque representative had tabled 69 amendments to Committee of the Regions opinions, and 80 per cent had been accepted. However, that does not necessarily mean that the CoR opinions were accepted by the legislators, or that they were effective in shaping legislation. It remains a criticism of the CoR that it lacks formal authority and its opinions may be disregarded. Indeed some critics of multilevel governance theory (MLG) have indicated the danger in assuming that participation in decision-making, for example by the CoR, implies the power to actually impact on agreed outcomes (Kohler-Koch, 1996:375).

One of the weaknesses of the Europe of the Regions idea is that the regions themselves are poorly formalised, in many cases lacking clear identity and institutional structures. 'Some states have no regional governments at all' (Keating & Hooghe, 1996:243), and circumstances differ widely, even in respect of issues such as the extent to which civil society is closely linked to local or regional governance. In Italy, for example, this is weak, while it is much stronger in Germany. Widely differing circumstances apply to, for example, Cornwall and the Scilly Isles, and Bavaria, or between Brittany and Catalonia. Furthermore, linkage between regions is weak despite the best efforts of the Commission, through its commitment to partnerships.

It seems more accurate to recognise the continuing pre-eminence of member states in the EU policy making. The representatives of member-state governments act as gatekeepers, as suggested above, in allowing regional authorities access. In Brussels, formal regional representation extends to an advisory role through the Committee of the Regions, or to participation in some deliberations of the Council where this is accepted by the national ministries involved. Even in terms of the implementation of regional policy, the involvement of central governments has not diminished – it may even have increased in recent times (Allen, 2000:254).

Nevertheless, theoretical explanations for European integration cannot entirely rule out the role of sub-state actors. In the previous chapter the concept of **multilevel governance** (MLG) was introduced and we can develop this further here, because the idea of MLG relates closely to regional development policy. Multilevel governance is a theory associated mainly with Hooghe and Marks (2001). The core arguments of the MLG perspective are presented in Discussion 6.5.

Discussion 6.5

Multilevel governance: the case for an alternative theory of EU policy making

MLG proposes that:

1. regional, state and supranational actors share control over many activities that take place in their respective territories;
2. states are one among a variety of actors contesting decisions that are made at a variety of levels;
3. there are transnational linkages between actors located in and representing different political arenas (Marks, Hooghe and Blank, 1996:346–7, cited in Bourne, 2003:290).

MLG assumes a dissemination of power between the European level represented by supranational institutions – albeit to some extent penetrated by individual member-state interests, and the states themselves – and sub-state or regional authorities. It suggests a complex interplay between the levels, with much blurring of the lines between them. The imprecise divisions between the various levels are inevitable given the complexity and variety of policy-making procedures, and the normative character of governance in Brussels, meaning a tendency for coalition building around usual routes to problem-solving, or pressure on interested parties to coalesce in a spirit of cooperation. The growth of regional development projects has meant an increased profile for the regions and created opportunities for local interests to not only interact with European level actors in EU institutions, but also to create partnerships in other regions, or with interest groups in Brussels. A feature of the European Union not explored in any detail in this book is the role of interest groups and lobbyists in policy making (see Greenwood, 1997; Mazey & Richardson, 1993; Pedler & Van Schendelen, 1994). Interest groups and advisory bodies are strongly represented in Brussels and may contribute to the channelling of regional interests, for example through representing large employers. In so doing they contribute to the culture of MLG.

MLG theory suggests that the state is under pressures from 'above' and 'below' and that policy making is a complex interplay of various actors at various levels. Keating and Hooghe draw attention to the role of economic change reducing the role of the state. They write that:

> policy making retreats into complex networks which do not correspond to formal institutions; and new and rediscovered forms of identity emerge at the sub-national and even at the supranational level (Keating & Hooghe, 1996:242).

Clearly, central governments do not have a monopoly on policy making. MLG theory can point to the prominent role of the Commission in pursuing Regional Development through Structural Funds, indicating once more the significance of neo-functionalist ideas about the autonomy of EU institutions and the limitations of state power. In essence, according to Bourne, MLG is important because it forces a re-examination of traditional perspectives and it evidently does 'capture something of an important new reality in EU policy making' (Bourne, 2003:292).

MLG does not entirely rule out the neo-functionalist view that supranational EU institutions can pursue policies independently, eventually co-opting support from state ministries, and achieving further policy objectives through functionalist spillover processes. MLG also holds that other actors contribute to policy formulation, and that some of these have specific local and regional interests. Networking and normative pressures all apply and to differing degrees in different policy areas. In some areas regional interests may bypass central government and channel opinion directly towards the European Parliament or the Commission. The Committee of the Regions may have a significant role in this respect. The profile of the regions of the EU has grown in Brussels, with more regional offices and more, though still not much, association between regions. There is no doubt that any description of European polity now has to take account of a regional dimension.

Indeed, regional policy has attained importance in relation to integration theory generally, as shown in the claim that it is an example of spillover effect, but also because regional policy has so markedly become a part of intergovernmental bargaining. The clearest example of this is the negotiations over EU enlargement, discussed in the previous section. Other areas of regional policy including such issues as transnational communication links and environmental policy have also featured in the interplay between state representatives. Policies are never made in isolation and functional intergovernmentalism remains a marked feature, perhaps even the dominant one, of EU politics. The growth of a regional dimension to policy making is likely to contribute further to the culture of intergovernmental bargaining that dominates policy processes, rather than undermine it. Whereas initially regional policy provided an important spur to MLG theory, the Berlin Summit in 1999, referred to above, at which the member states agreed to retain the majority of structural funding for themselves rather than permit redistributive aid towards the applicant states from Central and Eastern Europe, appeared to indicate that the pendulum had swung back. Intergovernmentalism was reasserting itself and the principles on which the Commission had constructed regional policy were substantially weakened (Allen, 2000:262). Indeed Allen says that 'historic' decisions are still constructed on the basis of intergovernmentalist deals. He concludes:

> Despite a great deal of sub-national activity associated with the structural funds, there is no really convincing evidence that this has weakened the intergovernmental character of policy negotiation (Allen, 2000:263).

At the end of the previous chapter it was argued that policy processes are different in different sectors. Indeed, even within the area of regions and regional policy we should perhaps clearly differentiate and highlight the two different contexts examined in this chapter. First, on the one hand we have considered regional development policy and the deployment of structural funds. In this area MLG theorists present a persuasive case that regional involvement in policy processes is considerable and the role of states can in some cases be more marginal

– although not in terms of the 'historic decisions' that settle the budgets for structural funding.

Secondly, on the other hand, where we considered the direct involvement of the regions and regional interests in policy making in general, for example through participation in the legislative process, we notice a decisive absence of regional authority. Opinion, yes, influence, maybe. But it is evident that the states remain in the driving seat. Where regions are concerned, the notion of the state as gatekeeper seems especially persuasive. Bourne quotes Pollack in arguing that regional as well as EU authorities are merely actors in an 'inter-governmental play' (Pollack, 1995:362).

In conclusion, it is important to place the foregoing in the context of globalisation and other trends happening beyond the reach of either regional authorities, or EU institutions. This book is concerned with how European integration is affected by globalisation. Keating and Hooghe make an important observation in respect of this:

> Regionalism and European integration have changed the national state in important ways. It is difficult, however, to isolate these from other factors pointing in the same direction – the internationalisation of markets; capital mobility; the rise of trans-national corporations; and neo-liberal ideology. Territorial politics in the European Union is complex (Keating & Hooghe, 1996:251).

This highlights the weakness of the state and the extent to which traditional state authority has been undermined. But it does not suggest that authority has shifted elsewhere in the triangular relationship between EU institutions – state – regional authority. Indeed, all are compromised by the profound economic and social consequences of neo-liberal globalisation. These are examined in the final four chapters of the book.

Keating and Hooghe comment on the new strains in EU polity, especially the tensions involved in adjustments to the discipline of EMU, and the fact that poorer countries may find themselves handicapped by not having traditional fiscal tools and currency adjustment to cope with economic downturns. The EU may instead find that it has to secure resource shifts to its poorer regions in order to compensate, but as we have seen from *Agenda 2000* and the limited access to structural funds granted to the new member states, these are not options the Union appears able or willing to pursue. Enlargement itself presents a second challenge, and a particularly serious one for the weakest regions. Keating and Hooghe comment that

> We have not seen the rise of a new territorial hierarchy. The national state has not been bypassed in favour of a Europe of the regions. The national state remains the primary actor in the EU. This does not mean, however, that policy making in this field can be explained simply by interstate bargaining (ibid.).

In fact, policy making is carried out through a complex of European, national state and regional interests, with varying state or regional engagement in different states. Keating and Hooghe call this 'the Europeanisation and regionalisation of national policy making' (ibid.).

The wider economic context afforded by an era of globalisation also underlies a cautionary conclusion from Allen (2000:262–4). He writes that structural funds are likely to continue to play an important role in an enlarged EU, but they can never provide the solution to wide economic disparities. Smaller states can benefit considerably from net transfers through structural funding – Ireland in the 1990s conclusively proves that – but in general, economic advancement by the CEECs will come from their improved economic performance, supported by European competition policy and by the coordinated economic policies of the member governments. It will depend on their successful adjustment to the changed circumstances of a more globalised, more neo-liberal economy. Allen points out that the apparent retrenchment by the 15 pre-enlargement member states may actually be the best and most realistic step for the longer-term stability of the Union, a Union which, he points out, 'was constructed, and has been sustained, by relatively coherent member states with relatively strong central governments' (Allen, 2000:263).

An examination of regional policy, which takes into account the wider economic forces mentioned by Keating and Hooghe, forces us to 'rethink our understanding of statehood based on the idea of bounded territorial spaces with impermeable borders' (Bourne, 2003:292). It is not like that.

Review   *Suggest a key weakness in the notion of a Europe of the Regions. What is multilevel governance theory?*
Suggest two ways that regional interests may affect policy processes in the European Union. What does this tell us about EU policy processes in general?

● ● ● ● ## Comparison of the EU–region relationship in Spain and Germany

The first section of this chapter points out that there are wide differences in the extent to which member states of the European Union accommodate a regional dimension to their governance. Briefly, Italy and France for example use sub-state authorities as merely administrative agents, while Germany, Austria and Belgium have fully developed federal systems. Spain has what one might describe as a quasi-federal construction, based on its 17 Autonomous Communities. The UK has taken some federalising steps since 1997, changes which partially address the highly centralised nature of UK governance hitherto, but nevertheless regional structures are virtually absent in England, where 48 million of the UK's population of 59 million live.

This section examines two examples of regional representation at the European level, looking at Germany and Spain. What is striking is that despite their federal and quasi-federal similarities, the experience of their regional representation in the European Union is very different. One might suspect that the explanation for this would lie in the EU–region relationship itself, but it does not. Much more significant is the quality of the relationship between the regional authorities and their central government authorities. For historical reasons, these are very different.

After the Second World War the German Basic Law or Constitution created the Federal Republic of Germany. The *Länder* have a generally good relationship with the federal government and the two accept the division of competence that exists between them. However, the *Länder* have a restricted level of competence:

> The *Länder* possess only a very limited range of exclusive responsibilities. [. . .] Their primary functions in the German federal system are [. . .] to work, through their federal level organ, the *Bundesrat*, alongside federal-level authorities in the co-determination of (most) federal-level legislation; and to implement (most) federal-level legislation with a large degree of discretion (Jeffery, 1997:58).

Furthermore, European Community affairs were traditionally viewed in Germany as constituting a part of foreign policy, and therefore solely in the domain of the federal government. However, this changed in 1992 and European policy has become 'domestic'. Jeffery reports on how the *Länder* successfully argued that EC policy impacts so directly on domestic concerns that it could not simply be regarded as part of foreign policy (Jeffery, 1997:59).

As is well known, ratification of the TEU was difficult and perhaps nowhere more so – the possible exception is Denmark – than in Germany, which actually was the last to ratify the Treaty. The *Länder* challenged the Treaty in the German Federal Constitutional Court, arguing that it ran counter to the guarantees to the *Länder* provided in the Basic Law. In fact, the Karlsruhe judgment, as it became known, ruled against the claim that the TEU would transfer authority to an entity that was 'more than intergovernmental'. The pillar structure of the TEU convinced the Court that the European Union was indeed more intergovernmental than state-like (see Bainbridge, 2002:343, and Jeffery, 1997:60). Nevertheless, the *Länder* did manage to secure certain guarantees through Basic Law amendments that would guarantee their right to participate in EC policy on the grounds that it was domestic, as opposed to foreign. These amendments included the provision that the *Länder* would have 'federal level competences' and that they would play a role in 'the codetermination and implementation of federal-level legislation' (Jeffery, 1997:61). The amendments also guaranteed that the *Länder* through the *Bundesrat* would be 'kept fully informed and be consulted in the process of formulation of Federal Government European policy'.

The success of the *Länder* in securing the concept of domestic European policy can be seen as evidence of the highly developed political culture in the German regions, a factor which in comparison with many other states (Italy for example) gives regional representation in Germany significant advantages. The *Länder* achievement in this respect contributed to the mood among European Union scholars to explore the existence of a 'Third Level' in European policy making. A further consequence was that the German experience over decades of both federalism and subsidiarity would feed debate in Europe on the extent to which the European Union might explore similar avenues, hence the inclusion of subsidiarity in the TEU. Certainly the *Länder* hoped that it might, and issued a declaration to this effect (Jeffery, 1997:64–5). However, the concept of subsidiarity has never been fully exploited and federalism has lost out to the more powerful intergovernmentalist preferences of member states.

Clearly, post-Maastricht, the German *Länder* managed to secure a role, if not centre stage, at least on the stage, on which European policy making is conducted by the federal government. What is significant is that in spite of this, the evolution of federal government in Germany does not signal the emergence of a Third Level across European policy making. The German context is simply not replicated elsewhere, with the possible exceptions of Belgium and Austria. The divided and weak Committee of the Regions, and the poorly developed regional polity in other states, including the near absence of a developed civic culture at the regional level in some (Putnam, 1993), means that the German sub-state experience is not likely to be easily replicated across the Union.

Jeffery concludes that one may bid farewell to the Third Level idea, and despite advances in Germany, the dominant authority remains the federal government, even though *Länder* participation in policy making is secure. In addition we have seen that the federal government has taken the opportunity provided by the TEU to offer *Länder* representatives voting rights on behalf of the federal government in some instances in the Council – in fact Basic Law amendments also guaranteed this right. This has not been the case where Spain is concerned. Indeed the last Spanish government, led by the conservative Popular Party, was especially unsympathetic to the claims from the Autonomous Communities for any greater devolution of authority from Madrid, and so the innovation agreed at Maastricht was never implemented in respect of the Spanish Autonomous Communities. In contrast, regional representatives from Germany, Austria, Belgium, Wales and Scotland have participated in Council meetings. For Spain, the PP permitted only observer status, which represented no particular advance on the pre-Maastricht protocol. It remains to be seen how the new PSOE (Socialist) government of Jose Luís R. Zapatero will respond to further calls from Spain's regions for their right to participate in the Council to be upheld. Early signs are that it is a concession he will make.

The key issue in the comparison between Germany and Spain is one of political stability and acceptance of the status quo. In Germany the Basic Law, after its European domestic policy amendments in 1992, is not questioned, and reform of the constitutional status of the *Länder* is not on the agenda. By contrast, in Spain a review of the status of the Autonomous Communities is never off it – at least not for the more assertive regions, the Basque Country, Catalonia and Galicia. These areas already have the most advanced form of autonomy in Spain – significantly more than the other Communities. Nevertheless they continue to ask for more and thereby a level of bubbling resentment persists that all Spanish governments have to contend with. The unfortunate consequence of this is that there is a degree of suspicion in relations between Madrid and the more assertive regional administrations. This breeds an atmosphere of mistrust and poor cooperation.

Paradoxically, the result is that the Spanish regions are less connected in Brussels and suffer from a degree of information gap, as opportunities for influence and opinion may be lost as they are not passed on by the central government. Since Brussels is above all controlled by central governments, especially in the Council and its various committees, access and participation by regions is dependent on the proactive goodwill of central government representatives. If this is not especially forthcoming, the regions find that they are less 'in the loop' than they might otherwise be. This is the Spanish experience.

The German *Länder*, by contrast, are more successful in two respects. Firstly, they are much better informed by central government agencies and representatives, the communication between them and the Federal government is much better. Secondly, they are more effective at networking across Europe with other regional interests, notably in Austria, Belgium, and elsewhere. The Spanish Autonomous Communities are less successful in this respect too.

In a detailed analysis of institutional adaptation to the process of **Europeanisation** in Germany and Spain, Tanja Börzel (2002) explores the cultural differences between German and Spanish governance. She contrasts the two with a description of Germany as 'co-operative federalism', while Spain, in contrast, exhibits 'competitive regionalism'. After the major steps in European integration in the 1980s and early 1990s, as we have already seen, regions in particular risked particular hardships consequent upon transformations in the European and global economies. The increasingly supranational dimension of European Community law appeared to impact severely on regions' freedom of manoeuvre, and not only that, but restrict the extent to which central governments could compensate for the economic consequences of greater harmonisation and internationalisation of markets. The regions had to discover ways to adapt to the changed circumstances introduced by the SEA, the TEU, the convergence criteria and the imminence of EMU. Börzel claims that this adaptation has occurred more easily in Germany than in Spain.

Changes in the German Basic Law were mirrored in Spain. In 1994 the Spanish government and the Autonomous Communities agreed on formal procedures which would permit the latter to participate in the decision-making and implementation of European policies. There were further steps over the next two years and the procedures were incorporated into law in 1997, but the Autonomous Communities did not have access to the Council, although they do have the right to determine the government's bargaining position where their 'exclusive competencies' (Börzel, 2002:1) are affected. Börzel points out that the constitutional changes in Germany merely brought European policy making into line with other areas where the *Länder* already had shared responsibility with the federal authorities. By contrast, in Spain changes which permitted regional participation in European policy making were comparative innovations in Spanish polity.

> Unlike in domestic policy-making, the Autonomous Communities have direct co-decision powers in central-state decision-making in Europe (Börzel, 2002:2).

Unfortunately, this dichotomy between the domestic and European policy arenas has meant that there has been little cooperative bargaining between the central and regional authorities. Börzel blames this on competitive nationalism, and implies that this malign force is operating not only in the Autonomous Communities, but also in Madrid, although she appears to pin responsibility mainly on the former:

Spanish competitive nationalism, [in] contrast [to German cooperative federalism] has been characterised by conflict and distrust. The *Comunidades Autónomas* compete rather than cooperate with the central state. Consequently the regions [have] attempted to bypass the Spanish government in European policy-making. [. . .] In Spain a new institutional framework had to be installed because up until [1997] competitive regionalism had prevented the emergence of the cooperative institutions necessary for the regions to participate in European policy-making (Börzel, 2002:2–3).

She goes on:

The German *Länder* and the Spanish *Comunidades Autónomas* have similar resources. But they have pursued opposing strategies in their attempts to redress the balance of power that has been upset by Europeanisation. Cooperative federalism induced the German *Länder* to pursue a strategy of cooperation with the state, which aimed at securing co-decision rights in the formulation and representation of the German bargaining position. The result of competitive regionalism in Spain, by contrast, was that the *Comunidades Autónomas* assumed a confrontational strategy which resorted to constitutional conflict and 'circumventing the state' in order to prevent further loss of power (Börzel, 2002:5).

We can conclude from the above that the different approaches in Spain and Germany stem from different experiences of regionalism within their body politic and different political cultures. Börzel says that in Germany the *Länder* adopted a cooperative strategy from the outset and calculated that this would best enable them to respond to their loss of power on account of Europeanisation. As a result the cooperative culture of German politics was enhanced by Europeanisation. Confrontation, by contrast, would prohibit institutional adaptation. Börzel says that the *Länder*, more than other regions, have the resources to circumvent their central authorities, but they choose not to, since to do so would undermine the federal government. But in Spain there were no pre-existing structures on which to build cooperation in European policy making. This made adjustment especially difficult, but the result was certainly that Spain proved much less adept at compensating for the losses incurred as a result of Europeanisation. However, the Spanish Autonomous Communities have noted the comparative success of the *Länder* in effective engagement with European policy making and have recently moved towards improved cooperation with the Spanish state.

Finally Börzel comments on other issues that have been discussed in this chapter. She says that even if all the best-resourced regional authorities (those in Germany, Austria, Belgium and Spain) were to develop a cooperative culture with their central governments, it would not signal any great improvement in the prospects for an independent and unified regional level of government in European affairs. And furthermore, she is cautious about the extent to which European-level competences are channelled downwards to the sub-state level:

While domestic legislative powers are transferred to the European level, the compensatory regional co-decision rights in European policy-making offer little benefit because they benefit the regional executives, not the legislatures. The erosion of the political power of the regional parliaments reinforces the general trend of deparliamentarisation, which is a trend that has come along with Europeanisation (Börzel, 2002:2–3).

This is a standard assumption – executives rule, legislatures follow (see Discussion 2.2). Certainly in the context of the EU, national legislatures are extremely weak, and while the powers of the European Parliament have greatly increased through co-decision (see Chapter 4) the ruling national executives in the Council are the most powerful legislators and decision-makers in the Union. This means that the criticism that European integration is an 'elite driven project' is hard to rebut. Furthermore, while the executive sets the rules, the costs and implementation responsibilities are passed down to state and sub-state authorities (Börzel, 2002:88). The experience in Germany has clearly shown, however, that the *Länder* have pursued a 'compensation-through-participation' strategy, consistent with their historical experience of cooperative federalism. Nevertheless, this strategy choice also contributed to the process of deparliamentarisation in Germany. Börzel describes German federalism as 'executive federalism' (Börzel, 2002:89). She also writes that the increased cooperation between the Autonomous Communities in Spain and the central government authorities, achieved by their following the more successful patterns of behaviour observed in Germany, equally demonstrates elite bargaining – the regional legislatures are left out of the process. This tendency has implications across Europe:

> Executive dominance in European policy-making – at the regional, national and European level – is major reason for the lack of transparency and accountability in European policy-making (Börzel, 2002:88).

It is also, I would suggest, a highly plausible explanation for the low turnout in elections to the European Parliament, and falling turnout in national elections too. The disconnection and disaffection of electorates is a widespread and serious challenge to democratic government.

Review   *What are the contrasts between the German and Spanish experience in responding to Europeanisation?*
What are the lessons that might be drawn for the wider European political process?

Summary

This chapter has made the following key points.

The practical significance of regional development policy

- Regional development policies through structural funding emerged as a response to key centralising initiatives such as the SEM and EMU.
- Structural funding initiatives and regional development policies can contribute to the creation of partnerships across the Union and between regions and EU institutions.

- Regional policies and structural funding initiatives can assist in connecting citizens to the aims and objectives of the Union.
- Regional development policy can be interpreted as an example of neo-functional spillover.
- The Committee of the Regions, created within the TEU, is an important conduit for advice and expertise from regional representatives to other EU institutions, but it lacks formal authority.

Funding EU regional policies

- Germany makes the largest individual contribution to EU funding, both in real terms and as a percentage of GDP.
- The 2004 enlargement challenges the entire basis of how the EU is funded and how its resources are deployed, since the new members are much poorer than the EU average.
- The logic of regional development policy would suggest that the EU should provide assistance to the new members.
- EU-15, and especially the Mediterranean states, have jibbed at this and the new member states are receiving much less than they might once have expected.
- EU funding and budgetary policy needs a complete overhaul.

Theoretical implications of regional development policy: multilevel governance

- The idea of a Europe of the Regions appeals to both federalists and some regions of the EU, but the idea is not well developed.
- Multilevel governance (MLG) suggests a dispersal of power across and between key actors at the European, state and sub-state levels.
- MLG forces a reassessment of conventional theories of policy-making processes and power relationships in the EU.
- Regional development policy has brought regional actors into both policy making and policy implementation.
- In broader policy areas, regional actors may have some influence but they have little power.
- States act as gatekeepers for regional influence on policy making.
- Policy-making processes vary considerably across and between sectors and issues.

Comparison of the EU–region relationship in Spain and Germany

- The German *Länder* achieved changes in the German constitution in 1992 which allowed them to fully participate in European policy-making processes. This suited a pre-existing culture of cooperation with federal government authorities.

- Germany demonstrates a style of government that we may call 'cooperative federalism', which could be adapted easily to accommodate European policy making.
- Spain has demonstrated a more 'competitive regionalism'. This proved unsuccessful in the arena of European policy making, because poor relations between Madrid and the regions diminished information flow and hindered effective partnership.
- The German model, while reasonably effective in Germany, cannot simply be exported to other, very different polities.
- Both the German and Spanish systems illustrate the weakness of regional parliaments. This is consistent with the Europe-wide problem of political processes being dominated by elites: executives rule, legislatures follow.

Key concepts: discussion and other definitions

Key concept 6.1   Subsidiarity

The principle that tries to ensure that decisions are taken as close as possible to the citizen (Cini, 2003:423).

This is an honourable and desirable concept – in theory. In practice, it has been a disappointment. The idea, as expressed above, is simple. It implies the existence of levels of authority, typically at the European, state, and sub-state levels. See Discussion 6.6 for a suggestion of how such a level-based principle of subsidiarity might, in theory, work.

In fact, in the Treaty there is no mention of any levels, other than the top two. A criticism of the concept of subsidiarity is precisely that: it doesn't get remotely close enough to 'the citizen'. In addition, given that so much EU legislation relates to the Single European Market (described therefore as 'Community Law'), subsidiarity only applies at the top level – so the citizen may indeed feel very remote from the decision-making process. The explanations that a proposal or directive 'is a Single Market issue' cuts little ice with sceptics.

A ruling on food production standards, ingredients or labelling might be argued on grounds of health and safety, animal welfare, or consumer law. Some people are quite happy for food standards to be set by Brussels, but not everyone is.

The concept of subsidiarity was introduced in the Treaty on European Union as a response to concerns expressed during the 1980s about the centralising character of many of the Community's most important policy initiatives. For example, the Single European Act could be interpreted as highly damaging to the interests of the regions, and in fact especially so for the periphery.

However, subsidiarity has tended to work, not for the benefit of regions, but for the benefit of states. Hooghe and Keating (1994) point out that the member-

---

Discussion 6.6

Subsidiarity across four levels – an illustration

(Level 3 and 4 illustrations are not based on reality or actuality)

Level One – European

If legislation is required to prevent industries from polluting the environment, for example by dumping effluent into a river that flows by a chemical works, then it would be best for the European Community to pass such legislation, rather than a local council. There should be, most would agree, one law, at European level, for the entire European Union and Single Market Area.

Level Two – State

If a state government wants to raise public sector pensions, then that should be of concern to the state authorities alone. The EU, arguably, has no legitimate interest in the decision. The state raises the pensions, and all state employees get the benefits.

Level Three – Region

The regional authorities may decree changes to the school day – for example to begin and end half an hour earlier if that is deemed advisable and acceptable to the teachers, the parents and the children. Such competence, for example, applies to German *Länder*.

Level Four – Local community/district council/city council

Should I want to build an extension on my house to accommodate a double jacuzzi and a sun lounge, then my local authority can decide whether to give me planning permission, or whether to tell me I can't do it because according to my architect's elaborate design, the sun lounge would overlook my neighbour's dining room.

---

state governments were able to exploit the principle of subsidiarity to take back control from the Commission over regional policy in the mid to late 1990s.

This is what the TEU says about subsidiarity:

> The Community shall act within the limits of the powers conferred upon it by this Treaty and of the objectives assigned to it therein. In areas which do not fall within its exclusive competence, the Community shall take action, in accordance with the principle of subsidiarity, only if and in so far as the objectives of the proposed action cannot be sufficiently achieved by the member States and can therefore, by reason of the scale or effects of the proposed action, be better achieved by the Community. Any action by the Community shall not go beyond what is necessary to achieve the objectives of this Treaty (Article 5, EC Treaty).

So it is clear that the principle in fact pushes responsibility to the state, and no further. Subsidiarity therefore enhances state powers, not regional powers. Jones (2001:62) comments that the principle is vague and open to interpretation. It is a 'broad principle rather than a clear guide'. It has been interpreted by some as a protection against federalism (Jones cites former British Premier John Major as an example) and as fully compatible with the logic of federalism by others.

Here's another definition:

> The principle that decisions should be taken at the lowest level consistent with effective action within a political system (Bainbridge, 2002:491)

Bainbridge refers to doubts about the usefulness of the concept given that it is too vague to be effectively interpreted by the courts. If the ECJ decides to interpret that vagueness in ways which appear to benefit the Community against the state, then that would cut across the entire basis of the principle and further politicise the ECJ, damaging its credibility.

The Treaty of Amsterdam attempted a clarification of subsidiarity by spelling out circumstances in which the Community may act, and emphasising the check as to whether desired outcomes could not be best achieved by state action as opposed to Community action. The key term here is proportionality – are the legislative proposals envisaged proportional to achieving the desired outcomes?

In conclusion, the question of subsidiarity remains somewhat vague. One weakness that echoes a point made previously in this chapter is that the question of subsidiarity may be a useful brake on over-zealous law-making in Brussels, but it passes responsibility from one elite to another – state executives. In a more ideal world, the concept might genuinely operate on a continuum from supranational executive to citizen. At the moment, it does not appear to do so. Nevertheless, the President of the Commission won't need to express a view on my application to build a sun lounge with a double jacuzzi.

Key concept 6.2 Europeanisation

The process by which authority over domestic, or state-level political and economic processes is relocated to the European arena.

This term is a relatively new one in the literature on the European Union. It is extensively used by Börzel (2002) and therefore referred to several times in this chapter. The context in which Börzel uses the term relates to the impact on regions, which is also how it is used in this chapter, hence the definition above.

This chapter has included the claim that the development of European regional policy, and specifically the rapid growth in the use of structural funding to boost economic and social improvements in less-developed regions of the Union, occurred as a response to criticism of several of the Union's more centralising policies. It was argued that the Single Market Project, and in particular the SEA, was a powerful shift of authority towards the Union and its supranational institutions. Indeed, the Single Market requires much greater levels of political control to enforce effective competition policy, health and safety legislation and environmental standards. At the same time, the pressures on the Community to be more competitive obliged the Union to exert much stronger influence over member states' economic policies. This became especially true in the run-up to Economic and Monetary Union, itself another example of a hugely centralising and integrating policy initiative. These policy trends are presented as examples of Europeanisation: the incursion of European policy on policy areas that were hitherto the responsibility of national or state governments.

Here's another definition:

> The strengthening of the European integration 'project' or the 'European construction' as a political ambition (Olsen, 2003:333).

This definition emphasises the 'project' nature of Europeanisation, whereas I have tended not to stress this aspect, being more concerned with the economic impacts in the context of regional policy. For example, the fiscal discipline imposed on member states by the Maastricht criteria was intended to prepare states for the launch of the euro in 1999. One of the consequences of the resultant austerity measures carried through by state governments was that their own capacity to provide fiscal support to their underperforming regions was compromised. Not only that, their entire budgetary planning and spending plans would be subject to tight controls imposed by the convergence criteria. The Commission could see that there were risks in this approach: one being that the reduction in support for poorer regions might lead to a political backlash, or that the states themselves might lose faith in the EMU project and choose to back out. The solution forthcoming from the Commission was to boost the funding provided by the Union to its poorer regions. This would compensate both the regions and their states for the efforts required to meet Commission targets in respect of the SEM and EMU.

The term Europeanisation is also applied in the following way:

> The domestic impact of European-level institutions (Olsen, ibid.).

For example, it is clear that the processes of introducing and consolidating the SEM and EMU involve substantial domestic impact of the Commission, the ECJ and the ECB, among others.

Here's another definition of Europeanisation:

> The Europeanisation of domestic institutions, politics and identities (Cini, 2003:418).

This definition is less helpful, because of its obvious tautology. Nevertheless, perhaps the implications are clear: Europeanisation changes things from the exclusively domestic or state-based to the European. This is the Full Monty in terms of upsetting opponents of European integration, since not only would it undermine local (and no doubt cherished) institutions, it alters the rules of politics and, worst of all, it introduces European *identity*, which for some is like having Beelzebub round for dinner.

Further reading

Bourne, A. (2003) 'Regional Europe', Chapter 18, pp. 278–93, in Cini, M. (ed.), *European Union Politics*, Oxford: Oxford University Press. This is an admirably clear and comprehensive overview of regional policy in the EU.

Börzel, T.A. (2002) *States and Regions in the European Union: Institutional adaptation in Germany and Spain*, Cambridge: Cambridge University Press. A detailed account of how state and regional authorities respond to increased Europeanisation. The study is based mainly on a comparison between the German and Spanish approach to the problem, but it also has implications for wider processes of governance, including questions of legitimacy and accountability.

Jeffery, C. (1997) *The Regional Dimension of the European Union*, London: Frank Cass.

Keating, M. & **Hooghe**, L. (1996) 'Bypassing the nation state? Regions and the EU policy process', in Richardson, J. (ed.) *European Union: Power and Policy Making*, 2nd edition. London: Routledge. Although written a few years before the advent of EMU, let alone enlargement, this is an excellent and prescient survey of the EU–region relationship, from a broadly MLG perspective.

Marks, G., **Hooghe**, L. and **Blank**, K. (1996) 'European integration from the 1980s: state-centric v multi-level governance', *Journal of Common Market Studies*, vol. 34, no. 5:341–78. This article is a clear statement on the changing role of the state in the EU, comparing the different perspectives of intergovernmentalism and MLG.

Film suggestion

Emanuele Crialese, *Respiro*, 2002, Italy

This remarkable and beautiful film depicts a remote community on the island of Lampedusa, off the south-west tip of Sicily. It is a place on the very margins of Europe. Years of regional development policy – as well as central government subsidies – may have delivered cosmetic changes (such as a fish-processing plant, for example), but ultimately not much changes. The fear is sometimes expressed that local identities and regional idiosyncrasies will somehow be eliminated by European bureaucracies and the continent will become bland and all the same. This absurd notion is hardly evident on Lampedusa. The same could be said of any number of communities all over Europe, including Britain.

The wider impact of globalisation on such places may be more evident, but is not new. Emigration and rural depopulation have been concerns for many decades.

Chapter 7

EU enlargement and the challenge to the state

Outline

- History and process of EU enlargement
- The rationale for enlargement
- The implications of enlargement – costs and benefits
- Further enlargements – how big can the Union get?
- Balkan enlargement in 2001
- The global context of enlargement

Key concepts

7.1 Human rights

7.2 Widening and deepening

Introduction

In May 2004 the European Union achieved a historic enlargement. Eight former members of the Warsaw Pact, plus Cyprus and Malta, joined the Union in the most ambitious and potentially most problematic of all enlargements to date.

The chapter title refers to the challenge to the state. In some ways 'states' would be more accurate. Enlargement presents a huge challenge to all concerned, to the individual state or states applying to join, to the states that joined in 2004, to the individual member states of EU-15, and to the institutions of the European Union. The complexity of the challenge, moral, political and economic, is the subject of this chapter.

The chapter begins with a brief overview of the history of EU enlargement before focusing on the process, using the 2004 enlargement as an illustration. The second section considers the rationale for enlargement and asks to what extent forces outside Europe affect choices regarding enlargement. The third part addresses the implications of enlargement in terms of costs and benefits, both for the states acceding to membership, and for the Union. This section includes reference to the theoretical argument over 'widening' and 'deepening' of the Union. Next, the chapter looks ahead to possible further enlargements. This may seem precipitous, given that the new occupants of the house have yet to settle in, but in fact there are other potential residents already knocking at the door, and perhaps others coming up the driveway. The house may be somewhat crowded, but most Europeans are used to living in a comparatively small, but crowded space. The chapter ends with a brief look at the global context.

Enlargement is a process which both highlights and tests some of the fundamental principles of the European Union. Not only does it involve the implementation of the *acquis communautaire*, it involves compliance with the basic values of the Union. This presents a challenge to all parties concerned, both from the Union side and in the candidate countries. All parties come under close scrutiny in respect of the principles of

> liberty, democracy and respect for human rights and fundamental freedoms, and the rule of law (Treaty of Rome, Article 6).

It can hardly be acceptable for the Union to apply judgements on candidate countries if the Union itself is wanting in the application of those same principles. Thus the process works both ways: it presents a challenge to the state applying, but also to the Union and its existing members. It highlights and reinforces the principles on which the European Union is based.

An important claim in the chapter is that the rationale for enlargement is consistent with the founding principles of the Community, but it has special significance where the 2004 enlargement is concerned, as well as perhaps future ones. Discussion 7.1 provides a brief history of EU enlargement. See also Figure 7.1.

Discussion 7.1

The expanding European Union

Founding members

1957 France, Germany, Italy, Belgium, Netherlands, Luxembourg

- *First enlargement* ('Northern')
  1973 United Kingdom, Denmark, Ireland
- *Second enlargement* (with Third enlargement 'Mediterranean')
  1981 Greece
- *Third enlargement*
  1986 Spain, Portugal

(German reunification 1990: German Democratic Republic merges with Federal Republic)

- *Fourth enlargement* ('EFTA')
  1995 Austria, Sweden, Finland
- *Fifth enlargement* ('Eastern')
  2004 Poland, Hungary, Czech Republic, Slovakia, Slovenia, Estonia, Latvia, Lithuania, Cyprus, Malta

Applications accepted and under negotiation

Bulgaria, Romania (provisional accession date 2007); Croatia

Invited to submit an application

Turkey

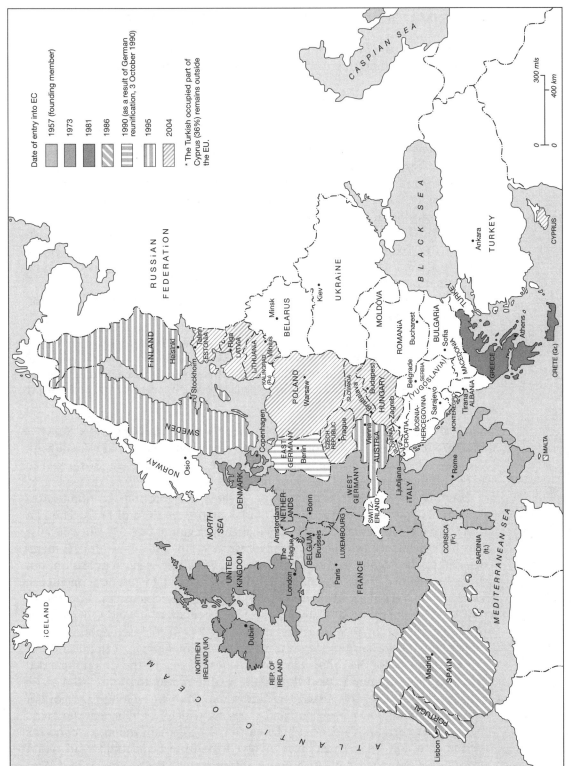

Figure 7.1 European Union post-2004 enlargement

Source: based on Urwin, 1997

● ● ● ● History and process of EU enlargement

An overview of the history of enlargement and a résumé of the process leading up to the 2004 enlargement will contextualise the discussion in the rest of the chapter.

History of enlargement

Enlargement used to happen slowly and in small doses. This no longer seems to be the case. The first enlargement of the Community, involving Britain, Denmark and Ireland, did not happen until 1973, 16 years after the signing of the Treaty of Rome, and 12 years after the accession countries first lodged an application to join. The process of accession was disrupted by de Gaulle twice vetoing the UK's accession, mainly in order to protect France's position of leadership of the Community. The main arguments during the negotiation process concerned the UK's preferential treatment of third parties, namely its Commonwealth partners, and agriculture.

Greece joined in 1981, fully 19 years after it first signed a Treaty of Association agreement. Greek membership

> . . . might have come sooner had it not been for the [. . .] military coup of April 1967. With the return of civilian government in 1974, Greece almost immediately applied for full membership, arguing that EEC membership would help underpin its attempts to rebuild democracy. The Community agreed, negotiations opened in 1976 and Greece joined in 1981 (McCormick, 2002:70).

Portugal and Spain were also ineligible until their dictatorships ended in 1973 and 1975 respectively. Accession negotiations for Spain in particular were difficult because of its large agricultural and fishing interests, but negotiations began in 1978 and membership was achieved in 1986.

Commission President Jacques Delors created the European Economic Area (EEA) to extend the Single European Market across the EC and EFTA. The EEA came into force in January 1994 but had already begun to lose relevance because four EFTA members, Austria, Sweden, Norway and Finland, applied for EC membership. In the event, Norway voted by a small majority against accession, but the others joined in 1995. EFTA was thereby reduced to just four members, Switzerland, Iceland, Norway and the micro-state, Liechtenstein. The fourth (EFTA) enlargement was a relatively uncomplicated affair. It would increase the Union population by 6 per cent and its GDP by 7 per cent, each applicant having a higher GDP than the Union average. The most significant implication of this enlargement for the Union was size: the area covered by the Union increased by 37 per cent, and now extended from the Mediterranean to north of the Arctic Circle and the borders of Russia. The Union moved to create a new category of structural funding for sparsely populated regions, which would benefit the Arctic regions of Sweden and Finland (see Discussion 6.2). Perhaps the major concerns for the accession states themselves involved the issue of neutrality. All had a history of non-involvement in military alliances since the Second World War, and Austria was barred from association with Western defence organisations by its post-war settlement, and the USSR considered the EEC to be the economic arm of NATO. However, with the demise of the Soviet Union, this was no longer an issue. Austria, Sweden and Finland remain outside NATO and have opted only for observer status in the Western European Union (WEU) – the security organ related to the EU and its emergent Rapid Reaction Force.

While not technically an enlargement of the Union (it did not increase the number of member states) the reunification of Germany may contain lessons that will be useful for both the Union itself and the new Eastern members that joined in 2004, not least in moderating any overly optimistic expectations concerning the benefits from joining. We return to this issue in the section on the implications of enlargement.

The process of enlargement

After the collapse of the Berlin Wall on 11 November 1989 and the fall of communism, the former communist states of Central and Eastern Europe wasted little time in expressing their ambition to join the EU. The Union itself responded to the historic and unexpected change of circumstances on its eastern borders by creating association treaties, called Europe Agreements, designed to provide support to countries embarking on the transformation to market economies and pluralist democracies. They comprised the promotion of freer trade between the signatories, industrial, technical and scientific cooperation, financial support and improved opportunities for political dialogue. By 1996 these had been agreed with all ten former communist states engaged in preparations to join the Union – the eventual 2004 entrants plus Bulgaria and Romania.

> The agreements provided for industrial free trade by stages over transition periods of up to ten years; some reduction of agricultural protection; and liberalisation of trade in services, of capital movement, and of the establishment of businesses (Pinder, 2001:130).

Pinder reports that trade responded well and so too did private investment in the form of foreign direct investment, especially in those countries perceived to be making the most rapid strides towards reform. The EU also provided PHARE (Poland and Hungary Aid for Economic Restructuring) assistance, initially to Poland and Hungary, but later extended to all the CEECs. PHARE, which currently supports candidate countries Bulgaria, Romania and Croatia, provides technical support, education and training as well as restructuring in agriculture, a large sector in all the applicant states pre- and post- the 2004 enlargement. Infrastructure spending accounts for a considerable portion of PHARE funding. PHARE has always been 'accession-driven', according to Jones (2001:482). Other states not yet formally candidates for accession to the Union are also part of the PHARE programme. These include Albania, Bosnia Herzegovina, and the Former Yugoslav Republic of Macedonia (FYROM).

The Copenhagen European Council of June 1993 set out the criteria for entry to the Union. These are minimum conditions that any potential applicant has

Discussion 7.2

Copenhagen Criteria: conditions for membership

In Copenhagen in 1993, the European Council agreed minimum conditions for membership of the European Union:

> . . . stability of institutions guaranteeing democracy, the rule of law, human rights and respect for and protection of minorities, . . . a functioning market economy as well as the capacity to cope with competitive pressure and market forces within the Union; [and] the ability to take on the obligations of membership, including adherence to the aims of political, economic and monetary union (Bainbridge, 2002:96).

Glenn (2003:218) synthesises this to three areas: political criteria, economic criteria, and meeting the demands of the *acquis communautaire* (the full set of EU treaties, norms, legislative acts and conventions). The last is often referred to as the 'conditionality principle' – since it is a key condition of membership that applicant states are able to apply the *acquis*, with exceptions or transition periods permitted in limited areas, such as EMU.

One might add to this list 'being a European country'. In 1987 Morocco applied to join the European Community. The application was rejected on the grounds that Morocco was 'not a European country', a condition of membership referred to under Article 237 of the Treaty of Rome, now Article 49 of the TEU.

A further *de facto* condition of membership is that a candidate state does not apply capital punishment. This was a stipulation in respect of Turkey's prospective application in the 1990s. Turkey has now rescinded the death penalty, a prerequisite to its lodging a formal application to join the EU. No European state outside the CIS now uses capital punishment. This condition is actually subsumed in the Copenhagen Criteria under 'human rights'. Thus it is that even if the Union were to make an exception to Article 237, currently neither the United States nor Japan need apply to join the EU.

to meet before an application to join may be considered. Together with the unsurprising, but not uncomplicated stipulation that an applicant must be 'a European country', the Copenhagen Criteria remain a useful yardstick against which to measure suitability for membership (see Discussion 7.2).

On 1 April 1994 Hungary became the first former communist state to lodge an application to join the European Union. Nine others subsequently did so, thus initiating the formal steps to joining (see Discussion 7.3). The major concern for the Commission was that applicants should meet the Copenhagen Criteria in all three fields of politics, economics and accommodation of the *acquis communautaire*. This would confirm the ability of the candidate countries to adjust to the Single European Market and conform to the statutes of company and property law, as well as the conventions of accountancy and the conduct of business in a capitalist system. The applicants needed to prepare for accession by implementing the provisions of the *acquis*, which consists of the full complement of EU legislative acts, incorporating all the treaties and treaty amendments. Pinder reports that this amounts to 'not far short of 100,000 pages of legislation' (Pinder, 2001:130). See Discussion 7.4.

In 1995 the Council agreed that the Union would proceed towards opening formal negotiations with the candidate countries after the Amsterdam Summit in 1997. It was in response to this that the Commission produced *Agenda 2000* which set out a commitment to enlargement and, significantly, a blueprint for

Discussion 7.3

Enlargement process

1. *Formal application*: submitted to the European Council.
2. *Opinion*: the Commission expresses an opinion. This sets out the economic and political implications of membership for the applicant state and assesses the prospects for the applicant state's capacity to adapt to membership. The opinion is addressed to the Council.
3. *Accession conference*: the Council formally invites the applicant state(s) to begin formal negotiations. A conference takes place between representatives of the Council, the Commission and representatives of the applicant state(s).
4. *Negotiations*: bilateral negotiations between the Commission and the applicant(s) examine each of the 31 chapters of the *acquis communautaire*; the Commission assesses progress and action required for compliance; chapters successfully dealt with are provisionally closed.
5. *Agreement*: upon successful closure of all chapters, the Commission makes a recommendation to the Council on enlargement.
6. *Parliamentary approval*: as part of co-decision procedure, the European Parliament gives approval to the application; an absolute majority is required in a vote of the parliament.
7. *Ratification*: all member states and the applicant states are required to ratify the enlargement, in some cases by referendum.

(Based on Glenn, J.G., in Cini, M. (2003) *European Union Politics*. Oxford. Oxford University Press.)

Discussion 7.4

Freedom of movement (for some)

A fundamental principle of the Treaty of Rome, Article 3.1(c) is the 'four freedoms'. These are the free movement of goods, free movement of persons, freedom to provide services and free movement of capital.

In 2001, preparing for the Eastern enlargement, the Council, under pressure from Germany and Austria, agreed a two-year delay in granting freedom of movement to citizens of new member states, but permitted national authorities to raise this by up to five years. Responding to political pressures from nervous and/or ill-informed electorates, most have done so.

After the Mediterranean enlargement there were similar fears about massive migration to richer parts of the Union. This did not happen. Admittedly, it could be argued that there was little migration after the 1986 enlargement precisely because of a similar restriction – freedom of movement of people was restricted for five years – but there are significant counter-arguments. The first is fundamental to the Treaty of Rome: it seems bizarre to suspend such a founding principle, and discriminatory to apply it to certain countries. It also fails to take into account labour market requirements – in several sectors there may actually be *demand* for labour that citizens of new member states might be able to meet.

Glenn (2003:222) also refers to exaggerated fears of mass migration. He reports that even in Germany after reunification only 7.3 per cent of East Germans moved to the former West Germany.

There is also a moral question: does not a restriction on movement pander to racist instincts? It ill behoves modern Germany, a country with an exemplary record in upholding the freedom of movement of people, and with a long-held positive approach to political asylum, and the accommodation of refugees, to support restrictions on the movement of citizens from countries on its borders, now members of the European Union.

reform of the Union that could enable enlargement to happen. Hitherto the focus of attention had almost entirely been on the applicant states while, privately if not publicly, it was acknowledged that the Union too needed to prepare for enlargement with its own programme of reform.

Agenda 2000 set out reforms to the structural funds referred to in the previous chapter, but an even more significant challenge was agriculture. Agricultural Commissioner Franz Fischler described the reforms set out in *Agenda 2000* as the most far-reaching changes to the CAP since its inception. *Agenda 2000* intended to increase the market orientation of the CAP and to reinforce its structural, rural and environmental elements (Jones, 2001:226). By March 1999 the Council had agreed cuts in CAP funding and a redirection of support away from production and towards a more market-oriented and competitive system, as well as one favouring protection of the environment, enhancement of food quality and the promotion of economic and social activities in rural areas. Jones reports that in spite of substantial reform during the 1990s, many critics of the CAP argued that the changes were insufficient. The Union had failed to adequately address problems of excessive and price distorting subsidies, over-production (especially of milk and sugar), and the substantial demands that agriculture continued to place on the Union budget. Furthermore, the reforms did not adequately address the challenges presented by the forthcoming enlargement. Like the Mediterranean entrants in the 1980s, the CEECs were not granted full access to CAP benefits, and the reforms indicated in *Agenda 2000* were in any case undermined by subsequent agreements between Germany and France (see Chapter 9), an indication of the power relationship between the Commission and the member states.

Agenda 2000 indicated that applicant states would need to work assiduously on meeting the demands of the *acquis communautaire*, the so-called conditionality principle, prior to accession and that afterwards there might be transition periods in some sectors, but that these were likely to be short. This marked a contrast between the Eastern enlargement and the Mediterranean enlargement in the 1980s, with which it is sometimes compared as there are superficial similarities: Greece, Portugal and Spain were all emerging from dictatorships, had substantially lower GDP than the EC average, and had large agricultural sectors. They also had considerable infrastructural weaknesses. However, whereas in the 1980s the accessions were accompanied by long transition periods in some areas of the Single Market, easing compliance and softening some costs of membership, these would not be available for the CEEC applicants, or would be available for only very limited periods. In fact, what transition periods have been applied are mainly to the benefit of the pre-enlargement 15, especially in relation to agriculture, and to freedom of movement (see Discussion 7.4).

More positively, *Agenda 2000* agreed considerable pre-accession assistance, €500m a year for agricultural development, and €1bn for structural aid. It also accepted that the ToA had not gone far enough with institutional reform of the Union. The weighting of votes in the Council and the composition of the institutions themselves required revision, so a further IGC would be necessary. This began in February 2000 and concluded in December, with the Treaty of Nice (see further discussion below). *Agenda 2000* also recognised particular challenges in the fields of employment, the environment, JHA, and EMU, but described these as difficulties that the whole Union and the candidate countries would have to debate and resolve together. Clearly in respect of EMU, the applicant states would not be expected to join at the outset, although they would need to accept the provisions relating to EMU in the *acquis* and be expected to join in the longer term.

Agenda 2000 also noted the scale of technology-related challenges to new member states, for both public utilities and enterprises. Many sectors, including technical research, trans-European networks, education and training, and environmental protection would require considerable expenditure and expertise to raise them to levels commensurate with standards expected in the Union. The Commission recommended that financial support be focused on fewer, larger, targeted programmes of proven value (Jones, 2001:476).

The Commission applied the Copenhagen Criteria (see Discussion 7.2) to assess the candidate countries' readiness to join the Union. The previous year, the Commission had sent out questionnaires with over 1000 questions to each applicant state, and included an assessment of the results in *Agenda 2000*. Nine of the ten met the political criteria – the exception was Slovakia – while in general terms there was progress, but not sufficient, with the economic criteria. Hungary and Poland had made the most headway in meeting the economic conditions, and the Czech Republic and Slovenia had also performed creditably. The overall conclusion was that the Union should prepare to open negotiations with all ten CEECs, plus Cyprus. At this time, Malta had not yet applied, and Turkey had not been accepted as a candidate country.

During 1997 it appeared that the Commission favoured a double-wave, or even a three-wave entry, and certain states appeared to be in the vanguard of negotiations. Negotiations for entry began in early 1998, initially with six applicants, Hungary, the Czech Republic, Poland, Slovenia, Estonia and Cyprus. Preparation for negotiations continued with the other five, Romania, Slovakia, Latvia, Lithuania and Bulgaria. Jones (2001:477–8) comments on how this process was well received by the six candidates placed in the 'fast track', but it went down badly with the others.

The Commission then produced regular reports on the progress towards accession and in 1999 reported positively on Slovakia's improvements but was downbeat about the Czech Republic, which appeared to have slipped back. The Commission then determined that it would approve all applications in principle but reach an assessment on each one on its individual merits. This would avoid any apparent favouritism towards 'first wave' entrants – which might in turn lead to their complacency, and equally it would avoid resentment among others that they were being placed in a 'second division'. So the first wave/ second wave approach faded. Instead, the Commission recommended applying the conditionality principle to the negotiation stage, which enabled negotiations to begin in early 2000 with all candidates that met the political criteria for membership. The two applicants in the weakest position were Bulgaria and Romania, where there were some significant unresolved issues, such as the conditions in childcare institutions in Romania, as well as doubts over the extent of both countries' readiness to fully participate in and contribute to a competitive market economy. There were also safety concerns in relation to nuclear power installations in Bulgaria. It became apparent that among all the applicant states, these two states were the back-markers. Overall, though, the picture was positive and the Commission appeared to accept the need for transition arrangements in some key areas.

> The report argued that transition periods in relation to the single market should be few and short, but in areas requiring considerable adaptation and important financial outlays (such as the environment, energy and infrastructure), transition arrangements could be much longer, provided that candidates demonstrated their commitment to catching up in these area (Jones, 2001:483).

The report indicated that the Council should commit to making a final decision on accession for all those countries meeting the necessary criteria in 2002. Thus the timetable for the Eastern enlargement emerged, and it looked as if there would, after all, be a 'Big Bang' enlargement. Strangely, though, there was still a lack of progress on the part of the Union itself in preparing for this enlargement. Nice, at the end of the year 2000, was meant to allay these concerns.

At the end of 2000, the Commission issued further positive assessments, especially regarding progress by Lithuania and Slovakia, but with reservations about the treatment of Roma minorities in several states. Problems remained in respect of widespread corruption and fraud, and most countries were weak in their judicial and administrative capacity (Jones, 2001:483–4). Again, the 2000 report confirmed that Bulgaria and Romania were lagging behind, though Bulgaria had achieved better progress than its northerly neighbour.

Nice duly produced another Treaty after a tortuous meeting of the European Council lasting five days and a record 41 hours. The Treaty was billed as being the essential enabling tool for the forthcoming enlargement, as it would finally introduce the institutional changes that a Union of 20 or more states would definitely require. Without reform of the voting system in the Council, for example, decision-making would be paralysed and the Union would grind to a halt. See Discussion 7.5.

However, Nice was a tortuous and at times acrimonious negotiation that involved several late sessions. Greeted in the morning after agreement as a

---

Discussion 7.5

Treaty of Nice: key institutional changes

- Extension of QMV in several areas
- New blocking limits in QMV system
- Increases power to European Parliament through increase in co-decision
- New rules governing the ECJ
- Preserves veto in granting subsidies to poorer member states until 2007
- Limit to size of Commission and number of seats in Parliament

triumph, the chickens came home to roost later on, as reported in Chapter 3. Vote weighting agreed at Nice was later challenged not only by the Draft Constitution but also by the subsequent Council meeting in Brussels in December 2003. In fact, the Nice settlement was unpicked, in particular to the disadvantage of Poland and Spain. The dispute left a bitter taste, but from this author's perspective, the error was committed at Nice.

Meanwhile, enlargement negotiations continued. The enlargement process dictates that negotiation of the 31 chapters of the *acquis communautaire* proceeds chapter by chapter, usually with the most unproblematic and straightforward chapters opened and closed first. The full list of the contents list of the *acquis* is in Discussion 7.6.

By the end of 2002, all ten applicant states had successfully completed the closure of the *acquis*, a considerable achievement. This enabled the Commission to offer Poland, Hungary, the Czech Republic, Slovakia, Slovenia, Estonia, Latvia, Lithuania, Malta and Cyprus an accession date of May 2004, subject to ratification by EU member-state parliaments – which was achieved without particular incident – and by the parliaments of the applicant states themselves. All ten conducted referenda on the decision to enter the EU. In some cases, a minimum turnout was required. In all countries, voters supported accession by comfortable majorities, although in a few the turnout was low.

Discussion 7.6

Acquis Communautaire

The *acquis communautaire* is the body of European treaties, laws, and norms. It comprises 31 chapters, all of which must be adopted, or be subject to transition agreements, by applicant states prior to accession to the EU. The *acquis* consists of almost 100,000 pages of documentation.

Chapter 1: Free movement of goods
Chapter 2: Freedom of movement for persons
Chapter 3: Freedom to provide services
Chapter 4: Free movement of capital
Chapter 5: Company law
Chapter 6: Competition policy
Chapter 7: Agriculture
Chapter 8: Fisheries
Chapter 9: Transport policy
Chapter 10: Taxation
Chapter 11: Economic & Monetary Union
Chapter 12: Statistics
Chapter 13: Social policy and employment
Chapter 14: Energy
Chapter 15: Industrial policy
Chapter 16: Small and medium-sized undertakings
Chapter 17: Science and research
Chapter 18: Telecommunications and information technologies
Chapter 19: Education and training
Chapter 20: Culture and audio-visual policy
Chapter 21: Regional policy and coordination of structural instruments
Chapter 22: Environment
Chapter 23: Consumers and health protection
Chapter 24: Cooperation in the field of justice and home affairs
Chapter 25: Customs union
Chapter 26: External relations
Chapter 27: Common foreign and security policy
Chapter 28: Financial control
Chapter 29: Financial and budgetary provisions
Chapter 30: Institutions
Chapter 31: Other

Photograph 7.1 The expanding European Union: Leaders from EU-15 were joined by their counterparts from the ten accession states for the Athens European Council summit in April 2003.

Review   *What are the minimum conditions that must be met in order for a state to seek membership of the European Union?*
What are the main steps in the enlargement process?

● ● ● ● The rationale for enlargement

The overarching contention of this section is that the rationale for enlargement consists of a number of positive goods – or benefits – relating to the governance of the European Union and its member states. Each one is a challenge to the Union, to the member states, and to the applicant states. The global context is also significant in a number of ways, especially in relation to security, which is examined below. Other angles of the global context are summarised at the end of the section. It is also argued that the rationale for enlargement is based on the founding principles established in setting up the EEC in the first place, relating first and foremost to peace and security. Only within the context of peace and security can economic prosperity develop.

The Treaty of Rome created the European Economic Community which, as Pinder points out, was a grand-sounding name for an organisation comprising just six states in Western Europe. However, as Pinder aptly describes it, the name was 'an aspiration not a fact' (Pinder, 2001:123), and the Treaty of Rome contained a provision that the Community would eventually expand into, as the famous phrase in the prologue implies, 'an ever closer union among the European peoples'. The Community has of course since changed its name, and the new name may still be to a degree more aspiration than fact, but it is nevertheless an extraordinary achievement that in less than 50 years the Union now comprises 25 states, and extends over an area that comprises most of Western and Central Europe as well as much of what is usually, but somewhat arbitrarily, described as Eastern Europe.

The foremost rationale for enlarging the Union is to promote *peace and security* in the European continent. As already indicated, this was the founding principle underlying the Schuman Plan and the establishment of the ECSC in 1951. The Union has certainly developed other rationales, including that of achieving economic prosperity through the single market in goods, services, people and capital, but peace and security is the *sine qua non* of European integration. Pinder emphasises the order of priorities, stressing the peace and security, and suggesting that the British preoccupation with the economic function of the Union has hindered the UK in playing a full part in the development of the Union (Pinder, 2001:1–3). He writes that different states inevitably bring differently nuanced interpretations of the balance of core purpose that underlies the Union, and he accepts that the new members joining in 2004 will also have varying perspectives. Nevertheless, for most of them peace and security will be the primary concern as they at last begin to play a full role in the continent from which they have, to a significant degree, suffered exclusion for over four decades.

Enlargement has powerful security implications. It consolidates partnerships between neighbouring states, where historically there has been conflict. Of course, security for the European Union, including the new members, has been achieved in partnership with NATO. After beginning formal negotiations to join the EU, all ten CEE applicants became members of the NATO Alliance.

Jackson and Sørensen write that the enlargement of NATO enhances regional security because it deters states from seeking alternative partnerships that may be counter to alliance interests, or from becoming involved in local conflicts perhaps rooted in ancient enmities (Jackson & Sørensen, 2003:91–6). Security also has an internal dimension, concerning in particular the fight against organised crime and international terrorism.

A second dimension to the rationale for enlargement of the Union concerns the *economic* potential of the region. The 2004 enlargement brings an increase of 74 million consumers to the Single European Market, with high growth levels and potential to boost intra-EU trade, especially for those EU-15 states that share borders with the accession states and those that have engaged with the CEECs in terms of inward investment. A further motivation for enlargement is the expectation that it will boost trade between the accession states and provide a significant boost to their relatively newly established market-based economies.

More detailed discussion of the economic implications of enlargement follow in the next section on benefits from enlargement.

A third aspect of the rationale for enlargement is the increased *political* authority gained by an expanded Union, now genuinely pan-European and representing 25 states. The enlargement enhances the profile and credibility of the European Union in international forums and raises its moral authority. The Union has transcended the old barriers of the Cold War period and enlargement makes a major contribution towards peace and reconciliation.

Enlargement affirms the founding goal of the EU, to establish 'ever closer union'. In so doing, it can have a beneficial and integrating effect, leading to further 'deepening' as well as 'widening', thereby consolidating the core objectives of the Union. Enlargement can breathe renewed vitality into the Union, leading to unforeseen but widespread benefits. Once it became clear that a major expansion of the Union was likely, a theoretical discussion emerged over the consequences for the Union in terms of its institutional design and competences. This centred on arguments over the relative strengths of **'widening'** the Union – bringing in new members and perhaps developing the concept of **'variable geometry'**, whereby an increasing number of states would decide which areas of policy they would select to participate in, and which they would prefer to remain aloof from. Variable geometry emerged post-Maastricht, with Britain, Denmark and Sweden opting out of the third stage of EMU (adopting the Single Currency), and Britain choosing not to adopt the Social Chapter governing some aspects of employment law. The Schengen accord was another example, with Ireland and the UK remaining outside the border-free Schengen Area. For supporters of the variable geometry idea, enlargement seemed to offer a logical opportunity to extend the principle. This led to the notion that widening the Union would therefore entail some loosening of its homogeneity in terms of policy application. Such an approach ran counter to the hopes and expectations of those of a more federalist persuasion, who argued that widening could happen, but not at the expense of the core achievements of integration. They argued that **'deepening'** of the Union's institutional design and its policy-making processes was the only way to ensure that enlargement did not weaken the basic structures of the Union.

Ultimately the latter argument prevailed and the Council affirmed in 1992 that along with enlargement there should be parallel developments in 'the internal development of the Union' (Bainbridge, 2002:541). The detailed assessment given to the incorporation of the *acquis* by applicant states prior to accession also affirmed that the process of widening should not in any way dilute the core homogeneity of Pillar I, and European Community law. See further discussion under Key concept 7.2, Widening and deepening.

Other political aspects of the rationale can be subdivided into four further categories: democratic principles; moral responsibility; human rights; and global role.

Democratic principles

The first of these relates to the principle of **democracy**. Enlargement consolidates and sustains democratic values, and in the context of the Mediterranean enlargements in the 1980s and the 2004 Eastern enlargement, this is especially important (McCormick, 2002:213). These involved 11 states emerging from the darkness of dictatorship. For all the states involved, as well as for the Union, a key dimension to accession was the need to consolidate embryonic democracies. For its members old and new, the EU represents a democratic polity and the rule of law.

Moral responsibility

A further political dimension from the EU perspective concerning enlargement is the issue of moral obligation. There is a moral imperative to permit accession to countries that are eligible to join. This stems from the commitment expressed in the Treaty of Rome affirming that membership is open to any European state that respects the core principles referred to at the beginning of this chapter: liberty, democracy, respect for human rights and fundamental freedoms, and the rule of law.

A second moral imperative surrounds the 2004 enlargement and is implied by Mayhew (1998) who writes about the arbitrary division of Europe agreed by the Allies at Yalta in 1944. The Yalta Agreement handed the Central and East European countries over to a despotic, totalitarian and foreign rule without even a minimal degree of consultation. This crime was compounded by the West's acquiescence over the subsequent several decades, exemplified by only derisory protest when Soviet tanks crushed popular uprisings in East Germany in 1953, Hungary three years later, and in Czechoslovakia when the tanks crushed the reformist regime of Alexander Dubček in 1968.

> No effective steps were taken [by the West] to show the Soviet Union that its treatment of the Hungarian uprising or the Czechoslovak 'spring' were unacceptable or to show real displeasure at the way the numerous revolts of the Polish workers and intellectuals were put down by national militias. Essentially the peoples of Central Europe freed themselves, at great cost and with practically no outside assistance, from Communist rule (Mayhew, 1998:5).

Indeed it is remarkable how many commentaries in the West now appear to claim that somehow the West prompted the liberation of CEE by spending vast amounts of money on arms and forcing the Soviet system to implode peacefully. This interpretation is regarded as laughable by individuals who actually lived through the popular revolutions in the countries concerned during the 1980s.

After 1989, Western politicians were extremely supportive of the CEECs and aid was immediately forthcoming. This prompted high expectations in the region that membership of the European Union would swiftly follow, but these hopes did not materialise. On the contrary, some members of the Community, especially the peripheral and Mediterranean states, appeared at best neutral about EU enlargement (Mayhew, 1998:11–12).

Part of the moral case must be that there is no good reason why others should not have access to the same rights, opportunities and benefits enjoyed by the EU at present. This is implicit in the commitment of the Treaty of Rome to allowing membership to countries that desire it and meet the criteria.

Human rights

The next aspect to the rationale for enlargement is also deeply political, and it concerns **human rights**. Following the Bosnian conflict, and in the context of the planned enlargement of the Union to include the CEECs, the Union affirmed the need to protect human rights. Both the Copenhagen Criteria and later the

Treaty of Amsterdam made specific reference to human rights, which were crucial issues for the accession process. The ToA established provisions for the 'suspension of a member state found guilty of "serious and persistent" breach of human rights' (Bainbridge, 2002:322). Jones offers a cautionary note, suggesting:

> although undoubtedly laudable, the references to human rights and non-discrimination in the treaty [of Amsterdam] could be little more than moral padding, aimed more at making the Union look virtuous, rather than a serious attempt to deal with discrimination and human rights abuses. But these references were significant in that they reflected a desire to explicitly link human rights considerations to the nature and objectives of the Union (Jones, 2001:79).

But the provisions referred to above were strengthened at the Nice Council in December 2000 which adopted a Charter of Fundamental Rights, incorporating the European Convention on Human Rights. This led to a fundamental addition to Community Law. It is highly significant in the context of the 2004 enlargement that the ECHR has been taken on by the Union, as human rights concerns proved a thorny issue in the accession process, especially in relation to protection of Roma minorities and, in some cases, aspects of the judicial system and treatment of prisoners. It is vital that the Union maintains a strong commitment in these areas, in order to ensure that, through enlargement, human rights are protected. It is likely that the Council's decision to institutionalise the Union's commitment to human rights was a direct consequence of the accession process for the former communist states.

Global context

Finally, a further rationale for enlarging the Union relates to the wider global context, to which the Union makes an increasingly powerful contribution. This relates to the desire on the part of the Union to exercise global responsibilities. Enlargement makes an important contribution to the wider role of the EU, extending its borders and greatly increasing its population. The global role of the EU has emerged more strongly in recent years, although Pinder suggests that something like it has always existed. It is far from uncontroversial, and many British eurosceptics scorn suggestions of a global role for the EU. But it is surely not fanciful to suggest that the Union seeks to provide a counter-balance to American **hegemony** in a globalising world, and that it seeks to pursue environmental and foreign policies that benefit the global community. It is clearly the case that the Union does have a global role, and it aspires to strengthen it. A characteristic of the emerging global responsibilities of the Union is that they are based around the concept of civil power, rather than military power. This is a novel idea, far removed from traditional realist perspectives of how power is exercised on the international stage (see Chapter 8). The concept of civil power is perhaps better suited to a post-Cold War environment. The global role of the Union is discussed in the final chapter, but it is reasonable to mention it here because it relates to the rationale for enlargement. The above considerations are summarised in Discussion 7.7.

Discussion 7.7

Rationale for enlargement/accession

1 Peace, stability and security

Enlargement assists in the

- establishment of a regional partnership based on mutual dependency and guarantees peaceful co-existence;
- deterrence of reactionary or opportunist alternative programmes;
- efforts to control and counter organised crime and international terrorism.

2 Economy

Enlargement seeks to promote

- participation in a single market based on the free movement of goods, services, people and capital;
- intra-EU trade as well as participation in global markets;
- economic growth;
- improved living standards.

3 Political

Enlargement provides

- enhanced credibility and authority of a wider Union.

as well as four further political dimensions:

- *Democracy*: enlargement consolidates emergent democracies;
- *Moral obligation*: it is a treaty requirement to offer membership to countries that meet the criteria; for historical reasons there is a particular moral responsibility in respect of the CEECs;
- *Human rights*: enlargement affirms a commitment to the protection of human rights throughout an enlarged Union;
- *Global role*: enlargement boosts the ambition of the Union to take on more global responsibilities concerning the environment and international justice; the EU role is based on the concept of a civil power.

Review   *What have been the major components of the rationales for enlarging the European Union? How have these rationales achieved a global significance?*
Do you think it is credible to claim that the EU, a regional grouping, can have global responsibilities?

● ● ● ● The implications of enlargement – costs and benefits

The challenge of enlargement

A central concern of most members of EU-15 during the negotiation process for the ten states that joined the Union in 2004 was that enlargement should not jeopardise the achievements of the Union thus far. An exception may have been Britain under the administration of John Major. McCormick writes that

> the Major government [. . .] supported the eastward expansion, but mainly to slow down the process of integration (McCormick, 2002:214).

It was a vain hope. For most, the enlargement would further integrate Europe and extend its achievements to a further 75m Europeans. The process of incorporating the *acquis* could not, therefore, be compromised. To do so would indeed risk the integrity of the Single Market by undermining its integration and substantially adding to problems of non-compliance. If the new member states were to be admitted under a less rigorous regime of company law or accounting practice, for example, it would undermine investment and damage the prospects of the CEE economies.

Enlargement profoundly altered the *geography* of the Union, bringing its eastern border to the former Soviet republics of Belarus and Ukraine, and extending the Union north-east to the Baltic states as well as across most of Central Europe, and increasing the area covered by the Union by 25 per cent, its population by 20 per cent.

The *economic challenge* of enlargement is considerable (see Discussion 7.8). Despite the area and population increases, GDP rose by only 4 per cent, as the economic performance of the accession states was, and remains, substantially below the Union average. For all ten, the combined GDP is approximately equal to that of Belgium. Enlargement lowered the per capita GDP across the Union by around 1.5 per cent. GDP figures should be treated with caution, because they are do not take account of the hidden, untaxed cash economy, which is large but variable throughout the accession countries, as it is in EU-15, but the broad picture is clear: there are immense gaps between the economies of the accession states and EU-15. Overall, the GDP average among the accession states is around 40 per cent of EU-15. But it is also important to recognise that there are huge variations between and within the accession states. Slovenia has a GDP of about 70 per cent of EU-15, while Bulgaria (admittedly not yet joining) has a GDP of around 23 per cent of EU-15. When Portugal joined in 1986, it was considered very poor – its GDP was 50 per cent of the then Community average,

---

Discussion 7.8

The challenge of enlargement in 2004: a snapshot

- Accession added 10 states to the Union – from 15 to 25
- Accession increased the geographical area of the Union by 19 per cent
- Population increased by 75m, from 378m to 453m, a 20 per cent increase
- GDP total of accession states (A-10) is 4 per cent of EU-15
- GDP per capita of A-10 averages 40 per cent of EU-15
- 2003 A-10 GDP annual growth is 5 per cent; EU-15 is 1.5 per cent
- 10 year projection of these figures would raise A-10 GDP to 50 per cent of EU-15 average
- A-10 employment in agriculture is 15 per cent (in Poland it is 18 per cent); in EU-15 it is 4.5 per cent
- A-10 agriculture contributes about 15 per cent of GDP; in EU-15, the figure is 2.5 per cent

while Spain's was 60 per cent. Poland, by far the largest of the accession states, with a population of close to 40 million, has a GDP of around 40 per cent of the EU-15 average.

Agriculture presents perhaps the greatest challenge. In all accession states, the contribution of agriculture to GDP is around three times higher than in EU-15, and in employment, four to five times higher. In total, about a fifth of the accession states' workforce is employed in agriculture, compared with 4.5 per cent in EU-15. Industry, on the other hand, employs more than the EU average. The strikingly weak part of the accession states' economies is services, which are poorly developed.

Mayhew (1998:184) points out a further challenge: the wide *cultural diversity* among the countries of CEE. Even among the three Baltic states, Estonia is Nordic and Protestant, Lithuania is Central European and Catholic. Should Romania join in the near future, it is predominantly Orthodox. Many of the accession states contain significant minorities, including Germans, Russians, Hungarians, and Roma. However, this cultural diversity is an asset, not a handicap, and in any case similar diversity already exists across the European Union. The point to grasp from this, both economic data and cultural observations, is that the 2004 enlargement is not a merging between the EU and one enormous, mostly economically and culturally homogeneous mass. The region is extremely diverse.

A further challenge presented by enlargement concerns *industrial restructuring*. One of the inheritances from the Soviet era is an *over*-industrialisation and the production of large quantities of often low quality coal, steel and chemical products. This has left a residue of environmental contamination that requires significant spending to correct, as well as major implications for employment. Similar problems have been faced by Germany since reunification in 1990, and despite massive financial transfers at the German tax-payers' expense, many problems remain. The German experience is salutary, and indicates that the physical and structural challenge of incorporating a former Soviet command economy into a modern European society is not a straightforward task. Cultural barriers persist in Germany 15 years after the collapse of the Berlin Wall, and this is in one country, with one language, and bar the aberration of communism in the GDR, one history. The conclusion is that the challenge of incorporating the accession states into the Union will be immense, unprecedented and not uniform across the region.

In Chapter 6, it was stated that accession presents significant challenges to the EU in relation to agricultural funding, the *CAP* and *structural funds*. There will be significant strains in this area. Cohesion funding will attempt to repair the environmental impact of 40 years of communism, and to assist in substantial infrastructural development. As already explained, this process began during the accession process, aided substantially by PHARE assistance, but now post-accession the funds available are not large. Some EU-15 members, namely the Mediterranean states already receiving support from structural funds, feared that increased assistance for new members would come from their budgets. But the settlement reached at Berlin in March 1999 put a ceiling on structural funding and ring-fenced the majority of the funds until 2006 for pre-enlargement members. The Council agreed €213bn for the existing member states and allocated €45bn to the accession states, plus €18bn for the Cohesion Fund (Bourne, 2003:287). The total EU budget was capped at 1.27 per cent of GDP, so there is little likelihood of further aid being directed towards the 2004 accession states, except by a unanimously agreed decision (Pinder, 2001:88). This is unlikely, so any extra resources will have to be paid for from new members' own domestic revenues. The danger in this is that the money allocated will be spread too thinly over ten countries and 75 million people. It is important that there are rapid and visible benefits to joining the EU, otherwise there could easily be a backlash. The backlash may already have begun, as already mentioned, with the poor turnout in European Parliament elections in June 2004.

Political benefits of enlargement

The benefits of enlargement do not flow in one direction only. Enlargement sceptics may point to the costs of enlargement and the dilution of voting rights in the Council that are consequent upon enlargement. They may also refer to the higher than average incidence of corruption, crime and hidden economy in some new accession states (as well as some EU-15 states). But a thorough investigation of the whole picture shows that there are considerable benefits from enlarging eastwards and, as implied at the end of the previous section, the alternative scenario would be inestimably more difficult. Mayhew also contributes the moral question:

> The discussion of the costs and benefits of accession is obviously affected by whether the current Union is considered as an exclusive club reserved for the [EU-15 members] or whether it is an open association of all democratic European states (Mayhew, 1998:185).

There are first of all many *political benefits* to an enlarged Union. Enlargement brings benefits in terms of *peace and security*, and greater prestige and more *influence* in international arenas. These aspects are and were significant drivers in the rationale for enlargement discussed above, so there is no need to repeat the discussion here.

Enlargement will assist in the overdue **rapprochement** between Poland and Germany, Germany and the Czech Republic, and Italy and Slovenia (see Discussion 7.9).

The unnatural partition of Europe, literally through the presence of a wall, a heavily guarded, electronically bugged, metal and wire fence, as well as mined forests and patrolled rivers, making any attempt to escape to the West a life-threatening enterprise, created a context within which there could be no proper recovery from the trauma of the Nazi era. Overcoming past hatreds would be the greatest prize of all in a reunited Europe.

Mayhew (1998:186) reports that after joining the Union in 1986 relations between Spain and Portugal improved significantly, as did the volume of trade between them. European integration has benefited from improved understanding and the healing of old sores in many bilateral relationships. Since 1989, it has

> ### Discussion 7.9
>
> ## Making friends
>
> After a presentation at the Katowitz Business School in Poland on the 'Future of Europe', in December 2003, a young student asked me 'Do you mean we Poles have to be friends with Germany?' Somewhat taken aback by the question, I replied 'Yes, frankly, that is the case. The Union is an association of states cooperating for a common future and it is necessary to build on the present to construct better opportunities for us all.'
> 'After what they did to us?' she replied.
> 'Yes, I'm afraid so. Europe has changed and it will change again after May 2004. We have to work together.'
> Quite so. It may be difficult, but we live in new times.

been clear that enlargement to the east would finally bring about the opportunity for the continent to reconcile itself with its past. This remains an aspiration, but an important one.

A further benefit of enlargement, clearly visible during the latter stages of the accession process, is that it can be a vector for *reform of the institutions* of the Union and its governance systems. Enlargement has forced the pace of change, although the changes were delayed until the last possible moment and some have yet to be settled. Given the scale of the Eastern enlargement, it has been impossible to delay difficult decisions indefinitely on questions of institutional reform and budgetary matters. It should also stimulate the Union towards greater transparency, and improved efficiency.

Another political benefit concerns *internal security* and crime. Mentioned above as a rationale for enlargement, it is evident that there are worries about an increase in criminality, human trafficking, organised underground criminal gangs, mafia and the rest. Mayhew argues that these problems are much more likely to be resolved through international cooperation post-enlargement and that without enlargement the risks from such activities would be incomparably greater. The same applies in terms of social disintegration, unemployment and migration. Improved economic prospects following enlargement will benefit not only the accession states, but in particular Germany, and its efforts to overcome social problems and high unemployment in the *Länder* of the former GDR.

Mayhew concludes that a failure in the enlargement process would greatly damage the prospects for recovery and could precipitate tensions in the Union itself, resulting in splits and even in its disintegration. Now that enlargement has been achieved, the prospects of this are remote, but it is perhaps a warning that it is vital to ensure that enlargement now succeeds.

Economic benefits of enlargement

Enlargement brings an expansion of the **Single Market** and access to more consumers requiring goods and services. The challenge remains to fully integrate the expanded market, but the opportunity is there. The implementation of the *acquis* has been and remains critical to this: **foreign direct investment** (FDI), as well as domestic investment, depends on business confidence in a common business environment. The Single Market, with its single regulatory framework, is a boost to the confidence of investors and consumers alike. It may be superficially attractive to argue that the implementation of the *acquis* is a burden on developing businesses, but it would be a wrong assumption. The *acquis*, as argued in the section above on the process of enlargement, brings improvements to the business environment that allow for common standards and common procedures, as well as common protection (See Discussions 7.10 and 7.11).

The larger part of GDP in EU-15 is from services, about 60 per cent. In the applicant states, as already stated, the agricultural sector is much larger than in EU-15, but so too is the manufacturing sector. This means that the new entrants

Discussion 7.10

Who's blocking your business?

It is a myth that the *acquis* imposes extra burdens and bureaucracy on business. Most bureaucracy in the EU is applied by over-zealous national or regional governments and not by the EU. One only has to recall the interminable queues of articulated trucks that used to block the roads at Irun, or at La Junquera, border towns between France and Spain, prior to Spanish accession to the Community in 1986. Suddenly, the queues were gone. The same applies to sending books to Poland. Prior to May 2004 books would be held by Polish customs, 'awaiting clearance' for weeks. If you want to get a residence permit or a driving licence in Italy the procedure may take months. There are even entire offices established years ago to help citizens to get *il permesso* for whatever it is you would like to do. These are not burdens imposed by the European Commission, or the *acquis communautaire*.

The SEM enables a single set of common rules to apply throughout the Union. This is immeasurably less bureaucratic than having 25 states all impose different and often contradictory rules of their own.

Discussion 7.11

'EU regulation strangles business competitiveness'

The complaint against EU regulation is often a covert appeal to get rid of legislation designed to protect workers' rights, for example the Working Time Directive which limits the number of hours worked, employee representation on Works Councils, benefits such as maternity and paternity leave, the minimum wage, and holiday entitlements.

Those who complain presumably also want to reduce health and safety provisions in the workplace, and remove advances that benefit the physically impaired or handicapped. They would repeal laws which make environmental protection in Europe the strongest in the world.

The argument is that employment law, consumer protection and environmental standards impair competitiveness. But the counter opinion is that they also result in much higher living standards and a minimum (but I would argue insufficient) level of attention to threats of ecological catastrophe.

provide a large market for the service sector of EU-15 businesses, especially in the personal finance sector and banking. Indeed several businesses have already made significant inroads into the accession states, including the Dutch bank ING and the Irish AIB. There has been substantial inward investment into the region by West European businesses, including Volkswagen, Siemens and ABB. In the services sector, French, Dutch and British supermarkets, especially Tesco, have made significant inroads. These businesses supply a growing local demand. Even the manufacturing companies, where several may indeed have relocated from high-wage, high fixed-cost domestic bases in Germany, supply local markets, and as Mayhew (1998:190) points out, the decision to relocate from Germany may have been a choice between South East Asia, Latin America, Eastern Europe, or closing down altogether. Global forces are acting on company choices and it is difficult to isolate such choices from the wider environment. In any case, many argue that businesses transferring some or all of their activities to lower cost regions bring benefits to the communities where they set up but also return revenues to their home bases, therefore sustaining home-based operations at the same time (Micklethwait & Wooldridge, 2000; Legrain, 2002).

Enlargement also brings other benefits to the *economic environment* of the European Union. It can be a stimulus to economic renewal, improved business opportunities, cross-border partnerships and reduction in restrictive practices – and even reform of the resilient CAP. Mayhew points out that privatisation and deregulation, long demanded by free-marketeers and *Economist* leader writers, is happening in France, Germany, Spain and elsewhere, to the benefit of a more vibrant economy, and that some relaxation of employment law and of restrictions on shop opening hours is happening in Germany. Traditionalists and defenders of 'family values', as well as environmentalists, may question the wisdom of such changes.

Benefits of enlargement to new member states

Historically speaking, different countries may have different priorities when seeking entry to the Union. Certainly for the EFTA entrants in 1995, the consolidation of their democracies was not an issue, and nor to anything like the same extent were security considerations. Britain joined the Union with a different set of objectives, it would seem, from some other states already in the Union, and others yet to join. There is not of course a single, monolithic view on what kind of union the EU should be, although some commonality may be emerging. However, there are certain core values, and the general opinion seems to be that the Union is an association of states united by certain supranational structures and common treaty obligations.

New members buy into the Union as it is presented. It is hardly sustainable that a new member, or even a group of new members, can argue for fundamental changes once they have taken on the obligations of the treaties. The Union can only grow and develop according to the common wishes of the overwhelming majority of its actors, and its constituent parts, the states, and their representatives. These are common understandings that the new members accept.

This section describes the benefits of enlargement to new members, with an orientation that is mostly, but not exclusively based on the 2004 enlargement.

For applicant states, a significant set of benefits are *political*. Accession has long been seen as a key step in consolidating democratic reform and thereby substantially reducing, if not eliminating altogether, the threat of atavistic and reactionary militarism. For Spain in particular, the transition to democracy has had to deal with underlying discontentment in some sections of the security forces, the military and a small minority of the population. With every year that passes, dictatorship becomes a more distant memory and the values of democratic civil society become more entrenched. This achievement is impressive, and is one now shared not only by Greece and Portugal, but by the eight former communist countries that joined the Union in 2004.

Eight of the 2004 entrants had recently emerged from communism, so their political motives for joining the Union were similar. Membership of the Union brings the means to protect democratic reform and consolidate newly established democratic institutions. In addition, the reform process since the overthrow of communism establishes a new culture of liberal democratic governance, which is consistent with the statutes and principles of the European Union. Mayhew points out a significant benefit that the accession process brings to applicant states, arguing that incorporating the *acquis communautaire* involves making fundamental changes to legal and political processes that affect the way governance is conducted:

> The process [of adopting the *acquis*] is not simply a legal one of approximating legislation. It is changing both the legal framework in which society and the economy operate and revolutionising the institutions of the state (Mayhew, 1998:362).

An example of this is the twelfth chapter of the *acquis* which concerns statistics. The *acquis* contains a blueprint for the effective management of statistical data in a modern democratic society, a fundamental necessity for efficient social, judicial, educational, health and many other services in a modern society. In summary, accession and membership plays a significant role in consolidating and modernising the changed political culture in new democracies.

Particularly for the 2004 entrants, and probably for future applicants too, there is also an important *security* gain to membership of both the EU and of NATO. In several instances, the states concerned joined NATO prior to joining the EU. Mayhew writes:

> The repeated requests by the [former communist CEECs], including those now run by 'post-communist' governments, to join NATO and the European Union reflect the worry of once again finding themselves 'free' but 'un-anchored' in a rapidly changing Europe. All governments in the region feel the need to be bound into NATO and the European Union for reasons of security as well as the more obvious political and economic reasons (Mayhew, 1998:179).

Particularly in the early 1990s, Russia was still regarded as a security threat, if not in the short term, at least potentially in the future. Therefore membership of NATO was an early political objective that would lock the new democracies into the Western alliance. In the event, Poland, Hungary and the Czech Republic joined NATO in March 1999, without any significant protest from Russia, which had itself begun to establish a closer relationship with NATO, especially in the fields of the non-proliferation of nuclear weapons and the fight against international terrorism. Bulgaria and Romania also applied to join the alliance. They had enhanced their credentials with NATO by providing logistical support during conflict operations in the former Yugoslavia, in both Bosnia and Kosovo. There was more Russian opposition to former members of the USSR joining NATO, but when the Baltic states of Estonia, Latvia and Lithuania applied to join the alliance, President Putin finally accepted their sovereign right to choose their own security policy. Thus the second post-Cold War NATO enlargement was agreed in November 2002, involving the three Baltic states, plus Bulgaria and Romania, and also Slovakia and Slovenia, bringing total membership to 26 (these seven actually joined in May 2004). This is also a striking achievement, so soon after the end of the Cold War. It also places considerable financial burdens on the new members, as they are required to restructure and modernise their armed forces in order to meet the standards required by the alliance. Nevertheless, NATO membership represents a good deal for the newly independent former Warsaw Pact members. NATO is the world's largest international security organisation, and membership comes with several perceived advantages, including access to advice and training, better military facilities and equipment, improved partnerships, a long-term security guarantee, and improved international credibility (see discussion concerning 'influence' below). In summary, NATO membership can be described as offering a security guarantee as well as other political benefits. Crucially too, it has sometimes provided a kind of ante-chamber to EU membership (as it also did for Spain, which joined NATO in 1982). Eight of the ten newest members of NATO are now EU members, and the other two, Bulgaria and Romania, are targeted for accession in 2007.

Is NATO so politically close to the Union that they are part of the same security architecture? This interpretation is questionable. A counter-argument is that the claimed security benefits of joining the Union in fact only apply to membership of NATO, and not to the Union at all. However, Mayhew (1998:195) says it is inconceivable that should a member state be attacked, others would not respond. Nevertheless, the Union's relationship with NATO might be subject to revision at some time in the future, perhaps affected by changes in the Union's own developing defence identity. However, security also has an internal aspect, and enlargement brings enhanced cooperation in the fight against organised crime, terrorism and other aspects relating to Pillar III of Maastricht, Justice and Home Affairs, and changes introduced by the ToA, especially concerning immigration and asylum. These issues are controversial, but in general terms greater integration and international cooperation assists in all these areas: enlargement offers improved opportunities to protect against crime.

Joining the Union also has important *economic* implications. The Union sustains, by statute, a liberal capitalist economy. This holds attraction for applicant states, as the perception is that the liberal market economy, with its privileging of private ownership and the free movement of capital, can deliver increased wealth, wider markets, and new opportunities for improved living standards after the privations of 40 years of communism. Of course, capitalism brings also increased competition, market instabilities and other risks. But the common consensus is that competition brings benefits to producers and consumers alike. These assumptions are contentious, but that is beside the point.

Membership also offers the prospect of eventual accession to the eurozone, which may be viewed as a significant benefit in a globalising economy, especially for states with small and vulnerable national currencies. Eurozone membership is also seen as helpful in attracting inward investment.

Mayhew writes that *foreign direct investment* will significantly increase in new member states. The flow of capital into the region increased during the accession period as enlargement became more certain. Spain and Portugal in the 1980s achieved similar benefit. Membership of the Union offers a more secure investment environment for the private sector and full integration into the SEM acts as a boost to trade, especially in services but also in consumer goods. This pattern was also noticeable following the Northern enlargement in 1973. The benefit to the CEECs should be more marked, because of lower fixed costs.

FDI brings related benefits including increased GDP, employment and a boost to local services and perhaps also supply industries (raw materials and components). It also brings technology transfer, infrastructure modernisation, improved education and training, and better management techniques. All are benefits that accrue to regions, not simply individual companies. FDI also brings increased levels of productivity.

Two cautionary notes apply here. One is that the extent of inward investment will in part depend on productivity. New member states will need to demonstrate improvements in this area. However, in the case of Volkswagen, its plants in the Czech Republic show productivity levels that are comparable with those in its home city of Wolfsburg. In some respects, productivity is part of a chicken-and-egg syndrome. FDI stimulates improved productivity, but FDI requires high productivity. It is in this respect that the availability and effective deployment of structural and cohesion funds has a key role. The second point is that FDI is never distributed evenly and some regions will benefit substantially, whereas others will barely benefit at all. That may lead to social tensions in more underdeveloped regions of the wider Europe.

Common membership of the EU will *stimulate trade* not only within but also between the new entrants. Despite their common 1945–89 experience, and their membership of CMEA, there was little trade between them during the communist era. CMEA was constructed around a command economy, heavily centralised to national needs. Trade between them developed slowly in the 1990s and should rise now, given that all are members of the SEM and should apply similar rules, standards and procedures.

Membership may also bring access to *structural funds* (European Regional Development Fund, European Social Fund, European Agricultural Guidance and Guarantee Fund). In the event, post-*Agenda 2000*, applicant states found that their access to structural funds would be less than they had hoped for, but nevertheless, as stated above, the Berlin Council agreed a total of €45bn for CEE applicant states before and after accession up to 2006 (Bourne, 2003:286–7).

A final advantage in joining the Union also has a political dimension – it is concerned with *influence*. Enlargement brings new member states the opportunity to participate in one of the world's largest trade blocs, and representation in the **Triad** economy of US/NAFTA, EU/EEA and Japan/Asia-Pacific region. The question of an alternative does not and did not arise: there was none (Mayhew, 1998:194).

> For [countries joining the Union] membership brings many advantages, which probably outweigh the loss of sovereignty, which in today's integrated world is worth little (Mayhew, 1998:195).

This is a key observation, and one that echoes claims already made in Chapter 2, Key concept 2.1 – see in particular quotations from Walker (1994), and Baun (1996). As Mayhew says, independence, or remaining outside the European Union, was not perceived as a valid option. All major political parties in all candidate countries supported membership. The eventual referenda held in each state delivered overwhelming Yes votes, although as noted previously turnout was low in some cases. For all CEECs, sovereignty was considered worthwhile only where it can be exercised from within democratic international organisations. Thus since the end of the Cold War the ten former members of the Warsaw Pact have sought and obtained membership of the Council of Europe, NATO and the European Union – with the exceptions of Bulgaria and Romania which are still negotiating entry to the Union. Clearly, the consensus was that independence spelt isolation and vulnerability.

The global dimension is significant. International institutions have become increasingly important in the global political economy, and as a result it is widely accepted that influence depends on partnerships and membership of international organisations. The WTO is a case in point, where the Commission represents the member states of the European Union as a whole, and is the largest single negotiating partner in the organisation. Similarly for states aspiring to join the European Union, membership provides not only access to the Single Market, but also the opportunity to play a part in determining how the market is actually governed. Writing about the EFTA enlargement Glenn comments that:

> applicants sought membership to be able to participate in European policy formulation, that is, to influence the rules of the game, a game they would be forced to play even if they were not full members (Glenn, 2003:214).

This is one of the attractions of membership, though clearly an insufficient one for some, such as Norway and Switzerland. Norway is a member of the EEA, and therefore has full access to the SEM, but it has no access to policy-making forums governing the market, such as the Council or the ECB. Switzerland voted against EEA membership but still has access to EU markets, at a cost. With no influence over EC law making, Switzerland is still obliged to make a contribution towards EU funds, an annual payment of €130m into the Cohesion Fund. The three non-EU EEA members pay €1bn over five years in exchange for market access (Castle, 2004).

The benefits from joining the EU are summarised in Discussion 7.12.

> ### Discussion 7.12
>
> ## Benefits to new member states from joining the EU
>
> The rationale for joining the European Union includes four dimensions:
>
> 1. *Political*: consolidation of newly created democratic institutions and the rule of law; support for the reform process; modernisation based on the *acquis*.
> 2. *Security*: in partnership with NATO, EU membership locks new democracies into western alliance, bringing defence and security benefits and long-term guarantees; enhanced cooperation in crime prevention and combating terrorism.
> 3. *Economic*: EU membership consolidates economic reform and engagement with market economy; access to wider markets; support for modernisation programmes; foreign direct investment; increased trade between 2004 entrants; eligibility for structural funding support, bringing improvements to infrastructure.
> 4. *Influence*: membership brings access to international forums and therefore opportunity to contribute to decision-making processes; EU has global significance; improved representation in international forums such as the WTO; ability to contribute to policy making inside the Union.

> **Review**   *What are some of the major challenges arising from the 2004 enlargement? (Note: they may also apply to other future enlargements.)*
> *What are the political benefits to the Union of enlargement?*
> *Suggest economic benefits to the Union that should follow from enlargement.*
> *What are some of the likely advantages to joining the EU for new members?*

● ● ● ● Further enlargements – how big can the Union get?

The Union started out as a group of six. It used to be described as 'a rich man's club'. It now comprises 25 states and has long since ceased to be derided as an exclusive narrow elite. The 2004 enlargement may be fairly quickly followed by another, as negotiations for the entry of Bulgaria and Romania began in early 2000, together with those who joined in May 2004.

● ● ● ● Balkan enlargement in 2007

As already pointed out, Bulgaria and Romania are even poorer than the states that joined in 2004. A GDP comparison places Bulgaria at 23 per cent of the Union average and Romania at 27 per cent. Romania is relatively large, with a population of almost 23 million, much larger than all the 2004 applicants bar Poland. Both have large agricultural sectors, with almost 40 per cent of the workforce in Romania employed on the land, compared with 26 per cent in Bulgaria.

Table 7.1 A Balkan enlargement in 2007?

	Population	GDP as % of EU	Employed in agriculture %
Bulgaria	8.2m	23	26
Romania	22.5m	27	41
Croatia	4.8m		

Both countries are still engaged in meeting the conditionality rule established at Copenhagen, the application of the *acquis communautaire*, and Romania still falls short in some political and economic respects. In June 2004 the Council officially announced that it had accepted an application to join from Croatia, and that negotiations would begin. Croatia faces considerable problems as well, and is still recovering from the trauma of war and the break-up of Yugoslavia in the early 1990s. For these states the likely accession to the Union is 2007, depending on progress in adopting the *acquis*. A Sixth Enlargement comprising Bulgaria, Romania and Croatia will be another major challenge and coming so soon after the Eastern enlargement, the timetable may be overly optimistic (see Table 7.1).

Nevertheless, the EU has set a precedent through the 2004 enlargement in its capping of structural funding to the new members and limiting their access to CAP support. These measures reduce the scale of the cost of accession to pre-enlargement member states. The Union faces a different task from the challenge of efficient structural funding and related cohesion or convergence strategies; although these challenges remain, the EU has effectively downgraded its expectations in these respects, and so reduced its commitments. The result is that greater responsibility for convergence is placed on the new member states themselves. For the Union, the new challenge is accommodating the widely divergent economic strengths of its members. It remains to be seen when any of the 2004 applicants join the euro, but probably not in the immediate future.

The EU has two immediate consolidation tasks: first, the euro – still in its infancy; second, the 2004 enlargement. Nevertheless, further enlargement, at least within five years, remains a probability.

A second EFTA enlargement

As we have seen, in theory any European state that meets the entry criteria may become a candidate for entry to the Union. This means that the current EFTA members, Switzerland, Iceland, Norway and Liechtenstein could become members, presumably without much difficulty from the EU perspective. In fact Norway has attempted to join three times, most recently as part of the 1995 EFTA enlargement, but accession was aborted after a narrow defeat for the Yes campaign in a referendum. Entrenched fishing and agricultural interests, plus historical antipathy in some of the Norwegian population towards Germany – and even towards Sweden on account of Sweden's neutrality during the Second World War – have made securing a vote for accession impossible. Small towns and rural communities are especially averse to joining the EU. Jones (2001:490) cites an opinion poll in March 2001 for *Nationen* newspaper declaring 56.2 per cent opposed to EU entry, with only 35.6 per cent in favour. On average a Norwegian government tries to join the Union every 20 years, so expect the next attempt around 2015. By that time the economy, now buoyed by substantial income from oil exports, may be in a less privileged state. That may tip the balance towards membership. Norway is of course a member of the EEA, and so has full access to EU markets, thus it is sometimes suggested that it has 'all the benefits and none of the costs': this is not the case, as explained above, since Norway is obliged to pay into the Cohesion Fund to help the EU's poorer states. Nevertheless, were Norway to join, it would immediately become a netcontributor to the EU budget.

Switzerland is a different case (see Chapter 3, pp. 89–90). The Swiss have never shown much interest in joining the EU, nor much enthusiasm for joining anything. Although a founder member of the solidly intergovernmental EFTA, Switzerland is not a member of NATO, nor the EEA. It only agreed to join the UN after a referendum as recently as 2002. Switzerland prefers commitments to bilateral intergovernmentalism, which is how it agrees its trading relationship with the EU. This works for Switzerland, a relatively small, highly industrialised market economy with major banking and pharmaceuticals sectors. After the Cold War ended, the Swiss government, backed by big business, took steps to join the Union and tested the waters of public opinion with a referendum on joining the EEA. The result was not as the government wished: EEA membership was rejected, and the application to join the EU withdrawn. A further referendum on EU membership was held in March 2001 and 76 per cent opposed entry (Jones, ibid.).

Liechtenstein, with a population of only 30,000, is too small to join the EU as a full member, and Iceland would probably follow any lead taken by Norway.

In conclusion, as regards a second EFTA enlargement, the verdict is that fresh applications are not likely in the short or medium term.

West Balkans

The next potential candidate group is the West Balkans, comprising four republics of the former Yugoslavia, Bosnia Herzegovina, Croatia, the Former Yugoslav Republic of Macedonia (see Discussion 7.13), and Yugoslavia itself – Serbia and Montenegro, which includes Kosovo, plus Albania. Croatia, as we have seen, is already an applicant negotiating entry. The others are some way behind. All were declared potential candidates at the Feira European Council in 2000. All receive EU financial assistance through the Stability Pact for South East Europe, and Stability and Association Agreements between the Union and each of the West Balkan states. Assistance programmes set up in 2000 scheduled €5bn between 2000–2006, but the funding is dependent on progress towards democracy. Pinder (2001:136) comments that the EU funding is a vital component in stabilising the region, while Jones says

> The Balkan outsiders currently fall far short of the political and economic criteria for EU membership (Jones, 2001:390).

Discussion 7.13

What's in a name?

The name Former Yugoslav Republic of Macedonia may seem a trifle unwieldy. In fact the FYROM has adopted this name as part of an attempt to improve relations with its southerly neighbour, Greece. Greece contains a northern province called Macedonia, and objected to the authorities in the former Yugoslav republic adopting the name Macedonia after the break-up of the Federal Republic of Yugoslavia. Greece feared territorial claims from its neighbour, but relations between the two have improved since the new name became official.

The region remains volatile. The support it receives from the EU is probably critical to its political development. But accession to the EU remains a long way off.

Turkey

The EU has long considered Turkey a potential member of the Union, signing an Association Agreement in 1963, although this was suspended during periods of military government. In 1987 the Turkish government applied to join the Community but two years later the Commission delivered the opinion that the application could not be considered since

> any decision to open negotiations . . . must be based on a strong conviction that a positive conclusion is possible, indeed probable, within a reasonable period (Commission, quoted in Bainbridge, 2002:520).

On various political and economic grounds, including stability and human rights, this was not possible where Turkey was concerned. Turkey's GDP is around half that of Greece, the Community's poorest member, and its population of 65 million would put enormous strains on the Community budget. Bainbridge reports that instead of accepting the application

> the Commission proposed an intensification of political, commercial and economic relationships within the framework of the Association Agreement (Bainbridge, ibid.).

By the mid-1990s the Turkish government was expressing impatience over the Union's lack of support for Turkish accession. The EU responded by confirming that Turkey was eligible to join, and stated that the customs union with Turkey was working satisfactorily but that there remained concerns over democratisation, human rights, relations between Greece and Turkey and a just and permanent settlement to the problem of the divided island of Cyprus. Progress has remained slow, and a resolution to the problems surrounding Turkey's accession are not likely to be settled in the short term.

Turkey presents particular challenges. It is a large country with particular security implications for the EU, as it borders Syria, Iran and Iraq. It is also overwhelmingly Muslim, which would in itself represent a significant difference to any previous accession. It has a large Kurdish minority, the treatment of which has been a long-standing concern to the EU and its member states. Glenn (2003:222) reports that various human rights groups, including Amnesty International, remain deeply concerned over the treatment of prisoners in Turkey and many do not see Turkish membership of the EU as imminent.

Turkish accession would have powerful security implications. Its position between Europe and the Middle East has always meant that it is a vital and strategic partner in NATO, but internal stability and problematic Greek-Turkish relations are serious concerns. These are dominated by the Cyprus question. Turkish Cypriots govern the north of the island, divided since 1974, while the south is under Greek Cypriot control. Cyprus's accession to the Union in 2004 was achieved in spite of there being no long-term settlement to the problem.

Interestingly, in geographical terms, Turkey is not even in Europe: 96 per cent of its territory is east of the Bosporus, therefore in Asia. However, the EU has always waived any concern about this given that Turkey is a member of the Council of Europe and of NATO (Bainbridge, 2002:521). (See reference to Morocco in Discussion 7.2.)

The Russian Federation and the CIS

The security implications of a possible Turkish accession are matched by similar concerns regarding the states of the former Soviet Union, including Russia itself, that now comprise the Commonwealth of Independent States (CIS). The CIS members that can legitimately be described as European are Armenia, Belarus, Georgia, Moldova, Ukraine, and the Russian Federation.

Russia, with its population of 150m and its vast geographical area (almost twice as large as China) is so big that it would destabilise the structure of the EU. Entry, according to Pinder, is 'not feasible' (Pinder, 2001:138). For the other CIS states, entry is not beyond the bounds of possibility, but in the meantime they face daunting challenges:

> These states face great problems in their efforts to transform themselves into market economies and pluralist democracies. At least for a long time ahead they must be regarded as partners in the EU's external relations, and not potential member states (Pinder, 2001:138).

All receive support from the EU through the TACIS programme, launched in 1991. TACIS is concerned with enterprise restructuring and development, administrative reform, social services, education, and as the biggest item, nuclear safety. The annual budget is €542m. TACIS runs in association with wide-ranging Partnership and Cooperation Agreements promoting trade, but these are significantly different to the Europe Agreements set up with the ten CEECs in the 1990s. Pinder reports that they contain no mention of membership of the EU, and the TACIS programme is much smaller than PHARE (Pinder, 2001:139–40).

Membership of the EU for some of the European CIS members is at least theoretically possible in the long term, although Jones, referring to the occasional references to EU membership by some politicians in some CIS countries, calls it 'currently not a realistic prospect' (2001:492). Russia is even more solidly in the 'not realistic' category. However, Falkner and Nentwich report that

> the EU's relationship with Russia, as with the Ukraine, is fundamental and will shape the destiny of the European continent (Commission, quoted in Falkner & Nentwich, 2001:270).

They argue that the EU urgently needs to develop tailor-made models of closer cooperation with all CIS European states, as well as their neighbours, in order to promote peace and human rights, and political as well as economic development in the region (Falkner & Nentwich, ibid.). Pinder also stresses the importance of the EU's relationship with Russia, arguing that it is one of the

> principal challenges facing the EU's common foreign, security and above all external economic policy. If a genuine partnership can be forged with Russia it would be a most important element in the EU's foreign policy and its relationship with the wider world (Pinder, 2001:141).

In conclusion, future enlargement policy is closely related to the wider international role of the Union. Its status as a regional power is indisputable and its global role is in the ascendance. Given the strategic importance of Turkey and the strategic and economic importance of Russia, the EU's relationship with its neighbours, whether candidates for entry to the Union or not, remains one of the most important policy areas for the EU.

Review   *Where are future enlargements likely to come from? What are the difficulties regarding them? Why don't Norway and Switzerland join the EU?*

●●●● The global context of enlargement

To what extent do outside forces affect the rationale for enlargement? The relationship to the global context in this chapter is mainly in relation to security issues. This is not surprising. For all the countries concerned, security concerns have been the overwhelmingly dominant feature of their history. Poland has suffered occupation at the hands of a succession of foreign powers, including Sweden and Lithuania, and in the twentieth century the country was left devastated by Nazi Germany and then occupied to all intents and purposes by Russia until the end of the Cold War. Thus external relationships are understandably priorities for the 2004 accession states, as they are for other prospective members, and for the emergent states in other areas struggling with the new post-Cold War environment, namely Russia itself, its CIS partners, and the states formed following the break-up of the former Yugoslavia.

It is not necessary to go through the arguments over security again; suffice to say that security remains a critical concern in a globalising economy, and may be an increasing concern, as terrorism internationalises, and risks from the arms trade and nuclear proliferation increase. Security issues in an increasingly complex and internationally linked global society are inescapable.

However, the global context is not simply one of security concerns. Economy is also important. The states joining the EU do so because they judge that it offers better economic prospects than the alternative of staying outside, or looking for other partnerships, or choosing a semi-detached relationship with the Union. In fact, as Mayhew observed (see above, p. 223), there were no alternatives. This is because the global environment, the global economy, implies that a policy of isolation is unlikely to bring rewards. Influence, access, partnerships, participation and engagement are all better options. This conclusion may be especially true for emergent democracies and developing economies. In the UK, the campaigners for the UK Independence Party, and some Conservatives, confidently assert that the UK should leave the European Union because it could manage perfectly well outside, as a free trading nation, in a close partnership with the USA, and that it would still have all the benefits of full participation in the Single European Market. All this is debatable. But it is certainly true that the UK is already a thoroughly globalised, medium-sized economy, and it is an advanced industrial state with a long-established democracy. Poland is not like that. Ireland has made huge strides in its economic development in the past 20 years. It has a population size similar to that of Norway, but it has no oil. It requires engagement with others.

The chapter has argued that the EU is developing an increasingly global role and that enlargement relates to this trend. The Union is a unique example of highly integrated political and economic international cooperation. Its international profile is unmatched by any other regional grouping. As a major regional power it has influence on other key actors in the international arena: its historical partner, the United States; its giant easterly neighbour, Russia and the CIS; the established industrial giant, Japan; the emergent, potentially very powerful states, China and India. This international role of the EU is examined in the final chapter. For now it is sufficient to note that the enlargement process places the workings of the Union in an international spotlight. It can therefore be a force for good in the world. The core values of the Union are given a public airing by the enlargement process. The Union can advertise what it stands for. It seems bizarre, but some of its opponents have attempted to portray the European Union as an echo of the old monolithic USSR. Such a grotesque parody insults the Union, but more importantly, insults the peoples of the states that endured, and overthrew, the Soviet occupation of their lands.

Enlargement does not take place in a vacuum. If the Union had not pursued its moral responsibility to offer membership to the countries of Central and Eastern Europe, had enlargement not happened in 2004, something else would have done. Europe would be a very different place. It would be idle to speculate on this for long, but in an increasingly internationalised political environment, where challenges are transnational and shared, the role of the EU is critically important. One could re-examine all the opposites of the positive goods discussed above and speculate on the alternative consequences. The EU has achieved its historic Eastern enlargement. It has done so while maintaining a reasonable relationship with the Russian Federation, which remains the world's second largest nuclear power, and has enormous economic potential. The states of the Union now bear responsibility to ensure that enlargement is a success. That, too, is inseparable from the global context.

Review   *Why is the global context relevant to the issue of enlargement?*

Summary

This chapter has made the following key points.

History and process of EU enlargement

- The 2004 Eastern enlargement is the greatest challenge of all enlargements to date
- Applications must meet the political and economic criteria established at Copenhagen
- Respect for human rights is a key condition for beginning negotiations
- Economic assistance is essential during the accession phase
- *Agenda 2000* established preconditions for enlargement
- The *acquis* provides a road map towards accession
- The *acquis* is a vital tool in political and economic development

The rationale for enlargement

Enlargement can help the Union to

- enhance peace and security
- achieve economic benefits within the SEM
- achieve political benefits ('deepening' as well as 'widening', enhanced democracy, fulfil moral obligations, consolidate EU's core values, including human rights, assist the Union in its global responsibilities)

The implications of enlargement – costs and benefits

- Enlargement presents huge challenges in terms of economic convergence and integration with the SEM and EU-15
- Political benefits include
  - security
  - rapprochement
  - institutional reform
  - internal security

- Economic benefits include
  - boost to the SEM
  - increased FDI
- Benefits to new member states include
  - political benefits, consolidation of reform, institutional development
  - enhanced security
  - economic development, FDI, improved trade, improved living standards
  - influence, participation in decision-making

Further enlargements – how big can the Union get?

- A Balkan enlargement is likely sooner rather than later
- The remaining EFTA states are not interested in joining the EU (for now)
- Serious obstacles remain before Turkey can join
- The EU must help to establish the core values of democracy and the rule of law in the West Balkans and in the CIS
- The EU–Russian Federation relationship is of vital importance in EU foreign policy

The global context of enlargement

- Security issues are global and inescapable
- The global economy makes partnerships essential
- The EU has a developing global role
- The EU can and must reinforce its core values through the process of enlargement

Key concepts: discussion and other definitions

Key concept 7.1   Human rights

The rights one has simply by virtue of being a human being (Donnelly, cited in Mansbach, 2000:483).

A right involves an entitlement that an individual can use to make a moral claim on others who are bound to respect that right. In this sense, violations of rights are fundamental wrongs (Mansbach, ibid.).

Human rights are individuals' fundamental moral obligations towards each other. Rights are fundamental in another sense: 'they logically and morally [. . .] take precedence over the rights of the state and society' (Donnelly, cited in Mansbach, ibid.).

Mansbach (2000:482) highlights the long history of institutionalised recognition of human rights, appearing as early as 1215 in the Magna Carta, and again in the English Bill of Rights (1689), the American Declaration of Independence (1776), and the French Declaration of the Rights of Man (1789). There are also disputes over cultural relativism, whereby some cultures may have a different interpretation over what constitute individual rights within a particular society, but the Nazi and Japanese atrocities of the 1930s and during the Second World War renewed the call for a strict interpretation of human rights. The Nuremberg trials, where Germans were convicted of crimes against humanity and war crimes, were widely regarded as a 'path-breaking precedent in human rights' (Mansbach, ibid.). In 1948 the UN adopted the Universal Declaration of Human Rights.

Nevertheless, as Mansbach points out, the issue of human rights did little to perturb the Cold War superpowers. The US tolerated systematic abuse of human rights by its allies, including Franco's Spain, Pinochet's Chile, Marcos's Philippines, Syngman Rhee's South Korea, Somoza's Nicaragua, Suharto's Indonesia and Mobuto's Zaire. The Soviet Union meanwhile routinely violated human rights, as did all the communist regimes in Eastern Europe; other communist regimes did the same in Cuba and China, notably during Mao Zedung's Cultural Revolution 1966–76. Still today human rights are a major concern in China more than 25 years after Deng Xiao Ping began the country's famed liberalisation. Abuse of human rights remains a major problem in the United States, notably in relation to the criminal justice system, the death penalty, and the treatment of detainees, especially at Guantánamo Bay and similar institutions established as part of the 'war on terror'. Many other countries are regularly reported as routinely and systematically flouting human rights: the issue remains as important now as it ever was. In Europe, Russia and Belarus are most often criticised on human rights grounds.

The issue of respect for human rights has long underpinned the European Union and its predecessor, the European Community. In the context of enlargement, human rights have special resonance. This is because respect for human rights has long been a precondition before a state can be accepted as a candidate for accession. As long ago as 1962, Spain, under Franco, and Portugal, under Salazar, both applied to join the European Community. Their applications were rejected on political grounds, with the lack of democracy and the lack of respect for human rights explicitly cited as reasons for the negative verdict.

The Preamble to the Treaty on European Union refers to

> the principles of liberty, democracy and respect for human rights and fundamental freedoms, and the rule of law (Treaty of Rome, Article 6).

This explicit reference was considered important in negotiations with the candidate countries leading up to the 2004 enlargement. Human rights concerns have consistently dogged Turkey's proposed accession to the Union. In December 1999 the Helsinki Council finally accepted Turkey as a candidate for accession, holding the view that granting Turkey this status might assist it in meeting concerns relating to human rights. The usual expectation is that states meet the political conditions established in the Copenhagen Criteria in 1992, which include 'the rule of law, human rights and respect for and protection of minorities', but in the case of Turkey, this was relaxed as an 'encouragement' to Turkey to do more to meet its obligations in this area.

The Treaty of Nice did not actually incorporate the European Convention on Human Rights, but the Convention is part of the European Union Charter of Fundamental Rights which was adopted by the tripartite Council-Commission-Parliament in 1977. The European Convention on Human Rights was created by the Council of Europe and is part of the judicial competence of the European Court of Human Rights, none of which are European Union institutions. However, it is significant in the development of the European Union that it now has not only explicit treaty commitments relating to human rights, but including since Amsterdam the authority to suspend any member state 'found guilty of serious and persistent' breach of human rights. The conjunction 'and' is interesting, and raises the question of whether the Union would suspend a member state for a single incidence of carrying out capital punishment. My expectation is that such an event would indeed provoke a dramatic reaction from the member states and suspension would follow. The death penalty has not been used in any member state since the late 1970s.

Bainbridge quotes from the ECHR:

> [The Convention guarantees] the right to life, liberty and security of person; the right to a fair trial, with the right to have the sentence reviewed by a higher tribunal; respect for privacy and family life; freedom of thought, conscience and religion; freedom of expression; freedom of the press; freedom of peaceful assembly and association; freedom from torture, inhuman or degrading treatment, slavery or forced labour; the prohibition of the death penalty; the right to leave or return to one's own country; and the elimination of discrimination in the enjoyment of rights and freedoms guaranteed under the Convention (European Convention on Human Rights, cited in Bainbridge, 2002:320).

The European Commission gives an opinion on matters relating to human rights in assessing applications to join the Union and these have been used as an argument against Turkish membership. The European Parliament has pressed for human rights clauses to be included in Europe Agreements. Meanwhile, the Parliament has taken a consistent interest in human rights cases, relating to complaints about abuses both within and outside the Union. It produces annual reports, and it works closely with human rights groups, including Amnesty International. The TEU formalised a procedure whereby complaints about human rights abuse could be brought before the European Parliament, and the establishment of an ombudsman is a further example of the emergence of European Union instruments to defend and protect human rights.

> ## Key concept 7.2   Widening and deepening
>
> Widening – bringing in more member states; deepening – consolidating the institutions and competences of the Union and increasing the extent of integration between member states

'Widening' and 'deepening' represent two contrasting approaches towards the development of the Union that emerged after the Cold War ended.

More federally inclined actors in the European project saw the opportunity to enlarge the Union eastwards as a significant step in fulfilling the promise of the phrase 'ever closer union'. But they also recognised that to enlarge the Union without institutional reform would put the entire enterprise, and not just enlargement, at risk. Enlarging the Union by up to 12 states could induce institutional paralysis. They preferred to accept widening, but they insisted that the institutions and instruments of the Union be developed in a way that would consolidate the achievements of the Union since its creation in the 1950s.

Others, among them the British Prime Minister John Major, saw enlarging the Union as an opportunity to bring the Single Market to the former communist states but also to 'slow down' the process of integration. This faction liked the idea of widening, but abhorred the prospect of 'deepening'.

Bainbridge highlights the tension between the opposing positions as articulated above. He says

> the prospect of enlargement and its alleged consequences are used to strengthen the case, on the one hand, for slowing down the integration process and, on the other, for speeding it up (Bainbridge, 2002:540).

In some respects the argument was an old-fashioned meeting between opposing aspirations for how to govern the Union: federalists v. intergovernmentalists. But this is an oversimplification because, as is normal in the affairs of the Union, neither side got exactly what it wanted. However, the 'no more deepening' faction was the biggest loser.

Bainbridge writes that the Commission reported to the Luxembourg Council in 1992 an unequivocal opinion:

> '. . . the accession of new members will increase [the Union's] diversity and heterogeneity. But widening must not be at the expense of deepening. Enlargement must not be a dilution of the Community's achievements'. The European Council itself concluded that 'if the challenges of a European Union composed of a large number of Member States are to be met successfully, parallel progress is needed as regards the internal development of the Union' (Bainbridge, 2002:541).

In fact within months the TEU established a new architecture of the Union, based on the pillar structure, which affirmed the supranational identity of European Community law and the enhanced status of the Single European Market. This, together with progress towards EMU, represented significant 'deepening'. On the other hand, Pillars II and III, CFSP and JHA respectively, affirmed the intergovernmental character of policy making in these areas. The apparent ring-fencing of Pillars II and III for intergovernmental control could, just, be regarded as 'no more deepening'. Enlargement, a separate policy, would enable 'widening'.

However, as will already be apparent from previous chapters, time never stands still where the EU is concerned. Further innovations followed Maastricht, including increases in the powers of the European Parliament and greater use of QMV through both the ToA and ToN, as well as significant weakening of Pillar III as elements of it were transferred to Pillar I. These changes furthered the deepening of the Union's structures. But at the same time, the Council gained powers at the expense of the Commission, which bolstered the intergovernmental character of policy formulation. This is why the characterisation of 'widening' v. 'deepening' as an argument between federalists and intergovernmentalists is an oversimplification. Governments managed to tilt the balance towards the Council (intergovernmentalist) during the post-1997 accession period, but the Union achieved 'deepening' at the same time.

Agenda 2000 managed to consolidate the enlargement process in a way which clearly indicates a deepening of the Union's policy-making formulae. It is an example of a policy instrument, as it formed, together with the *acquis*, an important tool in the accession process, both for the candidate countries and for the Union.

Pinder reports on how the Europe Agreements, negotiated with each candidate country in the early 1990s, eventually contained explicit reference to membership. They also contained the phrase 'ability to take on the obligations of membership including the aims of political, economic and monetary union' (cited in Pinder, 2001:130). Pinder goes on

> To allay fears that widening would result in weakening, there was also the condition that the Union should have 'the capacity to absorb new members while maintaining the momentum of integration' (Pinder, ibid.).

That is a fairly explicit commitment to both widening and deepening.

See related Key concepts 4.1 Intergovernmentalism, 4.2 Supranationalism and 5.1 Federalism. See also broader theoretical considerations in Chapter 5.

Further reading

Jones, R.A. (2001) *The Politics and Economics of the European Union*, Cheltenham: Edward Elgar. This text is excellent, detailed but extremely readable. Chapter 20, 'The Enlargement of the EU', pp. 462–93, on the process leading up to the 2004 enlargement, gives more detail than is provided here. See especially the description of the final stages of negotiation, on pp. 485–6.

Mayhew, A. (1998) *Recreating Europe*, Cambridge: Cambridge University Press. Chapter 7 is on the costs and benefits of enlargement. Although written several years before the Eastern enlargement took place, the conclusions Mayhew drew then remain valid today, and the text remains a classic.

Nugent, N. (2004) *European Union Enlargement*, Basingstoke: Palgrave Macmillan. A timely addition to the Palgrave European Union Series, of which Neil Nugent is the series editor, this book was published to coincide with the 2004 enlargment.

Film suggestion

Phillip Noyce, *Rabbit Proof Fence*, 2002, Australia

This film is about human rights. Though set in 1930s' Australia, human rights are universal so the film has a message applicable to any context.

Based on true events, the film depicts the impact of government policy in Australia in the 1930s to take half-caste children away from their families and to socialise them in white, Christian, Australian surroundings, provided by special detention centres. This racist policy brought the misery of the so-called 'stolen generations'. Unbelievably, the policy continued into the 1970s.

The film shows the plight of three half-caste girls kidnapped and forcibly removed from their families. The girls escape and undertake an extraordinary journey across the Australian Outback, following a rabbit proof fence in an effort to return home.

See a review of the film at:

http://www.bbc.co.uk/films/2002/10/16/rabbit_proof_fence_2002_review.shtml

and a fascinating interview about the personalities involved with the film at:

http://www.iofilm.co.uk/feats/interviews/r/rabbit_proof_fence_2002.shtml

Chapter 8

International Relations theory and the state

Outline

- The EU and 'new' regionalism
- International Relations theory
- Realism and neo-realism
- Liberalism and institutional liberalism
- International society
- International Political Economy (IPE)
  - Mercantilism
  - Neo-liberalism and globalisation
  - Marxism and reformism
- Hegemonic stability theory
- International Relations theory in context

Key concepts

8.1 Capitalism

8.2 Liberalism

8.3 Marxism

8.4 Hegemony

● ● ● ● Introduction

Chapter 5 surveyed theories of European integration. This chapter, focusing on International Relations theories, provides a second theoretical framework which can assist in understanding of the role of the state in the context of globalisation.

The chapter begins by pointing out that the field of IR is increasingly concerned with issues of regionalism and the role of regional organisations such as the European Union (EU), the North American Free Trade Agreement (NAFTA) and Asia Pacific Economic Cooperation (APEC), and other international groups such as the World Trade Organisation (WTO) and the G8. Indeed the EU has become a significant actor in international relations, as a phenomenon of global politics, as well as in IR theory itself. Following a brief introduction which locates the European Union in the context of the discipline of International Relations, several key strands of IR theory are surveyed. Naturally, this is a selective overview in a single chapter. It is important, however, to explain some basic concepts of IR theory which recur in the rest of the book.

The strand on neo-liberalism and globalisation is developed in later chapters, since it is clear that the phenomenon of globalisation is driving significant change in relation to the state. It is a vital feature, perhaps the dominant one, on the landscape of European political development, and naturally for globalisation studies.

International Relations, a sub-discipline of political science, traditionally attempts to explain how states relate to one another. In recent years the discipline has extended its scope to

> thinking about emergent transnational economic and social spaces and the forms of government that arise in such circumstances (Rosamond, 2003:123).

This trend is a response to evidence of a 'new regionalism' in recent years, of which the EU is an example. This regional integration is arguably a response to globalisation. It is evident that the EU has assumed greater significance as a global actor. IR then, has responded by looking at the role of transnational organisations as well as states.

IR theory provides a useful set of tools for the interpretation of diplomacy and for assessing the impact of globalisation. However, it is notable that trends such as regional integration could on the one hand call into question the relevance of an academic discipline which traditionally – and in America still – is overwhelmingly interested in interpreting international affairs as centrally, even exclusively – about bilateral relations between states. This chapter argues that this is not the case. An intelligent and comprehensive interpretation of the international environment requires a move beyond the Hobbesian fixation with state power and the notion that states are by definition independent and sovereign entities, whose primary function is to build up their military strength in order to ensure their survival, or their ability to dictate the affairs of others.

In the current environment the core precepts of classical IR, such as realism and neo-liberalism, are challenged by globalisation, but not rendered obsolete.

● ● ● ● The EU and 'new' regionalism

After the Second World War there was a proliferation of international organisations that displayed a decisively intergovernmental character and thus conformed neatly to the traditional assumption of IR theory that sovereign states are the essential foundation of international politics and the key actors in international affairs. Even contractual arrangements like the Bretton Woods Accords of 1944, or treaty-based innovations such as NATO, essentially left state sovereignty intact. The Treaty of Rome did not seem to significantly disturb this assumption, as the EEC consisted of six sovereign states whose independent governments had freely chosen to cooperate in the area of the economy, albeit with some measure of supranational institution building to underpin this cooperation. The EEC is a clear example, perhaps the best example, of regionalism, defined as 'state-led projects of institution building among groups of countries' (Rosamond, 2003:123).

Indeed, the evolution of the European Union has progressed integration to the point where the sovereignty of member states has clearly altered. In addition, geopolitical forces, such as the Cold War, further impacted upon state sovereignty as this book has already argued. Now with hindsight we can say that creating the ECSC and the EEC were the first steps in a process of significant regional integration in Europe. There is evidence of a similar process happening elsewhere, perhaps in response to globalisation, although in Europe regional integration obviously predates the burgeoning use of the term globalisation since 1991. What Rosamond (2003:123) calls 'new regionalism' is indicated by the North American Free Trade Agreement (NAFTA) founded in 1994, Asia Pacific Economic Cooperation (APEC) in 1989 and Mercosur in 1991 (Mercado Común del Sur: the South American common market). The United States appears keen to extend NAFTA to other countries in the Americas, and has visions of a Free Trade Area of the Americas (FTAA). How does this regionalism affect IR? In the European context the answer probably depends on the extent to which the EU has assumed the characteristics of a state, and how much of a global actor the EU has become. But also, it has pushed the discipline of IR towards accounting more for the role of transnational groups, or international institutions, and not just states.

International Relations scholars have paid increased attention to the EU as it has taken on further state-like characteristics referred to in Chapter 2 (see Discussion 2.4). It has, for example, a presence in the World Trade Organisation, in which the common interests of the Union are represented by the European Commission. In security matters the EU role is less developed, but it does have a developing profile in peacekeeping, with units from its Rapid Reaction Force (RRF) deployed in Sierra Leone and in Kosovo. The EU also has an institutional profile which is state-like: it has organs of governance, a headquarters, a civil service and external presence through trade missions and the like. It also has a legally constituted foundation, through its treaties, and a system of specifically supranational courts, and it may soon have a formal constitution. It has bilateral relations with NAFTA, and with other transnational organisations, including NGOs, as well as with states. Although often divided, it has an embryonic profile in terms of institutionalised foreign policy, through the CFSP and the office of High Commissioner for Foreign Affairs, currently Javier Solana. The most important innovation in recent years in the EU's state-like tendencies is the transition to a single currency among 12 of its members and the establishment of the European Central Bank in Frankfurt.

Not only does the EU demonstrate many features that are normally found only in states, it also demonstrates probably the best and most developed example of both regional integration and institution building. It is one of various international institutions to emerge as a key actor on the global stage. This observation comes with the caveat that, as explained in Chapter 4, the EU is not really a single institution. It is more accurately described as a transnational organisation comprising several member states and various institutions.

In summary, the EU is both an example of regionalism, and of institutionalisation. Transnational institutions are increasingly significant in international affairs and this has led to the emergence of institutionalism as a sub-area of IR theory, often referred to as liberal institutionalism. This is examined later in this chapter.

IR has much to contribute to any assessment of how globalisation impacts upon states and how as a part of this process states coalesce in multinational or transnational organisations. The foremost example of this phenomenon is the European Union, because it demonstrates a deeper economic and political integration, including the emergence of significant institutional development with both intergovernmental and supranational character, as discussed in Chapter 4. The EU has also developed a huge body of legislation contained in the *acquis communautaire*, amounting to some 97,000 pages. As an example of a transnational organisation, the EU is unique. No other body comes close in scope or complexity. It may offer something of a model to other regions coming to terms with globalisation. The final chapter assesses the potential for the 'EU as model' in more detail.

Review   *Why is the EU the best example of regionalism? What other examples are there? How is the EU 'like a state'? (See also Chapter 2.)*

International Relations theory

International Relations attempts to analyse and understand how states and international bodies relate to one another. Conflict, diplomacy and mutual responsibilities have marked the relationship between states since the concept of statehood was first established.

IR is a useful tool in assessing how globalisation impacts upon states and how, partly as a response to the issues highlighted by globalisation, states coalesce in transnational organisations. This has been true for decades and of course implies that globalisation should not be interpreted as something that has come about only since the end of the Cold War.

Jackson and Sørensen present a simple overview of the dominant IR theories, each of which is addressed in this chapter (see Table 8.1).

Table 8.1 International Relations values and theories

Focus	Theories
● Security Power politics, conflict and war	● Realism
● Freedom Cooperation, peace, and progress	● Liberalism
● Order and justice Shared interests, rules, and institutions	● International society
● Welfare Wealth, poverty, equality	● IPE theories

Source: box 1.2 (p. 6) from *Introduction to International Relations: Theories and Approaches* 2E (2003) by Jackson, R. & Sørenson, G. Reprinted by permission of Oxford University Press.

Realism and neo-realism

Realism assumes the primacy of the state in the conduct of international affairs (Weber, 2001:14). Realism is based on a traditional Westphalian concept of sovereignty that recognises no higher authority. For realists, and their successors, international relations are essentially a Hobbesian power struggle between independent states. States work towards maximising their power, mainly through military means.

Realist theories of IR owe much to Carl von Clausewitz, a Prussian officer who founded the modern theory of war, described in his treatise *On War*, published in 1832. Gray reports that in many European states governments did not have a monopoly of force until after the First World War, but nevertheless von Clausewitz was right 'to see the future of war in terms of conflicts between states' (Gray, 2003:73). Realist theory is associated with Morgantheau (1960). Classical realism was adapted by Waltz, the founder of neo-realism, in his seminal work *Man, the State and War* (1959). Realism holds that states are in permanent competition with one another. The role of government is first and foremost to ensure the survival of the state, hence government is obliged to prioritise military power, because without it a state is vulnerable to attack, and its very survival may be threatened. Furthermore, realism has a negative view of human nature. It holds that people are inherently disposed towards competitiveness and conflict.

Weber (2001) identifies the three core 'myths' that realist and neo-realists agree on. Weber uses the term 'myth' to describe a belief, based on observation or experience, that may or may not be true but is widely held to be true. The three myths that both positions agree on are:

> First, that the world is composed of sovereign nation-states; second, that there is no world government which means there is no international orderer; and third, that the absence of world government or an international orderer by definition means that international politics is anarchical (Weber, 2001:15).

These three conditions mean that states will behave conflictively. Both realists and neo-realists believe that there is no possible hope that states will give up

Table 8.2 Realism v. neo-realism

	Realism	Neo-realism
Interests of states	Survival	Survival
How to achieve survival	Increase power because world government is unachievable	Increase power because world government is unachievable
Human nature	Man is flawed and therefore prone to conflict. This explains why cooperation is never guaranteed and world government is unachievable	Man may or may not be flawed. Human nature is not essential consideration in explaining conflict
Anarchy	The environment in which sovereign states act	Describes the social relations among sovereign nation-states that causally explain why wars occur

Source: Weber, 2001:16.

power to international society or to international governance. It is in man's nature (and Weber highlight's Morgentheau's gender-exclusive use of the term 'man') to be conflictive, fundamentally flawed, 'tainted by original sin' (Weber, ibid.).

Neo-realism, as the name implies, advances the basic tenets of realism. Waltz claims that the absence of an 'orderer' means that the world is anarchic. He describes **anarchy** as 'the permissive cause of war'. In other words, wars happen because there is anarchy in relationships between states. However, a further difference between the neo-realist position and classical realism is that Waltz holds that conflict occurs not merely as a result of humans' innate disposition towards violence, nor even as a result of the defective nature of the state system, but as a consequence of social pressures, wealth inequalities and restricted access to scarce resources. In addition, the neo-realist position accepts that there may be a role for some kind of institutional arrangements between states that limits the risk of conflict. Thus the neo-realist position does not rule out the usefulness of international institutions, but retains the view that states participate in them purely out of self-interest, rather than on account of some lofty idealism or belief in an 'international society'.

Taking an overall view of the realist/neo-realist positions, one might view the concentration on military power to achieve political objectives with alarm, as 'the international system thus bred competition and insecurity' (Peterson, 1996:24). In response to this, and perhaps especially in the context of the acute dangers of armed conflict between the superpowers during the 1950s and 1960s (see Discussion 8.1), **détente** emerged as a preferred policy option in the 1970s. (See Table 8.2.)

After Richard Nixon became President in 1969 a new mood prevailed. He and the Soviet Premier Leonid Brezhnev opted for co-existence supported by treaty agreements to limit nuclear arsenals. They also established regular communication between Washington and the Kremlin. Détente indicated a form of institutionalised co-existence and by the mid-1970s appeared to make classical realism obsolete.

Discussion 8.1

Cold War 1950–69 – stability, or a close-run survival?

The following is a brief chronology of tensions and proxy conflicts between the USSR and the USA superpowers prior to the onset of détente between Presidents Nixon and Brezhnev in 1970.

1950–53 Korean War – conflict ends with partition of the country into two, the communist north and the capitalist south – an Asian echo of the German experience a few years previously. The war led to the US deploying troops in Europe on a permanent basis.

1953 Soviet troops suppress an uprising in the German Democratic Republic.

1956 Suez Conflict – Britain and France, backed by Israel, attempt to take back the Suez Canal from Egypt after President Abdul Nasser had nationalised it. The Soviets backed Egypt while the US looked on in alarm and eventually condemned its European allies for their dangerous adventurism.

1956 Soviet troops crush a popular rising in Budapest, Hungary.

1961 In order to stem the tide of East Germans fleeing to the West, Soviet and East German troops construct the Berlin Wall on the night of 12 August 1961.

1962 Cuban Missile Crisis – the USSR installs nuclear missiles in Cuba. Washington demands their immedi-ate removal. The ensuing stand-off is the most dangerous episode of the entire Cold War. Eventually the Soviets back down, but only after the US dismantles its own nuclear warheads in Turkey, aimed at the Warsaw Pact.

1965–74 Vietnam War – US troops relieve failing French forces in Indochina and the Vietnam War begins, ending in a catastrophic and costly defeat for the US.

1967 The Six Day War – the third Arab–Israeli conflict, in which the USSR and the US take different sides. Israel occupies the West Bank and Gaza, a situation still holding today.

1968 Prague Spring – the Warsaw Pact invasion of Czechoslovakia in summer 1968 puts paid to the uprising under the revisionist leadership of Alexander Dubček. Moscow applies the so-called Brezhnev Doctrine permitting Soviet intervention in allied states threatened by insurgency – an echo of the 1947 Truman Doctrine.

Given this litany of scary episodes, all under the shadow of a potential nuclear holocaust, it is remarkable that a form of nostalgia has emerged in some quarters for the 'security' of the Cold War. Clearly, some people have short memories, or else they choose to disregard history.

However, it is not uncommon to find the Cold War division between the two superpowers described as an explanation for the pre-eminent position of realism in IR theory. 'The East-West rivalry lent itself easily to a realist interpretation of the world' (Jackson & Sørensen, 2003:48), but a more nuanced perspective of the Cold War invites the view that détente undermined the traditional realist interpretation. McCauley (1998) describes four distinct phases of the Cold War – see Discussion 8.2.

If détente of the mid-1970s appeared to make classical realism obsolete, it was revived again in 1979 following the Soviet deployment of troops in Afghanistan, invited in by the crumbling pro-Soviet government. Cold War tensions increased under the newly elected US president Ronald Reagan, who took office early in 1981. Reagan demonstrated a greater readiness to confront the enemy than his predecessor, Jimmy Carter. He later characterised the Soviets as 'the evil empire' and sharply increased military spending. During his first term, arms

---

Discussion 8.2

Four periods of the Cold War

1945–53   **Stalin** – conservative and averse to taking risks.

1954–69   **Khrushchev** – more confident of growing Soviet power and not afraid to assert Soviet demands in bilateral relations with the US. The Cuban Missile Crisis in 1962 was the high watermark of danger in this period.

1970–79   **Brezhnev** and **Nixon** establish détente, involving arms agreements and improved East–West communication.

1980–85   Détente ends after the Soviet invasion of Afghanistan and the election of the more assertive US President, Ronald **Reagan**, in 1980. This period was again one of high risk, until Mikhail **Gorbachev** became Soviet leader in 1985 and initiated arms reduction talks. (Based on McCauley, 1998.)

---

spending rose by 40 per cent and from 5.2 to 7.0 per cent of GDP (Weinberger, 1984:279–80). Reagan began the Strategic Defence Initiative, dubbed 'Star Wars'. This, according to Walker (1994:274), alarmed the Europeans who feared an anti-continental ballistic missile system might lead to a cooling in the US commitment to Europe's defence. Europe might have become the sole target of the Soviet nuclear arsenal. European fears were increased by reports from the Pentagon that the Americans and the Soviets might countenance a limited nuclear exchange using short-range missiles in Europe (Walker, 1994:267). Given the tension in superpower relations in the early 1980s – communication between them virtually ceased – one can in retrospect identify this period as one of the most dangerous in the entire Cold War. Many European governments distributed leaflets advising citizens of what to do in the event of a nuclear attack.

> In Britain in 1982, the government issued less than reassuring pamphlets on how to build emergency bomb shelters, which included ludicrous drawings on how to take cover by lying in ditches with a coat wrapped around the head (Walker, 1994:268).

If war results not from single incidents, as one might be tempted to believe on the basis of the 'common knowledge' that the First World War was sparked off by the shooting of Archduke Ferdinand by a Serbian nationalist on a Sarajevo bridge, but from the confluence of several events and circumstances, the early 1980s was a spectacularly dangerous period. As well as Afghanistan and the arms spending spree that followed, several other episodes contributed to a pressure cooker atmosphere by late 1983. In Poland in December 1981 a military coup cracked down on the *Solidarność* Workers' Movement and installed martial law; Soviet air defences shot down the Korean airliner KAL-007 that had strayed into Russian airspace over Sakhalin on 1 September 1983; a month later the US invaded the former British colony and Commonwealth member, the Caribbean island of Grenada, to remove a pro-communist government. Walker (1994:276) reports the Soviet foreign minister Gromyko saying 'The world situation is now slipping towards a very dangerous precipice' on 8 September, while the Soviet

President, Andropov, in hospital on a dialysis machine, was filled with dread, suspecting that an imminent NATO exercise, Able Archer 83, could be the occasion of a full-scale strike against the USSR. This huge exercise, extending the length of the Iron Curtain, involved NATO shifting through various levels from conventional to full nuclear alert. Only at the last moment was it decided not to move President Reagan and Vice President Bush to take part in this test of US and NATO readiness for nuclear war. As the Soviets themselves were on heightened alert too, the period 2–11 November was arguably the most danger-ous point in the Cold War since the Cuban Missile Crisis in 1962. There was a real danger of a Soviet pre-emptive strike. With détente dead, the early 1980s demonstrated a renewed unilateralism on the part of the US, and a narrow realist interpretation of US interests. The Soviets, meanwhile, according to Walker, were perilously close to believing their own propaganda about Western intentions.

McCauley (1998:5–6) describes the period 1979–85 as a return to Cold War after a decade of détente. He cites the Soviet invasion of Afghanistan as 'arguably the most disastrous mistake Moscow made in foreign policy during the whole Soviet era'. The acute tension was eased only after the election of Gorbachev to the presidency of the USSR. Gaddis (1992:149) claims that Soviet policy changes after 1985 demonstrate the weakness of the fundamental tenet of realism that states will always seek more power. When Gorbachev became President he promptly revised the earlier Soviet commitment to ever increased military ex-penditure. However, Gaddis may be overstating his case, given that neo-realists accept the 'fungible' nature of power – weakness in one area may be compen-sated in other areas (Peterson, 1996:25) – and that in fact by permitting a weak-ening of military power relative to the United States, the Soviet Union was merely hoping to enhance its economic power. In this, of course, Gorbachev was far from successful. He set out to reform a system that could not be reformed. He was swept away by the momentous changes that engulfed the Soviet Union and its allies at the end of the decade. Fundamental to the collapse of the Soviet system was a deep social and economic malaise. Even in East Germany, consid-ered the strongest of the Soviet satellite economies, the strength of manufac-turing was overestimated, not only by the DDR itself for political reasons, but also by the Federal Republic of Germany both before and at the time of German reunification (Marsh, 1995:11).

Meanwhile, in Western Europe, both Moravcsik (1999) and Milward (2000) describe the European integration process as marked by national governments' choices to pool their efforts in order to achieve common benefits unavailable through separate and independent action. This perspective is consistent with a neo-realist interpretation of integration that participation in common structures may occur where such participation is of benefit to the state.

| **Review** | *What are the basic tenets of realism and neo-realism?* |
| | *Why does the ending of détente in 1979 appear to indicate a return to more a realist conception of international affairs?* |

● ● ● ● Liberalism and institutional liberalism

This section considers classical liberalism, and institutional liberalism, while leaving neo-liberalism to the later section on International Political Economy (IPE).

Classical **liberalism** offers an essentially positive view of human nature, unlike realism which sees human relations as competitive and conflictive. Liberalism promises to return 'the greatest happiness to the greatest number'. Liberalism argues that a commitment to free trade brings tangible benefits for all. The laws of supply and demand will ensure fair profits for all participants in a 'positive-sum game' with benefits all round.

Furthermore, liberals argue that protectionism in trading relationships is counter-productive (Peterson, 1996:30). Indeed the economic collapse of 1929 leading to the Depression of the 1930s is usually blamed on the 'beggar thy neighbour' **unilateralism** of the inter-war period. There were no significant multinational institutions in the field of economics, and the League of Nations proved ineffective. This situation contrasted sharply with the post-Second World War environment, when major institutions tasked with managing the world economic system based on partnerships became the hallmark of institutional liberalism. Hence the Bretton Woods Accords, the IMF, the IBRD (World Bank) and the General Agreement on Tariffs and Trade (GATT) established a framework for a form of controlled capitalism and a commitment to **free trade**. A significant dimension to the liberal economic regime post-Second World War was the fixed exchange rate system established in the Bretton Woods agreement.

Liberalism also carries with it the view that a liberal economic environment will sustain liberal democratic values, a factor which was especially attractive during the Cold War when the US was anxious to see the West European states built on such values in contrast to the communist bloc in the East. Thus liberalism is associated not only with **free market capitalism** but also with liberal democratic political systems, respect for human rights, a free press, independence of the judiciary and the rule of law. One might, however, object that this demonstrates complacency, as few states can truly claim to score consistently well in all these respects. Nevertheless, in general terms liberalism in trade is frequently linked to liberalism in other areas too, most obviously in liberal democratic political traditions. One might criticise these assumptions as self-serving cant. Gray points out that

> liberal regimes showed themselves to be fully as ruthless as totalitarian states. In order to defend democracy against dictatorship in the Second World War, the civilian populations of Dresden and Hamburg, Hiroshima, Nagasaki and Tokyo were incinerated (Gray, 2003:84).

Nevertheless, against the totalitarian dictatorships of Nazi Germany or Stalin's Russia, the liberal democratic model presents an attractive alternative, and one that has had considerable force in nourishing the process of European integration. The attraction of liberal democratic government has been especially apparent in enlargements involving states which endured long years of dictatorship,

© Bettmann/Corbis

Photograph 8.1 Hiroshima after the atom bomb, 6 August 1945. Liberal democracies have been prepared to target civilians in the fight for liberty. Radiators from buildings that disappeared from the face of the Earth after the blast litter the foreground of the picture.

namely Greece – which joined the EU in 1981, Portugal and Spain joining in 1986, and eight former communist CEECs joining in 2004. In all these cases, a significant motivation for accession was the belief that joining the EU would consolidate liberal democratic values, political stability and national security.

Liberalism continues to profoundly affect bilateral relationships between the US and the EU. Where trade disputes have arisen between the US and the Europeans these have usually been the result of some form of economic **protectionism**, especially in the case of agriculture. The EU has, for example, argued for the right to resist imports of US products that are genetically modified, arguing that European consumers do not want them. Similarly, US beef products are rejected by the EU on the grounds that the US tolerates the use of growth promoting hormones in cattle feed. There is, however, suspicion that some European beef production involves illegal use of these products. Both the US and the EU use hefty subsidies for agricultural production, and surplus production is routinely dumped on world markets with disastrous consequences for developing countries' agriculture. Subsidies distort world trade and adversely affect less developed countries who find that their prices are forced lower by cheap sub-sidised competitor products from intensively farmed produce in the US or in Europe.

Trade disputes have also afflicted other areas, most recently steel. The US slapped import restrictions on steel from developing countries, leading to fears that this would lead to a flood of cheap steel in the EU. The European Commission retaliated by placing import restrictions on US products. The case was investigated by the WTO, which ruled against the US. Washington then backed down and did not impose the threatened tariffs.

> The root cause of most bilateral conflicts has been deviation from the liberal prescrip-tion that each side eliminate barriers to economic exchange with the other (Peterson, 1996:31).

A central tenet of liberalism is that it brings benefits to all participants in the exchange process. Objections about increasing inequality because wealth is unevenly spread are traditionally met with the retort that everyone benefits. As the rich get richer there will be corresponding benefits to others lower down the hierarchy, a phenomenon that used to be described as 'trickle down theory'. Marxists and neo-Marxists traditionally debunk this and point to ample evidence of how liberalism merely accentuates divisions between rich and poor, north and south. This wealth divide has been accentuated by the modern variant on liberalism, neo-liberalism, which is examined below in the section on Inter-national Political Economy (IPE).

Core tenets of liberalism are summarised in Discussion 8.3.

Institutional liberalism, as the label suggests, is a branch of liberalism which emphasises the important function of international institutions in providing a rule-based system, thus a counter to the anarchic tendencies associated with realism. Institutional liberalism is strongly associated with the work of Robert Keohane (Keohane, 1989, 2002). Institutionalists highlight the increased role of international institutions in the conduct of international affairs (Peterson, 1996:27). The inter-war period that witnessed the calamitous slide towards fascism and war was marked by the relative paucity of international institutions,

---

Discussion 8.3

Core tenets of liberalism

Liberalism implies the following:

- A positive view of human nature
- Society is managed in order to return 'the greatest happiness to the greatest number'
- Fundamentals of economic liberalism privilege the benefits of a free trade environment; laws of supply and demand (Smith); laws of comparative advantage (Ricardo)
- A liberal economic environment sustains political liberties and liberal democratic values, comprising the rights and responsibilities of individuals, the right to private ownership of capital, and a pluralist political system.

the League of Nations being the one major exception and it ended in abject failure. Instead, in the ten years following the Second World War there was a proliferation of such bodies, including the UN, GATT, the International Bank for Reconstruction and Development (the World Bank), the IMF, the OEEC (which later became the OECD and included Canada and the USA, and later still Japan), NATO, the Council of Europe, the ECSC, the Commonwealth, and the Warsaw Pact (COMECON). The appetite for such bodies has not abated since. Apart from the transition of the ECSC to the EEC and eventually the EU, other prominent bodies include G-7, G-8, OPEC, ASEAN, the OAU, Asia Pacific Forum, the Arab League, APEC, Mercosur and countless others. An international environment characterised by the existence of so many international institutions naturally attracts the interest of IR theory.

However, the emergence of a significant role for international institutions does not signal the demise of more established positions in IR theory, such as realism. Neo-realism certainly accepts that states can apply self-interest and operate together, even allowing some sacrifice of their ability to act unilaterally (Peterson, 1996:27). Thus, international relationships are increasingly built on states cooperating and being interdependent.

Institutionalists also point to the increasing role of **multinational corporations** (MNCs). According to Peterson MNCs develop their own resources and agendas, and do so independently of states. Institutionalists reject the realist assumption that military-strategic policy is dominant, claiming that economic or trade issues can be just as important if not more so. Environmental considerations have also emerged as factors in international relations, often on account of the growing role of international **non-governmental organisations** (NGOs), such as Greenpeace, Friends of the Earth, and the Worldwide Fund for Nature. Furthermore there are human rights groups, such as Amnesty International, Médecins sans Frontières and Human Rights Watch, all of which impact upon international relations.

Peterson indicates that the philosophical foundation of institutional theory is more grounded in Locke than in Hobbes (Peterson, 1996:28). However, a weakening in institutional consensus emerged in the so-called 'regime theorists' who pointed to the strength of institutions like NATO, Bretton Woods and GATT as being founded on the hegemonic control of the US (see hegemonic stability theory below).

A further variation is represented by the term functional institutionalism. This highlights states' readiness to participate in international institutions because they recognise that their interests are best served through enhanced cooperation with other states. It may be, for example, possible to achieve economies of scale in the economic sphere – as in cross-border cooperation in high technology sectors, such as aerospace. This occurred in Europe with the advent of the Single European Market. In defence and security, partnership in NATO provides more effective security guarantees than would traditional realist isolationism. Institutions therefore enable states to more effectively secure their self-interests, especially when these self-interests are shared with other states. In a variation on this view, federalists hold that this is not a matter of choice, but of necessity.

The federalist approach recommends the creation of international institutions as the only way for states to achieve common objectives in the face of external developments, especially those related to globalisation (Pinder, 2001:6).

There is considerable debate about the role of institutions in the world economy. Institutionalists claim that the world is an arena of 'interstate cooperation' where the core actors are 'governments and the institutions to whom they delegate power' (Woods, 2001:289). States seek to defend and expand their own interests but see cooperation as the means to achieve this.

> The key condition for order is the existence of international institutions which permit cooperation to continue (Woods, ibid.).

Institutional theory is a branch of the liberal model of globalisation. Modern international institutions comprise delegated power from their participating states. The role of the institutions is to manage the contemporary environment – for which we might substitute the word globalisation – through compliance and regulation. Members establish rules and standards through negotiation, and markets are regulated by institutions (Woods, 2001:294).

It is claimed by enthusiasts for greater European integration, whether coming from a federalist or neo-functionalist perspective, with a history like the one that Europe has, and with historical tensions still able to precipitate horrors like wars in the former Yugoslavia in the 1990s, that whatever the future holds for Europe a return to greater reliance on separate states would be dangerous and potentially catastrophic. Thus institutional engagement holds clear attraction. Furthermore, it is clear from the list of significant institutions in Figure 8.1 that institutionalism is very much part of the contemporary order. The picture is not intended to be exhaustive: it includes a variety of organisations, some much more prominent than others. The figure is presented, however, in order to illustrate the different types and varying scope of international organisations in a simple framework.

It is important to recognise that international institutions come in various guises, perhaps with specific regional aims, and an intergovernmental character, such as NAFTA or ASEAN; a regional and at least partly supranational character, such as the European Union; or transnational and universal, such as Amnesty International (Jackson & Sørensen, 2003:118). Jackson and Sørensen also point out that international institutions may be created as a result of rule-based 'regimes' which govern state action in limited areas, such as shipping or aviation, or a combination of an institution and a rule-based regime, such as the WTO. Liberal institutionalists advance the view that institutions have advanced international cooperation. A clear example is the European Union, where

> 'EU countries cooperate so intensively that they share some functions of government, for example in agricultural and industrial policies; they have established the regulatory framework for a single market in the economic sector, and they are in the process of intensifying their cooperation in other areas. EU Europe, in other words, is a good test case for examining the importance of institutions. Institutional liberals do claim that institutions have made a significant difference in Western Europe after the end of the

		GOAL OF ORGANISATION	
		Specific	General
R E G I O N A L	Intergovernmental	NATO NAFTA APEC	OAU (Organisation of African Unity)
	Supranational	ECSC (European Coal and Steel Community)	(Parts of) EU (European Union)
	Transnational	Eurofer (European Confederation of Iron and Steel Industry)	European Movement
U N I V E R S A L	Intergovernmental	WHO (World Health Organisation) UNESCO (United Nations Educational, Scientific and Cultural Organisation) IAEA (International Atomic Energy Agency) WTO (World Trade Organisation)	UN (United Nations)
	Supranational	—	—
	Transnational	Greenpeace Amnesty International	WSF (World Social Forum) WFA (World Federalist Association)

Figure 8.1 A typology of international and transnational organisations

Source: box 4.8 (p. 118) from *Introduction to International Relations: Theories and Approaches* 2E (2003) by Jackson, R. & Sørenson, G. Reprinted by permission of Oxford University Press. Source material © Gyldendalske Boghandel, Nordisk forlag AlS, Copenhagen.

Cold War' (Keohane et al., 1993). Institutions acted as 'buffers' which helped absorb the 'shocks' sent through Western Europe by the end of the Cold War and the reunification of Germany (Jackson & Sørensen, 2003:119).

This positive assessment of the value of international institutions contrasts with the neo-realist perspective, which would assume that the ending of the Cold War would precipitate disorder and insecurity, and probably lead to war. Neo-realism highlights the relative security created by the Cold War balance of power. Without this, and the threat of nuclear annihilation, multipolarity emerges and its attendant instability and risk. The neo-realist Mearsheimer, who in 1990 predicted sharply increased instability in Europe with the ending of the Cold War, comments:

> Anarchy has two principal consequences. First, there is little room for trust among states [...] Second, each state must guarantee its own survival since no other actor will provide its security (Mearsheimer, 1990:12).

Mearsheimer's views appeared depressingly prescient as conflict occurred in the Baltic states during their secession from the USSR, and in the Caucasus, notably in Chechnya, and even more so in the disintegration of Yugoslavia, and in the Gulf War of 1991. However, while Mearsheimer and others predicted a multipolar world after the demise of the Soviet Union, what has actually emerged is nearer to a unipolar world (see Chapter 9). Certainly the end of the Cold War was followed by instability and significant wars. That these conflicts did not spread further may well be a result of the stabilising influence of international institutions. Indeed, while the European Union was criticised for its ineffectiveness in the former Yugoslavia, one might speculate on the consequences of such a war had the European Union simply not existed. Europe prior to 1914 may offer some guidance in such *'What if'* reflections on history.

Review *What are the basic tenets of liberalism in IR theory?*
What are the main characteristics of liberal institutionalism?

International society

The international society tradition is a midway position between the classical traditions of realism and liberalism in IR scholarship. It rejects any notion of agency on the part of states or governments and focuses on the foreign policy decisions of individual actors in government.

> It seeks to avoid the stark choice between (1) state egotism and conflict and (2) human goodwill and cooperation presented by the debate between realism and liberalism. On the one hand International Society scholars reject classical realists' singularly pessimistic view of states as self-sufficient and self-regarding political organizations which relate to each other and deal with each other only on an instrumental basis of narrow self-interest: international relations conceived as a state 'system' that is prone to recurrent discord, conflict, and – sooner or later – war. On the other hand, they reject liberalism's singularly optimistic view of international relations as a developing world community that is conducive to unlimited human progress and perpetual peace (Jackson & Sørensen, 2003:141).

International Society scholars examine the work of statespeople who are experts in statecraft. Statecraft encompasses foreign, military and trade policy, diplomacy, intelligence, spying, forming military alliances, the threat and use of armed force, negotiating and signing peace treaties and a great variety of international agreements and transactions. The International Society tradition accepts the realist contention of the pre-eminent role of sovereign states and the centrality of the concept of sovereignty. It also accepts the anarchic character of international relations but stresses how actors involved in foreign policy relations can cooperate to assuage the dangers inherent in this anarchy. The core contention of International Society (IS) is summed up in the following quotation, cited in Jackson and Sørensen (2003:1430), which emphasises the distinction between a 'system of states' (a realist concept) and a 'society of states' (a liberal concept):

> A system of states (or international system) is formed when two or more states have sufficient contact between them, and have sufficient impact on one-another's decisions . . . to make the behaviour of each a necessary element in the calculations of the other.

> A society of states (or international society) exists when a group of states, conscious of certain common interests and common values, form a society in the sense that they conceive themselves to be bound by a common set of rules in their relations with one another and share in the working of common institutions (Bull, 1995:9–13).

Jackson and Sørensen point out that after the demise of the USSR, in the new post-Cold War context, Russia moved towards participating in the Western-centred world of international organisations such as the G-8, OECD, IMF, EBRD and NATO. In so doing, Russia had to 'become a reliable partner in the Western-centred international society' (Jackson & Sørensen, 2003:143). Change in the international environment has nourished the development of the International Society perspective in other ways. The UN Charter Article 2 stresses the basis of international law as the sovereign equality of all members, and states that

> Members shall refrain in their international relations from the threat or use of force against the territorial integrity or political independence of any state [. . .] nothing [. . .] shall authorise the United Nations to intervene in matters which are essentially within the domestic jurisdiction of any state (United Nations Charter, quoted in Jackson & Sørensen, 2003:145).

However, this position – which matches a realist assessment of the integrity of the state – appears to have altered decisively in recent years. Jackson and Sørensen illustrate the point by citing the UN Secretary General Javier Perez de Cuellar speaking about human rights in 1991:

> It is now increasingly felt that the principle of non-interference with the essential domestic jurisdiction of states cannot be regarded as a protective barrier behind which human rights can be massively violated with impunity (UN Press Release SG/SM/4560, 24 April 1991).

This evolution in the UN perspective echoes an International Society view of politics as a human-centred activity, as opposed to state-centred. At the same time, International Society approaches IR from a historical and situational perspective, and stresses the normative nature of international relations and policy making. In refusing to make a choice between the optimism of liberals and the pessimism of realists, the IS approach demonstrates what may, according to Jackson and Sørensen, be its main strength.

A leading IS scholar, Martin Wight (1991) defines three International Relations traditions, realist, rationalist and revolutionist (see Figure 8.2). Wight stresses that the three traditions are not isolated from each other but are in a constant dialogue and each must be understood in the context of the others. IS theorists tend to have the most affinity for the rationalist position. Jackson and Sørensen point out that while history is important to IS theory, it is the history of ideas which matters most.

Wight points out that realism deals with how the world is, not how it ought to be. Realists have a pessimistic view of human nature, a Hobbesian 'state of nature' view of humankind. Extreme realism denies that International Society exists and denies the existence of international obligations beyond the state.

Realism	Rationalism	Revolutionism
• Anarchy	• Society	• Humanity
• Power politics	• Evolutionary change	• Revolutionary change
• Conflict and warfare	• Peaceful coexistence	• Anti-state utopianism
• Pessimism	• Hope without illusions	

Figure 8.2 Wight's three IR traditions

Source: box 5.6 (p. 146) from *Introduction to International Relations: Theories and Approaches* 2E (2003) by Jackson, R. & Sørenson, G. Reprinted by permission of Oxford University Press.

Rationalists on the other hand believe that human beings are reasonable and will enter into agreements and contracts for the common good, and can resolve the problem of anarchy by creating and abiding by international law. Rationalism is a middle ground between realist pessimism and the Utopianism of the revolutionists.

Revolutionists identify with the common good of all humanity, beyond the state. They are

> cosmopolitan rather than state-centric thinkers, solidarists rather than pluralists, and their international theory has a progressive and even a missionary character in that it aims at changing the world for the better (Jackson & Sørensen, 2003:147).

The revolutionist perspective believes in human perfectibility, and aims to create a world society consisting of every human being. Wight recognises that there are mid-positions between these three perspectives and gives the example of George Kennan, an influential commentator on US foreign policy during the Cold War. Kennan wrote

> I do not wish ever to see the conduct of this nation in [. . .] [i]ts foreign relations animated by anything else than decency, generosity, moderation and consideration for others (cited in Wight, 1991:120–21).

As Jackson and Sørensen point out (2003:149), Kennan recognised the importance of national interest in foreign policy, but he also stressed the legitimacy of other states' interests, even including rivals and enemies. Kennan is usually considered a moderate realist but such views are close to a rationalist perspective. Thus the rationalist position is associated with the mutual interests of order and justice.

International Society scholars are concerned with four dimensions. These are, first, ideas and how they shape human activity. Second, the dialogue between the different realist, rationalist and revolutionist perspectives, in which all three are considered and the relationships between them understood. The third dimension is history because only an understanding of history can assist us in seeing how events and ideas combine to shape the fourth dimension, which is the normative character of international relations. In other words, policy is shaped by human activity and this will tend towards conformity to established mores and patterns. We encountered similar normative pressures in looking at the role of institutions in the European Union in previous chapters.

The Cold War produced international order but, as we have already seen in the discussion of realism earlier in this chapter, at times during the Cold War the dominant superpowers behaved with cavalier irresponsibility (Bull, 1984:437). Bull describes war as an 'institution' and reports how war can in fact be stabilising. The nature of war, and its evolution as a rule-governed inter-state activity, may in fact reduce the likelihood of 'ubiquitous violence' (Bull, 1995:179). Jackson and Sørensen write that since 1945 wars between the Great Powers have been virtually non-existent. Instead, civil wars, secessionist wars, revolutionary wars and even wars against 'international terrorism' have been more common. Bull attributes this decline in the 'traditional war' to the norms of the UN Charter, which outlaws aggressive war, and to international public opinion which stands behind them (Jackson & Sørensen, 2003:156).

International Society, as has been stated, is concerned with both order and justice. Bull describes two forms of justice: commutative justice, which is about rules and reciprocity, and the equal treatment of all; and distributive justice, which is about ensuring that everyone has access to the benefits available from International Society. Distributive justice is about goods, and supports the notion that the poor deserve special treatment, perhaps through concessions and development aid. The Movement for Global Justice, the Fair Trade Movement and World Civic Forum are all NGOs which subscribe to the notion of distributive justice. Bull's main point

> is that world politics involves questions of both order and justice, and that world politics cannot be properly understood by focusing on either value to the exclusion of the other (Jackson & Sørensen, 2003:157).

A further aspect of the International Society approach to IR is the importance attached to examining statecraft and responsibility. As Wight's three traditions highlight realism, rationalism and revolutionism, there is an echo of this in three levels of responsibility that are central to statecraft:

> 1. devotion to one's own nation and the well-being of its citizens. 2. respect for the legitimate interests and rights of other states and for international law; and 3. respect for human rights (Jackson & Sørensen, 2003:158).

Jackson and Sørensen cite the Gulf War in 1991 as an example of statespeople exercising all three of these responsibilities by arguing that Saddam Hussein's invasion of Kuwait in August 1990 threatened other states' access to oil supplies from the Gulf Region and also the overall stability of various states in the region, including Saudi Arabia which joined the coalition to oust Saddam from Kuwait. In the second place, members of that coalition acted with the support of UN Resolutions which declared the occupation of Kuwait to be contrary to international law. Finally, the liberation of Kuwait would end the tyrannical oppression of Kuwaitis by the Saddam regime and the terms of settlement of the conflict would also protect the interests of persecuted minorities, notably the Kurds, living in northern Iraq.

The war in Bosnia-Herzegovina shortly afterwards, 1991–95, was more complicated in that the powers that eventually intervened had previously vacillated and applied different criteria at different stages. The EU was divided in its response to the unfolding crisis in the former Yugoslavia, while the UN attempted to steer a middle ground between non-intervention in what was arguably a civil war, and full military intervention. The UN attempted to provide safe havens for non-combatants, but this position proved untenable and gave way to a NATO intervention in 1995 with UN peace enforcement operations. The realist preference for non-intervention was undermined by the fact that Bosnia-Herzegovina became a sovereign state in 1992 and the conflict involved foreign intervention from Croatia and Serbia (Yugoslavia). Realists also argued that the war did not directly affect the interests of other states. However, the humanitarian case for intervention eventually became unanswerable, especially once the UN 'safe havens' had proved so disastrously unsafe. At Srebrenica, just 370 Dutch UN peacekeepers (the term is cruelly ironic as there was no peace to keep, Srebrenica was the heart of a war zone in Eastern Bosnia), woefully underequipped and exposed, were helpless as Bosnian Serb militias massacred 7,000 men and boys, many attempting to escape through the forests towards Tuzla.

> The Serb triumph over Srebrenica was the ultimate in international humiliation [. . .] the world had stood by and watched the biggest single mass murder in Europe since the Second World War (Silber & Little, 1996:350).

With the developing failure of the UN middle path, NATO began a partial engagement in 1994, finally threatening a full-scale intervention. This brought the warring parties to the negotiating table and resulted in the signing of the Dayton Agreement in late 1995. Silber and Little's brilliant and harrowing account, *The Death of Yugoslavia*, is a withering indictment of the failure of Western policy in the former Yugoslavia. They bitterly report that the abandonment of Srebrenica actually made the difficult task of drawing the maps at Dayton easier. But Jackson and Sørensen point out that the Bosnian War shows the complexity of modern statecraft:

> The Bosnia-Herzegovina case illustrates the deeply troubling moral choices that sometimes confront statespeople in a pluralist world in which they have a responsibility to safeguard their own country and its citizens but also a responsibility to defend international law and protect human rights around the world (Jackson & Sørensen, 2003:165).

International relations are both normative and ambiguous, and IR scholarship has to take account of international responsibility (rationalism) and humanitarian responsibility (revolutionism) as well as responsibility to one's own state and its citizens (realism).

Marxist critics of International Society point out that it virtually ignores economics and that it remains overwhelmingly state-centric. It should, they claim, prioritise human needs at the level of global society. Instead, International Society remains wedded to the 'ideology of the state'. Jackson and Sørensen report that Bull (1995:254–66) has suggested that the classical notion of the society of states may in fact be giving way to a more overlapping and complex network of different authorities and suggests five features of contemporary politics:

1. regional integration – the EU is the foremost example;
2. the disintegration of states, such as the former USSR and Yugoslavia;
3. the expansion of private international violence, in the form of international terrorism;
4. the growth of transnational organisations, including MNCs;
5. the increasing unification of the world through technological innovation and access to ICT.

Falk supports this assessment, claiming that:

> The reorganisation of international life has two principal features – increased central guidance and increased roles for non-territorial actors (Falk, 1985:651, quoted in Jackson & Sørensen, 2003:172).

In the remainder of this book, the contention that the state system is only a part of a wider world system with overlapping and related authorities, both above and below the state, is further established.

Review   *How does the International Society tradition in IR theory extend the basic tenets of the realist perspective?*

● ● ● ● International Political Economy (IPE)

Jackson and Sørensen refer to **International Political Economy** (IPE) as being centrally concerned with wealth and poverty and 'who gets what in the international economic and political system' (Jackson & Sørensen, 2003:57). IPE consists of three main contrasting approaches to International Relations. These are represented in Table 8.3.

Mercantilism

At the core of IPE traditions is the idea that international relations are conducted in both the economic and the political spheres and that any attempt to

Table 8.3 Three theories of IPE

	Mercantilism	*Economic liberalism*	*Marxism*
Relationship between economics and politics	Politics decisive	Economics autonomous	Economics decisive
Main actors/units of analysis	States	Individuals	Classes
The nature of economic relations	Conflictual, zero-sum game	Cooperative, positive-sum game	Conflictual
Economic goals	State power	Maximum individual well-being	Class interests

Source: box 6.11 (p. 192) from *Introduction to International Relations: Theories and Approaches* 2E (2003) by Jackson, R. & Sørenson, G. Reprinted by permission of Oxford University Press.

understand the nature of international relations has to take account of both. Classical realism focuses overwhelmingly on the politics of state security and has little to say about economics. **Mercantilism**, which is close to realism in many ways, argues that economics is important, but that it is subservient to politics. Indeed, economics serves the realisation of political objectives. The sovereign state is seen as the natural engine for economic growth and trade should – and is – conducted for the benefit of the national interest. This 'statist IPE doctrine' (Jackson & Sørensen, 2003:58) is 'often referred to as Mercantilism or economic nationalism'. Mercantilism privileges politics over economics and claims that a state may pursue its interests and build up its strength specifically through trade and prioritising wealth creation. This view diverges from classical realism, which holds that state power is built on strong military foundations.

The mercantilist view sees international relations as conflictual, and trade as a zero-sum game. Where one state benefits from trade, another loses.

Japan became a classic example of the mercantilist state, following the advent of democracy and a new constitution in 1952 by which the country recovered its sovereignty. Japan pursued a path of rapid capitalist development and built a strong manufacturing and export-oriented economy. By the 1960s and 70s Japan was running huge trade surpluses with both the US and Europe. Meanwhile, its military spending had been pegged at 1 per cent of GDP, a sum that in 1952 might not have seemed particularly great. Nevertheless the scale of economic growth in Japan enabled the country to become not only an economic power, but also a military one. Japan enjoyed the second largest national economy in the world after the US during the 1960s and 70s, and once the Single European Market emerged Japan consolidated its position as the third corner in the TRIAD of the global economy. The subsequent downturn in the Japanese economy during the 1990s, a product of the specific characteristics of Japanese capitalism and its weakness in the face of changes in global capitalism, especially banking, does not alter the fact that it was the dedicated pursuance of a statist approach that built Japan into the economic force it became for most of the latter half of the century. In summary, mercantilists support the notion of a powerful state and stress the primacy of politics over economics.

> Wealth and power are complementary, not competing goals. Economic dependence on other states should be avoided as much as possible. When economic and security interests clash, security interests have priority (Jackson & Sørensen, 2003:181).

Economic liberalism

The second IPE tradition is **economic liberalism**. This is not much different to the liberalism described earlier, stressing the mutual benefits of trade, the positive view of human nature and the intrinsic benefits of individualism in sustaining entrepreneurial activity. Liberal entrepreneurship is seen as a positive-sum game where everyone benefits, either in terms of profits or employment. Jackson and Sørensen describe both mercantilism and economic liberalism as fundamentally realist and liberal (Jackson & Sørensen, 2003:178).

The difference between classical liberalism and the economic liberalism of the past couple of decades is that the latter has been associated with the post-Cold War globalisation boom and the liberalising policy initiatives of the Reagan administration in the US and the Thatcher government in the UK in the 1980s. Both in the United States and in Britain, the liberalisation of capital markets and the subsequent freeing up of telecommunications networks to competition precipitated massive increases in capital flows and a boom in commerce that was to a large extent dependent on and intrinsically connected to the information communications technology (ICT) revolution. In this context, it is easy to see why the term neo-liberal is also used, as it implies a development from classical liberalism that takes account of changes in the political and economic environment following the end of the Cold War and the explosion in technology that came in the late 1980s and continued over the following 15 or so years.

Economic liberals argue that capitalism, and free trade in particular, offers many potential benefits to developing countries. They suggest that these benefits will accrue independently of the state as state power declines in relation to burgeoning private trade. Advanced capitalist society shows a weakening of the state position – an entirely desirable state of affairs. But in developing countries, in contrast, neo-liberalism tends to imply

> opposition to the development strategies based on import-substitution industrialization, which had dominated the period 1945 to the early 1980s. Here it is often linked to the 'Washington Consensus' (privatization and deregulation; trade and financial deregulation; shrinking the role of the state; encouraging foreign direct investment) and to the structural adjustment programmes promoted by the IMF and the World Bank (McLean & McMillan, 2003:368).

The consequences of this form of economic liberalism in developing countries appears to be the opening up of locally controlled or state-owned enterprises, and of land for primary extraction or for agriculture, to global markets and takeover by multinational corporations. Large areas of the Brazilian Amazon Basin for example are controlled by foreign multinational interests. Ellwood reports that

> In Asia, even before the crash of 1997, the region's 'economic miracle' had been built on a fast track liquidation of its natural resources. Pristine rainforests were plundered, rivers despoiled, seacoasts poisoned with pesticides and fisheries exhausted (Ellwood, 2001:94).

The industrialised societies' experience of neo-liberalism has tended to be very different (see Discussion 8.4).

Jackson and Sørensen caution against assuming that *laissez-faire* necessarily implies the absence of political regulation. It means instead that

> The state shall only set up those minimum underpinnings that are necessary for the market to function properly. This is the classical version of economic liberalism. At the present time this view is also put forward under labels such as 'conservatism' or 'neo-liberalism' (Jackson & Sørensen, 2003:185).

Discussion 8.4

Neo-liberalism in the USA and the UK: some surprising contradictions

Both Thatcher and Reagan, ideological soul-mates, pursued economic policies that owed much to the work of the economist Milton Friedman. Neo-liberal preferences promote a classical *laissez-faire* approach to running the economy, in other words the ideal of 'less government'. In a direct challenge to the **Keynesian** orthodoxy of the previous three decades, Thatcher and Reagan sought to reduce the role of the state, cut government responsibilities in fields as diverse as welfare, transportation, energy supply and economic planning. The free trade mantra would be 'leave everything to the markets', 'the markets know best' and 'you cannot buck the markets'. Thatcher, in her first term of office, reduced the power of the trades unions, which she saw as a blight on entrepreneurial activity. In her second term she began a programme of privatisation that would transform British society, transferring the major energy industries of coal, oil, gas and electricity to private ownership. In addition, other public utilities such as telecommunications and water, as well as road haulage, aviation and aeronautical engineering were privatised. The railways, widely viewed as a truly disastrous privatisation, she left to her successor, John Major. During the second Labour administration in 2003, in the midst of a crisis over rail safety and ballooning public investment in the private operators, the railways virtually returned to state control.

In the US, the Reagan administration pursued policies that would favour private corporations, reduce state control, cut red tape and maintain state involvement in education and welfare at a minimum. This agenda became known as **neo-liberalism**, but in many ways the term **neo-conservative** is perhaps more appropriate. On the positive side, under the leadership of Paul Volcker, the Federal Reserve used soaring interest rates to bring down inflation from 13.3 per cent in 1979 to 3.8 per cent three years later, after which it stayed (relatively) low. It was not lower taxes which enabled the economy to recover; it was lower inflation (Samuelson, 2004).

However, contrary to perceived wisdom, in two important respects, the neo-liberal orthodoxy of the Reagan administration did nothing to diminish the role of the state. The huge increases in military spending represented a massive investment of government money raised from taxation of private corporations and individuals. Defence spending represented a vast transfer from the public to the private, and was a massive boost to businesses like Boeing. Similarly, the huge increase in the US prison population during the past 20 years is a spectacular example of government-sponsored job creation. The US prison service employs as many people as Ford or General Motors, around half a million. For realists and conservative political theorists like Robert Nozick (1939–2002), this is consistent with the idea of the 'minimum state', as the state, for Nozick, has no business in any area of public life except in ensuring security and civil protection, and protecting private property, thus defence and criminal matters remain as core areas of government responsibility. Neo-conservatives would support such a contention, but neo-liberalism normally implies a minimum role for the state, allowing markets to function freely. This would include the assumption that taxation should be reduced and the Keynesian goal of income redistribution should be abandoned.

There are many ironies in the assumption that the US is a haven of free enterprise and minimalist government. As the example of Boeing illustrates, many large US corporations are hugely dependent on government largesse, especially in defence-related sectors. Hutton (2002) reports on the huge scale of government support for US corporations in various sectors, including automotive manufacturing, computer technology and defence. Schlosser (2001) describes how government road-building plans over 50 years, as well as low fuel prices, have coincided with the running down of state railways, benefiting not only the automobile and oil industries, but also the burgeoning fast-food industry (myriad fast-food restaurants at every highway intersection) and food processing. Hence the paradox: neo-liberalism, at least in the US, hardly represents the minimal state.

However, as Discussion 8.4 suggests, the implication of a minimal state may be at odds with reality. Perhaps what this discussion reveals is the extent of the emerging gap between neo-liberalism and the neo-conservatism of US policy, especially under George W. Bush and his mentor, Ronald Reagan.

Marxism

The third strand in IPE is **Marxism**. This is a system-changing position, as opposed to the system-maintaining stance of mercantilism and economic liberalism. Marxism is radical and reformist, offering what is essentially a critique of the capitalist world economy and of neo-liberal and neo-realist perspectives. Neo-Marxists (the term neo-Marxist is sometimes used to differentiate between classical Marxism and the specifically reformist post-Cold War position) hold that the contradictions between capital and labour described in classical Marxism are replicated in the unequal relations between rich and poor, developed and underdeveloped countries. Neo-Marxists argue that the underdevelopment of the Third World is both created and perpetuated by the industrialised rich countries. The latter sustain the global capitalist economy.

A reformist position contends that more importance should be attached to what is possible, rather than simply how things are. Reformism draws on Rousseau, author of the *Social Contract and Discourses* in 1762, in which he claims that the individual will make sacrifices for the common good. Reformism contains a mixture of idealism and holism, and seeks improvements to the actual state of affairs, highlighting environmental and ecological imperatives, inequalities between rich and poor, population pressures in LDCs. In contrast to neo-realists, reformists (and neo-Marxists) see states as part of the problem, not part of the solution. The accident at the Chernobyl nuclear plant in Ukraine in 1986, the arms industry, the 1991 Gulf War, the continuing conflict in Iraq, agricultural contamination and scares over E-coli, salmonella, BSE and its human variant Creuzfeldt-Jakob Disease (CJD), are all cited as evidence of (mainly) state-engendered crises. Reformists seek to promote international alliances along ecological or pacifist lines. The EU, according to Peterson, tends to divide reformists as to whether it is merely a tool of petty national interests or part of the solution to such difficulties. But blame for the deficiencies of international institutions should be laid firmly at the door of states:

> The major western states have resisted endowing international institutions with real substance, have refused to give real priority to means of anticipating international difficulties, still cling too much to the idea of national 'sovereignty', and above all react to crises too little, too unimaginatively, and too late (Shaw, 1994:166, cited in Peterson, 1996:33).

Various works have called for the moral content of foreign policies to supersede notions of national interest. One can cite the Brandt Commission (1983) and Galbraith (1993) as key examples. Reformism is highly eclectic, covering pacifists, ecologists, feminists, Marxists and advocates of 'critical theory'. The latter may be the most ambitious of all theories, as its ultimate aim is to transform the fundamental nature of international politics and create a world where there is not just increased cooperation between states, but the possibility of genuine peace (Mearsheimer, 1994:14, quoted in Peterson, 1996:33).

Reformists are diametrically opposed to neo-realists, and criticise the latter for failure to anticipate or even explain the end of the Cold War. Marxists, on the other hand, accept the collapse of the Soviet Union as a straightforward defeat for communism at the hands of capitalist homogenisation (Peterson, 1996:33), while holding to the view that the contradictions inherent within capitalism will eventually lead to its downfall. But perhaps the most important characteristic of the reformist perspective is that its advocates seek to reform existing institutions or create new ones. Soros (2002) has called for the creation of a new body to defend **public goods** such as environmental interests, human rights, labour rights, animal rights and social welfare. Such a body might be a form of parallel organisation to the WTO whose remit would remain the defence of private goods and free trade. If the two bodies could work together one could anticipate a more just and stable future. This discussion is developed in Chapter 12.

Hutton (2002) argues for a similarly ambitious measure of defending public goods, but says that this can and should happen through a reformed European Union and new initiatives inspired by the EU, for example in respect of financial regulation. He calls upon the EU to work towards defending and developing the regulatory powers of the UN in the field of public goods.

Marxism is sometimes criticised for its Utopian tendencies just as realism is condemned for being hopelessly defeatist. Between all these strands in IR theory, there are cross-overs and still more radical alternatives. Nozick, at least on the basis of his most famous contribution to political philosophy, *Anarchy, State and Utopia* (1975), might be seen as an extreme realist. At the opposite extreme is idealism. Idealism aspires to a form of world governance and is based on classical Utopian theory. Idealists believe that human nature is essentially good but that the existing world order has corrupted humankind's ability to shape the world in an equitable and just manner. Unlike reformism, which proposes changes to current structures, idealism starts from a perspective not dissimilar to the old joke about the American visitor to a remote village in Ireland asking for the best way to Dublin, and getting the response 'If I were going to Dublin I wouldn't want to be starting from here.'

Review   *What are the three main strands of IPE and how are they distinguished?*

● ● ● ● Hegemonic stability theory

A natural consequence of the statist approach implied in both realism and economic liberalism is the emergence of a global hegemon. A **hegemon** is 'a dominant military and economic power' (Jackson & Sørensen, 2003:196). A hegemon exercises influence beyond its state frontiers and may even assume direct political and economic control over other less powerful states. During the Cold War the balance of power between the USA and the USSR meant there were two superpowers each exercising hegemony, or political control and influence, over their quasi-empires, institutionalised by organisations such as NATO and the OECD on the one hand and the Warsaw Pact and COMECON on the other. After the end of the Cold War the US found itself as the sole surviving superpower. It seems pertinent to the discussion of IR to ask to what extent is the US really a hegemon in the current environment.

During the Cold War the US, for the most part pursuing a neo-realist line, provided a security guarantee through the nuclear deterrent and détente in Europe. Between 1947 and 1971 as we have seen, the Bretton Woods Accords provided a relatively stable economic environment in which the US could effectively ensure the compliance of its strategic allies in an expanding global economy and a benign trading environment. The dominance of the dollar and the model of the 'American dream' helped to gain the acquiescence of America's client states. The apparent success of the emerging institutional order boosted US hegemony, as America consolidated its military power, its political voice and its economic influence across the globe. The Cold War, indeed, was a significant period in the history of globalisation.

Nevertheless, in contrast to this benign interpretation with its touching faith in deterrence, one might take the view that the Cold War was the zenith of a realist power struggle between two superpowers. This struggle was primarily military. It included the creation of alliances with other states, and an arms race which created extraordinary levels of nuclear capability – arsenals large enough to destroy the planet several times over – and the conduct of proxy wars, notably in Korea and Vietnam (Bull, 1995:187). That the US was able to do this while at the same time developing its economic strength and achieving reasonably improved living standards for the majority of its citizens, ultimately contributed to the ending of the Cold War. The costs of military spending and the Americans' overwhelming lead in advanced technology by the 1980s, together with the Soviets' inability to provide adequate material comforts, finally brought about the implosion of the communist system between 1989 and 1991 – though there were other endemic social factors involved as well.

Hegemonic stability theory holds that an essentially anarchic world – in the realist sense – is rendered less dangerous and more stable by the existence of a hegemon. But the theory goes further: it is necessary to have a hegemon in order for a liberal world market economy to develop. Without it, liberal rules cannot be enforced (Jackson & Sørensen, 2003:196). Hegemonic stability theory places politics above economics and enforces conditions by which all states accede to the same liberal democratic values of the hegemon and as a consequence they accrue benefits. The theory also goes beyond economic liberalism, since it claims that should there be no hegemon the liberal world economy will be much more difficult to maintain, as narrow sectional interests will prevail, leading to protectionism and the break-up of world trade. It is therefore actually necessary for the United States, as the sole military *and* economic superpower of the post-Cold War period, to maintain its role.

In 1945

it was clearly in the United States' own interest to restore the liberal world economy based on new institutions which it could largely control. As the world's dominant industrial power, an open world economy was of great benefit to the US because it gave better access to foreign markets. Helping in the rebuilding of Western Europe and Japan was also important for American security reasons in its Cold War struggle with the Soviet Union. The United States was not interested in an unstable world, susceptible to Soviet influence, because that would be a threat to the United States' political and economic interests (Jackson & Sørensen, 2003:198).

Post-1945 the US provided the security guarantee within the context of which Western Europe could focus on economic growth and political development. This linkage across different areas is called fungibility – a key notion within hegemonic stability theory. Furthermore, the US accepted key imbalances in its post-war role. Not only did the US provide financial support to the reconstruction of Japan and Western Europe, it also accepted that Japan could retain a domestic market to which access by foreign imports was restricted, and Europe was able to subsidise and protect its agriculture (Jackson & Sørensen, 2003:198). Eventually this was reflected in US trade deficits. The US response was to follow a more self-interested set of policies, including the abandonment of the Bretton Woods regime by President Nixon. The 1970s was a decade of monetary instability, increasing protectionism and economic crisis.

Not only did Nixon ditch Bretton Woods, he also enabled US banks to lend freely on world markets, a move which according to Hutton (2002) undermined the World Bank and left developing countries at the mercy of fluctuating interest rates and volatile exchange markets. Two years later the Arab-Israeli Yom Kippur War brought a quadrupling of oil prices and a massive hike in inflation worldwide, and especially in Europe where manufacturing was highly dependent on oil. At that time energy use was especially profligate. The US turned its competitive fire on Europe, for so long its prodigy in a relationship Piening (1997) calls one of patron and client. No longer was this so.

The European response to a decade of turmoil was the rationalisation of the 1980s, after which European competitiveness in world markets improved. A prime issue was the development of the Single European Market. Far-reaching initiatives by the British Commissioner Lord Cockfield, his Italian colleague Paolo Cecchini and the French President of the Commission Jacques Delors created the Single European Market that would finally bring efficiencies and economies of scale that would raise productivity levels and enable Europe to cope better with the next wave of globalisation post-1990.

The question now uppermost is the extent to which the US is prepared to carry out its responsibility as a global hegemon in a way which actually brings stability and justice. In fact, the US hegemonic role is in decline, as Discussion 8.5 indicates. The economic stakes are much higher because the world has now entered a far more volatile and potentially dangerous phase of globalisation (Gray 1998, 2003). Like the unilateralist switch by Nixon in 1971, there is evidence of a similar line being taken by the George W. Bush administration since 2000, with a succession of policy decisions that appear to go against

Discussion 8.5

The travail of US hegemony

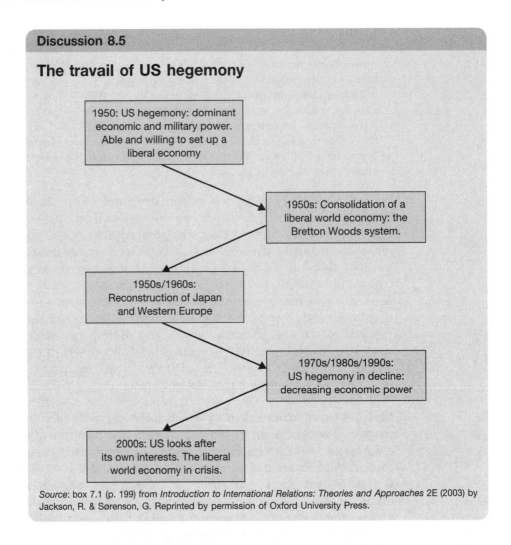

Source: box 7.1 (p. 199) from *Introduction to International Relations: Theories and Approaches* 2E (2003) by Jackson, R. & Sørenson, G. Reprinted by permission of Oxford University Press.

multilateral agreements, across many spheres of policy, including arms proliferation, chemical weapons limitation, trade, the environment and the ratification of the International Criminal Court. The US attempt to introduce tariffs on steel imports in defiance of WTO agreements in 2003 is a further example.

If the US abrogates its global role and seeks instead to pursue narrow sectional interests, then the world system could degenerate into anarchy. States are likely to adopt competitive agendas, enforcing protectionism and the abandonment of international agreements. A significant feature of America's historical role in Europe has been the linkage between the provision of security on the one hand, and economic and political development on the other. It is pertinent to ask to what extent this remains true a decade and a half after the end of the Cold War. We return to this in Chapters 9 and 10.

The argument presented in Discussion 8.5 is one of declining US hegemony, running approximately parallel to declining economic power. The contention that the US has experienced and is experiencing economic decline is based on the observation that its share of world trade is in decline, especially in comparison with the Asia-Pacific region, and it suffers from a ballooning trade deficit, having a substantial trade imbalance with both Japan/Asia-Pacific, and the European Union. However, for reasons indicated in the text alongside this, one should certainly not assume from this that there has been or is about to be an outright collapse in US ability to influence other societies and global affairs.

Strange (1987:5) argues that the strength of the US was manifested in its share of world output, of primary products, minerals and food, as well as manufactured goods and services. Furthermore, the US can rely upon its technological lead in 'information rich' key areas of the world economy, and the power it can wield through multinational corporations. The first part of this claim is less convincing now, as the US share of world output has declined. But the latter point probably still holds. In spite of the claim of a general decline in US hegemony since 1950 as illustrated in Discussion 8.5, US corporations still exhibit significant advantages and may still sustain a latent hegemonic role for the US. Also, Jackson and Sørensen point out that US cultural influence through movies, lifestyle and television remains a vital factor in preserving a leading role for the US (Jackson & Sørensen, 2003:199). This combination of influences permeates international institutions such as the WTO and the IMF. Nye writes about what he calls 'soft power', or 'co-optive power' meaning the ability

> to structure a situation so that other nations develop preferences or define their interests in ways that are consistent with one's own nation (Nye, 1990:191).

Such is the position of the hegemon. Such a position clearly implies a social and cultural dimension to hegemony, as well as an economic or political one.

Criticism of hegemonic stability theory is that it places too much emphasis on the role of the hegemon and downplays the role of other states. Jackson and Sørensen report that 'even the strongest hegemon can only achieve so much on its own' (Jackson & Sørensen, 2003:201) and that in fact stability requires cooperative efforts from a number of states with shared ideals. Thus the traditional hegemonic role is perhaps critical at the outset but the role changes as other states contribute to the liberal world order and draw benefits from free trade and liberal values. Another criticism, current at the present time, is that the US simply mismanages its role and instead of pursuing policies which would lead to qualitative improvements in living standards and international security, it instead responds to the wishes of a narrow sectional, domestic elite (Jackson & Sørensen, 2003:200; Gray, 1998; Moore, 2002; Chomsky, 2003).

On the other hand, a Marxist critique says that US hegemony is merely a phase of capitalist development and that as US power declined, or Europe and Japan caught up, economic crisis ensued during the 1970s. However, the US remained inextricably associated with a powerful set of values that became a new basis for its continuing hegemony, especially given that these were, and remain, values that other states would continue to support. Marxists also stress the inequality and hierarchy inherent in US hegemony. They point out the failure of US hegemony to be truly global. Gray (1998), not a Marxist by the way, highlights not only the diversity of types of capitalism, but also the fact that globalisation and the free market economy have barely penetrated vast areas of the globe, especially in the southern hemisphere, creating a north–south divide. This demonstrates the limited reach of hegemony, even in the context of the US pursuing policy preferences that have, and seek to have, global implications. Such policies are outlined in the next chapter.

This discussion of the US as hegemon is illustrative of the dynamic between economic and political power within the IR tradition of the International Political Economy (IPE). Jackson and Sørensen claim that one influences the other and that the relative decline of the US has not led to the breakdown of the liberal world economy, though Gray (1998) clearly implies that further, perhaps decisive, crises are not far ahead if the world remains wedded to a particular free market ideology driven through by multinational corporations and the political preferences of the '**Washington Consensus**'. The effectiveness of key actors on the world stage such as the UN and the WTO to act as forces for good seems to be dependent on the willingness of leaders of the TRIAD (US, EU, and Japan) to cooperate. Jackson and Sørensen imply a kind of *quid pro quo* in the relationship between state interests and those of the organisations to which they contribute. It is in their mutual interests to uphold the common framework. This remains the case today, though later chapters examine this claim in more detail, and with some scepticism.

As a final word on the interplay between politics and economics within the IPE tradition, there is a powerful recent example of this in the European context. A recent watershed political initiative within the EU is the Economic and Monetary Union project among 12 member states. It appears at first sight to be an economic initiative, having a profound impact on economic conditions and policy making, but it is perhaps primarily a political venture, driving further European political integration and designed to consolidate 'the European project'.

Review   *What is a hegemon? What is the central claim of hegemonic stability theory? How well does the US carry out its role as a global hegemon?*

● ● ● ● International Relations theory in context

This chapter has provided an overview of some leading theoretical positions from the discipline of International Relations. Figure 8.3 places these on a broad continuum in order that they may be seen in relation to each other on a scale that is approximately from right to left across the political spectrum.

Neo-realists, holding to the view that the primary actor in IR is the state, mount powerful criticisms of the chronic structural deficiencies of institutions such as the EU and the UN. However, they offer very little constructive reasoning on how international problems can be resolved. The realist/neo-realist perspective is, naturally and by its own definition, conflictive and unstable. In what may be interpreted as a defence of liberal institutionalism, Peterson argues:

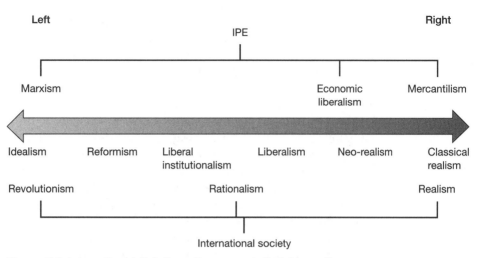

Figure 8.3 International Relations theory – a left–right continuum

> The integration of the global economy and the political fragmentation of East-West blocs mean that consolidating liberal democracy, stopping environmental degradation and checking nuclear proliferation will only be possible through collective, long-term international action (Peterson, 1996:197–8).

Thus states can better secure their prosperity and security through being embedded in powerful international institutions. Neo-realism on the other hand is, according to Peterson, right to insist that intense economic competition between states will remain central to the international system. Neo-realism has to draw on the insights of other schools, in particular institutionalism which has been largely vindicated by 1990s' experience. The European Union did not collapse following the end of the Cold War, though it undoubtedly faces fresh and daunting challenges, not least the latest and most complex enlargement in its history. Nevertheless, the EU may even have strengthened given the advent of EMU in 1999, though the Single Currency remains in its infancy and faces significant challenges. The increasing role of private sector actors and MNCs shows how economic and technological change moves ahead of political institutional development. The latter remains rooted in nineteenth-century concepts of 'national sovereignty' and 'national interest' (see Ito, 1990, quoted in Peterson, 1996:199, echoing Shaw, above).

Peterson says that the globalisation of production offers great incentives for the US, EU and Japan to work in closer harmony (Peterson, 1996:191, 199). While US influence is likely to remain significant, even as its hegemony declines, it is also possible that a combination of a neo-realist approach with support for liberal institutional initiatives is the best way for the US to pursue its interests. The Bush administration proved willing to take military action in Iraq without the unequivocal backing of the UN, but it may prove more difficult for America to act similarly in the future without UN backing. Meanwhile, the EU is split on this issue and it remains to be seen whether the Union can ever forge a common foreign and security policy, something which has remained an ambition but not a reality since Maastricht in 1992.

Clearly there are significant tensions in the state–international institution relationship. These were highlighted by the crisis over Iraq in 2003–4. Some have argued that institutions work better where the number of states involved is restricted, thus indicating that the 2004 and any future enlargements of the EU are likely to provoke serious instability (Keohane, cited in Peterson, 1996:199). The WTO is also perhaps handicapped by the sheer enormity of its task and its massive membership. However, at the core of the WTO is its multi-lateral character. It is in many ways a successful body, though much criticised. See Discussion 8.6 and further discussion in Chapter 11.

Perhaps the major weakness in institutional theory is the lack of coherent political power in institutions like the WTO. The very composition of inter-national institutions contributes to their weakness: they are composed of states. This is especially pertinent to current analysis of future direction of the EU. The extent to which the EU is a unified political authority or an assemblage of states who choose to act together in certain areas of policy, notably economics and

---

Discussion 8.6

The WTO and a liberal free trade environment

The WTO is an intergovernmental body with some limited supranational authority. It currently has 147 members. Negotiations are conducted multilaterally across a huge range of goods and services. It supports the ideal of a liberal, free trade environment. This is threatened if

- a major partner fails to adhere to the spirit of free trade, e.g. EU defence of CAP;
- a party to a trade agreement fails to accept agreed obligations, e.g. US attempt to impose restrictions on steel imports in 2003.

Solutions include:

- WTO authorisation of sanctions and/or fines
- retaliatory action by affected parties
- common cause between other trading partners, exerting pressure for change
- moral pressure to accept reform

However, the WTO has limited powers; it is at the mercy of its members; trade talks are fragile and long-drawn-out; progress has been uncertain:

- Seattle (1999) was a debacle, abandoned without progress

- Doha (2001) was judged a success: China joined the WTO; agreement was reached to launch a new 'Trade Round'
- Cancún, Mexico (2003): disagreements between LDCs and the rest derailed talks
- At the time of writing, July 2004, progress is largely stalled.

The Economist (17 November 2001) called the Doha deal a significant achievement with the 'potential' to be a good one. It at least averted the immediate risk of a collapse of the WTO and the multilateral trading system that it upholds. *The Economist* reported that the deal makes it 'marginally less likely that [the WTO] members will splinter into regional trade blocks' and that 'poor countries have the prospect of better access to rich country markets for their textiles and agricultural products'. It even goes so far as to say that 'for now, contrary to much conventional wisdom, the WTO is the poor countries' friend'. If this view is correct, it is imperative that future talks proceed equitably and reach a fair conclusion.

Nevertheless, critics of the WTO argue that its focus on free trade is wrong, and that fair trade, giving developing countries protection within global markets, is a much more equitable ambition.

trade post-EMU, is critical to understanding how the EU works now and how it will evolve in the future.

Given the weaknesses of international institutions, and their vulnerability to state-driven intransigence perhaps, reformists may have reasons to feel vindicated. Bilateral state-brokered solutions look increasingly unlikely to bring substantial benefits to the international system. Reformists tend to accept a significant role for major institutions like the EU and the WTO in developing long-term and cooperative policies. Nevertheless, the reformist critique of the EU, the World Bank, the IMF and the WTO are well-founded as there are evident weaknesses in these bodies (see Chapter 12). Economic and technological innovation as well as continuing political problems concerning democracy, legitimacy, resources and security, will demand reform and modernisation of existing institutions.

Peterson concludes that the EU/US relationship offers the potential for global leadership in the pursuit of a more stable peace and a more humane world. But there are risks, and they will not stay together purely out of nostalgia (Brittan, 1995, referred to in Peterson, 1996:204). This view may be challenged for its imperialist implications, especially in the light of recent US policy which has tended to reflect a more realist and unilateralist view in Washington. One might criticise the US in a number of areas from social welfare to the machinations of American democracy (Hutton, 2002). Or one might even accept the charge from Chomsky, a long-time critic of US foreign policy, who argues that the US is, by its own definitions of terrorism, a terrorist state (2003:188). Any such conclusion would indicate that the US has forfeited the right to be any kind of example to the rest of the world. Chomsky reports an American missile attack on a Sudanese pharmaceutical plant in 1998, when Bill Clinton was President, and which

> led to 'several tens of thousands of deaths', according to the only reputable estimates we have, estimates consistent with the immediate estimates of Human Rights Watch and later reports of knowledgeable observers (Chomsky, 2003:206).

Indeed there are signs that the partnership that Peterson wrote about in the mid-1990s is threatened. More recent events, and especially the US response to the attacks of 11 September 2001, have led to open disagreements, particularly over the decision to go to war against Iraq in 2003. Relations between Europe and America are clearly strained and the traditional partnership may not be taken for granted. It could be that the closeness of US/EU relations is another casualty of 9/11, despite the initial solidarity with the US after the attacks. If this is true, the role of the US as an international hegemon will experience further decline, in spite of the US being not so much a superpower as a 'hyperpower' (Hutton, 2002:352). The description may take account of the USA's military might, but it underestimates US weakness in other areas. Gray (2004) has written of the declining power of the US – a point developed in Chapter 12.

| **Review** | *To what extent do you think different schools of thought within IR are able to provide useful prescriptions for dealing with global problems? Where do the best hopes lie?* |

Summary

This chapter has made the following claims.

- **The European Union** is an example of a highly developed form of regionalism; this has given it global influence; it has some state-like characteristics which enhance its role in international relations.

- **Realism** is a classical tradition in IR theory. Realism holds that sovereign states are dominant players in international relations; states compete with other states in a win–lose environment and are therefore highly prone to conflict; the first function of government is to ensure state security; politics takes precedence over economics; there is no higher authority than the state, no orderer, and thus states exist in an anarchical environment; human nature is flawed and therefore wars happen.

- **Neo-realism** asserts that in the absence of an orderer, anarchy is the permissive cause of war; institutions may reduce the risk of war between states; war is a result not of man's inherent weakness, but of social factors such as inequalities and bad governance.

- **Liberalism** holds that people are naturally cooperative; free trade is a benefit and produces positive-sum gains; states that trade with each other tend not to go to war; liberalism brings political benefits such as representative democracy and social welfare; it privileges the role of individuals in enhancing their material well-being.

- **Institutional liberalism** privileges the role of international institutions over states; international institutions help to secure a stable and just international environment.

- **International Society** theory is concerned with both security and justice. It focuses on the role of people in foreign policy processes; policy making is normative; International Society theory covers realism, rationalism and revolutionism. It advocates interpreting international relations through the interrelating spectrum of state-centric realism, international law and institutionally-based rationalism, and matters of global justice that inform and nourish revolutionism.

- **International Political Economy** privileges the relationship between politics and economics; it encompasses three traditions that interpret this relationship differently:
  - **Mercantilism** is state-centric; it is concerned with power and asserts the dominance of politics over economics; political and military power can be established through competing effectively in trading relationships; states are competitive and conflictive.
  - **Neo-liberalism** is also state-centric and individualist; it is associated with the most recent phase of globalisation; it emphasises *laissez-faire* economics, privatisation and a reduced role for state authorities in the economy; neo-liberals assert the benefits of trade and competition. Neo-liberalism is associated with the 'Washington Consensus' which requires LDCs to adopt

the policy prescriptions of the IMF and the World Bank, under pressure from the conservative right in the US and its allies in MNCs.

  – **Marxism** rejects the state-centredness of other IPE traditions; it focuses on the needs of global society; economics is dominant; class relationships matter most.

  Reformism and Neo-Marxism tend to support an increased role for international institutions in global governance.

- **Hegemonic stability theory** argues that in a state-centric and anarchic world it is desirable to have a hegemon assert stability by getting less powerful states to accede to its policy prescriptions; this is achieved through the exercise of hegemony, or political, economic and cultural influence.

Key concepts: discussion and other definitions

Key concept 8.1   Capitalism

A distinct form of social organisation which is based on private ownership and control of the means of production where the latter is organised with the intention of creating a profit.

Legalised theft (Anon).

A distinct form of social organisation based on generalized commodity production, in which there is private ownership and/or control of the means of production (McLean & McMillan, 2003:62).

The *OED* describes capitalism as the condition of possessing capital and using it for production.

Capitalism is above all viewed as a social system and before the collapse of the Soviet Bloc in 1989–91 it was seen as opposing the alternative of communism. Indeed, the juxtaposition of capitalism and communism as opposing systems was a hallmark of the 'long' Cold War between 1917 and 1991.

Capitalism is dependent on 'free enterprise' and is based on the myth (we can call it a myth in the way that Weber (2001) uses the term 'myth' in *International Relations Theory: a critical introduction*, in other words it does not matter whether it is true or not, it is the 'commonly held assumption by its proponents') that 'free enterprise works' as the car window stickers of the 1970s used to remind us. In fact, during the 1970s in Britain there was rampant inflation and high unemployment, conditions which endured until the early 1990s. With un-employment reaching over 3m in 1990 the notion that capitalism 'works' had a certain irony.

Capitalism privileges certain features of economic management: private is perceived to be preferable to the public, so the role of the state in a capitalist system is generally kept to a minimum. This varies of course from state to state and there are many different forms of capitalism, as Hutton (2003) and Gray (1998) are anxious to point out. The USA favours a more minimalist role for the state than has Germany, for example, where high levels of taxation have sustained a high level of social welfare and state provision. Both, though, are capitalist economies.

Capitalism is deemed to be at the heart of global inequalities for its severest critics on the left. The capitalist system creates profit which reinforces wealth and power, thus inequality is a feature of capitalist economies. Supporters of capitalism see this as a natural and desirable situation and point to the oppor-tunities available in a capitalist system for entrepreneurs to behave in such a way that they too can make good profits and become wealthy. Another myth of capitalism is that anyone can benefit from the opportunities it presents: a humble sharecropper could one day become the President of the USA. Reality suggests otherwise, especially if the sharecropper is a Hispanic immigrant.

Capitalism has emerged as the dominant system of economic organisation in the age of globalisation. With the fall of communism, Francis Fukuyama famously declared that history was at an end, as any ideology, such as capitalism, required an opposite ideology to truly have conceptual relevance (Fukuyama, 1992). Once communism disappeared, as it practically did during the upheavals between 1989–91, capitalism stood alone. Of course, this argument is widely rejected, not least by neo-Marxists who point to the inherent contradictions within capitalism, and the added challenges presented by the threat of ecolo-gical catastrophe. Indeed, as modern capitalism, with its global reach, produces ever-widening wealth disparities, both within and between countries, and between the northern and southern hemispheres, critics of capitalism may become more vocal still.

The No Global Movement, the Campaign for Global Justice, and the World Social Forum are but three examples of broadly anti-capitalist mass movements. For some of their members, the most accurate definition of capitalism is the anonymous one offered above.

Key concept 8.2 Liberalism

The belief that it is the aim of politics to preserve individual rights and to maximise freedom of choice (McLean & McMillan, 2003:309).

Liberal theories of international relations are founded in the liberal philosophy of Locke (1632–1704), the utilitarianism of Bentham (1748–1832), the social reformism of J.S. Mill (1806–73), and the liberal economics of Adam Smith

(1723–90) and David Ricardo (1772–1823). More recent spiritual guidance has come from the political economist John Maynard Keynes (1883–1946), who advocated a liberal economy to meet social objectives, and recommended pragmatic government intervention in macroeconomic management, as well as public–private partnerships, in order to achieve a just and well-ordered society. Liberalism is a broad church and has spawned various offshoots, two of which are examined in this chapter.

Ricardo's theory of comparative advantage promoted the essence of free trade as follows: it is more efficient for states to specialise in producing the goods that their circumstances enable them to produce rather than try to produce everything. They can buy or exchange what they do not produce from others who do. This process of exchange, incorporating added value (which assists in profit accumulation) is to the advantage of all participants.

Liberalism is a reformist rather than system-changing political philosophy. It maintains a faith in the possibility of improving social conditions and, in keeping with its Enlightenment origins, believes in the ideal of continual progress. This embraces improvements not only in knowledge, but also in welfare and morality. McLean and McMillan (2003:309) point out the ambiguity in liberalism of its general concern for a more just and egalitarian society while at the same time extolling individual virtues and a culture of individualism, including the defence of private property. This empathy with the entrepreneurial characteristics favoured by capitalists can appear bourgeois to left-leaning or Marxist critics.

Liberal concerns to defend individual rights and private property are seen as a means to limit the powers of the state, but liberalism is sometimes criticised for taking insufficient account of the consequences of heavy concentrations of private power.

Liberalism is heavily influenced by discussions concerning representative government and government by consent. Thus the term liberal democracy, which is suffused with principles such as choice, alternative programmes, public discourse, open media, freedom of association, political pluralism and respect for human rights. These are core values to liberals and prerequisites to a healthy polity.

Key concept 8.3   Marxism

A tradition in Western political philosophy that is based on the work of Karl Marx (1818–83) and Friedrich Engels (1820–95). Marxism presents a socio-economic critique of capitalism, based primarily on an analysis of class relationships, and proposes political change to create a socialist alternative to capitalism.

Marxism is an Enlightenment tradition in Western philosophy based on the writings of Marx and Engels. Marx was in fact a trenchant critic of philosophy. He is perhaps best described as a social historian, and among his most significant works is a joint treatise written with Engels on the *Conditions of the English Working Classes*. The work describes the appalling conditions of the labouring (working) class in nineteenth-century cotton mills in Lancashire. Marx was less interested in philosophy than in a programme for change. Thus he produced, again with Engels, the *Communist Manifesto* (1848). The Communist Manifesto describes the opposing forces of capital (the bourgeoisie) and labour (the proletariat). Marx described human relations in terms of the value placed on labour and saw how the ruling class, who were the owners of factories – the means of production – paid workers a wage for their labour. However, ultimately the relationship was one of exploitation and could never be an equitable one. This situation was exacerbated by the intellectual strength of the ruling class, since it held not only the material strength, but also the intellectual force in society. In the midst of this tension is the paradox of the middle class, the bourgeoisie. Marx describes the bourgeoisie as positively revolutionary, enabling change in society, through its Enlightenment-inspired attack on old feudal certainties, the church and the ruling elite. Indeed, in assuming the mantle of the traditional ruling class, the middle classes unleashed human potential. The bourgeoisie could act as midwife for a communist utopia. Feudal, patriarchal ties to 'natural superiors' had hitherto held society back. Now, the bourgeoisie reduced human relations to 'a cash payment'. All things became commodities, having a commodity value that outweighed any aesthetic value. Crucially, though, people too became little more than commodities, exchanging their labour for a wage. The growth of the bourgeoisie therefore fundamentally altered the old order, and at the same time undermined the conservative instincts of family relations. The bourgeoisie thus became an enabling presence in the face of pressures for change.

The focus of interest for Marxism is the inherent contradictions within capitalism: the conflicting interests of labour and capital. Given that the working classes possessed an overwhelming numerical advantage, capitalism thus contained the seeds of its own inevitable demise. Marx also predicted a continual polarisation of the interests of labour and capital. In this critical respect Marx failed to anticipate the extent to which the new ruling elite would manage to 'buy off' the acquiescence of the working classes through improving their material well-being, through accepting worker representation through trades unions, or through improved working conditions. One might characterise this with the example of Ford workers managing to save enough of their wages to own Ford cars, and eventually, their own houses.

Marx regarded history as having a certain inevitable course. Marx called this 'historical determinism'. The working class would rise up against their oppressors. The capitalist system would be replaced by a workers' utopia based on the credo of 'from each according to his abilities to each according to his needs'. Such a society would be peaceful and harmonious and eventually would transcend even the need for states.

For further learning, read Marx K. & Engels F. with Jones, G.S. (ed.) (2002) *The Communist Manifesto*, Harmondsworth: Penguin Books.

Key concept 8.4   Hegemony (n); Hegemon (agent)

The exercise of power, or influence, of a dominant polity over other polities or regions.

Hegemony usually involves a range of political dimensions, including military authority, economic and cultural influence. Influence may extend to control, as in the case of Russia over the rest of the USSR during the Cold War. A hegemon is often a powerful state or region that has power over less powerful states or regions.

Hegemony may be exercised over a region, such as by Germany through the Deutschmark under the European Monetary System between 1979 and 1999; or it may be exercised over half the world, as by the superpowers during the Cold War; or over a state by a particular group within the state, such as Serbia over the rest of the Yugoslav republics, prior to 1988, or England over the rest of the United Kingdom.

A hegemon is usually a state or region within a state that has political, economic and cultural power over other states, or over other regions. However, the term might also be applied to the European Union, which exercises hegemony over its member states, and over various categories of other states that are not members, such as applicant states, other European states that are members of EFTA, as well as Russia and the CIS, the former Yugoslav Republics and Albania, or even the North African states Morocco, Algeria, Tunisia and Libya, all of whom are affected by the EU sphere of influence through trade and aid policies.

However, a traditional definition of a hegemon emphasises military power:

A hegemon is 'a dominant military and economic power' (Jackson & Sørensen, 2003:196).

Arguably a greater emphasis on economic power is more in tune with the current context of increased globalisation, and is clearly more relevant in the case of the EU. Thus Keohane defines the power of hegemons as based on

> control over raw materials, control over sources of capital, control over markets and competitive advantage in the production of highly valued goods . . . it must also be stronger on these dimensions taken as a whole than any other country (Keohane, cited in Strange, 1996:22)

Hegemony is power and influence over other states or communities that leads them to pursue policies that coincide with the interests of the hegemon. Hegemony is closely related to the concept of power (see Key concept 9.2) since it relates to the achievement of policy objectives through persuasion or, at the very least, influence.

A hegemon is 'a dominant state that uses its military and economic power to impose and maintain customs and rules aimed at preserving the existing world order and its position in that order' (Mansbach, 2000:539).

Strange (1996) argues that the discipline of International Relations tended to be overly preoccupied with the role of hegemons and therefore underestimated the dispersal of power and the different ways in which power is exercised. During the Cold War, hegemonic stability theory (HST) was considered as an explanation for détente, the stand-off between the two superpowers. HST certainly had merit during the détente years, but as suggested in this chapter, the Cold War was something of a high wire act, with significant risk of nuclear conflict. Also, given the proxy wars around the world and internal repression within many states during the Cold War, it is arguable that the 'peace' that pertained during the détente years of the 1970s was of a particularly volatile kind, and of little value in those corners of the world where conflict and human rights abuses were endemic.

Hegemonic stability theory tends to ignore the tendency for power to be dispersed or exercised through means other than the traditional use or threat of military force. Power and influence may emerge through trade and political capital built up over many decades, even by a group of states acting in concert, as is the case with the European Union. In other words, traditional notions of state power = hegemony do not square with alternative multilateral models, such as the EU.

Part of understanding the term hegemony is in recognising a continuum between influence and power, which probably comprises authority as well, as shown in Figure 8.4.

Examples are the hegemony exercised by the USA over its political and military allies post-1945; the hegemony of Russia over the other 14 republics of the USSR between 1917 and 1991; the hegemony of England over the other sub-state nations in the United Kingdom (Scotland, Wales, Northern Ireland).

Hegemony is exercised by a hegemon. The different dimensions of hegemony may show variable balance, for example in some instances political and economic power may be stronger than cultural power, as for example in the relationship between the USA and Latin American states during much of the twentieth century. A hegemonic relationship between the USA and Japan has persisted since 1945, but the cultural impact, though strong, is probably less significant than the political impact.

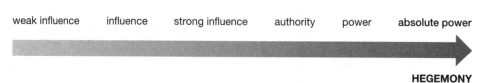

Figure 8.4 A hegemony continuum

There are many references to hegemony in this chapter. See in particular the section on hegemonic stability theory.

See also Key concepts 9.2 and 12.3 Power and soft power.

Further reading

Baylis, J. & **Smith**, S. (eds) (2001) *The Globalization of World Politics*, Oxford: OUP. This substantial edited collection contains a section on theories of world politics which covers key themes in International Relations theory. The book is an excellent resource and superb reading for students of globalisation.

Jackson, R. & **Sørensen**, G. (2003) *Introduction to International Relations: Theories and Approaches*, Second edition. Oxford: OUP. As will be apparent from this chapter, there are frequent references to this similarly excellent book. It covers all the main theoretical approaches of IR.

McLean, I. & **McMillan**, A. (2003) *Oxford Concise Dictionary of Politics*, Oxford: OUP. See the short essays on Liberalism, pp. 309–10 and Marxism pp. 337–9.

Weber, C. (2001) *International Relations Theory: A critical introduction*, London: Routledge. This sparkling and original book is a great introduction to the subject of International Relations. It covers significant strands of IR thinking that are not mentioned in this chapter and is a much more comprehensive overview of this fascinating area of study. The chapters most obviously related to the contents of this book are Chapters 2, Realism and 6, Globalisation. See film suggestions below.

Woods, N. (2001) 'International Political Economy in an age of globalisation', chapter 13, pp. 277–98 in Baylis and Smith (eds) *The Globalization of World Politics*, Oxford: OUP. One of many outstanding chapters in the Baylis and Smith text.

Film suggestions

The idea to recommend films to relate themes presented in different chapters is taken from another textbook. I owe a debt to the brilliant *International Relations Theory – A critical introduction*, by Cynthia Weber (2001). Not only do I think the book is a great introduction to the subject, it uses a dramatic and original device to illustrate the core messages of each chapter, what Weber calls the 'myths' of International Relations theory. She uses films to deliver the key concepts relating to IR theories and analysis of a film is fully integrated into the discussion in each chapter. I shamelessly recommend two films from her book, one to illustrate realism, one to illustrate liberalism. Weber bases her use of the film around globalisation, but the core myths within the chapter relate to liberalism, primarily the myth that a liberal, material society can satisfy human needs.

Cynthia Weber's book details explicitly how each film matches the myths. I unhesitatingly recommend the two films below but, to get the full benefit, you should see them in conjunction with reading the relevant chapters from Weber's book, not just this one.

Peter Brook, *Lord of the Flies*, 1968, UK

Based on the book of the same name by William Golding, this film should not be confused with a later American remake by Harry Hook in 1994. Weber (2001:34) warns against this and recommends reading Golding's book as a much better alternative.

Lord of the Flies is set during the Second World War and features a group of schoolboys aged between 5 and 12 who are being evacuated from the UK to escape bombing by the *Luftwaffe*. Their plane crashes on a remote island in the Pacific but no adults survive the crash. The film portrays the anarchy myth of Waltz's *Man, the State and War*, first written in 1954, the same year as Golding published *Lord of the Flies*.

The opening sequence of the film shows the changed environment for the schoolboys. Their world shifts from one of order, hierarchy, rules and the state, to the nameless island without any hierarchy, rules or order. Predictably the children begin by establishing these features as best they can, but the order and hierarchy they set up breaks down with disastrous consequences. The reality is that on the island, with no orderer (no adults), there is no means to enforce any system that the boys create. They live in a world of anarchy. The anarchy myth is aptly demonstrated. Competition and conflict bring shocking results.

Peter Weir, *The Truman Show*, 1998, USA

The eponymous hero of the film does not know it, but his entire life is conducted on a film set manipulated by Christof, a TV show producer. Truman's life, from conception to the end, is constructed entirely on screen for the entertainment of a worldwide audience. The set and everyone on it is artificial, an offshore neighbourhood in middle America. All the characters with whom Truman interacts, including his girlfriend, are actors.

The idea is that Truman's every need is met. He wants for nothing – he has everything except spiritual satisfaction and ultimately he has no real choice. He can only choose between material alternatives. The parallel to the perfect globalisation promise, the liberal dream of free America, is that ultimately, material needs cannot be satisfied and without personal or spiritual challenge, Truman's life is meaningless. In other words, liberalism is a sham. The obsessive individualism, the daily comforts, the material satisfaction, the daily provision of purchasable needs, fails to create what the advertisements always imply: happiness.

In the wider context of globalisation, one can argue that globalisation underlines the central ambiguity in liberalism: how does liberalism propose to counter the concentration of private power that liberalism implies? Christof, the TV producer, and his media empire are a parody of a great all-consuming and manipulative multinational corporation – unlimited in its power.

Weir's film is a great show, terrifically entertaining, wildly original, and a wonderful satire on modern materialism.

Chapter 9

Globalisation and the European Union in transition

Overview

- The meaning of globalisation
- Globalisation as process
- The EU response to globalisation

Key concepts

9.1   Globalisation

9.2   Power

● ● ● ● Introduction

This chapter examines the concept of **globalisation** and assesses the EU response to the forces underlying the phenomenon. The term is relatively new; it does not even appear in my two-volume *Shorter Oxford English Dictionary* published in 1983. Now, entering the word globalisation into the Google search engine suggests 2,890,000 websites containing definitions of the word, and it has passed into everyday usage. A search with Amazon.com, a business readily identified with the modern phase of globalisation, reveals 3,877 titles on the subject. Despite, or perhaps because of its widespread use, there seems little agreement on what it actually means and none on whether it is a force for good, or bad.

The lack of clarity is widespread, but sceptics who question the usefulness or accuracy of the term seek to distinguish between what is 'internationalisation' and what is 'globalisation'. This chapter begins with an attempt to establish this difference, and therefore some understanding of what globalisation is, and continues with a necessarily selective examination of different writers' assessments of what globalisation means.

The second part of the chapter gives a brief history of key stages in the development of the International Political Economy, partly to illustrate that globalisation, as it is often understood, is not as new as is sometimes assumed. This is complicated by the scepticism expressed in the first part, because on the one hand one might argue that the entire concept of globalisation is a myth, therefore it cannot have any history. That is not the view taken here: there are aspects of globalisation, and claims made about globalisation, that have significant historical precedent. By outlining some of these we may better understand how the modern idea of globalisation has emerged. Looking at some history also highlights some of the weaknesses in the arguments presented by globalisation theorists and those who support the project of globalisation.

The word 'project' is important. Gray (1998) refers to globalisation as a 'political project', a view adopted throughout this book: globalisation, as currently conceived, is a project designed to achieve certain outcomes, namely the world-wide assimilation of national economies into a neo-liberal *laissez-faire* economy, with minimal government interference. This project is driven by the political preferences of leading policy makers in the world's largest national economy, the US. It has also gained support elsewhere, notably in the UK. It proposes that the complete liberalisation of capital markets, freeing these from government interference, and the undermining of state responsibilities in education and welfare, brings benefits to all, national economies and individuals alike. It is worth elaborating what 'all' means here: advanced industrialised economies, developing or underdeveloped countries; individuals in comfortable employment, or even those actually living on welfare, or in poverty. All will benefit from the project to create a single global economic system, run – but barely managed – by markets.

The third and final part of the chapter examines the response of the European Union to the dominant features of globalisation in recent years, but this too is complicated by the fact that the EU has responded – and needed to respond – not only to characteristics of globalisation, but also to other developments which relate more accurately to internationalisation. The European Union, as the chapter title implies should be interpreted as 'in transition'. Always underpinned by a process rather than a single unchanging institutional framework, the idea of the EU in transition is a continuation of themes explored earlier in the book: the European integration process, the development of the Single European Market, Economic and Monetary Union, the transition from EC to EU, various enlargements including the historic Eastern enlargement which brings former Cold War adversaries together, and now the response to contemporary globalisation and major changes in the international environment following the terror attacks on New York and Washington in 2001. The European Union has always been a moving feast. The claim is made that it is now necessarily in transition once more, discovering its role post-9/11 and how best to respond to the latest challenges presented by a still fast-changing environment.

A core claim of the chapter is therefore that there is a difference between globalisation and internationalisation which is not always apparent from a tendency to confuse the two, not least in common parlance. A second claim supports the interpretation presented by Gray, that globalisation is a US-inspired political project. The role of the United States in establishing policy regimes sympathetic to the project of globalisation is illustrative of a wider US hegemony, one that requires a counter policy from the European Union. This issue is addressed in the final chapter of the book.

The terms hegemon and hegemony are used frequently in this chapter. If you are not sure what they mean, look again at Key concept 8.4.

The meaning of globalisation

Hirst and Thompson (1999) are among the 'globalisation sceptics'. Their focus is an analysis of *economic* globalisation which promotes the notion of a globalised economy. This is the dominant strand in globalisation theory. Hirst and Thompson seek to separate economic globalisation, and its consequent globalised economy, from other phenomena which are frequently assumed to be integral to economic globalisation, such as recent developments in **politics** and **culture**. These are areas affected by increased internationalisation, but

> without the notion of a globalized economy many of the other consequences adduced in the domains of culture and politics would either cease to be sustainable or become less threatening (Hirst & Thompson, 1999:3).

Hirst and Thompson identify the core claims of globalisation before questioning whether these claims do, in fact, stand up to scrutiny. Their conclusion is that globalisation is based on unsound assumptions and is therefore largely a myth. They summarise the assumptions of globalisation theorists as follows:

> It is widely asserted that we live in an era in which the greater part of social life is determined by global processes, in which national cultures, national economies, and national borders are dissolving. Central to this perception is a rapid and recent process of economic globalisation. A truly global economy is claimed to have emerged, or be in the process of emerging, in which distinct national economies and therefore distinct national strategies of economic management are increasingly irrelevant. The world economy has internationalised in its basic dynamics, it is dominated by uncontrollable market forces, and it has as its principal economic actors and major agents of change truly transnational corporations that owe allegiance to no nation state and locate wherever on the globe market advantage dictates (Hirst & Thompson, 1999:1).

Hirst and Thompson's study identifies five claims against the globalisation thesis sketched above. These are presented as Discussion 9.1.

Part of the scepticism is a response to the assumption from globalisation theorists that the phenomena described are global: the word globalisation overstates the geographical impact of capital flow, the spread of markets, and the reach of international trade. As Goldmann (2001) observes, the term 'internationalisation' might be more accurate, since globalisation is concentrated in the Triad, and therefore in the northern hemisphere, virtually excluding two thirds of the world's population. This is true even if we include the Pacific coastal regions of Asia in an extended Asia Pacific notion of the third leg of the Triad (Japan/Asia Pacific). In fact, 'approximately 75 per cent of the world's exports and 60 per cent of manufacturing output and almost all transnational activity' is located in and between these three (Triad) regions (Griffiths & Wall, 2001:150). In short, globalisation is not global at all.

Discussion 9.1

The case against economic globalisation

1. The present highly internationalised economy is not unprecedented: it is one of a number of distinct conjunctures or states of the international economy that have existed since an economy based on modern industrial technology began to be generalised from the 1860s. In some respects, the current international economy is less open and integrated than the regime which prevailed from 1870 to 1914.

2. Genuinely transnational companies appear to be relatively rare. Most companies are based nationally and trade multinationally on the strength of a major national location of assets, production and sales, and there seems to be no major tendency towards the growth of truly international companies.

3. Capital mobility is not producing a massive shift of investment and employment from the advanced to the developing economies. Rather, foreign direct investment (FDI) is highly concentrated among the advanced industrial economies and the Third World remains marginal in both investment and trade, a small minority of newly industrialising countries apart.

4. As some of the extreme advocates of globalisation recognise, the world economy is far from being genuinely 'global'. Rather trade, investment and financial flows are concentrated in the Triad of Europe, Japan and North America and this dominance seems set to continue.

5. These major economic powers, the G-3, thus have the capacity, especially if they coordinate policy, to exert powerful governance pressures over financial markets and other economic tendencies. Global markets are thus by no means beyond regulation and control, even though the current scope and objectives of economic governance are limited by the divergent interests of the Great Powers and the economic doctrines prevalent among their elites (Hirst & Thompson, 1999:2).

Goldmann refers to globalisation as a 'faddish term of the 1990s' (Goldmann, 2001:18). If it was faddish, we might have expected it to have gone away by the middle of the following decade, but it clearly has not. Goldmann summarises four ways in which the term is defined, as given in Discussion 9.2.

If Goldmann, as well as Hirst and Thompson, is right, and globalisation is a myth, then why be concerned to offer counter-arguments? Unfortunately, just because it is a myth does not mean that it barely amounts to a string of beans. On the contrary it has a powerful appeal to business leaders and political elites who have engineered a culture of acquiescence in the project of economic globalisation. Hirst and Thompson write that

> extreme views [in support of globalisation are] relatively coherent and capable of being developed into a clear ideal-typical conception of a globalized economic system. Such views are important in that they become politically highly consequential. The most eloquent proponents of the extreme view [of economic globalisation] are very influential and have set the tone for discussion in both business and political circles (Hirst & Thompson, 1999:3).

They continue:

> The advocates of 'globalization' have proposed the further liberalization of the international economy and the deregulation of domestic economies. This advocacy has had serious effects in Asia and in emerging financial markets, leading to economic crisis, unemployment and impoverishment. The view we attack may have been dented by

Discussion 9.2

Goldmann's four ways in which globalisation is defined

In one usage, [globalisation] refers to the *latest phase of capitalism* in which corporate transnational activities have made national economies increasingly integrated or amalgamated with each other. Whether resulting from market dynamics or from political will, globalization is an economic phenomenon in this usage. The central fault line, as it has been put, comes between those who emphasise macro-economic benefits and those who focus on social adjustment costs.

Globalization is also used in the sense of *cultural equalization* by the diffusion of particular cultural products, lifestyles and consumption patterns across the entire world in conjunction with the dissemination of rationalism, instrumentalism, and a concomitant way of organizing society.

In another use [. . .] globalization is pictured as an *individual level*, everyday phenomenon. It refers 'neither to values nor to structures' but

> to processes, to sequences that unfold either in the mind or in behaviour, to interactions that evolve as people go about their daily task and seek to realize their particular goals (Rosenau, 1997:80).

There is a fourth approach, according to which *globalization is a broad process* within which economic penetration, cultural assimilation, and sequences of interaction are special instances. I take David Held to exemplify this approach when he defines globalization as

> the stretching and deepening of social relations and institutions across space and time such that, on the one hand, day-to-day activities are increasingly influenced by events happening on the other side of the globe and, on the other, the practices and decisions of local groups or communities can have significant global reverberations (Held, 1995:20).

Held adds that politics today unfolds 'against the background of a world permeated by the movement of goods and capital, the flow of communication, the interchange of cultures and the passage of people' (Held, ibid.:21).

Goldmann goes on to argue that types 1 to 3 above are aspects of internationalisation and the fourth sense, deployed by Held, is the same as internationalisation (Goldmann, 2001:18).

the Asian crisis, but it is not dead. It remains strong in the developed countries, where it has sustained the rhetoric of 'competitiveness' and the belief that the extensive welfare states of Northern and Western Europe are a constraint on economic performance that they can no longer afford in an internationalized economy. These myths still need puncturing before they do impossible damage to both social stability and economic performance (Hirst & Thompson, 1999:4).

Micklethwait and Wooldridge (2000) do not share these concerns. They write an impassioned defence of globalisation, describing it as positive and liberating, offering opportunities to millions. They claim that any malign effects are caused, not by globalisation, but by poor governments and human incompetence, or worse. Their argument is that the rules of economics will prevail and that supply will follow demand, the consumer is king, and the profit motive will ensure that business responds to consumer needs, and will do so responsibly. A criticism of their book *Future Perfect: The challenge and hidden promise of globalisation* is that while its focus is on economic globalisation, it conflates the project of globalising the world economy with cultural benefits which have more to do with internationalisation than with the political project of achieving economic globalisation. That over 125,000 Chinese are studying in British universities is a sign of internationalisation, not the economic project of globalisation. The same is true of the increase in home PCs and use of the Internet – though still pitifully low in many poorer and less-developed regions. Many of the cultural benefits that we may experience on a daily basis are not products of unfettered global capitalism, they are the result of increased internationalisation, trade and cross-border communication: such things are not globalisation.

In an international economy, national economies still have control and businesses are nationally located even while they have subsidiaries and sales operations in different states. Hirst and Thompson reserve the phrase multi-national corporations (MNCs) for this kind of business. Transnational corporations on the other hand are not nationally rooted: they are global, footloose and beholden to no state control. These are the future, according to extreme globalisation theorists. Under conditions of globalisation, business relocates to a higher plain, above the state. Markets and production become the key logic of global business and global society. This creates a basic problem for state authorities: their role in governance is sharply reduced. Transnational companies are to all intents and purposes 'unreachable' and have no loyalty to states, only to markets. Under globalisation, by definition markets become difficult to regulate. Capital circulates, businesses move to where the profit motive dictates. These consequences are developed further in the next chapter, but central to this notion is the idea that the state is in decline.

Scholte argues that globalisation calls into question the traditional role of the state and says 'it is arguably dangerous to give methodological territorialism further lease on life in a globalising world' (Scholte, 1999:18), thus calling into question the entire discipline of International Relations. This book rejects this view, and argues that states have been and remain significant elements within the process of globalisation. Meanwhile Giddens, like Held cited above, says that globalisation theory indicates the declining significance of space and time, given the

> intensification of worldwide social relations which link distant localities in such a way that local happenings are shaped by events occurring many miles away and vice versa (Giddens, 1990:64).

This has become a classic definition by a major globalisation theorist. For Giddens economic globalisation is 'a reality and not just a continuation of, or a reversion to, the trends of previous years' (1998:30). He argues that the most important change is the

> expanded role of world financial markets, increasingly operating on a real-time basis. Over a trillion dollars a day is turned over in currency exchange transactions. The proportion of financial exchanges in relation to trade has grown by a factor of five in the past fifteen years (Giddens, ibid.).

Giddens argues that this massive increase in capital movement is evidence that globalisation is real, but he also says that

> Globalisation [. . .] is not only, or even primarily, about economic interdependence, but about the transformation of time and space in our lives. Distant events, whether

economic or not, affect us more directly and more immediately than ever before. Conversely, decisions we take as individuals are often global in their implications. The dietary habits individuals have, for example, are consequential for food producers, who might live on the other side of the world (Giddens, 1998:30–31).

This may be true but it suggests something of an overstatement of the power of individuals. It reminds one of the clichés from chaos theory known as

> the butterfly effect, where it is claimed that the flapping of the wings of a butterfly can, given time, effect the direction of a hurricane on the other side of the planet (http://www.webslave.dircon.co.uk/alife/chaos.html).

The 'time-space distantiation' thesis implies inevitability about 'systems' being outside human control. This is, as Hirst and Thompson suggest, a council of despair. It is especially pernicious because it implies that there is no need for governments to try to span the gap between the national and the global. Supporters of globalisation 'deny both the need for strong supranational governance and the possibility of supranational level action. They are pessimists of the intellect and of the will' (Hirst & Thompson, 1999:237). In fact, state governments must be proactive in shaping a response to issues raised by the globalisation project, but as is argued in Chapter 11, they have tended to run shy of confronting the 'inevitability' of their own powerlessness.

Gray (1998) argues that globalisation is a process driven by the ascendancy of neo-liberal political economy emanating from what is often questionably referred to as the Anglo-Saxon world. President Reagan in the US and Prime Minister Thatcher in the UK introduced policy changes in the 1980s which effectively deregulated the financial and telecommunications sectors. These changes resulted in an explosion of capital movement, and they also coincided with rapid ICT innovation. The launch of the World Wide Web in 1990 was a further decisive boost to the process. Gray's main argument is that the project of globalisation is designed to ensure the ascendancy of neo-liberal and free market policies worldwide.

So far we have concentrated on the economic aspects of globalisation. The expansion of capital flow, the growth of multinational corporations and the increased incidence of cross-border trade in and between the three regions comprising the Triad during the 1990s contributed to widespread belief in the notion that globalisation was different to anything that had ever happened before. In fact, Goldmann (2001) and Hirst and Thompson (1999) dispute this as well: the scale of capital flow was greater as a proportion of GDP between 1870 and 1914 than it has been since 1990. Trade was if anything more global during those pre-First World War decades.

However, it can also be argued that globalisation is complex and multifaceted. Giddens (1990) refers to four 'overlapping trends'. The first is the communications revolution; the second is the so-called 'weightless economy', meaning financial and knowledge-based services, becoming increasingly globalised. Third, the profound change brought about by the collapse of the Soviet Union in 1990–91. The fourth trend is the societal and cultural changes impacting on everyday life. The combination of these four dimensions represents, according to Giddens, a major transition in human history over the past 20–30 years.

One can argue that the underlying force behind this transition is both economic and political. All four of Giddens's trends have significant political and economic implications, but it is the economic impact of globalisation that is reshaping political relationships between different states, as well as affecting the wider society. It may be helpful to think of globalisation in terns of the impact it has on **power** – and particularly the power of governments, since central to the globalisation thesis is that states lose power.

Here it is perhaps useful to digress slightly and clarify the use of the meaning of the word **politics**, and the related word power, since these are important in the context of globalisation. Politics is human behaviour concerned with the exercise of power. This power might be over the allocation of scarce resources, for example. Finer (1970) holds that what defines political behaviour depends on the nature of the predicament one is faced with. Furthermore, politics occurs where alternative choices – we may call them policies – are available. In such instances, choice of one policy as opposed to an alternative depends on the distribution of power between the factions involved, factions which have different preferences. Power is 'the capacity to achieve desired results' (Finer, 1970:12–13). It follows from this that some predicaments provoke political behaviour and demand a political solution, and power is a key component in the prosecution of one particular set of actions as opposed to an alternative set of actions. Power is of course understood in its widest sense, encompassing influence and authority, not simply the ability to coerce through violence, for example. Finer points out that 'authority is a source of power' (Finer, 1970:14). This discussion is important in the context of globalisation because the argument around the meaning and implications of globalisation is so often bound up with questions of who exercises power, over whom, and how, as evidenced in the title of George Monbiot's book *Captive State: the corporate takeover of Britain* (2000).

The discussion of globalisation is deeply political. It is concerned with governance, who governs and how. It is also economic: economics is about the production and distribution of resources – or wealth, especially given the vast sums of capital that are daily traded on foreign exchange markets, or the wealth of the largest companies. The United Nations reports that there are over 600,000 transnational corporations with 800,000 foreign affiliates; these made estimated sales of $15.7 trillion, and have total foreign assets of $21.1 trillion. The biggest transnational corporation by foreign assets, America's General Electric, had $141.1 billion of them in 1999 (UN Conference on Trade and Development 2001, World Investment Report, cited in Legrain, 2002:136). The distribution of wealth and power is central to globalisation. If extreme advocates of globalisation are correct, wealth and power are *outside the reach* of governments. Furthermore, matters like handling environmental impact are also outside the scope of government control, because markets, and consumers, will approve companies that behave in an environmentally responsible way, and punish those that do not by taking their custom elsewhere.

Rosenberg (2000) is sharply critical of globalisation theory in general and Giddens in particular. He accuses Giddens of underestimating the contemporary relevance of classical theory. In particular, Giddens's work contains an alarming tendency to marginalise both the human contribution and the impact on people of the processes he describes, whereas Marx and Weber consistently created paradigms that were human-centric. Giddens appears to credit globalisation with an extra-human dimension that indulges a sense of helplessness, anomie and impersonalisation. Rosenberg also attacks inconsistencies in Giddens' elevating the 'time-space distantiation' notion to a new social theory. Indeed, one might suggest that globalisation is far more prosaic: it brings a variety of problems and opportunities. A feature of globalisation is the emergence of significant new power elites, some institutional, some based in 'market forces', but all essentially enabled and nurtured by state government policy. The argument here is that states have acquiesced in the process of globalisation: this claim is developed in Chapter 11.

It is sometimes claimed that globalisation is actually Americanisation (see Discussion 9.3). In the sense that the globalisation project, as described here, is primarily US-driven, the claim is not entirely unjustified. It stems from America's overwhelming political and economic power. Strictly speaking it cannot be dissociated from US-corporate power; given that many large MNCs are indeed based in the US, the claim for Americanisation makes more sense than the hard-globalisation thesis which suggests corporations become de-located from states. US policy and the lobbying of corporate interests in America created market deregulation in the 1980s and 90s. Since the end of the Cold War the US has emerged not only as the only superpower, but also – more dangerously for some

---

Discussion 9.3

Globalisation as 'Americanisation'?

Where globalisation is narrowly defined in economic terms, the argument that globalisation is in fact Americanisation is sustainable, based on the claim that the US is a global hegemon, seeking to exert political power over its allies and others alike. The US neo-liberal agenda is intended to boost American interests and influence. This view, consistent with Gray (1998), may be interpreted as Americanisation. Nevertheless, Gray argues that it is destined to fail as the social consequences overwhelm the changes introduced in the name of liberalisation. Ultimately, there will be a counter-reaction, and a decline in US power.

A second view of Americanisation refers to fears that a process of cultural assimilation is occurring worldwide. This opinion holds that the impact of American symbols and icons, brands, corporations and lifestyle, is such that American interests accumulate unchallenged power. The US-dominated entertainments industry, the enormous wealth of US corporations, and the global spread of the English language are cited as evidence of a process of Americanisation. This argument is part of the 'we're all becoming the same' idea. However, following the arguments already presented in this chapter, this view of globalisation is actually about internationalisation, not globalisation. Seen in this light, it appears to exaggerate what is actually happening.

The USA is not all-powerful in business. Half of the world's top 500 multinational corporations are

Discussion 9.3 (*continued*)

actually *not* American. Japan has had a profound impact on management systems in the US as well as in Europe:

> In the management literature, especially in US business schools, Japanese methods of management are analysed and western firms are strongly recommended to adopt just-in-time stock control, consensus-seeking among groups of workers and managers, a longer-term corporate strategy and a more research-oriented use of human and financial resources (Strange, 1996:75).

The world's most popular sport, either in terms of participation or as a TV-indulged hobby, is football, a game which hardly registers in the USA. Cultural exchange crosses borders in all kinds of ways, many having nothing whatsoever to do with America: the popularity of Arabic and North African music in France stems from French colonial history and migration patterns – and is very much part of an internationalisation of culture. That London is a multi-ethnic world city with scores of different language communities is an example of trans-ethnic and international interaction, and is barely related to the USA. It is true that English is a global language but it belongs to no one. It is spoken by many communities of speakers and its spread has become functional, and by no means an expression of American cultural dominance.

The UN, the EU, OPEC, the WTO and ASEAN are significant multinational institutions which may have increasing global influence in the future. They may even become significant brakes on the expansion of American power. There is also an emergent international network of hundreds of **non-governmental organisations**. Many of these have global reach, such as Oxfam, Greenpeace or Amnesty International. None are remotely 'American'. The Internet, created by scientists employed by the US Pentagon, has long since outgrown its inventors. It is an international tool, like the English language, barely controllable and belonging to no one. The Roman Catholic Church, despite scandals and internal disputes, remains a highly influential supranational organisation. The growth in Islam is not part of a growing trend towards Americanisation: on the contrary, it may even be part of a counter-culture against American values.

Finally, there are other forces that have a thoroughly global dimension but are by no means illustrative of a trend towards Americanisation. The internationalisation of problems is an example of a worldwide phenomenon leading to raised consciousness. The field in which this is most apparent is the environment where both NGOs and UN-related organisations are key actors in the process. Goldmann (2001:26) refers to the 1972 Stockholm Conference on the Human Environment being a watershed for the introduction of environmental concerns into international law. It spawned the United Nations Environment Programme (UNEP), and was followed by the Brundtland Commission on sustainable development. Internationally brokered agreements on the ozone layer and the disposal of hazardous waste have been achieved and a number of other organisations are cited by Goldmann as having significant environmental interests, including the WTO, OECD, NATO and OSCE. The Stockholm Conference was also effective in putting the environment on the agenda of the EEC (Goldmann, ibid.). The point is that the significant inroads made by environmental agencies are part of internationalisation and yet are in many respects counter to US policy.

An example of a policy move that is counter to US trends is the case of SUVs – Sports Utility Vehicles, or 4-wheel drive trucks – in Europe. The Clinton Administration gave these two-tonne monsters tax breaks despite their having CO_2 emissions up to four times higher than conventional cars. The growth in sales of such vehicles in Europe in recent years might be taken as an example of 'Americanisation' – they have long been popular in the US with automakers and the public alike. However, Paris councillors, the Mayor of London, and the UK government's senior advisor on transport, have called for higher taxes on SUVs, and the French government plans a higher purchase tax to take account of their environmental impact and appalling safety record. The traffic, so to speak, is not all in one direction (Judd, 2004).

See also Key concept 10.2.

© Jacques Langevin/Corbis Sygma

Photograph 9.1 Where's the World Bank? A Cambodian villager stands on a boat on Tonle Sap Lake near the Phtout lake village.

observers – a 'hyperpower' (Hutton, 2002:352). US-led military engagements in the Persian Gulf in 1991 and Bosnia in 1994 bolstered the sense of US global power. The increasing cultural hegemony of the US film and entertainments industry throughout the Triad has added to the sense of American shaping of the global environment. The rhetoric emanating from US politicians post-9/11 also helps to sustain an image of the US as 'leader of the free world' – a point underlined by the US launching a war against Iraq with a small number of allies despite the absence of specific backing from the UN Security Council, in so doing cutting short UN-initiated weapons inspections. The sense, indeed, is one of a unipolar world, not the multipolar one promised by the end of the Cold War (Peterson, 1996).

A not untypical response to the question 'What is globalisation?' is that globalisation is the internationalisation of markets.

> We drive German cars, listen to Japanese hi-fis, eat French food, drink Colombian coffee, wear Italian clothes, buy Chinese toys, chat on Finnish mobile phones, work on computers made in Taiwan and use American software (Legrain, 2002:5).

This list shows consequences of globalisation but it tells us little about the nature of the political economy in an era of globalisation. Instead, it lists outcomes in certain areas of the world, mainly in the Triad and the NIEs in the Asia Pacific region. These consequences stem from internationalisation of markets, and of production. They indicate increased trade, and arguably are related to the economic project of globalisation as described above. Such material gains are evidence of prosperity, but the prosperity is dramatically uneven. There are colossal variations both between countries and within them. More importantly, one should attempt an understanding of globalisation that is more sophisticated than simply highlighting some outcomes for some consumers.

Finally, Gray presents an approach to globalisation that is firmly in the IPE tradition. In *False Dawn* he analyses the unfolding consequences of the globalisation project, but claims it is merely a phase in human development. Globalisation supporters have suggested that the global economy coincides with the 'end of history' and that markets now take care of human needs. For Gray, this assumption is another folly of the Enlightenment, convinced of the certainty of human improvement. Gray claims that the appalling conflicts of the twentieth century show that things deteriorated, and continue to do so, in part because of the invention of systems that we cannot control.

> Sovereign states today act in an environment so transformed by market forces that no institution – not even the largest transnational corporation or sovereign state – can master it. In this environment the most unmanageable forces spring from a torrent of technological innovations. It is the combination of this unceasing stream of new technologies, unfettered market competition and weak or fractured social institutions that produces the global economy of our times (Gray, 1998:76).

Indeed, things *can only get worse*. Gray describes globalisation as

> the worldwide spread of modern technologies of industrial production and communication of all kinds across frontiers – in trade, capital, production and information (Gray, 1998:55).

In a later book, *Straw Dogs*, he call globalisation 'the chaotic drift of new technologies' (Gray, 2002:175). He accompanies this with the claim that globalisation 'consumes modern values'. Globalisation is a complex and multifaceted phenomenon. It has a range of economic, political and social consequences, which are the subject of the next chapter. Here, we turn to the history and development of globalisation.

Review

What is globalisation?

What are some of the criticisms of globalisation, as suggested by Hirst and Thompson, for example?

What is power and how does it relate to discussions about globalisation?

Suggest some possible arguments against claiming that globalisation represents a social theory.

Is globalisation just 'Americanisation'?

What is Gray's view of globalisation?

● ● ● ● Globalisation as process

This section sketches a brief history of the background to globalisation and provides an explanation of the context of **multilateralism** – the approach to governance of the world economy that assumes a central role for states acting together, usually through international institutions. It is central to the final chapters of this book to address questions raised by the principle of multilateralism, to consider whether it can work for common benefit of all humanity, or whether, in fact, it does not work at all. It is important to understand the principle of multilateralism in order to more fully assess the implications of globalisation.

The claim that globalisation should be understood as a process stems from the view that its origins go back to when humans first put a boat into the sea and distant communities traded with each other. This section holds that the current phase of globalisation is part of the development of international trade, which of course has a long history (see Discussion 9.4). One might suggest that an ancient phase in the history of globalisation was characterised by the famous trading route known as the Silk Road that stretched from Cadiz in Southern Spain through Europe and across China to Shanghai on the Pacific Coast. It became established during the early Roman Empire and parts of it before then. There were other routes too, carrying trade in spices, cloth and artisan treasures between Europe and the Far East from 200BC. The Romans established trading routes throughout most of Central and Western Europe as well as North Africa. The middle ages saw another boom in trade, especially between Europe and Asia, one for which a link can be made to the age of empire building, the colonialist phase throughout the seventeenth, eighteenth and nineteenth centuries, during which international links were consolidated by political ties. Industrialisation post-1800 also boosted international trade and vice versa. As a proportion of GDP, international capital flows were as high in the late nineteenth century as they were in the 1980s, so globalisation is nothing new (Gray, 1998; Hirst & Thompson, 1999).

There are grounds for suggesting that the modern phase of globalisation began with the end of the Second World War. The evidence for this is that the United States emerged from the war stronger, while Europe and Japan lay in ruins. The United States was in a position to shape the development of the post-war economy, and did so, in ways which laid the basis for American hegemony over much of the globe. However, this project was based on multilateralist principles (Clark, 2001). American interests lay in setting up a liberal order under the framework established by the Bretton Woods Accords (see Chapter 1). But US policy was not focused only on its relationship to Western Europe, or even on the threat from the Soviet Union. Clark writes:

> Given the geography of the United States, and the lack of direct threats to its security, its objectives tend to be 'milieu goals', rather than national interests narrowly defined in response to direct threats to its territorial security (Clark, 2001:173).

Clark is writing before the September 11 terror assaults on the World Trade Center and the Pentagon – later we consider how this changed US policy. He continues:

Discussion 9.4

Globalisation as process

- 200BC–400AD The Silk Road – trade routes between Western Europe and the Roman Empire across the southern continent and into Asia, linking the entire Eurasian landmass. Trade encompassed Indian subcontinent, China, and Japan
- Roman Empire – AD50–410 Rome controlled most of Northern Britain, Western and Central Europe, the Mediterranean and North Africa
- 400–700 Dark Ages – retrenchment, decline in trade
- 700–1066 Viking expansion, growth in trade
- 1066 Norman Conquest

Medieval Europe – trade across the Holy Roman Empire

- 1750–1800 Industrialisation begins
  Age of Empire and colonialist expansion
- 1871–1914 Growth in international trade during *La Belle Epoque*

British Gold Standard keeps currencies stable and sustains international payments system

- 1914–18 First World War
- 1929 Wall Street Crash
- 1922–33 Fascism emerges across Europe
- 1933–45 Third Reich – rise of Nazi Germany
- 1939–45 Second World War
- 1944 Bretton Woods Conference
- 1947 GATT launched; OEEC created; IBRD and IMF created
- American Marshall Aid sponsors reconstruction of Western Europe; aid to Japan

- Post-war period multilateralist US foreign and economic policy
- 1949 NATO created
- 1951 ECSC launched
- 1960s GATT Kennedy Round
- 1971 US abandons Bretton Woods Accords – decline of multilateralism
- 1973 First OPEC oil price shock
- 1970s turbulence in international capital markets; rising unemployment; instability in currency markets; rising inflation and unemployment
- 1979 Second OPEC oil price shock
- 1979 EMS introduced
- Late 1980s liberalisation of financial and telecommunications markets in US and UK; privatisation of public utilities (gas, telephone, electricity, coal and water industries)
- 1989–91 Revolutions in Eastern Europe precipitate end of Cold War
- Sharp increase in international capital flows
- World Wide Web launched; massive increase in markets, especially in telecoms, technology and property sectors
- Asian Crisis from 1995; property values in freefall in Japan; Indonesia, world's fourth largest country, in turmoil
- 11 September 2001 – attacks on World Trade Center and Pentagon
- Chinese annual economic growth of around 9 per cent (9.9 per cent in first quarter of 2003 – compare US growth in late-1990s of around 2.9 per cent (Yueh, 2003).

The goal of creating a liberal and multilateral international order is the best expression of this set of American interests. 'Given its size, wealth, and geographical position between the two great oceans', is one such opinion, 'the United States inevitably has global commercial interests that are best served when barriers to trade are few and when economic relations among states are governed by law' (Mead, cited in Clark, ibid.).

From this perspective, then, the US view of multilateralism was to establish a world economic order spanning both oceans, and comprising Japan in the East and Europe in the West. Thus the reconstruction of both Japan and Europe was part of an American multilateralist objective. In Chapter 1, the trauma of

European history was explained as underlining the core rationale for European integration. For Japan, the history was no less calamitous and was equally formative in terms of the impact on Japanese reconstruction, and the Japanese willingness to be part of the post-war American multilateral world order.

Japan, which had been a virtually closed nation for 200 years, awoke from the Tokugawa Shogunate after 1853 and gradually resumed contact with the outside world, initially through a host of unequal trading agreements foisted upon the country by the USA. Eventually the Meiji Era 1868–1912 began a rapid industrialisation, culminating in the Japan–Russia war of 1904–5, in which Japan, with US support, was victorious. Japan had previously annexed Korea from Chinese control and its territorialist expansion mirrored that of empire-building European states during the nineteenth century.

After opposing Germany in the First World War, Japan felt aggrieved that it did not benefit much from the post-war settlement. Following the great Kanto Earthquake in 1923, and the inauguration of Emperor Hirohito three years later, Japan embarked on a period of nationalist aggression which led inexorably towards war. The Manchurian Incident sparked off a decade of conflict with China, culminating in the horror of the Nanking Massacre in 1937 (Chang, 1997). The appalling violence of the Japanese contribution to the Second World War, including the kamikaze attacks on Pearl Harbor in 1941 which brought the USA into the war, was ended only by the mechanised slaughter wrought against the country by the firebombing of its cities and the dropping of atomic bombs on Hiroshima and Nagasaki in August 1945.

This was the background to the American project post-1945; US policy was marked by a multilateralist approach central to Marshall Aid and to the reconstruction of Europe, as well as Japan.

> That multilateralism was chosen in 1945 was [. . .] a reflection of American preferences; that it could be implemented was a reflection of American power. For both these reasons, the history of post-1945 multilateralism became inextricably linked with American foreign and economic policy (Clark, 2001:176).

Clark points out the consistency between this account and that of hegemonic stability theory, examined in the previous chapter, referring to Gilpin (1987) and Keohane (1984).

The institutions established post-1945 would enable a more stable economic environment to prevail in the second half of the twentieth century. Japan and Germany and all of Western Europe thus became embedded within the capitalist economy that eventually would lead to the global domination of the Triad, the core of the so-called global economy 50 years later.

Political and economic integration followed through the establishment of international organisations ranging from the OECD and the G-7 to NATO and the EEC/EU, as well as the UN itself. All lent credibility to the notion of a multilateralist international order, even during the uncertain years of the Cold War. However, multilateralism was not especially regularly applied, nor consistently successful. GATT for example was not fully operational at the outset and the Bretton Woods Accords were unilaterally suspended by the US in 1971. Critics of multilateralism note its flaws, given the imbalances between a hegemon and its allies. Indeed, multilateralism can also be viewed as a way not simply to exert control over one's enemies, or potential sources of either political or economic instability, but also over one's allies. Clark cites an analogy that indicates that the end of the Cold War changed nothing:

> 'It is as if two horses were running round a track [and] one broke its leg, and the other kept on running anyway' (Cumings, cited in Clark, 2001:172).

He continues:

> The mistake too many have made is in assuming that the second horse was running *because* of the first. There is now a chorus of support for this broad outlook. [. . .] It insists that 'America's post-war grand strategic aims were essentially unconnected to the superpower rivalry' and thus survived intact at the Cold War's end (Layne, 1998:9). It picks up on the theme that multilateralism had more to do with America's strategy for dealing with its friends, than its strategy for dealing with its foes (Clark, 2001:172).

US policy continued in the post-Cold War period as one of containment (of foes) and hegemony (over allies). Nevertheless, as the Cold War ended Clark says there were ambiguities over US policy, as it sought greater burden-sharing from its allies. Critics of multilateralism attacked it from both sides, as nothing more than an instrument of US hegemony, or as 'the US not doing enough'.

With the collapse of the Soviet Union, the USA was left as the one remaining superpower, but US policy barely changed. Some predicted the emergence of a multipolar world (Peterson, 1996). Others have described the US as a 'hyperpower', dominating the latest phase in the history of globalisation (Hutton, 2002; Haseler, 2004). In 1991 the US led a transnational force against Iraq to evict Saddam Hussein from Kuwait, and then intervened in 1994 in Bosnia following the abject failure of the Europeans to sort out the chaos in their own backyard. These events are referred to again in Chapter 12, where it is argued that US policy *has now changed*, in particular since the terrorist attacks of 11 September 2001. It is argued that since 9/11, and possibly before, the US has abandoned multilateralism. This presents a new context, which is the focus of the final chapter.

However, while it is argued that US policy barely changed with the ending of the Cold War, globalisation entered a new phase, driven by the launch of the World Wide Web and dominated by dramatic improvements in information communications technology (ICT). For the industrial world, and for many beyond, no one could remain untouched by the development of a new phase of capitalism, which some called globalisation.

Amid the truly planet-wide complex of mutual dependencies and obligations, there has also emerged a global social, or, in marketing parlance, 'societal' aspect to globalisation. This new dimension is barely formalised, but it would appear to owe its existence to increased communications through technology, travel and mass tourism as well as better education. It is perhaps part of the cultural dynamic within globalisation, but has increasingly political consequences. It includes the grass-roots emergence of an international global justice movement.

This concentrates on raising awareness of humanitarian concerns, and emphasises the need for a growing understanding of responsibility for our planet. Even outside the formal campaign groups established to promote concerns of this kind, there is in general a much greater knowledge about environmental issues and obligations. This has given rise to World Summits in Rio de Janeiro, Kyoto and more recently Johannesburg. Such gatherings tend to produce vague commitments rather than truly enforceable limits, but nevertheless they indicate an increased awareness of mutual responsibilities. Nevertheless, it is hard to be particularly impressed by binding progress, universally applied and monitored, in these areas. Doubts about the effectiveness of such summits increased in 2001 when the US under George W. Bush refused to ratify the Kyoto commitment to reducing carbon emissions, then Japan and Australia added their concerns that Kyoto was not worth supporting if the US – the world's greatest polluter – was not going to commit to the process.

The prospect of failure of Kyoto contributed to the emergence of serious and violent protest against capitalism, and the G-8 in particular. Summits in Seattle, Washington, Gothenberg and Génova have all been marked by mass protest and civil disorder. Governments are going to have to find better ways to meet public concerns on issues such as debt, HIV-AIDS, environmental threats, and underdevelopment. Perhaps governments find it easier to negotiate in more familiar territory, such as the economic and the military spheres, the traditional domains of often bilateral and almost always intergovernmental negotiation. However, there are signs of a more multilateral approach in some forums, particularly the EU and the WTO, and the UN has always intended to be a multilateral organisation, although it is handicapped by the veto powers of the permanent members of the Security Council (Chomsky, 1992). This view is summarised below by Clark, citing Cox, in asking whether

> the UN could function as a world organisation if it came to be perceived as the instrument of its most powerful member (Cox, cited in Clark, 2001:177).

It may be that more institutional innovation is required in order to confront the problems of the new millennium. The potential for such innovation is examined in Chapter 11. Here it is sufficient to say that globalisation has contributed to increasing interest, much of it stemming from NGOs and reformists dissatisfied with what they perceive as the misuse of power by states. Goldmann writes of the 'internationalisation of problems' (Goldmann, 2001:26–32), a point beyond dispute. He argues for a similar internationalisation of the response, and reformists and many NGOs agree on the need to reach international solutions to global problems. The notion of global civil society is one which is beginning to generate serious and widespread debate, while multilateralism is likely to once more become a hallmark of international affairs.

On the other hand, Held (1995) argues that globalisation has instead provoked a retrenchment behind traditional nationalistic and ethnically rooted allegiances. It is in the nature of globalisation that it will provoke such widely differing and even conflicting responses. This, then, adds to the complexity of governance in the post-industrial, postmodern phase of globalisation.

Review   *Identify candidates for earlier phases in the development of globalisation.*
What is the significance of multilateralism to the development of globalisation?
What criticisms can be levelled at multilateralism?
Suggest an explanation for the view that globalisation is a process.

The EU response to globalisation

In Chapter 4 we saw how the project to create the Single European Market was in large measure driven by states. Various writers (Jones, 2001; Baun, 1996; Kapteyn, 1996; Bourke, 1996) have referred to the important role of multinational corporations in bringing about the Single European Market. The close involvement of corporations in EC policy making is well documented (Mazey & Richardson, 1993; Greenwood, 1997; Pedler & Van Schendelen, 1994). MNCs have engaged with the integration process and had significant impact on the EU response to pressures from the external trading environment, notably competition from the USA and Japan, as well as growing competitiveness throughout the Asia Pacific region, especially the emerging 'tiger economies'.

During the 1980s European productivity was growing less rapidly than its Triad rivals. The SEM, and eventually EMU, was a response. Moravcsik (1999) and Milward (2000) describe how EC governments pursued policies that actively promoted internationalisation, albeit for Milward in order to maintain a modern welfare state, while for Moravcsik to promote commercial interests. The process of European integration has been driven by states, and steps towards integration only occur when they coincide with national interest. Moravcsik argues that the entire Single European Market project has been driven by intergovernmental bargaining in which state representatives pursue their individual goals. Governments have discovered that cooperation and integration best serve their purposes, although Goldmann (2001) adds that 'spillover' is significant in producing unintended or even unforeseen consequences. Spillover theory argues that policy in one area necessitates and inspires policy in another area, thus nourishing the integration process, but the role of the state is still paramount in the European Union (see Chapters 4 and 5). The Treaty of Nice reaffirms the role of states and the intergovernmental aspects of the EU policy process, although it shifts the balance of power in the Council towards the larger members.

This section looks at the wider context of how the EU has responded to changes in global capitalism, especially in relation to SEM initiatives, such as the liberalisation of telecommunications and capital markets. The key point is that the European Union has set out from the mid-1980s to engage further with global markets and to remain competitive. The removal of restrictions on capital movement, for example, facilitated cross-border mergers and acquisitions as well as joint ventures which have enabled significant economies of scale, especially in terms of research and development. Several industries with long lead-times and high development costs could only remain competitive through significant rationalisation, pooling of resources, technology sharing and joint ventures. The Eurofighter aircraft, the European Space Agency, satellite technology, Airbus Industries, the automotive and pharmaceuticals sectors, as well as air transport – in 2004 KLM and Air France merged their operations – have all shown high levels of intra-SEM collaboration. The stimulus came in the 1980s. The Cecchini Report released in 1988, building on the White Paper prepared by the UK Commissioner Lord Cockfield in 1985, identified impediments to the effective workings of the Single European Market, and set a date for SEM completion by the end of 1992. The report utilised a survey of over 11,000 companies and estimated that the effective completion of the SEM would provide a boost to growth in the region of 5 per cent.

As the SEM was created, a further dramatic project was emerging from the Maastricht summit in 1992: Economic and Monetary Union (EMU). The Single Currency would begin in 1999 with notes and coins launched three years later. The motives for EMU were similar to those for the SEM. It was predicted that EMU would provide cost savings and a boost to growth, as well as a fundamental and logical step in the completion of the Single Market, while at the same time there were powerful counter-arguments. On both sides of the euro debate the arguments are probably overstated. The euro is a formidable political symbol, representing the singular success of European integration. This fact alone would seem to be sufficient to convince eurosceptics that the euro is undesirable, while for those of a more federalist persuasion, it is something to celebrate. At root, and from the perspective of multinational corporations operating in many different markets, the Single Currency is a logical development and EMU does indeed offer a framework that is more predictable and less costly, thus aiding strategic planning as well as day-to-day operations management.

Although EMU has had the backing of corporate Europe, and corporate America and Japan too, Tsoukalis (2000), and others such as Jones (2001) and Baun (1996), emphasise that the drive towards EMU was primarily a political project partly in response to German reunification. Tsoukalis sounds a sceptical note, referring to the extent to which the negotiations leading up to the launch of the EMU project at Maastricht were detailed in some respects such as the economic convergence criteria, but deliberately vague in other respects, such as the extent of political influence on the independent ECB. Tsoukalis complains that much was left for future decision – a not untypical strategy where policy innovation is concerned in the EU. Furthermore, he warns that while the EU is nowhere near an optimal currency area, the question of how the ECB would handle an economic slump or a shock in a participating economy is unanswered. There is no exit strategy: in 1997 the former leader of the British Conservative Party, William Hague, memorably described EMU as 'a burning building with no exits'. Nevertheless, Tsoukalis accepts that 'if EMU is successful, it will most likely bring with it a much stronger and more integrated EU, in both economic and political terms' (Tsoukalis, 2000:177). In the context of globalisation, that is an important hope, especially if one believes that for globalisation to be successful, it requires a counterweight to US domination. Discussion 9.5 summarises common arguments for and against EMU.

Discussion 9.5

For and against Economic and Monetary Union

Arguments for EMU include:

- Boost to intra-EU trade
- Reduced transaction costs
- Price transparency
- End to hedging (fixing a higher price to allow for possible currency fluctuations)
- Increased currency stability
- Stable and low interest rates, and low inflation
- Logical step towards completion of SEM
- Boost to political integration and global influence of EU

Arguments against EMU include:

- The SEM is not an optimal currency area
- A 'one size fits all' interest rate is a recipe for instability
- Giving monetary powers to an ECB is an unacceptable loss of national sovereignty
- Inflation, interest and exchange rates can just as effectively be managed by national authorities
- Lack of public support

- A single currency without a single political community is a recipe for chaos
- There is no 'exit strategy' and the single currency is a risk too far
- Economic union is inevitably a precursor to political union, which is not wanted

Other arguments have also been suggested, especially in the UK. Pro-euro enthusiasts have argued that London's status as a financial and share trading capital would be undermined by remaining outside the eurozone. So far there is little evidence of this happening. Pro-euro campaigners also argue that inward investment will fall, but there is little evidence of this either (see Discussion 11.4). On the anti-euro side, campaigners have emphasised threats to sovereignty. It is claimed that Britain would lose the right to have the Queen on its banknotes, and even that the monarchy itself would be threatened. See also discussion on euroscepticism and Key concept 3.2 in Chapter 3.

There is another dimension to the EMU project that should be highlighted. Hutton (2002) reports that in 1999 the US dollar 'accounted for 77 per cent of all international loans and 83 per cent of all foreign exchange transactions' (Hutton, 2002:199). This meant that 'the international finance system had been shaped to extend US financial and political power, not to promote the world public good' (ibid.). The advent of the euro was also designed to create a potential rival to the dollar, and four years later Monbiot (2003) reported that there were signs of this happening. He suggested that the emergence of a euro-denominated market for oil could have major repercussions for the relative strength of the dollar and the fledgling European currency. Once the euro is established in this key market it is more likely to become a significant reserve currency, a factor which would certainly affect the euro/dollar relationship in financial markets.

For some, the European integration process is part of the 'problem' of globalisation. For others, it is part of the solution. Wallace and Wallace (2000) claim that the EU has acted as both a shelter from, and accelerator of, global processes. Christiansen (2001:511) summarises the global context of European integration from both perspectives. On the one hand, the EU offers opportunities for globalisation to flourish through its single market and its support of a liberal trade environment. This especially suits multinational corporations which benefit from improved access to key markets. The result is that wealth becomes concentrated in those markets. States, under pressure from MNCs, reduce their commitment to welfare, pursuing instead maximum efficiency and price stability. Both the Single Market Programme that led to the SEM in 1992, and the austerity measures required to meet the TEU convergence criteria prior to EMU forced governments to apply downward pressure on public spending.

> Supranational institutions have little to put in place instead and the trend is towards an unevenly regulated market place (Christiansen, ibid.).

It follows that European integration is creating a supranational legal order designed to meet the needs of economic integration. It is therefore 'not the result of an explicit programme of political integration' (ibid.). Anti-globalists therefore criticise the EU for meeting the wish-list of private corporate interests while neglecting democratic, political control. The accusation is that the EU has failed to set up adequate tools for the regulation of markets. In addition, its decision-making lacks transparency and is overly complex. Issues of transnational governance are not adequately debated. Christiansen says that those who want to see more political responses to these problems are faced with a dilemma:

> A more efficient EU, better able to respond to the challenges of globalisation, is likely to be more centralised and even less responsive to the preferences of citizens and elected governments. Yet the 're-nationalisation' of economic policy-making, where voters could directly register their influence, risks to reduce the effectiveness of political authority over internationalised markets still further (Christiansen, 2001:511)

The EU may attempt to create social policies and extend citizens' rights but such measures are secondary to the greater aim of market liberalisation. This has been achieved to a remarkable extent in the EU: capital mobility and market access are hardly any less than in a state. Businesses and the public sector are as a result exposed to powerful competitive pressures.

Furthermore, the EU has reduced the extent to which individual states may act unilaterally. Switzerland and Norway remain outside the EU precisely in defence of their perceived sovereign interests. Similarly, the UK, Denmark and Sweden have opted out of EMU, fearing that the Single Currency represents one more narrowing of options in respect of economic and fiscal policy. EMU, and European integration, is seen not as part of the solution to problems caused by globalisation, but part of the problem.

Christiansen summarises the counter position: that European integration should be regarded as a protection against globalisation. Advocates of greater integration see the EU as being a forum for debate as well as a policy maker on the implications of globalisation. They believe that essentially the EU provides states with a multilateral mechanism to confront the challenges of globalisation. It offers an institutional response to the process of economic liberalisation that states acting alone are unable to provide. Furthermore, though it is not uniformly developed across all policy areas, the EU provides a supranational polity that can respond to the pressures exerted by global forces.

Its development may have been led by the market, but eventually an effective legal order, a system of political rights and duties, and a political community have been established. Both states and firms are now subject to rules and regulations that go much further than anything which is available at the global scale. Indeed, global environmental and social regulation receives much impetus from the political consensus among the EU member states (Christiansen, 2001:512).

Indeed, this process has generated political debate that goes far beyond Brussels and engages the wider public at a state and sub-state (regional) level. Ultimately as Woods (2001) argues, the transnational market is regulated by the collaboration of supranational institutions and national governments. There is a growth in 'supranational polity'. The EU is a prime example of this, where Brussels is a centre of information and opinion exchange between policy makers, industrialists, NGOs, lobbyists and a wide assortment of public and private interest groups from around the world. See Discussion 9.6.

Discussion 9.6

The EU response to globalisation

Christiansen (2001) presents two perspectives on the EU relationship to globalisation. The first is the view that the EU is an integral and contributory dimension to process of economic globalisation. The main arguments are as follows:

- The SEM was created at the behest of multinational corporations
- MNCs are the major beneficiaries of the Single Market
- Power is concentrated in central regions
- The EU pursues policies of economic integration to boost markets and market efficiency
- EMU and the Single Currency are central to this process
- EU legal order is based on economic imperatives, not political ones
- Environmental, social and citizenship rights are secondary and piecemeal
- Market liberalisation has remained the core of the European integration process
- The EU lacks transparency, is overly complex and undemocratic

An opposite perspective holds that the EU is a counter-force to globalisation. The main points of this argument are as follows:

- European integration allows individual states to have powerful representation in multilateral forums where they can therefore have real influence and genuinely participate in decision-making, often in relation to matters central to the globalisation debate
- The EU provides a regulatory framework to mitigate the more damaging consequences of economic liberalisation
- The EU can and does exercise control at a supranational level
- The EU is a rule-based system that obliges third parties, both private and public, to meet its agreed environmental and social standards, as well as rules regarding international trade
- The EU is a counterweight to US power in the international environment
- In multilateral negotiations the EU has permitted representatives from individual member states to present their opinions, thus significantly enhancing their influence in international trade and other matters
- The EU has established, though not uniformly, a political community

It is clear that the two great federating initiatives of the past twenty years, the SEM and EMU, have not only had the support of multinational corporations, but are indeed significant responses to and contributions to the process of globalisation. Now the European Union finds itself still adjusting to EMU, and also wrestling with the challenge of the 2004 enlargement. The constitutional and institutional settlement of the Union is by no means complete. It is for this reason that the Union is still regarded as a 'work in progress'. It is in transition – accommodating its own major initiatives of recent years, and simultaneously adapting to changed circumstances in the international environment. Among the latter, two phenomena stand out. First globalisation itself and second, the terror attacks of 11 September 2001.

European integration offers the opportunity to assuage the worst impacts of a globalising world and in particular gives European states the forum they require in order to respond to global competition, environmental and social pressures, and the more unfettered capitalist instincts of the US. Certainly the SEM was established on the basis of economic imperatives, but the EU has developed a supranational polity able to provide an effective legal order, a system of political rights and duties, and a political community. In addition, as Christiansen points out, the integration process provides a counterweight to the economic interests of the US, the remaining superpower. It is hard to see how individual states acting alone would counter pressures for market access from US companies supported by the US government. The EU regularly resists such demands, often in areas associated with environmental protection, health and safety standards and labour regulations (Christiansen, 2001:512). Schlosser (2001) reports on the 'Europe days' in the US's largest meat processing company, IBD, where the workers welcome the days when they are producing meat for the EU because the line speeds are slowed down resulting in fewer injuries to the unfortunate workers. The normal speed is 400 head of cattle per hour passing through on their way to becoming pre-packed hamburgers. On 'Europe days' the throughput is half that.

The EU offers a forum for its members to express their views from inside a large and powerful economic block, as well as a paramount political entity in various international forums, particularly the WTO. It is unlikely that small and medium-sized states would achieve as much by acting alone, whereas in concert with others their views can be heard. To the extent that the EU represents a political community, one may point to its profile and influence as a significant benefit for its member states in the context of globalisation.

The EU has also provided leadership in matters relating to the environment, demanding higher levels of protection through lower emissions of carbon gases than the US is prepared to accept, as the Kyoto World Summit in 1997 demonstrated (Satoh, 1998:7). The US subsequently reneged on the Kyoto deal, but there is still hope that all other signatories will abide by it and meet the targets it lays down for reducing carbon emissions, modest though they are. Despite, or perhaps because of its rejection of Kyoto, the pressure remains on the US to respond to its environmental responsibilities. Bridges reports an acceptance.

that some environmental problems, such as the phenomenon of 'global warming', are so immense and so impossible for any one country, or even small groups of countries, to tackle that a concerted, synergistic approach by all governments is required (Bridges, 1999:179).

Bridges reports that the EU has engaged in a highly developed dialogue on environmental questions with Japan, following the 1991 EC–Japan Joint Declaration. This has led to joint research on protection of tropical forests, acid rain and global warming. Similar dialogues have since been established with China and South Korea.

Bridges describes some of the sensitivities regarding the tendency on the part of the EU, and European nation states acting bilaterally, to link aid and development projects in Asia with environmental issues (Bridges, 1999:80–81). However, he reports considerable improvements in the extent of European and Asian bilateral and multilateral contacts since the end of the Cold War, as political dialogue has developed (Bridges, 1999:180).

One of the most significant characteristics of the globalisation project, indeed a mantra for those sympathetic to the process, is its association with so-called free trade. In several sectors including steel, aeronautical engineering, aviation and intellectual property, and for a variety of reasons, the EU and the US have regularly risked trade wars between them while maintaining subsidies to domestic producers or even erecting trade barriers. Critics are right to point out the extent to which the US and the EU, using their immense power inside the WTO, have been able to distort the free trade ideal by engaging in systematic and long-term protectionism.

The most spectacular hypocrisy pertains in the agricultural sector. The EU has selectively disregarded principles of free trade to defend its agricultural and agrochemical sectors. At the heart of this convenience is the ongoing anomaly of the Common Agricultural Policy, a system of subsidies to farm production, guaranteeing incomes and maintaining prices above world levels. When the European Economic Community was established, the US tolerated the emergence of the CAP as a price worth paying since without it, it is unlikely that the political impetus towards European integration would have been as strong. CAP was successful to the extent that it made Europe self-sufficient, but ultimately it created surpluses that would be dumped on world markets, depressing developing countries' exports and distorting world prices. CAP offers a powerful example of the rejection of free market principles, so comprehensively does it defend and promote the interests of European farmers. While recent reforms have hinted at decoupling subsidies from production, they do not go far enough, or quickly enough. Rieger (2000:179–80) describes the CAP regime as 'a planned economy [. . .] a highly segmented system of governance [. . .] operating through both national and supranational mechanisms'.

Baldwin et al. report the failure of the Seattle WTO meeting at which agriculture was a major barrier to an agreement.

> The EU came under continued heavy fire from the Cairns Group (of agricultural exporters) on [. . .] the CAP. Agriculture had dominated the Uruguay Round but

refused to go away even after negotiations were complete. The EU and the US were still at loggerheads, and both defended their positions on agriculture aggressively. The EU insisted that it had transformed the CAP considerably since the MacSharry Reforms of 1992. The US usually retorted that the Union's refusal to commit itself to the elimination of trade distorting farm support was holding up reform elsewhere. Into this cauldron, several years later, came the US Farm Bill of 2002, which reversed the prevailing US policy direction and sharply increased support for American farmers (Baldwin et al., 2003:37).

The rhetoric of free trade does not match the reality of EU and US agriculture policy. It is also significant how agriculture demonstrates that state governments dictate policy and are quite capable of defending their interests against free market competition. Equally the EU can and does resist US policy preferences in the WTO: it has held out against accepting US exports of genetically modified foods and beef produced with the aid of growth-enhancing hormones.

In conclusion, the EU response to globalisation has been driven by economic imperatives, but there has also been a powerful dynamic towards the creation of a political community that may better respond to some of the major challenges presented by global capitalism. The European integration process is a significant response to the increased powers of 'markets' at the expense of traditional state authorities.

Chapter 12 has more on the EU response to globalisation, especially in the context of the fall-out from September 11.

Review   *How has the European Union responded to globalisation?*
What arguments are there to support the view that the EU response has been inadequate?
What counter-views are there which suggest that the EU has in fact been able to respond positively to globalisation?
Which opinion do you think is nearest to the truth?

Summary

This chapter has made the following key points.

What is globalisation?

- Giddens's definition is commonly found in the literature: 'The intensification of worldwide social relations which link distant localities in such a way that local happenings are shaped by events occurring many miles away and vice versa' (Giddens, 1990:64).
- *Economic* globalisation is a US-driven political project to promote a neo-liberal global economy.

- Globalisation is primarily driven by economic imperatives; it assumes the emergence of transnational corporations; it privileges the role of private businesses in free markets, identifying and responding to consumer needs.
- The notion of globalisation is contested, especially on the grounds that it is neither unprecedented, nor global, but also because it risks serious social and political upheaval.

The process of globalisation

- Globalisation is best understood in the context of the history of trade; it is one of a series of stages in human development, somewhat arbitrarily identified as ancient (200BC–AD400), medieval (1400–1700), colonial (1750–1945), industrial (1800–1950), modern (1945–90), postmodern (1990–present).
- The claim that globalisation is simply Americanisation is questionable. In many respects US business is not dominant, but the US remains a major political and economic power. It is unlikely that the US can continue to act with impunity in international affairs, as multilateralism remains an essential *modus operandi* for the international environment.

The EU and the response to globalisation

- The EU has pursued policies that are both a response to globalisation and a stimulus to it. In particular the advent of the Single European Market and the liberalisation of intra-EU trade has both facilitated characteristic features of globalisation and assisted the global competitiveness of European industry.
- The EU has also sought to achieve political consensus and the creation of supranational institutions that can attempt to ameliorate some of the adverse consequences of globalisation.
- The EU is seen by some as an integral part of the globalisation process, especially on the grounds that its core function is to liberalise trade within the SEM; EMU is also an expression of the EU's acceding to the pressures to establish a global economy.
- An opposite view is that the EU provides a multilateral framework that can respond to globalisation and limit negative consequences; the EU provides a forum for reaching agreement on important political issues; it has a significant body of legislation providing social and environmental guarantees; it is a counterweight to US power.
- The EU Common Agricultural Policy uses approximately half of its total budget. The CAP is a market-distorting protectionist regime that provides guaranteed incomes for many of its farmers at the expense of others, often the smaller, weaker ones. More damagingly, CAP has created subsidised surpluses that damage exports from developing countries; the EU has dumped the surpluses on world markets with dire consequences for farmers in LDCs.

Key concepts: discussion and other definitions

> ## Key concept 9.1   Globalisation
>
> The process of increasing interconnectedness between societies such that events in one part of the world more and more have effects on peoples and societies far away (Baylis & Smith, 2001:7).

The emergence of the word globalisation into popular discourse has been driven by the ascendancy of the neo-liberal political economy emanating from what is often questionably referred to as the Anglo-Saxon world. Reagan and Thatcher introduced policy changes in the 1980s, effectively deregulating the financial and telecommunications sectors. These changes resulted in an explosion of capital movement, while they also coincided with unprecedented ICT innovation, especially following the launch of the World Wide Web in 1990.

This book also argues that after 1945 significant international institutions were established which have been key players in the progress of globalisation. The Bretton Woods Accords (1944) established an economic framework which aimed to facilitate stability in world markets, even while the US pumped millions of dollars into Western Europe through Marshall Aid, and simultaneously financed the reconstruction of Japan. The institutions created at Bretton Woods provided the framework for the development of post-war capitalism, while the reconstruction of the European and Japanese economies was vital to establishing trading partners to the US, and political partners in the emerging Cold War. US policy provided the foundations for the current phase of globalisation.

The definition above, similar to others from Giddens (1990) and Held (1995) cited at the beginning of the chapter, is the kind of definition that critics such as Goldmann, and Hirst and Thompson, object to on the grounds that it overstates the globality of trends in the international economy. In fact, the processes said to constitute globalisation are concentrated among OECD countries in the northern hemisphere. Indeed, it is hard to accept the notion of the world being a 'single place' in economic or social terms. Bauman (1998) argues that globalisation excludes to a far greater extent than it includes, and uses the metaphor of 'tourists' and 'vagabonds' to represent those who benefit from globalisation, and those for whom the benefits remain completely out of reach (see next chapter).

Another critical take on the concept interprets it as essentially a modern form of colonialism:

> Globalisation is what we in the Third World have for several centuries called colonization (Khor, 1995, quoted in Baylis & Smith, 2001:15).

This is unsurprising, since the pressures to accept the arguments in favour of the economic project of globalisation, including the ascendancy of markets, comes primarily from the West, even allowing for the curiously common habit of appropriating Asia Pacific, and Japan in particular, into 'the West'. The claim is based on the not unreasonable observation that it is companies that drive globalisation and the majority of these are Western, or at least Triad-based. On the other hand, others argue that multinational corporations bring employment, raise living standards and provide spin-off benefits in terms of infrastructure and education to developing countries (Legrain, 2002; Micklethwait and Wooldridge, 2000).

Business, and marketing in particular, tends to adopt a narrow interpretation of what globalisation means:

> Globalisation is the successful attempt by companies to sell the same product or service simultaneously in many different markets around the world (Hindle, 2000:106).

Even from a business perspective, this is surely a gross oversimplification. Most businesses tailor their activities to specific markets and only very few products are in fact the same in all markets. A brand may have a uniform identity, but within brands lie considerable degrees of product adaptation to the distinctive demands of different markets.

Here's another definition:

> A social process in which the constraints of geography on economic, political, social and cultural arrangements recede, in which people become increasingly aware that they are receding and in which people act accordingly (Waters, 2001:5).

This is a variation on Giddens's definition above, and has the merit of not proclaiming much beyond the decline in geographical constraints for (some) people. There is an implication here, at least, that not everyone is affected equally. However, one would have to admit that the definitions discussed so far are somewhat tame and neutral. Caroline Lucas, Member of the European Parliament and leader of the Green Party in the UK, offers a more polemical definition:

> [Globalisation is] 1. The process by which governments give away the rights of their citizens in favour of speculative investors and transnational corporations. 2. The erosion of wages, social welfare standards and environmental regulations for the sake of international trade. 3. The imposition worldwide of a consumer monoculture. Widely but falsely believed to be irrevocable. See also financial meltdown, casino economy, Third World Debt and race to the bottom (Lucas, 2000).

Lucas combines her definition with perceived consequences and presents a critique of globalisation. The first sentence above echoes the thesis put forward by Strange (1996), while the second matches Gray (1998), and her third, claiming that globalisation imposes a worldwide monoculture, is similar to views expressed in Monbiot (2000). These and other listed consequences are rejected by writers such as Legrain (2002) and Micklethwait and Wooldridge (2000); see Chapter 10.

Key concept 9.2   Power

Power is 'the capacity to achieve desired results' (Finer, 1970:12–13).

The ability to make people (or things) do what they would not otherwise have done (McLean & McMillan, 2003:431).

McLean and McMillan claim that power is often classified into five principal forms: force, persuasion, authority, coercion and manipulation, but that only the final two are uncontroversially forms of power.

Power, therefore, is the ability to affect outcomes according to one's preferences. In the political context, power is understood in its widest sense, embracing influence as well as authority. In some instances power may include the threat or use of force, or the potential to use force. In other instances, a power may be based on economic or cultural strength, rather than military strength. The former Soviet Union was first and foremost a military power; from 1952 for over 30 years Japan developed as a global economic power, not as a military power, since its military freedom of action was sharply limited by the Japanese constitution.

Power is linked to, and backed by, authority, which is often referred to as 'legitimate power' (McLean & McMillan, 2003:433). The state has the authority to enforce the law of the land, and this authority is broadly recognised and accepted by a sufficiently large number of the population to be effective and uncontroversial. Such authority deems it to be, for example, a civic responsibility to pay taxes. If anyone refuses to pay taxes, or evades them, the state authorities may invoke sanctions such as seizure of property, fines or imprisonment.

Influence is a powerful tool in political contexts and can be overt, as in the influence that the US has in international diplomacy, or subtle, as might be the influence of a small state over larger ones in a transnational institution such as the European Union. An example might be the extent of Swedish influence over other member states in respect of environmental protection, where Sweden might press for more stringent standards on harmful emissions to the atmosphere.

Power is the ability of a person or group of persons so to affect outcomes that their preferences take precedence over the preferences of others (Strange, 1996:17).

Strange stresses that power is dependent on how those exercising it perceive their interests, and different groups have very different perceptions of what they consider to be in their interests. Strange is writing from the perspective of seeing power as being highly dispersed in the globalising political economy.

Mansbach refers to the psychological aspect of power:

> A psychological relationship in which one actor influences another to behave differently than it would have if left to its own devices (Mansbach, 2000:545).

Mansbach stresses that power is intangible and cannot, for example, simply be equated with military strength. It would be wrong to assume that having nuclear weapons for example necessarily leads to achieving one's objectives in international affairs. The United States, for all its military might, could not achieve what it wanted in Vietnam.

A further dimension to power is in the contrasting notions of **hard power** (military might, and associated with unilateralism) and **soft power** (moral authority, trading influence, ability to persuade – characterised by multilateralism). See also Key concept 12.3, Soft power.

Further reading

Baylis, J. & **Smith**, S. (eds) (2001), *The Globalization of World Politics*, Oxford: OUP. This is an edited collection of essays on many aspects of globalisation. It is a brilliant collection of essays on wide-ranging themes, perfect for dipping into. Two chapters in particular relate to the ground covered in this chapter: Chapter 1, by Scholte, J.A., 'The globalisation of world politics' for a good introduction to the subject, and Chapter 23, Christiansen, T. 'European and regional integration'.

The next two books are well-known classics in arguing the case against globalisation. The first is a simple introduction to core issues. It is published by the campaigning magazine, *New Internationalist*.

Ellwood, W. (2001), *The No-Nonsense Guide to Globalization*, London: New Internationalist. This is probably the simplest critical introduction to the whole idea of the globalisation project. A very short book, it is perfect for a quick grasp of the commonest arguments against globalisation.

Klein, N. (2001), *No Logo*, London: Flamingo. A more detailed book, this is an uncompromising assault on the power of global brands, including criticism of employment practices and marketing by various household names. *No Logo* has become a standard-bearer for the No Global movement, although many of its central claims remain heavily contested. Klein calls for governments to respond to the march of globalisation and to confront the power of large corporate interests and their global selling strategies.

Every case demands an opposite view; see Chapter 10 for titles by Micklethwait & Wooldridge, and Legrain.

The next two books appear to accept the inevitability of globalisation but take issue with its present form and direction. Gray presents a fierce denunciation of the neo-liberal political project driven by the US. Given the overwhelming power of the US his book is hardly optimistic. Hutton on the other hand appears to argue that there is a ready alternative to the US-preferred model.

Gray, J. (1998), *False Dawn: the Delusions of Global Capitalism*, London: Granta. A powerful critique of the US inspired neo-liberal political project to extend free market capitalism across the globe. Gray writes with impeccable style and provides a wealth of evidence to support his core thesis. *False Dawn* is a great polemic and a powerful tract against the neo-liberal orthodoxy emanating from Washington, and supported to a considerable extent elsewhere among G-8 countries.

Hutton, W. (2002), *The World We're In*, London: Little, Brown. Will Hutton, like Gray, develops a stinging critique of current US policy, before mounting an impassioned defence of the European social welfare model. The weakness of the book is in part its title: it's much less about the world than it is about the US and the EU, but also in its somewhat rose-tinted view of the success of the EU. Hutton's arguments, though they are seductive, are perhaps weakened by an underestimation of Europe's own deep-seated economic and social problems. Compared with Gray, Hutton is an optimist.

Tsoukalis, L. (2000), 'Economic and Monetary Union', in Wallace, H. & Wallace, W. (eds), *Policy Making in the European Union*, Oxford: OUP, Chapter 6, pp. 149–78. This is a single chapter account of the implications of EMU. Tsoukalis provides a critical background to the introduction of the euro and argues that the measure was primarily political and elite-driven. EMU leaves many questions unanswered, in particular how it will manage divergent economies and how the ECB, the independent agency tasked with managing the single currency, will handle any coming crisis.

Film suggestions

Krzysztof Kieslowski, *Dekalog 10: 'Thou shalt not covet thy neighbour's goods'*, 1998, Poland

Kieslowski made a series of short films based on the Ten Commandments. A central tenet of capitalism is the ownership of private property. Modern consumer culture requires individuals' commitment to material values. This leads to value itself being ascribed to ownership, to possession. This is readily observable, especially in rich, contemporary capitalist countries. Marketing has become the core management function, being the range of activities that contribute to creating the Attractiveness of products and services, the Interest of consumers, the Desire of consumers to own the product and the Action from consumers in buying the product (AIDA). From this one might draw the conclusion that for most consumers, the progress of globalisation is desirable. This film is a parody on acquisitiveness. *Dekalog 10* is a black comedy on the potentially destructive consequences of the materialist value of ownership.

> Two brothers [. . .] discover a stamp collection in their dead father's flat. As the collection's significance (and value) dawns on them, they are forced to turn the flat into a mini Fort Knox, replete with security systems, Rottweilers and window bars. But are they guards or prisoners? (Hammond, 2003:296).

The brothers' new-found acquisitiveness – they need a further stamp to make their collection even more valuable – plays havoc with their judgement, their relationship and their daily lives. Their situation is not so distant from that of the 'golden ghettos' of many rich neighbourhoods, anxious and remote from the outside world. Some essence of humanity is perhaps distorted by wealth, especially when conspicuous wealth co-exists with conspicuous poverty.

Michael Busse/Marie Rosa Bobbi, *Storming the Summit – The Bloody Days of Genoa*, 2002, Germany/Italy

This is a short film about the violence surrounding the G-8 Summit in July 2001, when 300,000 protesters descended on the summit, demanding changes to the direction of globalisation. To control the crowd 20,000 Italian police were called in, attacking protesters while various hooligans from England, Germany and other countries went on the rampage through the city, destroying property and lighting fires.

The film is obtainable from German United Distributors, Programmvertrieb GmbH, Richarzstr. 6-8a, D-50667 Koln. Email: Bettina.oebel@germanunited.com

Chapter 10

Globalisation and its consequences

Overview

- Postmodernism
- Gray and the challenge to the Enlightenment
- The consequences of globalisation
- Future perfect? In defence of globalisation

Key concepts

10.1 Postmodernism

10.2 Culture

Introduction

This chapter examines the consequences of globalisation, but it begins with a further exercise in contextualisation. Briefly, major historical periods may, with the obvious caveat that these are simplified frameworks, be delineated as shown in Discussion 10.1 – with the contemporary phase of globalisation coinciding with the current postmodern period. Therefore we begin the chapter with a brief overview of postmodernism.

This contextualising of globalisation is continued by relating it to the Enlightenment, which was referred to in Chapter 1. John Gray, as we have seen, criticises the legacies of the **Enlightenment**, in particular the conviction that humankind is able to employ rationality and science to achieve ever improved material well-being, as well as what he sees as the political project of globalisation. Gray condemns this as a continuation of the false claims or myths of the Enlightenment tradition. His argument is summarised in the second part of this chapter.

The third section presents different perspectives concerning the political, social and cultural consequences of globalisation. Mostly they are critical, but not exclusively so. In fact the final section is largely a defence of globalisation highlighting in particular the benefits in terms of individual freedoms, improved choice and the opportunities for better living standards, not only in developed countries but also in the Third World.

> **Discussion 10.1**
>
> ## Epochs
>
> 1600–1789 Pre-industrial – **Feudalism**: society governed by monarchy, aristocracy and the church
>
> 1700–1850 – **The Enlightenment** – an intellectual counter-culture; reformist; celebrates man's potential, science and learning; challenge to *l'ancien régime.*
>
> 1800–1900 – **Industrial Revolution** – Age of Empire
>
> 1900–1950 – **Modern industrial** period – characterised by Fordism, classical 'scientific management' theories (Taylor); bureaucratic management (Weber); behaviourism (Mayo, Fayol).
>
> 1950–1990 – **Late-modern** – post-Fordism; growth of small business culture (SMEs); growing service sector; ideological struggle between Marxism and liberal democracy – Cold War
>
> 1990 onwards **Post-industrial, postmodernism** – advance of ICT; challenge to established grand theories, such as Marxism and liberalism – 'end of ideology' (Fukuyama, 1992). Growth of service sector, especially retail and leisure, financial and professional services.

● ● ● ● Postmodernism

Postmodernism is generally understood as a movement in literature and the visual arts, including architecture. However, the term postmodernity is also used, specifically as a social theory and referring chronologically to the postmodern, post-industrial context. There is much cross-over between the two terms, as postmodern culture is understood to have superseded modern culture. A striking example of the postmodern in architecture is Frank Gehry's Guggenheim Museum in Bilbao, a modern arts space constructed in a derelict port and shipbuilding area. Postmodernism, as described by Lyotard (1979), also implies something that has developed from modern industrial society, meaning it is post-industrial, and characterised by technology that has advanced to a post-mechanical age, and where most employment is in the tertiary, or service sector rather than in primary extraction or agriculture, or secondary manufacturing. Postmodernism, then, is located in the most advanced, post-industrial societies. According to Macey, Lyotard's *La condition postmoderne* is the key postmodernist text in philosophical terms; it is concerned with

> the effects on human knowledge of computerisation and the more general idea of a post-industrial society, but associates the postmodern primarily with contemporary incredulity towards the grand narratives of progress, socialism and the Enlightenment. [. . .] Lyotard's rejection of the grand narratives unsettles the stability of the traditional notions of reason and rationality (Macey, 2000:307).

See Discussion 10.2. Macey refers to critics of postmodernism, such as black writers and feminists who say that Lyotard's willingness to abandon the grand narratives is premature as the grand narratives of black liberation and feminism

Discussion 10.2

The decline of the grand narrative

Lyotard refers to the postmodern as 'incredulity towards meta-narratives' (1987:74). The idea of a grand narrative, an overarching theme, as an explanation of how society evolves, is rejected. Marxism, with its faith in historical determinism is the primary example, but equally trust in the certainty of human progress, developed since the Enlightenment, is now abandoned. The grand narrative of the Enlightenment has been adhered to with almost spiritual faith, a belief in the modern project that would deliver continual scientific, technological and moral progress. This faith became in effect the new religion for humanists. Further, this decline of a grand narrative

> can be seen as the effect of the blossoming of techniques and technologies since the Second World War, which has shifted the emphasis from the ends of action to its means; it can also be seen as the effect of the redeployment of advanced

liberal capitalism after its retreat under the protection of Keynesianism during the period 1930–1960, a renewal that has eliminated the communist alternative and valorised the individual enjoyment of goods and services (Lyotard, 1987:82–3).

This observation is especially interesting in a contemporary culture that extols celebrity (and some would say mediocrity) to the extent that a footballer can be transferred for €35m from the world's richest football club to the second richest, not on account of his likely contribution to the team, but because of his 'marketability' as an international fashion icon.

The emergence of economic globalisation as a policy goal fits well with the context of postmodernism: note the decline of Keynesian economics, the absence of a communist alternative, the valorisation of individual enjoyment of goods and services – and of individualism 'narcissism', according to Lasch (1979).

have only just begun. Others, such as Habermas (1980, 1985), argue that postmodernism is in fact anti-modernism and that it rejects the positive promise of modernity in its celebration of eclectic irrationalism (Macey, ibid.). Meanwhile, Lasch (1979, 1995) condemns postmodernism as 'an expression of the rampant individualism of a culture of narcissism which has lost all sense of values' (Macey, ibid.).

The sociologist Zygmunt Bauman (cited in Macey, 2000:309) refers to modernity as 'a long march to prison' and argues that its promise was never fulfilled. Now the task of intellectuals is to discover new forms of emancipation rather than surrendering to the seductions of postmodern consumerism. Bauman seems to view postmodernity

> not as a new age chronologically separable from modernity, but rather a new attitude towards modernity characterised by self-criticism, self-denigration and anxiety and relatedly the breakdown of social forms and institutions providing order and solidarity in the modern world such as the modern nation-state (Ross, 2001:59).

Macey refers to the work of the Belgian economist Ernest Mandel who considered that

> in the post-war period market capitalism and then monopoly capitalism have been superseded by a third technological revolution that gives rise to an era of *Spätkapitalismus* or late capitalism. This era is characterised, according to Mandel, by an unprecedented fusion of science, technology and production as the new technologies of nuclear energy and computers extend industrialisation to all sectors of the

economy and society. The importance of manual and physical labour declines as continuous flows of production and computerised control come to dominate industry and accord a new importance to intellectual workers such as scientists, laboratory workers and technicians (Macey, 2000:308).

The consequence of this is that society moves from an era characterised by the production of commodities to an era where the manipulation of knowledge is paramount in the workplace. Furthermore, the workplace changes too: from being a fixed location or factory, the workplace may become less fixed, and more transitory as mobility of employment increases. Work becomes free from a daily location; experts or consultants work remotely using new technologies, or are more or less permanently on the move according to need. Computerisation and improved communication technologies are highly influential in these changes.

Such developments have coincided with what the British sociologist Stuart Hall has called 'new times', with the end of the Cold War and the publication of Fukuyama's influential tract, *The End of History* (1992), the core thesis of which chimed with the 'end of the grand-narrative' notion. Fukuyama saw ideology as finished, once communism imploded in 1989.

Bauman views postmodernity as the 'result of the modern age reaching its self-critical, often self-denigrating stage' (1993:2).

© Lyn Wait

Photograph 10.1 The Guggenheim Museum – the postmodern delivers a post-industrial future to the port city of Bilbao in Northern Spain.

The claim is not so much that the advanced technological societies have entered a new age, but rather that faith in modernity and the project of modernity has dissipated. This is essentially a cultural fact (Ross, 2001:33).

Bauman identifies other features of postmodernity. He refers to the 'decline of the modern nation-state' and the rise of what he calls 'neo-tribes' (1993:141). He explains that, unlike classic tribes, 'neo-tribes do not last longer than their units ("members")' (ibid.). Each single neo-tribe is 'doomed to an episodic and inconsequential existence'; but what is neither episodic nor inconsequential is the 'postmodern condition in which the neo-tribes become the dominant mode of [. . .] sociality as such' (Bauman, 1993:142). This notion of the decline of the modern nation state as a source of collective identity is obviously connected to the thesis of globalisation, introduced in the previous chapter. The neo-tribes are represented by experts, technocrats, accountants, financiers, private investors, personal finance advisors, corporate executives, marketing gurus and other business specialists, as well as legal advisors and sundry other free operators, unbound by government or by state boundaries. Contemporary economic globalisation has released a new class of technocrats and experts that profit from a liberal business environment and whose interests, at least in the short term, appear to coincide with those of the most powerful businesses. Bauman argues that the globalisation hypothesis that the global economy is run, in fact, by extraterritorial authorities, is correct. This view is also held by Strange (1996) and Monbiot (2000).

> The way in which the world economy operates today (and *there is today a genuine world economy*), as well as the extraterritorial economic elites who operate it, favour state organisms that *cannot* effectively impose conditions under which the economy is run, let alone impose restraints on the way in which those who run the economy would like it to be run . . . (Bauman, 1993:231).

In other words, states cannot control the global economy. This for Bauman generates extreme risk and serious adverse social consequences, as well as a state of affairs within which 'no-one now seems to be in control' (Bauman, 1998:58). As we shall see in the next chapter, this book argues, following Gray and Strange among others, that national governments have effectively *given up* that control.

Bauman provides a powerful metaphor to describe postmodernism. His thesis is that postmodernism engenders anxiety and instability and this is characterised by the contrasting experience of two human types, the tourist and the vagabond. The material benefits of post-industrial capitalism are readily available to the tourist, whose travelling is by choice, in comfort and generally welcomed by their hosts. On the other hand, the vagabond is denied these benefits, and remains poor, dispossessed and seemingly condemned to cross frontiers in search of basic comforts (Bauman, 1997:83–95; 1998:77–102). See Discussion 10.3.

Postmodernism supposes fundamental changes in social relations. This is why the grand theories that have dominated sociology for over a century are so fundamentally challenged. Marxism, with its defining feature of class conflict,

Discussion 10.3

Tourists and vagabonds

Bauman uses a metaphor to describe the post-modern existence. He says we are all postmoderns, 'plotted on a continuum' between the poles of 'perfect tourist' and 'vagabond beyond remedy' (Bauman, 1997:93). Tourists move around freely, and are welcome wherever they go. Vagabonds wander in a vain search for security and hospitality. Their lot is to be cast as outsiders. What determines one's place on this continuum is the 'degree of freedom in choosing . . . life itineraries' (ibid.). In our postmodern society, Bauman argues, we are all

> on the move; none of us can be certain that he or she has gained the right to any place once and for all and no one thinks that his or her stay-ing in one place forever is a likely prospect . . . (ibid.).

Nevertheless, it is clear that tourists are the 'winners', but they are grossly outnumbered by the 'vagabonds', the losers from globalisation, a process which divides as it unites. Nor should one assume that all vagabonds are aimlessly wandering the planet. Many, perhaps most, are actually locked into their locality, unable to move. This is part of the curse of geography. The idea that globalisation creates a 'borderless world' (Ohmae, 1990) or renders geography irrelevant (O'Brien, 1992), is patently false. Many remain irretrievably rooted to their village or shanty town. Others, the elite, are mobile through choice.

Photograph 10.2 'Vagabonds' on the move. Refugees read a booklet entitled 'How to request asylum in France?'

is rejected as an anachronism now that we are in a post-industrial society. Information technology, robotics and the provision of services have replaced traditional mechanical machinery and the manufacture of products as the mainstay of employment. Callinicos (1989) rejects this interpretation and holds that social relations have barely altered, although on the surface things appear to have changed:

> Our world is being remade. Mass production, the mass consumer, the big city, the big-brother state, the sprawling housing estate, and the nation-state are in decline: flexibility, diversity, differentiation, mobility, communication, decentralisation and internationalisation are in the ascendant. In the process our own identities, our sense of self, our own subjectivities are being transformed. We are in a transition to a new era (Callinicos, 1989:4).

However, Callinicos rejects the arguments of post-Marxists such as Ernesto Laclau and Chantal Mouffe for whom the classical Marxist emphasis on class struggle as the agency of change should be abandoned. They argue that 'the postmodern epoch is fundamentally different from the industrial capitalism of the nineteenth and twentieth centuries' (Callinicos, 1989:4).

Post-Marxists argue that the notion of class and class struggle is outdated. A new post-capitalist society has emerged, with different challenges, social movements and new conflicts that supersede that between capital and labour. But Callinicos (1989:121) suggests that the idea of a post-industrial society is 'nonsense'. He states:

> I do not believe that we live in 'New Times' in a 'post-industrial and postmodern age' fundamentally different from the capitalist mode of production globally dominant for the past two centuries (Callinicos, 1989:4).

Nor does Callinicos accept the notion that the working class has declined. In fact there 'has been considerable *growth* of the industrial working class on a global scale' (1989:125). Wage-labour 'has if anything become a more pervasive feature of social experience in the past half century, with the decline of peasant agriculture and the growing involvement of women in the labour market' (1989:127).

Callinicos suggests that postmodernism is merely a symptom, an expression of disillusionment on the Left in politics, and a symptom of the opportunities for a consumption-oriented lifestyle available to 'upper white-collar strata' by neo-liberal capitalism in the Reagan-Thatcher era (1989:6–7). Therefore changes are superficial: the fundamental explanations of Marxism are still valid.

Review   *What is postmodernism? What in particular does it represent in relation to established social theory?*
Can you identify connections between postmodernism and globalisation theory?
Why does Callinicos reject postmodernism?

● ● ● ● Gray and the challenge to the Enlightenment

This short section presents a summary of John Gray's *Straw Dogs*. Like Bauman, Gray highlights anxieties and contradictions inherent in contemporary post-modern globalisation. But Gray does not stop at an analysis of postmodernity. In *Straw Dogs* his target is virtually the entire post-Enlightenment legacy, comprising humanism, Marxist 'scientific socialism' and neo-liberalism. The Enlightenment was characterised by scepticism towards Christianity and an antipathy towards religious authority. This, together with a new confidence in reason and science, gave impetus to a form of humanism that, like Christianity, exalted the human condition. Marxism and liberalism, both products of the Enlightenment, have dominated Western philosophy ever since. Liberalism emerged from and contributed to not only the Enlightenment but also the French Revolution which, as argued in Chapter 1, spurred a variety of responses including national consciousness and militarism, as well as rebellion, liberalism, Marxism and ultimately feminism and various other liberation movements. These are the tracks of Western political thought throughout the past 250 years.

The central claim in Gray's *Straw Dogs* is that human beings cannot be masters of their own destiny, as Christianity proclaims that they should be, or as the Enlightenment similarly tempted us to believe. Gray rails against the iniquities of Christianity, and points out that the Enlightenment was a reaction against theism. It sought to place man above God in the hierarchy, in fact it emphasised rationality, egalitarianism and the pursuit of knowledge as the one true path, virtually independently of Christian belief. But according to Gray, the spirit of the Enlightenment, the pursuit of knowledge and the conviction that humankind was on a path towards endless improvement, is just as mistaken as the old promises of Christian faith. Both Christianity and the Enlightenment make the same error in presupposing that free will can enable us to reach nirvana. Both assert man's fundamental difference from other animals. This is mistaken.

> For Christians, humans are created by God and possess free will, for humanists they are self-determining beings. Either way, they are quite different from all other animals (Gray, 2002:41).

Gray describes both neo-liberalism and Marxism, superficially opposite ends of a philosophical spectrum, as Enlightenment ideals (see Discussion 10.4). Both are wrong. *Straw Dogs* argues that there is no guarantee of endless progress, and in fact technology has advanced to the point where it is simply not controlled and we are therefore in an age of unprecedented uncertainty. He describes globalisation is 'the chaotic drift of new technologies' (2002:175).

The warnings in highlighting the dangerous reliance on technology, illustrated in Discussion 10.4, are just as relevant now as they should have been in Soviet times. As Gray points out, the 'cult of technological immortality has not died out' (Gray, 2002:139). The giant US food corporation Cargill carries out massive deforestation works in Brazil's Central Amazon Basin in order to boost soya production, much of it to feed cattle for beef production and

Discussion 10.4

Enlightenment projects: the devastation of the environment

Gray says that Marx was animated by the conviction that 'Humans are destined to be masters of the earth' (Gray, 2002:168). He believed that 'scientific socialism' would free humankind from the toils of labour and the constraints of the state. Scarcity, private property, the family, the state, and the division of labour would wither and disappear. Gray writes:

> If 'scientific socialism' resembles any science, it is alchemy. Along with other Enlightenment thinkers, Marx believed that technology could transmute the base metal of human nature into gold (Gray, 2002:167).

Technology, in the Enlightenment tradition, has long been seen as a tool to master nature. Gray targets the dying embers of the great socialist experiment, Soviet Russia, to illustrate his point. He refers to Federov, the nineteenth-century Russian thinker, for whom nature was the enemy because it condemned the human personality to extinction. The only worthwhile human project was a titanic struggle for immortality. It seems incredible that such fantasies could ever have any influence, and yet according to Gray, Federov's thinking was one of the early intellectual currents to shape the Soviet regime. The Bolsheviks believed man was destined for dominion over nature. The effects of this mindset endured throughout the Soviet era with devastating consequences for the environment.

The practical effects of the Marxian-Federovian cult of technology were ruinous. Inspired by a materialist philosophy, the Soviet Union inflicted more far-reaching and lasting damage on the material environment than any regime in history. Green earth became desert, and pollution rose to life-threatening levels. No advantage to mankind was gained by the Soviet destruction of nature. Soviet citizens lived no longer than people in other countries – many of them a good deal less.

Resistance to Federovian policies was one of the forces that triggered the Soviet collapse. The explosion in the nuclear reactor at Chernobyl galvanised protest all over the country. Much of the opposition to Gorbachev focused on his scheme for re-directing some of Russia's rivers, which would have flooded large parts of Siberia and – as a consequence – altered the world's climate. Mercifully, Gorbachev was toppled, and this grandiose folly never came to pass. Even so, the Soviet legacy to Russia was a devastated environment – a legacy that its semi-criminal, slash-and-burn capitalism has only made yet more catastrophic (Gray, 2002:138–9).

consumption in the US. The damming of the Yangtze River in China is on a similar scale to some of the great follies of Soviet central planning. Such projects develop their own momentum, and actions by one multinational corporation prompt similar actions by competitors, anxious not to lose out in 'global markets'.

It is not difficult to accept Gray's thesis that technology, created by humankind, now controls human society. The twentieth century produced advances in technology that enabled killing on a scale utterly unprecedented in any other epoch. 'Humans are weapon making animals with an unquenchable fondness for killing' (ibid., 92). The Nazis launched a war that resulted in the deaths of around 41 million Europeans (Davies, 1996:1328). This figure excludes the approximately 6 million Jews murdered in the gas chambers during the Holocaust. 'Between 1917 and 1959 over 60 million people were killed in the Soviet Union' (Gray, 2002:95) as a matter of *public policy*.

What makes the Twentieth Century special is not the fact that it is littered with massacres. It is the scale of its killings and the fact that they were premeditated for the sake of vast projects of world improvement (Gray, ibid., 96).

That, surely, is the most chilling point. There is an echo here of Bauman, who has written extensively on the Holocaust. Macey writes that for Bauman

the Holocaust is neither a 'Jewish problem' nor a 'German problem' [...] Bauman insists that it was a project born of and implemented in a modern rational society, and that it is therefore a problem of modern rational society. Modern civilization was not the Holocaust's sufficient cause, but it was one of its necessary causes. Rational bureaucracy, scientific planning and scientific rationality in the service of absolute modern power created it (Macey, 2000:35–6).

Gray says that man has created technology and machinery which not only has been used to exterminate millions of human beings in a modern industrialised society, but we also have used technology to create systems of weaponry over which ultimately we have only limited control, in part because it is almost impossible to prevent nuclear proliferation and the development of further weapons of mass destruction. Other technologies have contributed to levels of environmental despoilation that equally threaten the survival of the planet. That our very survival is threatened is indicative of our status as animals, subject to the constraints imposed upon us by factors that we cannot control. The Enlightenment taught us to believe that we could control our environment, and that this distinguished us from other animals. Humanism, like Christianity, purports that there are qualitative differences between human beings and other living organisms.

Over the past 200 years philosophy has shaken off Christian faith. It has not given up Christianity's cardinal error – the belief that humans are radically different from all other animals (Gray, 2002:37).

Gray argues that this is a delusion. However, we are not the same as other animals, in fact we have disadvantages compared to them – we demonstrate traits that are absent in other animals:

It is when [humans] believe they have left their animal nature behind that [they] show the qualities that are theirs alone: obsession, self-deception and perpetual unrest (Gray, 2002:132).

Gray ends *Straw Dogs* by reminding us that

other animals do not require a purpose in life. [...] The human animal cannot do without one. Can we not think of the aim of life as being simply to see? (Gray, 2002:199).

Gray, then, rejects the view that modernism by definition takes us forward, that it progresses the human condition. This is the context in which the globalisation project has emerged. For Gray, neo-liberal globalisation is simply another step in the flawed traditions of the Enlightenment. In contrast it is striking how advocates of contemporary globalisation present it as liberating and potentially able to meet the common demands of consumers, unbound by limitations of time and space. This is Enlightenment confidence of a super-charged variety. Gray interprets it as absolute folly.

Modernism has evolved into a late capitalism that is still marked by confidence in a better future, just like the preceding grand narratives. Economic globalisation is touted as the one true path towards a global improvement, for advanced as well as for industrialising and pre-industrial societies. The link to the Enlightenment is explicit:

> Globalization offers the chance to fulfil (or at least come considerably closer to fulfilling) the goals that classical liberal philosophers first identified several centuries ago and that still underpin Western democracy (Micklethwait & Wooldridge, 2000:xxii).

Micklethwait and Wooldridge describe the real point of globalisation as enhancing freedom:

> Globalization increases people's freedom to shape their identities, independent of those of their ancestors; to sharpen their talents by pursuing education anywhere in the world. The same global bazaar that allows consumers to buy the best that the world can offer also allows producers to find the best partners (ibid.:xxvii).

This view looks remarkably Triad-centric, even allowing for the fact that the consumers may be Chinese, Japanese or Korean, or other Asians. This positive interpretation of a postmodern globalising world is remarkably different from the stark imagery of Bauman, or the fears of Gray.

Review   *What is the central argument in* Straw Dogs? *Why is it relevant to contemporary globalisation?*

● ● ● ● The consequences of globalisation

Gray and the neo-liberal project

In **False Dawn** (1998), Gray's attack has a narrower focus. He concentrates on the 'neo-liberal political project' pursued by US and UK governments. He emphasises that globalisation proper, as a social, cultural and economic phenomenon, must be distinguished from the American neo-liberal political project of a global free market:

> Much current debate confuses globalisation, an historical process that has been under-way for centuries, with the ephemeral *political project of a worldwide free market* [my italics]. Properly understood, globalisation refers to the increasing interconnection of economic and cultural life in distant parts of the world. It is a trend that can be dated back to the projection of European power into other parts of the world in imperialist policies from the sixteenth century onwards (Gray, 1998:215).

Yet, arguably, there is a connection between globalisation proper, comprising social and cultural dimensions, and the global advance of neo-liberal ideology. The link relates to the discussion in the previous section, that the Enlightenment spawned political ideologies, including classical liberalism – a direct antecedent to the contemporary neo-liberalism favoured by advocates of globalisation. This book focuses mainly on the neo-liberal dimension to globalisation, thus its economic orientation. The wider cultural implications are not analysed in any detail, but see Key concept 10.2.

Goodman et al. argue that neo-liberalism generates inequality:

> One of the most important changes of the 1980s was the relative decline in the demand for less-skilled workers resulting in both relatively lower wage levels and a lower likelihood of being in employment. If this continues, it will be a powerful force for a continued increase in inequality. Continued mechanisation and globalisation point in this direction (Goodman et al., 1997:281–2).

Inequalities are stark both within countries, and between them. The richest 2.7m Americans earn as much as the poorest 100 m; the per capita income in the richest country, Switzerland, is 400 times that of Mozambique (Landes, 1998:xx). The US and its closest allies, through successive elected governments of apparently different political hues in different OECD countries, continue to support this policy prescription, or at the very least, they acquiesce in it. Gray is concerned about the social consequences of the neo-liberal agenda. Where the UK is concerned, he cites increasing inequality, family breakdown and upheavals within entire communities as direct consequences of a decade of adherence to the policy prescriptions of neo-liberals after 1979. Worldwide, the same agenda has marginalised huge numbers of people, increased migration, and created rising incidence of criminality and higher rates of incarceration (Ladipo, 2001). Bauman calls this the 'criminalization of poverty' (1998:125).

In *False Dawn*, Gray targets the US-driven political project of neo-liberal capitalism. He makes an important distinction between this and the

> globalisation of economic and cultural life that began in Europe in the early modern period from the fifteenth century onwards, and is set to advance for centuries (Gray, 1998:23).

It is important to keep this distinction in mind, and to remember that Gray is not opposed to globalisation *per se*. His target is contemporary economic globalisation, the same as Hirst and Thompson (1999) (see previous chapter). Gray claims that economic neo-liberalism is promoted as a global ideal by the USA, the world's sole remaining superpower. Gray sees the United States as the world's 'last great Enlightenment regime' (1998:2) by which he means a state committed to promoting its idea of a global order, a 'universal civilisation' governed according to American norms and values. He interprets the former Soviet Union as a 'rival Enlightenment Utopia, that of a universal civilisation, in which markets were replaced by central planning' (Gray, 1998:3). Pre-eminent among the American norms or values are a commitment to free-market capitalism (economic neo-liberalism) and political democracy, which he calls the 'Washington consensus'. According to this, 'democratic capitalism' will be accepted worldwide and there will be a global free market. Different economic and political cultures will be subsumed in a single orthodoxy. Gray thinks this American dream of a free-market liberal utopia is completely wrong.

> A utopia that can never be realised; its pursuit has already produced social dislocation and economic and political instability on a large scale (Gray, 1998:22).

He provides examples from three countries, the UK, New Zealand and Mexico, where the experiment with the neo-liberal free markets has been conducted with particular zeal by political elites.

> In each country the free market acted as a vice within which the middle classes were squeezed. It enriched a small minority and increased the size of excluded underclasses. It inflicted serious damage on the political vehicles through which it was implemented. It used the powers of the state without scruple, but corrupted and in some measure de-legitimated the state's institutions. It scattered or destroyed its initial coalition of political support. It fractured societies. In its aftermath it set the terms within which oppositional parties were compelled to operate (Gray, 1998:53–4).

Gray highlights one of the contradictions of Thatcherism in its relationship to the nation state. He argues that neo-liberal economic policies stripped the state of most of its leverage over economic policy, while the rhetoric of Thatcher's administration was staunchly nationalist, especially in its relationship towards the European Union. Privatisation 'prised open the British economy to world markets as never before' (Gray, 1998:35). Economic globalisation was held up as a holy grail, while the nation state was similarly lauded as an invulnerable symbol of supreme importance. While the EU was condemned as an assault on sovereignty, neo-liberals proclaimed that one could not 'buck the markets'. Gray sums this up as follows:

> The sovereign nation state was glorified at just the historical moment when those who elevated it declared it to be economically redundant (Gray, 1998:36).

Russia shows the impossibility of forcing the world economy to adopt one universal, global model. 'Neither the economic nor the political institutions of any other country can be transplanted to the unique circumstances of post-communist Russia' (1998:135). He argues that Russia needs to develop its own form of capitalism, 'not the free-market of recent western textbooks, but a capitalism in which extensive state intervention coexists with large areas of unregulated entrepreneurial activity' (ibid.). Furthermore, he says that the failure of the 'shock therapy' tactics between 1991 and 1994 to rapidly transform the Russian economy from the Soviet system into one of *laissez-faire* capitalism proves his point.

> Shock therapy, which had been the only available economic strategy, ceased to be politically viable. Its social costs had become insupportable (Gray, 1998:147).

In the Western Enlightenment tradition, there is a general assumption that political and economic processes, being conducted within the context of continual scientific discovery, will lead to improving living conditions and an improved state of knowledge. On the contrary, Gray takes issue with this cosy humanist assumption and says that the present phase of globalisation is not only dangerous, it is built on an entirely wrong premise. Gray argues that

As it is presently constituted, global capitalism is inherently unstable. A world-wide free market is no more self-regulating than the national free markets of the past. Barely a decade old, it already contains serious imbalances. Unless it is reformed radically, the world economy risks falling apart in a replay [. . .] of the trade wars, competitive devaluations, economic collapses and political upheavals of the 1930s (Gray, 1998:209).

Gray criticises proponents of the free market for their assumption that it will advance liberal values. Soros supports this view, writing that:

It is dangerous [. . .] to place excessive reliance on the market mechanism. Markets are designed to facilitate the free exchange of goods and services among willing participants, but they are not capable, on their own, of taking care of collective needs such as law and order or the maintenance of the market mechanism itself. Nor are they competent to ensure social justice. These 'public goods' can only be provided by a political process (Soros, 2002:6).

The question of **public goods** is developed in Chapter 12. Here it is enough to emphasise the deficiency of relying on markets alone to sustain well-being. On the contrary, free market capitalism undermines liberal values and imposes 'massive instability on developing countries' (Gray, 1998:210). Throughout his writing, Gray takes issue with the 'one global civilisation' thesis and says that globalisation makes it harder for different civilisations to live in peaceful co-existence. It is therefore a threat to peace between states, because 'the present international economic system contains no effective institutions for conserving the wealth of the natural environment'. He goes on to argue, as he does in *Straw Dogs* (2002), that

sovereign states will be drawn into a struggle for control of the world's dwindling resources. In the [twenty-first] century ideological rivalries between nation states may well be succeeded by Malthusian wars of scarcity (Gray, 1998:211).

The process, then, leads back to conflict, precisely the position the widespread commitment to integration that dominated the political elites after the Second World War was designed to avoid.

Not everyone, of course, shares Gray's apocalyptic vision. Indeed Micklethwait and Wooldridge (2000) and Legrain (2002) write that the major threat to stability and living standards for developing countries as well as for the rest of the world comes not from more globalisation, but from a retreat from it. These perspectives are examined later in this chapter.

To summarise, Gray accepts that globalisation is an irreversible process, and reserves his strongest attacks for the assumption that there is but one 'true path', the neo-liberal free trade agenda. By looking at different contexts, he hopes to demonstrate the error in the neo-liberal assumption that a global economy can be imposed from above on the basis of the policy preferences of the elite in Washington.

End of history, end of geography?

The collapse of the Soviet system and the end of the Cold War in 1991 appeared for some to signal the end of the Manichean struggle between left and right, between the two great protagonists of the Enlightenment, Marxist communism and liberal capitalism. This was interpreted as the death throes of ideology, since any ideology needs a counter-ideology, and now with neo-liberal capitalism ascendant and unopposed, there was no more ideology. Fukuyama described this as the 'end of history' (Fukuyama, 1992). This interpretation has proved premature. For Bauman, the end of the Cold War brought a decisive change in the process of globalisation:

> when the curtain was eventually torn apart, it uncovered an unfamiliar scene, populated by bizarre characters (Bauman, 1998:64).

This 'unfamiliar scene' is the current phase of globalisation. The 'bizarre characters' are the multiple agencies that exert power and influence where once states had a virtual monopoly. States responded by seeking new alliances through the European Union, NATO, NAFTA and the WTO, while national groups sought to escape from federal cages such as the Soviet Union, the Federal Republic of Yugoslavia and Czechoslovakia.

Bauman goes on to claim that corporate and financial interests, or markets, have a vested interest in the weakness of the state, since weakness would make regulation less likely. Meanwhile, Bauman believes that globalisation masks two distinct but mutually reinforcing tendencies, the global rich and the local poor. This is the true meaning, for Bauman, of 'glocalisation'.

Meanwhile the inherent contradictions within capitalism remain and, if anything, globalisation has put these tensions into sharper relief, not only between the owners of capital and workers, but between north and south. Other tensions abound too, not least environmental and demographic. For Bauman 'the end of

BALLARD STREET Jerry Van Amerongen

Mrs. Nimmers uses localism to combat globalism.

Figure 10.1 Glocalisation . . .

Source: reprinted by permission of Jerry Van Amerongen and Creators Syndicate, Inc.

geography' (Bauman, 1998:12) is a more apt description of globalisation than 'end of history' but the 'borderless world' is more real for those elites who have traditionally been able to cross borders and so conquer distance. Bauman argues that the compression of space is a class-stratified phenomenon, thus indicating a partial acceptance of Giddens's claim about globalisation in a contemporary postmodern, globalised world. Giddens writes that globalisation is

> not only, or even primarily, about economic interdependence, but about the transformation of time and space in our lives (Giddens, 1998:30–31).

Crucially, Bauman argues that tourists may be freed from the 'tyranny of place' but others, vagabonds, are constrained by their localities, their poverty of resources, above all their lack of access to clean water. Geography, it would appear, is all too real.

Bauman argues that the elites, the tourists, have

> *chosen* isolation and pay for it lavishly and *willingly*. The rest of the population *finds itself* cut off and *forced* to pay the heavy cultural, psychological and political price of their new isolation (Bauman, 1998:21).

The consequence of such isolation is that localities are 'losing their meaning-generating . . . capacity' (Bauman, 1998:2–3). This has devastating and alienating consequences, including the effect of driving 'locals' to react with neo-tribal and fundamentalist political tendencies in a vain attempt to respond to or to resist globalisation. One can perhaps posit a link here between this isolation and the drift towards fundamentalist or simplistic, even terrorist, solutions to the problems generated by globalisation. Developing the metaphor described above, Bauman adds:

> There are no tourists without the vagabonds, and the tourists cannot be free without tying down the vagabonds; the vagabond is the '*alter ego* of the tourist' (1998:93–4).

Globalisation, therefore, creates 'extraterritoriality' for the elites, which

> feels like intoxicating freedom, [while] the territoriality of the rest feels like home ground, and ever more like prison – all the more humiliating for the obtrusive sight of the others' freedom to move. [. . .] the condition of 'staying put', being unable to move at one's heart's desire and being barred access to greener pastures, exudes the acrid odour of defeat, signals incomplete humanity and implies being cheated in the division of splendours life has to offer (Bauman, 1998:23).

This description seems ever more apt as the fashion for the wealthy youth of the West to find 'experience' in travelling to exotic places as part of their 'education' attains new heights of popularity every year. The 'gap year' is a postmodern experience, and one that emphasises the chasm between tourists and vagabonds. The tourists are safe and secure and have a return ticket and insurance. The poor, if they move around at all, are not in control of their destinies. They are like cork at the mercy of the ocean waves, except that they may actually sink.

Globalisation brings a dislocation between agent and result: policies pursued in the name of globalisation bring consequences which are pushed to the margins, as the forces that drive globalisation – governments, corporations, private interests, distance themselves from responsibility for the social consequences. Bauman refers to the absence of control, since not even the elite is in control of the consequences of globalisation (Bauman, 1998:58). This is the ultimate consequence, the essence of postmodernism. Control itself becomes anonymous and intangible. Hirst and Thompson (1999) argue similarity – economic globalisation weakens the very instruments that society needs in order to function. Stability is sacrificed in pursuit of an ideological principle, that government should *intervene less*. Instead of a connection between action and result, or agent and consequence, there is a

> no man's land, stretching beyond the reach of the design-and-action capacity of anybody in particular (Bauman, 1998:60).

Bauman underlines that the weakness of the modern state appears as both cause and effect (1998:60). Giddens is less apocalyptic. Instead he writes that the nation state

> is not disappearing, and the scope of government, taken overall, expands rather than diminishes as globalisation proceeds (1998:32).

Giddens claims that some states such as the post-communist countries of Eastern Europe have increased sovereignty since the collapse of the USSR. Others meanwhile have given up powers in traditional areas of economic management, especially through adopting more 'market-oriented' approaches, for example through pursuing privatisation policies. The decline of the classical Keynesian approach has reduced the role of governments and the old geopolitical frameworks of international relations have altered. Nevertheless, governments retain considerable economic power, often through partnership and cooperation with other states in international institutions.

Another way to consider the consequences of globalisation is to focus on economic differentials between rich and poor. While globalists argue that the liberalisation of international trade has lifted millions out of poverty (see Figure 10.4 below), the assumption is based on the definition of poverty as subsisting on less than $1 a day. This seems a somewhat arbitrary figure. It is doubtless true that many millions of people have achieved material improvements in their lives through improved wages, notably in China, India and throughout the Asia Pacific Region, so much so that

> the neo-liberal account suggests that economic globalization is the only effective path leading to global poverty reduction, while the causes of enduring inequality are to be located principally in the failure of countries to integrate fast enough or deep enough into the world economy. More rather than less, globalization is the principal remedy for eradicating global poverty (Held & McGrew, 2002:80).

Critics reject this view, arguing instead that poverty and inequality are getting worse as the benefits of economic globalisation are unevenly spread across the globe and within countries. Held and McGrew cite a number of studies that demonstrate increasing pay inequalities within industrialised countries as well as arguments about how the $1 a day figure is calculated, and whether it is a

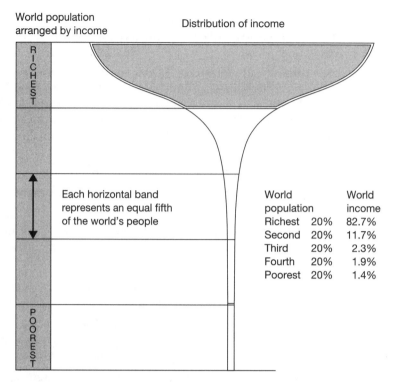

Figure 10.2 The 'champagne glass' pattern of inequality between the world's rich and poor

Source: Wade, 2001. Reprinted by permission of openDemocracy.net.

useful measure, and further studies showing a widening gap in terms of health as well as income.

> In 1960, the income of the richest 20 per cent of the world's people stood at about 30 times that of the poorest 20 per cent; by 1997 the corresponding figure was 74 (UNDP, 1997, cited in Held & McGrew, 2002:81).

Robert Wade produced the famous champagne glass image to demonstrate the stark wealth differentials between the world's poorest and richest (see Figure 10.2). Held and McGrew say this matters because

> the accelerating gap [. . .] reinforces patterns of global exclusion and disempowerment, while also making globalization ethically, if not politically, unsustainable. [. . .] This architecture, which divides humanity into elites, the bourgeoisie, the marginalized, and the impoverished, cuts across territorial and cultural boundaries, rearranging the world into the winners and losers of globalization (Held & McGrew, 2002:81).

Further comment on this, and on Wade's champagne glass, is provided in Discussion 10.5.

Soros, who describes himself as 'an ardent supporter of globalisation' (Soros, 2002:7) is well aware of its shortcomings:

Discussion 10.5

Held & McGrew on the globalisation of poverty

Economic globalization is the principal causal mechanism which determines patterns of global inequalities, mobile capital relocates jobs and production in the world economy, trade intensifies international competitive pressures, and global finance constrains the welfare and redistributive capacities of states. This produces four mutually reinforcing dynamics: the increasing segmentation of the global workforce into winners and losers from productive and financial integration; the growing marginalization, exclusion and impoverishment of the losers both within and between states; the erosion of social solidarity, as welfare regimes are unable, or politically unwilling, to bear the costs of protecting the most vulnerable; and the intensification of economic polarization and exclusion within, between and across states. Neo-liberal economic globalization is responsible, according to its critics, for nothing less than the globalization of poverty and social exclusion [. . .].

The globalization of poverty threatens not only to erode human security, but also to undermine the globalization project itself. As the unevenness of globalization divides the world and nations into polarizing zones of affluence and poverty, inclusion and exclusion, empowerment and disempowerment, it generates a deepening fragmentation of world order which finds expression in, among other things, increased number of failed states, transnational terrorism, the rise of fundamentalisms, transnational organized crime and ethnic/religious conflicts. Unless neo-liberal economic globalization is tamed, so the argument goes, a 'new barbarism' will emerge as conflicts spill over into the global 'zones of peace' fuelled by intensifying poverty, exclusion, disempowerment and inequality (Held & McGrew, 2002:2–3).

The richest 1 per cent of the world's population receive as much as the poorest 57 per cent. More than a billion people live on less than a dollar a day; nearly a billion lack access to clean water; 826 million suffer from malnutrition; 10 million die each year for lack of the most basic healthcare. These conditions were not necessarily caused by globalisation, but globalisation has done little to redress them (Soros, 2002:10).

The response to the globalisation of poverty according to Held and McGrew, citing a UN Development Report (1999), must be to create a reformed and robust system of global governance that can regulate global markets. The 'Washington Consensus must give way to the Monterrey Consensus', a reference to the UN Financing for Development Conference in 2002. Priority must be given to human security and development over the requirements of global markets.

The assault on inclusive models of capitalism

An important claim in Gray's *False Dawn* (1998) is that the US-driven project of neo-liberal capitalism is presented as the one and only model for capitalist development. Its advocates employ the power of international institutions like the IMF to instruct developing countries on how to meet the demands of the free market economy. The prerequisites for 'respectability' in the global economy are privatisation of public utilities and other industries, market liberalisation, attracting foreign capital, and the complete removal of tariff barriers. According to Chomsky American geostrategic policy in the Middle East is in lockstep with economic policy. He reports that the huge US subsidy to Israel in 2003 was conditional, not on the implementation of the road map to peace with Palestinians, but on an economic plan to force a neo-liberal (economic) order on Israel through the imposition of

> [a]n economic plan that will slash public sector jobs and wages and lower taxes, measures that have been dubbed 'an economic road map' [. . .] a [plan] which is welcome to the Israeli business sector but which led immediately to a strike by 700,000 workers (Chomsky, 2003:174).

A clear consequence of the neo-liberal orthodoxy is the reduction in welfare provision by state authorities. Gray (1998) and Hutton (2002) argue that there are many models of capitalism and it is impossible to prescribe a single overarching system as appropriate for all circumstances. Gray describes the different contexts in which the neo-liberal experiment has been imposed and reports on its dramatic failures in all instances, while Hutton interprets the progress of economic globalisation as an ideological assault on pre-existing models of capitalism, notably the corporatism favoured in Japan and the social welfare model of post-war Germany. The neo-liberal free market project was recast from traditional liberalism as a political-economic ideology, economic neo-liberalism, by Reagan in the USA and by Thatcher in the UK. This assault is concerned, above all, with the 'drive to install the market principle' (Hutton, 1997:9), and to roll back the state:

> The vocabulary of Western liberalism – of freedom, choice, independence and even morality – has been captured and recast into thought categories consistent only with competitive economic individualism. Freedom is defined as the freedom to buy and sell; choice as the right to exercise choice in markets; independence is independence from the state; moral conduct is the exercise of individual choice (Hutton, 1997:9).

This 'ideology behind it all', Hutton argues, is morally and economically bankrupt. To find an alternative, Hutton looks back to Keynesian economics. This contrasts sharply with what Hutton considers the ultra-competitive, short-termist, individualist, free-market, casino capitalism championed by New Right neo-liberals like Hayek, Nozick, Friedman and their political followers Reagan and Thatcher. Hutton proposes a cooperative model of stakeholder capitalism, that is consensual, managed, and long-termist. Hutton demonstrates that all have a 'stake': industry leaders, banks and finance, workers and the state, and that there are common objectives to reach common or shared benefits. Hutton argues that the successful post-war economies, such as Germany and Japan, were not modelled on free-market principles.

How successful are Germany and Japan? Of course, under the changed course of global capitalism in recent years, these economies have been exposed as vulnerable. The consensus on which their successful economies were created has been severely undermined (but see Discussion 10.6).

Germany has been under sustained pressure to reduce the 'inflexibilities' in its labour market, and reduce labour costs, reported by the *Economist* (26 June 2004) as the highest in the developed world, bar Norway. The pressures from

Discussion 10.6

Germany under pressure – coping with reunification

Germany faces significant difficulties in adjusting, not only to the demands of contemporary free market capitalism, but above all – and this point is often neglected in references to German economic woes – to the monumental task of reunification in 1991. It is worth recalling what reunification entailed. The FRG expanded on 3 October 1990 from 248,000km^2 to 346,000km^2, an increase of 30 per cent, and from 64 million inhabitants to 82 million, a rise of 20 per cent. What did the GDR consist of as the Wall came down and reunification became inevitable less than a year later? It had a shattered economy, almost no properly functioning markets, a broken infrastructure, derelict factories and decrepit manufacturing and an appalling level of environmental degradation, as well as very different social and educational expectations from those the Federal Republic had become used to. It also had a grossly inflated *Ostmark*, exchanged at parity with the *Deutschmark*, when the true value would have been nearer eight to one. This triggered inflation and unsustainable levels of consumption in the German economy, already adjusting to a 7.5 per cent increase in taxation and sharply increased public spending to pay for reconstruction. Germany is still adjusting to this. It seems highly unlikely that any other country in the world could have come close to managing such an extraordinary state of affairs with anything like the degree of success that has been achieved – and this with almost no external assistance. The result so far represents a monumental achievement, but there is little doubt that the task ahead remains immense. A new difficulty is a growing nostalgia, ironically dubbed *Ostalgie* in Germany, for the Communist GDR. Boyes (2003) reports on how East Germans are not hugely impressed by the reality of life under global capitalism, as huge wage differentials persist between for example Hamburg, and Mecklenburg a few miles to the east. Unemployment, insecurity and lack of local opportunities appear to be creating a German *mezzogiorno*, and these problems shows every sign of worsening before they improve.

the globalising economy are such that the special corporate, state and federal government partnership that has provided Germany with Europe's strongest manufacturing economy and a strong balance of payments surplus is threatened by a lack of inward investment, and worse, a flight of capital to cheaper labour markets.

Meanwhile Japan has different problems. Japanese capitalism has been built around a traditional web of interests encompassing state, corporations and banking, all deeply interlinked so that every nook and cranny of Japanese society is bound by all three. In a changed globalising economy, Japanese banking in particular has faced the full rigour of competition in international markets. A greater requirement to see short-term returns and the free movement of capital, together with persistently high yen exchange rates have placed the sector under immense pressure. Already suffering from recession after 1991, Japan experienced a chronic loss of confidence, exacerbated by the Asian Crisis which followed the sharp devaluation of the Thai baht in July 1997 (Krugman, 2000). Japan struggles in the face of the onslaught from free market pressures in which capital transfers have accelerated in a far more liberal financial system than existed prior to the late 1980s. Japan finds itself far less insulated from global markets and less able to rely on its huge trading surplus with the US and Europe.

It is in banking above all that Japan has felt the harsh winds of free market capitalism, but in other respects too, such as the tendency for Japanese capitalism to build up enormous holding corporations where profitable enterprises support less profitable ones and where supply contracts are regarded as lifelong commitments, the typically secure structures have been greatly weakened. The evidence is all too plain, with more people out of work, declining order books for small and medium-sized enterprises and a rising level of insecurity in the population at large. Large companies, with their typical competitive advantage and extensive overseas markets, tend to have accommodated the changing global environment more successfully. It is the smaller more local businesses which have suffered.

One should not exaggerate the impact on Japan. The country has not gone into the economic meltdown that many Western observers on the right anticipated, and despite Japan being effectively a complete basket case as far as neo-liberal economic orthodoxy is concerned. The typical structures of Japanese capitalism remain very different to the usual set of US preferences. In spite of this, Japan still works. Certainly the corporate-led social inclusiveness of Japanese capitalism is having difficulty in adjusting to changed circumstances. Zero interest rates can hardly be pushed lower, and property prices have taken an enormous hit in the past decade. An unemployment rate of 4.7 per cent in 2004 may not seem excessive by European standards, but in Japan it is worryingly high. However, after a decade of stagnation, the Japanese economy, like that of neighbouring South Korea, is registering positive.

Worryingly, though, Japan seems in thrall to the US-policy prescription, and the word *gaiatsu* has been coined to mean pressure from outsiders (to conform to Western policy expectations). While condemning Japan to imminent collapse, the standard US/UK apologists for neo-liberalism conveniently ignore the extent to which they, and the US in particular, have enjoyed a long economic boom based largely on consumer credit and soaring property prices, and continue to tolerate shockingly high wealth differentials while their economies are loaded with debt. Credit card debt is unheard of in Japan, as it is in most of continental Europe. In 2004, 75 per cent of credit card debt in the entire European Union was in the United Kingdom (*Independent*, 1 May 2004).

It is not only critics of globalisation that indicate that there are major costs associated with the neo-liberal project. Chomsky quotes extensively from a US National Intelligence Council report on projections over the coming years. The NIC expects globalisation to continue on its course but

'Its evolution will be rocky, marked by chronic financial volatility and a widening economic divide'. Financial volatility very likely means slower economic growth, extending the pattern of neo-liberal economic globalisation (for those who follow the rules) and harming mostly the poor. The NIC goes on to predict that as this form of globalisation proceeds, 'deepening economic stagnation, political instability, and cultural alienation [will] foster ethnic, ideological and religious extremism, along with the violence that often accompanies it', much of it directed against the United States. 'Unsurprisingly,' Kenneth Waltz observes, the weak and disaffected 'lash out at the United States as the agent or symbol of their suffering' (Chomsky, 2003:209).

Local crises with global implications

The Asian Crisis of 1997 onwards can also be viewed as part of the wider impact of the economic globalisation project. Krugman (2000) reports on a domino effect in developing markets affected by the enormous volatility of capital flow post-1990. He cites various examples of stock market growth and heavy investment into developing markets that produced unsustainable short-term booms in the economies of Mexico, Brazil, Argentina and several LDCs in the Asia Pacific region. Ultimately the major cause of the eventual bursting of the bubble in all these locations was that the investments were based on nothing substantial. The same can be said of the more sector-specific crashes in so-called dot.com businesses in the early 1990s and in the grossly over-inflated telecommunications sector.

In Mexico the signing of NAFTA in 1992, the free trade agreement with the United States, was a continuation of a market liberalisation begun in 1982. Gray reports that the Mexican government of Carlos Salinas (1988–94) was hailed as 'a model of successful modernisation by all sectors of American opinion' and was praised by *Newsweek* for having transformed Mexico into 'a US sunbelt state' (Gray, 1998:46). Mexico became for the US a neo-liberal experiment that could not be allowed to fail. However, Gray reports that Salinas had his doubts:

> When you are introducing strong economic reform, you must make sure that you build the political consensus around it. If you are at the same time introducing additional drastic political reform, you may end up with no reform at all (Salinas, quoted in Gray, 1998:47).

As things transpired, Salinas' PRI regime was consumed by the policies of economic insecurity that its free market policies had fuelled. Gray reports:

> Engineering the free market in Mexico enhanced economic and social inequalities in what had long been one of the world's most unequal societies. In 1992, the richest 10 per cent of Mexicans received 38 per cent of the country's income, the poorest half only 18 per cent. Two thirds of all income is distributed to 30 per cent of the population. [. . .] The lowest 30 per cent of the Mexican population receives only 8 per cent of national income. The minimum wage in 1993 was less than half of what it was in 1975 (Gray, 1998:48).

Mexico found itself on a conveyor belt to social and economic disintegration. Gray writes that the reforms of the 1980s onwards widened inequalities and destroyed the growth of a middle class which had been occurring for 40 years. The process accelerated once NAFTA was established and 'moved into a new gear with the austerity programme instituted in the wake of the devaluation crisis of 1994' (Gray, 1998:49). In fact, the peso collapsed and the Clinton administration rushed out an IMF loan to prevent savage losses for American investors in the fragile Mexican economy and to stem the risk of a ripple effect sending markets into a tailspin.

A million jobs were lost in 1995. Political chaos ensued, but meanwhile NAFTA had opened up Mexican business to a takeover by US corporations, among them Wal-Mart and K-Mart, as grocery shopping became concentrated in the hands of American-style supermarkets (Gray, 1998:49–50). Gray says there is no way back for Mexico – its economy, and its political environment, has been transformed by the neo-liberal experiment.

Krugman reports that the massive US/IMF intervention did stabilise Mexico, but that the lessons from the crisis were not learnt (Krugman, 2000:57–9). The investment that preceded the collapse was based not on indigenous growth but on speculation. Krugman writes that the rescue that was forthcoming for Mexico might not be available for other economies, similarly affected. That is how it proved. Argentina and Brazil followed with similar crises and even worse effects. When in 1997 Thailand devalued the baht, no one initially took much notice. High levels of investment in what were cunningly described as 'emerging markets' reached spectacular levels in the early 1990s (Krugman, 2000:85). After the Mexican debacle of 1994–95, Southeast Asia was the respectable place to invest, in anticipation of high yields. The result of high levels of foreign investment was an explosion of available credit, which in turn brought fresh investment.

> Some of this took the form of actual construction, mainly office and apartment buildings, but there was also a lot of pure speculation, mainly in real estate, but also in stocks. By early 1996 the economies of Southeast Asia were starting to bear a strong family resemblance to Japan's 'bubble economy' of the late 1980s (Krugman, 2000:86).

Eventually, soaring investment and a consumer boom among a newly affluent population led to a surge in imports. Then rising wages and a fall in exports created a dramatic rise in imports, and a ballooning trade deficit. Thailand and Malaysia in 1997 reported trade deficits of between 6 and 8 per cent of GDP, similar to Mexico before the Tequila crisis (Krugman, 2000:87). In short, investor returns went sour, speculators went bankrupt, and lenders stopped lending. However, the central bank found that as foreign currency stopped coming in, the demand for baht to pay for imports continued unabated. The result was the central bank had to buy foreign currency to support the baht, which proved unsustainable and eventually the government had to let the currency go into free fall.

Recession spread from Thailand across Southeast Asia, and further damaged Japan. Krugman reports that devaluation, as happened to Britain in 1992 when sterling was forced out of the ERM, can be an effective launch to recovery when the markets hold their nerve. In Asia, the markets did not manage to do so. Instead there was a contagious loss of confidence that spread throughout the region. See Figure 10.3.

Malaysia and Indonesia followed:

> Within three months Indonesia was in even worse shape than the rest of Southeast Asia, indeed on its way to one of the worst economic slumps in world history; and the crisis had spread not just across Southeast Asia but all the way to South Korea, a faraway economy whose GDP was twice as large as that of Indonesia, three times as large as that of Thailand (Krugman, 2000:96–7).

The contagion was not because of high levels of mutual investment between Thailand and South Korea, or even between Thailand and Indonesia. The contagion came because of a sudden loss of confidence in the speculators in North America, Europe and Japan. Economic globalisation and the free flow of capital

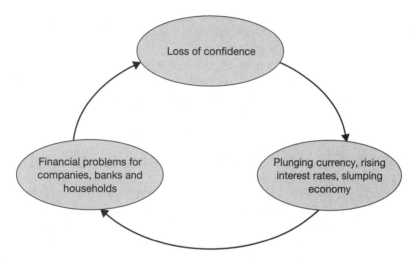

Figure 10.3 The vicious circle of financial crisis

Source: illustration, p. 94 from *The Return of Depression Economics* by Paul Krugman. Copyright © 1999 by Paul Krugman. Used by permission of W.W. Norton & Company, Inc.

are central to the chronic instabilities unleashed on developing countries. This is a core plank in the critique of neo-liberal economic globalisation. It is hugely speculative, and thus profoundly risky.

Krugman concludes that the battering that Southeast Asia took in the late 1990s cannot be blamed only on crony capitalism, or even on bad government. In fact, they had taken the neo-liberal medicine and were responding in orthodox ways. They had become vulnerable because they had opened up their markets, so becoming 'better' free market economies. They had taken advantage of their popularity with international lenders to run up substantial debts with the outside world. The debts intensified the feedback in loss of confidence to financial collapse and back again – see figure above – and the vicious circle became more intense. Worst of all, the new debts were in dollars – that brought the house of cards down.

Finally, a less widely noted impact of globalisation has been the changes in the legal environment. International law is largely dominated by Anglo-American international law firms, and increasingly shaped by Anglo-American legal practices. Sassen refers to the spreading influence of US law, especially in matters relating to international finance and contract law, 'Certain US legal practices are being diffused throughout the world – for instance the legal device of franchising' (Sassen, 1996:19).

Given the primacy in international law of US preferences, it is evident that transnational legal instruments have emerged as stronger in the context of international law than domestic, state-level jurisdiction. Sassen refers to the 'strategic geopolitical role' of highly developed states and the 'hegemony of neo-liberal concepts of economic relations, with [their] strong emphasis on markets, deregulation, and free international trade' (Sassen, 1996:17). These are precisely the areas that correspond to the political project of globalisation, serving the interests of US and UK preferences.

Review	*What are Gray's main complaints about what he describes as the political project of neo-liberal globalisation?* *How might globalisation lead to a renewal of inter-state conflict?* *What are some of the consequences identified by Bauman? What other consequences have been observed elsewhere?*

Future perfect? In defence of globalisation

A counter view to the concerns expressed above is presented by Micklethwait and Wooldridge in their book *Future Perfect: the challenge and hidden promise of globalisation* (2000). It is worth summarising some of their key arguments.

They write about the liberating potential of global capitalism from a strongly neo-liberal perspective. They argue that the greatest threat associated with globalisation is that it is forced to retreat, and that problems of inequality, poverty and hunger are the result of politicians meddling, Third World debt, protectionism – especially in agriculture – and low levels of investment in education. Globalisation is a liberating force that brings wealth and opportunity to people in the remotest parts of the globe.

In contrast to Gray, Micklethwait and Wooldridge praise the potential of technology to assist in the realisation of untold benefits. Technology is presented as the great enabler of the liberating potential of globalisation. They mention, for example, the volume and speed of capital movements.

> Both sides of the globalization debate admit that the one trillion dollars that profit-seeking foreign investors poured into the developing world during the 1990s had more effect (for good or ill) than all the cumbersome government-aid programs of the previous three decades (Micklethwait & Wooldridge, 2000:xxi–xxii).

Given what we have seen concerning the Asian Crisis reported by Krugman (2000) this is a surprising assumption. Volume of investment is no guarantee of long-term benefit. Nevertheless, technology, comprising anything from the obvious such as telephones and computers, to frequent and cheap air travel, as well as the humble air conditioning unit, has served to transform the business prospects and the lives of countless millions of people in developing countries. Pride of place though, according to Micklethwait and Wooldridge, should go to the mobile phone. They describe how access to mobile phones opens up business opportunities for remote villages, whose farmers can find out the latest market prices for their produce.

This does not explain how they should respond, however, when they discover that dumped produce from developed countries has caused those market prices to fall through the floor. But there is little doubt that certain technologies can radically improve standards of living and the opportunities to do business.

Micklethwait and Wooldridge are on stronger ground when examining the Asian Crisis, considered from the perspective of Paul Krugman in the previous section. Krugman opined that faced with a crisis, developing economies should be able to use capital controls to ride out short-term problems, although he is quoted by Micklethwait and Wooldridge as saying that such controls should be 'an aid to reform and not an alternative' (Krugman, cited in Micklethwait & Wooldridge, 2000:59). Micklethwait and Wooldridge reject capital controls and explain that the crises in Thailand and a few months later in Korea stemmed mostly from the still relatively closed nature of Thai and Korean banking and the lack of genuinely open capital markets. In other words, the Asian Crisis was the result not of too much economic globalisation (neo-liberal free market capitalism) but *too little*. Even so, Korea bounced back and the stock market reached new highs in 1999. But Micklethwait and Wooldridge fear that the lessons have not been properly learned and there is still a lack of complete openness to foreign banking. The South Korean economy is still dominated by the *chaebol*, the huge conglomerates that comprise large numbers of disparate companies sustained by a network of ties between the constituent parts. The *chaebol* and the relative lack of openness shade into various degrees of nepotism and corruption that undermine South Korean capitalism and mean that it is still vulnerable to a repeat of the 1997–99 crisis.

Micklethwait and Wooldridge write that

> countries that get rid of capital controls and liberalize their banking systems see more efficient investment because markets allocate money better than bureaucrats do. Research by the Milken Institute has demonstrated that economies fare best when capital is cheap, plentiful, and just as important, allocated fairly (Micklethwait & Wooldridge, 2000:55).

They go on to report a Milken Institute study which concluded that the three most open emerging markets were the ones least affected by the Asian Crisis of 1997–99, Singapore, Taiwan and Hong Kong. The bottom four places went to Indonesia, South Korea, Russia and Bulgaria, all of which – with the exception of Bulgaria – were devastated by the crisis. Nevertheless, Micklethwait and Wooldridge agree that 'financial markets are horribly volatile' (Micklethwait & Wooldridge, ibid.). In explaining the crisis, they also point to over-expansion, property speculation and overcapacity creating a fear of deflation across the region. Asian companies borrowed too much short-term money, most of it denominated in foreign currency. As previously noted, the banks got nervous about their declining foreign currency reserves and eventually refused to extend loans further. Crisis ensued.

A further explanation for the crisis was unsustainable exchange rates, too much borrowing and inadequate standards of accounting and supervision, and finally poor quality and availability of information. In sum, Micklethwait and Wooldridge blame weaknesses in the emerging markets themselves, not the international financial system in which they were operating. And in any case, they point out that Alan Greenspan, Head of the Federal Reserve, reported to Congress in September 1998 that even the most badly damaged East Asian economies only lost about one sixth of their per capita growth over the preceding decade and their average incomes remained two and a half times those in China and India (Micklethwait & Wooldridge, 2000:59).

Discussion 10.7

Five myths of globalisation

1. **Size trumps all**
   Big mega corporations are getting bigger and they run the global economy; small companies are routinely swallowed up by the power of multinational corporations.

2. **The triumph of universal products**
   Globalisation means reduced choice; everything becomes homogenised as monopolies supply only what they want consumers to buy; diversity is lost.

3. **The rules of economics have to be rewritten**
   Globalisation and technology changes everything; old assumptions about business cycles are redundant; prices can only go up; everything is different.

4. **Globalisation is a zero-sum game**
   Globalisation produces big winners and big losers; jobs will be stripped away as companies relocate to places where labour is cheap; globalisation is a race to the bottom in terms of working conditions; only the rich profit; international trade ruthlessly exploits developing countries.

5. **The disappearance of geography**
   Businesses can relocate easily; home bases will be lost; companies will become rootless.

(Based on Micklethwait & Wooldridge, 2000:97–118).

Micklethwait and Wooldridge identify five myths about globalisation that are commonly paraded by its critics. These are summarised in Discussion 10.7.

Micklethwait and Wooldridge contest each of these common criticisms. First of all, there is plenty of evidence that size is far from everything in business. They point out that

> the proportion of American output coming from big companies rose gradually from 22 per cent in 1918 to 33 per cent in 1970, but it did not change between then and 1990, and surely, given the arrival of the technology industries, it must have fallen since then. In Germany, Japan and Britain, the proportions all fell pretty dramatically between 1970 and 1990 (Micklethwait & Wooldridge, 2000:101).

Just as significantly, big companies tend not to be very good at remaining on top. Micklethwait and Wooldridge write that companies fall from grace, and even disappear. In the 1970s just three automobile companies ruled American roads, Ford, Chrysler and General Motors. The market is much more competitive now and Chrysler has merged with Germany's Daimler Benz – although the merger is more a German takeover than a merger. Telecommunications and media are both far more competitive than they were 20 or 30 years ago. Microsoft may be massive, but there are ten thousand other software companies. The US toy industry, once dominated by Mattel and Hasbro, now has Lego, Sony and Nintendo. Toys "R" Us face competition from Wal-Mart and other supermarkets, as well as e-toys.com.

The same is true in European markets. There are big companies, but they are not without competition. Even the food sector, dominated by four, or perhaps five, supermarkets in Britain is changing fast and new niche providers have appeared and local competition is increasing.

Micklethwait and Wooldridge report on mergers and acquisitions, pointing out that while the

> numbers of such ventures have increased, most will fail. They usually bear witness to inflated expectations as well as inflated acquisition prices. Roughly two out of every three mergers do not work; the only winners are the shareholders of the acquired company who receive for their shares more than they are subsequently proved to be worth (Micklethwait & Wooldridge, 2000:102).

Global mergers are more difficult still because they bring together different cultures and different management structures and pay scales.

The second myth concerns the claim that globalisation creates uniformity, a homogeneous one world product, and a lack of local identity. This myth is common, but in fact there are very few truly global companies producing global products. Micklethwait and Wooldridge quote a Coca-Cola executive as suggesting 'McDonald's, Mercedes Benz and BMW, and Sony, but that's about it' (Micklethwait & Wooldridge, 2000:104). One might add Kodak, Nestlé, and Coca-Cola itself to this list, and perhaps Volkswagen, but there are indeed only a few. And even of those mentioned, it is questionable whether they are truly transnational, or global. As was suggested in the last chapter, the reach of most MNCs is across the Triad and to neighbouring countries, rather than genuinely worldwide. The other dimension to this myth concerns whether the products are the same. Micklethwait and Wooldridge describe how products vary for different markets but this seems a trivial observation. A McDonald's cheeseburger is still a McDonald's cheeseburger even if it has *teriyaki* sauce on it in Tokyo. The important constant is the brand name. Nevertheless, the point is taken: globalisation creates opportunities for more producers, more service providers and more products in more markets. The European airline industry is a case in point: the sector has opened up massively, mainly as a result of EU competition law.

Myth number three charges that the business cycle is dead and in fact the laws of economics need to be redrawn. There does not seem to be much evidence for this claim. Stock markets grew exponentially in the early 1990s before collapsing back in the second half of the decade. They have staged a tentative recovery in the past three years. Property prices in the UK took a dramatic fall in the early 90s but have assumed stratospheric growth in the past five to six years. Few expect that to continue; the cycle is still likely to make its mark. As for the other 'laws' of economics, there seems no evidence to suggest that we should abandon the assumption that markets operate on the basis of supply and demand. There is still a certain undeniable logic in the law of comparative advantage. Micklethwait and Wooldridge estimate that while the World Wide Web is undoubtedly a major innovation that impacts profoundly on business, they are surely right when they argue that the invention of the electric light was greater still. One could probably suggest the same for the invention of the telephone, or perhaps even, as suggested elsewhere by Micklethwait and Wooldridge, air conditioning in some countries.

The fourth myth is the zero-sum game assumption. Legrain writes that

> between 1990 and 1998 the number of Chinese living on less than a dollar a day fell by 150 million. That is the fastest fall in poverty the world has ever seen (Legrain, 2002:15).

Legrain produces a passionate defence of globalisation – which incidentally he describes as 'a process of integration and internationalisation, one that was happening during the Cold War and has continued since' (Legrain, 2002:11). The zero-sum myth is rejected on the grounds that millions benefit all around the globe. Globalists argue that 'in the past quarter century of intensive globalisation, major progress in advancing human development has been achieved' as shown in Figure 10.4. There are losers in the globalising economy, but Micklethwait and Wooldridge, and Legrain, assert that they are heavily outnumbered by the people whose lives are materially improved by their countries' engagement in international trade. Legrain argues that the wretched poverty of many African subsistence farmers cannot be blamed on globalisation since 'They don't trade, so they can't be harmed by it' (Legrain, 2002:10).

Micklethwait and Wooldridge argue that businesses cannot simply relocate to where labour is cheapest. Their argument relates to markets and productivity. Businesses prefer to be close to their markets, so transport costs are low, and they require high productivity, which is most likely where there is a ready supply of appropriately skilled and educated workers. Thirdly, businesses tend to require a high quality infrastructure in the area where they set up operations. All these factors mean that it is no simple matter to uproot and relocate from an advanced industrial home base at the heart of one's major market, to a developing country on the other side of the world. Nevertheless, some European businesses might

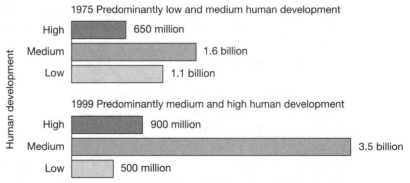

Data are in terms of number of people and refer only to countries for which data are available for both 1975 and 1999.

Figure 10.4 How the structure of human development in the world has shifted

Source: feature 1.1 (p. 11) from *Human Development Report* (2001) by the United Nations Development Programme, © 2001 the United Nations Development Programme. Used by permission of Oxford University Press.

relocate some production to the new member states of the EU, where labour costs are substantially less. However, a business making such a move would also need to consider possibly adverse reactions in its home market.

It is also important to recognise that most European businesses are relatively high technology specialist producers of goods and services. Many require more skilled workers, scientists and technicians than did traditional labour-intensive manufacturing industries of the past. This also means that labour is a lower proportion of total costs than it used to be. The result is that employment in OECD countries naturally has a different profile to most employment in NICs, where manufacturing tends to be more labour intensive and less specialist or highly trained.

Micklethwait and Wooldridge say that the creation of NAFTA in 1992 had a negligible effect on employment in the US, despite claims that employment would disappear into low-wage Mexico at the expense of American workers. It is also important to emphasise that globalisation creates jobs: where rationalisation has occurred, workers have tended to find new employment, especially in the service sector, and retailing in particular.

The most important defence of globalisation is contained in the argument that it opens up opportunities for development and improvement in living standards in LDCs. Micklethwait and Wooldridge write that

> In 1960, the average wage in developing countries was just 10 per cent of the average manufacturing wage in the United States; in 1992, despite all that terrible globalisation, it had risen to 30 per cent. The reason lies in [a] concept that anti-globalists cannot handle: globalisation helps the whole pie get bigger (Micklethwait & Wooldridge, 2000:102).

The point is underlined by reference to enduring laws of economics. Adam Smith's principle of the division of labour holds that the more people specialise in what they do best, the more productivity is improved. Secondly, the bigger the market, the more refined the division of labour can become. That principle should protect employment in OECD economies and developing economies alike.

In addition, David Ricardo's principle of comparative advantage affirms that the whole point of international trade is to allocate resources to the country that can use them best. Micklethwait and Wooldridge accept that this process has costs, but in the long run there are more winners than losers. They go on to refer to the question of fair trade, which is often raised in relation to the myth of globalisation being a zero-sum game. They assert that the best way developed countries could assist in creating a fairer trading environment would be to open up their own markets and in particular in agriculture. There are many tariff barriers that harm Third World producers. In addition:

> Much of the money that the west spends supporting manufacturing (some sixty billion dollars in the European Union alone) goes to the sort of basic industries that could represent a step up the development ladder for poor countries (Micklethwait & Wooldridge, 2000:113).

Rich countries tend to impose tariffs on imports from LDCs that are much higher than those imposed on other rich countries. In short, Micklethwait and Wooldridge argue for more free trade, and quote an UNCTAD report that if the rich countries lowered these tariffs it could add $700 bn to the exports from the developing world. These are the real issues of fair trade.

The final myth argues that geography is no longer an issue. Here Micklethwait and Wooldridge agree with the claims made in response to the 'end of geography' claim earlier in the chapter. Essentially businesses have good reasons to stay rooted in their home markets and the overwhelming majority do so. Businesses also recognise the value of clustering in key areas, so sectors become identified with specific locations. Above all, even in a globalising economy, most trade is conducted within the frontiers of the state. In the US, some 96 per cent of the total volume of business is conducted within the USA.

It is striking that Micklethwait and Wooldridge barely mention the environment in 386 pages. In contrast, Soros and Legrain do. They call for much greater proactive engagement by governments, through international and multilateral institutions, to establish and enforce measures to protect an already seriously degraded global environment.

Review *What explanation do Micklethwait and Wooldridge give for the Asian Crisis of 1997–99?*
What are the five myths of globalisation? How do Micklethwait and Wooldridge respond to them?

Summary

This chapter has made the following key points.

Postmodernism

- Postmodernism rejects the 'grand narratives' of Marxian or liberal theory.
- Postmodernism is characteristic of advanced post-industrial societies.
- Bauman refers to the 'absence of control' in postmodern society.
- Callinicos rejects the claim that Marxism is no longer relevant and says globalisation is a phase in the development of capitalism.

Gray and the challenge to the Enlightenment

- The Enlightenment repeats the cardinal error of Christianity in that it overestimates the status and competence of humankind relative to other animals.
- Technology has brought disaster and ultimately is not within human control.
- Humans, like all animals, are subject to the environment in which they live, and while humans can destroy that environment, they cannot control it.

- The neo-liberal project is one more stage in the Enlightenment tradition.
- A counter view is that globalisation enhances freedom.

The consequences of globalisation

- Gray and the neo-liberal project
  - Neo-liberalism generates increased inequality.
  - The neo-liberal project pursues an unobtainable utopia (Gray).
  - Neo-liberalism fractures societies and creates chronic instability.
  - The state is severely undermined by the pursuit of neo-liberal policy.
  - An unregulated market risks economic collapse and political upheaval.
  - States will struggle for control of dwindling resources.
  - There are no effective institutions to protect the environment.
  - The neo-liberal experiment will end in conflict and wars over scarce resources.
- End of history? End of geography?
  - Bauman describes the impact of economic globalisation through his tourist/ vagabond metaphor, in which elites travel by choice, while the poor cannot control their destinies.
  - Globalisation brings about a dislocation between agent and result – the state frees markets but cannot control them.
- The assault on inclusive models of capitalism.
  - There cannot be *one* model of capitalist development (Gray).
  - Germany and Japan are major economies experiencing great difficulties in adjusting to the changed economic environment created by neo-liberalism.
- Local crises with global implications.
  - Mexico suffered a currency crisis but was rescued by an IMF bail-out.
  - Nevertheless there was a ripple effect that hit Argentina and Brazil.
  - The Asian Crisis of 1997–99 was caused by reckless speculation and the lack of proper control on accounting practices; it triggered a major loss of confidence among investors, causing a ripple effect throughout Asia, as well as Russia.

Future perfect? In defence of globalisation

- Technology is liberating.
- The Asian Crisis was caused by insufficient access for foreign banks and a lack of openness in financial markets generally.
- Complete market deregulation is the best way to ensure stable economic development.
- Globalisation promotes diversity and choice.
- The laws of economics are basically unaltered.
- There are losers under globalisation, but many more winners.
- Location and proximity to markets still matter and most companies remain based in their home countries.

Key concepts: discussion and definitions

Key concept 10.1   Postmodernism

A wide variety of cultural practices and theoretical discourses associated with the experience of postmodernity (Macey, 2000:305).

Postmodernist debate is mainly a product of the 1970s although the term is actually much older. It has been used to describe a reactionary tendency within modernism, and was associated with Pop Art of Lichtenstein and Warhol. Eco and Rushdie have been described as postmodernist writers.

As reported in the chapter, in philosophical terms postmodernism is linked to Lyotard's *La Condition Postmoderne* which is concerned with the effects of modern computer technology on industrialised society, while Baudrillard's *Simulacra and Simulations* (1981) calls into question the existence of reality itself by pointing out that in some senses Disneyland is more 'real' than the real America in which it was built (Macey, 2000:307). Postmodernism, for Bauman is one of many possible accounts of postmodern reality. Bauman writes that it

> merely articulates a caste-bound experience of the globals – the vociferous, highly audible and influential, yet relatively narrow category of extraterritorials and globetrotters. It leaves unaccounted for and unarticulated other experiences, which are also an integral part of the postmodern scene (Bauman, 1998:101).

Thus, in his usual evocative language, Bauman relates postmodernism directly to his metaphor of tourists and vagabonds. The globals are the postmodernists; the other postmoderns, the great majority, are excluded. But Bauman goes on to point out the helplessness of the postmodernists when faced by what they cannot easily relate to:

> [The postmodernists] are rather helpless, when facing the realities of militant Islam, the ugliness of Mexico City hovels, or even the black squatting in a gutted South Bronx house. These are huge margins, and one does not know how to deal with them (Burszta, cited in Bauman, 1998:101).

The term postmodernism, now firmly associated with the post-industrial and computerised age, has become part of the discourse on globalisation. Meanwhile, it is also commonly applied to film media too. See for example the film suggestions below.

Key concept 10.2   Culture

The context in which any given human society exists, and expressed by symbols, icons, language, education, entertainment, fashion, consumer goods, and other commonly accepted manifestations of identity.

The cultural dimension to globalisation is clearly visible and affects our daily lives. The implication is that globalisation represents a culture that overlays or co-exists with pre-existing more local cultures. This view is implied by the notion of 'Americanisation', addressed in Discussion 9.3.

Culture is represented or personified by symbols and icons: therefore the culture of globalisation for some people at least might be represented by the ubiquitous McDonald's hamburger chain. Culture is composed of countless manifestations, but in the context of globalisation some appear to stand out. Here we briefly consider entertainment; branding; language; media and television.

Macey (2000:78) refers to the culture industry as meaning the entertainments sector. Indeed the extraordinary reach of the Hollywood film studios and US entertainment corporations that promote actors as well as films are a significant symbol of globalisation. France has stood firm in WTO negotiations to defend its right to insist on limitations on access to French cinemas of American movies, and has local content laws on commercial radio stations, seemingly attempting to resist the onslaught from American popular cinema and music. In the face of the overwhelming financial power of Hollywood, European film makers and distributors have collaborated in the making and distribution of European films. Without such partnerships, it is unlikely the industry would survive, and especially unlikely that it would produce innovative and good quality films.

Products, and specifically brands, take on a fetishist quality in the contemporary culture. The mobile phone has become not only a communications tool, but a fashion accessory. Marx wrote of the alienation induced by commodity fetishism in the first volume of *Kapital*. Individuals too become commoditised, appropriated by marketing firms and the media, generating personality cults around anyone from royalty to footballers. Perhaps the most striking example of the cultural impact of globalisation is in the ascendancy of brands, the most important asset of multinational corporations. Once not so long ago companies were valued according to their tangible assets, their property, machinery, and intangibles like expertise, goodwill and reputation forming a lesser and vague part of any estimation of value. Now the major asset of businesses is the calculated value of their brand names, based on considerations like depth of penetration in international markets, reputation and influence over competitors, longevity, and scope of appeal to consumers. With a visit to any shopping mall, a commercial break on a TV channel, air travel, or even a day out at a sports event, one is assailed by branding culture. This is not to say that branding is new: some of the strongest brand names have a history that extends to a hundred years or more, such as Ford, General Motors, Mercedes Benz, Kodak, Sony and Coca-Cola.

Language is also an important feature of globalisation culture, notably the spread of English, even where *it is not understood*. It is striking how Japanese youth's like to wear T-shirts emblazoned with English words, usually assembled in a grammatically logical fashion, but containing no meaning, or at most a meaning so obscure as to be meaningless. The point is that the English language is the symbol, not what the words actually convey. Where English is actually used to convey meaning, it has extraordinary reach. It continues to consolidate its position as a worldwide lingua franca, spoken by 1.25 billion people out of a population of 6.25 billion (Crystal, 1997, p. 5). The 5 billion who don't speak English would probably like to, except where basic food and security needs are more pressing daily concerns.

Television, a significant stimulus to the growing material discontent of East Germans during the 1970s and 80s despite attempts by the communist authorities to jam Western radio signals, arguably contributed to the downfall of communism. Its contribution to the dissemination of modern globalisation is many times greater. Half the world's population watched the 2002 World Cup Final on television. TV images present a world that is for many remote, but becomes tantalisingly 'real' through the flickering of a screen. Television does for globalisation what marketing gurus have explained is the whole point of advertising: to create Awareness, Interest, Decision and Action (AIDA), where action is the purchase of the product or service.

Television, like the Internet, becomes a propaganda tool for militant extremists too. The visual impact of planes crashing into the twin towers of the World Trade Center was a terrifying demonstration of the power of international terrorism. We know the cliché that the media provides the terrorist with the oxygen of publicity. Media coverage of terrorist attacks enables the threat of terrorism to spread far and wide. Gray (2003) has described the paradox of Al Qaeda, an anti-modern organisation using modern technology to convey its message. The same can be said of Islamic militants who supply a TV channel with grotesque video-footage of a hostage being beheaded, hoping that the film will be broadcast worldwide (Cockburn & Gumbel, 2004).

Further reading

Gray's *False Dawn* is recommended here too, but it was also included in the list of recommended books in the previous chapter. Look also though at the other Gray book widely referred to in this chapter:

Bauman, Z. (1998) *Globalisation: the human consequences*, Cambridge: Polity. This is a short book, written in Bauman's uncompromising style. See in particular Chapter 4, 'Tourists and Vagabonds'.

Eagleton, T. (2004) *After Theory*, London: Penguin. A brilliant, wide-ranging and highly readable work of cultural theory. Eagleton takes issue with postmodernist thinking, but with pretty much everything else as well; never afraid of challenging the big issues, including popular culture, faith and fundamentalism, morality and reason, love and death.

Gray, J. (2002), *Straw Dogs*, London: Granta. *Straw Dogs* is a powerful attack on the idealism of Enlightenment thought, and in particular it contains powerful comment on the relationship between technology and 'progress'. The book is also a sweeping overview of the Western philosophical tradition. It is lively, disturbing and even 'exhilarating' (as the back cover says).

Held, D. & **McGrew**, A. (2002) *Globalization/Anti-Globalization*, Cambridge: Polity. This is an excellent account of the arguments over globalisation, ultimately arguing a cogent case for a multilateral response to the challenge of the neo-liberal project of economic globalisation.

Hutton, W. (1997) *The State We're In*, London: Vintage. See especially chapters 9 and 12, 'Why Keynesian economics is best' and 'Stakeholder capitalism'.

Two extremely readable books that mount a strong defence of globalisation are:

Legrain, P. (2002) *Open World: The Truth about Globalisation*, London: Abacus. Legrain also defends globalisation but is more critical. He takes on Naomi Klein, George Monbiot and other globalisation critics. The book is especially good because it offers no panacea, ending with an agenda to make globalisation work better (see Chapter 12 in this book).

Micklethwait, J. & **Wooldridge**, A. (2000) *A Future Perfect: The Challenge and Hidden Promise of Globalisation*. London: Heinemann. This is a positive defence of the benefits of globalisation. Read the Introduction and Chapter 1, which set up the basic arguments of the book. Also look at Chapter 6 'The Five Myths of Globalisation'.

Film suggestions

The first two films below are suggested more for their atmosphere than any message or specific content. My point in putting forward *Mulholland Drive* and *City of God* is primarily to represent the mood of postmodernism, and in the latter case, the polar extreme of Bauman's continuum from global tourist to local vagabond.

David Lynch, *Mulholland Drive*, 2001 USA/France

Not especially a film about globalisation, though you could argue that the characters are mostly beneficiaries of a relatively comfortable middle-class Los Angeles suburb, although hardly at ease with themselves or their surroundings. They demonstrate a certain *anomie*. Their lives are decorated by postmodern symbols, and ultimately bound up with fears and anxieties. The film belies the usual Hollywood structure – it is a long, rambling suspense movie, with a plot that is often difficult to follow. As Andrew says, Lynch indulges in gratuitous tricks which don't make the film especially easy to follow. Nevertheless, it is beguiling viewing, intriguing camera work, great music, and typical David Lynch.

Geoff Andrew writes:

> Originally intended for TV, *Mulholland Drive* is much in the mould of Twin Peaks and Lost Highway. Lynch's characteristically bizarre noir focuses (probably too strong a word!) on a young beauty (Elena Harring) who loses her memory after a car accident and hides out in a house where she's found and befriended by the absent owner's helpful niece (Naomi Watts), new to LA in the hope of becoming an actress. Meanwhile, a hot young film director (Justin Theroux) is having trouble with the Mob trying to influence his choice of leading lady. Despite too many detours into nonsensical narrative cul-de-sacs, and too many shots that slowly travel towards corners down darkened corridors to the accompaniment of ominous rumbles, this works well enough as unsettlingly nightmarish suspense. That is, until it suddenly and stupidly decides to switch characters' identities, leaving one with a so what feeling of *déjà vu* (Andrew, 2002:811).

Mulholland Drive has also been criticised as misogynistic, so any recommendation here comes with various health warnings. But is this postmodern cinema? Definitely.

Fernando de Mereilles, *City of God* (Cidade de Deus), 2003, Brazil

A shocking film made in a shanty district of Rio de Janeiro. This Rio is no carnival. It presents a portrait of urban dislocation, neglect and hopelessness. It is almost unremittingly bleak. *City of God* is a film version of Bauman's vagabonds, of the most geographically fixed kind. The film shows gang violence among children and young adults among the *favelas* of the eponymous City of God – though there is no God here. A violent, gut-wrenching film, this is the very bottom of the marginalised left-behinds of contemporary globalisation.

If you can hack the shocking nature of the sheer brutality of these children's existence, it is a stunning piece of cinema – much of the filming uses long single takes on a video-8. The opening shot in which children chase a cockerel through the narrow crowded streets is wonderful, though somewhat alarming for the cockerel.

The film is based on the book *Cidade de Deus* by Paulo Lins:

> a chronicle of the author's experiences living amid gang warfare in a housing project built to isolate the impoverished from the city's wealthy tourist sector. It documented the lives, deaths and escapes of various people among the drug dealing and brutality of the streets. (Source: http://www.cnn.com/2004/SHOWBIZ/Movies/02/28/sprj.aa04.fernando.meirelles.ap/)

The reference above to tourists is apposite, for the film is an acute portrayal of the vagabond end of Bauman's metaphor. Another comment on the film from a BBC review describes it as:

> Shocking, frightening, thrilling and funny, 'City of God' has the substance to match its lashings of style. Cinema doesn't get more exhilarating than this. (Source: http://www.bbc.co.uk/films/2002/12/02/city_of_god_2003_review.shtml)

Visit the website for more details.

Pawel Pawlikowski, *The Last Resort*, 2000, UK

This short film (73 minutes) is a fairly harrowing yet poignant account of life in Britain for an asylum seeker, a Bauman vagabond. Tanya arrives, with her son, from Russia in the fairground resort of Margate. She seeks asylum and a new life in Britain. The film goes far beyond the tabloid headlines and demonstrates in documentary style the experiences of asylum seekers in the UK.

For an enthusiastic review of the film see http://jigsawlounge.co.uk/film/lastresort.html

James Dearden, *Rogue Trader*, 1998, UK/US

The film is about Nick Leeson, played by an earnest and hyperactive Ewan McGregor, and is based on Leeson's own book. Leeson was dispatched by Barings Bank to Singapore to invest in futures on the Singapore International Money Exchange in 1995. The film is not without significant weaknesses, but it is entertaining. It serves a purpose in this book demonstrating the vulnerability of massive capital investments in developing markets, and the addiction to high profitability based on pure speculation, as well as the lack of proper monitoring of a young employee who gets in way too deep. The collapse of Barings, the world's oldest private bank, was a major scandal in terms of poor supervision by senior management. For many the story was a convenient allegory of post-Thatcher casino capitalism.

Chapter 11

Globalisation, the state and multinational corporations

Outline

- The acquiescent state
- Multinational corporations in the global economy
- Business, governments and governance
- MNCs, trade and globalisation

Key concepts

11.1 Transnational/multinational corporation

11.2 Washington Consensus

● ● ● ● Introduction

The chapter begins by looking at the role of states in the progress of globalisation. The core claim is that governments have actually engineered their own 'altered states' in ways which have diminished their roles, but in other ways have contributed to what Milward calls 'the survival of the nation state' (Milward, 2000). For Giddens globalisation is '[not] a force of nature [. . .] States, business corporations and other groups have actively promoted its advance' (1998:33). Much of the liberalisation that has been a central characteristic of contemporary globalisation has been carried out by governments. State governments have thus played a central role in undermining the very sovereignty which, in a curious irony, many politicians treat as an almost non-negotiable family treasure where possible encroachment from the European Union is concerned.

The second section looks at the contribution of multinational corporations (MNCs) to the process of globalisation. That multinational corporations have an important role in the process of globalisation is well understood. Simply in terms of product innovation, especially in terms of technology and communication, the corporate role is immense. This chapter is concerned with other aspects of the MNC role, notably in the promotion of trade, foreign direct investment and employment, as well as the influence of multinational corporations on governance.

It is argued that MNCs play a leading role. It is abundantly clear that multinational corporations are, by definition, large. However, it is important not to exaggerate their power, as they remain subject to consumer choice and competitive pressures, most mergers and acquisitions fail, absolute monopolies are rare and comparisons between turnover of MNCs and the GDP of countries are fatuous.

The third section claims that corporations play an increasingly significant part in governance, and in particular were closely involved in the creation of the Single European Market. MNCs clearly benefit from the SEM, but they are also obliged to conform to the EC *acquis* regarding consumer protection, labour law and environmental regulations. They are also subject to the supranational authority of the Commission and the ECJ. What is arguably more significant, however, is that in some contexts MNCs are more powerful than in others, especially in developing countries, where MNCs, often acting in tandem with international institutions and local elites, can wield tremendous power. The consequences can be socially and environmentally damaging. This relative freedom for MNCs has been central to the neo-liberal project, and has been strongly supported by major international institutions such as the World Bank and the IMF.

It is also argued that MNCs have played a major role in relationships within the triangle comprised by the US government, the EU and the corporate sector. There is a remarkably integrated relationship between the corporate sectors and government on both sides of the Atlantic as well as in other parts of the world, notably in Japan and China.

The final section of the chapter examines the relationship between MNCs, trade and foreign direct investment. It is pointed out once again that the global economy is not as global as is often claimed. Two reasons account for this judgement; firstly, most trade and FDI occurs within the Triad; secondly, the overwhelming majority of business is intra-regional rather than inter-regional.

The acquiescent state

The state has not been a passive victim of globalisation. Globalisation, as Giddens says, is not a 'force of nature'. It does not *by itself* strip away the traditional powers of national governments. Indeed, globalisation does not have agency: it cannot *do* anything. There are actors within the globalisation process that impact upon others, on states, on shareholders, on businesses, on individual workers and farmers. Who those actors are is often assumed to be an unanswerable question: are they faceless bureaucrats, remote capitalists in ivory towers, board members in faraway places? This chapter argues that much of the time they are a great deal nearer: they may be our own elected representatives in government. It is important to get away from the notion that globalisation has nothing to do with governments. There is perhaps every risk of this conclusion, given the claim for example, referred to in the previous chapter, by Bauman that 'no-one seems now to be in control' (Bauman, 1998:58). Bauman goes on:

> Globalisation is not about what we all, or at least the most resourceful and enterprising among us, wish or hope *to do*. It is about *what is happening to us all* (Bauman, 1998:60).

This is an important quote in understanding Bauman's perspective, but it is necessary to understand why globalisation, apparently, has divested *us* of power, influence, or role. Various writers come to similar conclusions about the state. It is less powerful than it once was. Its sovereignty has been chipped away, or bitten off in large chunks. The state is a much reduced entity in global affairs. Realists must be concerned, as perhaps realism now only has meaning for the truly powerful, the single hegemon in a unipolar world, not the multipolar one that might have emerged when the Cold War ended. Indeed, Hutton (2002), Strange (1996), Monbiot (2000), Hirst and Thompson (1999) have all written of the declining role of the state. Others, including extreme globalists like Ohmae (1990), have argued that it has become an irrelevance.

Why has this happened? The key point is that state governments have engineered their own reduced roles. Privatisation of public utilities, the shrinking of state provision in sectors such as health and welfare, the reduced role of local authorities in provision of local services, the delivery of entire sectors of the economy to private businesspeople and private shareholders, the loosening of controls on capital movements, the liberalisation of the telecommunications sector just as it was about to expand massively in terms of technological competence as well as reach, the handover of the World Wide Web to private interests, the removal or reduction of tariffs, the removal of frontier controls, the liberalisation of markets in goods and services, and many other initiatives, have been carried out as conscious acts of policy by governments. We are a long way from the post-war Keynesian corporatism that was the hallmark of European governance throughout four decades after the signing of the Bretton Woods Accords in 1944. This, by the way, is not an argument of political point-scoring with hindsight. I am not suggesting that the old state monopoly telephone companies should never have been privatised: privatisation clearly made a massive contribution to the technological advances of the 1990s and the tumbling prices for telecoms services. Instead, the point is that in many ways, privatisation being one of them, state governments divested themselves of authority.

Strange (1996:10) comments that the demand for capital in order to finance technological innovation has escalated, and points out that the supply of that capital is a critical factor dominated not by state authorities, but by private markets. This is an important change affecting the international political economy, and one that clearly marks a shift in power, or at the very least a significantly changed role, for traditional state-based actors such as governments or the IMF. Capital markets are dominated by MNCs, as some of the largest private finance houses, banks and insurance companies are highly international in terms of their overseas commitments, assets and engagement with foreign markets. Technology has enabled capital to be increasingly located offshore, out of the reach of traditional government authorities. This can be interpreted as evidence of weakened state authority.

Government has retreated towards the realist notion of the state's core functions being security, defence and not much else. Whatever remains is subject to marketisation under the mantra of 'consumer choice'. Even security is increasingly a partnership with the private sector, as increased fear of crime has led to a spectacular growth in private security services. The policy changes outlined in the previous paragraph have not arisen out of nothing. They have been pursued above all by the United States, zealously adopted in the UK during the 1980s and 90s, and introduced in many other states as part of the political project of neo-liberalism, the driving force of economic globalisation. In other words, governments have followed policy prescriptions that enabled the neo-liberal political project of *laissez-faire* capitalism to dominate the global economy.

Bauman, Strange, Monbiot and Gray, from different perspectives, all argue that the state has to a large extent ceded authority to 'global markets', often difficult to identify, and difficult to control. National governments have also shaped the development of the European Union, reasserting the primarily inter-governmentalist character of the Union. It is governments and their representatives that shape EU policies, and it is governments that ultimately determined the final text of an unsatisfactory Constitutional Treaty in June 2004. It is governments that agreed to keep the CAP in place until 2013, despite the continued damage its subsidising regime inflicts on farmers in developing countries. It is also national governments that shape other international bodies with a global brief, such as the UN or the WTO.

Governments have acceded to the policy preferences of the **Washington consensus**, explained as 'privatisation and deregulation, trade and financial deregulation; shrinking the role of the state; encouraging foreign direct investment' (McLean and McMillan, 2003:368). The result is that authority and decision-making has passed away from states to what Bauman describes as 'bizarre characters' (1998:64). Strange summarises the shift in power away from states as follows:

> The impersonal forces of world markets, integrated over the post-war period more by private enterprise in finance, industry and trade than by the cooperative decisions of governments, are now more powerful than the states to whom ultimate political authority over society and economy is supposed to belong (Strange, 1996:4).

She argues that in a changed international environment states no longer compete for territory, but for market share. As a mechanism to achieve greater market penetration, states search for allies in order to achieve 'the added bargaining power conferred by a larger economic area' (Strange, 1996:9). She also underlines significant changes in the underlying structures of capitalism during the 1980s that were vital to the technological advances of recent years, notably, changes in the supply side of capital, where a newly liberalised environment provides the necessary credit to support innovation. Together with greater mobility of capital, this new financial architecture is able to meet the accelerating demand from business. Business responded with a growth framework that was described by Ray Vernon in his product life-cycle (PLC) theory. The process Vernon describes is enabled by the new capital architecture described above, and it presents an explanation for the dramatic internationalisation of business (see Figure 11.1).

A key feature of Vernon's PLC theory is that it explains the continual need for credit, effectively supplying the lifeblood of the capitalist system.

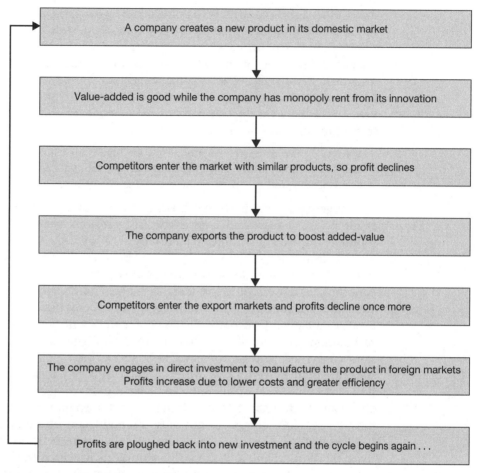

Figure 11.1 Vernon's product life-cycle theory
Source: adapted from Vernon & Wells, 1968.

Strange highlights three challenges to traditional assumptions of economics, social and political science, and international relations.

> The first premise is that politics is a common activity; it is not just confined to politicians and their officials. The second is that power over outcomes is exercised impersonally by markets and often unintentionally by those who buy and sell and deal in markets. The third is that authority in society and over economic transactions is legitimately exercised by agents other than states, and has come to be freely acknowledged by those who are subject to it (Strange, 1996:12–13).

As a consequence of these changes, there will be a growing 'asymmetry among allegedly sovereign states in the authority they exercise in society and the economy' (Strange, 1996:13) and the process of capital liberalisation weakens the authority of all states, large and small, as the world move towards a more globalised economy. States become 'victims of the market economy' (Strange, 1996:14). Politics can no longer be considered as the conduct of relations between states:

many other agents contribute to political processes. The contention is that power has moved from its traditionally perceived location, states, to markets. However, this complicates affairs because of the intangible nature of markets – and it complicates the position of states too, because in an outcome perhaps not entirely intended, states themselves become subject to the power of markets. This is, according to Strange, an uncomfortable situation for social scientists perhaps used to thinking that power pertains to someone, or some social or economic institution such as government.

> Markets do not fit this conception. They are impersonal, intangible, not even necessarily to be found in one place. They do not have rational preferences and can behave unpredictably and in a perverse manner (Strange, 1996:29–30).

Strange cites Soros in saying markets operate on a 'reflexive principle'. The result is, as Bauman and Gray argue (see previous chapter), that we live in unstable, unpredictable times. The Asian Crisis followed a boom time that won plaudits from the IMF and the White House and far beyond. Strange identifies transnational corporations (she prefers this term to multinationals – see Key concept 11.1) as exercising considerable 'parallel power' alongside states (Strange, 1996:65). The influence of companies over labour policy, regional funding, taxation and environmental policy is potentially significant. The extent to which corporations are able to exert power over states is relative to the power of the state concerned, and as we have seen, in the new political economy, some states are more powerful than others. Significantly too, in some states there may be a closer shared set of interests, and shared policy objectives, between corporations and traditional state authorities. Thus, for example, the Washington consensus since 2000 comprises not only the politicians and officials surrounding the President, but also Pentagon interests, the interests of oil company executives, the World Bank and the IMF, institutions in which the US has a decisive voting power. A policy consensus based on the exercise of power is not confined to Washington:

> State managers are often part of international elites, which include representatives from international organisations and key industrialists and financiers, that set the political conditions for the advancement of globalisation and which benefit, for example, from access to new goods and services, cheaper travel and technological advances. Many of those that are vulnerable to the shocks and crises that globalisation inevitably produces, on the other hand, are not politically powerful and may be further marginalised by processes of global integration (Newell, 2002:2).

Newell argues that globalisation disperses power in radically uneven ways, and not simply between states, or on a north-south basis, but also within states and between different groups in society.

In summary, governments and their representatives have created globalisation as we currently experience it, and are part of the uneven spread of power that has led to significant marginalisation for some communities, as well as tangible advances in material prosperity for others. Governments must take control of globalisation by coalescing around a set of interests that are common to the great mass of humanity, rather than of short-term benefit to narrow 'globalised' elites. States acting alone can achieve little, and the experience of regional integration in Europe in particular shows a historical acceptance by most EU countries that partnership and integration, and the politics of consensus building, is a more productive policy choice than unilateralism. Isolation or reliance on bilateral agreements is likely to increase polarisation, and undermine international forums such as the WTO and the UN.

If Bauman is right, and no one seems to be in control, it is governments that must act to recover lost authority. We return to how this might be achieved in the final chapter, which examines the prospects for improved institutional responses to the globalisation.

Review   *What is meant by the claim that states have acquiesced in the process of globalisation?*

● ● ● ● Multinational corporations in the global economy

A multinational corporation is a business that operates in several countries having made significant capital investment in international markets, typically creating manufacturing capabilities as well as sales operations in those markets. From a management perspective, MNCs engage in international marketing as opposed to mere export marketing. MNCs operate in several countries. Nevertheless, the term multinational corporation is disputed on the grounds that most have production facilities in only a few countries, while supplying many markets. On these grounds the term transnational corporations (TNC) might seem more appropriate. However, the term transnational corporation is also suggested, by Hirst and Thompson (1999) for example, as meaning businesses that have become truly global in that they are no longer nationally rooted. Such businesses are extremely rare; few businesses are genuinely global (see previous chapter). However, some observers such as Hindle observe that this may be changing:

> More and more multinationals will shift the operation and control of key business functions away from their head office. They will be following companies like IBM which recently opened a regional head office in Singapore with 1,000 employees to watch over its growing activities in the area and said that it must accelerate the transfer of its white-collar professionals outside the United States. This diffusion of power will speed up in 2004 into what will become the third age in the global strategy of multinationals (Hindle, 2003:109).

Moving head office responsibilities to different locations would indeed be a sea-change in the structure of international business. If this is occurring, it will certainly extend the boundaries of the Triad and signal a shift towards what Hirst and Thompson (1999) could see little evidence of in the late 1990s. Since the absence of genuinely transnational corporations was signalled as one reason for claiming that globalisation is a myth, then we have to acknowledge that if Hindle is right, we may see the emergence of more transnational corporations in future. In any case, globalisation is not static; it is a process, and trends are important.

In Chapter 9, Discussion 9.2 considered whether globalisation is actually Americanisation. This view is based on the apparent domination of American business and on the clear superpower status of the US in political and economic spheres. American business is probably less dominant than is often assumed. For example, in a rating of multinational corporation (MNC) size by foreign assets, US businesses account for half of the top ten, but Royal Dutch Shell, Toyota, Volkswagen, Nestlé and DaimlerChrysler are not US companies (Griffiths & Wall, 2001:148). DaimlerChrysler was created by the merger of Germany's Daimler Benz and Chrysler of the US. In fact this merger would be more accurately described as a takeover by the German company. A more comprehensive method of assessing MNC size using a transnationality index based on a combination of ratios assessing foreign assets/total assets, foreign sales/total sales and foreign employment/total employment provides a top ten dominated by European companies and two Canadian ones, but none are from the US. Similarly, half of the top 20 MNCs by turnover are not American.

Moreover, companies are subject to consumer choices and fashions change. Even the mighty McDonald's reported losses in two consecutive quarters in 2003 as consumers in the US became more conscious of the health implications of a diet substantially composed of burgers and chips. Also, mistakes happen: Enron was the world's sixth largest company by turnover in 2002, but within six months it had ceased to exist, buried under a corporate scandal of false accounting. The point is twofold: the US indeed has many large and powerful corporations, and many have subsidiaries in international markets, but large numbers of powerful companies are not American. Secondly, businesses may not be as powerful as is often assumed by writers such as Ellwood (2001) or Monbiot (2000). This point is developed below.

There are, however, certain sectors that are overwhelmingly dominated by US companies, and these are especially high profile: this book is written using Microsoft software and an American company, Dell, built the computer (in Ireland). Unless you are of that unusual breed of Europeans who seek out European films, the last movie you watched was probably made in Hollywood and presented to you in an American-owned multi-screen cinema. In addition, the financial services industry is overwhelmingly American, as is telecommunications, notwithstanding the size and success of European companies like Nokia, the world's largest mobile phone manufacturer, and Vodafone. The truth is that globalisation is complex and to dismiss it as Americanisation is an oversimplification (see Discussion 9.3). Nevertheless, Hutton (2003:202–3) points out that financial deregulation was achieved in the 1970s and 80s as a result of US pressure, and in the 1990s the US engineered the global deregulation of the telecommunications sector. In both financial services and telecoms the US dominated the market and was able to pick off local suppliers with relative ease. There was an orgy of takeovers and mergers in the 1990s (see Figure 11.2). Capital investment in the telecommunications industry and in so-called dot.com businesses created an enormous bubble that left millions of investors wishing they

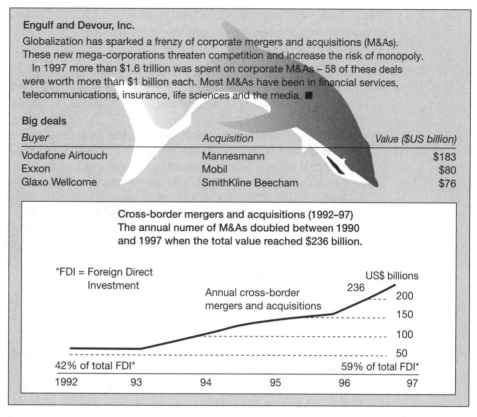

Engulf and Devour, Inc.
Globalization has sparked a frenzy of corporate mergers and acquisitions (M&As).
These new mega-corporations threaten competition and increase the risk of monopoly.
  In 1997 more than $1.6 trillion was spent on corporate M&As – 58 of these deals
were worth more than $1 billion each. Most M&As have been in financial services,
telecommunications, insurance, life sciences and the media. ■

Big deals

Buyer	Acquisition	Value ($US billion)
Vodafone Airtouch	Mannesmann	$183
Exxon	Mobil	$80
Glaxo Wellcome	SmithKline Beecham	$76

Cross-border mergers and acquisitions (1992–97)
The annual numer of M&As doubled between 1990
and 1997 when the total value reached $236 billion.

*FDI = Foreign Direct
    Investment

Annual cross-border
mergers and acquisitions

US$ billions
236
200
150
100
50

42% of total FDI*   59% of total FDI*
1992   93   94   95   96   97

Figure 11.2 Engulf and devour

Source: figure 1.1 (p. 26) from *Human Development Report* (1999) by the United Nations Development Programme,
© 1999 the United Nations Development Programme. Used by permission of Oxford University Press.

had been less impressed by the glossy prospectuses and excited sales talk. Hutton
summarises the post-boom and bust situation:

> 62 per cent of global information technology business originates in the US and
> American companies [own] 75 per cent of the global software market [. . . there are
> . . .] one hundred and eighty commercial satellites in orbit in space; all but half a
> dozen are American owned. The US controls the information age as it does the world
> financial system (Hutton, 2002:207).

The frenzy of mergers and acquisitions (M&As) in the 1990s was a clear illustration of the impact of liberalised capital markets. Figure 11.2 shows the scale of
such growth. Ellwood writes that the enthusiasm for mergers and acquisitions
creates monopolies and reduces consumer choice. In some areas this may happen, but as reported in the previous chapter, around two thirds of acquisitions
fail and it is far from certain that consumer choice is adversely affected, although
a sectoral analysis would be required to assess the full impact.

Companies may pursue growth strategy either organically, based on increased
sales and investment, or through mergers and acquisitions. Legrain implies

that the former strategy works best for the best-run businesses, and cites Tesco, Wal-Mart and Starbucks as examples (Legrain, 2002:134). Many others try to buy success by gobbling up their rivals:

> The late 1990s witnessed an unprecedented merger boom. At its peak, in 2000, the value of mergers and acquisitions completed worldwide topped $3.7 trillion, of which cross-border deals came to $1.1 trillion. The ten biggest mergers of all time have all happened since 1998.
>
> [. . .] In computing, Compaq bought Digital Equipment and is hooking up with Hewlett-Packard. In mobile phones, Britain's Vodafone snapped up America's Airtouch in 1999 and then swallowed Germany's Mannesmann for $173 billion in 2000 – the biggest takeover ever. Deutsche Telecom acquired Voicestream and One-2-One (now T-mobile), while France Telecom bought Orange. In America's telecoms market, SBC Communications has taken over two of the other six Baby Bells spun off from AT&T: Pacific Telesis and Ameritech. Bell Atlantic and GTE combined to form Verizon; WorldCom took over MCI. In Aerospace Boeing bought McDonnell Douglas. In retailing, America's Wal-Mart's purchase of Britain's Asda was followed by the French marriage of Carrefour and Promodès . . . (Legrain, 2002:134–5).

Legrain continues this account for almost an entire page. He also highlights the enormous size of MNCs:

> Together the top one hundred non-financial multinationals owned $2.1 trillion in foreign assets in 1999, and $5.1 trillion in total assets. They had sales of $4.3 trillion and employed 13.3 million people. The biggest, ranked by foreign assets, is America's General Electric, which had $141.1 billion of them in 1999. Second was Exxon Mobil with $99.4 billion; third Shell, with $68.7 billion (Legrain, 2002:136).

This is enough to tell us what we already know, multinational corporations are big. But Legrain argues that these figures should be understood in a broader perspective.

> General Electric was worth a whopping $370 billion at the end of January 2002. The company with the biggest sales in 2000, America's Exxon Mobil, had a turnover of $206 billion; it also made the biggest pre-tax profits, of $27.5 billion. These are staggeringly large figures. Yet relative to the market and the economy as a whole, they are still pretty small. Exxon Mobil's profits are a mere 0.3 per cent of US national income and 0.09 per cent of world income. GE's market capitalisation was only 2.7 per cent of the total value – $13.6 trillion – of companies quoted on American stockmarkets and 1.4 per cent of the world total of $26.3 trillion. In fact, the top hundred quoted US companies account for a much smaller share (46 per cent) of America's total stockmarket capitalisation in 2000 than they did in 1980 (62 per cent) (Legrain, 2002:139).

The last point is striking, because it belies the common view that big business just gets bigger. But there are other assumptions too, that multinational corporations bring only negative consequences. Legrain defends them as 'not the demons they are made out to be' (Legrain, 2002:137). They pay their employees more than the national average, and the gap is widening. They create jobs faster than their domestic counterparts and they spend heavily on research and development.

Foreign companies account for a remarkable 12 per cent of all R&D spending in America, 19 per cent in France and 40 per cent in Britain (Legrain, ibid.). They also spend a higher proportion of turnover in R&D. Finally, they export more than domestic firms do.

No one disputes that multinational corporations are an integral part of the globalisation process. The sales of multinationals' foreign affiliates equate to 37 per cent of total global GDP (UNCTAD report, cited in Griffiths & Wall, 2001:149). These affiliates also account for 32.5 per cent of world exports. Comparing turnover to GDP, half of the world's largest 'economic units' are multinationals, not countries. 'Only fourteen nation states have a GDP which exceeds the turnover of Exxon, Ford or General Motors' (ibid., 150). Bauman presents similar evidence concerning the size of MNCs:

> The sheer size of the main players in global markets today far exceeds the interfering capacity of most if not all elected state governments – those forces amenable, at least in principle, to ethical persuasion. General Motors had in 1992 an annual turnover of $132.4 billion, Exxon of $155.7 billion, Royal Dutch/Shell of $96.6 billion, against the Gross National Product of $123.5 billion of Denmark, $112.9 billion of Norway, $83.8 billion of Poland and $33.5 billion of Egypt . . . The five biggest 'non-national' companies had a joint turnover just twice as big as the whole of Sub-Saharan Africa (Bauman, 1997:56).

Such figures may be startling, but should also be treated with caution. Legrain (2002) argues that the comparison between turnover and GDP is bogus, given that turnover may have little relation to profit. The comparison simply does not compare like with like, and should not therefore be used to imply that MNCs are more powerful than states. A more honest comparison would be between companies' value-added (i.e. profit) and countries' GDP. In this case, only two companies make it into the top 50 creators of value-added or GDP. The two largest companies by this measure, Wal-Mart and Exxon Mobil, created value-added equivalent to the GDP of Chile and Algeria respectively. The US economy is 200 times greater than that of Wal-Mart, Japan 100 times greater and China 20 times greater.

> Even small countries like Belgium, Sweden and Austria are three to five times larger than the largest multinational. The value-added created by the largest fifty corporations represents only 4.5 per cent of the value-added of the fifty largest countries (Legrain, 2002:140).

Legrain says that comparing the power of companies with states is fatuous. Businesses have to attract customers, are subject to criticism in the media or from campaign organisations that can damage sales. Brands may be popular, but they may also lose popularity quickly. Legrain points out that MNCs do not control armies, cannot declare war, cannot raise taxes or call on people's atavistic sense of nationalism in the way that states may do so. Even the largest multinational corporations have to pay taxes in small states like Luxembourg. They also have to abide by consumer legislation, environmental standards and trading agreements in their largest markets. Legrain says that all the combined clout of Wall Street's financial institutions could do nothing to avenge the attacks on the Word Trade Center, but the US could.

> Even states that fail to deliver the basics for their citizens – like food and security, let alone prosperity and freedom – rarely disappear. The only 'companies' that have powers remotely comparable to those of states are the drug cartels. Colombia's earn billions of dollars a year, control parts of the country, have private armies and operate outside the law (Legrain, 2002:140–41).

Above all, companies exist in a competitive environment. All businesses are constrained by competition and the need to attract and retain customers. Globalisation has hugely increased competition in many sectors, including computers, telecommunications – remember the days when any telecoms service had to be bought from a state-owned monopoly charging relatively much higher prices? – energy, air transport, and even retailing. Despite a decade of restructuring, and many joint ventures, the automotive sector remains fiercely competitive, and heading for turbulence: there is a worldwide overcapacity in car production of 25 per cent (Maxton, 2003). Indeed, it is significant that the fortunes of large companies ebb and flow. Many companies that were enormous once have disappeared. Others have failed to keep pace in competitive environments. Others grow inexorably, like Microsoft, founded in 1975, or Oracle, set up in 1979, AOL in 1985. Other household names that are products of the most recent phase of globalisation are Vodafone, Starbucks, and Dell. Nokia, the world's largest mobile phone maker, was founded in 1865 as a forest industry enterprise, but barely heard of outside its native Finland until 20 years ago. A similar case is Sweden's IKEA founded in 1943. Legrain points out that the numbers of businesses competing in a sector may not be the best indicator of the level of competition. He reports that there are many vitamin makers in the US, yet the US Department of Justice found eight of them guilty of running a cartel. In contrast, there are only two companies making big passenger aircraft, Boeing and Airbus, and they compete fiercely.

In summary, MNCs are large and powerful but they are subject to the choices made by consumers. If we don't like supermarkets, we don't have to use them. See Discussion 11.1 for a summary of the weaknesses of big business.

A further key role of multinational businesses is their role in **foreign direct investment**. Encouraged as a central plank in neo-liberal economic policy, FDI is seen as essential to establishing a more global economy. Nevertheless, despite massive increases in FDI since the early 1990s, it is striking how most of it occurs between OECD countries, and in particular Triad economies. This aspect of the MNC role in globalisation is examined more closely later in this chapter.

Review   *In what respects are MNCs perhaps not as powerful as is sometimes claimed?*

Discussion 11.1

The weaknesses of big business

Even the largest multinational corporations are not invulnerable:

- Consumer choice/brand switching can rapidly undermine business performance.
- Businesses operate in a competitive environment and can rapidly lose market share.
- Consumer boycotts, adverse publicity, well-orchestrated campaigns can damage company reputation and sales.
- Well-organised campaigns by NGOs and campaign groups have exposed and altered corporate policy in several high profile instances: Shell/Brent Spar oil platform, McDonald's/'healthy eating', Nestlé/formula milk in LDCs, Nike and Gap/working conditions.
- Mergers and acquisitions fail in two thirds of all cases.
- Large companies hit on hard times and may even disappear altogether.
- New companies emerge as leading players, especially in new technologies and services.
- Businesses are obliged to accept the legal environments in which they operate, including payment of taxes, adherence to environmental and labour regulations, health and safety, and

consumer law. These restraints are enforced by legislative authorities such as states, the European Commission, the ECJ, ECHR; and quasi-legal authorities such as ILO, WTO, WHO, and the International Court of Justice.

- Businesses pay tax – where they reduce their tax liability through avoidance it is up to governments to close loopholes that make this possible.
- Turnover does not equal profit.
- MNCs on average pay higher wages than local businesses.
- Shareholders can influence company policies, e.g. executives' remuneration packages; shareholder influence is probably growing.
- Media coverage can also have major effect on MNC policies, e.g. need to improve vehicle safety, security and fuel economy.

However, MNC policies may be less affected by public opinion and consumer response in less developed countries, especially in relation to environmental impact. Campaign groups such as Greenpeace, Friends of the Earth, *New Internationalist* magazine and other environmental organisations play an important role in raising public awareness of international issues.

● ● ● ● Business, governments and governance

Part of the criticism of multinational corporations is their proximity to and influence on governments and governance. This is an important challenge and should be addressed. Critics of the corporate sector (Monbiot, 2000; Klein, 2001; Ellwood, 2001) have described globalisation as a 'race to the bottom' in which governments compete to loosen controls on MNCs and lower taxation in order to attract investment. Hutton (2002) points to the tighter regulatory environment in Europe, but global frameworks are required, especially in respect of taxation and the elimination of avoidance mechanisms employed by the hyper-rich and by many large corporations:

Global taxation measures – harmonizing corporate taxes, preventing companies from shifting their money to tax havens, and levying a tariff on all international currency transaction – would forestall one of the world's gravest impending problems: the erosion of the tax base as states offer ever more generous terms to the ultra rich in order to attract their money (Monbiot, 2000:355).

Further corrective measures are referred to in the next chapter. Meanwhile, the US has propelled a neo-liberal free trade agenda to the benefit of large corporations, many of which are US-based. This is broadly advantageous to the US economy as it ensures continued market leadership in key sectors. Free trade suits the largest companies, especially when they already have a technological lead, as they can improve their position by access to new international markets while benefiting from economies of scale not available to local competitors. Hutton (2002) refers to financial services, ICT and intellectual property as sectors where the US companies already have a decisive lead. Multinational corporations can have a decisive influence on policy choices. For many reasons, especially employment implications, and because of the success of lobbyists, and a form of mutual elite dependency, state governments are reluctant to impose heavy restrictions or penalties on the activities of MNCs. This is overwhelmingly the case in developing countries, where the penetration of government by MNC influence is extremely strong. However, several states acting in concert, such as in the EU, are more likely to impose limits, especially in matters of environmental or labour protection. MNCs of course lobby at both national and multinational institutional levels. As mentioned in Chapter 4, lobbying is a regular part of Brussels life, with coalitions of industrial interests, as well as representatives of single multinational businesses, playing an important role in informing and influencing the policy objectives of the European Commission (Greenwood, 1997).

Despite Monbiot's scepticism (2000), lobbying should not merely be interpreted as 'big business getting what it wants'. Rather, it is a vital part of the democratic process, and it coincides with lobbying from other bodies such as the ILO, and NGOs, including environmental pressure groups, which are able to mobilise public opinion to their cause. It is in the interests of the European Union to create and maintain effective balances between the interests of employers, employees, consumers and various other lobby organisations that contribute to decision-making at the European level. Governments must shape policy not at the whim of MNCs, but in consideration of wider society interests.

There are high levels of public concern over the environmental and health implications of MNC activity, especially in the food industry. In the wake of disease outbreaks concerning E-coli, bovine spongiform encephalopathy (BSE), foot and mouth disease, avian flu and swine vesicular disease, there is increased demand for more stringent monitoring of food production and food safety generally. Technological progress has impacted on food production as much as on any other industry and MNCs are increasing the mass production of food, including genetically modified products. Schlosser reports that

> In 1987 ConAgra took over the Elders Company in Australia, the largest beef company in the country that exports more beef than any other in the world. Over the past decade, Cargill and IBP have gained control of the beef industry in Canada. Cargill has established large scale poultry operations in China and Thailand. Tyson Foods is

planning to build chicken-processing plants in China, Indonesia and the Philippines. ConAgra's Lamb Weston division now manufactures frozen french fries in Holland, India, and Turkey. McCain, the world's biggest french fry producer, operates fifty processing plants scattered across four continents (Schlosser, 2001:230–31).

Public concern demands the engagement of governments and international institutions charged with protecting public interests. For years in Britain food production and food safety concerns remained under the supervision of the Ministry of Agriculture, Fisheries and Food. Only since the change of government in 1997 and the devastating impact of BSE and foot and mouth outbreaks has this obvious conflict of interests been addressed. Now food safety concerns are part of the remit of a Ministry for Consumer Affairs. Food production and food consumption are prime areas for external regulation. It is extraordinary that such issues could be considered outside the remit of government, whether at a national or supranational level, as is the implication of the extreme globalist perspective.

Unquestionably, multinational corporations have played, and continue to play, a significant role in questions of governance. Hocking and Smith describe US corporations as significant actors in their own right, acting as a third corner of the EU/US government/US corporate triangle. The balance between them is not one of traditional corporate dependency on government. On the contrary, commerce is not subordinated to national interests. This is further evidence that MNCs play a vital role in shaping changes in the global economy. Indeed, MNCs played a significant part in the emergence of the Single European Market in the 1980s. They were enthusiastic supporters of market integration, envisaging that the SEM would offer increased market opportunities and higher profits.

The SEM also created opportunities for the corporate sector to influence policy making more easily than if they had to deal with a whole variety of separate national governments. Mazey and Richardson (1993) state that major MNCs have established their own offices in key centres, and Brussels in particular, to lobby the EU decision-making process, rather than to rely on professional lobbyists acting on their behalf, though they may do this as well. Identifying separate national interests is often significantly less relevant than identifying sectoral interests and working in partnership with other private companies. Hocking and Smith highlight the complexity of the business and political environment and the increased role of the corporate sector in governance:

> From [the] implications of intense interpenetration and internationalisation if not globalisation arise a number of very significant questions. If there is a growing focus not only on traditional matters of commerce but also on 'behind the border' issues of regulation and operating conditions; if there is a complex interaction between the concerns and the strategies of government and business; and if there is difficulty in identifying the 'us' and 'them' implied by notions of foreign economic policy, then the roles of government and business are central to the exploration of multilevel policy-making and implementation. Matters of business strategy and competitiveness at the firm level are difficult to separate from issues of strategy and competitiveness at the national or continental levels. The need is thus for an analytical approach which can cater for the complexity and for the policy consequences (Hocking & Smith, 1997:124).

US firms operating in Europe could rely on their previous experience of dealing with the EC and with European institutions, or newer entrants to the European market could benefit from partner companies' knowledge and experience, or they could use sector representatives to supply relevant information and to lobby on their behalf. Such groupings are especially well established in the electronics and pharmaceutical sectors. The US federal government can also assist firms in the development of their European interests.

The main point here is that the SEM represents an opportunity for American as well as European companies. Trade organisations representing US interests in Europe were among the most enthusiastic supporters of the SMP (Hocking & Smith, 1997:132). A further byproduct of the SMP was the stimulus to Japanese FDI in Europe, no less than American. Japanese corporations saw fresh opportunities. They responded quickly to the potential commercial successes. The UK in particular benefited from a major influx of Japanese capital investment, especially in the automotive and electronics sectors. The UK is also the preferred base for American MNCs, with Germany the second most likely location. Around 70 per cent of US exports and FDI goes to the UK and Ireland, and to Germany and the Benelux states.

Significant factors in the choice of destination for FDI include the English language, the ready acceptance of US goods and services, and the generally welcoming business environment. France, in contrast, Disneyland Paris notwithstanding, appears to be a less positive recipient of US engagement.

The corporate sector has of course had a huge influence on the European integration process, quite independently of the role or influence of states. This is evidenced by the support of MNCs for the integration process, for the SEM and also for EMU.

The Single Market has also been a factor in several important mergers. Mergers are driven by business imperatives, not the niceties of political discourses on sovereignty. Mergers have taken place between European firms, such as KLM and Air France, or the acquisition of Mannesmann by Vodafone, or have involved extra-European entities, as with Daimler Benz and Chrysler, or Renault and Nissan. The two-way relationship between the corporate sector and the market should not be underestimated:

> Business has managed to rapidly form intra-European organisations through various takeovers, mergers or by finding new locations, sometimes outside Europe. Companies have therefore undoubtedly constituted a driving force for European integration, which by its nature is less concerned with the problem of state controls than with the actual liberalisation of the market (Kapteyn, 1996:147).

However, Kapteyn goes on to stress that business interests direct their strategic planning towards a global rather than a European context.

Bourke researched EU/Japanese relations and found that the major force of integration between them came from corporate links. Most of the initial period from 1973 to 1985 in EU/Japanese relations was based purely on trade, but from the mid-1980s onwards it was characterised by trade and investment (FDI) (Bourke, 1996:2). In terms of trans-territorial links, Japanese companies operating inside the EU created the majority of EC/EU links with Japan. He also reports that many of these links are forged regionally, at the sub-state level. However, the core players are firms.

> While the EU defines membership in terms of states, participation in the global economy is conducted through firms (Bourke, 1996:200).

Bourke suggests that globalisation may present a greater challenge to relations between states and within transnational groups like the EU than it does to states themselves. He claims that MNCs are better at establishing international bonds than are bodies that integrate states. If this is true, the implications are profound for the future of multinational institutions involved in international governance (Bourke, 1996:204).

A final point relating to the corporate-government relationship concerns the process of control over the corporate sector. While business supported the creation of the Single Market, the outcomes associated with it are not all running in one direction and in support of the free market globalisation objectives of the corporate sector. The existence of a Single European Market, controlled and regulated by a body of multilaterally agreed legislation, ensures that there are common norms, standards and rules to which businesses must conform. All businesses, from the smallest sole trader to Wal-Mart, operating in the European Single Market are obliged to conform to EU legislation. The existence of such a multilateral framework, under the supranational authority of the Commission and the European Court of Justice, and now also the Fundamental Charter of Human Rights, ensures that businesses meet standards and act within the law. If there were no Single European Market, it goes without saying that businesses would more easily be able to dictate on their terms what product standards, consumer law and environmental protection they should conform to.

The relatively high level of legislative restraint on corporate activity in the Single European Market is, however, not replicated anywhere else. Even in the United States, the environment in which business operates is less regulated, a point often argued in favour of removing those restraints on business that are said to raise costs to uncompetitive levels and adversely affect productivity in the European Union, and in some countries in particular, notably Germany. There is substantial pressure on the EU to comply with the neo-liberal agenda that seeks a less regulated business environment. Such pressures should alarm anyone concerned about the social and environmental impact of corporate activity.

Outside Europe, and in particular in developing countries, MNCs may have much greater leeway to behave in ways that would not be tolerated in Europe, for example in relation to primary extraction of oil, minerals, water and timber. As part of the policy prescriptions linked to financial support from the World Bank, or in order to conform to conditions stipulated by the International Monetary Fund, developing countries have been obliged to liberalise their capital markets and privatise state interests, including land and resources. This has given multinational corporations an open door to control significant resources in developing economies (see Discussion 11.2).

Discussion 11.2

Cochabamba fights back

In Bolivia's third city, Cochabamba, ordinary people took back their water from a corporate conglomerate, after the World Bank had pressurised the Bolivian government into privatising the public water supply. Having refused credit to the public water company, the bank demanded that a monopoly be given to Aguas del Tunari, part of International Water Limited, a British-based company half-owned by the American engineering giant Bechtel.

Granted a forty year concession, the company immediately raised the price of water. In a country where the minimum wage is less than $100 a month, people faced increases in their water bills of $20 a month – more than water users pay each month in the wealthy suburbs of Washington, home to many World Bank economists. In Cochabamba, even collecting rainwater without a permit was now illegal.

So they organised; young and old, activists and those who, as Marcela Lopez Levy wrote, had previously been 'too busy surviving to get involved'. She spoke to Marcelo Rojas, who became one of the leaders. 'I had never taken an interest in politics before' he said. 'My father is a politician, and I thought it was all about cutting deals. But to see people fighting for their water, their rights, made me realise there was a common good to defend'. [. . .] He was arrested and tortured by the police, as were many young people who built barricades and protected the old when the authorities attacked. They took over their city and they won. The government tore up the contract, and the company cleared its desks (Pilger, 2002:12–13).

Governments, in an effort to meet interest payments on loans, have felt obliged to direct their economies towards international trade at the expense of providing for local needs. A switch away from local food production to a cash crop economy in a country like Ghana, Kenya, Ethiopia, Indonesia or Brazil can be disastrous given the vagaries of international markets in agricultural products, or even primary resources such as wood. If control of such interests passes into the hands of foreign multinationals the problems are made worse. Even businesses that are not involved in exploiting primary resources or in agricultural production are able to benefit from more lax environmental controls than apply in rich countries, as well as less restrictive labour legislation, and lower social costs. Pilger reports on the shocking wages and working conditions of workers in a factory in Indonesia, making clothes for Gap destined for sale in Britain and America. He writes that many of the workers in Jakarta factories were migrants from the countryside where cash-cropping had destroyed self-sustaining agriculture. The underlying point is that the policies that made Indonesia a 'model pupil of globalisation' according to the IMF, just weeks before the Suharto dictatorship collapsed in 1998, opened up the country to FDI and foreign MNC involvement, including subcontracting in sectors like shoes. Pilger says 'Nike workers get about 4 per cent of the retail price of the shoes they make, which is not enough to buy the laces' (Pilger, 2002:16).

The Single European Market may approximate a level playing field; the global economy does not.

> **Review**   *Suggest ways in which MNCs contribute to breaking down traditional state-based policy making. Have MNCs have contributed to the process of European integration? If so, how? If not, why not?*

● ● ● ● MNCs, trade and globalisation

An obviously key dimension of globalisation is trade. The volume of trade and the proportion carried out by and between MNCs indicates the scale of their involvement in the process.

However, while trade between Triad members is clearly an indication of an international economy, Legrain points out that the world economy is less global than it seems. The Triad is actually less a free trading area than three related regional hubs that together account for some three quarters of all trade, but most economic activity is contained *within each of the three hubs*.

> The EU trades a mere 11 per cent of its collective output with the rest of the world; NAFTA trades just over 8 per cent; and Japan, 11 per cent. The rest of the world is linked to one or several of these regional hubs through a tangled web of bilateral (or regional) trade agreements (Legrain, 2002:111–12).

A consequence of increased trade, rarely referred to by advocates of free trade and further globalisation, is a greater cost on the environment (see Discussion 11.3).

While it is still the case that most multinational companies are Triad based, there has been some spread in their location from the core OECD economies.

Discussion 11.3

Who pays for trade?

The communications technology revolution of the last 25 years, [. . .] coupled with improvements in air freight and cheap ocean transport, [have enabled] companies to move their plants and factories wherever costs are lowest. Improved technology and cheap oil has led to a massive increase in goods being transported by air and sea. According to the Boeing Aircraft company, world air traffic cargo tripled from 1985 to 1997 and is predicted to triple again by 2015. The global shipping business which now consumes more than 140 million tonnes of fuel oil a year is expected to increase by 85 per cent in the next decade. And costs are falling too. Ocean freight unit costs have fallen by 70 per cent since the 1980s while air freight costs have fallen three to four per cent a year on average over the last two decades.

These cheap transport rates in reality are 'cheap' only in a purely financial sense. They reflect 'internal' costs – the costs of production, packaging, marketing, labour, debt and profit. But they don't reflect at all the 'external' environmental impact of this accelerated use of fossil fuels. Moving more goods around the planet increases pollution and contributes to carbon dioxide in the atmosphere, a major source of global warming and climate change. These environmental costs are basically ignored by business. This is one of the main reasons why environmentalists object to the globalisation of trade. Companies make the profits, they complain, but society has to pay the bill (Ellwood, 2001:18–19).

As recently as the mid-1980s, the turnover of MNCs was heavily concentrated in the US, Canada, UK, Netherlands and Germany, but now the spread includes Asia, especially Japan, and the so-called 'Tiger' economies of Singapore, Taiwan, South Korea and Hong Kong. South America too has seen a big rise in MNC activity. Fortune 500 ranks companies by turnover and reports that in 1998 185 out of the top 500 were US-based, 100 were Japanese and 170 were European. South Korea had nine and China six (Jeannet & Hennessey, 2001:17–18). The result is a huge increase in indigenous provision to supply the MNCs, spurring growth in regions that have traditionally lagged behind.

Figure 11.3 shows trade flows within the Triad. It demonstrates the trade deficit of the United States, which imports a far higher proportion of goods from Europe, and in particular from Japan, than it exports. In some ways this is not surprising: it suggests that US business is inclined to sell inside its own enormous domestic market rather than seek to sell into historically 'difficult' markets like Japan. The term 'manufacturing value added' (MVA) indicates the difference between production costs and selling costs, and again demonstrates that MVA is considerably higher in Japan and Europe than in the US. However, it is important to recognise that US multinationals operating in Europe contribute to European exports and will have a correspondingly limiting impact on the export capability of their parent companies in the US.

There may be a greater propensity to export in Europe than there is in the US out of historical habit and economic necessity. Legrain reports that foreign companies in Ireland exported 89 per cent of their output, compared with 34 per cent of the output from domestic companies. In the US domestic

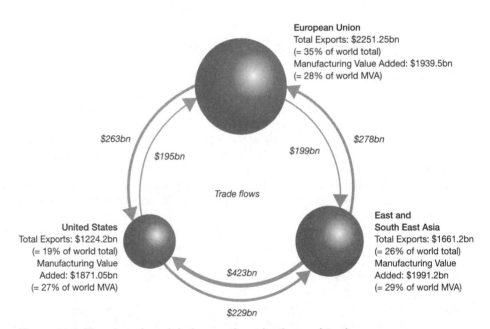

European Union
Total Exports: $2251.25bn
(= 35% of world total)
Manufacturing Value Added: $1939.5bn
(= 28% of world MVA)

$263bn $278bn

$195bn $199bn

Trade flows

United States
Total Exports: $1224.2bn
(= 19% of world total)
Manufacturing Value
Added: $1871.05bn
(= 27% of world MVA)

East and
South East Asia
Total Exports: $1661.2bn
(= 26% of world total)
Manufacturing Value
Added: $1991.2bn
(= 29% of world MVA)

$423bn

$229bn

Figure 11.3 The changing global map of production and trade

Source: © Peter Dicken, 2003. Reprinted by permission of Sage Publications Ltd.

© Touhig Sion/Corbis Sygma

Photograph 11.1 Toyota invested £700m in a manufacturing facility at Derby in the UK, in 1992.

firms exported 15.3 per cent of output and foreign owned ones only 10.7 per cent. Naturally, foreign firms operating in the US target their products at the US market. It is clearly the case that multinational corporations contribute to the integration of the world economy and Figure 11.3 shows the extent to which the Triad are locked into reciprocal trade. It is hardly surprising that a major economic downturn in one region has considerable impact elsewhere. Such evidence is sometimes used to argue that the world economy is indeed truly global but, as already stated in Chapter 9, the world economy is really a Triad economy, extending across wider regions, but still excluding large areas of the world, especially most of the southern hemisphere.

While it is still the case that the overwhelming majority of MNCs are concentrated in the Triad of NAFTA, the EU, and Japan, the Triad is 'widening'. In particular, the Asia Pacific region, comprising ASEAN, South Korea and China, has a growing proportion of trade. In Europe too, the growth in investment in the CEECs that joined the Union in 2004 indicates an eastern widening of the European leg of the Triad (see diagram, Figure 11.4).

The significance of MNCs in promoting increased internationalisation if not globalisation is also demonstrated in the dissemination of ideas, especially in respect of management theory and practice (Micklethwait & Wooldridge, 2000:68). Corporations are increasingly involved in education and training. Micklethwait and Wooldridge refer to corporate universities, such as McDonald's Hamburger University. The illustration is perhaps an unfortunate one, as the Hamburger University is not so much a university in the usual sense of the term,

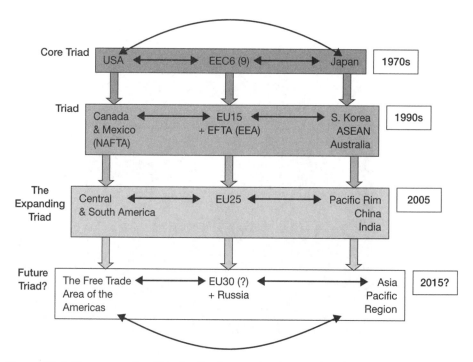

Figure 11.4 The expanding Triad – the increasing internationalisation of trade

but is unsurprisingly a training centre for McDonald's employees and managers. Its primary function would appear to be the preparation of staff in customer service and in understanding the culture of the organisation. It is, however, an example of the cultural dimension of globalisation.

Nevertheless, it is fair to argue that MNCs bring people together as producers and consumers and as such make a significant contribution to internationalisation in ways that go far beyond the massive increase in capital flow since the late 1980s. Foreign direct investment, the rising number of MNCs with plants in different continents and the impact on employment and management practices are all significant vectors in establishing closer links between the different continental legs of the Triad.

Because MNCs by definition are located in different markets, they eschew traditional state-based categorisation. It is true that most MNCs retain a strong identity with their home base and display the character of their home base organisation, but at the same time many have been proactive in building powerful linkage between the European and US corporate sectors. A consequence of this is that any assumption of inter-state competition is often inaccurate as far as MNCs are concerned, where suppliers are widespread and markets are interdependent. It has long been said that if the US economy sneezes, the UK catches a cold. The same is even more true for the UK/EU relationship, as 58.5 per cent of Britain's merchandise exports go to other EU member states (Legrain, 2002:191). The close relationship between Triad members is demonstrated not only by trade between them, but also by foreign direct investment.

By the late 1980s US foreign direct investment (FDI) in the Single European Market (SEM) approached $175 bn, and European investment in the US was even higher (Hocking & Smith, 1997:123). US firms operating in the SEM were estimated to have created 2.5 million jobs and to be running at a turnover of $500 bn. This is a clear indication of the extent of the US stake in the EU economy and how the success of the Single European Market is vital for US interests. Interdependency is a modern-day reality as never before.

The overwhelming proportion of FDI comes from American and European companies, around 85 per cent, and 70 per cent of this is invested in the US and the EU (Legrain, 2002:112). In 2000, Britain was the biggest single source and third biggest recipient of FDI in the world, with the US the largest recipient and third biggest source. Japanese companies used to be big players in FDI, but the 1990s' downturn in the Japan economy has knocked back the Japanese share. Developing countries received only 19 per cent of FDI in 2000, down from a peak of 41 per cent six years earlier. The biggest beneficiaries are China, Brazil and Mexico, while the poorest get very little (Legrain, ibid.). Heavy FDI into the European Union is of course associated with access to the SEM of 450m consumers. Most EU countries are major recipients of FDI but Britain, Ireland and the Netherlands are the most dependent on this capital inflow, while the new members from CEE are desperate to attract foreign capital to boost their development. Some such as Hungary, the Czech Republic, Poland and Slovakia have thus far been conspicuously successful in attracting investment from other European as well as American and Japanese corporations.

The accountancy firm Ernst & Young reported a significant upturn in FDI projects in the European economy in 2003, particularly in the UK and France. It is notable that Britain's non-participation in the euro seems not to be adversely affecting inward investment. Some highlights from the Ernst & Young report are shown in Discussion 11.4.

Bourke also emphasises the major role of multinational corporations in globalisation. He claims that companies drive the process, which he describes as 'neo-liberal internationalisation' (Bourke, 1996:198), based on cooperative alliances across the globe. However, echoing concerns expressed at the end of the previous section, Bourke points out the lack of countervailing regulatory power within the system. Existing forums based on intergovernmentalism, and functional and institutional theory, take insufficient account of non-governmental, non-state actors, such as MNCs. Presumably a realist theory of international relations is deficient in this respect too, though Bourke does not say so explicitly.

> International political economy provides valuable correctives to this defect by stressing that the important power interlocutors need not be states. However, a geopolitical dimension is also necessary to explain the politics of access (Bourke, ibid.).

The implication from this is that the multilateral institutional arm of governance must be strengthened. This is dealt with in the final chapter.

Review *Where are most MNCs located? Is this changing? Where is most trade located? How have MNCs contributed to developing transcontinental relationships?*

Discussion 11.4

UK and France lead recovery in European foreign direct investment, says Ernst & Young

- The year 2003 saw a 2 per cent rise in the number of foreign direct investments in Europe compared with 2002. Britain and France led the way, with most FDI inflow to Britain coming from the US, while France benefited largely from intra-European investment. The UK's better growth rate remains a significant draw for investors, although most of the increase was accounted for by expansion of existing projects.

- The accession states saw a decline in inward investment, but this should be understood in the context of significant previous investment in previous years in the lead-up to membership.

- Neither membership nor non-membership of the eurozone appeared to have a significant effect on FDI.

- The largest growth by project type was in manufacturing, while sales and marketing operations showed a decline.

- Most investment into CEECs was in expansion of existing projects, notably in Russia, Hungary, Poland, Czech Republic, Romania, Slovakia and Bulgaria.

- Toyota Motor Group was the highest ranking investor with 12 projects in 2003, followed by Nestlé and Robert Bosch (9 each), and Coca-Cola Corp, DaimlerChrysler Corp, and General Electric Co, all with 8.

Based on: http://www.ey.com/global/content.nsf/UK/Media_-_04_05_27_DC_-_European_Investment_Monitor

Summary

This chapter has made the following key points.

The acquiescent state

- State authorities have been active participants in the process of globalisation
- Economic globalisation has resulted in the decline of traditional state authority
- Governments have engineered their own reduced authority
- Marketisation has reduced the state role
- Economic globalisation disperses authority in unequal ways and some states remain more powerful than others

Multinational corporations in the global economy

- Multinational corporations are significant players in global capitalism; their pursuit of wider markets to achieve higher profits has a massive impact on the development of globalisation
- MNCs are large but they are essentially governed by law and are subject to consumer choice and a competitive environment; they are not all-powerful; most mergers and acquisitions fail

Business, governments and governance

- Businesses are close to governments and are highly active in lobbying and influencing policy
- In the EU there is a close relationship between institutions and MNCs as well as sectoral interests
- MNCs played a significant role in the emergence of the SEM
- MNCs play a key role in the EU/US/corporate relationship
- The SEM imposes significant restrictions on businesses in terms of employment law, consumer legislation, health and safety, and environmental protection
- Businesses are subject to much less restraint outside the EU, especially in LDCs

MNCs, trade and globalisation

- Increased trade and FDI are characteristics of globalisation
- Both are mostly Triad-based
- The Triad has expanded from its original heart of US/EU-9/Japan

Key concepts: discussion and other definitions

Key concept 11.1 Multinational corporation (MNC)

A large-scale business entity with production and sales operations in several different countries and regions.

Jeannet and Hennessey describe multinationals as 'companies that manufacture and market products or services in several countries' and add further clarification with 'Typically, an MNC operates a number of plants abroad and markets products through a large network of fully owned subsidiaries' (Jeannet & Hennessey, 2001:17).

Multinational companies typically require senior managers to provide strategic management. This involves making decisions about the entire enterprise and deciding what the company should do, rather than how things should be achieved at a local level. This distinction is between strategic management at a corporate level and operations management at a subsidiary level (Hannagan, 2000:124). Multinational companies are normally organised into separate divisions with relatively independent subsidiaries in various countries, each one of which is treated as a cost centre, or a strategic unit within the whole.

The United Nations Conference on Economic Development (2001) reckoned there are about 60,000 multinational firms with over 800,000 affiliates abroad. The term multinational corporation is normally used interchangeably with multinational firm, and sometimes transnational corporation. Some writers, such as Strange (1996), prefer the term transnational corporation because most firms remain firmly located in their home base and merely extend operations into different markets. What drives businesses to produce and sell beyond their national frontiers is the ambition to extend their market reach. In this respect, their engagement is strictly market oriented and therefore the term multinational a misnomer.

This book uses both terms, and specifically TNC when referring to views expressed by Strange.

Key concept 11.2   Washington consensus

Privatisation of state assets; trade and financial deregulation; shrinking the role of the state; encouraging foreign direct investment. The term implies that these policies reflect the preferences of US governments as well as the World Bank and the IMF, both of which are also based in Washington.

Privatisation and deregulation, trade and financial deregulation; shrinking the role of the state; encouraging foreign direct investment (McClean and McMillan, 2003:368).

The Washington consensus 'dictates that social betterment is impossible without unending economic growth' (Gray, 1998:175). It takes no account of the environmental consequences of unending economic growth. The mantra 'growth is good' has long dominated IMF prescription for developing countries, but even in 1997 the World Bank was abandoning its previous commitments to minimal government and arguing that an effective state was a prerequisite to social development (Gray, 1998:202).

The 'Washington consensus' is intimately linked to the 'neo-liberal project' according to Held and McGrew:

> The neo-liberal project – the Washington consensus of deregulation, privatization, structural adjustment programmes (SAPs) and limited government – has consolidated its hold within key western capitals and global institutions such as the International Monetary Fund (Held & McGrew, 2000:4).

An orthodox Marxist perspective holds that the G-7 (Canada, France, Germany, Italy, Japan, UK and US), together with the World Bank, act as imperialist enforcers of the capitalist system in which capital investment is the major tool through which to establish control over the economies of developing countries. Thus the Washington consensus has emerged as merely a new phase in capitalist development.

Callinicos refers to 10 points that constitute the Washington consensus, arguing that these represent a worldwide neo-liberal agenda:

> fiscal discipline, public expenditure priorities, tax reform, financial liberalisation, competitive exchange-rates, trade liberalisation, foreign direct investment, privatisation, deregulation, and property rights' (Callinicos, 2003:2).

Callinicos stresses the intimate relationship between the US government and the IMF/World Bank in pursuing these objectives, and the extent to which the aspirations involved were pursued by the Democratic administration of Bill Clinton and by the Third Way agenda adopted by Blair in the United Kingdom after 1997. Callinicos describes Anthony Giddens as Blair's 'court philosopher' (Callinicos, 2003:3). Callinicos says that the 1999 World Trade Organisation conference in Seattle was meant to progress the neo-liberal agenda, but it collapsed because 40,000 uninvited guests turned up to protest about the environment, Third World debt and fair trade. Arguments between the US and the EU were not resolved and the 'neo-liberal juggernaut (was) temporarily, at least, halted' (Callinicos, 2003:5).

The independence of international organisations is a prerequisite to their effectiveness in representing common interests. Callinicos points to the apparently timely removal from office of Joseph Stiglitz, chief economist to the World Bank, on the eve of the Seattle Conference. Stiglitz emerged as an arch critic of development policies subsumed under the Washington consensus. His book *Globalization and its discontents* (2002) is a powerful indictment of the Washington orthodoxy. He also presents a compelling prescription for the reform of globalisation. Other notable critics are Paul Krugman, George Soros, Noam Chomsky and Jeffrey Sachs.

Gray thinks the Washington consensus is a fleeting moment:

> The Washington consensus will not last forever. It will undoubtedly be shaken by economic shocks and geopolitical shifts. It is an episode in the search by the United States for a post-Cold War identity, no more stable or enduring than any other aspect of American opinion or policy. As the example of the World bank's changing view suggests, it is already being questioned (Gray, 1998:205).

Indeed in a later reprinting of *False Dawn*, Gray argues in a new foreword that the Washington consensus, and what he calls 'global laissez faire' (Gray, 2002ii: ixx–xxi), is all but over, as the US government now overtly favours increased protectionism. He cites the attempt to impose steel tariffs as an example.

The term 'Washington elite' is also used, meaning those advising the George W. Bush administration, and containing some leading figures in the Bush government, as well as members of the IMF and World Bank. After September 11, the Bush administration adopted a more hard-line neo-conservative policy in pursuit of US global hegemony (Chomsky, 2003); see Chapter 12. A pressure group with a decidedly realist character had emerged as a significant force behind Republican Party policy-making: The Project for an American Century argues for a world order based on American values and preferences. Visit http://www.newamericancentury.org/ for more details.

Further reading

Callinicos, A. (2003) *An Anti-Capitalist Manifesto*, Cambridge: Polity. Callinicos gives a Marxist critique of the neo-liberal project of economic globalisation. A condemnation of the Washington consensus, Callinicos argues that only a radical programme of Marxist reform can bring global justice.

Dicken, P. (2003) *Global Shift: Reshaping the Global Economic Map in the 21st Century*, London: Sage Publications Limited. An outstanding and comprehensive textbook on the theories, consequences and characteristics of economic globalisation. The book includes various case studies, as well as discussions on inequality, development, the environment and governance.

Monbiot, G. (2000) *Captive State: The Corporate Takeover of Britain*, Basingstoke and Oxford: Pan. Monbiot charts the increased power of big business and the extent to which government has transferred authority to corporate interests, leaving society less protected and more vulnerable to corruption.

Schlosser, E. (2001) *Fast Food Nation*, London: Allen Lane/Penguin. As well as being a tremendously entertaining read about all aspects of the fast-food industry, this thoroughly researched book provides an interesting account of the triangular relationship between America's major fast-food retailers, the major players in the meat supply industry, and government. Reading this book could change your life: you might never eat another hamburger again.

Stiglitz, J. (2002) *Globalization and its discontents*, London: Penguin. A stinging indictment of the management of globalisation by a former Chief Economist at the World Bank.

Strange, S. (1996) *The Retreat of the State: The Diffusion of Power in the World Economy*, Cambridge: Cambridge University Press. Susan Strange provides a detailed presentation of a multidisciplinary approach to the role – and decline – of the state. She also points out how the state has been an active participant in its own reduced authority.

Film suggestions

These films portray the bad side of business: the first shows the ruthless pursuit of personal gain in a highly competitive business; the second shows the callous indifference of a major corporation to the sufferings of an entire community poisoned by its activities; the third shows a clash of civilisations where 'progress' and profit override ancient customs and the land rights of Aborigines. The last shows the modern corporation as exhibiting psychopathic tendencies. The common thread in all four films is that the corporate environment is shown in a poor light.

James Foley, *Glengarry Glen Ross*, 1992, US

David Mamet's play about the wheeling and dealing of real estate salesmen in Chicago gets dedicated playing from a splendid cast (Jack Lemon, Al Pacino, Alec Baldwin). 'Always be closing' is the motto in a high pressure atmosphere where the claustrophobic competition to succeed exposes character flaws in the protagonists of the story. The job requires a complete lack of integrity but the world created by this environment is a house of cards.

See http://www.eufs.org.uk/films/glengarry-glen-ross.html for a review.

Steven Soderbergh, *Erin Brockovich*, 2000, US

Erin Brockovich (Julia Roberts) plays a single mother with attitude in this David and Goliath story of a multinational company getting its come-uppance from a determinedly investigative legal assistant who seeks justice for a community disastrously affected by chromium contamination in the water supply of residents around the Hinkley plant of the giant Pacific Gas & Electricity Corporation. The eponymous Brockovich gets a job with the small law firm of Ed Masry (Albert Finney) and pursues her quarry with total conviction, not afraid to use her sex appeal wherever it might bring her closer to nailing the corporate guilt. The facts are basically true – it led to the biggest class action settlement in US legal history. The film is a powerful indictment of corporate greed and disregard for human pawns. It is also well acted and well scripted.

Werner Herzog, *Where the Green Ants Dream (Wo die grünen Ameisen träumen)*, 1984, Germany

This film is more than an attack on corporate greed, although the core of the story is an oil company attempting to drill in the sacred ancestral lands of two Aboriginal tribes. The case ends up in the high court, and the institutional settings of modern Australia present a painful contrast to the ancient traditions of Aboriginal culture.

The film is visually stunning and contains an interesting cameo of a white drop-out who rails against the Enlightenment faith in progress in a scene that might have been scripted by John Gray. *Where the Green Ants Dream* is 'a contemporary environmental morality tale'. http://www.bfi.or.uk/showing/nft/featurearchive/herzog/tour-films.html

Mark Achbar, Jennifer Abbott, Joel Bakan, *The Corporation*, 2004 Canada

This film, in documentary format, and featuring Michael Moore, Naomi Klein, Noam Chomsky and Milton Freidman as themselves, is a meticulous study of corporate conduct set against a checklist of behavioural characteristics considered typical of a psychopath. One sequence explores the Cochabamba case (see Discussion 11.2 on p. 368). The absorbing film is both disturbing and thought provoking, and as one critic remarked, it could do for the corporation what *Jaws* did for sharks. There is also a book accompanying the film. For more details, visit http://www.thecorporation.tv/

Chapter 12

Multilateralism and the European Union as a global actor

Overview

- Multilateralism and international institutions
- After September 11
- The European Union as a global actor
- Responding to globalisation
- Conclusion: a cosmopolitan social democracy

Key concepts

12.1 Multilateralism

12.2 Transatlantic partnership

12.3 Hard/soft power

● ● ● ● Introduction

This chapter argues that governments must commit afresh to a multilateral future through international organisations that can secure a just and secure system of global governance. This is a daunting challenge given the extent to which the legitimacy and effectiveness of the major international governmental organisations (IGOs) is constrained by the preferences of the most powerful states, mainly located in the economically dominant northern hemisphere.

This book has focused mainly on the European Union, but has also made frequent references to other leading IGOs, namely the United Nations, the World Bank, the International Monetary Fund and the World Trade Organisation. Other organisations also play a significant role in shaping the globalisation process, such as the G-8, the OECD, NAFTA, OPEC and NATO. In nine of these ten bodies, the leading players are North American and West European. Japan, despite being the world's second largest state economy and in many (but not all) respects 'a model world citizen' (Piening, 1997:151), is a minor player. No other state outside Western Europe or North America has a significant role, except in OPEC, a cartel consisting of the major oil-producing nations, and heavily dependent on the preferences of its largest customer, the United States. Most of these institutions were designed in the aftermath of the Second World War to reflect nineteenth-century powers. Only Germany was marginalised in the wake of the catastrophe of Nazism. Even the European Union, often attacked as a Franco-German product, is as Siedentop (2000) has commented, a French design. It has remained mostly inclined towards French preferences for intergovernmentalism, rather than German federalism (see Chapter 5).

This chapter begins by looking at the role of international governmental organisations and assesses how they are affected by the globalisation process. It examines the extent to which they are hostage to state interests. IGOs by definition tend towards **multilateralism**, but many are undermined by unilateralist politicking by member states. A further characteristic of IGOs is that power is not spread equally. Some states, like the animals in Orwell's *Animal Farm*, are 'more equal than others'.

The second part of the chapter is concerned with the response to the terror attacks against the USA in September 2001. Using arguments from Robert Keohane, the case is made for a return to a multilateral and institutional response to the challenges presented by globalisation, now including the 'globalisation of informal violence' (Keohane, 2002). US policy in particular is critically examined, with an assessment of both unilateralist and multilateralist policy responses.

The third part of the chapter examines the EU response to globalisation, especially in the context of Europe/America relations. The section begins by underlining the major weaknesses of the Union. It is argued that resolving these problems is a prerequisite to the EU making a meaningful contribution to the task of reforming and improving the international system. The prospects for the transatlantic relationship are considered, especially in the context of the so-called 'values gap' between Europe and America, and in the light of possibly divergent strategic interests.

The chapter ends with an assessment of how international institutions, including the European Union, might respond to the current challenges. In an era of international terrorism, and other challenges to international stability, as well as the threats posed by chronic disease, failing states and climate change, reform has become an imperative. Governments must cooperate to create and sustain policies that promote public goods such as sustainable development, fair trade, environmental protection, human rights and international justice.

The final model discussed in the book is described by Held and McGrew (2002) as 'cosmopolitan social democracy'. This is a multilateral approach to international governance that attempts to bring together several of the major strands in globalisation theory, including liberalism, institutional liberalism and reformism (see Chapter 8 and Figure 12.2).

The core argument of this chapter is that while the end of the Cold War changed little, the combined effects of the election of George W. Bush, the 9/11 attacks on the United States, and the 2003 war on Iraq have brought fundamental changes to the international environment, and to the US/EU relationship. The **transatlantic partnership** faces particular strains, but given the divisions within the Union itself, and the continuing ascendancy of the neo-conservative right in the US, it is difficult to predict the outcome.

The European Union, the world's most sophisticated and long-lasting example of regional integration, with 25 member states and 453 million citizens, is threatened by its own weaknesses and contradictions. It must enhance both its soft power and its legitimacy. Only through harnessing its economic mission to a commitment to fundamental human rights and respect for the environment can the Union secure lasting political credibility. Only on this basis can the Union hope to exert a force for good in shaping globalisation. The Union must seek to translate its commitments in these areas into its multilateral relationships with allies and trading partners throughout the world, including the United States.

This is an ambitious ideal, especially since the Union itself is probably at a crucial point in its history. It will need to plot its future course with care, since while it might aspire to offer positive examples to others, only the most ardent devotee of the Union could fail to recognise that it has major problems. The Union is plagued by contradictions and hypocrisies, as well as internal divisions. These may even threaten its undoubted achievements over the past several decades. We live in interesting times.

Multilateralism and international institutions

Globalisation has brought problems and benefits. It has impacted significantly on the development of multinational institutions, and on states. The advanced industrialised countries of the OECD have actively pursued the liberalisation of the world economy. They have acquiesced in both the negative consequences of globalisation and the deficiencies of international institutions. The role of states has altered, becoming more multifaceted and definitely more international. It is beholden on state governments to search for multilateral approaches through international institutions that can effectively address the challenges presented by globalisation.

According to a traditional realist framework, states conduct their affairs with other states. While this is still true, they are also intimately involved with various international institutions, delegating representatives and participating in collective decision-making. It is through these international organisations that states maintain their international profile. International institutions have replaced the battlefield as the arena in which (most) states flex their muscles.

Institutionalism is a fragile concept. In June 2004 the UN finally adopted a new resolution pointing a way forward for Iraq, under a sovereign interim government from 30 June 2004. This agreement followed three years of marginalisation of the UN in international affairs, and even 14 years of division since the Iraqi invasion of Kuwait in 1990.

> The issue of Iraq has dogged the [Security] Council and sabotaged its cohesion from the moment of Saddam Hussein's invasion of Kuwait in 1990 and harsh sanctions were imposed (Usborne et al., 2004).

The sanctions were always controversial, with some claiming that ten years of UN sanctions cost half a billion civilian lives (Pilger, 2002). Nor is it only the

UN that has suffered in recent years. After the early optimism of the Doha WTO meeting in 2001 little progress has been achieved on a new trade round for the benefit of developing countries, as Doha promised. Multilateral institutionalism has had a tough time, but the new UN initiative over Iraq may be an attempt at a fresh start, seeking to create international energy behind the fraught process of nation building in an Iraq so deeply traumatised by decades of dictatorship, war and occupation.

In the UN, the WTO, NATO and the EU, it is states that decide policy direction, and states that determine sanctions against those who 'break the rules'. Alternatively, states delegate authority to specific supranational authorities to take action on their behalf. For example, the WTO may apply sanctions against any member in breach of trade agreements; the ECJ may rule against companies operating a price-fixing cartel; the Commission may impose financial penalties on a member state in breach of EC environmental legislation. Exceptionally, the European Council (composed of heads of government) may even suspend a member state if it is seriously in breach of the spirit of the treaties. This happened in February 2000 when the other 14 members of the Council voted unanimously to impose sanctions on Austria because it had formed a coalition government that included the allegedly racist Freedom Party under the leadership of Jörg Haider.

In the UN the enforcing of sanctions depends on the most powerful: any one of the five permanent members of the Security Council may veto a UN resolution. In those international institutions of which the USA is a member, such as the UN, the IMF, the World Bank, NATO and the WTO, the US frequently appears to act as a hegemon. This view may be disputed, but despite changed circumstances, America still has a sufficient military and technological lead, as well as control over significant resources and powerful economic and political influence, to justify the term hegemon (Jackson & Sørensen, 2003). See also Discussion 12.1.

International institutions are run by their member states. This form of institutionalism is amenable to a neo-realist interpretation, since the state remains the core actor, participation by states is effectively voluntary, and sanctions are limited. However, an international system so comprised is somewhat fragile if states are determinedly neo-realist in their approach. Neo-realism may permit some level of cooperation and participation in international organisations, but it does so from a strongly state-centred foundation. A more stable institutionalism depends upon a stronger multilateralist consensus, as pertained for much of the post-Second World War period. There have been significant departures from multilateralism, however, but none as marked as that of the US since 2000. Under George W. Bush, even before 9/11, the US had been strikingly unilateralist. Hence the claim that institutionalism is fragile, if not fractured.

Different IR perspectives were outlined in Chapter 8 and there is no need to repeat any overview here. Suffice to say there is proximity, but not fusion, between neo-realist and neo-liberal standpoints. The neo-realist position holds that states struggle to defend their individual interests in what is still essentially an anarchic environment – because there is no higher, international authority.

Discussion 12.1

Institutions are weak and undemocratic

The United Nations

The UN is ostensibly a democratic, one-member-one-vote organisation, but some are more powerful than others. Resolutions depend on the backing of the Security Council, within which any one of the five permanent members (Britain, China, France, Russia and the United States) can veto a resolution. Furthermore the UN has no executive power in terms of enforcement of its resolutions, or the decisions of its International Court of Justice. See also Discussion 12.4.

World Trade Organisation

The WTO has 147 members. It has a dispute settlement procedure which can enforce sanctions against members that break agreements. However,

in negotiating those agreements the 'big players' can hold out for what suits their interests, as the EU and the US to a lesser extent have done over agricultural subsidies; the WTO has a limited role in matters relating to the environment, and has on occasions backed 'free trade' over environmental and social measures.

The World Bank and the International Monetary Fund

The World Bank and the IMF are subject to the weighting of votes according to the capital invested by the members; this gives rich OECD members over 60 per cent of the voting strength. The US has a weighting of 17.5 per cent, sufficient to veto policies or loans of which it disapproves. LDCs are often in a 'take it or leave it' situation when seeking financial support.

Neo-realism accepts, however, that states operate within an international structure and will cooperate so long as their interests are served. The international structure may involve weaker states in alliance with stronger ones in order to enhance their security. Critical to neo-realism is the notion that states will always seek to preserve their autonomy, even when forming alliances.

Jackson and Sørensen summarise the relationship between neo-realism and neo-liberalism as follows:

> During the 1980s some neorealists and neoliberals came close to sharing a common analytical starting point that is basically neorealist in character: i.e. states are the main actors in what is still an international anarchy and they constantly look after their own best interests. Neoliberals still argued that institutions, interdependence, and democracy led to more thoroughgoing cooperation than is predicted by neorealists. But many current versions of neorealism and neoliberalism were no longer diametrically opposed (Jackson & Sørensen, 2003:52).

Multilateral governance can only be effective where the institutions involved are not subject to the wishes of powerful minorities pursuing a dedicatedly neo-realist – or even worse, classical realist – agenda, or it can be effective where sufficient numbers of states, especially the more powerful ones, perceive that their individual interests will best be served by operating through multilateral channels.

It is important, however, not to overestimate the extent of a straightforward cleavage between multilateralism and unilateralism. While it is possible to observe a consensus for multilateralist preferences in international affairs after the

Second World War – specifically on account of the formation of the UN, the Bretton Woods Accords and the institutions they created – it is evident that the US, as a superpower and hegemon, was content with such a multilateralist framework all the while it could serve US interests. Indeed, Roosevelt insisted on the UN Security Council offering the veto to its five permanent members (Pollack, 2003:119). By 1971 the relative decline of the US was apparent and the Nixon administration began to pursue a more unilateralist foreign and economic policy, beginning with the effective ending of the Bretton Woods fixed exchange rate regime. US declining power was evident from its growing trade deficit with Europe and Japan, the comparable nuclear strength of the USSR, and the morass into which the US had descended in Vietnam (Pollack, 2003:120).

From 1971 onwards the US pursued a policy of engaging with multilateral organisations on a selective basis, where there was an identifiable coincidence with domestic interests, for example in respect of the economy and the WTO, or foreign policy interests, and commitment to NATO, and NATO enlargements in 1999 and 2004. Pollack reports that this selective approach pertained through various US administrations, including that of Bill Clinton, who had to contend with a Republican Congress which, together with the Pentagon, resisted multilateral restraints on US military action. Two examples are the US decision not to support the 1996 Land Mines Treaty, which aimed to outlaw the anti-personnel mines, and the selection of targets in the Kosovo campaign. In 1997, although personally committed to the Kyoto Protocol, the measure was not forwarded to an obviously hostile Senate. The Senate also defeated the Comprehensive Test Ban Treaty on nuclear weapons testing. In other words, there was plenty of evidence of unilateralism in the US before George W. Bush arrived in the White House in 2000.

A further caution is that following 9/11 it is not the case that the US pursued a *solely* unilateralist response. While it is true that the support offered by NATO was not taken up, and within days of the terror attacks the Bush administration made the war against terrorism its highest priority. However, it pursued this priority

> through the maintenance of a large international coalition. [. . .] Within days of the 9/11 attacks, the administration began to assemble a wide-ranging coalition against terrorism, including Russia, Pakistan, Saudi Arabia, and a NATO alliance which for the first time invoked Article 5 of the NATO Treaty. At the same time the administration moved quickly to mend US relations with the UN, including the rapid payment of back dues and the confirmation of John Negroponte (as UN Ambassador). The following year, seeking support for a potential US war against Iraq, Bush announced that the US would return to UNESCO following a 20-year absence (Pollack, 2003:123).

Nevertheless, as argued below, the US response to 9/11 has been less than multilateralist, tending to be based more on an assumption of US leadership with others invited to follow. US policy hardened later, as signalled in the *National Security Strategy* document in September 2002. This argued for unilateral action against perceived threats to American interests, even in the absence of UN (multilateral) backing.

Discussion 12.2

Power and weakness

Robert Kagan (2002) argues that support for multilateral rules and institutions is inversely proportional to state power. From this he claims that great powers 'often fear rules that may constrain them more than they fear the anarchy in which their power brings them security and prosperity'. Great powers therefore favour military responses over multilateralist alternatives which might constrain their sovereign decision to use force. Weaker states, like contemporary Europe, lacking the military alternative, prefer multilateralist options and the constraint on the use of force.

Pollack (2003) says that Kagan's account does seem to reflect the Bush administration's willingness to use force and readiness to act without authorisation from the UN, both in Afghanistan and in Iraq post 9/11, and especially since September 2002 when the administration released its National Security Strategy which argued for the use of pre-emptive force against so-called 'rogue states' (Peterson & Pollack, 2003, 134–5). This was in marked contrast to continental European preferences.

Europe is turning away from power, or to put it a little differently, it is moving beyond power into a self-contained world of laws and rules and transnational negotiation and cooperation. It is entering a post-historical paradise of peace and relative prosperity, the realisation of Kant's 'Perpetual Peace'. . . The means by which this miracle has been achieved have understandably acquired something of a sacred mystique for Europeans, especially since the end of the Cold War. Diplomacy, negotiations, patience, the forging of economic ties, political engagement, the use of inducements rather than sanctions, the taking of small steps and tempering ambitions for success – these were the tools of Franco-German rapprochement and hence the tools that made European integration possible (Pollack, 2003:124).

Kagan's view is that the European integration experiment has led Europe to attempt to export its achievement of multilateralist consensus to the rest of the world.

Pollack reports on the common assumption that the US is unilateralist and the EU multilateralist (see Discussion 12.2). This interpretation has some merit, but as already shown in the preceding paragraphs concerning the US, it is an oversimplification. The EU, much like the US, is selectively multilateralist where it suits the common interests of the member states and in particular the more influential larger ones. Certainly there has never been a common shared consensus on the extent to which Europe should be multilateralist, or supportive of supranational institutional development (see Chapters 4 and 5). Different states hold different priorities. In recent years the UK, usually picked out as unsympathetic to greater integration, has supported binding EU rules on trade liberalisation in financial services and telecommunications, interestingly enough sectors where the UK has a significant lead over the rest of the member states. Germany has opposed a Commission proposal on corporate takeovers, anxious to defend traditional German ownership structures which may include *Länder* participation, or preferential share ownership. France has fought to defend high levels of state subsidy; it has wanted to secure exceptions on audiovisual material in the WTO; it has consistently resisted reform of the CAP. Italy has objected to a common arrest warrant. The UK holds out against any EU involvement in taxation or social security and welfare. CFSP has never been much more than an ambition, and certainly not one common to all member states. In foreign policy the EU has demonstrated widely divergent policy preferences, most obviously over the disintegration of the former Yugoslavia and more recently over the US decision to go to war against Iraq in March 2003. Different states pursued different policies, driven not so much by popular opinion at home, but by governing elites determining national interest.

The UK supported the US, arguably out of tradition, out of loyalty, or from some moral conviction that this was the right thing to do. Critics contend that the Blair government pursued long-term commercial and strategic interests in backing the US, including access to reconstruction contracts and oil supplies from Iraq, potentially the Middle East's second largest oil producer. The Shröder government in Germany, having won an election on its anti-war stance, continued to oppose military intervention that did not have UN backing. France also went against the US, as it has historically tended to do, seeking instead to present a strongly independent French or European position with a closer identification with Arab interests in the Middle East and Gulf region. Italy and Spain, under right-wing prime ministers, supported Bush, presumably for reasons of ideology as well as anticipated rewards. Most of the new member states joining the EU in 2004 also lined up behind Bush's 'coalition of the willing', perhaps out of historical duty given their sense of debt to the US for its opposition to the great oppressor, the Soviet Union, throughout the Cold War. Clearly there was some justification in US Secretary of State for Defence Donald Rumsfeld's assertion that the European Union was divided between 'Old Europe' and 'New Europe' (see Discussion 12.3).

Both the US and the EU have taken highly selective approaches to negotiating trade within the WTO. Agriculture is the most obvious area of self-interest overriding common principles supportive of multilateralist agreement, but many other areas have proved problematic. Since 1995 the WTO has had the authority to approve countermeasures against states that break agreements through its Dispute Settlement procedures. The WTO has ruled against US imposition of steel tariffs, the EU's refusal to accept hormone-treated beef from the US, while GM food remains a serious point of dispute within the current Doha Round. Pollack concludes, however, that

> The EU remains, on the whole, a strong supporter of multilateral rules and institutions. Such support, however, reflects not an ideological or instinctive respect for multilateralism *per se*, but a sophisticated and instrumental calculation by EU member governments regarding the types of multilateral rules and institutions most conducive to the satisfaction of the Union's domestic and international preferences (Pollack, 2003:127).

Review   *Why is institutionalism 'fragile'? How true is Kagan's characterisation of the EU as multilateralist and the US as unilateralist?*

Discussion 12.3

Old Europe/New Europe

In February 2003 the US, backed by the UK, sought a further UN resolution to attack Iraq. When such a resolution was not forthcoming, Bush went ahead anyway. Nor was the UN the only international organisation undermined by US/UK policy over Iraq in 2003. When the UK Prime Minister Tony Blair backed George Bush rather than follow the European Union lead from France and Germany, his decision made it so much easier for other European leaders, notably Aznar in Spain, Berlusconi in Italy and Millar in Poland, to follow Blair's endorsement of US policy, despite the overwhelming public opposition in those three countries. Romania and Bulgaria did likewise. This division in European ranks made it possible for Donald Rumsfeld, US defence secretary, to portray Europe as divided between 'Old Europe' and 'New Europe', and to list a number of European countries among his 'coalition' members, a vital step in appealing to the undecided among his domestic audience.

As Bush crowed about the 'international community' represented by his 'coalition', the US in fact embarked on a war in which 95 per cent of the effort was from the US itself, backed by a small contingent from the UK and tiny ones from others. Language, as Orwell pointed out, is easily manipulated in times of war. While elite politicians of a similar ideological bent or with similar geostrategic interests hurried to support Bush, no doubt expecting reconstruction contracts and oil supplies in the future, populations in these European countries showed massive majorities against what their political leaderships had endorsed. Blair's lead and the agreement from a handful of other European states (whether members of the EU, 2004 entrants or applicants) severely damaged the credibility of the EU both within the organisation and beyond. Not for the first time, the aspiration to present a common foreign and security policy seemed hopelessly far from reality.

● ● ● ● After September 11

The end of the Cold War left the United Sates as the sole surviving superpower. The US led the coalition against Saddam Hussein's occupation of Kuwait in the Gulf War. The US also led the foreign engagements in Bosnia and in Kosovo. There has been a pattern of American response to what it sees as deviant behaviour in maverick leaders or 'failed states', but the nature of US military action has shifted towards a more unilateralist position. The 1991 Gulf War was authorised by the UN Security Council; the US acted in Bosnia after the Srebrenica massacre had underlined the failure of the UN to resolve the crisis – in which the EU had been utterly ineffectual. In Bosnia, NATO engagement was uppermost and the peace-making role of the Contact Group, comprising Germany, Russia, the UK, France and the US, and eventually Italy, was also decisive in reaching the Dayton Accords that ended the war. In Kosovo, again the US was critical to ending the Serb ethnic cleansing that threatened to overwhelm the Kosovo Albanians, but NATO was also involved. The eventual ending of the conflict involved effective diplomacy on the part of the EU, in particular its Special Envoy, the Finnish President Martti Ahtisaari, together with Russia (Peterson, 2003:90).

Since 9/11 there has been a different complexion to US military action. President Bush refers to the 'international community', but since the terror attacks of September 11, the approach has been that 'the US leads/others follow', and the UN in particular has been marginalised.

> Initially, some commentators thought 9/11 might change the Bush administration's approach to multilateral issues such as climate change. But [. . .] even in the fight against terrorism, its approach has been that America should lead and others should assist. Beginning with its decision not to seek UN Security Council authorisation to use military force against Afghanistan, and continuing with its decisions to prosecute members of the Taliban and Al-Qaeda in national rather than international tribunals, and in 2003, to invade Iraq, the US has not been willing to accept significant multi-lateral decision making (Bodansky, 2003:67).

Indeed, not even NATO's offer of support in Afghanistan was taken up, bar a modest British contribution and some logistical and infrastructural support. Bush has preferred to build what he termed a 'coalition of the willing' to prosecute the 'war on terror'; multilateralism has been downgraded. Peterson and Pollack refer to Bush's January 2002 State of the Union address as pivotal in a shift towards American unilateralism. The references to an 'axis of evil' alarmed America's European allies and their concerns were increased by the absence of hard evidence linking Saddam Hussein to Al-Qaeda. In fact 'staunch US ally Saudi Arabia was sometimes alleged to be a more important sponsor of state terrorism' (Peterson & Pollack, 2003:8). US policy appeared to represent a hardening of a military response as opposed to

> Europe's instinctive predisposition towards 'civilian power' methods: patient diplomacy, aid and trade instruments, reinforcing multilateralism. More generally Bush's speech appeared to signal a shift from the measured, restrained and coalition-focused language and behaviour shown by his administration in the first days after 9/11 to a brand of headstrong American unilateralism (Peterson & Pollack, 2003:8).

The shift in US policy had major implications for the EU, NATO and the UN. Donald Rumsfeld, US Secretary for Defence, described the international coalition against terrorism as 'a shifting alliance' that will be 'opportunistic' and 'temporary' with the US always prepared to 'abandon certain allies along the way out of sheer pragmatism, just as they will abandon us' (Rumsfeld, cited in Peterson & Pollack, 2003:9).

The effect according to Peterson and Pollack

> was to shatter any notion that the transatlantic alliance was special, time-honoured, and permanent, bound together by a shared history and common values. It was widely agreed that NATO was a prime victim of 9/11. It was less clear that the US could 'win' a war on terrorism without the EU, especially given its growing competence in justice and home affairs questions and ability to seize or block the assets of international terrorist organisations. The rise of a new common enemy in the form of international terrorism often seemed to have the opposite effect on transatlantic cohesion as did the Soviet threat during the Cold War (Peterson & Pollack, ibid.).

But Europe itself, and the UN, were divided. In the Security Council it was clear that France and Britain took opposite views. Ultimately, as Britain backed the US but the Security Council would not countenance a fresh resolution authorising force in February 2003, the US launched its invasion anyway. Its 'coalition of the willing' included the UK, Spain, Italy and Poland. Other new members of the EU also backed the US. The EU and the Security Council were hopelessly split.

Robert Keohane writes that the internationalisation of informal violence – a phrase he prefers to the more generally applied single word terrorism – is a product of globalisation and part of its multidimensional character. Innovative thinking is required to meet this and other challenges from contemporary globalisation.

9/11 highlights the need to reinterpret globalisation more broadly, beyond its narrow economic focus. This book has tended towards the Gray interpretation of globalisation as a political project designed to promote a neo-liberal economy, consistent with the Washington consensus. However, by emphasising various consequences of globalisation, especially in Chapter 10, we are inevitably drawn into a wider interpretation. The reaction to American values, so often celebrated by George W. Bush in a virtually meaningless homily to 'freedom', now includes acts of extraordinary violence such as 11 September 2001.

After 9/11 the context of globalisation changed. Keohane argues that 9/11 forces a rethinking about security viewed in terms of territorial space.

> Globalisation means, among other things, that threats of violence to our homeland can occur from anywhere. The barrier conception of geographical space, already anachronistic with respect to thermonuclear war and called into question by earlier acts of globalised informal violence, was finally shown to be thoroughly obsolete on September 11 (Keohane, 2002:276).

The reassessment has three dimensions. Firstly, no state is safe from infiltration by terrorists, and from terror attack, the traditional defence of frontiers against foreign threats is rendered anachronistic, and non-state actors operating within the borders of liberal states can be as coercive and fear-inducing as states. Secondly, the globalisation of informal violence can be analysed by exploring patterns of asymmetrical interdependence and the implications of power. Essentially, this means who holds power over whom and how power affects relationships between states, non-state actors, and institutions. Thirdly, the US response to the attacks tells us a lot about the role of multinational institution in world politics.

Keohane claims that 9/11 radically alters the traditional realist arguments *against* military intervention. He points out that Morgenthau and Waltz were opponents of the Vietnam War. Their arguments were based on the view that Vietnam posed no direct threat to US interests, and was in effect too far away. In the contemporary context of the 'war against terror' this argument no longer holds. The US has assumed a policy of conducting a war against terror that embraces the possibility of pre-emptive action against states deemed to harbour a terrorist threat. With the United Nations withholding support from any notion of pre-emptive strikes, the US has pursued a more unilateralist course, in Afghanistan in October 2001, and in Iraq in March 2003.

The United States, for all its military superiority, is shown to be vulnerable in the face of international terror. Keohane refers to significant asymmetries in confronting terror, summarised in Discussion 12.4.

Discussion 12.4

Asymmetries and the globalisation of informal violence

Keohane highlights important asymmetries in the globalisation of informal violence.

1 Asymmetry of information

A paradox of globalisation is that in an information society which is also open, potential terrorists may themselves accumulate detailed knowledge about targets while state authorities have poor knowledge of the potential terrorists.

2 Asymmetrical beliefs

The use of suicide bombings would appear to depend upon the promise of eternal life to those prepared to play the role of martyrs to a fundament-alist cause. Attacks of this kind are more difficult to prevent and often more savage in their results, especially as civilians are usually the targets. The motivation for such attacks is not consistent with the secular beliefs widely held in the societies attacked by Al-Qaeda.

The US and its allies have enormous advantages in terms of military resources, economic influence, material benefits, technology and political influence. They can also convey their preferred messages worldwide, using a wide variety of broadly sympathetic media. Therefore the asymmetries mentioned above are exceptional, but nevertheless they provide some short-term advantage to those organisations intent on carrying out random acts of violence. (based on Keohane, 2002:276–7).

Keohane argues that 'we have overemphasised states and we have over-aggregated power' (Keohane, 2002:277). We have correspondingly underestimated our vulnerability, a point which becomes more startlingly evident after September 11.

What should the response be? 'Institutionalist theory implies that multilateral institutions should play significant roles wherever interstate cooperation is extensive in world politics' (Keohane, ibid.). But the US response to 9/11 marginalised the international institutions. NATO support was offered, but not accepted.

> [Even] before 9/11 the Bush administration had been pursuing a notably unilateralist policy with respect to several issues, including global warming, trade in small arms, money laundering, and tax evasion (Keohane, 2002:278).

Keohane argues that a more multilateralist approach is essential post 9/11. It will not do for the US to pursue its objectives alone, as in Afghanistan, and then call on the UN to clear up the chaos that is left following military action to remove the Taliban, suspected of harbouring Al-Qaeda. Questions remain over the legality of the war in Iraq in March 2003 and over the subsequent occupation. Throughout the process, the US has sought to present its actions as backed by a coalition of states, although it has not had UN backing. The removal of the UN weapons inspection team under Hans Blix before he had finished work was roundly condemned and led to intense friction between the US and Germany and France in particular, as well as tension within the UN Security Council. However, from a US perspective, the war against terrorism [. . .] increases incentives for unilateral action and bilateral diplomacy. Threats of terrorism generate incentives to retain the ability to act decisively, without long deliberation or efforts at persuasion (Keohane, 2002:280).

Clearly 9/11 showed signs of opening up a chasm between the US and international institutions, including the EU – although it also brought into equally sharp relief differences between EU member states. Keohane highlights the US move towards unilateralism in its reluctance to accept UN involvement in any action against Afghanistan and its insistence in February 2002 that the US might renew its war with Iraq with or without UN backing. He suggests that

> a cynical interpretation of United States policy towards multilateral institutions would suggest that American policymakers want to retain freedom of military action for themselves, but to delegate tedious political issues – such as [the reconstruction of] Afghanistan – to the United Nations. When the inevitable political failures become evident, blame can then be placed at the door of the UN (Keohane, 2002:280).

Keohane concludes that 9/11 and the globalisation of informal violence clearly underlines the fact that globalisation has certainly not rendered the state obsolete, but it does indicate that the state will increasingly require the backing of international institutions in order to legitimise unilateral action by states. This is debatable, because it presupposes that the international community can restrain a hegemonic superpower, something which has not been much in evidence since 9/11, with many critics arguing that not only was the intervention in Iraq illegal, but also the prior attack on Afghanistan was too, since there was no UN Security Council backing. Furthermore, Chomsky uses an FBI report on the lack of firm knowledge that the planning of 9/11 by Al-Qaeda was carried out within Afghanistan, and that everything was based on mere supposition, to argue that the assault on Afghanistan was illegal in international law (Chomsky, 2003:200).

Nevertheless, it seems reasonable to claim that even a dominant superpower will be unable to defend its own interests if it becomes entirely isolated from the world community, especially if the measures taken to defend its interests appear counter-productive or too costly in material and human terms.

Keohane predicts a further consequence of 9/11 may be a blurring between humanitarian intervention and security. Military actions in failed or failing states may be increasingly interpreted as both self-defence and humanitarian (Keohane, 2002:282). He highlights an essential moral dilemma for the US, and one 9/11 surely forces us to confront, even though it is uncomfortable:

> Individual freedom, economic opportunity, and representative democracy constitute [core values]. The ability to drive gas-guzzling SUVs does not. In the end 'soft power' depends not merely on the desire of people in one country to imitate the institutions and practices prevailing in another, but also their ability to do so. Exhibiting a glamorous lifestyle that others have no possibility of attaining is more likely to generate hostility and a feeling of 'sour grapes' than support. To relate successfully to people in poor countries during the twenty-first century, Americans will have to distinguish between their values and their privileges (Keohane, 2002:282–3).

This is surely correct, and applies no less to America's allies in Britain and the rest of Europe, and elsewhere. The heart of the matter is responsibility: Bauman's demand (2002) for a more inclusive and responsive approach from OECD countries to those left at the margins of globalisation is particularly pertinent in the new context created by the 9/11 attacks.

The European Union should return to first principles and search for an answer to the question that was raised after 9/11, but never answered: Why did they do this? Perhaps it would be constructive to see the 9/11 attacks and the increase in international terror as part of the wider political and economic context, the inequalities and injustices in the world, including several of the consequences of the political project of neo-liberal *laissez-faire* capitalism described in Chapter 10. Much international terrorism is indisputably linked to the most serious simmering dispute in international affairs, the continuing conflict over Israel-Palestine. The EU has a role in focusing attention on the underlying causes of international terror as well as the struggle against terror itself. We return to this EU role in the final section of this chapter.

Chapter 7, on EU enlargement, refers to the ascendancy of human rights as a core principle of the Union. A further consequence of 9/11 has been the shifting of human rights concerns, by both the EU and the US, to the backburner (Light, 2003:80). Prior to 9/11, Russia was under considerable pressure over human rights issues, particularly in relation to the conduct of the war against separatists in Chechnya. President Putin was quick to line up in support of the coalition against terror, and in return perhaps the critical gaze has moved away from Russian abuses. In other respects too, human rights have been flouted in the wake of 9/11, not least in the US itself (see Discussion 12.5).

In summary, despite the initial solidarity expressed after the atrocities of 9/11, significant differences have arisen between the European Union and the United States, as well as divisions within the EU itself. The disunity in the Union is profound and settling current differences should be a priority. While the direction of EU policy is uncertain, some, such as Haseler (2003), have speculated on a redrawing of the transatlantic partnership (see below). Others have argued that retaining the EU/US relationship is vital:

> The problems confronting the international community at the dawn of the twenty-first century pose infinitely more complex questions than mankind has faced hitherto. The construction of a sustainable, stable, secure, just – and terror free – world requires every ounce of cooperative energy the two sides of the Atlantic can bring to bear. Hanging together is not just an option. It is an imperative (Howorth, 2003:26).

Of course a close partnership between the EU and the US is desirable, and perhaps vital in the struggle to contain terrorism and deal with its underlying causes. Unfortunately the neo-conservative ascendancy in the US has decisively shifted policy away from these goals. The rhetoric espoused by the Bush administration assumes not only that military force will win a 'war on terror', but that any attempt to merely contain terrorism, or to address causes, is a sign of weakness. Halper and Clarke (2004) underline the risks confronting the world as a direct consequence of the flawed US response to 9/11:

Discussion 12.5

Moral authority and human rights post-9/11

Arguably the United Nations has been damaged by the unilateralism of the US, but for many the US lost moral authority by acting outside the remit of the UN, and has compounded the problem with treatment of detainees that breaches the Geneva Conventions. It is clear that for many Europeans as well as Moslems, the treatment of prisoners at Guantánamo Bay in Cuba and elsewhere raises major concerns.

President Bush obtained from his lawyers an opinion that he is not bound by US laws or by international commitments prohibiting torture, and that Americans committing torture under his authority cannot be prosecuted by the Justice Department.

> This opinion rests on the argument that national security considerations override both US law and international treaties. [...] It deliberately overrode the norms the military had previously been trained to regard as mandated by the Geneva Conventions. The world now knows how overriding the norms at the top, overrides them all down the line.
>
> The Bush administration's civilians had been complaining about how law, international treaties and conventions, and military norms and inhibitions were interfering with their determination to seize and hold anyone they pleased in secret prisons, declare them without legal rights even when they were American citizens, torture them whenever they wanted, and keep them forever, if they liked. They wanted these instructions removed.
>
> Their complaints sounded like the complaints of Adolph Eichmann, when he described during his trial in Israel the irksome bureaucratic, admin-

istrative and legal obstacles he ran into in wartime Germany in carrying out his genocidal responsibilities (Pfaff, 2004).

The extract is from William Pfaff, who writes for the *International Herald Tribune*. It indicates why US moral authority has been undermined in recent times. Revelations of torture and humiliation of Iraqi prisoners at Abu Ghraib prison in Baghdad caused international outcry and damaged the reputation of the US, especially in the Arab and Moslem communities. It has also arguably helped terrorist organisations with recruitment. The US has compounded the problem by insisting that neither its military personnel nor private contractors working for the US could be indicted on any charges by the International Criminal Court, which the US refuses to recognise.

It is striking that Robert Kagan, described by Halper and Clarke as 'one of the principal architects of the neo-conservative belligerence that has brought us to this state of affairs', acknowledges that 'America, for the first time since World War II, is suffering a crisis of international legitimacy' (Kagan, cited in Halper & Clarke, 2004:297).

The significance of this is that it highlights Europe's responsibility to respond in a way that is supportive of international law and international institutions, including the ICC. The UK government was sharply criticised for its failure to exert pressure on the US authorities to either charge or release four British citizens held for over two years at Guantánamo Bay without access to lawyers or to family visits.

> Instead of a carefully calibrated approach [...] drawing on a mix of instruments – political, intelligence, police, special forces and so on – America has gone to war with an idea 'terrorism' – and now finds itself on the cusp of a 'clash of civilisations' with the Islamic world (Halper & Clarke, 2004:298).

It is as if the fantasy created by Huntington's notion of this global split between competing cultures (Huntington, 1996) is becoming a reality in the wake of subsequent policy failures. Halper and Clarke contrast the British experience in Northern Ireland, which was always based on a policy of containment, with the absolutist nature of the Bush administration's response to Al Qaeda's September 11 attacks. See Discussion 12.6.

Discussion 12.6 illustrates the context in which the response to 9/11 should be judged. In the opinion of many commentators, after the initial solidarity with the US that followed the attacks, the shift towards unilateralism has made the world more divided and more dangerous. It is all the more vital that the European Union responds adequately and constructively.

Discussion 12.6

US neo-conservative policy failures in Afghanistan, Iraq and the Middle East

The military assault of Afghanistan toppled the Taliban but did not result in the capture of Osama Bin-Laden, identified as the originator of the 9/11 attacks, nor in destroying Al-Qaeda, blamed for 9/11 and subsequent outrages.

As the US administration became fixated on the war on terror, it lost sight of other key concerns such as the threat from nuclear proliferation, the alleviation of poverty and disease, or relations with China and Russia based on an open and democratic economic order, or the maintenance of space as a demilitarised zone (Halper & Clarke, 2004:299). Meanwhile, Pakistan has become an unwilling host for a resurgent Taliban, and Afghanistan has witnessed a nineteen-fold increase in opium production. The post-conflict aid to Afghanistan has been minimal and reconstruction is grossly under-resourced.

Washington has portrayed itself as a government at war and claimed wartime powers, resulting in significant erosion of civil liberties and a massive increase in surveillance operations, arrest, and detention without trial. Halper and Clarke argue that the British, Spanish, Italians and Germans have historically treated terrorism as a 'problem management issue' (ibid., 301), in contrast to declaring war against 'an idea', a war that has no identifiable enemies and has no way of reaching any kind of conclusion. The 'war on terror' contrasts with the last great US military confrontation, the Cold War, where the USSR was a state and the West knew where it was.

Halper and Clarke argue that the invasion of Iraq in March 2003 was based on an elaborate deception:

In order to make the case for the decade old neo-conservative objective of attacking Iraq, a web of deception was needed: that Saddam Hussein had, and intended to use, weapons of mass destruction (WMDs); that Saddam Hussein protected and supported al-Qaeda; and were he not removed the weapons might be provided to al-Qaeda, which could use them against the United States.

These claims, in effect, transformed the issues at hand by turning the possible existence of these threats into 'proven' facts. The process, which anthropologists call the 'discursive construction of reality', uses language to create a reality different from that which existed prior to the use of the language. In this case, prominent neo-conservatives fashioned a dialogue, a linguistic environment, that caused many to believe that the claims were rooted in fact, which was not the case (Halper & Clarke, 2004:306–7).

But the strategy appears to have been broadly successful in persuading the domestic audience that it was appropriate:

Just before the second anniversary of 9/11, polls showed that 70 per cent of Americans believed that the 9/11 hijackers were Iraqis, that Saddam Hussein used chemical weapons against [US] troops and that the link between Saddam and al-Qaeda had been proven (Halper & Clarke, 2004:303).

The invasion of Iraq was presented as part of a wider strategic objective of regime change throughout the Middle East. Not only did the US government assume that the fall of Saddam would eliminate the threat from Iraq, it was also assumed that democracy would follow as night follows day. Furthermore the removal

Discussion 12.6 (*continued*)

of Saddam would have a domino effect throughout the Middle East and various Islamic states would choose governments consistent with US preferences and conforming to US models of democracy. The neo-conservatives in Washington have asserted the supremacy and universality of American values and pursued this 'exceptionalism' through

> an aggressive, militarized diplomacy [. . .] [They] have transformed exceptionalism into an aggressive, oppressive quality, which is singularly counter-productive in terms of America's interaction with the world (Halper & Clarke, 2004:310).

The assumption that American values will sweep over the Middle East seems impossibly naïve. It ignores the cultural traditions of the area as well as local preferences, and it also illustrates a staggering failure to learn from history. Previous attempts by the US to 'remake South East Asia in the American image or the Europeans to remake the non-European world' (ibid.) clearly carry no message to those who assume the US can use force to remodel the entire Middle East.

Halper and Clarke emphasise that the most successful episodes for American diplomacy have always been built on consensus with others and through working within international organisations. In contrast, current policy is dividing America's allies and, damaging multinational institutions, as well as undermining US interests, for example consumers are reportedly shunning American exports. A rise in anti-Americanism is tangible almost everywhere, not least in Europe. Terrorism has increased, with Israel in particular subject to a horrific increase in attacks, part of a shocking escalation in the cycle of violence involving Palestinian radicals and the Israeli Defence Force.

It seems beyond doubt that US actions have stimulated Islamic radicalism in Iraq, Syria, Saudi Arabia, Pakistan, Egypt, Sudan, and on the West Bank, and accelerated terrorist designs on the US homeland. Moreover, emigration, failing businesses, and fear, have radicalized Israeli politics; it finds itself less stable and certainly less secure in the aftermath of the Iraq war and the downgrading of the administration's commitment to the peace process (Halper & Clarke, 2004:313).

Review   *What is the challenge to the state in the era of globalisation?*
What is Keohane's assessment of the impact of 9/11 on the United States? How should states and institutions respond?
What do Halper and Clarke find problematic about the US response to 9/11?

● ● ● ● The European Union as a global actor

This section examines the role of the EU in the wider global context. It addresses the purpose of the Union and its future direction and considers the prospects for the continuation of the **transatlantic partnership**. In several chapters of this book we have seen that while the US/EU relationship has been at times tetchy and difficult, the US has for the most part supported EU integration. There may be some shift in this support now, as the US arguably sees the EU as a potential rival and it may be in the interests of a more unilateralist USA to feed some of the internal disagreements and tensions within the Union.

We begin by highlighting some problems facing the Union and briefly examine whether the EU is actually up to the task of resolving them. Then we look at three assessments of the nature and prospects of the EU/US partnership, the last of which is an exercise in prediction based on Haseler (2003). As this book has made clear, the EU has a number of serious and outstanding problems, some of which are summarised in Discussion 12.7.

Discussion 12.7

Union? What Union?

Will Hutton, writing in the *Observer* newspaper on 30 November 2003, identifies a crisis of unity within the Union. He refers to divisions over the euro, the constitution, defence, and a creeping nationalism throughout the EU, and problems over transatlantic relations. These problem areas are summarised below:

1 The euro zone

The Stability and Growth Pact has been repeatedly breached by Germany and France in a brazen disregard of the rules for managing the eurozone economy. Hutton's complaint is not that the EU finance ministers failed to agree on sanctions against the two largest economies in the eurozone, but that they failed to agree on what should be done about the failing Stability and Growth Pact. The mechanism for managing the euro is now due for revision, but not whole scale reform, early in 2005.

2 The Constitution

The planned Constitutional Treaty, which is in fact less than a constitution, although approved by the European Council in June 2004, requires ratification by all member states, something which is not certain, particularly in an increasingly eurosceptic Britain. There is no 'Plan B' in the event of a rejection by a single member of state.

3 Defence and CFSP

Hutton reports on agreement between France, Germany and the UK to enhance defence cooperation. The measure may be a sensible ambition, but it is alarming to other member states that the big three

pursue such a significant policy development through trilateral negotiation.

4 Immigration

The EU has an ageing population, a possible pensions crisis on the horizon, and important skill shortages in various sectors. However, it is tending towards further restrictions on entry from third countries and is even restricting the free movement of persons between EU-15 and new member states. These measures are dangerous sops to racists and nationalist romantics. In London half of all NHS nurses and a quarter of all doctors are foreign born. Without migration, the British health service would collapse. There are still substantial shortages of skilled personnel in many other areas of the British and European economies, plus countless less skilled jobs that migrants could usefully fill and send money home to their families (Legrain, 2002:329).

5 US/EU relations

Hutton says the US, traditionally supportive of European integration, now sees the EU as a rival, and most worryingly, one of a more multilateralist persuasion. The US increasingly prefers to foster divisions within the Union (Old Europe/New Europe).

In conclusion Hutton writes 'Europe is in its worst shape for years. The British always take the view that nothing is more certain than a powerful EU steamrollering our interests and national identity alike. It's all very much more fragile, and could so easily come apart. There is only so much battering, criticism and friendlessness any institution can take before it breaks. Europe is no different' (Hutton, 2003).

Hutton's concerns are not overstated. Indeed, another concern contains perhaps the biggest threat of all: the need to re-establish public support for the European project. The institutions of the European Union are facing considerable strain, as Hutton makes clear. If the challenges outlined in Discussion 12.7 can be overcome, then public support should follow. If not, then the prospects for the Union are poor, as Hirst and Thompson indicate:

> The future of Europe as a whole may be decided by differences within the European Union that prevent it from acting to unite the European continent. [. . .] Self protective policies at national level will most probably prevent progress to the economic and political integration of Europe. Europe will only develop if its national leaderships and its central institutions are able to exploit the advantages that the pooling of sovereignty and the resources of the largest trade bloc in the world make possible (Hirst & Thompson, 1999:247).

These are high stakes and clarity of vision and purpose is vital. The need for European unity in the context of contemporary globalisation is also important in order to present a balance against US hegemony and unilateralism. It is significant that the EU, unlike a state, is by its very nature a testimony to multilateralist politics. It has evolved as a set of international institutions based on commonly negotiated rules and treaties. It involves the delegation of authority to supranational authorities, in particular the ECJ. It also involves significant delegation to the Commission in international forums such as the WTO, and to global negotiating forums such as the Kyoto Conference of Climate Change. It is therefore perhaps to be expected that the EU might be more comfortable with the emergence of new multilateral systems than the United States, a single sovereign state. Peterson and Pollack argue that thoughtful critics of American foreign policy, such as Nye (2002), argue for a stronger US commitment to multilateralism and assert that the Bush administration's aversion to multilateralism is 'myopic and ultimately self defeating for a US that seeks to exercise global leadership' (Peterson & Pollack, 2003:127).

The European Union must exercise a role in influencing the US. Given the size of the Union, the commercial importance of the Single Market, its status and its political authority, it is in a position to have this influence. Often criticised for its military weakness, the EU has the potential to compensate through the exercise of 'soft power' – economic strength, support for economic development, commitment to multilateralism, diplomacy and persuasion, and moral authority grounded in a commitment to human rights and environmental responsibility. This soft power can be especially effective if it is utilised in an even-handed way in conflict zones such as the Balkans or the Middle East. It is through the exercise of soft power that the Union has the potential to influence and ultimately persuade the United States that an excessive reliance on hard power without a moral dimension is counter-productive. However, if the Union's own internal divisions continue, it will be severely weakened and unable to carry out this responsibility.

Peterson and Pollack (2003:129) refer to the possibility that an EU-25 will be even less united and less effective as an action-oriented institution than EU-15 prior to the 2004 enlargement. It may even become more of a 'framework organisation like the OSCE' (Peterson & Pollack, 2003:129). They also highlight continuing divisions over common defence and security policy, exposed in the 1990s over Bosnia, and painfully obvious once again over Iraq in 2003. They point out, however, that in other contexts CFSP has been much more successful, over the Middle East, North Korea and Zimbabwe. Nevertheless, overall, the EU's overwhelmingly intergovernmental character and its

> political deficiencies and debilities [. . .] make it unlikely that a European vision of international order will provide a serious alternative to that of the United States in the foreseeable future (Rieff, cited in Peterson & Pollack, 2003:139).

In determining the future role of the European Union in international affairs, and the transatlantic partnership in particular, three contrasting views stand out. First, Peterson and Pollack claim that the biggest threat to the transatlantic relationship is something of a dead heat between American unilateralism and European disarray (Peterson & Pollack, 2003:140). They argue that the 'values gap' which comprises arguments over issues like the death penalty, the environment, abortion, religion and gun control, is a distant second. They estimate that ultimately the EU and the US are bound more closely to each other than to any other part of the world, with the possible exceptions of Canada, Australia and New Zealand. Nevertheless, even if the partnership survives, there have been enough trade disputes and political differences over the years to suggest that it is unlikely to be a particularly harmonious future.

There are two other interpretations. One is that indeed the values gap is considerable and growing, and is wide enough to present a serious threat to the transatlantic relationship. Micklethwait and Wooldridge write about fundamental differences, not only between the US and continental Europe, but between the US and Britain too. Hutton (2002) has written about the different values that affect the way society is governed on each side of the Atlantic. Micklethwait and Wooldridge summarise the growing gap between the former Cold War partners in reductive terms: America is more right wing than Europe.

> There are fundamental differences in values between Europe and America that will drive the continents apart (Micklethwait & Wooldridge, 2004:18).

They argue that these are not differences that can be papered over simply by a change in occupancy at the White House. Democrats and Republicans appeal to similar constituencies and thus in the US;

> the centre of (political) gravity is further to the right. Look at any poll of attitudes towards the basic questions of politics – the size of capitalism, spending on defence, crime and punishment, attitude to multinational institutions like the United Nations – and America takes a more rightwing approach than any other developed country. Even set alongside Britain, its nearest equivalent, America tolerates a far higher degree of inequality, with 1 in 6 households earning less than a third of median income (in Britain the figure is closer to 1 in 20). Its incarceration rate is five times higher than that of Britain, Europe's toughest sentencer; America spends much less on government in general, but twice as much on defence per head; it brings religion into politics far

more often. The gap is even more extreme if you compare America with France or Germany (Micklethwait & Wooldridge, ibid.).

These conclusions appear more than justified by the 2004 re-election of George W. Bush, despite a stuttering economy, a record current account deficit and continuing difficulties in the quagmire of post-Saddam Iraq. The US is more isolated abroad than at any time since the end of the Second World War, but Bush was re-elected by a decisive majority. According to the former Republican conservative and academic Niall Ferguson, the reason is quite clear:

Bush [. . .] loses no opportunity to attest to his born-again Christian faith [. . .]. [M]oral over-simplifications [. . .] characterised his first term – typified by key phrases like the 'axis of evil', the 'war against terror' and 'the onward march of freedom' [and these phrases] resonate irresistibly with a critical mass of Americans right across the country. He is, as is too seldom understood in Britain, fundamentally 'a messianic American Calvinist', someone for whom all setbacks are merely a divine test to which a 'faith-based' president can only react with obstinate resolve (Ferguson, 2004:39).

Gray also describes the huge differences between America and Europe over religion. He describes Europe as 'post-Christian' and the US as

a country of widespread, intense and often fundamental religiosity [where] just under 70 per cent of Americans believe in the devil, compared with a third of the British, a fifth of the French and an eighth of the Swedes. Around a quarter of Americans are born-again Christians for whom diabolical possession is not a metaphor but a literal reality (Gray, 1998:126).

This chasm in political attitudes between America and Europe could be tolerated during the Cold War when there was a common enemy and a common purpose, but that unifying element has dissolved. President Bush and Prime Minister Blair have attempted to replace it with another far less easily identifiable enemy, the international terrorist. This is no easy task. Public opinion in Europe thinks that the handling of the threat of terror since 9/11 has been inept and dangerous. Furthermore, the shifting political sands begin to expose not only gaps in thinking and attitudes between American and European voters, but an emergence of new conceptions of where Europe's interests lie. This may lead to fundamental policy revisions concerning Europe's role in the global political economy.

Any reassessment of Europe's role lies at the heart of the third possible course for the transatlantic partnership. This focuses on strategic interests, where differences may prove the undoing of NATO, the cornerstone of the Western Alliance since 1949. Haseler (2003) writes that while 9/11 changed everything for the Americans, the end of the Cold War had already altered European perspectives. Fundamentally, European reliance on the US was much reduced by the collapse of the Berlin Wall, since the essential purpose of NATO disappeared with the Soviet Union. Haseler argues that the Bosnian crisis brought home to the Europeans the need for greater coordination in matters of defence and security. Meanwhile NATO remains useful to the US all the while it is American-led.

The US performance in the Gulf War and then in Bosnia and Kosovo reinforced an emerging confidence among conservative opinion in America that

Washington could assert hegemony virtually anywhere it pleased, as a world policeman. There was a growing confidence in a strategic vision based on 'hard power', a concept described by Joseph Nye (Nye, 1990). This analysis, fuelled by Huntington's vision of the world as two opposing civilisations (Huntington, 1996) was taking root as terrorists struck the twin towers and the Pentagon on September 11 (Haseler, 2003:9). In September 2002 the Bush administration released the *National Security Strategy* document, containing the notion of 'full spectrum dominance' whereby the US would be able to resist any challenge from anywhere in the world. It also affirmed that the world's only superpower would act where possible with others, but 'alone when necessary'. In February 2003 Bush outlined a vision of a democratic Iraq as a focal point for a reordering of Middle East. Haseler highlights the divisions within the UN as France won support from Russia, China and Germany in opposing US intention to go to war, with President Chirac arguing that an attack on Iraq was not central to the war on terror and that it 'would produce a host of mini Bin Ladens' (Haseler, 2003:12). The logic of the pre-emptive strike was first implemented in Iraq a month later.

Haseler argues that for many Europeans the divisions over the war on terror merely compounded growing doubts over the divergence of US policy from the European vision on matters such as trade, the environment, the ICC and the preferred model of capitalism.

> The fundamentalist religious rhetoric in the Bush world view grated on secular European ears [while] what was seen as Europe's cynicism and disregard for the full extent of the trauma of 9/11 did not play well on American sensibilities (Haseler, 2003:13).

Haseler goes on to argue that there are different strategic objectives between the US and Europe. First, the EU is much less concerned about Russia other than to build a closer relationship with Moscow; the US has oil interests in the Middle East which are not necessarily the same as Europe's interests; Europe has a long historical interest in a more even-handed approach to the Arab-Israeli conflict (Israel-Palestine) than the US is prepared to contemplate; and finally that Europe will have to look after its own security needs more independently of the US than was ever the case during the Cold War. Haseler predicts that the Franco-German alliance will once again draw in Italy and Spain who are

> not natural Atlanticists like the British foreign policy elite, and can be expected to align themselves with Franco-Germany. Over time the Eastern Europeans will lose their sentimental attachment to America because of its role in freeing them from Soviet rule, and democratic Russia should pose less and less of a threat (Haseler, 2003:16).

Thus, according to Haseler, the map of Eurasia will be redrawn as Europe constructs a new security arrangement (see Discussion 12.8).

Central to Haseler's estimation of the future direction of EU security policy is the claim that EU geostrategic interests diverge significantly from those of the US. The British position in this possible realignment of the EU/US strategic relationship is interesting, especially in the light of the Blair government's steadfast support for the US over Iraq, while Shröder in Germany and Chirac in France

Discussion 12.8

A new European security architecture

Stephen Haseler highlights the German decision to cooperate with France in defence matters as a major shift in European thinking on matters of security. He calls it a 'switching of sides', as Germany has always been Atlanticist on defence issues. Haseler predicts an emerging security architecture based on the European Union's Rapid Reaction Force, an agreed nuclear strategy (with two nuclear powers), a beefed-up military committee and command in Brussels, the Galileo satellite system, and its own joint intelligence committee. Eventually CFSP will accommodate more majority voting and achieve a higher profile under a single EU foreign affairs spokesperson.

This vision is achievable because it will support Europe's fundamental reliance on 'soft power', rather than 'hard power'. Europe has no interest in playing the expensive role of world policeman and will not require the hugely overblown budget of the Pentagon. While European defence budgets will need to increase, the priority will be to achieve specialisation among member states, a proper European procurement policy and a priority for new expenditure to go into counter-terrorism and intelligence.

NATO can be redesigned as a primarily political alliance stressing the underlying political, social and cultural unity of Europe and America, and retaining the clause in which 'each signatory remains committed to come to the defence of the others in case of attack'.

Britain will need to decide where it lines up: as a major player and nuclear power in a new Europe, or alone in an uncertain world dependent on its unequal **'special relationship'** with the USA (based on Haseler, 2003:16–21).

lined up against Bush in defence of the UN and the principle of multilateralism. Prime Minister Blair's pro-Washington stance baffled many natural Labour supporters, and led some to label him 'Bush's poodle'. Haseler says the government's support for US policy was sustained with the

> fervour of the true believer and was most evident among Britain's security establishment (its diplomats, intelligence officials and senior military). This establishment was infused with a lingering Atlanticism and 'NATO-think', but there were also vested interests at work (Haseler, 2004:167).

Haseler refers to 'spooks and submarines' affirming that the 'spooks' (British intelligence services) and 'submarines' (meaning the Royal Navy's nuclear Trident submarine fleet lobby) have significant need to retain an intimate relationship with the US, given that senior figures in the UK's intelligence service have access to Washington's intelligence networks, and Trident submarines are dependent on essential US help with servicing (Haseler, 2004:167–8). Labour government policy has appeared to look both ways, though, as five years previously Blair had signed a potentially historic agreement with Chirac at St Malo to establish a much closer foreign policy and defence relationship between Britain and France, and one that would also include Germany in a formidable troika, enabling an EU defence identity that was separate from NATO and could act independently. Indeed the Helsinki Summit in 1999 confirmed the establishment of the EU's Rapid Reaction Force.

These developments are clear indications of divergent strategic interests between Europe and America, although Haseler reports (ibid., 175) that Blair later backtracked from St Malo, which prompted Shröder to move a German and French initiative for a European Defence Union that would be outside the EU, and created, like the Schengen Agreement, between a few states but open to others to join. This would put European defence policy firmly in Franco-German control and the scope of EU defence concerns would remain much more limited than that of the United States.

Chomsky argues that the current US policy to develop Ballistic Missiles Defence (BMD), sometimes dubbed 'Son of Star Wars', is to enable the weaponisation of space. Nor is it purely a defensive shield. Canadian military planners advised their government, according to Chomsky, that BMD is

> 'arguably more in order to preserve US/NATO freedom of action than because the US really fears (a) North Korean or Iranian threat'. China's top arms control official was revealing nothing new when he observed that 'once the United States believes it has both a strong spear and a strong shield, it could lead them to conclude that nobody can harm the United States and they can harm anyone they like anywhere in the world' [. . .] the National Security Strategy (is determined) that no potential challenge to US hegemony will be tolerated (Chomsky, 2003:226–7).

BMD represents a new generation of defence hardware that may risk a new international arms race (Hari, 2003). Chomsky underlines the return to realist principles in international affairs:

> China's interpretation of BMD is shared by US strategic analysts, in virtually the same words: BMD 'is not simply a *shield* but an *enabler* of US action' a Rand Corporation study observed. Others agree. BMD 'will facilitate the more effective application of US military power abroad', Andrew Bacevich writes in the conservative *National Interest*: 'by insulating the homeland from reprisal – albeit in a limited way – missile defence will underwrite the capacity and willingness of the United States to "shape" the environment elsewhere'. He cites approvingly the conclusion of Lawrence Kaplan in the liberal *New Republic* that 'missile defence isn't really to protect America. It's a tool for global dominance'. In Kaplan's own words, missile defense is 'not about defense. It's about offense. And that's exactly why we need it'. It will 'cement US hegemony and make Americans the "masters of the world"' (Chomsky, ibid.).

Such observations present a sharp contrast to the European 'soft power' alternative. Only a decisive reversal in American policy could restore the prospects of a close EU/US strategic partnership. Such a restoration seems unlikely not only from the European perspective but from an American one as well: US unilateralism has enhanced US frustration at the EU's indecisiveness, divisions and military weakness. The US has long demanded a greater European commitment to defence spending, and a greater commitment to NATO. Neither seems probable, at least not on terms acceptable to the US. For these reasons Haseler's anticipation of a separation if not a divorce seems justified. Outright breakdown is not likely, because of the current intensity and breadth of cross-fertilisation in areas of commerce, not least the high levels of FDI and MNC activity referred to in Chapter 11, the mutual dependence in terms of trade, and ultimately the need for a continued defence alliance, albeit under changed structures, and cooperation in confronting terror and international crime.

Nevertheless, Haseler's estimation that the EU could enhance its profile as an independent military entity, albeit backed by a 'soft power' approach, is dependent on a much enhanced CFSP. It would mark a decisive step forward from the divisions of 2003 were this to be achieved within the five year timeframe indicated by Haseler.

Beyond the EU's relationship with America, the Union has a major role in other regions. It has, as indicated above, a special interest in seeing stability and justice established in the Middle East, due to the geographical proximity of the region to Europe's southern flank, and on humanitarian grounds. Europe having a large Moslem minority ensures that a solution to the Arab-Israeli conflict remains a domestic interest for the EU as well as an important foreign policy concern.

In its relations with Russia and the Caucasus there is also a close European interest in EU sponsorship of stable and secure democratic development. EU relations with Russia are a significant dimension to European foreign policy, especially in the context of the 2004 enlargement.

In a globalising world, the EU also has strong and growing trading relationships with China, India and the Asia Pacific region. The Association of South East Asian Nations (ASEAN) may even look to the EU as a potential model for greater political cooperation in an emerging Asian trade block. ASEAN though is a highly disparate group, comprising states with widely differing population sizes and economic strength (see Discussion 12.9). The organisation was founded as a loose pact to promote economic and social development and to establish more common understanding between members. ASEAN has nothing comparable to the EU in terms of institutional or legislative integration and remains a strictly intergovernmental association. In 1992 it launched a free trade area aiming at complete liberalisation over a 15-year period. With a population of 400 million it is comparable to the EU, but the disparities among its members are highly pronounced.

Brunei is one of the world's richest nations, Vietnam one of the poorest. Singapore is the second smallest ASEAN member, with just 0.75 per cent of the region's population, but contributes around 10 per cent of its gross national product (GNP). Indonesia in contrast has almost 47 per cent of the population but contributes just 30 per cent of the GNP. There has also been interest in currency union in Asia, particularly between Japan, South Korea and China, though

---

Discussion 12.9

The Association of South East Asian Nations (ASEAN)

Brunei, Cambodia, Indonesia, Laos, Malaysia, Myanmar, Philippines, Singapore, Thailand, Vietnam.
Selected statistics (2002) (www.aseansec.org/home.htm)
GDP: $610 billion
GDP per capita: Brunei $12,090; Singapore $20,515; Vietnam $439; Indonesia $819

there remain formidable obstacles to such an innovation. Nevertheless, increasing Chinese foreign direct investment, especially in South Korea, and massively increased trade involving China, whose economy is expanding at around 9 per cent a year, means that the Asia Pacific region remains a significant growth area. This may in itself contribute to pressures for greater regional economic integration. China is the EU's third most important non-European trading partner, and is estimated to become the world's largest economy within a generation. The EU runs a considerable trade deficit with China, but EU exports of high technology products are a vital feature of the expanding economic relationship. Politically, China is of major significance to the EU, not least because unlike Japan it is a nuclear power. The major potential disruption to EU/China relations is concern over human rights, where ever since the Tiananmen Square incident of 1989, when troops crushed a massive pro-democracy demonstration, the Union has been wary of China's human rights record. Given that the EU has a commitment to tying human rights issues into international agreements, the issue remains a central element to Union relations, not only in China but throughout Asia. Even in relations with Japan, the EU has used bilateral meetings to raise concerns over the continuing use of the death penalty.

The Lomé Convention was the centrepiece of EU external relations with the African, Caribbean and Pacific states from 1975. In 2000 it was replaced by the Cotonou Agreement. It provides for a multilateral partnership governing trade and aid between the EU and 77 states. The content of the agreement is not dissimilar to the Lomé Convention. The Lomé Convention and Cotonou Agreement help to build closer ties between the EU and ACP states, and the volume of exports to Europe has increased over several decades, but these instruments have been criticised for

> promoting economic dependence, and for perpetuating the flow of low-profit raw materials from the ACP to the EU, and the flow of high-profit manufactured goods from the EU to the ACP. Questions [have also been] raised about the extent to which they have helped ACP states invest in their human capital, and helped them to develop greater economic independence (McCormick, 2002:216–17).

Jones also refers to criticisms of the Lomé Convention on several grounds, including the weak negotiating power of ACP states, EU funding did not match ACP population growth, debt rescheduling would have been more useful to many states than any gains from Lomé, projects were often poorly adapted to local conditions, inadequately monitored and reviewed and many ACP states had poor development records (Jones, 2001:420).

In negotiating a successor to Lomé, the EU sought to build in broader political and economic objectives such as good governance and human rights, as well as more liberal trading relationships between ACP states and greater participation of non-state actors within ACP countries. The Cotonou Agreement combines trade with aid, and aims to facilitate preferential access to EU markets, increased development funding and the emergence of regional free trade agreements.

The Union also maintains a network of agreements, called the European-Mediterranean Conference, with its southerly near-neighbours Algeria, Jordan, the Palestinian Authority, Lebanon, Syria, Egypt, Tunisia, Israel, Morocco and Turkey. A series of more limited arrangements apply with Asia and Latin America, called the Generalised System of Preferences, though this is more limited than the Lomé Convention accords. The GSP establishes preferential entry to many imports from developing countries which has reduced discrimination and boosted trade. Pinder says the system is not as good as it should be because in competitive product areas quotas are maintained for different products in different states, but nevertheless the GSP system has helped to strengthen links with LDCs (Pinder, 2001:15).

Jones reports that the EU and its member states provide about 55 per cent of the total international development assistance and over two thirds of grant aid to developing countries, more than the combined total of the US and Japan, but less than a fifth of this aid is channelled through EU institutions. EU development policy is 'a mixture of enlightened self-interest and altruism' (Jones, 2001:413), as the developing world is an important trading partner to the EU, accounting for about one third of its imports and exports.

In summary, the European Union maintains institutionalised multilateral relationships with many countries in the developing world and as such has a significant profile, as well as considerable responsibility, in promoting trade, political and economic development, and respect for human rights. However, its role should not be exaggerated. Jones cautions that:

> It seems unlikely that national aid programmes will be superseded by EU programmes in the foreseeable future. Nevertheless, the need for greater coordination between the aid policies of the EU and of member states is increasingly recognised. Because development policy is an aspect of the EU's external relations, the emergence of a stronger common foreign and security policy would also enhance the prospects for the convergence of EU and national aid policies (Jones, 2001:428).

As in the security domain, the EU demonstrates more potential for a decisive role in development than actual confidence that this can be achieved given current circumstances.

In conclusion, the onus is on the Union to unite around its common values and to use its powerful economic position to better influence the United States. Both the EU and the US need to forge a closer partnership, but also to incorporate other regions with shared interests in shaping outcomes that benefit humanity, not merely Western interests. There is a risk that a renewed transatlantic partnership would merely look like a new cultural imperialism. Instead, it must be within a genuine multilateral and international framework, encompassing a strengthening and democratisation of existing international institutions and, where necessary, the creation of new ones. This is the subject of the next section.

Finally, Europeans and Americans need to return to the question of why 9/11 happened, and examine the underlying causes that bring such profound hatred against what are frequently described as 'Western values'. European soft power can play a major role in fashioning a constructive approach and in balancing the excessive reliance on hard power that writers such as Nye (2003) have observed in the United States response to 9/11.

Review	What fundamental weaknesses threaten the future of the EU?
	Suggest three interpretations of how the transatlantic relationship might develop.
	How does the EU relate to the wider world?

● ● ● ● Responding to globalisation

This final section of the book is about the reform of existing institutions in order to better face the challenges of globalisation. The European Union is vital to this task, providing a counter-balance to a mostly unilateralist and hegemonic United States. The EU should seek changes to the ascendancy of the 'one path' notion of neo-liberal free market orthodoxy. For the Union to successfully play this role it must first overcome its own weaknesses (see Discussion 12.7) and establish a coherent defence and security identity. It probably also requires that the UK decide where it wishes to position itself in the architecture of the international political economy. If the UK does decide to remain in the EU, it must commit to the European cause. If on the other hand the UK continues to marginalise itself within the Union, and to behave more like an adjunct of US interests, especially in relation to foreign and security policy, it will stifle the Union's international role, and hobble its internal development.

This means that there are three major obstacles to the European Union effectively contributing to the process of reshaping contemporary globalisation: its inherent weaknesses, its deficient CFSP, and its internal divisions, centred mainly on the UK. If the Union is able to resolve these issues, it might at last fulfil its destiny of playing a political role that is commensurate with its economic status. None of this implies that the Union needs to become a federal state. It is far more likely to endure as an association of states that have pooled sovereignty in significant areas, and have delegated authority to specific supranational institutions. It used to be said that the Union was an economic giant, but a political pygmy (Piening, 1997:31). This is no longer accurate: the regional power of the Union is immense and its voice in international affairs has grown considerably. The advent of the Single Currency and the Eastern enlargement undoubtedly enhance the political role of the Union, but it remains the case that the EU has greater potential influence than actual impact. The cornerstone of turning potential into reality is probably CFSP: only once that is genuine will the Union finally have a political voice to match its global economic profile (see Figure 12.1, and Table 12.1).

The argument presented in this section is that the Union should have a decisive role in reforming some of the international institutions that are central to the management of the emerging global economy. The approach adopted is consistent with the rest of the book in that arguments are largely based on existing published work and again readers are referred to the original sources for more detailed accounts.

Soros argues that the WTO has actually been reasonably successful in meeting its brief to develop world trade, to establish binding agreements, and to assist

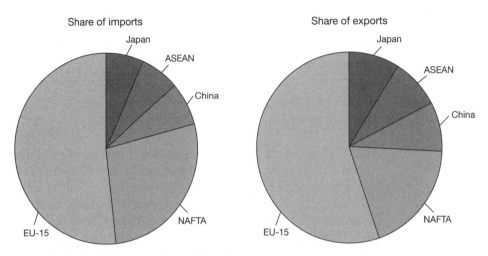

Figure 12.1 The EU share of world trade

Source: compiled from World Trade Organisation Website, 2004, http://www.wto.org. All figures are for 2003.

Table 12.1 GDP: Selective comparisons

	Total	*Per capita*	*Population*
European Union	$11,847 bn	$26,327	453m
NAFTA	$12,822 bn	$29,888	429m
United States	$11,278 bn	$38,620	292m
Japan	$4,366 bn	$34,350	127m
China	$1,463 bn	$1,120	1,300m

Source: Based on 'The World in 2004' (2003). © The Economist Newspaper Limited, London 2003.

in bringing many developing countries into the global economy. It has successfully pursued **private goods** in a liberal/neo-liberal trading environment. It also has the potential, if its members devote their energies to the cause, to create a Doha Trade Round that is genuinely beneficial to developing countries. Soros says Doha is encouraging but needs to be 'complemented by a set of financial incentives for voluntary compliance with international rules and standards' (Soros, 2002:55). It can be argued that the WTO, a one-member-one-vote organisation, is at least theoretically a great deal more democratic than the World Bank or the IMF. The Cancún talks broke down in 2003 when the LDCs, led by Brazil, India and China, walked away from what Ernesto Zedillo, a former president of Mexico, characterised as 'rich countries' obscene agricultural protectionism' (Zedillo, 2003:93). Zedillo gives a sombre assessment of the chances of Doha restarting, but argues that the WTO needs to go back to first principles and argue for a 'grand vision for the multilateral trading system, one that fosters growth and development' (Zedillo, ibid.). It goes without saying that the EU, or more particularly its member states that are the masters of the CAP, is crucial to achieving this objective.

The WTO is heavily criticised by anti-globalisation campaigners and writers such as George Monbiot and Naomi Klein, while others who may be described as constructive critics, such as Soros and Legrain, argue that simply getting rid of the WTO is not the answer. They accept that 'the need for fundamental reform of the WTO is undeniable' (Shrybman, 2003:123). Soros, echoing arguments presented previously in this book from Gray, writes that

> The globalisation of markets without a corresponding strengthening of our international political and social arrangements has led to a very lopsided social development (Soros, 2002:7).

Soros argues for a strengthening of political institutions. He commends international trade and global financial markets for being very good at generating wealth but they cannot take care of other social needs such as the

> preservation of peace, alleviation of poverty, protection of the environment, labour conditions, or human rights – what are generally called *'public goods'*. Economic development, that is, the production of private goods, has taken precedence over social development, that is, the provision of public goods (Soros, 2002:14).

Soros argues that the rules-based system of the WTO should be complemented by an incentives-based system for the provision of **public goods**. Like Micklethwait and Wooldridge (2000) and Legrain (2002), Soros does not blame globalisation for the worst ills in the world:

> By far the most important causes of misery and poverty in the world today are armed conflict, oppressive and corrupt regimes, and weak states – and globalisation cannot be blamed for bad governments (Soros, ibid.).

But Soros criticises the US for pursuing hegemony without a moral foundation. The US wields hegemonic power, spending 37 per cent of all military spending (Soros, 2002:157) and

> [it] occupies a dominant position in the global economy. In so far as anybody is in charge of economic policy it is the United States. The United States can do anything it wants, but practically nothing can happen without its consent [. . .] the United States is the unquestioned hegemon in the world today (Soros, 2002:150).

Soros says that after 9/11 the US has consolidated a realist, unilateralist approach, with US Attorney General John Ashcroft even going so far as to declare any opposition to anti-terrorist measures as 'an unpatriotic act that gives aid and comfort to the enemy' (Soros, 2002:160). It is in this context that Soros calls for a global society with a moral foundation. He writes that markets are amoral, based on untrammelled pursuit of self-interest, and military might is not necessarily right. A global society

> requires the United States to abide by the same rules that apply to others. Moreover it requires the [US] to exercise leadership in strengthening our international institutions, rules, laws and standards. Since the sovereignty of states stands in the way of enforcing most rules, laws and standards, it must be willing to offer inducements and incentives for voluntary compliance. Of course the United States cannot be expected to do this on its own, but it must take the initiative to secure the cooperation of other countries (Soros, 2002:167).

Soros recommends a reform of the IMF and the World Bank that incorporates a mechanism to provide multilateral development assistance and public goods on a global scale (see Discussion 12.10). Hutton argues along similar lines:

> The world needs a genuine supranational financial institution that monitors economic performance and stands ready to provide hard currency in times of difficulty; instead it has the IMF, an adjunct of the US treasury (Hutton, 2002:458).

Legrain, who like Soros is essentially supportive of many of the achievements of globalisation, is well aware of some of its downsides and the iniquities that it has done little to remedy. He proposes various initiatives. First, and controversially for opponents of international trade, he proposes abolishing all trade barriers, estimating that the result would add $2,800 bn to the world economy, $1,500 bn of which would go to poor countries, taking 320 million people out

---

Discussion 12.10

Soros's SDR proposal

Soros proposes a fund based on the Special Drawing Rights (SDR) system, to provide development assistance on a global scale. The proposal is designed to

> make a substantial amount of money available almost immediately, to finance the provision of public goods on a global scale as well as to foster economic, social and political progress in individual countries [. . .] SDRs are international reserve assets issued by the IMF to its members and convertible into other currencies. LDCs would benefit both directly through the addition to their monetary reserves and indirectly from the provision of public goods on a global scale (Soros, 2002:73).

Richer countries would contribute allocations to the fund, proportional to their wealth, eliminating the risk of free-riders contributing less than they should. Contributions would require substantial increases on the current aid provision made by OECD countries. The Monterrey Conference on Financing Development estimated that meeting UN development targets of 2015 would require an additional $50 billion per year, and seriously addressing the need for public goods a further $20 billion (Soros, 2002:74). LDCs would use their SDRs to augment their monetary reserves, and donations would be allocated to LDCs on the basis of their programmes being approved. Programmes would include partnerships with private investment. The SDR system would be monitored and controlled by an advisory board within the IMF but independent of it. Its role would be to recommend and prioritise development programmes that are consistent with defending public goods. The scheme would:

1. Increase the amount available for international assistance – it could go a long way towards meeting UN 2015 development targets.

2. Ensure a more equitable distribution of the burden of development assistance.

3. Remove some of the deficiencies of international assistance as currently administered, notably:

   a An independent board would ensure that the needs of recipients take precedence over the needs of donors.

   b The stranglehold of intergovernmental dealings would be broken; recipient governments would no longer be gatekeepers.

   c Donor coordination would be enhanced.

   d Recipients would have a greater sense of ownership and involvement.

   e There would be a feedback system that would reinforce successes and eliminate failures.

Source: based on Soros, 2002:183–4.

of poverty. The main area for decisive action is ending agricultural subsidies and eliminating tariffs on foods and clothing in rich countries. LDCs themselves should lower tariffs between them. A second barrier that needs lowering is freedom of movement of persons. Migrant labour in the G-7 is not only good for developing countries, as some of the wages earned are sent back to family members, but benefits the rich countries' economies, where there are labour shortages, skills shortages, jobs that local people do not want to do and a worsening demographic problem emerging on account of ageing populations. Legrain also recommends the use of prudent capital controls to protect markets from the kind of turbulence witnessed in the late 1990s.

Legrain argues that scrapping TRIPs (trade-related aspects of intellectual property) is desirable but not likely as the US fought so hard for this in the Uruguay Trade Round and it is now embedded in the WTO, but patent protection, especially in respect of drugs for the treatment of HIV/AIDS, is morally unjustifiable. Legrain argues for patent protection to be loosened, while environmental protection must be strengthened. At present the WTO has a limited role in this area and, arguably, tends to favour free trade over environmental concerns. Shrybman writes that any government which violates WTO rules is liable to sanctions, often too severe for even the wealthiest governments to ignore (see Discussion 12.11).

Legrain argues for an institution with similar powers to the WTO to be created alongside it, complete with a secretariat and a budget paid for by a form of Tobin Tax – a tax on currency exchange operations. A World Environment Organisation is an absolute priority (see Discussion 12.12). It would create a united forum over and above some 200 separate multilateral agreements already in place, monitored or created by a huge number of different bodies. Legrain calls the Bush government's rejection of Kyoto 'shameful and reckless' (Legrain, 2002:330). A WEO would drive research and provide information and provide a forum for dispute settlement. Shrybman argues that such a body, he calls it a Global Environmental Organisation (GEO), would have supranational authority and play a supportive role to the WTO, legitimising the use of trade and economic sanctions.

Discussion 12.11

The WTO and the environment

In the (WTO's) first trade complaint (a challenge by foreign gasoline companies to US Clean Air Act regulations) the Environmental Protection Agency was given two options. Either remove the offending statute or face trade sanctions in the order of $150 million a year.

A similar fate befell European food-safety regulations (in 2000) when the WTO ruled that a European Community (EC) ban on hormone-treated beef violated several rules. The Organisation ordered the EC to remove its import controls and, when it refused, it authorised trade sanctions worth more than $125 million as the price of its defiance (Shrybman, 2003:121).

Discussion 12.12

Defending the planet: the need for a World Environment Organisation

During the 1990s the so-called Tiger economies of Southeast Asia, Thailand, Taiwan, Singapore, Malaysia and South Korea were pressured by the IMF to open up their capital markets, attract inward investment and foreign multinationals, including those interested in exploiting primary resources. There has been no control over the environmental impact of these countries taking the IMF medicine. According to Ellwood, the IMF regional report for 1997, written just before the collapse of the Thai baht precipitated the Asian Crises, singled out Thailand's 'remarkable economic performance' and 'consistent record of sound macroeconomic policies' (Ellwood, 2001:22). Not only the subsequent crash, but also the environmental impact of neo-liberalism in Asia, demands a more sobering assessment:

In Asia, even before the crash of 1997, the region's 'economic miracle' had been built on a fast-track liquidation of its natural resources. Pristine rain-forests were plundered, rivers despoiled, seacoasts poisoned with pesticides and fisheries exhausted. In the Indonesian capital Jakarta more than 70 per cent of water samples were found to be 'highly contaminated by chemical pollutants' while the country's forests were being hacked down at the rate of 6 million acres (2.4 million hectares) per year. In the Malaysian state of Sarawak (part of the island of Borneo) 30 per cent of the forest disappeared in a mere two decades, while in peninsular Malaysia 73 per cent of 116 rivers surveyed by authorities were found to be either 'biologically dead' or 'dying' (Ellwood, 2001:94–5).

Legrain also calls for debt cancellation to 'free poor people from debts that they cannot pay' (Legrain, 2002:332). Debt relief should come with strings attached: any resources freed up should be directed towards helping the poor. The World Bank should be turned into a development agency that offers grants, not loans. Financial assistance should be channelled through aid organisations, NGOs, and local and private concerns properly monitored, so avoiding undesirable 'gatekeeping' by unscrupulous governments who redirect aid away from the projects for which it is intended. Legrain also calls for more aid from rich countries.

> It is an outrage that the richest country on earth, the US, gives a mere 0.1 per cent of its national income to help less fortunate foreigners – and a large part of that is military assistance to Israel and Egypt. The extra $5 billion that President Bush has promised to spend in 2004–6 is still not enough. In 1965 America gave 0.6 per cent of its GDP. EU governments do better. They give 0.33 per cent of GDP, which they have pledged to raise to 0.39 per cent. They should meet the UN target of giving 0.7 per cent of GDP. [. . .] NATO countries spent $4 billion bombing Yugoslavia but had difficulty finding $50 million to help Montenegro's economic reforms. The Bush administration [determined] to spend $379 billion on defence in fiscal 2003 but a mere $10 billion on overseas aid (Legrain, 2003:332–3).

Finally Legrain argues that governments in rich countries should do more to protect their own most vulnerable citizens through increased spending on skills training for those who lose their jobs. Legrain's proposals are summarised in Discussion 12.13.

Discussion 12.13

Making globalisation work better

1. Abolish trade barriers and protectionist measures imposed by rich countries.
2. Facilitate easier movement of persons seeking genuine employment, or faced with political persecution.
3. Provide for restrictions in capital movements to limit sudden capital flight from developing countries.
4. Loosen patent protection, especially in pharmaceutical sector for the treatment of chronic disease.
5. Create a supranational World/Global Environmental Organisation to work in partnership with the WTO. Trade agreements, as well as trade sanctions, should be linked to environmental impact.
6. Debt relief for the world's poorest countries.
7. The World Bank should provide development grants, not loans.
8. Large increases in aid budgets.
9. Improved support for the most vulnerable in developed countries.

(Based on Legrain: 2003)

Review   *What should the role of the EU be in reshaping globalisation?*
What are Soros's main concerns in respect of the US? What does he propose?
What other measures could improve the future impact of globalisation?

● ● ● ● Conclusion: a cosmopolitan social democracy

There have been many material benefits from globalisation. Many people in advanced societies and also in less developed countries have experienced real improvements in living standards. Technological advances have brought liberating opportunities in the workplace, in education, in leisure and in health. But there are also many associated problems that require innovative thinking and determined, coordinated action. Hunger, chronic disease, AIDS-HIV, crime, human trafficking, child exploitation, international terrorism, environmental degradation, and the risk of nuclear proliferation are concerns that no civilised advanced society can turn away from. It should be obvious that globalisation requires multilateral and institutional responses. The status quo is not an option.

Any notion that a single state can act as a global hegemon and world policeman, exerting its will through overwhelming use of military power, leading others to compliance or forcing them into submission, is completely unrealistic and dangerously counter-productive. Equally, the headlong pursuit of military strength and economic growth without regard for the environmental consequences indicates that humans have mutated into ostriches and lemmings armed with nuclear missiles.

Discussion 12.14

The weakness of the United Nations and the International Court of Justice

In July 2004, the International Court of Justice at The Hague, a UN body, gave a judgment in respect of a security fence or wall erected by the Israeli Defence Force as a barrier against illegal entry into Israel by extremists planning terror attacks on the Israeli state. The barrier has been built on Palestinian land. The ICJ ruled that the barrier is illegal, that it effectively annexes Palestinian land, that it violates the rights of ordinary Palestinians, that it should be removed and that Palestinian farmers living near it should be compensated. It also called upon the USA and Britain to exert pressure on Israel to comply with the demands of the Court. However, since the sole judge in a jury of 15 to dissent from the Court's verdict was the American, and since the UK tried to prevent the Court taking any decision at all, and since the USA has a long history of using its veto in the UN Security Council on resolutions directed against Israel, it would seem very unlikely that the Security Council will oblige Israel to comply. Alone, the Court cannot force compliance with its judgments. For this reason the ICJ is described in Chapter 8 above as only a quasi-judicial authority.

The example illustrates the weakness of even supreme international institutions such as the United Nations and the International Court of Justice.

Yet the organisations created after the Second World War that laid the foundations for a multilateral system of governance will remain the basis for effective governance in a global environment. International governmental organisations (IGOs) such as the EU, the WTO, the World Bank and the UN, will be prominent actors in an international civil society that promotes common public goods in a climate of international justice. However, such grand ambition requires the commitment of the richest and most powerful states to promote internal reforms in these organisations and where necessary to create others that can meet the challenge. In the wake of the deep divisions exposed by the 2003–4 Iraq crisis it is difficult to be especially optimistic about the imminent emergence of an effective multilateral response to current threats, in spite of the urgent need for a sustainable defence of planet-wide interests. See Discussion 12.14.

And yet there is no alternative. Bauman (2002) has spoken of the need for solidarity with those for whom the material benefits of post-industrial capitalism remain mere dreams, in particular the poor, the dispossessed and those seemingly condemned to cross frontiers in search of basic comforts, those whom he describes as vagabonds, as opposed to tourists, whose travelling is by choice, in comfort and generally welcomed by their hosts. Bauman claims that tolerance of the weak is not enough. We should be concerned that not only is Bauman right, but even a cursory reading of the media in Europe at this time tells us that we are not even at the stage of tolerance. Prejudice and misinformation is far more evident. The current *zeitgeist* is one of problematising otherness, apportioning blame to migrants and denying hospitality to those seeking shelter. How else can it be that the term 'asylum seeker' has attained such pejorative implications for the mass of the population in Europe?

The weakness of current institutions and the lack of coordinated and enforceable environmental protection demands decisive initiatives from governments. Governments remain the key actors in international relations and the key constituents in international organisations, but not in a traditional intergovernmental territorially bound fashion.

> Political space for the development and pursuit of effective government and the accountability of power is no longer coterminous with a delimited political territory. Forms of political organisation now involve a complex deterritorialization and reterritorialization of political authority (Held & McGrew, 2002:124).

Held and McGrew argue that state power is undergoing a transformation as the functions of states are rearticulated and reconstituted at the intersection of regional and global networks and systems, themselves in a state of flux. Their position is 'neither globalist nor sceptic, but transformationalist' (ibid., 126). Discussions of 'loss of sovereignty' miss the point, being based on a zero-sum interpretation of international relations. The reality is much more complex, more nuanced and more variable. Contemporary globalisation means there can no longer be any clear-cut distinction between domestic and foreign affairs, just as in many spheres of governance there can no longer be a clear demarcation between states.

> In a world in which global warming connects the long-term fate of many Pacific islands to the actions of tens of millions of private motorists across the globe, the conventional territorial conception of political community appears profoundly inadequate (Held & McGrew, 2002:129).

Reform and institutional innovation therefore requires action by governments with a commitment to cooperation as the only viable way to enhance their own legitimacy, the legitimacy of the institutions to which they contribute, and better prospects for global justice. States are increasingly unable to operate with sovereign independence. Indeed the state system is undergoing a metamorphosis and sovereignty has been transformed.

> It has been displaced as an illimitable, indivisible and exclusive form of public power, embodied in an individual state, and embedded in a system of multiple, often pooled, power centres and overlapping spheres of authority. There has been, in other words, a reconfiguration of political power (Held & McGrew, 2002:125–6).

As a state-centred system gives way to a more complex and multi-layered global politics Held and McGrew propose a model that draws on a range of perspectives on the globalisation phenomenon (see Figure 12.2). They argue that there are points of overlap between liberal internationalism, institutional reformism and global transformist thought. This creates what they call the terrain of cosmopolitan social democracy. See Table 12.2.

Cosmopolitan social democracy

[Cosmopolitan social democracy] seeks to nurture some of the most important values of social democracy – the rule of law, political equality, democratic politics,

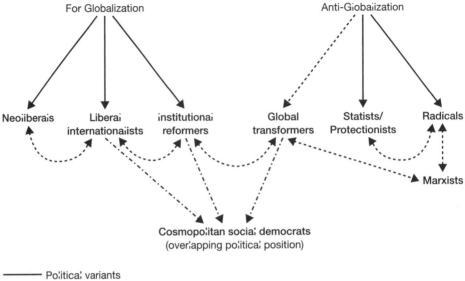

Figure 12.2 **Variants in the politics of globalisation**
Source: Held & McGrew 2002:99.

social justice, social solidarity and economic effectiveness – while applying them to the new global constellation of economics and politics (Held & McGrew, 2002:131).

The project of cosmopolitan social democracy can combine impartial international law, transparency and accountability, legitimacy and democracy in global governance. It can be founded on a commitment to social justice, human rights, gender equality, security and a more equitable distribution of resources. It requires effective regulation of the global economy through the public management of financial capital flow and trade, and the provision of global public goods. It requires the engagement of principal stakeholders. Held and McGrew argue that the identification of common ground between different positions in the globalisation/anti-globalisation debate 'provides a basis for a little optimism that global social justice is not simply a utopian goal' (Held & McGrew, 2002:131).

They identify further grounds for optimism through signs of greater engagement by intergovernmental organisations with a wider range of stakeholders and the increased salience of global issues such as human rights and environmental protection, as evidenced by the emergence of an International Criminal Court, greater acceptance of fundamental principles of human rights, widespread but not yet universal acceptance of the threat posed by climate change, and an emerging acceptance of the concept of international law. Multi-layered governance is a clear reality:

Table 12.2 Towards cosmopolitan social democracy

Guiding ethical principles/core values	Global social justice, democracy, universal human rights, human security, rule of law, transnational solidarity.
Short-term measures	*Governance* Reform of global governance: representative Security Council; establishment of Human Security Council (to coordinate global development policies); Global Civil Society Forum; strengthened systems of global accountability; enhancement of national and regional governance infrastructures and capacities; enhanced parliamentary scrutiny. *Economy* Regulating global markets: selective capital controls; regulation of offshore financial centres; voluntary codes of conduct for MNCs Promoting development: abolition of debt for highly indebted poor countries (HIPCs); meeting UN aid targets of 0.7 per cent GNP; fair trade rules; removal of EU and US subsidies of agriculture and textiles. *Security* Strengthening global humanitarian protection capabilities; implementation of existing global poverty reduction and human development commitments and policies; strengthening of arms control and arms trade regulation.
Long-term transformations	*Governance* Double democratisation (national to suprastate governance); enhanced global public goods provision; global citizenship. *Economy* Taming global markets: World Financial Authority; mandatory codes of conduct for MNCs; global tax mechanism; global competition authority. Market correcting: mandatory global labour and environmental standards; foreign investment codes and standards; redistributive and compensatory measures; commodity price and supply agreements. Market promoting: privileged market access for developing countries; convention on global labour mobility. *Security* Global social charter; permanent peacekeeping and humanitarian emergency forces; social exclusion and equity impact reviews of all global development measures.
Institutional/political conditions	Activist states, global progressive coalition (involving key Western and developing states and civil society forces), strong multilateral institutions, open regionalism, global civil society, redistributive regimes, regulation of global markets, transnational public sphere.

Source: Held & McGrew, 2002:132–3.

Since 1945 there has been a significant entrenchment of cosmopolitan values concerning the equal dignity and worth of all human beings in international rules and regulations; the reconnection of international law and morality, as sovereignty is no longer merely cast as effective power but increasingly as legitimate authority defined in terms of the maintenance of human rights and democratic values; the establishment of complex governance systems, regional and global; and growing recognition that the public good – whether conceived as financial stability, environmental protection, or global egalitarianism, requires coordinated multilateral action (Held & McGrew, 2002:135).

An important step would be for a coalition of authorities embracing state authorities and international institutions such as the World Bank to engage more closely with **non-governmental organisations** (NGOs) with expertise and experience in environmental protection, the promotion of sustainable development and the protection of human rights. In the WTO the development agenda should be re-energised, fair trade should be prioritised over free trade, and trade agreements need to be established in harmony with environmental interests.

Held and McGrew argue for the creation and maintenance of a further coalition of political interests comprising European countries with strong liberal and social democratic traditions, liberal groups in the United States that are supportive of multilateralism and the rule of law, developing countries committed to freer and fairer trading system, NGOs campaigning for greater justice and democracy, and economic forces that are concerned to establish a more stable economic environment. Europe should have a particularly constructive role given its social democratic traditions and its experience of multilateralism over more than half a century:

> As the home of both social democracy and a historic experiment in governance beyond the state, Europe has direct experience in considering the appropriate designs for more effective and accountable suprastate governance. It offers novel ways of thinking about governance beyond the state which encourage a (relatively) more democratic – as opposed to neoliberal – vision of global governance. Moreover, Europe is in a strategic position (with strong links west and east, north and south) to build global constituencies for reform of the architecture and functioning of global governance (Held & McGrew, 2002:135).

It would be entirely wrong however to 'broker a crude anti-US coalition of transnational and international forces' (Held & McGrew, 2002:136). On the contrary, US political society is complex and it is important to recognise the existence of progressive social, political and economic forces seeking to advance a rather different kind of world order from that championed by the Republican right (Nye, 2002). Held and McGrew emphasise that any EU strategy to promote a broad coalition behind 'a new global covenant' must enlist the support of progressive forces within the United States while at the same time

> [resisting] within its own camp the siren voices now calling with renewed energy for the exclusive re-emergence of national identities, ethnic purity and protectionism (Held & McGrew, 2002:136).

The survival of the state is not in question: merely the extent to which coalitions of states are prepared to act together to defend common interests, and to recognise and act upon broader human and planet-wide interests. Governments have acquiesced in the advance of globalisation, but they can no longer abdicate responsibility. They should instead work creatively towards reasserting democratic control to defend the interests of the wider society. Governments must be proactive in shaping policy responses more conducive to the common good, rather than shaped by and for sectional interests or regional interests.

There is also, as Chomsky has commented, an emergence of what he calls a 'second superpower' (Chomsky, 2003:235), comprising an unprecedented growth in global justice movements, meeting annually in the World Social Forum, aided by technological advances and better communication. There is much greater concern for civil and human rights of minorities, of women, and of concern for future generations, the latter driving a growing environmental movement. The force will become irresistible and is a cause for optimism.

Taking the long view of globalisation – as the consequence of centuries of entrenched human relationships, or a neo-Marxist perspective that interprets globalisation as a late stage in capitalism – there is reason to assume that feminism can significantly reshape politics in the twenty-first century. Campbell (2004) has raised questions about the impact of feminism, asking what it was that feminism has been up against. She comments on the limited and pessimistic interpretation of women's liberation being encapsulated by the contraceptive pill, gains in the workplace through improved technology, and access to education achieved through legislative changes. She argues that it is more significant that women mutinied against mass disappointment when men had maximum access to women's bodies, and that feminism challenged the bans and restrictions that built professions in men's image. She says

> [I]t wasn't evolutionary failure that made women poorly paid, it was the historic compromise between capital and labour [and] deals that put women at the bottom of the pay scales. Feminism exposed rape as not an excess of desire but a desire for dominion and domestic violence as a strategy for control (Campbell, 2004).

Campbell comments on how the idea of feminism is now felt in global institutions like the UN who accept that the era of patriarchy is losing its legitimacy. Feminism can reach parts of politics that other political movements do not reach:

> It changes the very conception of politics with its great innovation – the idea that the personal is political [. . .] Its project is not just about resources rights and redistribution, it is about a revolution in relationships (Campbell, ibid.).

This opens up the possibility that feminism can contribute or provoke a reassessment, not just of gender relations, but of all relationships, including that between all human society and the planet. Feminism is not a political party, nor even simply an idea. It is a progressive way of thinking that can have major global implications. See Discussion 12.15.

States and international institutions cannot retreat from the painstaking task of responding to the perils and opportunities brought about by globalisation. Globalisation offers significant opportunities as well as acute risks. States and international organisations such as the EU and the WTO that comprise states, have major stakes in realising the benefits and reducing the risks.

Commentaries following the re-election of George W. Bush have speculated on the possibility that the second term may in fact produce a more emollient United States, more inclined to seek support from its allies and from international institutions. It remains to be seen whether this indeed happens. Whatever the policies of a second Bush presidency, it is surely of paramount importance that common positions are adopted to confront the challenges faced by states and institutions. The future is likely to bring a far more multipolar world and

Discussion 12.15

Globalisation and gender issues

There are different feminist perspectives on global governance. One is liberal-feminism, which attempts to secure increased representation by women in the global policy-making process. The new Spanish PSOE government in 2004 honoured a pre-election pledge by creating a cabinet half of whom were women. Liberal-feminists argue for consensual norms based on discussion and bargaining and greater involvement of women's NGOs.

A second perspective focuses on structure and agency and provides an analysis of how an embedded nature of social relations underpins governance and power relations. Marxist-feminists take gender to be a specific form of social inequality that operates in the workplace and in the private realm of home, family and social milieu. The state is patriarchal not only because most key roles are held by men, but because the state perpetuates a division of realms between the public and the private.

Gender issues have long been politicised as in the feminist slogan the 'personal is political', where women's 'role' is predetermined by existing gender relationships, social expectations and institutionalisation of the status quo. Women's demands for equality before the law, parity in pension arrangements, property relations and defence against discrimination at work are ongoing issues that achieve a global profile in an era of increased internationalisation. Women's NGOs are increasingly active in diverse policy-making forums and networks beyond the state. International governmental organisations such as the World Bank and the UN have sponsored programmes with gender-related objectives, in particular micro-lending initiatives from the Bank and the Fourth UN Conference on Women held in Beijing in 1995. Issues such as the impact of SAPs, segregated labour markets, women's contribution to economic growth, equal pay for equal work, reproductive rights and domestic violence have all achieved more attention through engagement of IGOs with the increasing number of NGOs with an interest in women's rights and wider gender-related concerns.

Feminist critiques of neo-liberalism point to the NIEs of East Asia where 'the family firm, touted by scholars as the engine of Asian economic success, is rooted in gender ideologies and held together by the waged and unwaged labour of women' (Cheng & Hsuing, cited in Steans, 2002:90).

Steans emphasises the assumptions about the 'naturalness' of gender roles and women's responsibility for childcare, for example. Rules and norms reflect the preferences of powerful states and dominant social elites. The women's movement has challenged the consequences of neo-liberalism in NIEs that have increased the marginalisation and exploitation of women and increased female poverty (Steans, 2002:99).

There are significant criticisms even of high-profile initiatives such as the Beijing Conference. Spivak has warned that events like Beijing are merely 'well-organised ideological apparatus used to demonstrate an ostensible unity between North and South, when the North organises the South and the UN supports development policies which nurture post-Fordism' (and therefore conform to OECD expectations and norms, rather than the local needs of the people affected) (Spivak, 1996).

Meanwhile, gender issues tend to be marginalised within governance networks and processes but there are signs that gender issues are becoming more closely integrated into a wider acceptance of a global human rights agenda. Women's rights to health and education have long been part of a development agenda, and this is moving towards a wider acceptance of fundamental human rights informing policy making in relation to the globalisation of economic processes. This is the domain in which women's NGOs are mainly active in articulating the views of the poor and marginalised, and in communicating with policy makers at national and IGO levels. (For a more detailed account, see Steans, 2002.)

one that cries out for a fresh commitment to multilateralism and respect for common interests.

It would be a mistake, however, to assume that the response to globalisation has to come only from governments and institutions. Ultimately, individuals have to recognise that the personal really is political: how we lead our lives, conduct our relationships, how we behave as consumers, the questions we ask about the products we buy and the food we eat – these are matters over which we have more choice than is popularly assumed. Engagement, learning, thinking and acting as responsible global citizens, should lead to a deeper commitment to make a difference.

Summary

This chapter has made the following key points.

Multilateralism and international institutions

- International institutions are composed of member states; they are dependent on state authorities reaching common consent on how best to reform and manage the institutions in order to achieve common benefits.
- International institutions can only function effectively when they are not subject to domination by powerful states.
- The US has been a selective advocate of multilateralism since the Second World War; the EU has also been selectively multilateralist; the characterisation of the US as unilateralist and the EU as multilateralist is an over-simplification.
- The Iraq Crisis in 2003 split the European Union.

After September 11

- After the Cold War ended the US continued to be selectively multilateralist, but in some areas a greater tendency towards unilateralism appeared.
- After 9/11, US policy became decisively unilateralist, tending to reflect a greater reliance on US hegemony and requiring others to follow America's lead.
- Keohane argues that the US must return to constructive engagement with international institutions, as neither isolationism nor unilateralism is a viable option.
- The US has undermined its efforts against terror by losing moral authority.
- 9/11 alters traditional realist arguments against war because the threat is more difficult to identify and is not bound by geographical constraints.

The European Union as a global actor

- Major weaknesses and divisions threaten the future of the European Union.
- An integrated, united EU can use 'soft power' to influence the United States and others.

- Peterson and Pollack contend that the economic and cultural ties that bind the EU and the United States are strong enough to ensure lasting partnership.
- Others point to a major 'values gap' between America and Europe.
- Haseler predicts a reshaping of the European security architecture based on fundamentally different strategic interests between the US and Europe.
- US hegemony, unilateralism and hard power contrasts with the soft power and multilateralist preferences of the EU.
- The EU has political and economic interests in its international relations with other regions, including ACP through the Cotonou Agreement.

Responding to globalisation

- The EU must work to improve the institutional response to globalisation.
- The WTO, by and large, successfully promotes private goods, but public goods have been neglected.
- The current lopsided social development must be countered by a multilateral commitment to the promotion of public goods.
- Soros presents a proposal to reform the IMF and the World Bank, incorporating an SDR mechanism geared towards promoting public goods.
- A World Environment Organisation should be created to work in partnership with the WTO, guaranteeing a link between trade agreements and responsibility for the environmental implications.
- State governments remain the core actors in the international system, although they will face increasing pressures to respond to the demands of ordinary citizens and NGOs since these represent an emerging civil power that demands more constructive multilateral and just responses from governments.

Conclusion: cosmopolitan social democracy

- Globalisation can and should be made to work for the common benefits of all humanity.
- Sovereignty and the role of states has much altered in a multi-layered, more complex global environment.
- Cosmopolitan social democracy brings together different strands of the globalisation debate in a coalition of interests seeking a more just and stable global environment.
- Gender equality is a key component in the emerging human rights agenda.
- The European Union can have a decisive role in coalition building, together with progressive and liberal interests in the United States, and economic interests seeking a more stable commercial environment.

Key concepts: discussion and other definitions

Key concept 12.1   Multilateralism

A form of governance intended to provide international stability within the international state system based on cooperation, common principles and shared sovereignty between states.

Multilateralism implies cooperation and partnership between sovereign states.

Multilateralism emerged as a preferred approach to the management of the international political economy after the Second World War. The innovations introduced at Bretton Woods were designed to ensure that the competitive use of currency devaluation and trade tariffs employed during the 1920s and 1930s would not be repeated, thus avoiding the traumas that occurred in the international system.

Multilateralism emerged as the dominant approach to international governance until the early 1970s when the US unilaterally abandoned the Bretton Woods fixed exchange rate between the dollar and European currencies. Selective multilateralism then took over. The approach was further undermined after the election of George W. Bush in 2000, and even more so after the September 11 attacks.

Multilateralism may be viewed differently on each side of the Atlantic, as Howorth notes:

> The Europeans have a 50-year apprenticeship in structured multilateralism, and instinctively perceive the international system as a process of genuine institutional bargaining, informed by accepted rules, in which the pooling of sovereignty is recognised as offering more positive rewards than can be obtained through its jealous retention or mere assertion. The US, on the other hand, sees multilateralism as one approach among many, only to be entered into if it clearly yields greater rewards than are attainable by going it alone (Howorth, 2003:14).

The process of globalisation has entailed an increasing density of transnational politics, an expanding international jurisdiction, and a deepening impact of suprastate regulation. This has, according to Held and McGrew, led to a qualitative, structural shift in how global affairs and trans-boundary problems are governed. 'These developments represent the evolving infrastructure of a fragile system of global governance – a new complex multilateralism' (Held & McGrew, 2002ii:8).

Held and McGrew indicate that the end of the Cold War appeared to offer fresh opportunities for a new multilateral approach, and it undermined the previous ascendance of a hegemonic interpretation of power relationships based on Cold War divisions. Given the absence of a world government, as the challenges in international relations became more complex and multifaceted, it appeared that multilateralism offered a way to achieve better global governance.

Global governance does not presuppose a global government. It does, however, transcend the classic post-war multilateralism of the Bretton Woods institutions. It instead involves multi-layered and regional dimensions; it is pluralist, meaning that authority is dispersed; it has variable geometry, with different levels of engagement around the world; it is complex, featuring many institutional actors that overlap and interact; state authorities are not replaced; indeed they are strategic sites 'for suturing together these various infrastructures of governance and legitimizing regulation beyond the state' (Held & McGrew, 2002ii:9).

The significance of multilateralism is underlined by the complexities of global governance: it is inconceivable that agreements can be reached on matters as diverse as nuclear non-proliferation, international crime, climate change, and counter-terrorism without multilateral agreement. Equally, the prospects for concluding a successful trade round in the WTO are undermined by bilateral agreements that make multilateral agreement more difficult.

Key concept 12.2 Transatlantic partnership

The political and economic relationship between the United States of America and the European Union.

For the entire post-1945 period, the transatlantic relationship between the US and Europe has been central to international affairs in the Western world. Given the central power of the United States in international capitalism, and the status of the EC/EU as a key market for US exports, it is unsurprising that the relationship has consolidated the essentially Western character of capitalism and emerged as a model for the rest of the world. This contributes to the claim that capitalism itself has an imperialist character, and merely consolidates a pre-existing world order established under colonialism. Thus the Western world may be considered hegemonic, creating and consolidating dependency relationships in the developing world.

This view may be challenged by the emergence of other capitalist models, notably in Japan and more recently in China and in other parts of Asia.

The transatlantic partnership was established on the basis of more than mere economic exchange, however. The cultural ties between Europe and America go back to the original settlement of North America by European emigrants, particularly from Britain (hence the currency of the phrase the Anglo-Saxon world, meaning English-speaking) establishing a culture with many of the same roots as those of the old continent. More importantly, after the Second World War transatlantic relations were built on a military-strategic imperative in the context of the Cold War. The United States built a 'patron-client relationship' (Piening, 1997:94) with Europe, which in 1945 was in no position to reconstruct itself without American assistance. As with Japan, it was not until the 1970s that this relationship began to change towards one of partnership. The US role as hegemon diminished in the latter part of the twentieth century, although as this chapter makes clear, post-9/11 American policy has been much more assertive once more in attempting to consolidate a hegemonic relationship, not only with Europe, but with the entire world.

The transatlantic relationship has never been especially constant in terms of warmth of relations or closeness in geopolitical ambition. During the Cold War, the perceived threat from the USSR was the glue that kept Europe dependent on and engaged with America. Germany in particular became the focus of this dependency, with the permanent location of US troops on German soil. France, on the other hand, especially under President de Gaulle, was less welcoming of US influence in Europe and maintained a more distant relationship, at one time (in 1966) withdrawing France from the military command structure of NATO. French suspicion of the UK's so-called 'special relationship' with the US contributed to de Gaulle twice vetoing a British application to join the EEC. Meanwhile, Britain, for historical, cultural and political reasons, has always had a more intimate relationship with Washington, maintained in particular by the Foreign Office.

NATO has until recently been the cornerstone of the transatlantic partnership, but even this may be threatened by changes in the geostrategic system. It is ironic that the different national perceptions of the value of the transatlantic partnership may undermine European unity, given that for at least 40 years the United States sponsored and supported the European integration project.

Key concept 12.3   Soft power

Soft power is how a state uses influence to affect the policy choices of other states; soft power contrasts with hard power which is based on military strength.

Soft power concerns how one country uses *influence* to affect the policy choices of others.

> The ability to get others to want what [you] want (Nye, cited in Keohane, 2002:199).

Keohane (2002:95) refers to soft power as the exercise of influence, such as the way the US has influenced others through institutional involvement with the UN and NATO, for example. He also cites the adoption by others of US standards as international benchmarks, such as the US approach to the

> honest regulation of drugs, as in the Food and Drug Administration (FDA); transparent securities laws and practices, limiting self-dealing, monitored by the Securities and Exchange Commission (SEC) (Keohane, 2002:199).

Soft power rests on the attractiveness of some actors and their norms and principles to others. Soft power is relative to norms, and so 'those actors who conform to widely admired norms [. . .] gain influence' (Keohane, 2002:213).

Peterson and Pollack equate soft power with civilian power, 'patient diplomacy, aid and trade instruments, reinforcing multilateralism' (2003:8).

Soft power contrasts with hard power, normally interpreted as the ability to coerce others to do your will. Coercion is based on the use or threat of force, and so states that are militarily powerful may exercise hard power over other states. The traditional view of hegemony is based on hard power assumptions although, as explained in Key concept 8.4, hegemony normally implies a range of dimensions, embracing both hard and soft power.

Although it is an oversimplification, the EU is sometimes described as a 'soft power' in contrast to the 'hard power' of the US. The respect in which this characterisation is most accurate is in the relative weakness of the EU as a military power, but this can be reflected in a positive manner, as in successful peacekeeping ventures by limited forces, such as the EU has achieved in Macedonia (Peterson & Pollack, 2003:11).

Nye (2003) has written of the negative consequences of massive reliance on hard power over soft power. In commenting on the enormous military might of the United States, spending nearly half of the total military spending in the world, Nye says that the 'dazzling' success of America's four-week war against the Saddam regime 'was extremely damaging to America's attractiveness in the world' (Nye, 2003:63). Nye emphasises the unilateralist direction of US policy and argues that the US must re-learn the virtues of soft power.

'September 11th showed globalisation is more than just an economic phenomenon. It has been shrinking the natural buffers that two oceans provided to America' (Nye, ibid.). 9/11 according to Nye represents the 'privatisation of war'. He writes that after 9/11 a struggle ensued between unilateralists and multilateralists in US policy making and the unilateralists won. They underestimate the importance of soft power, which uses persuasion, rather than coercion.

> Hard power, the ability to coerce, grows out of a country's military and economic might. Soft power arises from the attractiveness of a country's culture, political ideals and policies. When America's policies are seen as legitimate in the eyes of others, its soft power is enhanced. Hard power will remain crucial in a world of states trying to guard their independence, and non-state groups willing to turn to violence. But soft power will become increasingly important in preventing the terrorists from recruiting supporters from among the moderate majority, and for dealing with the transnational issues that require multilateral co-operation for their solution (Nye, 2003:64).

This view is surely critical in searching for a just and acceptable response to contemporary challenges, including international terror. Nye reminds us that legitimacy is a form of power, and that humans live not only by the sword, but also by the word. He points out that even the Cold War was not won by hard power alone, but by Western soft power undermining the Soviet Union from within. Legitimacy is everything.

Further reading

Chomsky, N. (2003) *Hegemony or Survival? America's Quest for Global Domination*, London: Hamish Hamilton. A powerful polemic against US foreign policy, drawing on all of Chomsky's many years as a keen observer and critic of US actions in Latin America, the Gulf and beyond. Chomsky maintains that the US has consistently pursued its own interests at any cost to others and that in recent times it has chosen a clear strategy of 'total spectrum dominance' based on a policy of consolidating US hegemony.

Ellwood, W. (2001) *The No-Nonsense Guide to Globalization*, London: New Internationalist. This is among the recommended texts at the end of Chapter 9. See in particular the last chapter, 'Redesigning the global economy'.

Halper, S. and **Clarke**, J. (2004) *America Alone: the Neo-Conservatives and the Global Order*, Cambridge: Cambridge University Press. This is an extremely detailed analysis of the takeover of US policy by neo-conservative thought over the past quarter-century, culminating in the decision to invade Iraq in 2003. One of the major interests in the book is the poverty of debate, the failure of the media to inform the public and to effectively analyse policy, or to report on what has been a virtual coup from the inside where American polity is concerned. Halper and Clarke track the course of US unilateralism and see the current administration as more isolated than any US leadership since the Second World War. A striking thing about this book is that its authors are conservatives and mainstream Republicans. This quotation is from the dust-jacket of the book:

> Halper and Clarke have crafted an engrossing tale about the roots and impact of neo-conservatives on American policy. The book is must reading not only for what it says about how they did it, but also for documenting the paucity – in the US government and beyond – of meaningful debate about the potential risks as well as benefits of mounting 'preventive war' in response to the events of September 11, 2001 (Chester A. Crocker, Former Assistant Secretary of State for African Affairs, 1981–89, and Professor James R. Schlesinger, Professor of Strategic Studies, Georgetown University).

Haseler, S. (2004) *Super State: The New Europe and Its Challenge to America*, London: I.B. Tauris. This book develops ideas in the paper extensively referred to in this chapter (Haseler, 2003). Haseler writes that Europe is on the verge of becoming a serious rival to the USA, as it uses its size, its market strength, the euro, and emergent defence identity in the European Rapid Reaction Force to assert its independence from its former protector. Europe is prepared to be a partner to the US, but is no longer able to accept America as the 'leader of the free world'. Haseler predicts the break-up of NATO as well as the emergence of a more consolidated European political power, leading the European Union closer to becoming a super-state, but one composed of diverse states with individual identities, but common interests. These interests, especially in relation to security, will be different to those of the United States.

Held, D. & **McGrew**, A. (2002) *Globalization/Anti-Globalization*, Cambridge: Polity. This is a concise, erudite and powerfully argued account of the major positions in the globalisation debate. See especially the final chapter, 'Reconstructing World Order: Towards Cosmopolitan Social Democracy', pp. 118–36, outlining the concept of cosmopolitan social democracy. The book makes a good companion to a more detailed Held and McGrew edited collection, *Governing Globalization* (2002), also published by Polity.

Keohane, R. (2002) *Power and Governance in a Partially Globalized World*, London: Routledge. This is a collection of essays by the prominent exponent of liberal institutionalism, Robert Keohane. Often complex and detailed, but always profoundly thought-provoking, Keohane addresses not only many of the core assumptions of International Relations theory, but the relevance of the discipline itself. The final chapter is a fascinating response to the terror attacks on Washington and New York on 11 September 2001. Keohane suggests that International Relations might be renamed global politics and that liberals must redouble their efforts to find multilateral institutional responses to the new dangers posed by the globalisation of informal violence. Read particularly Chapter 12, 'The globalisation of informal violence, theories of world politics, and the "liberalism of fear"', pp. 272–87.

Legrain, P. (2002) *Open World: The Truth about Globalisation*, London: Abacus. This book is also recommended at the end of Chapter 10. Look in particular at the final chapter for a more detailed account of proposals for making globalisation work better.

Peterson, J. & **Pollack**, M. (eds) (2003) *Europe, America, Bush*, London and New York: Routledge. This is an outstanding set of essays on the triple impact on the transatlantic relationship of Bush becoming President, 9/11 and the US invasion of Iraq in 2003. Immensely readable, informative and thought-provoking, this is a great book.

Soros, G. (2002) *George Soros On Globalisation*, Oxford: Public Affairs Limited. George Soros, financier and philanthropist, the man generally credited with evicting the UK from the ERM in 1992, writes a polemic against US hegemony and a plea for globalisation with a moral dimension. This short, dynamic read contains a detailed description of his SDR proposal. He finishes by asking that anyone who objects to his proposal should 'come up with a better idea'.

Film suggestion

Francis Ford Coppola, *Apocalypse Now*, 1979, US

Apocalypse Now is Coppola's masterpiece, and possibly the best film made about the Vietnam War. David Cannon, reviewing the film, refers to its massive over-budgeting (it cost $29m though it was budgeted at $12m) and production overrun (by three years) as a fitting parallel with the war itself (http://www.film.u-net/Movies/Reviews/Apocalypse_Now.html).

The film is about chaos. It is also about the weakness of hard power (see Key concept 12.3). In a story loosely based on Joseph Conrad's *Heart of Darkness*, Captain Willard (Martin Sheen) is sent on a mission from Saigon up the Mekong River to assassinate Colonel Kurtz (Marlon Brando), a renegade officer who is waging his own private war, worshipped by a platoon of followers deep in the heart of the Cambodian jungle. The river journey highlights the indiscriminate horror of the war, a Napalm attack on a defenceless village so that a power-crazed US Army captain can indulge his passion for surfing ('I love the smell of Napalm in the morning'), the butchering of a family whose boat is searched by Willard's nervous, drug-taking escorts, and when Willard gets close to Kurtz, the madness is tangible, not only in Kurtz himself, but Willard's own mission to take him out. The entire war is insane, prosecuted by the United States, the world's greatest industrial, economic, political and military superpower, with 750,000 soldiers embroiled in the morass of a hopeless, stupid, brutal and doomed adventure.

Visually stunning, with a superb soundtrack, and at least from Sheen a brilliant acting performance (he suffered a heart attack at the beginning of filming), this film is worth seeing on many counts.

In terms of this book, it serves as a useful metaphor for chaos and how wrong choices may mean that chaos is faced down by still more chaos, even under the guise of 'legitimate' state-waged war. Hard power alone means critical weakness. Kurtz is unacceptable to the US military because he has abandoned the rules, the assumption that legitimate war is waged by and between states. Kurtz is anarchic, so he must be removed. In the final frame of the film, the USAF destroys the compound in a massive air attack as Willard leaves, his mission completed. Willard's own confusion is clear. Who is he working for and why? The horror is everywhere, the morass of a pointless and savage war extending over years, where there are no rules, only chaos and more horror.

Two short reviews of the film can be found at

http://www.channel4.co.uk/film/reviews/film.jsp?id=100565
http://www.eufs.org.uk/films/apocalypse_now.html

Note: The longer 2000 version of the film, *Apocalypse Now Redux*, is probably not an improvement on the original, in most critics' judgement.

Apocalypse Now might be interpreted as the ultimate celluloid call for multilateral institutional responses to globalisation. I couldn't think of a better one, but I'll keep looking.

Glossary

Numbers after terms in the glossary refer to broader discussion in the Key terms sections at the end of each chapter.

Acquis communautaire The body of treaties, laws and norms, comprising all legislation, of the European Union.

Anarchy An absence of formal authority. Within the context of International Relations theory, realism holds that inter-state relations are inherently anarchic since states are competitive and there exists no higher authority to regulate tensions and the ensuing conflict between states.

Atlanticism/Atlanticist A term applied to British foreign policy perspectives implying a inclination for policy making which conforms to United States preferences, and builds on the paramount importance of close relations with the USA. The term may sometimes occur in relation to other European governments, especially the Federal Republic of Germany during the Cold War. See also Special relationship.

Benelux A short-form name for Belgium, the Netherlands and Luxembourg.

Capitalism (8.1) A distinct form of social organisation which is based on private ownership and control of the means of production where the latter is organised with the intention of creating profit.

Civic nationalism A form of elite-driven nationalism that is tolerant of diversity and marked by a recognition of different ethnicities, even multiculturalism.

Cold War The stand-off between the rival powers emergent from the Second World War, the USA and the USSR. The antagonism was based on opposing political and economic models and military rivalry, exacerbated by a nuclear arms race which prevailed throughout most of the Cold War period 1945–91. See also Détente.

Common policy Areas of EU law that are applied to all member states without derogation. Common policy applies to all so-called Pillar I or Community Law as defined in the Treaty on European Union (1992), but may be extended to other areas by treaty provision, which requires unanimous agreement in the Council.

Competence A term used to describe powers exercised by the European Union in specific policy areas.

Confederalism A loose form of federal arrangement where states participate in a matrix relationship based on bilateral agreements with little evidence of binding supranational structures. Relations are conducted on an intergovernmental basis.

Constitution The body of rules and the set of precedents which combine to determine how governance is conducted within a state. It defines the roles of the institutions of the state. It may also be accompanied by a Bill of Rights setting out the rights of citizens.

Council of the European Union Formerly known as the Council of Ministers, the Council is the primary legislative organ of the European Union, responsible for law making. It delegates certain legislative powers to the Commission and in many areas has a co-legislator role with the European Parliament. The Council is comprised of many councils, each with specific areas of policy responsibility and headed by the ministerial representatives of the member states.

Culture (10.2) The context in which any given human society exists, and expressed by symbols, icons, language, education, entertainment, fashion, consumer goods, and other commonly accepted manifestations of identity.

Deepening See Widening and deepening.

Democracy A system of representative government which in the Western tradition presupposes a pluralist political system where voters have a free choice between different political parties presenting alternative political programmes. Democracy also presupposes freedom of the press as well as basic human rights including freedom of speech, thought, belief and association, and the right to set up political parties and campaign groups.

Demos The public, the masses, within a political system, especially one based on the principles of representative democracy.

Détente An easing of strained relations between the Soviet Union and the United States. The term applies especially to the period 1970–79, when relations between the Cold War rivals were stable and marked by a reduction in tension following the acute dangers of the 1960s. Détente was marked by arms control, bilateral communication, and acceptance of the doctrine of mutually assured destruction (MAD), thereby significantly reducing the risk of conflict. Détente came to an abrupt end with the deployment of Soviet troops in Afghanistan in 1979.

Dictatorship (1.2) An authoritarian form of government that does not have democratic legitimacy and is not subject to the law. See Totalitarian.

Economic liberalism A theory of political economy associated with the writings of Adam Smith (1723–90). Economic liberalism promotes free trade on the assumption that states that trade with each other are less likely to come into conflict and that common interests will emerge. Economic liberalism also assumes a minimal role for the state, namely to provide security and the rule of law. See also Institutional liberalism.

Enlightenment (The) An international, though primarily European, intellectual movement established throughout the eighteenth century and grounded in a belief in progress, rationalism and the capacity of human invention, thought and science to deliver continual and improving benefits. The Enlightenment encompasses a broad spectrum of thought and, while not an outright rejection of religion, it did challenge the notion of religious authority as the sole source of knowledge.

Ethnic nationalism A form of popular nationalism promoted by the mass of a specific racial group, whose members are united by a common sense of identity, shared language and culture, and belief in their destiny.

European Central Bank (ECB) The primary authority responsible for the management of Economic and Monetary Union and the Single Currency, the euro. The ECB is managed by a governing council composed of the governors of the participating central banks, and an executive board (the President, the Vice President and four other members appointed by the member states after consultation with the governing council and the European Parliament).

European Commission A central institution of the European Union with a combination of executive, administrative, legislative and judicial responsibilities, sometimes referred to as the 'civil service' of the Union.

European Council The executive body of the European Union consisting of the heads of government (in the case of France and Finland the heads of state) as well as the President of the Commission. The Council is responsible for major initiatives and the direction of Union policy, including the principles and guidelines of foreign and security policy.

European Court of Justice (ECJ) The primary judicial authority of the European Union, responsible for adjudicating on possible breach of European Union treaties, and on the conduct of EU institutions.

European integration process (3.1) The dynamic of political change that has led national governments in Europe to cooperate in creating institutional innovations in order to achieve desired outcomes that would be less easily realised without such cooperation.

Europeanisation (6.2) The process by which authority over domestic, or state-level political and economic processes is relocated to the European arena.

European Parliament The directly elected assembly of the European Union. It has a co-legislative role with the Council as well as reviewing and advisory functions in framing EU policies. It also plays a key role in the financial affairs of the Union.

Euroscepticism (3.2) Strongly critical view of the European Union and the integration process in general, tending towards hostility towards the Union, or even opposition to EU membership.

Exchange Rate Mechanism (ERM) Part of the European Monetary System (EMS) created in 1979 to assist stable exchange rates between European currencies.

Federalism (5.1) A system of integration which suggests that everybody can be satisfied by combining national and regional/territorial interests within a complex web of checks and balances between a national or federal government and a multiplicity of regional governments.

Foreign Direct Investment (FDI) Capital flow from one country to another, and intended to promote business development either through support to lending institutions such as banks or directly to businesses involved in the production and sale of goods and services. Most FDI stems from private businesses, but governments, international institutions and aid organisations are also involved, especially where infrastructural projects are concerned. FDI is described in terms of inflow and outflow.

Free market capitalism Social organisation based on private capital and the conduct of commercial exchange with minimal regulatory or state interference. See also *Laissez-faire*.

Free trade Commercial exchange, primarily between private companies, where there is minimal intervention by regulatory authorities and where states do not impose tariffs or barriers which may discourage such exchange. Free trade is governed only by markets and the laws of supply and demand.

Functionalism An approach towards unity that is based less on the creation of supranational structures than on piecemeal steps towards common policy using technical cooperation for common benefits. Functionalism, as articulated by its primary exponent David Mitrany, has a global rather than regional perspective.

Globalisation (9.1) The process of increasing interconnectedness between societies such that events in one part of the world more and more have effects on peoples and societies far away (Baylis & Smith, 2001:7).

Governance Processes of rule making, monitoring and implementation conducted by various interconnected actors and institutions, and affecting local, state and global communities. 'The range of actions and institutions that supply order' (Rosamond, 2003:119).

Hard power (12.3) How a state uses military strength to affect the policy choices of other states; hard power is directed towards limiting the options of others. See also Soft power.

Hegemonic stability theory The notion that stability in the international state system requires the existence of powerful states able to exert influence and control over several less powerful states in such a way that they limit states' tendency to engage in conflict. HST is widely contested, but it was considered especially applicable to the Cold War context where the hegemonic role of the USA and the USSR over their respective spheres of influence imposed a kind of acquiescent calm.

Hegemony (8.4) The exercise of power, or influence, of a dominant polity over other polities or regions.

Human rights (7.1) The rights one has simply by virtue of being a human being. The General Assembly of the United Nations adopted the Universal Declaration of Human Rights in 1948, which has remained the basis for understanding and defining human rights ever since.

Institutional liberalism A school of thought within International Relations theory which supports a liberal view of political economy, but emphasises the centrality of international institutions in facilitating efficient trade and the conduct of international affairs.

Intergovernmentalism (4.1) An approach to policy making based on the principle of negotiation between one or more sovereign states pursuing their individual interests but tending towards cooperation to common advantage.

International Political Economy (IPE) A branch of International Relations theory which itself contains a wide range of positions including mercantilism, economic liberalism, Marxism and reformism. These perspectives share an understanding that international relations are dependent on both political and economic drivers, and that the two are closely interrelated. It is impossible to conceive of the political dimensions to inter-state affairs without taking account of economic factors, and vice versa.

International Relations (IR) A sub-discipline of political science concerned with the theory and practice of inter-state relationships within the state system. In addition, IR increasingly takes account of the role of international institutions and the role of the states which comprise them.

Keynesian economics A mix of economic and social policy based on the writings of the British economist John Maynard Keynes (1883–1946). Keynes advocated a partnership between private interests and the responsibility of the state to promote social welfare for the common good. Keynesianism implies macroeconomic management of the economy but has never fully resolved the problem of maintaining full employment or curbing inflation.

Laissez-faire An approach to economic management based on the principle of minimal regulatory or state interference, where commercial exchange is controlled only by the laws of the market place. The role of the state is to uphold only the basic rights of ownership that are central to a capitalist system.

Legislature An institution, usually a parliament, within a system of governance that makes legislation, or enacts laws.

Liberalism (8.2) The belief that it is the aim of politics to preserve individual rights and to maximise freedom of choice.

Marxism (8.3) A tradition in Western political philosophy that is based on the work of Karl Marx (1818–83) and Friedrich Engels (1820–95). Marxism presents a socio-economic critique of capitalism, based primarily on an analysis of class relationships, and proposes political change to create a socialist alternative to capitalism.

Mercantilism A school of thought within International Political Economy (IPE) which privileges the role of the state in promoting its domestic producers and exporting, as opposed to a broader liberal interest in developing bilateral trade with other states. Mercantilism is wholly competitive and promotes exports while discouraging imports. Mercantilism presupposes that trade can both enrich and empower the state and can provide the means for it to become a military power. Mercantilism has sometimes been described as a 'beggar thy neighbour' approach to trade.

Multilateralism (12.1) A form of governance intended to provide international stability within the international state system based on cooperation, common principles and shared sovereignty between states.

Multilevel governance Supranational, state and sub-state levels of policy making and policy implementation.

Multinational corporation (MNC) (11.1) A large-scale business entity with production and sales operations in several different countries and regions.

Nation A relatively homogeneous group, usually ascribed a specific ethnicity, and sharing common identity, culture, traditions, history, beliefs, myths and sense of destiny. Sometimes used synonymously with *state*, as in United Nations.

Nationalism (2.2) 'An ideological movement for the attainment and maintenance of autonomy, unity and identity on behalf of a population deemed by some of its members to constitute a "nation"' (Smith, 1995:149–50).

Neo-conservatism A trend among the Republican elite in the US that supports the notion of American supremacy in world affairs, primarily through the adoption of an aggressive foreign policy, increased defence spending and the ambition to achieve 'total spectrum dominance' through a missile defence system and overwhelming military strength. Neo-conservatives also support the right of the US to engage in 'pre-emptive military action' against perceived threats, even without the support of the United Nations. Although the neo-conservative ascendancy in the US has a much longer history, these shifts in US thinking have been especially pronounced since the terror attacks on New York and Washington in September 2001. 9/11 provided the pretext for Washington's 'War on Terror' and a more forthright and unilateral approach to international relations.

Neo-functionalism (5.2) A theory of regional integration that maintains that political integration and the growth of authority at the supranational level occur as a long-term consequence of modest economic integration. Integration in one sector creates pressures for integration in related sectors, and so on. This process is called functional spillover.

Neo-liberalism A branch of liberalism associated with the post-Cold War period of globalisation and marked by the increased capital flow, burgeoning technology and the reduction in the role of the state in the macroeconomic management of the economy. Gray (*False Dawn*, 1998) described neo-liberalism as a political project pursued by the US and the 'Washington consensus' that sought a free market with minimal government intervention throughout the world. By 2002, however, in a new preface to *False Dawn*, Gray says that the US had abandoned this quest and reverted to government intervention, notably by trying to impose tariffs on steel imports.

Neo-realism A development of realism associated with the writings of K.N. Waltz, in which the basic tenets of realism are retained but greater attention is paid to the international system that emerges as a consequence of the interaction of states. Neo-realism also pays more attention to the social factors which may underlie conflict between states.

Non-governmental organisations (NGOs) Campaign organisations, independent of governments, with specific sectoral objectives directed at social or environmental improvement, such as Oxfam, Amnesty International or Greenpeace.

Nostalgia The combination of constructed memories that leads to an idealistic or fantastical vision of the past consisting of exaggeratedly benign and positive interpretations of history.

Politics The process by which decisions are taken and power distributed. In its most common usage, politics relates to the ways in which states are governed and societies are organised. Politics concerns the representation, and suppression, of interests and may also imply the permanence of 'latent disagreement' (McClean & McMillan, 2003:423).

Postmodernism (10.1) A wide variety of cultural practices and theoretical discourses associated with the experience of postmodernity which itself is associated with post-industrial society.

Power (9.2) 'The capacity to achieve desired results' (Finer, 1970:12–13).

Private goods A range of interests pertaining to individuals and associated with free enterprise and the right to accumulate profit. These interests include wealth, property and ownership.

Protectionism The imposition of tariffs and duties and other impediments to trade, including the banning of certain imports, ostensibly to protect the interests of home producers.

Public goods A range of interests of universal benefit to humankind and relating to the long-term sustainability of life on earth. These include environmental protection, basic human rights, labour protection, health and safety, food standards and animal rights. Public goods are sometimes contrasted with private goods.

Qualified Majority Voting (QMV) Where a vote is required in the European Council or in the Council of the European Union (formerly the Council of Ministers) the weighting of votes per member state reflects to some extent the populations of the states, so larger states have more votes. The Dublin Summit in 2004 agreed a formula which would take direct account of population size by insisting that not only was a qualified majority of votes required to approve legislation, but that proposals also required the support of states with 60 per cent of the Union population, the so-called 'double majority'.

Racism Prejudice or discrimination against members of an ethnic group on grounds of ethnic origin or skin colour; the tendency to privilege one's own ethnic community over another or others. Racism may include verbal and physical abuse, intimidation and even extreme violence against individuals or their communities.

Rapprochement Meaning the resumption of harmonious relations and used especially of the settlement between two states after a long period of historical enmity.

Realism A branch of International Relations theory which holds that the state is the primary actor in international relations and that the primary motivating factor in policy making is the enhancement of state power, especially military power. Realism sees inter-state relations as competitive within an essentially anarchic environment where there is no higher authority than the state. Realist thinking includes an approach to statecraft which encompasses the philosophical traditions of Machiavelli, *The Prince* (1513) and Hobbes, *Leviathan* (1651).

Regionalisation The *de facto* emergence of an international economy in which regional power blocs co-exist and compete. Regionalisation is seen as a key characteristic of contemporary globalisation.

Regionalism (1) 'State-led projects of institution building among groups of countries' (Rosamond, 2003:123). The European Union, NAFTA and ASEAN are examples of such regionalism, each involving significant levels of inter-state (intergovernmental) cooperation. (2) The term may also denote the demands for greater local autonomy and the assertion of specifically local preferences at the expense of the state. See Borzel (2002ii).

Republicanism The belief that the state should be a republic, i.e. not be governed by, or headed by, a monarchy.

Secularism The formal separation of church and state authorities. In a secular state the church has no role in the affairs of government, nor in education provided by the state.

Single European Market (SEM) The totality of economic activity within and between member states of the European Union (the internal market). The development of the Single Market began with the establishment of the European Coal and Steel Community in 1951. The Single European Act of 1986 set a target for completion of the Single Market by 1992. The SEM is intended to uphold the four freedoms of movement of goods, services, people and capital as well as remove both physical and technical barriers to trade, such as customs checks, discriminatory standards, tariffs and duties. The SEM also envisages the harmonisation of VAT rates throughout the internal market.

Soft power (12.3) How a state uses influence to affect the policy choices of other states. Soft power contrasts with *hard power* which is based on military strength.

Sovereignty (2.1) The ability of a state, or a constitutionally recognised body acting on behalf of the state, to exercise authority over its territory and its people without being subject to any higher authority.

Special relationship The close bilateral relations between the UK and the USA since 1940. The view that a unique bond exists between the two countries stems from cultural, linguistic and political affinities, but has also been marked by interest-based policy making. This has meant that while the relationship has often been trumpeted, especially in Britain, as a defining characteristic of US–UK relations, it has never been an equal relationship and has varied in intensity according to events and the personalities involved.

Spillover A feature of the neo-functionalist approach to European integration whereby integration in one area of policy leads to integration in a related area. For example, the Single European Act led to the opening up of borders between member states, which precipitated a need for more inter-state cooperation in policing.

Stakeholders Individuals and organisations directly affected by and with a direct interest in matters of private and public policy, ranging from entire communities through employees to owners and investors.

State (1.1) A political entity that is coterminous with a territory and represented by a government that is recognised as having legitimate authority, or sovereignty, over that territory and the people who live in it.

State nationalism A form of nationalism initiated by elites anxious to build the nation according to a specific national image and marked by the dominance of a particular ethnicity.

Subsidiarity (6.1) The principle that tries to ensure that decisions are taken as close as possible to the citizen. In reality though, subsidiarity mainly applies to decision-making at one of two levels, the supranational European level, or the state level. There is little direct EU involvement at a sub-state level.

Supranationalism (4.2) An approach to policy making and enforcement through which a higher authority can enforce legislation and determine policy practice in those states which are bound by its legal framework.

Totalitarian A word used to describe a particularly brutal form of dictatorship (see Dictatorship). Regimes of this kind typically employed the organs of state (government, police and military) to maintain a tight hold on three critical areas of society: thought (including religion or its absence, and all forms of expression), politics (including single-party government, the police and the military) and the economy (state ownership or private ownership subject to state control). Totalitarian regimes include those of Hitler (Nazi Germany), Stalin (Soviet Union), Pol Pot (Cambodia), Saddam Hussein (Iraq) and Kim Il Jung (North Korea).

Transatlantic partnership (12.2) The political and economic relationship between the United States of America and the European Union. This partnership was a particular hallmark of the Cold War (1945–91).

Triad (The) The three-cornered structure of the major locations of international trade, represented by the USA and NAFTA, the European Union, and Japan and the East Asia Pacific region. Approximately 80 per cent of all trade is conducted within and between the Triad and it is the home of the great majority of multinational corporations. The term was originally coined by Ohmae (1985).

Unilateralism A tendency to abrogate or ignore international agreements and institutions. Unilateralism is associated in particular with an extreme realist position in the conduct of international affairs and tends to eschew compromise or any assumption that finding common ground can bring mutual advantage.

Variable geometry An approach to European integration which envisages different levels of engagement with new policy initiatives, depending on individual state preferences. This is similar to what has been described as an *à la carte* Europe.

Washington consensus (11.2) Privatisation of state assets; trade and financial deregulation; shrinking the role of the state; encouraging foreign direct investment. The term implies that these policies reflect the preferences of US governments as well as the World Bank and the IMF, both of which are also based in Washington.

Widening and deepening (7.2) Widening – bringing in more member states; deepening – consolidating the institutions and competences of the Union and increasing the extent of integration between member states.

Xenophobia The unreasonable fear or hatred of other races or communities.

References

Allen, D. (2000) 'Cohesion and the Structural Funds: transfers and trade-offs' in Wallace, H. & Wallace, W. (eds), *Policy Making in the European Union*. Oxford: OUP.

Andrew, G. (2002) 'Mulholland Drive' in *Time Out Film Guide 2003*. London: Penguin.

Ardagh, J. (1995) *Germany and the Germans*. Harmondsworth: Penguin.

Armstrong, K. & Bulmer, S. (1998) *The Governance of the Single European Market*. Manchester: Manchester University Press.

Arnull, A. (2003) 'The Community Courts', Chapter 12, pp. 179–91, in Cini, M. (ed.) *European Union Politics*. Oxford: Oxford University Press.

Bainbridge, T. (2002) *The Penguin Companion to the European Union*, 3rd edition. London: Penguin.

Baldwin, M., Peterson, J. & Stokes, B. (2003) 'Trade and economic relations', pp. 29–46 in Peterson, J. & Pollack, M. (eds) *Europe, America, Bush*. London and New York: Routledge.

Baudrillard, J. (1981) *Simulacra and Simulations*, tr. Paul Foss, Paul Patton and Philip Beitchmann. New York: Semiotext(e).

Bauman, Z. (1993) *Postmodern Ethics*. Oxford: Blackwell.

Bauman, Z. (1997) *Postmodernity and Its Discontents*. Cambridge: Polity.

Bauman, Z. (1998) *Globalization: the human consequences*. Cambridge: Polity.

Bauman, Z. (2002) 'The fate of humanity in the post-Trinitarian world', address to CongressCATH 2002, *Translating Class, Altering Hospitality*, Centre for Cultural Analysis, Theory & History, University of Leeds, 20–23 June 2002.

Baun, M. (1996) *An Imperfect Union: the Maastricht Treaty and the New Politics of European integration*. Boulder, CO: Westview.

Baylis, J. & Smith, S. (eds) (2001) *The Globalization of World Politics*. Oxford: Oxford University Press.

Blacksell, M. (1997) 'State and nation: Germany since reunification' in *Europa*, no. 3, Article 5, 1997.

Bodansky, D. (2003) 'Transatlantic environmental relations' pp. 59–68 in Peterson, J. & Pollack, M. (eds) *Europe, America, Bush*. London and New York: Routledge.

Bourke, T. (1996) *Japan and the Globalisation of European Integration*. Aldershot: Dartmouth.

Bourne, A. (2003) 'Regional Europe', Chapter 18, pp. 278–93, in Cini, M. (ed.) *European Union Politics*. Oxford: Oxford University Press.

Börzel, T.A. (2002) 'Member state responses to Europeanization' in *Journal of Common Market Studies*, vol. 40, no. 2: 195–214.

Börzel, T.A. (2002ii) *States and Regions in the European Union: Institutional Adaptation in Germany and Spain*. Cambridge: Cambridge University Press.

Boyes, R. (2003) 'Hello Lenin: Ostalgia for the old East Germany' in *The Times*, 23 July.

Brandt Commission (1983) *North South – A Programme for Survival*. London: Pan Books.

Bridges, B. (1999) *Europe and the Challenge of the Asia Pacific*. Cheltenham: Edward Elgar.

Brittan, L. (1995) 'The EU–US relationship: will it last?', speech to the American Club of Brussels, 27 April.

Bull, H. (1984) 'The Great Irresponsibles? The United States, the Soviet Union and world order', in Matthews, R.O., Rubinoff, A.G. & Stein, J.C. (eds) *International Conflict and Conflict Management*. Scarborough: Prentice-Hall Canada.

Bull, H. (1995) *The Anarchical Society: a Study of Order in World Politics*. 2nd edition. London: Macmillan.

Bullmann, U. (1997) 'The Politics of the Third Level', Chapter 1, pp. 3–19, in Jeffery, C. *The Regional Dimension of the European Union*. London: Frank Cass.

Burgess, M. (2003) 'Federalism and federation', Chapter 5, pp. 65–79, in Cini, M. (ed.) *European Union Politics*. Oxford: Oxford University Press.

Callinicos, A. (1989) *Against Postmodernism*. Cambridge: Polity.

Callinicos, A. (2003) *An Anti-Capitalist Manifesto*. Cambridge: Polity.

Campbell, B. (2004) 'Feminism is a revolution in human relationships' from a speech at the Cheltenham Festival of Literature, reported in the *Independent*, 12 October.

Campbell, J. (2003) *Margaret Thatcher: Iron Lady*. Jonathan Cape.

Castle, S. (2004) 'High cost of being out of the EU, but locked in', *Independent*, p. 5, 16 June.

Chang, I. (1997) *The Rape of Nanking*. London: Penguin.

Chomsky N. (1992) 'A view from below', pp. 137–50, in Hogan, M.J. *The End of the Cold War: Its Meaning and Implications*. Cambridge: Cambridge University Press.

Chomsky, N. (2003) *Hegemony or Survival: America's Quest for Global Dominance*. London: Hamish Hamilton.

Christiansen, T. (2001) 'European and regional integration', pp. 494–518, in Baylis, J. & Smith, S. (eds) *The Globalization of World Politics*. Oxford: Oxford University Press.

Cini, M. (2003) 'Intergovernmentalism', Chapter 7, pp. 93–108, in Cini, M. (ed.) *European Union Politics*. Oxford: Oxford University Press.

Clark, I. (2001) *The Post-Cold War Order: The Spoils of Peace*. Oxford: Oxford University Press.

Cockburn, P. & Gumbel, A. (2004) 'Korean is beheaded as warning over troop deployment', *Independent*, 23 June.

Crystal, D. (1997) *English as a Global Language*. Cambridge: Cambridge University Press.

Davies N. (1996) *Europe: a History*. Oxford: Oxford University Press.

Denman, R. (1997) *Missed Chances: Britain and Europe in the Twentieth Century*. London: Orion.

Dicken, P. (2003) *Global Shift: Reshaping the Global Economic Map in the 21st Century*. London: Sage.

Dinan, D. (1999) *Ever Closer Union: an Introduction to European Integration*. Basingstoke: Palgrave.

Droz, J. (1967) *Europe Between Revolutions, 1815–48*. London: Fontana.

Egeberg, M. (2003) 'The European Commission', Chapter 9, pp. 131–47, in Cini, M. (ed.) *European Union Politics*. Oxford: Oxford University Press.

Ellingham, M. & Fisher, J. (2002) *The Rough Guide to Spain*. London: Rough Guides/Penguin.

Ellwood, W. (2001) *The No-Nonsense Guide to Globalization*. London, Oxford: New Internationalist, Verso.

Evans, G. with Newham, J. (1998) *The Penguin Dictionary of International Relations*. London: Penguin.

Falk, R. (1985) 'A new paradigm for international legal studies', in Falk, R. Kratochwil, F. & Mendlovitz, S.H. (eds) *International Law: A Contemporary Perspective*. Boulder, CO: Westview.

Falkner, G. & Nentwich, M. (2001) 'Enlarging the European Union: the short-term success of incrementalism and depoliticisation', Chapter 13, pp. 260–82, in Richardson, J. (ed.) *European Union: Power and Policy Making*. London: Routledge.

Ferguson, N. (2004) 'The depressing reality of this messianic President's new empire', *The Independent*, 4 November.

Financial Times (2004) 'Missed Targets', 22 January, p. 12.

Finer, S. (1970) *Comparative Government*. London: Allen Lane/Penguin.

Forsyth, M. (1981) *Unions of States: The Theory and Practice of Confederation*. Leicester: Leicester University Press.

Fukuyama, F. (1992) *The End of History and the Last Man*. London: Hamish Hamilton.

Fusi, J.P. (1990) *El País Vasco: Pluralismo y nacionalidad*. Madrid: Alianza Universidad.

Gaddis, J.L. (1992) *The United States and the End of the Cold War*. Oxford: Oxford University Press.

Galbraith, J.K. (1993) *The Culture of Contentment*. London: Sinclair-Stephenson.

Gellner, E. (1983) *Nations and Nationalism*. Oxford: Blackwell.

George, S. (1998) *An Awkward Partner: Britain in the European Community*. Oxford: Oxford University Press.

Giddens, A. (1990) *The Consequences of Modernity: Self and Society in the Late Modern Age*. Cambridge: Polity.

Giddens, A. (1998) *The Third Way: the Renewal of Social Democracy*. Cambridge: Polity

Gilpin, R. (1987) *The Political Economy of International Relations*. Princeton, NJ: Princeton University Press.

Glenn, J. (2003) 'EU enlargement', Chapter 14, pp. 211–28, in Cini, M. (ed.) *European Union Politics*. Oxford: Oxford University Press.

Goldmann, K. (2001) *Transforming the European Nation State*. London: Sage.

Goldmann, K, Hannerz, U. & Westin, C. (eds) (2000) *Nationalism and Internationalism in the Post-Cold War Era*. London and New York: Routledge.

Goodman, A, Johnson, P. & Webb, S. (1997), *Inequality in the UK*. Oxford: Oxford University Press.

Gowland D., O'Neill B. & Dunphy R. (2000) *The European Mosaic: Contemporary Politics, Economics & Culture*. Harlow: Addison Wesley Longman.

Gowland, D. & Turner, A. (1999) *Reluctant Europeans: Britain and European Integration, 1945–96*. Harlow: Longman.

Gray, J. (1998) *False Dawn: The Delusions of Global Capitalism*. London: Granta.

Gray, J. (2002) *Straw Dogs*. London: Granta.

Gray, J. (2002ii) *False Dawn: The Delusions of Global Capitalism*. Revised Edition, London: Granta.

Gray, J. (2003) *Al Qaeda and What It Means To Be Modern*. London: Faber and Faber.

Gray, J. (2004) 'Power and vainglory' in *The Independent* Review, p. 3, 19 May.

Greenfield, L. (2000) 'Democracy, ethnic diversity and nationalism' in Goldmann, K., Hannerz, U. & Westin, C. (eds) *Nationalism and Internationalism in the Post-Cold War Era*. London and New York: Routledge.

Greenwood, J. (1997) *Representing Interests in the European Union*. London: Macmillan.

Griffiths, A. & Wall, S. (2001) *Applied Economics*. London: Financial Times/Pitman Publishing.

Haas, E.B. (1958) *The Uniting of Europe: Political, Social, and Economic Forces, 1950–1957*. Stanford, CA: Stanford University Press.

Habermas, J. (1980) 'Modernity versus postmodernity', tr. Seyla Ben Habi, *New German Critique*, 22. Winter 1981.

Habermas, J. (1985) *The Philosophical Discourse of Modernity: Twelve Lectures*, tr. Frederick G. Lawrence. Cambridge: Polity Press.

Habermas, J. (2001) 'Why Europe needs a constitution', *New Left Review*, 11, Sept–Oct.

Halper, S. & Clarke, J. (2004) *America Alone: the Neo-Conservatives and the Global Order*. Cambridge: Cambridge University Press.

Hammond, W. (2003) Dekalog 10: 'Thou shalt not covet thy neighbour's goods', p. 296, *Time Out Film Guide*. London: Penguin.

Hari, Y. (2003) 'The second nuclear age may be more difficult to survive than the Cold War', *The Independent*, 23 May, p. 18.

Haseler, S. (2003) 'Rethinking NATO: A European declaration of independence', *European Essays*, no. 26. London: Federal Trust.

Haseler, S. (2004) *Super State: the New Europe and Its Challenge to America*. London: I.B. Tauris.

Held, D. (1995) *Democracy and the Global Order: From the Modern State to Cosmopolitan Governance*. Cambridge: Polity.

Held, D. & McGrew, A. (2002) *Globalization/Anti-Globalization*. Cambridge: Polity.

Held, D. & McGrew, A. (eds) (2002ii) *Governing Globalization*. Cambridge: Polity.

Hindle, T. (2000) *Guide to Management Ideas*. London: Economist Books.

Hindle, T. (2003) 'The Third Age of Globalisation', pp. 109–10, in *The World in 2004*. London: Economist Newspapers Limited.

Hirst, P. & Thompson, G. (1999) *Globalization in Question*. Cambridge: Polity Press.

Hocking, B. & Smith, M. (1997) *Beyond Foreign Economic Policy*. Pinter.

Hoffman, S. (1995) *The European Sisyphus: Essays on Europe 1964–94*. Oxford: Oxford University Press.

Holmes, R. (2003) 'Set Cornwall free', letter in *The Independent*, p. 21, 12 December.

Hooghe, L. & Keating, M. (1994) 'The politics of European regional policy', *Journal of European Public Policy*, vol. 1, no. 3: 367–93.

Hooghe, L. & Marks, G. (2001) *Multi-level Governance and European Integration*. Boulder, CO: Rowman and Littlefield.

Howorth, J. (2003) 'Foreign and defence policy cooperation' pp. 13–28, in Peterson, J. & Pollack, M. (eds) *Europe, America, Bush*. London and New York: Routledge.

Huntingdon, S. (1996) *The Clash of Civilizations and the Remaking of the World Order*. New York: Simon and Schuster.

Hutton, W. (1997) *The State We're In*. London: Vintage.

Hutton, W. (2002) *The World We're In*. London: Little, Brown.

Hutton, W. (2003) 'Union? What Union?', *Observer*, 30 November.

Ignatieff. M. (2000) *Virtual War: Kosovo and Beyond*. London: Chatto & Windus.

Ito, Kan (1990) 'Trans-Pacific anger', *Foreign Policy*, vol. 80, no. 2: 131–52.

Jackson, R. & Sørensen, G. (2003) *Introduction to International Relations: Theories and Approaches*, 2nd edition. Oxford: Oxford University Press.

Jeannet, J.-P. & Hennessey, H.D. (2001) *Global Marketing Strategies*. Boston, MA: Houghton Mifflin.

Jeffery, C. (1997) *The Regional Dimension of the European Union*. London: Frank Cass.

Jones, R.A. (2001) *The Politics & Economics of the European Union*. Cheltenham: Edward Elgar.

Judd, T. (2004) 'Urban 4 × 4 drivers should pay more tax, says transport chief', p. 14, *The Independent*, 28 June.

Kagan, R. (2002) 'Power and Weakness', *Policy Review*: 113 (available at http://www.policyreview.org/JUN02/Kagan_print.html)

Kapteyn, P. (1996) *The Stateless Market*. London: Routledge.

Katzenstein, P. (1996) 'Introduction', in P. Katzenstein (ed.), *The Culture of National Security: Norms and Identity in World Politics*. Ithaca, NY: Cornell University Press.

Keating, M. & Hooghe, L. (1996) 'Bypassing the nation state? Regions and the EU policy process', in Richardson, J. (ed.) *European Union: Power and Policy Making*, 2nd edition. London: Routledge.

Kedourie, E. (1966) *Nationalism*. London: Hutchinson & Co.

Keohane, R. (1984) *After Hegemony: Cooperation and Discord in the World Political Economy*. Princeton, NJ: Princeton University Press.

Keohane, R. (1989) *International Institutions and State Power: Essay in International Relations Theory*, Boulder, CO: Westview.

Keohane, R. (2002) *Power and Governance in a Partially Globalized World*. London: Routledge.

Keohane, R. & Hoffman, S. (eds) (1991) *The New European Community*. Boulder, CO: Westview.

Keohane, R., Nye, J. & Hoffman, S. (eds) (1993) *After the Cold War: International Institutions and State Strategies in Europe, 1989–91*. Cambridge, MA: Harvard University Press.

Khor, M. (1995) Remarks to the International Forum on Globalisation (New York, November).

Klein, N. (2001) *No Logo*. London: Flamingo.

Kohler-Koch, B. (1996) 'Catching up with change: the transformation of governance in the European Union', *Journal of European Public Policy*, vol. 3, no. 3:359–80.

Krugman, P. (2000) *The Return of Depression Economics*. New York and London: Norton.

Ladipo, D. (2001) 'The rise of America's prison industrial complex', in *New Left Review*, vol. 7, Jan/Feb: 109–23.

Landes, D. (1998) *The Wealth and Poverty of Nations: Why Some Are So Rich and Others Are So Poor*, New York and London: Norton.

Lasch, C. (1979) *The Culture of Narcissism*. New York and London: Norton.

Lasch, C. (1995) *The Revolt of the Elites and the Betrayal of Democracy*. New York and London: Norton.

Layne, C. (1998) 'Rethinking American grand strategy: hegemony or balance of power in the twenty-first century?', *World Policy Journal*, vol. 15, no. 2.

Legrain, P. (2002) *Open World: The Truth about Globalisation*. London: Abacus.

Levy, C. (ed.) (1996) *Italian Regionalism: History, Identity and Politics*. Oxford: Berg.

Lewis, H. (2003) 'The Council of the European Union', Chapter 10, pp. 148–65, in Cini, M. (ed.) *European Union Politics*. Oxford: Oxford University Press.

Light, M. (2003) 'US and European perspectives on Russia', pp. 69–84, in Peterson, J. & Pollack, M. (eds) *Europe, America, Bush*. London and New York: Routledge.

Lucas, C. (2000) http://www.greenparty.org.uk/reports/2000/meps/globalisationspeech.htm

Lyotard, J.-F. (1979) *The Post Modern Condition: A Report on Knowledge*, tr. Geoffrey Bennington and Brian Massumi. Manchester: Manchester University Press.

Lyotard, J.-F. (1987) 'The postmodern condition' in Baynes, K. et al. (eds) *After Philosophy*. Cambridge, MA: MIT Press.

Macey, D. (2000) *The Penguin Dictionary of Critical Theory*. London: Penguin.

Mansbach, R.W. (2000) *The Global Puzzle: Issues and Actors in World Politics*. Boston, MA: Houghton Mifflen.

Marks, G., Hooghe, L. and Blank, K. (1996) 'European integration from the 1980s: state-centric v multi-level governance', *Journal of Common Market Studies*, vol. 34, no. 5:341–78.

Marsh, D. (1995) *Germany and Europe: Crisis of Unity*. London. Mandarin.

Maxton, G. (2003) 'A rough road', pp. 119–20 in *The World in 2004*. London: Economist Newspapers Limited.

Mayhew, A. (1998) *Recreating Europe: The European Union's Policy towards Central and Eastern Europe*. Cambridge: Cambridge University Press.

Mazey, S. & Richardson, J. (eds) (1993) *Lobbying in the European Community*, Oxford: Oxford University Press.

McCauley, M. (1998) *Russia, America and the Cold War 1949–1991*. Harlow: Addison Wesley Longman.

McCormick, J. (2002) *Understanding the European Union: a Concise Introduction*. Basingstoke: Palgrave.

McDonald, F. & Dearden, S. (1999) *European Economic Integration*. Harlow: Longman.

McLean, I. & McMillan, A. (2003) *Oxford Concise Dictionary of Politics*. Oxford: Oxford University Press.

McRae, H. (2004) 'The biggest boom in history could see China overtake the UK by next year', in *The Independent*, p. 40, 8 April.

Mearsheimer, J. (1990) 'Back to the future: instability in Europe after the Cold War', *International Security*, vol. 15, no. 1: 5–56.

Mearsheimer, J. (1994) 'The false promise of international institutions', *International Security*, vol. 19, no. 3: 5–49.

Micklethwait, J. & Wooldridge, A. (2000) *A Future Perfect: The Challenge and Hidden Promise of Globalisation*. London: Heinemann.

Micklethwait, J. & Wooldridge, A. (2004) 'US-Europe gap wider than the Middle East', *Japan Times*, 25 June 2004.

Milward, A. (2000) *The European Rescue of the Nation State*. London: Routledge.

Mitrany, D. (1943) *A Working Peace System*. London: Royal Institute of International Affairs.

Monbiot, G. (2000) *Captive State: the Corporate Takeover of Britain*. Basingstoke and Oxford: Pan.

Monbiot, G. (2003) 'The bottom dollar', *The Guardian*, 22 April.

Moore, M. (2002) *Stupid White Men*. Harmondsworth: Penguin.

Moravcsik, A. (1993) 'Preferences and power in the European Community: a liberal intergovernmentalist approach', *Journal of Common Market Studies*, vol. 34, no. 4:473–524.

Moravcsik, A. (1999) *The Choice for Europe: Social Purpose and State Power from Messina to Maastricht*. University College London.

Moravcsik, A. (2001) 'A Constructivist research programme for EU studies, in *European Union Politics*', vol. 2, no. 2:226–49.

Morgantheau, H.J. (1960) *Politics Among Nations: the Struggle for Power and Peace*, 3rd edition. New York: Knopf.

Morrow, F. (2003) 'Srebrenica: a cry from the grave', p. 1138, *Time Out Film Guide*. London: Penguin.

Newell, P. (2002) 'Globalisation and the future state', *IDS Working Papers,* no. 141, pp. 1–34, Brighton, Sussex: Institute of Development Studies.

Nozick, R. (1975) *Anarchy, State and Utopia*. Oxford: Blackwell.

Nye, J. (1990) *Bound to Lead: the Changing Nature of American Power*. New York: Basic.

Nye, J. (2002) *The Paradox of American Power: Why the World's Only Superpower Can't Go It Alone*. Oxford and New York: Oxford University Press.

Nye, J. (2003) 'America's soft learning curve', pp. 64–5, in *The World in 2004*. London: Economist Newspapers Limited.

O'Brien, R. (1992) *Global Financial Integration: the End of Geography*. London: Pinter.

Ohmae, K. (1985) *Triad Power: The Coming Shape of Global Competition*. New York: Free Press.

Ohmae, K. (1990) *The Borderless World*. London and New York: Collins.

Øhrgaard, J.C. (1997) 'Less than supranational, more than intergovernmental: European political cooperation and the dynamics of intergovernmental integration', *Millennium: Journal of International Studies*, vol. 26, no. 1.

Olsen, J.P. (2003) *Europeanization*, ch. 21, pp. 333–48, in Cini, M. (ed.), *European Union Politics*. Oxford: Oxford University Press.

Padoa-Schioppa, T. (2003) *Transforming Sovereignty*. European essay, no. 28. London: Federal Trust.

Parker, G. (2004) 'Brussels points the finger at lax states' in *Financial Times*, 22 January, p. 6.

Pedler, R.H. & Van Schendelen, M.P. (1994) *Lobbying the European Union*. Aldershot: Dartmouth.

Peterson, J. (1996) *Europe and America: Prospects for Partnership*. London: Routledge.

Peterson, J. (2003) 'The US and Europe in the Balkans', chapter 7, pp. 85–98 in Peterson, J. & Pollack, M.A. (eds) *Europe, America, Bush*. London and New York: Routledge.

Peterson J. & Bomberg, E. (1999) *Decision Making in the European Union*. Basingstoke: Macmillan.

Peterson, J. & Pollack, M.A. (eds) (2003) *Europe, America, Bush*. London and New York: Routledge.

Pfaff, W. (2004) 'Torture as an instrument of the Bush administration', *Japan Times*, 16 June.

Piening, C. (1997) *Global Europe: The European Union in World Affairs*. Boudler, CO: Lynne Reinner.

Pierson, P. (1996) 'The path to European integration: a historical institutionalist analysis', in *Comparative Political Studies*, vol. 29, no. 2: 23–62.

Pilger, J. (2002) *The New Rulers of the World*. London: Verso.

Pinder, J. (2001) *The European Union: a very short introduction*. Oxford: Oxford University Press.

Pollack, M. (1995) 'Regional actors in an intergovernmental play: the making and implementation of EC Structural Funds', in S. Mazey and C. Rhodes (eds) *State of the European Union, vol.3: Building a European Polity*. Boulder, CO: Lynne Reinner, and London: Longman.

Pollack, M. (2003) 'Unilateral America, multilateral Europe?', pp. 115–27, in Peterson, J. & Pollack, M.A. (eds) *Europe, America, Bush*. London and New York: Routledge.

Preston, P. (1996) *A Concise History of the Spanish Civil War*. London: Fontana.

Putnam, R.D. (1993) *Making Democracy Work – Civic Traditions in Modern Italy* Princeton, NJ: Princeton University Press.

Rieger, E. (2000) 'The Common Agricultural Policy: polities against markets', chapter 7, pp. 179–210 in Wallace, H. & Wallace, W. (eds) *Policy Making in the European Union*. Oxford: Oxford University Press.

Rosamond, B. (2000) *Theories of European Integration*. Basingstoke: Palgrave Macmillan.

Rosamond, B. (2003) *New Theories of European Integration*, in Cini, M. (ed.), *European Union Politics*. Oxford: Oxford University Press.

Rosenau, J.N. (1997) *Along the Domestic-Foreign Frontier: Exploring Governance in a Turbulent World*. Cambridge: Cambridge University Press.

Rosenberg, J. (2000) *The Follies of Globalisation Theory*. London: Granta.

Ross, P. (2001) *Contemporary Social Issues in Modern Britain*. York: York St John College.

Sandholtz, W. and Stone Sweet, A. (eds) (1998) *European Integration and Supranational Governance*. Oxford: Oxford University Press.

Samuelson, R. (2004) 'One pillar of Reagan's success goes unsung', *The Japan Times*, 12 June.

Sassen, S. (1996) *Losing Control? Sovereignty in an Age of Globalization*. New York and Chichester: Columbia University Press.

Satoh, Haruko (1998) *The UK and Japan: A Special Relationship into the 21ˢᵗ Century*. London: Royal Institute of International Affairs, Briefing Paper no. 46.

Savater, F. (2004) 'ETA n'osera plus commettre d'attentat', *Le Figaro*, 15 April.

Schlosser, E. (2001) *Fast Food Nation*. London: Allen Lane/Penguin.

Scholte, J.A. (1999) 'Globalisation: prospects for a paradigm shift', in M. Shaw (ed.) *Politics and Globalisation*. London: Routledge.

Scully, R. (2003) 'The European Parliament', chapter 11, pp. 166–78, in Cini, M. (ed.) *European Union Politics*. Oxford: Oxford University Press.

Shaw, M. (1994) *Global Society and International Relation*. Cambridge: Polity.

Shrybman, S. (2001) 'Honor the earth', pp. 119–123, in Ellwood, W. *The No-Nonsense Guide to Globalization*. London, Oxford: New Internationalist, Verso.

Siedentop, L. (2000) *Democracy in Europe*. London: Allen Lane.

Silber, L. & Little, A. (1996) *The Death of Yugoslavia*, revised edition. London: BBC/Penguin.

Smith, A.D. (1986) *The Ethnic Origins of Nations*. Oxford: Blackwell.

Smith, A.D. (1991) *National Identity*. London: Penguin.

Smith, A.D. (1995) *Nations and Nationalism in a Global Era*. Cambridge: Polity.

Soros, G. (2002) *George Soros On Globalisation*. Oxford: Public Affairs Limited.

Spivak, G. (1996) '"Woman" as theatre: United Nations Conference on Women, Beijing, 1995', *Radical Philosophy*, vol. 75, Jan-Feb: 1–7.

Steans, J. (2002) 'Global governance: a feminist perspective', in Held D. & McGrew, A. (eds) *Governing Globalization*. Cambridge: Polity.

Stiglitz, J. (2002) *Globalization and its Discontents*. London: Penguin.

Strange, S. (1987) 'The persistent myth of lost hegemony' in *International Organization*, vol. 41:551–74.

Strange, S. (1996) *The Retreat of the State: the Diffusion of Power in the World Economy*. Cambridge: CUP.

Strøeby Jensen, C. (2003) 'Neo-functionalism', Chapter 80–92, in Cini, M. (ed.) *European Union Politics*. Oxford: Oxford University Press.

Thatcher, M. (1988) *Britain and Europe: Text of the Speech Delivered in Bruges by the Prime Minister on 20 September 1988*. London: Conservative Political Centre.

Tomaszewski, J. (2000) 'From internationalism to nationalism? Poland 1994–96' in Goldmann, K., Hannerz, U. & Westin, C. (eds) *Nationalism and Internationalism in the Post-Cold War Era*. London and New York: Routledge.

Tsoukalis, L. (2000) 'Economic and Monetary Union', in Wallace, H. & Wallace, W. (eds) *Policy Making in the European Union*, chapter 6, pp. 149–78. Oxford: OUP.

Urwin, D. (2003) 'The European Community: 1945–85', Chapter 2, pp. 11–27, in Cini, M. (ed.), *European Union Politics*. Oxford: Oxford University Press.

Usborne, D. (2004) 'Rise of moral issues produces a shift right beyond democrats', *The Independent*, 4 November.

Usborne, D., Brown, C. & Penketh, A. (2004) 'The Re-United Nations', *Independent*, p. 1, 9 June.

Vernon, R. & Wells, L.T. (1968) 'International trade and international investment in the product life cycle', *Quarterly Journal of Economics*, May.

Wade, R. (2001) 'Inequality of World Incomes: What should be done?', http://www.openDemocracy.net

Walker, M. (1994) *The Cold War*. London: Vintage.

Wallace, H. & Wallace, W. (eds) (2000) *Policy Making in the European Union*. Oxford: OUP.

Waltz, K. (1959) *Man, the State and War*. New York: Columbia University Press.

Waltz, K. (1979) *Theory of International Politics*. Reading, MA: Addison Wesley.

Waters, M. (2001) *Globalization*. London: Routledge.

Weber, C. (2001) *International Relations Theory: A Critical Introduction*. London: Routledge.

Weiler, J.H.H. (2000) 'To be a European citizen', in Goldmann, K., Hannerz, U. & Westin, C. (eds) *Nationalism and Internationalism in the Post-Cold War Era*. London and New York: Routledge.

Weinberger, C. (1984) *Annual Report to the Congress, Department of Defense, Fiscal Year 1985*, pp. 279–80. Washington DC.

Wight, M. (1991) *International Theory: The Three Traditions*. Leicester: Leicester University Press.

Wilkinson, R. (2002) 'Global monitor: the World Trade Organisation', *New Political Economy*, vol. 7, no. 1: 129–41.

Woods, N. (2001) 'International political economy in an age of globalization', chapter 13, pp. 277–98, in Baylis, J. & Smith, S. (eds) *The Globalization of World Politics*. Oxford: Oxford University Press.

Woodward, K. (ed.) (1997) *Identity and Difference*. Sage/Open University.

Young, H. (1991) *One of Us: a Biography of Mrs Thatcher*. London: Macmillan.

Young, H. (1998) *This Blessed Plot: Britain and Europe from Churchill to Blair*. London: Macmillan.

Yueh, L.Y. (2003) 'China's Economic Growth with WTO accession: Is it sustainable?' Asia Programme Working Paper No. 1, May. London: Royal Institute of International Affairs.

Zedillo, E. (2003) 'Doha or Die', *The World in 2004*, London: Economist Newspapers Limited.

Index